D1345486

Advances in
Potato Pest
Biology and Management

Edited by

Geoffrey W. Zehnder
Auburn University
Auburn, Alabama

Mary L. Powelson
Oregon State University
Corvallis

Richard K. Jansson
Merck Research Laboratories
Three Bridges, New Jersey

Kandukuri V. Raman
ISAAA
Cornell University
Ithaca, New York

APS PRESS
The American Phytopathological Society
St. Paul, Minnesota

Reference in this publication to a trademark, proprietary product, or company name by personnel of the U.S. Department of Agriculture or anyone else is intended for explicit description only and does not imply approval or recommendation to the exclusion of others that may be suitable.

Library of Congress Catalog Card Number: 93-74778
International Standard Book Number: 0-89054-164-7

©1994 by The American Phytopathological Society
Second printing, 1997

Printed in the United States of America on acid-free paper

The American Phytopathological Society
3340 Pilot Knob Road
St. Paul, Minnesota 55121-2097, USA

CONTENTS

PART XI.   *Potato Pest Management: A Global View*

ABOUT THE BOOK AND EDITORS

The book *Advances in Potato Pest Management,* published in 1981 (Hutchinson Ross Publishing Company) and edited by James Lashomb and Richard Casagrande, has been an invaluable reference for workers in potato pest management. However, many technological advances have occurred within the past decade and their application in potato pest management research has created a need for an updated reference work in this discipline. As a first step in synthesizing recent efforts in potato pest management research, an International Conference on Potato Pest Management was held in Jackson Hole, Wyoming in October, 1991. *Advances in Potato Pest Biology and Management* is a compilation of information presented at the conference and, as is stated in the preface of the 1981 book, is "intended to provide a broad survey of the state of the art of potato pest management".

Lashomb and Casagrande wrote in 1981 that "pest management in most crops is more of a philosophy than a reality because as yet we have had insufficient time to study the major components and interaction of crop ecosystems". Many of the novel pest management strategies presented in the following chapters are a result of an additional decade of research effort on these interactions, and others reflect new technologies that have become available since 1981. Although there is no question that we have progressed a great deal, we recognize that much work remains to be done before these new strategies and technologies are realized as viable, cost-effective approaches in commercial potato production.

The editors of the book are: Geoffrey W. Zehnder, Associate Professor of Entomology at Auburn University, Auburn, AL; Mary L. Powelson, Professor of Plant Pathology, Oregon State University, Corvallis, OR; Richard K. Jansson, Senior Research Fellow, Agricultural Research and Development, Merck Research Laboratories, Three Bridges, NJ; and K.V. Raman, Center Director, ISAAA (International Service for the Acquisition of Agri-Biotech Applications), and Professor, Department of Plant Breeding and Biometry, Cornell University, Ithaca, NY.

FOREWORD

In the remarkably brief period of 4 centuries the potato has emerged from its native home in the Andean region of South America, and become one of the four major food crops of the world, along with rice, wheat, and maize. This dramatic increase in the importance of the potato was due primarily to its rapid development as a basic food crop in many European countries, from where it has spread throughout the world.

During the past 40 years some significant trends have developed in world potato production. In the industrialized countries the area planted has slowly declined, but higher productivity has resulted in relatively stable total annual production. In the developing countries the area planted to potatoes has increased considerably, and productivity has also risen steadily. Today these developing countries produce approximately 30% of the world potato crop, compared with only 7% just 40 years ago.

While potato yields have been increasing dramatically, it is important to note that much of this progress has been due to the widespread and abundant use of agricultural chemicals, particularly for insect pest and disease control. Today, the world's potato crop receives a greater total amount of pesticides than does any other food crop we grow. If the potato continues to be grown more extensively in developing countries, it would not be practical or economically sound merely to recommend a wider use of the conventional chemical control measures developed in the industrialized countries. We must search for more viable alternatives. What new production technologies must be developed and implemented in order to realize more of the invaluable contribution that the potato can make to the conquest of hunger, while at the same time maintaining the quality of the environment, and conserving our natural resources in a sustainable agriculture?

As we approach the biologic limits for what our planet can support, we must define and develop technologies to meet this challenge. In the chapters of this book, *Advances in Potato Pest Biology and Management*, a number of specific potato production technologies are described and discussed. They range from some historical, forgotten practices (that should be reexamined for their potential contribution to a modern agriculture), to some of the marvelous new discoveries made on the research frontiers of biotechnology and genetic engineering (that promise incredible solutions to traditional problems). These technologies are proposed for integrated pest and disease control systems that promote both agricultural productivity and sustainability.

The data, results, and recommendations presented in this book provide valuable guidelines for evaluation and further experimentation in the fields of potato farmers all over the world. Only in this way can valid potato production strategies be defined and implemented in each of the widely variable environments where potatoes are grown in the world.

We are living in one of the most exciting and critical periods in the history of mankind. The authors of the following chapters of this book have accepted the challenge of providing the multidisciplinary, technologic base for increasing potato production and productivity in a sustainable agriculture. By building on this base, we can realize even more of the potato's potential for feeding an expanding world population during the next millennium.

John S. Niederhauser
Professor, Department of Plant Pathology
University of Arizona, Tucson

1990 World Food Prize Recipient

ACKNOWLEDGMENTS

This book, *Advances in Potato Pest Biology and Management*, is an outgrowth of the *International Conference on Potato Pest Management*, that was held in Jackson Hole, Wyoming on 12-17 October, 1991. The conference was attended by researchers and extension personnel from various land grant universities, government agencies, international research centers, and industry to address current knowledge and to identify research needs related to management of insects, diseases and nematodes of potato. Weed pests of potato were not addressed at the conference, however we hope that future conferences on potato pest management can be organized to include this component. Conference participants numbered approximately 200, and included people from 27 states in the U.S. and from Australia, Belgium, Canada, Denmark, Dominican Republic, Ecuador, England, Netherlands, and Peru. We acknowledge the text processing assistance of Lisa McKay in development of the camera-ready chapter manuscripts, and we thank the following conference sponsors without whom the development of this book would not have been possible:

INTERNATIONAL POTATO CENTER

UNIVERSITY OF FLORIDA, IFAS

POTATO ASSOCIATION OF AMERICA

VIRGINIA POLYTECHNIC INSTITUTE
AND STATE UNIVERSITY

SOUTH FLORIDA POTATO
GROWERS EXCHANGE

IDAHO POTATO COMMISSION

ENTOTECH, INC., A NOVO
NORDISK CO.

RHONE-POULENC AG. CO.

MERCK, SHARP & DOHME

UNITED AGRI-PRODUCTS CO.

ATOCHEM NORTH AMERICA

SANDOZ CROP PROTECTION

AG-CHEM, INC.

CIBA-GEIGY CORP.

BASF CORPORATION

ECOGEN, INC.

CARNATION CO.

DOW-ELANCO

GOWAN CO.

MYCOGEN, CORP.

MOBAY CORP.

NOR-AM CHEMICAL CO.

ROHM & HAAS CO.

ORE-IDA FOODS, INC.

PART I

Introduction

POTATO PEST MANAGEMENT:
A DECADE OF PROGRESS

James Lashomb
Department of Entomology
Cook College, Rutgers University
New Brunswick, New Jersey 08903

More than a decade has passed since the first interdisciplinary book on potato pest management was published (1). As is manifested in this volume, astonishing progress has been made within the past ten years in potato insect and disease management worldwide. Using Smith's (3) description of the evolution of crop protection (cited in 2), the current state of potato pest management may be perceived as moving from the crisis phase (e.g., in potato-growing areas where recurring insecticide failures have resulted in increasing pest densities), into the integrated control phase. In the case of potato pest management today, we are beginning to view the concept of sustainable agriculture as a shared philosophy, and we also see the emergence of new plant protection tools from biotechnology.

This chapter briefly highlights the major advances in potato pest management during the past decade, all of which are discussed in great detail in the chapters that follow. The purpose of this discussion is to illustrate the recent direction taken in potato pest management research. As observed by some of the earliest societies to cultivate the crop (see Thurston, this volume), scientists in the 1990s recognize the need for holistic, integrated potato pest management systems. Today, these systems can include a variety of techniques ranging from those used hundreds of years earlier in low input, sustainable systems to those developed through sophisticated biotechnology approaches. As demonstrated in various chapters of this book, solutions to pest problems on potato require the coordination of multidisciplinary programs and efficient technology transfer to the grower.

Our knowledge of potato pest biology has increased dramatically in the past decade, and this has been critical to the development of new crop management strategies. For example, great progress has been made in understanding the biology and phenology of the Colorado potato beetle, a yield-limiting insect pest of potato in many areas. This knowledge has led to the development of new cultural and biological control methods that are described in several chapters of the book. Similarly, additional chapters are devoted to advances that have been made in our comprehension of the biology of other potato insects pests and pathogens (fungi, bacteria, viruses and nematodes), and in the development of biointensive insect, disease and nematode management strategies.

The recent meteoric progress in computer technology has impacted pest management in potato by facilitating greater cooperation between biologists and computer specialists. This liaison has led to the development of models to estimate the effects of pest damage to crops, and in the evolution and implementation of expert systems for pest and crop management decision-making. Recent advances in modelling and expert systems in potato pest management are discussed in three chapters of the book.

Our experiences in potato pest management (or lack thereof) during the past decade has taught us the pitfalls of using synthetic pesticides on a scheduled basis, without concern for consequences in terms of the rapid development of pest resistance and/or the public's reaction to related environmental issues. Several chapters discuss recent advances in understanding the mechanisms involved in the development of resistance to pesticides, and in the development of current and future strategies for managing pest resistance to chemical pesticides and biological insecticides, such as *Bacillus thuringiensis* (applied by foliar spray and by introducing Bt-expressing genes into potato plants).

The difficulties associated with incorporating pest resistance factors into commercially-acceptable potato cultivars using traditional plant breeding methods are well known. Several chapters in this volume discuss recent progress that has been made in the development of pest-resistant potato cultivars with the potential for commercially-acceptable yields and quality. These advancements were possible, in part, because of recent studies on the biochemistry of wild potatoes, and on the mechanisms involved in the phenomenon of plant resistance to pest attack.

What is now possible in gene recombination technology could only be dreamed about ten years ago. Today, when conventional breeding for potato insect resistance fails or is slow to develop, the process can be enhanced by inserting foreign genes into the potato genome. A significant portion of the book (six chapters) is devoted to recent advances in biotechnology that will facilitate the development of pest-resistant potato cultivars and biopesticides.

The International Potato Center (CIP) has done much to promote the growing of potato in developing countries, primarily through its interdisciplinary research efforts to develop technologies for control of major worldwide potato pests without overreliance on pesticides. The CIP philosophy and several of its major research programs are discussed in the section on *Potato Pest Management: A Global View*.

4

Looking back on the past decade of progress in potato pest management, I believe that several if not many of our serious potato pest problems will be solved given another decade of similar progress. With a continuance of research funding that this important crop deserves, I am confident that a publication on potato written ten years hence will report on the widespread use of many potato crop management strategies presented herein, and will present strategies for the future that we have not yet considered.

Acknowledgment

This is New Jersey Agricultural Experiment Station publication #F-08246-01-93, supported by state funds and the U.S. Hatch Act.

Literature Cited

1. Lashomb, J. and R. Casagrande (eds). 1981. Advances in potato pest management. Hutchinson Ross, Stroudsburg, Pa.
2. Metcalf, R. and W. Luckman. 1987. Introduction to insect pest management. John Wiley and Sons. New York.
3. Smith, R.F. 1969. The new and old in pest control. Proc. Acad. Nazion. Lincei, Rome (1968) 366:21-30.

ANDEAN POTATO CULTURE: 5,000 YEARS OF EXPERIENCE WITH SUSTAINABLE AGRICULTURE

H. David Thurston
Department of Plant Pathology
Cornell University
Ithaca, NY 14853

The latest key word in agriculture - and many other circles - is *sustainable*. Everyone is for sustainability; radical environmentalists, chemical companies, biotechnology types, and even the public and politicians. I like the definition that Peter Gregory gave in his talk:

Sustainable agriculture is the successful management of resources for agriculture to satisfy changing human needs while maintaining or enhancing the quality of the environment and conserving natural resources.

I would like to pose the following question: can we learn something about sustainable agriculture from the long history of potato culture in the Andes? I believe that the Incas and their predecessors had a rather successful, productive, sustainable agriculture for millennia. Most archeologists believe that humans began crop production perhaps 10,000 yr ago. Some authorities suggest that potatoes may have been cultivated that long ago, and they certainly have been cultivated for thousands of years in South America. Many of the successful practices of these ancient farmers have been forgotten or abandoned in developed countries, but are still used by many traditional, indigenous, subsistence, or partially subsistence farmers. Although there is considerable evidence showing that traditional farmers experiment and innovate, most of the useful traditional practices and materials used in agriculture were probably developed empirically through millennia of trial and error, farmer selection, and keen observation (16).

Much of the information in this paper, although altered and rewritten, is from the book *Sustainable Practices for Plant Disease Management in Traditional Farming Systems* by H. D. Thurston which was published in 1992 by Westview Press, Boulder, CO.

Today there are many concerns about modern potato culture; that it is highly energy-intensive, the genetic base is narrow, and emphasis on increasingly high yields and efficiency leads to monoculture, and sometimes to excessive erosion, pollution, and excessive pesticide residues. A historical perspective on the practices and genetic materials used by traditional potato farmers through the centuries may help us to learn to better conserve energy, maintain natural resources, and reduce chemical use.

Systems that have lasted for thousands of years certainly justify serious study. The potato originated in the Andes Mountains of South America, so a look at the farming systems there should be of value in understanding how Andean farmers managed potato culture and potato diseases. Until recent population pressures put serious strains on the systems, many Andean farming systems appeared to have a high degree of sustainability, stability, resilience, productivity, and efficiency. Andean farmers were not always interested in the highest yields, but rather were more concerned with attaining stable, reliable yields. They minimized risks and seldom took chances that might lead to hunger, starvation, or losing their land. Most pest management practices used by Andean traditional farmers consisted primarily of cultural controls. Andean farmers managed pests by using a diversity of potato cultivars and crops species, fallowing, rotation, multiple cropping, organic amendments (resulting in biological control), raised beds, sanitation, tillage manipulations, and time of planting. Disease resistance of the landraces or traditional cultivars is a highly important legacy. An examination of some of these traditional technologies used for potato production in the Andes can give us some guidelines leading to sustainability.

The Waru Waru System of the Andes

Raised fields, raised beds, ridges, and mounds have been used widely for millennia by traditional farmers all over the world. Over 82,000 ha of remnants of raised fields or raised beds called "waru waru" or "caballónes" are found at an elevation of 3,800 m near Lake Titicaca bordering Peru and Bolivia (7,8). Some of these raised fields may be 2,000 yr old. When a few of the raised beds were rebuilt according to specifications obtained from archeological studies, potato yields were 15 T/ha from raised beds, while the regional average was less than 5 T/ha. In addition to better water management, the waru waru contributed to flood control, frost control, and disease management. Organic matter from crop residues, muck from the bottom of the canals surrounding the waru waru, and human and animal manure were added to the raised beds which probably contributed to disease suppressive soils. Fish thrived in the canals between raised beds, and ducks also were raised. The Bolivian and Peruvian governments now help farmers to reconstruct raised beds. Thus, farmers in the Andes are learning a forgotten technology from their traditional ancestors.

The Management of Nematodes Using Fallowing and Rotation by the Incas of Peru

The origin of the destructive potato-cyst nematodes (*Globodera rostochiensis* and *Globodera pallida*) is generally accepted to be the South American Andes. Although the Inca Indians did not know nematodes existed, they did know how to effectively control them. Fallowing is often more effective in reducing pathogen populations in combination with crop rotations. In Peru, before the arrival of the Spanish, farmers of the Inca empire used fallow and rotations for potatoes. The Inca empire had a highly organized system of land tenure and access to land. In the early 1600s, one Inca writer, Poma de Ayala (15), listed 32 different Inca classifications of agricultural land including land for fallow and for rotation. In fact, the Spanish justified their take-over of Indian lands by suggesting that there was lots of unused land in the Andes and that the concept of land as property did not exist, because so much land was tied up in the long Inca fallows.

Rotations of 6 to 8 yr are still used today by some indigenous communities in the Andes. These traditional Andean farmers not only fallow, but use other crops in their rotations. A typical rotation/ fallow practice is to cultivate fields for only 1 to 3 yr before returning them to a long fallow of 8 or more years. Farmers usually plant potatoes in the first year and other Andean tubers such as oca (*Oxalis tuberosa*), mashua (*Tropaeolum tuberosum*), or ullucu (*Ullucus tuberosum)*, for one or two subsequent years. Mashua, a tuber crop used in rotation with potatoes by ancient Peruvian farmers, contains isothiocyanates, which, incidently, are nematicidal compounds (10). In Cuyo-cuyo, Peru, local farmers today still plant mashua interspersed among other tuber crops (11). Nonhosts probably played an important role in the management of the potato cyst nematode. Cornell scientists have found that nematode densities in the soil decline 30-50% annually when a nonhost crop is grown (1). Thus, the strategy of the Andean farmers to rotate with nonhosts of the potato cyst nematode is also a sound nematode management practice.

Through centuries of trial and error the Incas and their predecessors must have learned that this 7 or 8 yr rotation/fallow gave the best potato crops. Studies in Rothamsted, England demonstrated that a 7 yr fallow reduced potato cyst nematode populations below their economic threshold so that a profitable crop could be grown (12,13). In the Andes of Peru today, where the traditional long rotation/fallow periods are no longer used, some of the highest populations of potato cyst nematodes in the world are found. To the Spanish, the Inca system for distribution of land and their long fallow/rotation practices probably seemed to be senseless. Long fallow periods were abandoned in many areas of Peru, and serious losses due to the potato cyst nematodes have occurred in Peru ever since their abandonment. Thus, after the conquest, the Spanish not only lost the agronomic benefits of fallowing and rotation, but the potato cyst nematodes became increasingly more prevalent and destructive.

Storage Practices for Potatoes in the Andes

An Inca storage practice for potatoes was to place storages at high altitudes in the Andes mountains, to utilize cold temperatures which would prevent deterioration. In the 1600s the Spaniard Bernabé Cobo (14) stated:

"The placing of these storages at high altitudes, was done by these Indians, in order that the contents of the storages were protected from water, humidity, and rotting".

Traditional potato storage in Peru probably dates back thousands of years. The Incas and even pre-Inca civilizations in Peru apparently had large, state-organized storage networks in addition to the stores of individual farmers. According to the calculations of archeologists (4), Inca storehouses in the Mantaro Valley of Peru had the capacity to store about one and a half million bushels of grain, tubers, or other food. Extensive Inca storages were found near Cuzco and Huancayco in Peru. Both cities are at high elevations with cool temperatures. Traditional farmers in the Andes today prevent insect damage by storing potatoes with leaves of the Eucalyptus trees or the plant muña (*Mintostachus mellis*). These aromatic plants have insect repellent qualities.

When the Spaniards arrived in the Andes they found the Indians using another practice for long-term storage of potatoes. Bernabé Cobo (14) wrote the following in 1653:

"There are some wild bitter potatoes called "afora" that are not eaten in fresh form, but that are good for chuño. The chuño is so hard it even keeps for years. It does not rot or deteriorate."

For millennia Andean Indians have been freeze-drying bitter, frost-resistant potatoes grown at 3,600 to 4,400 m above sea level to produce chuño (16). Potatoes are spread out to freeze at night when freezing temperatures are expected. After freezing, men and women trample the potatoes, and the water released by freezing is squeezed out. Subsequently, the chuño is spread out in a field and sun-dried. Chuño will keep for years in storage if properly dried. Chuño is still important in the highlands of Peru. An ancient Inca proverb extols the value of chuño:

"Stew without chuño is like life without love."

The Use of Copious Quantities of Organic Matter

Many traditional farmers, such as those in China, Rome, Greece and South and Central America have added considerable quantities of organic material to the soil. One of the tasks farmers had during the time of the Incas in Peru was to carry manure to their potato and maize fields. Soils of Peruvian terraces, many still in use today, are maintained by the application of manure and compost and by periodic fallowing. These practices were probably used prehistorically also. Von Hagen (17) quoted Cieza de León as describing Inca practices in the 1500s as follows:

> *"They bring back the droppings (guano) of birds to fertilize their corn fields and gardens, and this greatly enriches the ground and increases its yield, even if it once was barren. If they fail to use this manure, they gather little corn."*

Llama trains transported guano for fertilizer from islands off the Peruvian coast to the highlands during the time of the Incas. Indians also fertilized with manure from corralled llamas and other cameloids, green manures, and ashes according to the Spanish. Fish such as anchovies or sardines were often planted with a grain of maize to provide moisture and fertilizer at the time of planting (5). Historically, many agricultural systems incorporated large quantities of organic matter into the soil and this practice was probably a major key to their sustainability. This incorporation generally resulted in less soilborne disease, in addition to other valuable agronomic benefits.

Selection of Potato Varieties

Scientific breeding of potatoes for disease resistance probably did not begin until after the potato late blight epidemic in Ireland in 1845. However, traditional farmers have been selecting for disease resistance for thousands of years. A major center of diversity for potatoes is found around Lake Titicaca in Peru and Bolivia, where today the greatest diversity of potato germplasm in the world is found. Resistance has been found in South

American potato germplasm to almost every disease for which pathologists and breeders have sought. However, there is a danger that the potato "landraces" selected during thousands of years of cultivation by traditional farmers will be replaced by a few improved varieties developed by agricultural scientists. Sixty percent of the potato varieties in commercially developed valleys, such as the Mantaro Valley of Peru, are improved varieties, while away from these areas only about 25% are new varieties (3).

In the Andes traditional potato growers often grow a large number of potato varieties in the same field. In addition, farmers may have a number of separate plots in different locations and at different altitudes, which have different environmental conditions. Over 2,000 named potato varieties were grown in Peru. In one isolated Peruvian valley with about 1,000 habitants, Brush (2) found over 50 potato varieties. De Murúa (6) wrote that when Inca farmers found a new type of potato, or other root crop, or maize they would have a celebration which included singing, dancing, drinking, and a procession. Such activities would certainly indicate an extremely strong interest in plant selection and improvement.

Natural plant communities rarely have the serious plant disease epidemics that occur frequently in the intensive and extensive monocultures of our modern agriculture. Genetic erosion due to a few new varieties of crop plants replacing landraces is a major concern today in the international agriculture community. I have certainly done my part to contribute to genetic erosion, as I worked for 11 yrs in Colombia, South America with the Rockefeller Foundation in cooperation with the ICA (Instituto Agropecuario Colombiano - Colombian Agricultural Institute) potato and plant pathology research programs. This and subsequent ICA programs introduced many new and successful potato varieties in Colombia. Currently, less than 15% of the potato area in Colombia is cropped with old varieties, and these persist mainly because of their outstanding cooking quality and taste (9). Although the new varieties are often much higher yielding, and may have other desirable characteristics, this rapid change to newer potato varieties threatens the survival of varieties selected for centuries by indigenous populations. A similar scenario could be given for several of the worlds major food crops such as wheat, rice, and maize. Thus, many of these invaluable genetic resources embodied in landraces that were developed in a long evolutionary process may eventually disappear.

In the long run the CGIAR centers may make one of their major contribution by collecting and safeguarding diversity in the germplasm of the world's major food crops. Future generations may find that the preservation of potato germplasm alone may more than justify all the financial support given to the entire CGIAR system. Survival of the diversity incorporated in the many traditional landraces and their wild relatives, most found in developing countries, is seriously threatened by numerous human activities. Loss of these irreplaceable reservoirs of genetic material would constitute a tragedy for mankind. There are hopeful signs that the value of such germplasm is becoming appreciated, although financial support for its preservations is still pathetically small.

Epilogue

In conclusion, yes – we scientists can learn from indigenous and ancient traditional agricultural systems. In the future, as energy supplies based on petroleum become scarcer, this knowledge will become more important. To improve agricultural systems in both developed and developing countries, it is essential that the agricultural practices of traditional or indigenous farmers be thoroughly understood and compared with alternative or new practices that might be better than some of the old. If changes in indigenous systems are necessary or needed, a thorough understanding of these systems is imperative as a first step before changes are initiated. Often, existing traditional practices provide effective and sustainable means of disease control. Traditional practices and landraces have had profound effects on "modern agriculture", as most of our present practices and varieties evolved from these ancient techniques and plant materials. We scientists can contribute to the improvement of traditional systems, but a more respectful attitude regarding traditional knowledge would help.

The potato can supply more nutritious food faster and with less land than almost any other crop now widely grown. For me, it is positively heartbreaking to travel through areas of the developing world which are obviously well adapted for potatoes, or in the low, warmer elevations, adapted for cassava or sweet potatoes, and see people attempting to eak out a meager living growing maize, rice or other cereals.

Finally, a few summary observations on this fine conference.

- I was most pleased to see the inclusion of cultural practices in IPM programs for potatoes and note their increasing importance.
- Even the most advanced research, such as transgenic potatoes with pest resistance, when put into practice, will benefit from, and last longer, when combined with sustainable cultural practices.
- The increased emphasis on biological control, reflected in the papers given at this meeting, can only benefit the potato industry in the long run.

- I hope that weeds, rats, and other important pests will be included in the next meeting.
- The international makeup of this meeting is important and encouraging. We can learn from each other and can avoid or prepare for significant problems occurring in other areas.

Literature Cited

1. Brodie, B.B. 1984. Nematode parasites of potato. Pages 167-212 in: Plant and Insect Nematodes, Nickle, W. ed. Marcel Dekker, Basel.
2. Brush, S.B. 1977. Farming the edge of the Andes. Nat. History 86:32-40.
3. Brush, S.B. 1986. Genetic diversity and conservation in traditional farming systems. J. Ethnobiol. 6:151-167.
4. D'Altroy, T.N., and Harstorf, C. 1984. The distribution and contents of Inca State storehouses in the Xauxa Region of Peru. Am. Antiquity 49:334-349.
5. Del Busto, J.A. 1978. Peru Incaico. Liberia Studium, Lima. 385 pp.
6. De Murúa, Martin. 1987. Historia General de Peru. Historia 16, Madrid. 583 pp.
7. Erickson, C.L. 1985. Applications of prehistoric Andean technology experiments in raised field agriculture, Huatta, Lake Titicaca: 1981-1982. Pages 209-232 in: Prehistoric Intensive Agriculture in the Tropics, Farrington, I.S. ed. BAR Intl. Ser. 232, Oxford.
8. Erickson, C.L., and Candler, K.L. 1989. Raised fields and sustainable agriculture in the Lake Titicaca basin of Peru. Pages 230-249 in: Fragile Lands of Latin America: Strategies for Sustainable Development, Browder, J.O. ed. Westview, Boulder, CO.
9. Gomez, P.L., and van der Zaag, D.E. 1986. The role of the national potato programme in Colombia. Potato Res. 29: 245-250.
10. Johns, T., and Towers, G.H.N. 1981. Isothiocyanates and thioreas in enzyme hydrolisis of *Tropaeolum tuberosum*. Phytochemistry 20:2687-2689.
11. Johns, T., Kitts, W.D., Newsome, F., and Towers, G.H.N. 1982. Anti-reproductive and other medicinal effects of *Tropaeolum tuberosum*. J. Ethnopharmacology 5:149-161.
12. Jones, F.G.W. 1970. The control of the potato-cyst nematode. R. Soc. Arts 117:179-199.
13. Jones, F.G.W. 1972. Management of nematode populations in Great Britain. Pages 81-107 in: Proc. Tall Timbers Conf., Tall Timbers Res. Sta., Tallahassee, FL.
14. Mateos, P.F. ed. 1956. Obras de Padre Barnabé Cobo de la Compania de Jesus. Biblioteca de Autores Españoles, Atlas, Madrid. 952 pp.
15. Poma de Ayala, F.G. 1987. Nueva Cronica y Buen Gobierno. Murra, J.V., Adorno, R., and Urioste, J.L., eds. Historia 16, Madrid. 1384 pp.
16. Thurston, H.D. 1992. Sustainable Practices for Plant Disease Management in Traditional Farming Systems. Westview, Boulder, CO. 279 pp.
17. von Hagen, V.W. ed. 1959. The Incas of Pedro de Cieza de León. Harriet de Onis (trans.) Univ. Oklahoma Press, Norman. 397 pp.

PART II

Advances in Potato Pest Biology and Management: Insects

BIOLOGY AND MANAGEMENT OF SOIL INSECT PESTS OF POTATO IN AUSTRALIA AND NEW ZEALAND

J. N. Matthiessen
CSIRO Division of Entomology
Private Bag P.O. Wembley
Western Australia 6014
Australia

S. E. Learmonth
Horticultural Research Centre
Western Australian Department of Agriculture
Manjimup
Western Australia 6258
Australia

Australia and New Zealand are distinctive in having prominent in almost all potato-producing areas one or more of several soil-dwelling insects that are pests of potato. There are three main pests, all of which are Coleoptera: African black beetle, *Heteronychus arator* (Fabricius), whitefringed weevil, *Graphognathus leucoloma* (Boheman), and potato wireworm, *Hapatesus hirtus* Candèze. Minor pests include the coleopterans, small lucerne weevil, *Atrichonotus taeniatulus* (Berg), garden weevil, *Phlyctinus callosus* Boheman, false wireworms (Tenebrionidae), various pasture scarabs (Scarabaeidae) and wireworms (Elateridae), and the orthopterans, field cricket, *Teleogryllus* sp. and mole cricket, *Gryllotalpa* sp. Potato moth, *Phthorimaea operculella* (Zeller) occurs in both countries but because it is not strictly a soil-dwelling insect, it is not included here. None of the species are specific associates of potato, but rather are pasture-dwelling generalist feeders that have the potential to inflict economic levels of damage to crops such as potatoes that have a higher value than the pasture they temporarily replace during typical rotational usage of land.

History of Control and Research

In the past, prophylactic applications of organochlorine insecticides were made to ensure that the risk of attack by the main soil insect pests was minimized. It would appear that, largely as a result of the effectiveness of such insecticides in reducing losses, there was little stimulus to research in detail their biology and pest status. Furthermore, soil insects are widely recognized as being particularly difficult to study. The combination of these two factors seems to have been the principal reason why, until recently, research on soil insects in potato crops in Australia and New Zealand was directed almost exclusively towards field testing of chemical insecticides. These factors, and the apparent lack of a broad range of soil insect pest problems in potato crops in other parts of the world, mean that there is a paucity of information both on details of the biology of soil insects that are pests of potato and attempts at devising alternatives to insecticides for their management.

A recent upsurge in research on the biology and management of the main soil insect pests of potato in Australia has a common history related to concerns about the environmental consequences of overuse of persistent agricultural chemicals. While it is desirable to reduce the use of organochlorine insecticides, the limited or inconsistent efficacy of less persistent chemicals (26, Learmonth *et al.*, unpublished) and the low tolerance to insect damage on potato ensured continued use of these substances.

A radical change in approach was applied in Australia in 1987 when exports of meat were found to be contaminated with residues of organochlorine insecticides. In several parts of Australia, the contamination was traced back to use of the insecticides in potato production which is commonly rotated with pasture land (12,21). Approval for the use of those insecticides in agriculture was immediately withdrawn. This, in turn, precipitated a fundamental re-appraisal of approaches to control the main soil insect pests of potato. This chapter reviews the major soil insect pests of potato in Australia and New Zealand in the context of developments that occurred since the commencement of the post-organochlorine insecticide era.

Biology of the Main Pests

African black beetle. As the name suggests, African black beetle is native to Africa where it is recorded mainly as a pest of maize (5), but also of potato (27). It is subterranean in all stages of its life cycle, but adults fly actively and can be readily caught in light traps (28).

The adult stage is particularly damaging, attacking tubers and also severely reducing yield by severing of stems on young potato plants. Tubers are also attacked by larvae. Outside of Africa, the Australian and New Zealand region is the only area where African black beetle occurs. In New Zealand, it occurs only on the North Island, whereas in Australia, it occurs in coastal regions in the southeast from southern Queensland to South Australia, and in the southwest corner of Western Australia (1).

The biology and ecology of African black beetle has been extensively studied in New Zealand in pasture, where it is a pest in periodic outbreaks (19). The studies in New Zealand culminated in construction of life tables (18) and a simple population dynamics model which was used effectively to illustrate the basic mechanism behind the periodic pasture-damaging population outbreaks (19).

Larvae of African black beetle are generalist feeders on soil organic matter and plant roots (16). Roots of grasses, where adults tend to aggregate and oviposit (20), are a more favorable food source than those of legumes. While the eggs are tolerant of high soil moisture, the first of the three instars is not (18). In the moist temperate climate of New Zealand, this is the key mortality factor that diminishes when spring has lower rainfall than usual, leading to pasture-damaging outbreaks, particularly if there is a succession of dry years (19).

In southwestern Australia, where African black beetle reaches its greatest pest potential in potato crops, the insect is widespread in pastures and turf, but appears to be only a limited or sporadic pest in those habitats. General accounts of the life-history of African black beetle in southwestern Australia (15) suggest a similar univoltine seasonal pattern to that in New Zealand. The markedly different climates between the two areas, particularly the dry conditions of spring in the Mediterranean climate of southwestern Australia, which would cause outbreaks in New Zealand, suggested that direct extrapolation of New Zealand results was not appropriate. Studies on the biology of African black beetle in undisturbed annual pasture were undertaken to establish basic population parameters and relate them to its pest characteristics in potato crops (24).

African black beetle adults emerge in summer-autumn (January-May) and overwinter as reproductively immature and semi-mature adults. Final maturation and oviposition occurs in spring (September-November). Fecundity averages approximately 12 eggs per female and survival through the three larval instars is estimated at greater than 80% (24). Major losses from a local population occur through emigration of adults soon after emergence, and large fluctuations in African black beetle abundance in southwestern Australia are neither a measured nor anecdotal phenomenon.

Light trapping is currently showing that African black beetle flight activity is greater and more continuous during the adult emergence period (Learmonth, unpublished) than in New Zealand where flight is mainly in sporadic swarms (28). It appears that adult dispersal is a major population-regulating factor in southwestern Australia and the mechanism by which the dispersing adults (or their progeny) are lost to the population is currently under investigation (Matthiessen, unpublished).

Whitefringed weevil. Whitefringed weevil is of South American origin and the adults, which are innocuous to potato, are surface-dwelling, flightless and parthenogenetic. The subterranean larval stage is severely damaging to potato tubers. Note was made of whitefringed weevil damaging potatoes in Chile (3), but there are no subsequent references to it being a pest of potato in South America. Whitefringed weevil was first recorded as a pest of various underground crops in the southeastern USA in the 1930's and its life cycle was studied in general terms (29). Sparse information on the biology and seasonal development of the damaging larval stage appears to have largely been a consequence of the difficulty of sampling the small early stages (11), and also the effort required to culture the species in the laboratory (2).

In Australia and New Zealand, whitefringed weevil can cause some damage in pasture (7), but generally it is benign in that habitat. In tropical northeastern Australia, whitefringed weevil is more likely to be a serious problem if a potato crop follows too soon after a peanut crop (8) because population development is greatly favored by legume food (7,25).

Recently, the development of whitefringed weevil larvae has been examined in the laboratory (9). There are eleven larval instars, with the first instar being a non-feeding stage capable of prolonged survival. Total larval development requires over 300 days at 25.5°C. A wet sieving/flotation method for extracting all instars of whitefringed weevil from soil core samples was recently developed (22) and used to study the phenology of its populations in pasture in southwestern Australia (23).

Whitefringed weevil adults occur from summer to early winter (December-June), but upsurge in the numbers of first instars only occurs after the onset of winter rains in April. The winter rains induce germination of the annual pasture species, which includes the protein-rich legume subterranean clover *Trifolium subterraneum* L. It appears that it is only the few adults present after the rains begin that contribute significantly to the next generation (23). The principal reasons for this can be linked to the weevil's requirement for fresh legume food to attain high fecundity (7,25), and a combination of high humidity to ensure egg survival and immersion in water to stimulate egg hatch (10). In the Mediterranean environment of southwestern Australia these factors coincide only during the moist winter period (April-October).

During winter, whitefringed weevil populations are composed of mostly (95%) first instars present in high abundance (several hundred/m^2). Larval growth occurs in the spring-summer period (September-January). High mortality from unknown causes also occurs during this period which can reduce densities of late instars to 10/m^2 or less. The presence of some late-instars throughout the year suggests that a portion of the population does not complete development in the one year.

Requirements by whitefringed weevil for moisture and warmth (10,29), and its generally poor adaptation to the dry Mediterranean environment (23), suggested that in regions with a dry summer, high levels of soil moisture from irrigation might favor the development of populations. Matthiessen and Learmonth (unpublished) found that irrigation of otherwise undisturbed whitefringed weevil-infested annual pasture for the duration of the dry summer in southwestern Australia (November-April) increased larval survival by 2 to 3-fold but the rate of larval development was not affected. They also found that first instars of the following generation appeared in late summer, about two months earlier than usual. This probably resulted from induction of oogenesis by the unseasonal availability of high-quality food plants enhanced by high survival and rapid hatching of eggs, all results of the unseasonal moisture from irrigation.

Despite the enhanced survival of whitefringed weevil larvae caused by irrigation, there were fewer larvae in an adjacent non insecticide-treated irrigated potato crop compared with the irrigated pasture (Matthiessen and Learmonth, unpublished). This suggested that pre-plant cultivation which occurs in winter when whitefringed weevil larvae are mainly first instars helped to reduce weevil populations. Thus, the pest potential of whitefringed weevil is probably not enhanced by irrigation in potato crops, but it may be where irrigation occurs but cultivation does not or is infrequent, such as in alfalfa, *Medicago sativa* L.

Potato wireworm. The elaterid beetle, *H. hirtus*, which in Australia is known as the potato wireworm is an endemic species, most commonly found in the state of Victoria in southeastern Australia. Its natural habitats are grassland and forested areas. The early larval stages require high soil moisture for survival and they are most likely to be found in low-lying or poorly-drained areas. Larvae take several years to develop and this, along with its patchy occurrence, has precluded detailed studies of its biology or population ecology in its natural habitat.

Recently, a study of the life-history of the potato wireworm was undertaken on potato in Victoria, as a response to the withdrawal of the organochlorine insecticides (13). Removal of randomly selected soil cores (20x20x20 cm) was inadequate for sampling this wireworm because of the low density of insects present. Its phenology was determined by sampling larvae, primarily using halved potato tubers as baits. Ten larval instars were identified, most of which were present in the field throughout the year.

Within crops, larvae were attracted to seed pieces, and fed on them before tubers formed. In the absence of insecticides, the proportion of seed pieces damaged ten weeks after planting was indicative of the proportion of harvested tubers damaged. This method of sampling, however, was too late to be of use to potato growers because preventative insecticide applications are required before planting. Consequently, baits consisting of one-half of a potato tuber were buried in the ground (15 cm) for 18-35 days before planting, depending on season, to assess wireworm abundance and determine the need for insecticide treatments. Attack of these bait tubers by wireworms gave a reliable estimate of areas infested with wireworms, and wireworm abundance, while emphasizing the patchy distribution of wireworms. The proportion of baits attacked reliably forecasted the proportion of tubers damaged in nontreated crops, thereby providing a simple method for assessing the risk of damage to the subsequent potato crop.

Adult wireworms were often found under the bark of trees (*Eucalyptus* spp.) or under lumps of earth in ploughed potato fields. Dissection of adults showed that the testes in males had enlarged by early spring (September), and egg development in females occurred between early October and mid-November. It was inferred that most oviposition occurred in late November and December. No adults were found on the soil surface after late November.

Interactions With Potato

African black beetle and whitefringed weevil. Following withdrawal of the organochlorine insecticides, growers continued to apply replacement chemicals before planting and incorporate them into the soil. As before, the effectiveness of insecticide treatments was also assessed indirectly by measuring insect damage and yields, rather than by estimating insect abundance. Consequently, attempts to enhance the reduced efficacy of the substitute chemicals were restricted by availability of only limited empirical information.

Recently, Matthiessen and Learmonth (unpublished) determined the nature of damage caused by African black beetle and whitefringed weevil on potato. Sampling was carried out both in sections of crops treated with the standard chlorpyrifos insecticide treatment and in nontreated sections. The primary objectives of the sampling were to determine: the type of damage to potato plants by the soil insects; the timing of the damage in relation to plant phenology and the insect stages present; the degree of damage; and differences in damage between insecticide-treated and nontreated crops. Sample units consisting of 50 cm sections of the hilled-up rows were selected and dug to expose all the insects and plant parts. Hills were divided into nine zones (Fig. 1). As plant parts (seed piece, stems, tubers) and insects were encountered, their location in the soil hill, level of damage and associated insects were recorded in the appropriate zone of the hill.

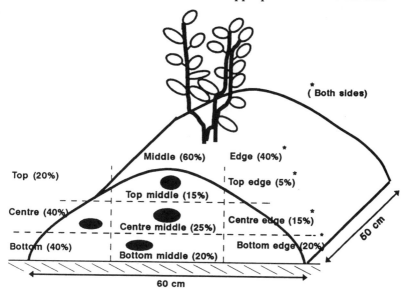

Fig. 1. Diagrammatic representation of a sample segment in a potato-growing hill showing the data-recording sections and the proportion of the exposed face that each comprised.

Fifty samples were taken in each treatment at regular intervals during the growth of potato crops. The distribution of insects, tubers and damage in the soil was determined relative to the proportion of the total cross-sectional area of each section (Fig. 1). In this way, a quantitative evaluation of where tubers, insects, and the location of the greatest intensity of insect attacks occurred was obtained.

Neither potato tubers nor soil insects were uniformly distributed in the soil profile. Tubers were concentrated in the middle and lower sections of the hill at around twice the density of a uniform distribution. They were under-represented by between 2-5 fold in the top and edge sections. African black beetle was present in upper middle areas of the soil profile at densities approaching twice that of a uniform distribution, while it was under-represented by 2-4 fold in the bottom and edge sections. Whitefringed weevil had an almost opposite distribution, being present in the lower middle sections of the soil profile at a density of about 2 fold greater than a uniform distribution. In turn, they were under-represented (by up to 11 fold) in the top and edge sections.

The effects of the two species on potato tuber damage in nontreated crops reflected their contrasting distributions. After taking into account the nonuniform distribution of tubers in the soil profile, African black beetle damage in the top middle sections was up to 3 fold higher than would be expected from a uniform distribution, and was 2-30 fold lower in bottom edge sections. Damage from whitefringed weevil was up to 3 fold greater than a uniform expectation in the bottom middle sections, and 4-40 fold lower in top edge sections of the soil profile.

The numbers of insects present were usually reduced by insecticide treatment, although African black beetle populations were reduced more than those of whitefringed weevil. This may have been due in part to the distribution of the two species in the soil profile. Despite their contrasting distributions, however, comparison of the relative distribution of live insects in insecticide-treated crops with that in nontreated crops revealed a consistent pattern of change. For both species, the insecticide caused a reduction in the proportion of the insects in upper and outer sections of the soil profile, and an increase in the lower and more central sections, despite attempts to uniformly disperse the insecticide by rotary hoeing.

Because of the concentration of the potato tubers in the deeper and middle parts of the potato hill, the insecticide-induced change in the relative distribution of insects impacted positively on their potential to damage tubers. The damage impact of African black beetle in the bottom section of the soil profile increased by as much as 16%. In the case of whitefringed weevil, the increased damage impact was about 8% in the same section. The general trend for both insects was that the insecticide treatment reduced the relative intensity of tuber damage in the upper sections, and increased it in the lower sections of the soil profile. Thus, although the soil-incorporated insecticide generally reduced the abundance of the pest insects, there was a relative increase in the proportion of those remaining in areas of the soil profile containing most tubers. Consequently, tuber attacks were not reduced by the same proportion as insect abundance.

The ability of African black beetle to cause stem damage was dramatically reduced by the pre-plant application of insecticide, and this in turn had a major effect on protection of gross tuber yield. However, the damage resulting from both species directly attacking tubers was more difficult to reduce. Both species made multiple attacks on tubers and damaged multiple tubers. Furthermore, the noxious effect was heightened by their tendency to cause tuber damage continuously from the time of tuber formation. In the case of African black beetle, immigration of newly-emerged adult beetles into potato from surrounding pastures during summer-autumn was also implicated as a cause of tuber damage in insecticide-treated crops.

Management Options

New sampling methods and knowledge of the biology and phenology of African black beetle and whitefringed weevil in pasture and potato crops presents two key advances. Firstly, it has opened up possibilities of more strategically directing insecticidal management. Secondly, it has made possible direct evaluation of the effectiveness of management strategies on populations of the pest insects, both in pasture and in potato crops, rather than relying on indirect evaluation by product assessment at harvest. Several alternative management options are currently being tested by the authors.

The first departures from traditional control methods have initially been directed at reducing adult abundance before oviposition occurs. In the case of African black beetle, foliar application of insecticides directly to pasture in late winter without incorporation into the soil has substantially reduced the subsequent abundance of larvae and consequently that of the new adult generation in summer, when most damage to potato occurs. Similar trials are being carried out against whitefringed weevil adults in the early autumn to limit oviposition at that time. While this technique does not eliminate the use of chemical insecticides, it targets what appears to be the most vulnerable period in the life cycle of each species. This approach eliminates the need for incorporation of insecticide into the soil and the concomitant deleterious effects of a rotary hoe on soil structure.

New knowledge concerning the impact of the soil insects on potato crop growth and the deficiencies of current soil-incorporated insecticide treatments also suggest ways of enhancing the efficiency of the more traditional control methods. In the case of whitefringed weevil, it appears that current soil-incorporation methods do not get sufficient amounts of the insecticide deep into the soil where they can kill the larvae which prefer deeper parts of the soil profile. Learmonth (unpublished) is currently working on a method for "injecting" some of the insecticide deeper into the soil at the time of planting.

In the case of African black beetle, advances have revealed constraints to the management tactics for that species. For example, it is clear that the high level of flight activity by emerging adults in the warm summer-autumn leads to re-invasion of crops during their growth. This flight activity occurs after pre-plant applications of insecticides, which usually reduce the abundance of African black beetle and protect the crop against the stem damage caused by this insect. The immigrants are generally not apparent, and cause tuber damage that is only revealed at harvest. Further studies using light traps to determine the full extent and nature of African black beetle flight activity are currently being carried out. An outcome may be the development of a warning (alert) system of African black beetle flights, to enable potato growers to check their crops to assess whether supplementary insecticide applications will be required.

Other management options that are being explored are cultural and biological controls. Cultural control options are aimed at crop rotation or associated methods to break the direct pasture-to-potato cycle. This method is being promoted in Queensland, specifically to break the peanut/potato continuum (8).

Greatest early promise with biological control has been the use of selected strains of the fungus *Metarhizium anisopliae* (Metchn.)Sorokin against African black beetle (Matthiessen & Milner, unpublished). Classical biological control options for African black beetle have previously been examined in New Zealand, but with little success or promise (4).

For potato wireworm, a soil-incorporated application of chlorpyrifos before planting was found to be an effective substitute for organochlorine insecticides in reducing tuber damage (13). Granular, controlled-release formulations of chlorpyrifos were not effective. The less persistent insecticides, however, have been found to be inconsistent against wireworms (26), and it was suggested that chlorpyrifos may have repelled wireworms from the potato tubers rather than killed them (13). Because of the successful use of potato tuber baits to assess wireworm populations before potatoes are planted, it was proposed (13) that growers could use the method to determine the need for insecticides, and to delineate the infested patches so that treatment could be restricted to only those areas that need it. Similar strategies have been developed elsewhere (see Jansson, et al. [this volume] for more detailed investigations on wireworm control strategies).

Epilogue

Future research on the biology and management of soil insect pests of potato in Australia and New Zealand will be aimed at building on the recent significant advances in our knowledge, and further developing the new control strategies that were stimulated by the withdrawal of the organochlorine insecticides. In the case of African black beetle, strategic applications of insecticide to pasture in late winter before the spring oviposition should help to limit pre-plant soil incorporation of insecticides and their associated deleterious effects on soil structure. The potential for invasive flights of African black beetle, which until recently was not well understood, presents a substantial challenge for management of this pest. Ongoing research is identifying the full significance of invasive flights, as well as seeking means of countering them. Because of the discovery of infective strains of *M. anisopliae* against African black beetle, biological control offers a significant opportunity for this pest that is being actively pursued in field tests.

Whitefringed weevil also presents a substantial challenge in that, despite recent advances in the understanding of its biology and ecology, there are unpredictable aspects that have thus far restricted the impact of alternative control methods, such as strategic pre-oviposition applications of insecticide to pasture. Further research to detail its biology pertinent to such control methods is being pursued. Techniques for developing deeper pre-plant application of insecticide to counter the propensity of this pest to attack deeply set tubers are also underway. A recent development that may have wider implications is the finding that the soil fumigant metham sodium has high insecticidal activity against whitefringed weevil. Despite its high cost, some growers are currently using this fumigant for this purpose. Additionally, laboratory tests of entomopathogenic nematodes as biological control agents against whitefringed weevil have yielded LC_{50} values about an order of magnitude above the current economically viable nematode concentrations (Matthiessen & Curran, unpublished), but further testing is warranted.

Biological studies on the potato wireworm are considered to be an adequate basis for developing and testing new management methods.

Baiting areas before planting potatoes offers a practical method that growers and pest monitoring services could adopt to forecast pest potential (see 14). Strains of *M. anisopliae* infective against this wireworm have recently been isolated, and field tests, initially in pasture, are determining infection and mortality under field conditions. Ultimately, *M. anisopliae* may be combined with baiting to provide an effective nonchemical control program in the future.

Acknowledgments

We thank the many colleagues in various entomological research and extension institutes in Australia and New Zealand who provided information on soil insects in their respective regions, in particular Dr. Paul A. Horne of the Plant Research Institute, Victorian Department of Agriculture and Rural Affairs, for information on potato wireworm and comments on the manuscript.

Literature Cited

1. Allsopp, P. G., and Hitchcock, B. E. 1987. Soil insect pests in Australia: control alternatives to persistent organochlorine insecticides. SCA Tech. Rep. No. 21. Australian Agricultural Council, Canberra. 123 pp.

2. Bass, M. H., and Barnes, E. E. 1969. A laboratory rearing technique for the white-fringed beetle. J. Econ. Entomol. 62:1512-1513.

3. Berry, P. A. 1947. Investigations on the white-fringed beetle group in South America. J. Econ. Entomol. 40:705-709.

4. Cameron, P. J., and Thomas, W. P. 1989. *Heteronychus arator* (F.), black beetle (Coleoptera: Scarabaeidae). Pages 17-21 in: A review of biological control of invertebrate pests and weeds in New Zealand 1874 to 1987. P. J. Cameron, R. L. Hill, J. Bain, and W. P. Thomas, eds. Tech. Comm. No. 10, CAB International Institute of Biological Control, Oxford. 424 pp.

5. Drinkwater, T. W. 1982. The control of the black maize beetle, *Heteronychus arator* (Col.: Scarabaeidae), in maize in South Africa. Phytophylactica 14:165-167.

6. East, R. 1977. Effects of pasture and forage crop species on longevity, fecundity, and oviposition rate of adult white-fringed weevils *Graphognathus leucoloma* (Boheman). N. Z. J. Exp. Agric. 5:177-181.

7. East, R. 1982. Interactions between whitefringed weevil *Graphognathus leucoloma* and legume species in the northern North Island. N.Z. J. Agric. Res. 25:131-140.

8. Fay, H. A. C., Brown, J. D., and De Faveri, S. 1989. Progress towards a management strategy for whitefringed weevil on the Atherton Tableland. Pages 17-21 in: Proceedings of a soil-invertebrate workshop. L. N. Robertson, and P. G. Allsopp, eds. Dept. Prim. Industries, Queensland. 106pp.

9. Gough, N., and Brown, J. D. 1991. Development of larvae of the whitefringed weevil, *Graphognathus leucoloma* (Coleoptera: Curculionidae), in northern Queensland. Bull. Entomol. Res. 81:385-393.

10. Gross, H. R., Mitchell, J. A., Shaw, Z. A., and Padgett, G. R. 1972. Extended storage of eggs of whitefringed beetles. J. Econ. Entomol. 65:731-733.

11. Harlan, D. P., Stewart, J. R., and Mitchell, J. A. 1970. A portable mechanical shaker for collecting larvae of the white-fringed beetle from soil. J. Econ. Entomol. 63:1018-1019.

12. Horne, P. A. 1988. Contamination of pasture by insecticides. Pages 109-114 in: Proc. 5th Australasian Conf. Grassl. Invert. Ecol., Melbourne.

13. Horne, P. A., and Horne, J. A. 1991. The life-history and control of *Hapatesus hirtus* Candeze (Coleoptera: Elateridae) in Victoria. Aust. J. Agric. Res. 42:827-834.

14. Jansson, R. K., Seal, D. R., and Lecrone, S. H. 1993. Biology and management of wireworms on potato. Pages xxx-xxx in: Advances in Potato Pest Biology and Management. G. Zehnder, R. K. Jansson, M. L. Powelson, and K. V. Raman, eds. APS Press, St. Paul, Minnesota.

15. Jenkins, C.F.H. 1965. The black beetle. J. Agric. West. Aust. 6:39-42.

16. King, P. D. 1977. Effect of plant species and organic matter on feeding behaviour and weight gain of larval black beetle, *Heteronychus arator* (Coleoptera:Scarabaeidae). N. Z. J. Zool. 4:445-448.

17. King, P. D., Meekings, J. S., and Mercer, C. F. 1982. Effects of whitefringed weevil (*Graphognathus leucoloma*) and black beetle (*Heteronychus arator*) populations on pasture species. N.Z. J. Agric. Res. 25:405-414.

18. King, P. D., Mercer, C. F., and Meekings, J. S. 1981. Ecology of black beetle, *Heteronychus arator* (Coleoptera: Scarabaeidae) - population studies. N. Z. J. Agric. Res. 24:87-97.

19. King, P. D., Mercer, C. F., and Meekings, J. S. 1981. Ecology of black beetle, *Heteronychus arator* (Coleoptera: Scarabaeidae) - population modelling. N. Z. J. Agric. Res. 24:99-105.

20. King, P. D., Mercer, C. F., and Meekings, J. S. 1981. Ecology of black beetle *Heteronychus arator* (Coleoptera: Scarabaeidae) - influence of pasture species on oviposition site preference. N. Z. J. Zool. 8:119-122.

21. Learmonth, S. E., and Sproul, A. N. 1988. Pasture rotation - the main source of insect pest problems in Western Australian potato crops. Pages 163-168 in: Proc. 5th Australasian Conf. Grassl. Invert. Ecol., Melbourne.

22. Matthiessen, J. N. 1989. Sampling whitefringed weevil and African black beetle in the potato/pasture system in south-western Australia. Pages 33-35 in: Proceedings of a soil-invertebrate workshop. L.N. Robertson, and P.G. Allsopp, eds. Dept. Prim. Industries, Queensland. 106pp.

23. Matthiessen, J. N. 1991. Population phenology of whitefringed weevil, *Graphognathus leucoloma* (Boheman) (Coleoptera:Curculionidae) in pasture in a mediterranean-climate region of Australia. Bull. Entomol. Res. 81:283-289.

24. Matthiessen, J. N., and Ridsdill-Smith, T.J. 1991. Populations of African black beetle, *Heteronychus arator* (F.) (Coleoptera:Scarabaeidae) in a mediterranean-climate area of Australia. Bull. Entomol. Res. 81:85-91.

25. Ottens, R. J., and Todd J. W. 1979. Effects of host plant on fecundity, longevity, and oviposition rate of whitefringed beetle. Ann. Entomol. Soc. Am. 76:837-839.

26. Stewart, K. M. 1981. Chemical control of wireworms (Elateridae) in potatoes. N.Z. J. Exp. Agric. 9:357-362.

27. Venter, R. J. H., and Louw, M. 1978. *Heteronychus arator* (Fabricius), a potentially dangerous pest of potatoes (Coleoptera: Scarabaeidae). Phytophylactica 10:99.

28. Watson, R. N. 1979. Use of a modified light trap to improve catches of black beetle, *Heteronychus arator* (Coleoptera: Scarabaeidae), and black field cricket, *Teleogryllus commodus* (Orthoptera: Gryllidae). N.Z. Entomol. 7:92-97.

29. Young, H. C., App, B. A., Gill, J. B., and Hollingsworth, H.S. 1950. White-fringed beetles and how to combat them. U.S. Department of Agriculture Circular No. 850, 15pp.

BIOLOGY AND MANAGEMENT OF WIREWORMS ON POTATO

Richard K. Jansson [1] and Dakshina R. Seal
Tropical Research and Education Center
University of Florida
Institute of Food and Agricultural Sciences
Homestead, FL 33031

There are numerous species of wireworms that attack potato worldwide. However, because of similarities in their biologies, common management approaches apply to most, if not all, species. The biology of wireworms, with particular reference to those species that attack the sweet potato, *Ipomoea batatas* (L.) Lam., was recently reported and reviewed (8, 9, 49-55). Others have reviewed the biology and management of wireworms on potato (44), and for these reasons, readers are referred to these papers for additional information. Additionally, the reader is referred to Keaster et al. (28) for a listing of research publications on the Elateridae through 1982.

Currently, little is known about the wireworms that attack potato in many regions of the world because this group of pests has been neglected in recent years. This point was made especially clear in a recent survey of potato researchers concerning their knowledge of wireworm problems on potato. The results of this survey are presented herein. The survey also identified the research needs and gaps in our knowledge of wireworms. Some of the most common research needs included: (1) the development of reliable sampling plans and economic thresholds for wireworms; (2) knowledge about the biology of wireworm species, including their identification; and (3) development of integrated pest management (IPM) programs for these pests which includes the use of cultural control strategies. Many of these gaps were recently filled for the corn wireworm, *Melanotus communis* (Gyllenhal), which is the predominant species attacking potato in southern Florida. A case study reviewing the

[1] Current Position: Senior Research Fellow, Merck Research Laboratories, Merck & Co., P.O. Box 450, Hillsborough Road, Three Bridges, NJ 08887-0450

development of a management program for this wireworm is presented later in this chapter.

Survey of Wireworm Problems on Potato

Researchers were polled regarding their knowledge of the status of wireworms as pests of potato in their representative regions of the world. Over 125 questionaires were distributed to researchers, of which 78 (62.4%) were returned. The results presented below are the responses of those researchers that returned the questionaire. Researchers were asked the following questions:

1. What is the pest status of wireworms on potato in the respondent's area? i.e., major pest, minor pest, not a pest, unknown?
2. Estimate the percentage of the total crop loss to potato due to wireworm injury and damage.
3. What are the principal wireworm species attacking potato in the respondent's area?
4. What factors are responsible for the development of wireworm outbreaks on potato?
5. What are the predominant chemical insecticides used by growers for wireworm control?
6. Has the respondent observed a recent increase in wireworm population build- up and concomitant damage to potato crops?
7. What are the most important control methods, other than chemical insecticides, recommended for wireworm management? Are growers currently using these alternative methods?
8. What natural enemies of wireworms are present in your area?
9. What are the major gaps in the knowledge base of wireworms on potato?

Outcome of the Survey

Composition of the respondents. Of the 78 respondents, 55 were from the United States. The remaining 23 respondents were from Australia (Western Australia and New South Wales), Canada (Quebec, Prince Edward Island, and New Brunswick), Colombia, Costa Rica, England, Finland, Germany, Hungary, India, Indonesia, Mauritius, New Zealand, Nigeria, Peru, Poland, Scotland, and Tunisia. Many of these respondents were asked to comment on wireworm problems outside of their country. For example, researchers with the International Potato Center (CIP) located in Colombia, Peru, India, Indonesia, Tunisia, and Mauritius were asked to respond to questions based on their knowledge of a particular region of the world.

Pest status. In general, wireworms were considered a minor pest of potato in most regions of the world. Only 6 respondents, one from Australia and five from the United States (Florida, Georgia, Idaho, Tennessee, and Utah), (7.7%) considered wireworms to be a major pest of potato. Fifty one respondents (65.4%) considered wireworms to be a minor pest. The remainder of the respondents (26.9%) indicated that wireworms were not a pest or, in some cases, they did not know their pest status.

Crop loss. Several researchers investigated crop loss due to various wireworm species, including, *Limonius canus* LeConte (18, 42, 62, 64), *L. californicus* (Mann.) (18, 64), *Ctenicera pruinina* Horn (62, 64), and *Melanotus communis* (Gyll.) (24). However, for the most part, little is known about the impact of most wireworm populations on crop loss. Results from the survey indicated that significant crop loss did not occur in most of the regions from which information was available. Significant crop loss was only reported in the United States and in Australia; however, signficant crop loss may also occur occassionally in parts of Canada, the United Kingdom, and New Zealand when conditions amenable to wireworm outbreaks on potato are present. In Australia, significant crop loss occurs only in Victoria and not in Western Australia. In the United States, crop loss is generally sporadic and varies both within and between states (Fig. 1). Crop loss has been most devastating (11-25% loss) in Florida (especially southern Florida) and Georgia, and can be significant (7-10% loss) in California, Idaho, and Nebraska. Crop loss (5-7% loss) may also occur in Virginia, Michigan, Pennsylvania, New Jersey, Wyoming, and Utah. Potato crop loss from wireworms is reportedly insignificant ($<$ 5%) in all other states. It should be noted that estimates on crop loss by the respondents were subjective and not necessarily based on experimentation.

Elaterid species attacking potato. Arnett (2) noted that there are 73 genera and 885 species of Elateridae in the United States and Canada. Keaster et al. (28) listed publications on 398 genera of Elateridae worldwide. The respondents listed thirty species of wireworms in 10 genera as pests of potato. An additional six species and two genera not

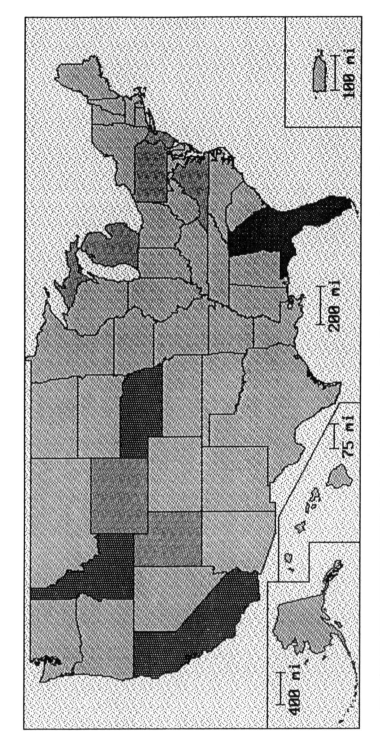

Fig. 1. Crop loss due to wireworms in the United States. Shading denotes the estimated levels of crop loss due to wireworms. Levels are (from lightest to darkest) 0-4, 5-7, 8-10, and 11-25% crop loss. Estimates based on respondents' perspectives only.

34

listed by the respondents were also listed as pests of potato by Radcliffe et al. (44). Other species not reported in the survey, but known to attack potato include *Ctenicera puncticollis* Motsch., *Agriotes fuscicollis* Miwa, and *Melanotus caudex* Lewis in Japan (30, 48). Thus, at least 39 species of wireworms may attack potato worldwide. These species are presented in Table 1. Some of these species are widely distributed, whereas others are of only regional or local importance. In general, the predominant pest species of potato vary from region to region; none of the species were circumglobal in their distribution. With such a large number of species attacking potato, any generalizations on life history and control are compromised.

Interestingly, 25 respondents (> 32%) indicated that they did not know the predominant wireworm species attacking potato in their region. Other respondents knew the genera of wireworms that attacked the crop; however, species identifications were not known. Thus, there is an obvious need to identify wireworm species attacking potato in many parts of the world. The importance of identification of wireworm pests was recently illustrated in Georgia (54), where a species previously reported to be an important wireworm pest was found to be low in abundance and a species previously unrecorded as a pest on sweet potato in Georgia was found to be the major wireworm pest (54). Such presumptions could seriously impair management tactics because of species differences in biology and behavior.

Factors that enhance wireworm outbreaks. Several factors were listed as important for developing outbreaks of wireworms on potato. The most common factor associated with wireworm outbreaks was the cropping history of the field. Potatoes are most vulnerable to wireworm outbreaks when they follow a favorable host in the rotation, such as grasses, permanent pasture, or sod within 1-3 years. Other crop associations important for enhancing wireworm outbreaks in potato include: small grains, alfalfa, weedy fields, sagebrush (California), alfalfa (New York and California), sugarbeet (Utah), peanut, and sweet potato (Georgia). The impact of the previous crop on wireworm incidence and damage to potato has been demonstrated in Florida (24, 34). They showed that wireworm populations and concomitant damage to potatoes were significantly greater in potatoes that followed sorghum-sudangrass than in those that followed mechanical fallow.

Another factor noted as important in enhancing wireworm problems on potato was soil drying. When soils dry out, wireworms presumably seek moisture from potato tubers. Recent studies in southern Florida confirm this belief. Wireworm feeding activity differed in soils with differing soil moisture levels. In general, the drier the soil, the greater the incidence of wireworm feeding (56).

Table 1. Wireworm species reported to attack potato.

Species	Common Name	Origin of Report
Aeolus mellillus		ME, KY, IL
Agriotes spp.		India, Central America
Agriotes fuscicollis Miwa		Japan
Agriotes lineatus (L.)	Lined click beetle	England
Agriotes mancus (Say)	Wheat wireworm	Canada, ME, NE, NY, IL, Central America
Agriotes obscurus	Dusky wireworm	Scotland, England, Canada
Agriotes sputator		England
Agrypnus variabilis (Candeze)		New Zealand, Australia
Athous haemorrhoidalis		England
Conoderus sp.		Indiana
Conoderus spp.		SC
Conoderus amplicollis (Gyll.)	Gulf coast wireworm	Southern U.S.
Conoderus exsul (Sharp)		New Zealand
Conoderus falli Lane	Southern potato wireworm	NC, FL
Conoderus lividus		KY, IL
Conoderus rudis (Brown)		GA, FL
Conoderus scissus		AL, GA
Conoderus verspertinus (F.)	Tobacco wireworm	NC, NJ, TN
Ctenicera sp.		ID
Ctenicera aeripennis destructor (Brown)	Prairie grain wireworm	ND
Ctenicera pruinina (Horn)		OR, WA, ID, NE, UT, CA
Ctenicera puncticollis Motsch.		Japan
Ctenicera strangulata (White)		New Zealand
Hapatesus hirtus Candeze		Australia
Hemicrepidius memnonius		IL

36

Table 1 (continued)

Horistonotus uhlerii Horn	Sand wireworm	Southern U.S.
Hypolithus abbreviatus (Say)	Abbreviated wireworm	Midwestern U.S.
Hypolithus bicolor		Canada
Limonius sp.		IN
Limonius agonus (Say)	Eastern field wireworm	Canada, DE, MA, NH, PA
Limonius canus LeConte	Pacific Coast wireworm	CA, ID, OR, UT, WA
Limonius dubitans		IL
Limonius ectypus		NY
Limonius infuscatus Motsch.	Western field wireworm	UT, WA
Limonius subauratus LeConte	Columbia Basin wireworm	WA
Melanotus sp.		ME, CO
Melanotus spp.		MI, NE, NJ
Melanotus caudex Lewis		Japan
Melanotus communis (Gyll.)	Corn wireworm, community wireworm	FL, NC, NY
Melanotus communis-dietrichi		KY, IL
Melanotus cribulosis		IL
Melanotus depressus		IL
Melanotus lanie-opacicollis		IL
Melanotus pilosus		IL
Melanotus similis		IL
Melanotus verberans		IL

Chemical control. Over the past 50 years, there have been numerous studies on the efficacy of soil insecticides and fumigants at controlling various species of wireworms on potato. A brief literature search found over 50 refereed publications on chemical control of wireworms on potato since 1937. These studies tested various types of chemicals ranging from chlorinated fumigants, arsenicals, and chlorinated hydrocarbon insecticides to modern synthetic insecticides.

The survey found that twelve chemical insecticides are currently being used for wireworm control on potato (Table 2). Phorate (Thimet), fonofos (Dyfonate), ethoprop (Mocap), and diazinon are currently the most commonly used chemical insecticides for wireworm control. Of the insecticides listed, phorate, disulfoton, parathion, aldicarb, carbofuran, fonofos, fensulfothion, and diazinon have been used for wireworm control on potato since the 1960's. In addition, chlorpyrifos and ethoprop have been used on potato since the 1970's. With such a large numbers of relatively old chemical insecticides and a lack of newer insecticides, there is a need to develop soil insecticides for wireworm control as current insecticides are lost over time due to their reduced effectiveness, removal from the crop by the Environmental Protection Agency, or lack of re-registration.

Insecticide resistance in various wireworm species has been reported (4, 20, 21, 39, 43, 47), and resistance of *M. communis* to phorate in potato has been suspected (25). None of those surveyed indicated that insecticide resistance in wireworms was a problem in their area.

Many respondents indicated that insecticides are not used for wireworm control. In New Zealand, insecticides are currently not used

Table 2. Chemical insecticides commonly used for wireworm management.

Chemical insecticide	No. of respondents indicating usage
Phorate (Thimet)	26
Fonofos (Dyfonate)	22
Ethoprop/Ethoprophos (Mocap)	19
Diazinon	14
Disulfoton (Di-Syston)	7
Carbofuran (Furadan)	6
Chlorpyrifos (Lorsban)	4
Aldicarb (Temik)	3
Fensulfothion (Dasanit)	3
Oxamyl (Vydate)	2
Parathion	1
Terbufos (Counter)	1

despite the potential severity of the pests. Their use is not recommended because modern insecticides fail to have the long residual activity necessary for adequate efficacy. Other respondents indicated that insecticides were not used because (1) wireworms were not a problem, or (2) the cost of insecticides was prohibitive (developing countries).

Resurgence of wireworm problems? Ten of the 78 respondents (12.8%) noted that wireworm problems may be increasing. Wireworms are becoming increasingly more important in certain parts of Idaho, California, Delaware, Kansas, North Carolina, Nebraska, Washington, Canada, and Australia. Reasons suggested for the recent increase in wireworm problems included: changes in the farming systems, especially the increased rotation with grasses; and the removal of insecticides with long residual activity in the soil.

Alternate control strategies. Respondents listed several alternate control strategies that growers may be using for wireworm management. These included: use of appropriate rotation schemes and avoidance of planting of potato after favorable hosts; use of pre-plant sampling schemes to identify problematic fields and switching to other crops in these fields; fallowing of infested fields; and control of alternate weed hosts. Cultural practices have long been recognized as important components in wireworm control. Delayed planting of potato (19, 45) or its off-season cover crop (24, 34), crop rotation (37, 38, 46, 52, 58), fallowing during the off season (34), and flooding (7, 32) can reduce wireworm incidence and damage to crops. Most respondents indicated that growers had integrated some alternative tactics into their crop production systems, although these approaches were not integrated specifically for wireworm management in all cases.

Natural enemies of wireworms. A dearth of information was obtained from respondents regarding the presence of natural enemies of wireworms in potato. Although several natural enemies were listed, including birds, various carabid beetles, *Metarhizium* sp., *Beauveria* sp., certain mammals, and other wireworm species, no published reports are available on any of these organisms. Various wireworm species are known to be cannibalistic and predacious (3, 14, 29). Other natural enemies reported in the literature include Carabidae and Staphylinidae (17), a bethylid parasite (22), and entomopathogenic nematodes (11, 65). Morris (35) found that the prairie grain wireworm, *Ctenicera aeripennis destructor* (Brown), was not susceptible to two entomopathogenic nematodes, *Heterorhabditis bacteriophora* Poinar and *Steinernema carpocapsae* (Weiser). Similarly, preliminary tests in southern Florida found that the corn wireworm, *M. communis*, was also not susceptible to these nematodes (R.K. Jansson and S.H. Lecrone, unpublished).

Gaps in wireworm knowledge base. Numerous research needs were emphasized by the respondents. The most important gaps in the knowledge base included: (1) improved methods for sampling wireworms and predicting crop loss due to wireworms, including the development of economic thresholds; (2) information on the population dynamics/biology of wireworms that attack potato in a given region, including studies on seasonal movement of larvae, adult movement, feeding activity of larvae, factors affecting adult oviposition, and the effects of soil conditions on larvae; (3) identification of wireworm species attacking the crop in a given region; (4) development of integrated pest management (IPM) programs for wireworm control, including the incorporation of appropriate crop rotation schemes and other cultural practices; (5) development of varieties with resistance; (6) survey for and impact of natural enemies on wireworms; and (7) insecticide resistance and development of replacement chemical insecticides for wireworm control. Of these, the first three needs were listed as most important for a wide variety of species.

The above-mentioned gaps in the knowledge base were also true for potato production systems in southern Florida in 1986. Studies were conducted over a 6 year period to develop a management program for *M. communis* on potato in southern Florida. The following is a case study on the biology of this wireworm and the management program that we developed.

Biology of *M. communis*

Few studies have been conducted on the biology of *M. communis*. We report here some of our recent studies conducted in southern Florida on the biology of this pest.

Adult activity. *M. communis* adults were more active during the night than during day. During the day, adults hid under plant matter and in soil crevices. A similar behavior was observed in the laboratory when adults were placed in plastic boxes with the bottom covered with moistened paper towels. Adults were active until they hid on the underside of the paper. In a field study, 50 pitfall traps were placed in a harvested potato field. Traps were checked twice a day at 0600 and 1700 EST for several weeks. Most adults were found in samples collected at 0600 EST; few adults were found in samples collected at 1700 EST.

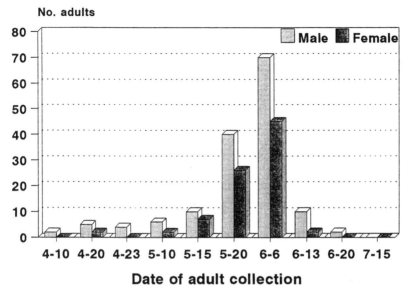

No. adults

Fig. 2. Emergence pattern of *M. communis* adults from soil in southern Florida in 1990.

Emergence pattern of *M. communis* adults. In April 1990, about 6,000 larvae were collected from different potato fields in Dade County, FL. These larvae were reared in plastic tubs (34 cm deep, 30 cm diam) filled with Perrine marl soil. Five hundred larvae were placed in each tub along with a sufficient amount of carrot and/or potato tuber pieces as food. The tubs were checked for adults twice monthly for six months. Most adults emerged in late May to early June (Fig. 2). Males emerged before females. Similar results were also found in two studies that monitored flight activity patterns of *M. communis* over several years in southern Florida (10, R. K. Jansson et al., unpublished).

Oviposition behavior. *M. communis* females laid most eggs at night; few eggs were laid during the day. Eggs were laid in soil crevices or under dead plant material in shady areas of fields and in woodlands. Most eggs were laid in batches; single eggs were rarely laid. Females oviposited between 50 and 130 eggs. The oviposition period ranged from April to August. Peak oviposition was observed in either April (1989) or May (1990).

Larval behavior and abundance. First instar larvae did not disperse from the site of oviposition. First instars were gregarious;

larvae dispersed after the first molt, which occurred within 15-20 days after oviposition in the laboratory (24 ± 2°C). Small larvae (1st-3rd instars) fed on small rootlets and organic matter in the soil. Older larvae (> 4th instar) were often cannabalistic, but fed mostly on potato tubers, roots of weeds, and organic matter.

Small larvae rarely made holes in mature tubers. Third instars made very narrow and shallow holes (1 mm) when reared on potato and carrot. Older larvae made deep holes (3.1 ± 0.05 mm diam.; 2.1 ± 0.1 mm deep) on matured tubers.

Small larvae were most abundant in soil samples in May and June; medium-sized larvae (3rd-5th instars) were most abundant in June; large larvae were most abundant between April and June (Fig. 3). No small larvae (1st instars) were found in August. Late instars (> 3rd) were found most of the year.

Vertical distribution and movement of larvae. An understanding of larval movement of wireworms in soil is important for evaluating the effectiveness of sampling methods, and for targeting placement and timing of soil-applied chemical insecticides. Several studies determined vertical movement of larvae of different wireworm species (5, 15, 27, 31, 36, 57). Nothing is known about movement of *M. communis*. In potato fields, *M. communis* larvae were found up to 40 cm below soil surface in a harvested potato field in April, 1990 (57). Below 40 cm, the Perrine marl soil changes to a Rockdale (Krome very gravelly loam/coral rock) base. Most wireworms were recorded at a depth between 21-31 cm in the soil. About 90% of small larvae (1st-3rd instar) were observed between 0-20 cm in the soil. First instars were rarely observed in deeper soil zones (> 20 cm deep).

During the growing season, wireworms migrated upward to developing tubers (57). Few wireworms were recorded around the tubers within 5-9 weeks after planting. Most wireworms were recorded around tubers within 2 - 4 weeks before harvest. In March and April (harvest), most wireworms were observed within 20 cm of soil surface (Table 3). Wireworms moved down in the soil after April when harvesting ceased.

Wireworms prefer cooler moister soil in southern Florida in the absence of a food source. In an experiment, 20 late instars (> 5th instar) were released on the surface of a cement box (55 x 55 x 60 cm) filled with Perrine marl soil. Wireworms moved deeper in each box over time (57). In a complementary study, larvae were released at the bottom of the box, and none of the wireworms moved above 20 cm from the bottom of the box up to 5 weeks after release (57). After 7 weeks, only two larvae moved up 30 cm from the bottom of the box.

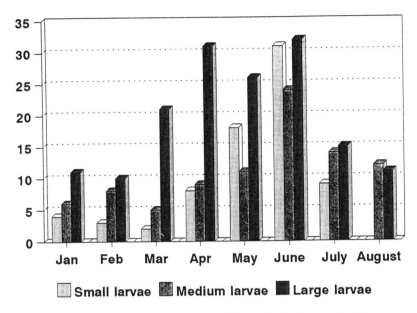

Small larvae   **Medium larvae**   **Large larvae**

Fig. 3. Seasonal abundance of *M. communis* larvae in Perrine marl soil between January and August of 1990 in Homestead, Florida.

Table 3. Vertical distribution of *M. communis* in Perrine marl soil in different months of the year in southern Florida.

Depth	Mean number of wireworms per sample		
(cm)	April	July	October
10	0.28b	0.14b	0.05b
20	1.34a	0.36a	0.15a
30	0.09c	0.33a	0.17a

Means within same column followed by the same letter are not different ($P < 0.05$); Waller-Duncan K-ratio t test.

Movement of wireworms is also affected by the feeding activity of larvae. When larvae are in a feeding stage of development and food is available, wireworms direct their movement toward the food source. When rolled oat baits were placed 10 cm below the surface of the soil in the cement box (as above), 40% of larvae released at the bottom and 70% of larvae released on the surface were found in or near the bait (57). Stone and Foley (59) reported greater upward movement than downward movement in *Limonius californicus* (Mannerheim) when food was present. Larvae in a nonfeeding mode, however, did not move even in the presence of food. Doane (12) observed that when most *Ctenicera destructor* (Brown) larvae were in an appetitive phase, they responded to germinating food.

Lateral distribution and movement of larvae. Samples collected around potato plants found that larvae of all sizes (small, medium and large) were more abundant within a 10 cm radius of plants than between the zone extending from 10 to 20 cm of the plant (D.R. Seal and R.K. Jansson, unpublished). No larvae were found in the soil between the rows.

In an experiment in cement boxes (60 x 50 x 130 cm) containing Perrine marl soil (15-20% moisture), about 30, 20, 10, 10, and 10% of wireworms moved 20, 30, 60, 80, and 120 cm laterally, respectively, after 1, 2, 3, 4, and 5 weeks, respectively (D.R. Seal and R.K. Jansson, unpublished). Lateral movement was similar in soils with a high (20%) organic matter at the same moisture level. In a very moist soil (40-45%), no wireworms moved beyond 30 cm laterally even after 5 weeks. In this soil, mortality was 40, 30, 40, 60, and 80% after 1, 2, 3, 4, and 5 weeks.

Feeding behavior of larvae. Larvae of all stages fed periodically on carrot and potato tubers. Feeding activity varied over time and between 18-60% of larvae were in a feeding stage. (D.R. Seal and R.K. Jansson, unpublished). Larvae that fed on carrot made fewer feeding holes when transferred to potato tubers than those that were starved before the experiment. In a food preference test that compared carrot, potato, corn seed, and rolled oats, more larvae fed on carrot followed by rolled oats, corn seed and potato (D.R. Seal and R.K. Jansson, unpublished). Another experiment found that feeding activity of this wireworm varied with soil temperature and the moisture content of the soil (56).

In a potato field planted in December 1990, wireworm larvae rarely fed on developing tubers one month after planting. Numbers of wireworm damaged tubers increased during the growing season. A significant increase in wireworm feeding holes on tubers was recorded 11 weeks after planting (Table 4). Numbers of feeding holes increased considerably each week thereafter until harvest (D.R. Seal and R.K. Jansson, unpublished). Toba and Turner (61) developed a sampling method in which wireworm damage to tubers was monitored after plant emergence. These studies indicate that the time of the season when tubers are examined might have a significant impact on inferences on the severity of the population because feeding damage increases as the season progresses.

We have classified wireworm feeding holes as deep (> 1 mm), shallow (< 1 mm), and healed (shallow feeding scars). Deep and shallow holes are the result of recent feeding; healed holes are old scars caused by previous wireworm feeding. An evaluation of these types of holes during the season found that numbers of deep holes were greater 7 weeks after

Table 4. Abundance of wireworms and wireworm damage holes on different sampling dates in a potato field in southern Florida.

Variable (Mean/sample)	Weeks after planting		
	7	9	11
Mean no. of wireworms	0.00+0.01	0.05+0.01	0.10+0.02
Mean no. of damaged tubers	0.61+0.12	1.32+0.18	10.75+0.72
Mean no. of deep holes	0.43+0.12	0.65+0.12	14.99+1.21
Mean no. of shallow holes	0.48+0.20	0.59+0.13	1.63+0.28
Mean no. of healed holes	0.02+0.02	0.27+0.10	0.91+0.18

planting than other hole types, when numbers of wireworm per sample were = 0.05 (D.R. Seal and R.K. Jansson, unpublished). Numbers of deep feeding holes peaked 11 weeks after planting when numbers of wireworms per sample were = 0.10. Few healed holes were found on all sampling dates indicating that wireworms fed mostly on tubers closer to harvest.

In a laboratory study, we found that each feeding hole was made by an individual wireworm (D.R. Seal and R.K. Jansson, unpublished). After feeding, wireworms moved away from the tuber and rested. Few wireworms were observed around damaged tubers. *L. carlifornicus* larvae were also found to move away from baits placed in the field after feeding ceased (63).

Wireworm Management in Southern Florida: A Case Study

M. communis has been the single most important constraint to potato production in southern Florida for many years. Other species identified, but of little or no consequence to the crop include: the southern potato wireworm, *Conoderus falli* Lane, *C. rudis* (Brown), gulf coast wireworm, *C. amplicollis* (Gyll.), and *C. scissus*. The pest status of *M. communis* is linked to the farming system used by growers. After harvest, growers typically plant a sorghum-sudangrass hybrid cover crop in the fields for the summer. This cover crop is extremely attractive to elaterid adults which move into established sorghum-sudangrass fields and oviposit. The cover crop is then mowed and disced into the soil in the fall before potatoes are planted. Larvae which hatch from eggs then attack the developing tubers. This rotation has been followed for many years in southern Florida, thereby enhancing the perennial wireworm problem on the crop each year.

During the past several years, growers have typically relied on soil insecticides applied before planting (fonofos or parathion) and in the furrow at planting (phorate) to manage wireworm populations. Applications of these insecticides were routinely made without knowledge of the wireworm densities present in fields. For this reason, a forecasting system of wireworm crop loss was developed to help growers optimize and reduce insecticide use, reduce environmental contamination, and increase grower profits. In addition, a cultural control method was developed to reduce the reliance on chemical insecticides.

Cultural control of wireworms (off-crop management). As noted above, potato fields are planted with a cover crop during the summer to improve the tilth of the soil, reduce soil compaction, and minimize weed problems in the following potato crop. Most recently, growers have relied on the use of a sorghum-sudangrass hybrid, *Sorghum bicolor* (L.) Moench x *S. arundinaceum* (Desv.) Stapf var. *sudanese* (Stapf (Hitchc.), as a cover for their fields. Unfortunately, this grass is very attractive to adult elaterids. A recent study (34) found that the wireworm abundance and damage to potato was correlated with the length of time that the cover crop was present in fields during the summer. Based on their study, we conducted an experiment to determine the effects of planting date (late vs. early) and mowing on the abundance of wireworms and their concomitant damage to potato tubers. We found that wireworms were 14- to 45-fold more abundant in plots planted early than in those planted later in the summer (24). Also, crop loss due to wireworm feeding was $1,800 to $3,400 per ha higher in potatoes that followed early-planted cover crop than in those that followed late-planted cover crop. Thus, delaying the planting of the summer crop resulted in a significant decrease in wireworm abundance and associated crop loss. Mowing of cover crops (early or late) had little impact on wireworm abundance and associated crop loss (24). Based on these data, growers have adopted the use of a late-planted cover crop to reduce wireworm problems in potato.

Forecasting system for predicting wireworm damage. The need for predicting wireworm-associated crop loss in potato has long been recognized (33). One of the major gaps in the knowledge of *M. communis* in southern Florida was a useful sampling plan for estimating wireworm population densities and predicting concomitant damage to the crop at harvest. Several researchers developed sampling plans for wireworms on potato (23, 26, 40, 41, 60, 61). Early studies developed sampling plans by randomly collecting soil samples and recording the numbers of larvae found in each sample. However, because most wireworm species are extremely aggregated in fields, these methods required an excessive number of samples to reliably estimate wireworm populations. Recent studies in southern Florida confirmed this finding (26). As a consequence, researchers developed alternate sampling approaches including the use of sequential sampling plans (41) and plans that used food baits. Many researchers have examined the use of food baits as a sampling tool (1, 6,

12, 13, 16, 49, 51, 55, 63, 66). Jansson and Lecrone (23) tested various food baits for preplant sampling of wireworms in potato fields in southern Florida. They found that rolled oat baits were the most attractive food bait for sampling *M. communis* larvae (23). They subsequently determined the numbers of rolled oat baits that were needed to reliably estimate wireworm numbers in potato fields before planting (26).

Rolled oat baits were used to develop economic thresholds for wireworm larvae before planting. Various wireworm densities were established in research plots in potato fields by varying the time of year that the summer cover crop was planted. Previous research demonstrated that wireworm abundance and damage to potato was related to planting date and the length of time that the cover crop was present in potato fields during the summer (24, 34). Research plots with various cover crop planting date/mowing combinations were sampled for wireworm abundance before potatoes were planted in the fall. Plots were then planted with potato and harvested the following spring. Wireworm injury and damage to size A and B potatoes at harvest were related to wireworm numbers per bait before planting. (Table 5). The average for two years (1988 and 1989) was then used in a model to simulate economic loss from wireworms (R.K. Jansson et al., unpublished).

Table 5. Regression relationships between wireworm injury and damage (%) to potato tubers of different sizes and mean no. of wireworms per rolled oat bait sample in 1988 and 1989 in southern Florida.

Year	Size	Injury or damage	Regression Equation	P	r^2
1988	A	Injury	Y = 3.71+2.29X	0.001	0.73
1989	A	Injury	Y = 7.87+1.26X	0.005	0.25
1988	A	Damage	Y = 1.61+1.11X	0.0001	0.62
1989	A	Damage	Y = 4.93+1.64X	0.003	0.27
1988	B	Injury	Y = 0.23+0.20X	0.001	0.30
1989	B	Injury	Y = 0.48+0.08X	0.05	0.13
1988	B	Damage	Y = 0.02+0.01X	0.007	0.21
1989	B	Damage	Y = 0.27+0.05X	0.09	0.10

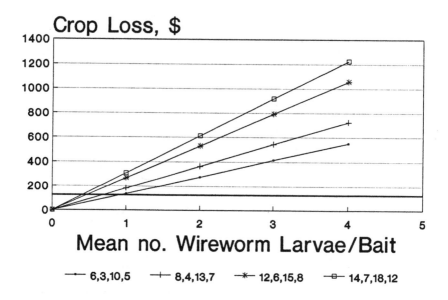

Crop Loss, $

Legend:
— 6,3,10,5   —+— 8,4,13,7   —*— 12,6,15,8   —□— 14,7,18,12

Fig. 4. Relationship between crop loss ($/ha) and mean no. of wireworm larvae per rolled oat bait under four different crop price scenarios (see below).

Crop loss scenarios were developed based on price of U.S. No. 1 and 2 size A and B. potatoes, injury and damage of wireworm larvae to tubers, and mean numbers of wireworm larvae per bait (Fig. 4). The following equation was used to calculate crop loss:

$$CL = [(wwia \times p1a) - (wwia \times p2a)] + [wwda \times p1a] + [(wwib \times p1b) - (wwib \times p2b)] + [wwdb \times p1b]$$

where *wwia* and *wwib* are the number of harvest units (22.7 kg bag) injured by wireworms for size A and B potatoes, respectively; *wwda* and *wwdb* are the number of bags damaged by wireworms for size A and B. potatoes, respectively; and *p1a, p2a, p1b,* and *p2b* are prices per bag for U.S. no. 1 A, U.S. No. 2 A, U.S. No. 1 B and U.S. No. 2 B potatoes, respectively. The prices selected for the model were within the range of seasonal average prices growers had been receiving for their crop between 1987 and 1990. Four levels of pricing ranging from the highest to the lowest prices were used: $6, 10, 3, and 5; $8, 13, 4, and 7; $12, 15, 6 and 8; and $14, 18, 7 and 12 per bag for U.S. No. 1 A, U.S. No. 1 B, U.S. No. 2 A, and U.S. No. 2 B potatoes, respectively.

Table 6. Economic thresholds for *M. communis* (mean no./rolled oat bait) in potato fields before planting. Thresholds are presented for each of four price scenarios and three control cost scenarios.

Potato prices U.S. no. and size				Cost of wireworm control/ha, $		
1 A	2 A	1 B	2B	50.01	111.73	148.76
6	3	10	5	0.4	0.8	1.1
8	4	13	7	0.3	0.6	0.8
12	6	15	8	0.2	0.4	0.6
14		7	18	12	0.2	0.4 0.5

Economic thresholds were computed using three different control cost scenarios. Management options currently available and their costs include fallowing ($24.70/ha), scouting (pre-plant sampling [$25.31/ha]), pre-plant broadcast application of chemical insecticide ($24.70/ha) and its associated application cost ($12.35/ha), and in-furrow at planting application of chemical insecticide ($61.72/ha). Three control scenarios typically used include: (1) fallowing ground during the summer and scouting the following fall ($50.01/ha); (2) the above with an application of chemical insecticide in the furrow at planting ($111.73/ha); and (3) all of the above with the addition of a pre-plant broadcast application of insecticide ($148.78/ha). Economic thresholds for each of these control scenarios were then computed for each of the four potato pricing scenarios where the threshold equals the numbers of wireworms per bait that caused an amount of crop loss equal to the cost of control. Table 6 shows 12 economic threshold levels for this wireworm (4 price scenarios x 3 control cost scenarios). The economic threshold developed is simple, and can be adjusted to account for changes in potato prices and control costs in the future. Such a model will allow growers to have more flexibility in deciding their management options for wireworms in the future.

Acknowledgment

We thank S. H. Lecrone for technical assistance and Dan Williams and Sons, Alger Farms, C. F. Daigle Jr. for permission to use their potato fields. This research was supported by a grant to R.K.J. from the South Florida Potato Growers Exchange.

Literature Cited

1. Apablaza, J.U., Keaster, A.J., and Ward, R.H. 1977. Orientation of corn-infesting species of wireworms toward baits in the laboratory. Environ. Entomol. 6:715-718.

2. Arnett, R.H., Jr. 1985. American insects: A handbook of the insects of America north of Mexico. Van Nostrand Reinhold Co., New York. 850 pp.

3. Begg, J.A. 1957. Observations on the life-history of the eastern field wireworm, *Limonius agonus* (Say), under laboratory conditions. Rept. Entomol. Soc. Ontario 87:7-11.

4. Brett, C.H., Jones, G.D., Mount, D.A., and Rudder, J.D. 1966. Wireworms in sweet potatoes; resistance to cyclodiene insecticides and control with a midsummer application of insecticide over foliage. J. Econ. Entomol. 59:99-102

5. Bryson, H.R. 1935. Observations on the seasonal activities of wierworms (Elateridae). J. Kansas Entomol. Soc. 8:131-140.

6. Bynum, E.D., Jr., and Archer, T.L. 1987. Wireworm (Coleoptera: Elateridae) sampling for semiarid cropping systems. J. Econ. Entomol. 80:164-168.

7. Campbell, R. E., and Stone, M. W. 1938. Flooding for the control of wireworms in California. J. Econ. Entomol. 31:286-291.

8. Chalfant, R.B., and Seal, D.R. 1991. Biology and management of wireworms on sweet potato. Pages 303-326 in: Sweet potato pest management: a global perspective. R.K. Jansson, and K.V. Raman, eds. Westview Press, Boulder, Colorado and London. 458 pp.

9. Chalfant, R.B., Jansson, R.K., Seal, D.R., and Schalk, J.M. 1990. Ecology and management of sweet potato insects. Annu. Rev. Entomol. 35:157-180.

10. Cherry, R.H., and Hall, D.G. 1986. Flight activity of *Melanotus communis* (Coleoptera: Elateridae) in Florida sugar cane fields. J. Econ. Entomol. 79:626-628.

11. Danilov, L.G. 1974. Susceptibility of wireworms to the infestation by the nematode, *Neoaplectana carpocapsae* Weiser, 1955, str. agriotos. Bull. All-Union Res. Inst. Plant Protection 30:54-57.

12. Doane, J.F. 1981. Evaluation of a larval trap and baits for monitoring the seasonal activity of wireworms in Saskatchewan. Environ. Entomol. 10:335-342.

13. Doane, J.F., Lee, Y.W., Klinger, J., and Wescott, N.D. 1975. The orientation response of *Ctenicera destructor* and other wireworms (Coleoptera: Elateridae) to germinating grain and to carbon dioxide. Can. Entomol. 107:1233-1252.

14. Dobrovsky, T.M. 1954. Laboratory observations on *Conoderus vagus* Candeze. Fla. Entomol. 37:123-131.

15. Fisher, J.R., Keaster, A.J., and Fairchild, M.L. 1975. Seasonal vertical movement of wireworm larvae in Missouri: influence of soil temperature on the genera *Melanotus* Escholtz and *Conoderus* Escholtz. Ann. Entomol. Soc. Am. 68:1071-1073.

16. Foster, D.G., and Ward, C.R. 1976. Wireworm bait traps in grain sorghum. Texas Agric. Exp. Stn. PR-3425.

17. Fox, C.J.S., and MacLellan, C.R. 1956. Some Carabidae and Staphylinidae shown to feed on a wireworm, *Agriotes sputator* (L.), by the precipitin test. Can. Entomol. 88:228-231.

18. Gibson, K. E. 1939. Wireworm damage to potatoes in the Yakima Valley of Washington. J. Econ. Entomol. 32:121-124.

19. Gibson, K. E. 1956. Cultural practices affecting wirewom injury to potato. J. Econ. Entomol. 49:99-102.

20. Gunning, R.V., and Forrester, N.W. 1984. Cyclodiene lindane resistance in *Agrypnus variabilis* (Candeze) (Coleoptera: Elateridae) in northern New South Wales. J. Aust. Entomol. Soc. 23:247-248.

21. Guthrie, F.E., Rabb, R.L., and Mount, D.A. 1963. Distribution and control of cyclodiene-resistant wireworms attacking tobacco in North Carolina. J. Econ. Entomol. 56:7-10.

22. Hall, D. G. 1982. A parasite, *Pristocera armifera* (Say), of the wireworm *Melanotus communis* (Gyll.) in south Florida. Fla. Entomol. 65:574.

23. Jansson, R.K., and Lecrone, S.H. 1988. Evaluation of food baits for pre-plant sampling of wireworms (Coleoptera: Elateridae) in potato fields in southern Florida. Fla. Entomol. 72:503-510.

24. Jansson, R.K., and Lecrone, S.H. 1991. Effects of summer cover crop management on wireworm (Coleoptera: Elateridae) abundance and damage to potato. J. Econ. Entomol. 84:581-586.

25. Jansson, R.K., Lecrone, S.H., and Cherry, R.H. 1988. Comparative toxicities of fonofos and phorate to different populations of *Melanotus communis* (Gyllenhal) in southern Florida. Can. Entomol. 120:397-400.

26. Jansson, R.K., Lecrone, S.H., and Seal, D.R. 1989. Food baits for pre-plant sampling of wireworms (Coleoptera: Elateridae) in potato fields in southern Florida. Proc. Fla. State Hort. Soc. 102:367-370.

27. Jones, E.W., and Shirck, R.H. 1942. The seasonal vertical distribution of wireworms in the soil in relation to their control in the Pacific Northwest. J. Agric. Res. 65:125-142.

28. Keaster, A.J., Jackson, M.A., Ward, S.S., and Knause, G.F. 1988. A worldwide bibliography of Elateridae. Missouri Agric. Exp. Sta., University of Missouri-Columbia, Columbia. 294 pp.

29. Kring, J.B. 1959. Predation and survival of *Limonius agonus* Say (Coleoptera: Elateridae). Ann. Entomol. Soc. Am. 52:534-537.

30. Kuwayama, S., Sakurai, K., and Endo, K. 1960. Soil insects in Hokkaido, Japan, with special reference to the effects of some chlorinated hydrocarbons. J. Econ. Entomol. 53:1015-1018.

31. Lafrance, J. 1968. The seasonal movements of wireworms (Coleoptera: Elateridae) in relation to soil moisture and temperature in the organic soils of southwestern Quebec. Can. Entomol. 100:801-807.

32. Lane, M.C., and Jones, E.W. 1936. Flooding as a means of reducing wireworm infestations. J. Econ. Entomol. 29:842-850.

33. MacLeod, G.F., and Rawlins, W.A. 1935. A comparative study of wireworms in relation to potato tuber injury. J. Econ. Entomol. 28:192-195.

34. McSorley, R., Parrado, J.L., Tyson, R.V., Waddill, V.H., Lamberts, M.L., and Reynolds, J.S. 1987. Effects of sorghum cropping practices on winter potato production. Nematropica 17:45-60.

35. Morris, O.N. 1985. Susceptibility of 31 species of agricultural insect pests to the entomopathogenic nematodes *Steinernema feltiae* and *Heterorhabditis bacteriophora*. Can. Entomol. 117:401-407.

36. Nadvornyi, V.G. 1971. Vertical migrations of wireworms (Coleoptera: Elateridae) in cultivated lands of the Smolensk region. Redobiologia 11:46-57.

37. Nash, K.B., and Rawlins, C.A. 1941. Wireworm studies in several potato rotation systems. J. Econ. Entomol. 34:287-290.

38. Nettles, W.C. 1940. Effects of substitute crops and rotations on wireworm control. J. Econ. Entomol. 33:644-646.

39. Norris, D.M. 1957. Failure of soil insecticides to control the southern potato wireworm *Conoderus falli* Lane. Bull. Entomol Soc. Am. 3:40.

40. Onsager, J.A. 1969. Sampling to detect economic infestations of *Limonius* spp. J. Econ. Entomol. 62:183-189.

41. Onsager, J.A. 1974. A sequential sampling plan for classifying infestations of southern potato wireworm. Am. Potato J. 51:313-317.

42. Onsager, J. A. 1975. Pacific coast wireworm: relationship between injury and damage to potatoes. J. Econ. Entomol. 68:203-204.

43. Onsager, J. A., and Maitlen, J. C. 1966. Susceptibility of wireworms to aldrin in eastern Washington. J. Econ. Entomol. 59:1120-1123.

44. Radcliffe, E.B., Flanders, K.L., Ragsdale, D.W., and Noetzel, D.M. 1991. Pest management systems for potato insects. in: CRC Handbook of pest management in agriculture, 2nd edition. Vol. 3. D. Pimentel, ed. CRC Press, Boca Raton.

45. Rawlins, C.A. 1939. Planting dates as affecting wireworm injury to potato tubers. J. Econ. Entomol. 32:761-765.

46. Rawlins, C.A. 1940. Biology and control of the wheat wireworm, *Agriotes mancus* Say. Cornell Univ. Agr. Expt. Sta. Bull. 738.

47. Reid, W.J., Jr., and Cuthbert, F.D. 1956. Resistance of the southern potato wireworm to insecticides. J. Econ. Entomol. 49:879-880.

48. Sakurai, K. 1952. On the wireworms injurious to potatoes and their control in Hokkaido. Oyo-Kontyu 8:34-41.

49. Seal, D.R. 1990. Biology and management of wireworms affecting sweet potato in Georgia. Ph.D. Dissertation, University of Georgia, Athens.

50. Seal, D.R., Chalfant, R.B., and Hall, M.R. 1991. Distribution and density of wireworms and their damage in relation to different cultivars of sweet potato. Proc. Fla. State Hort. Soc. 104:284-286.

51. Seal, D.R., Chalfant, R.B., and Hall, M.R. 1992. Effectiveness of different seed baits and baiting methods for wireworms (Coleoptera: Elateridae) in sweet potato. Environ. Entomol. 21:957-963.

52. Seal, D.R., Chalfant, R.B., and Hall, M.R. 1992. Effects of cultural practices and rotational crops on abundance of wireworms (Coleoptera: Elateridae) affecting sweet potato in Georgia. Environ. Entomol. 21:969-974.

53. Seal, D.R., McSorley, R., and Chalfant, R.B. 1992. Seasonal abundance and spatial distribution of wireworms (Coleoptera: Elateridae) in Georgia sweet potato fields. J. Econ. Entomol. 85:1802-1808.

54. Seal, D.R., and Chalfant, R.B. 1993. Bionomics of *Conoderus rudis* (Brown) (Coleoptera: Elateridae): a newly reported pest of sweet potato in Georgia. J. Econ. Entomol. (in press).

55. Seal, D.R., Chalfant, R.B., and McSorley, R. 1993. Seasonal abundance and mathematical distribution of wireworms and wireworm damage holes in sweet potato fields in Georgia. J. Econ. Entomol. (in press).

56. Seal, D.R., and Jansson, R.K. 1994. Feeding behavior and growth of *Melanotus communis* (Gyllenhal) (Coleoptera: Elateridae): effect of moisture, temperature, and food. J. Econ. Entomol. (in press).

57. Seal, D.R., and Jansson, R.K. 1994. Vertical movement of *Melanotus communis* (Gyllenhal) (Coleoptera: Elateridae) larvae in laboratory and field conditions. J. Econ. Entomol. (in press).
58. Shirck, F.H. 1945. Crop rotations and cultural practices as related to wireworm control in Idaho. J. Econ. Entomol. 38:627-633.
59. Stone, M.W., and Foley, F.B. 1955. Effect of season, temperature, and food on the movement of the sugar-beet wireworm. Ann. Entomol. Soc. Am. 48:308-312.
60. Toba, H.H., and Turner, J.E. 1976. Why sample for wireworms. Pages 31-33. in: Proceedings of 15th annual Washington State conference and trade fair. Moses Lake, Washington.
61. Toba, H.H., and Turner, J.E. 1981. Seed piece examination: a method for sampling wireworms on potatoes. J. Econ. Entomol. 74:718-720.
62. Toba, H.H., and Turner, J.E. 1981. Wireworm injury to potatoes in relation to tuber weight. J. Econ. Entomol. 74:514-516.
63. Toba, H.H., and Turner, J.E. 1983. Evaluation of baiting techniques for sampling wireworms (Coleoptera: Elateridae) infesting wheat in Washington. J. Econ. Entomol. 76:850-855.
64. Toba, H. H., Turner, J.E., and Powell, D. M. 1981. Relationship between injury and damage to potatoes by wireworms. Am. Potato J. 58:423-428.
65. Toba, H.H., Lindegren, J.E., Turner, J.E., and Vail, P.V. 1983. Susceptibility of the Colorado potato beetle and the sugarbeet wireworm to *Steinernema feltiae* and *S. glaseri*. J. Nematol. 15:597-601.
66. Ward, R.H., and Keaster, A.J. 1977. Wireworm baiting: use of solar energy to enhance early detection of *Melanotus depressus*, *M. verberans*, and *Aeolus mellillus* in midwest cornfields. J. Econ. Entomol. 70:403-406.

COLORADO POTATO BEETLE:
DIVERSE LIFE HISTORY
POSES CHALLENGE TO MANAGEMENT

Donald C. Weber and David N. Ferro
Department of Entomology
University of Massachusetts
Amherst, MA 01003

The Colorado potato beetle (CPB), *Leptinotarsa decemlineata* (Say), has a diverse and flexible life history. Its dispersal, diapause, feeding, development and reproduction vary greatly over its geographic range, and also within local populations. This mosaic of responses to biotic, abiotic and xenobiotic environmental factors has given it the status of a superpest in the north temperate zone. Reliance on chemical control has been remarkably unsuccessful, provoking pesticide resistance and environmental contamination in an increasing number of regions. The development of alternative management tactics will prove a challenge to potato growers and researchers. This chapter reviews the expanding research on CPB, with an emphasis on cultural controls, as a basis for sustainable and environmentally-sound management strategies for this pest.

An International Superpest

CPB first shifted from its native hosts in southwestern North America to cultivated potato approximately 150 years ago. This host range expansion facilitated its spread to much of the rest of the continent, and then to Europe and Asia via its introduction to France in 1921. The distribution of CPB in North America covers about 8 million km^2, an enormous expansion of its original geographic range (32). The Old World geographical range now includes at least 6 million km^2, and is still spreading eastward into Asia (36). CPB may soon shift to expanding potato monocultures in areas of Mexico where it presently feeds on wild *Solanum* hosts (6). The beetle is capable of occupying diverse environments within temperate and subtropical regions. Climatically favorable regions it does not yet occupy include most of China, temperate Soviet east Asia, Korea, Japan, areas of the Indian subcontinent, parts of North Africa and Asia Minor, and the temperate Southern Hemisphere (36,65,73).

The CPB is oligophagous, feeding principally on the nightshade genus *Solanum*. Original hosts were buffalobur (*Solanum rostratum* Dunal), *Solanum elaeagnifolium* Cavanilles, and *Solanum angustifolium* Miller in the southwestern USA and Mexico. The principal cultivated food throughout most of its range is the potato; eggplant and tomato are other crop hosts. The CPB has also expanded its host range to include several non-crops, namely *Solanum dulcamara* L. in northeastern USA and Europe, *Solanum carolinense* L. in the southeastern USA, *Solanum sarrachoides* Sendtner in the western USA, and *Hyoscyamus niger* L. in USA and Europe (26,28,32,33). There is considerable geographic variation in host utilization by CPB, both in the original and expanded portions of its geographic range (30,31,32).

Reproduction And Development

Depending on the latitude, climate and host availability, CPB may have one, two or three generations per year. Developmental studies have found a generation time from egg to adult of as little as 21 days, with a developmental threshold of about 10°C and an optimal temperature range of 25° to 30°C (16). However, temperature-development relationships differ among populations (55). Mating is multiple and polygamous, with partial sperm precedence and male guarding of mated females (5,54). There is a female contact sex pheromone of unknown structure which prompts mating by males (34). Lab studies have shown oviposition to be variable, with females typically laying a total of 500 to 1000 eggs in masses of 20 to 60 eggs on the undersides of foliage (33,44,48,69). The female is almost always inseminated prior to hibernal diapause; therefore, the postdiapause female need not mate prior to dispersal and reproduction in the spring (17,57).

Diapause occurs in the adult and may be hibernal or aestival. Photoperiod is the primary factor triggering hibernal diapause, which is preceded by a period of feeding without reproduction (10,12). Diapause results from exposure to short days, although the critical photoperiod ranges from 12 to 16 hours (longer in the north) (13,31). Food quality and temperature are also important in inducing both hibernal and aestival diapause (11,26,56). In northern latitudes, the beetle burrows in the soil, typically to about 20 cm depth, but sometimes up to 50 cm (40,62,70). In southern parts of North America, adults diapause at the soil surface (32). The burrowing habit provides protection against extreme winter temperatures. Exposure to -8°C or lower temperatures will result in beetle mortality (38,51,65). CPB overwintering mortality is inversely related to depth of diapause in the soil in New Jersey, Massachusetts and Turkey (24,40,70). Mortality is also correlated with late diapause and low prediapause weight (21,46).

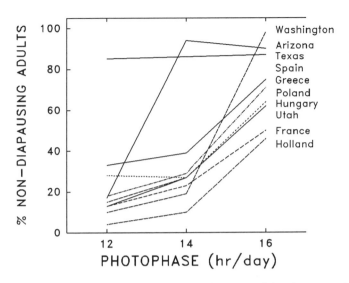

Fig. 1. Diapause response of European and American Colorado potato beetle populations to photoperiod (13,31).

Both European and American populations show marked geographic variation in diapause induction, and one south Texas population was found to be insensitive to daylength (Fig. 1)(13,20,31). Even within a single population, when maintained on optimal food, there may be enormous variation in response in terms of diapause and reproduction. The result is that each generation of CPB typically contributes to the diapausing population underground (21,31,56). It has been demonstrated that beetles may remain in diapause over 2 or more winters (2), and may diapause more than once (48,62).

Pesticide Resistance

In the agricultural context, the resistance of CPB to insecticides is its most spectacular attribute. Shortly after its shift to potato and migration eastward in North America, insecticides became the main CPB control method. In fact, the first widespread application of insecticides in agriculture was against CPB. Development of several new pesticides and modern application technologies were prompted by this pest (19). Starting with its evolution of resistance to DDT in the mid-1950s, the CPB has developed resistance to all major classes of chemical insecticides (18). Factors that apparently favor resistance development are:

1) Use of too-low thresholds for control, prophylactic treatments, or an eradication mentality. Relatively high damage thresholds are feasible

in many growing regions because the potato plant is capable of withstanding substantial defoliation, particularly after bloom (14,25,77).

2) Failure to develop and use alternatives to chemical control, including crop rotation and biological control. Cultural and biological control can reduce the number of chemical applications significantly.

3) Occurrence of two or more generations per year. None of the areas experiencing serious resistance have univoltine populations.

4) Lack of non-crop hosts to act as reservoirs of susceptible beetles. The presence of solanaceous weeds in the western and southeastern USA may have partly mitigated resistance development.

The Long Island growing area of New York (USA) represents perhaps the worst case for these conditions encouraging resistance. Nonetheless, resistance is almost as serious in other parts of the eastern USA (18,60), and has also been detected in many areas of Canada (43) and Europe (4,18,53,76). As the beetle invades new territory in Asia, this scenario may be repeated. Agricultural privatization in central and eastern Europe and former Soviet republics may encourage more intensive chemical control, which in turn will promote resistance development if prudent management of CPB is not practiced.

The failure of chemical controls over large portions of the CPB's distribution has prompted increasing research into the mechanisms and management of pesticide resistance. The biochemical diversity of response to different classes of pesticides is astounding (9). Kennedy and French (37) and other researchers have developed straightforward resistance monitoring techniques which avert unexpected control failures and may assist in conserving the dwindling resource of pesticide susceptibility. The long-term strategies for averting additional pesticide resistance, including resistance to foliar-applied or transgenic microbial controls, may involve a variety of strategies for optimal CPB suppression (22,50).

The clear lesson of resistance is that non-insecticidal tactics must be thoroughly integrated into CPB management strategies of the future. Much research is now focusing on biological and cultural controls (27), including plant resistance (59).

Biological Controls

Natural enemies have been inadequate for control of CPB in commercial crops. Our limited knowledge about natural enemies, and the historical reliance on chemical controls, have limited their usefulness. Endemic natural enemies include *Myiopharus* spp., tachinid larval-pupal parasitoids; three species of pentatomid stink bugs which prey on the larvae; the coccinellid egg predator *Coleomegilla maculata* (DeGeer); the carabid *Lebia grandis* Hentz, a pupal ectoparasitoid as well as predator of CPB eggs; and *Beauveria bassiana* (Balsamo) Vuillemin, a fungal pathogen. Ferro evaluates these and other biocontrol agents in detail (15).

Cultural Controls

Cultural controls include crop rotation, delayed or early planting, trap cropping and disruption of overwintering habitats.

Crop rotation generally delays colonization of early-season CPB (39,74), and may result in reduced numbers of pesticide applications needed for control, and a delay in the development of pesticide resistance (49). Rotation works best where fields are well separated from one another, and in regions not heavily planted to potatoes. We have seen great success with this tactic at a site in Berkshire County, Massachusetts, which is outside a major potato-growing area. The grower was able to alternate potato and non-host plantings either across a major river, or to fields several km apart. Crop rotation may be less successful in an area with much potato acreage, particularly when conditions encourage abundant spring dispersal of overwintered adults. The very warm spring of 1991 in the Connecticut River Valley potato-growing region of Massachusetts stimulated early spring emergence of overwintered beetles, well before many potato fields had been planted. The resulting regional flight of large numbers of beetles began in late May, reducing the potential benefit of crop rotation.

Late planting aims to delay crop emergence until after post-diapause beetles have emerged and left the field by flight, thereby avoiding early beetle colonization. Simulation models indicate that, if adult beetle feeding on the crop is delayed by 10 or more days, a dramatic reduction in the second generation larval population is possible, compared with a beetle population feeding on a crop planted at the normal time (Fig. 2). Because the first generation of summer adults (the offspring of the overwintered colonizers) emerge later in the season on the late-planted crop, the shorter photoperiod stimulates reproductive diapause, largely eliminating the second generation larval impact on the crop.

Early planting has been recommended for CPB management in North America and in Europe (8,63). The purpose is to use rapidly-maturing varieties for an "early in, early out" approach which also eliminates the second summer generation, in this case by removal of the crop. In some areas, this practice may be jeopardized by a cold, wet period after spring planting which results in increased incidence of plant disease. Altered planting and harvest dates (both early and late) also may be inappropriate in some regions because of the phenology of other

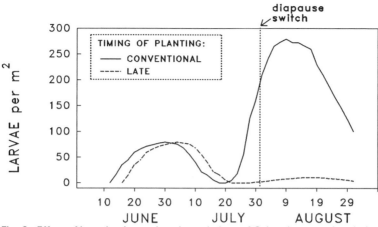

Fig. 2. Effect of late planting on larval populations of Colorado potato beetle (model output adapted from 68). "Diapause switch" refers to critical photoperiod, after which emerging beetles will not reproduce.

pests and diseases.   Even in areas where it may be practical, altered planting seasons may not be compatible with grower practices or specific market "windows."   Boiteau (3) cites the possible benefits of regional simultaneity in planting dates for New Brunswick because of the redistribution of beetles from early-planted to late-planted crops, followed by increased fecundity on the younger foliage.

Trap cropping may be effective in intercepting newly-emerged, overwintered beetles which would otherwise colonize the main crop (71). Even if a trap crop is not planted, potato rows bordering last year's crop or overwintering areas may arrest many beetles, thereby functioning as a trap crop which may be monitored and treated (50).   In experimental trap cropping of Massachusetts CPB moving into a field from aggregations in woody borders (69), we have reduced colonizing numbers by approximately one-half.   However, many overwintered adults newly emerged from diapause do not remain on potato plants which they encounter (35), a behavior which may limit efficacy of trap cropping.   It is possible that antifeedants can be combined with trap cropping and microbial controls in the early season for a stimulo-deterrent approach to CPB behavior modification (1).   Late-season trap-cropping has also been used experimentally to intercept beetles dispersing away from senescing potatoes (45).

Overwintering CPB aggregations also may be targeted for disruption. In Massachusetts, beetles concentrate in the soil of woody field borders to diapause (70). These or other diapause sites may be disrupted. Milner et al. (45) and Wyman et al. (75) report on the application and removal of straw mulch to produce cold-shock mortality in diapausing beetles. Diapause may also be disrupted by soil tillage (28). Other potential tactics involve increasing disease inoculum, spring trap cropping adjacent to aggregations, or simple confinement of emerging beetles with spunbonded row covers. These controls must be developed with attention to potential impacts on natural enemies. The predator *Coleomegilla maculata* overwinters in woody vegetation along field borders (29), and the parasite *Myiopharus* overwinters inside the diapausing CPB adult (42). Therefore both species may be adversely affected by these or other CPB disruption tactics aimed at diapause aggregations.

Dispersal

Knowledge of CPB dispersal, and the factors which encourage or discourage it, is very important for cultural management programs. The phenology of dispersal is key to the success of altered planting date and crop rotation strategies. The effectiveness of trap-cropping depends both on its attractiveness to the beetle and on its arrestant qualities. The magnitude of movement to and from non-crop hosts has implications in the short term for population dynamics of the beetles and pest management of the crop. In the longer term it may also be important in averting resistance, depending on specific genetic mechanisms and the magnitude of gene flow between crop and non-crop populations. More generally, knowledge of dispersal is an important component in understanding CPB evolutionary history and gene flow among populations.

The beetle is capable of walking at approximately 1 cm/s (58), and may move several hundred meters in the field in this manner. Walking speeds in the field are strongly affected by vegetation; 1 cm/s was the maximum observed on bare ground, while speeds were at least 10 times slower in grass turf and in a tall wheat crop (47). For walking beetles, Visser and coworkers have cited non-specific plant olfactory cues as attractants to hosts (64). However, other workers have questioned whether these are important in the field, and have emphasized chance encounter and visual cues for host-finding (35).

CPB flight is encouraged by high temperatures, sunlight, and other factors detailed below. Compared with walking, flight increases the speed of dispersal to between 2 and 3 m/s, yielding a range of several km (69, 70a). Given favorable meteorological conditions, CPB can fly more than 100 km, as evidenced by its incursions across the North Sea to Scandinavia (72). Its spread through North America (61) and Asia (36) has also exceeded 100 km in some years, although this could result from repeated short flights or human-assisted transport. CPB flight behavior was highly variable among our Massachusetts test populations, and flight probably varies in importance from region to region. For instance, CPB flight is rarely seen in the Netherlands (13).

Flight plays a major role in the life history of the CPB in Massachusetts. As documented by Voss & Ferro, there appear to be three distinct types of flight in CPB which differ in characteristics as well as in function (66). Both sexes perform all three types of flight behavior.

Short-range or *trivial* flight occurs within the host habitat. This is a low-altitude flight with frequent turning. Trivial flight may serve to spread eggs within a field, or for mate-finding by males. For both sexes this flight serves a short-range bet-hedging function (52) and allows sampling of the habitat for higher-quality resources.

Long-range or *migratory* flight is straight-line, often downwind flight which initially is not involved with host location. That is, the beetle is not searching for food immediately after take-off. The factors affecting the duration of this refractory period are not known. Long-range flight is most frequently performed by post-diapause adults which do not encounter food upon emergence. These adults have enormous energy reserves, and may fly several km with little difficulty. Long-range flight may also occur later in the season, although our field data show that it is considerably less frequent. A proportion of overwintered adults also undertakes long-range flight following feeding and reproduction.

Subsequent (summer) generations of beetles require food after pupation to enable flight. They feed and reproduce on the crop, and may subsequently undertake long-range flight. Because this may involve departure from an apparently suitable habitat, this dispersal may be attributed to a large-scale type of bet-hedging in which the insect has an incentive to distribute offspring not just within a habitat, but among different habitats as well.

The third type of flight which can be distinguished is *diapause flight*. This is a specialized type of flight which in Massachusetts takes the beetle from its summer habitat (typically potato) to a wooded site or uncultivated border area where it burrows into the soil to diapause. Diapause flight is low-altitude, directed flight which often starts with a spiraling ascent from the crop to approximately 5 m altitude, and a subsequent orientation to tall vegetation. Beetles flying to the woody borders appear to drop to the soil immediately upon contact with tree foliage. They are uninterested in feeding, and commence digging immediately. This results in an extremely clumped distribution of overwintering adults at wooded borders. Diapause flight is preceded by a period of reproduction on the crop, then a period of feeding with no oviposition. Beetles that emerge late in the season (after early August in western Massachusetts) neither reproduce nor undertake diapause flight; they must diapause in the crop habitat or walk to overwintering sites.

Seasonality of dispersal. Fig. 3 represents the seasonal occurrence of different types of CPB dispersal in northeastern USA. In the spring (late May and early June in western Massachusetts), overwintered beetles rarely fly if they emerge directly into a host habitat such as a planted potato field. They feed, and females begin oviposition about 5 days later. If emerged beetles do not initially find host plants (either because they overwintered outside the previous year's crop, or because the crop has been rotated or planted late) beetles will first walk in search of host plants. If temperature and solar radiation are high, these beetles will undertake long-range flight in search of hosts (7,41). These long-distance flights may continue for about two weeks, and result in movement of several km (17).

During mid-summer, the majority of flight is of the trivial type within the host habitat or between adjacent fields. This applies to post-diapause beetles as well as subsequent generations which have already found food plants and reproduced. A small proportion of beetles, after feeding and reproducing, depart apparently favorable habitats by long-range flight.

During the late season, beetles emerging from pupation before the critical photoperiod for diapause induction (early August in western Massachusetts) reproduce and feed for several days, may engage in trivial flight, and then cease reproduction. After additional feeding, they then may undertake a diapause flight to nearby wooded borders, where they burrow into the soil and spend the winter. In contrast, adults emerging after the diapause switch (68)(see Fig. 2) do not reproduce or fly. Depending on the distance to habitats reached by diapause flight and the phenology of late-season beetle eclosion, the overwintering sites may contain beetles which walked to the site, flew to the site, or a mixture of both.

Flight mill experiments. Using a computer-linked flight mill system (70a), we were able to test the flight of 12 beetles simultaneously, and to compare beetles of different age, sex, and food regimes. In tests with overwintered females (17), we have shown that starved beetles flew more frequently, and for greater duration and distances, than those fed potato foliage. Beetles were flown for one hour per day, and held at 25°C with 16:8 L:D photoperiod. Starved overwintered females flew almost four times as much as fed overwintered females (Fig. 4). The situation was much different for summer generation females reared and flown under the same long-day conditions. Fed summer females flew approximately the same times and distances as fed overwintered females, but starved summer females were incapable of flight.

We also performed experiments with overwintered beetles in which diet was switched 10 days post-emergence (either starved then fed potato, or fed potato then starved) (69). After the diet switch, feeding immediately arrested flight behavior in previously starved beetles. Beetles starved after 10 days of feeding flew less than 25% as much as those initially starved. This latter treatment mimicked the situation in which a temporary trap crop was encountered by beetles soon after emergence, and indicated that overwintered beetles, when starved subsequent to feeding, were less likely to undertake lengthy flights.

EARLY SEASON

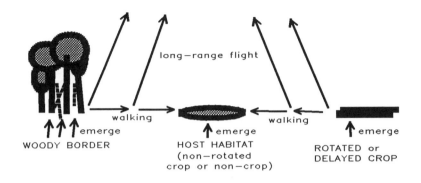

long—range flight

walking   walking

↑ emerge   ↑ emerge   ↑ emerge
WOODY BORDER   HOST HABITAT   ROTATED or
                (non—rotated   DELAYED CROP
                crop or non—crop)

MID-SEASON

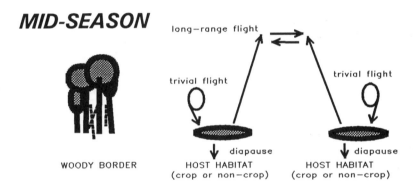

long—range flight

trivial flight   trivial flight

WOODY BORDER   ↓ diapause   ↓ diapause
                HOST HABITAT   HOST HABITAT
                (crop or non—crop) (crop or non—crop)

LATE SEASON

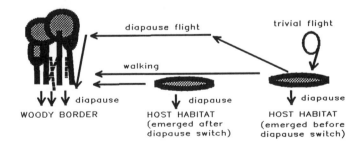

diapause flight   trivial flight

walking

↓↓↓ diapause   ↓ diapause   ↓ diapause
WOODY BORDER   HOST HABITAT   HOST HABITAT
                (emerged after (emerged before
                diapause switch) diapause switch)

Fig. 3. Phenology of dispersal in Colorado potato beetle, northeastern USA.

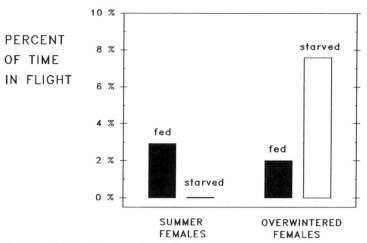

PERCENT OF TIME IN FLIGHT

Fig. 4. Flight of Colorado potato beetle females for first ten days after emergence, one hour per day on flight mill. Fed beetles were provided with potato foliage and moist dental wick; starved beetles only the wick.

Implications of dispersal patterns. The physiological readiness for flight after diapause, and the lack of flight readiness immediately after adult eclosion, suggests that a sudden mid-season disappearance of host plants was not common in the evolutionary history of CPB. Conversely, it suggests that dispersal to locate new host habitats after diapause has been important. The question of when such behaviors evolved in CPB—whether they are adaptations or preadaptations to potato crop ecosystems—can only be addressed by investigating the beetle's rela-tionship to ancestral hosts, particularly the spatial and temporal distribution of plant resources useful to the beetle. This will give a better understanding of the factors inherent in the CPB's dispersal and diapause behaviors.

Life-History Strategy

The CPB, through its variable dormancy and dispersal mechanisms, appears to employ all four possible permutations of the now/later, here/elsewhere dichotomies for reproduction. This bet-hedging strategy minimizes the risk of catastrophic loss of offspring (52,67), and is suited to agricultural settings where habitat loss and high mortality from pesticide applications are commonplace. Along with its ability to adapt to crop hosts and a variety of pesticidal controls, its diverse and flexible behavior has made the CPB a complex and challenging insect to control. Therefore, success in managing the CPB must rely on cultural tactics more sophisticated than simple crop rotation. For example, early trap-cropping combined with diapause disruption may greatly enhance the value of crop rotation and/or late planting.

Knowledge Is Power

There are many exciting recent developments in CPB research that address essential needs for understanding its life history and for effective management. Certain aspects of CPB biology and behavior are still not well understood, including dispersal behavior and the variable patterns among CPB in different crop and non-crop systems. Additional research needs to investigate how diapause behavior may be exploited to suppress damaging populations on crops.

Although host-plant relationships have been studied extensively in the lab, more work is necessary to investigate the importance of non-crop hosts in the field. In some areas, solanaceous weeds may play an important role in the population dynamics of CPB and in its susceptibility to insecticides. Studies to characterize CPB antifeedants and sources of plant resistance are essential to add to the array of existing management tactics. In the management of insecticide resistance, it is important that we gain an understanding of the genetics and mechanisms of resistance.

Cultural and biological controls must be the foundation for sustainable CPB management programs in the future. Cultural controls such as crop rotation already play a major role in many growing regions. However, diverse cultural controls have the potential for a much stronger impact on CPB management. Biological controls should play an important role in the management of CPB, but they cannot fulfill this function unless we increase our knowledge of both native and exotic natural enemies, and decrease our reliance on broad-spectrum chemical controls. Finally, given the geographical diversity of CPB life histories, management programs should be tailored specifically to each growing region.

Acknowledgment

We thank Peter Follett, Ruth Hazzard, Tibor Jermy, Árpád Szentesi and Geoff Zehnder for their helpful comments, and Quan Chang Yuan and Árpád Szentesi for translations from Russian and Hungarian respectively. A Switzer Environmental Fellowship provided general support to DCW during the study period.

Literature Cited

1.   Alford, R.F. Deployment strategies for antifeedants in management of Colorado potato beetle. This volume.

2.   Biever, K.D., and R.L. Chauvin. 1990. Prolonged dormancy in a Pacific Northwest population of the Colorado potato beetle, *Leptinotarsa decemlineata* (Say) (Coleoptera: Chrysomelidae). Can. Entomol. 122: 175-177.

3.   Boiteau, G. 1986. Effect of planting date and plant spacing on field colonization by Colorado potato beetles, *Leptinotarsa decemlineata* (Say), in New Brunswick. Environ. Entomol. 15: 311-315.

4.   Boiteau, G. 1988. Control of the Colorado potato beetle, *Leptinotarsa decemlineata* (Say): learning from the Soviet experience. Bull. Entomol. Soc. Can. 20(1): 9-14.

5.   Boiteau, G. 1988. Sperm utilization and post-copulatory female-guarding in the Colorado potato beetle, *Leptinotarsa decemlineata*. Entom. Exp. Appl. 47: 183-187.

6.   Cappaert, D.L. 1988. Ecology of the Colorado potato beetle in Mexico. Masters Thesis in Entomolgy, Michigan State University, East Lansing.

7.   Caprio, M.A., and E.J. Grafius. 1990. Effects of light, temperature, and feeding status on flight initiation in postdiapause Colorado potato beetles (Coleoptera: Chrysomelidae). Environ. Entomol. 19: 281-285.

8.   Casagrande, R.A. 1987. The Colorado potato beetle: 125 years of mismanagement. Bull. Entomol. Soc. Am. 33: 142-150.

9.   Clark, J.M., and J.A. Argentine. Biochemical mechanisms of insecticide resistance in the Colorado potato beetle. This volume.

10.   de Kort, C.A.D. 1990. Thirty-five years of diapause research with the Colorado potato beetle. Entomol. Exp. Appl. 56: 1-13.

11.   de Wilde, J. 1978. Seasonal states and endocrine levels in insects. Pp. 10-19 in Environmental Endocrinology, ed. I. Assenmacher and D.S. Farner. Springer, New York.

12.   de Wilde, J., C.S. Duintjer and L. Mook. 1959. Physiology of diapause in the adult Colorado beetle (*Leptinotarsa decemlineata*). I. The photoperiod as a controlling factor. J. Insect Physiol. 3: 75-85.

13.   de Wilde, J., and T.H. Hsiao. 1981. Geographic diversity of the Colorado potato beetle and its infestation in Eurasia. Pp. 47-68 in Advances in Potato Pest Management, ed. J.H. Lashomb and R. Casagrande. Hutchinson Ross Publ. Co., Stroudsburg, Penna.

14.   Dripps, J.E., and Z. Smilowitz. 1989. Growth analysis of potato plants damaged by Colorado potato beetle (Coleoptera: Chrysomelidae) at different plant growth stages. Environ. Entomol. 18:854-867.

15.   Ferro, D.N. Biological control of Colorado potato beetle. This volume.

16.   Ferro, D.N., J.A. Logan, R.H. Voss and J.S. Elkinton. 1985. Colorado potato beetle (Coleoptera: Chrysomelidae) temperature-dependent growth and feeding rates. Environ. Entomol. 14: 343-348.

17.   Ferro, D.N., A.F. Tuttle and D.C. Weber. 1991. Ovipositional and flight behavior of overwintered Colorado potato beetle (Coleoptera: Chrysomelidae). Environ. Entomol. 20: 1309-1314.

18.   Forgash, A.J. 1985. Insecticide resistance in the Colorado potato beetle. Pp. 33-52 in Proceedings of the symposium on the Colorado potato beetle, XVIIth International Congress of Entomology, ed. D.N. Ferro and R.H. Voss. Res. Bull. 704, Mass. Agric. Expt. Sta., Amherst, Mass.

19. Gauthier, N.L., R.N. Hofmaster and M. Semel. History of Colorado potato beetle control. Pp. 13-33 in Advances in Potato Pest Management, ed. J.H. Lashomb and R. Casagrande. Hutchinson Ross Publ. Co., Stroudsburg, Penna.

20. Goryshin, N.I., T.A. Volkovich, A. Kh. Saulich, N.N. Shakhova. 1985. Experimental analysis of seasonal development of Colorado beetle (*Leptinotarsa decemlineata*) in the forest-steppe zone. I. Characteristics of the photoperiodic reaction. Zool. Zh. 64: 1349-1359.

21. Goryshin, N.I., T.A. Volkovich, A. Kh. Saulich, N.N. Shakhova. 1986. Experimental analysis of seasonal development of Colorado beetle (*Leptinotarsa decemlineata*) in the forest-steppe zone. II. Field tests and phenological observations. Zool. Zh. 65: 528-539.

22. Gould, F. Resistance management strategies for transgenic plants. This volume.

23. Gulidova, L.A. 1986. Control of Colorado beetle in private plots. Zashchita Rastenii 1986(4): 52.

24. Gürkan, B., and A. Boşgelmez. 1984. Potato beetle (*Leptinotarsa decemlineata* Say) population dynamics. Bitki Koruma Bülteni 24: 119-136 (in Turkish with English abstract).

25. Hare, J.D. 1980. Impact of defoliation by the Colorado potato beetle on potato yields. J. Econ. Entomol. 73: 369-373.

26. Hare, J.D. 1983. Seasonal variation in plant-insect associations: utilization of *Solanum dulcamara* by *Leptinotarsa decemlineata*. Ecology 64: 345-361.

27. Hare, J.D. 1990. Ecology and management of the Colorado potato beetle. Ann. Rev. Entomol. 35: 81-100.

28. Hare, J.D., and G.G. Kennedy. 1986. Genetic variation in plant-insect associations: survival of *Leptinotarsa decemlineata* populations on *Solanum carolinense*. Evolution 40: 1031-1043.

29. Hazzard, R.V., D.N. Ferro, R.G. Van Driesche and A.F. Tuttle. 1991. Mortality of eggs of Colorado potato beetle (Coleoptera: Chrysomelidae) from predation by *Coleomegilla maculata* (Coleoptera: Coccinellidae). Environ. Entomol. 20: 841-848.

30. Hsiao, T.H. 1978. Host plant adaptations among geographic populations of the Colorado potato beetle. Entom. Exp. Appl. 24: 437-447.

31. Hsiao, T.H. 1981. Ecophysiological adaptations among geographic populations of the Colorado potato beetle in North America. Pp. 69-85 in Advances in Potato Pest Management, ed. J.H. Lashomb and R. Casagrande. Hutchinson Ross Publ. Co., Stroudsburg, Penna.

32. Hsiao, T.H. 1985. Ecophysiological and genetic aspects of geographic variations of the Colorado potato beetle. Pp. 63-78 in Proceedings of the symposium on the Colorado potato beetle, XVIIth International Congress of Entomology, ed. D.N. Ferro and R.H. Voss. Res. Bull. 704, Mass. Agric. Expt. Sta., Amherst, Mass.

33. Jacques, R.L. 1988. The Potato beetles: The genus *Leptinotarsa* in North America. E.J. Brill, New York, 144 pp.

34. Jermy, T., and B.A. Butt. 1991. Method for screening female sex pheromone extracts of the Colorado potato beetle. Entomol. Exp. Appl. 59: 75-78.

35. Jermy, T., Á. Szentesi, J. Horvath. 1988. Host plant finding in phytophagous insects: the case of the Colorado potato beetle. Entomol. Exp. Appl. 49: 83-98.

36. Jolivet, P. 1991. The Colorado beetle menaces Asia (*Leptinotarsa decemlineata* Say 1824) (Col. Chrysomelidae). L'Entomologiste 47: 29-48.

37. Kennedy, G.G., and N.M. French. Monitoring reisitance in Colorado potato beetle populations. This volume.

38. Kung, K.-J.S., M. Milner, J.A.Wyman, J. Feldman, and E. Nordheim. 1992. Survival of Colorado potato beetle (Coleoptera: Chrysomelidae) after exposure to subzero thermal shocks during diapause. J. Econ. Entomol. 85, in press.

39. Lashomb, J.H., and Y.-S. Ng. 1984. Colonization by Colorado potato beetle, *Leptinotarsa decemlineata* (Say) (Coleoptera: Chrysomelidae) in rotated and nonrotated potato fields. Environ. Entomol. 13: 1352-1356.

40. Lashomb, J.H., Y.S. Ng, G. Ghidiu and E. Green. 1984. Description of spring emergence by the Colorado potato beetle, *Leptinotarsa decemlineata* (Say) (Coleoptera: Chrysomelidae), in New Jersey. Environ. Entomol. 12: 907-910.

41. Le Berre, J.-R. 1952. Contribution to the study of determination of flight in the Colorado beetle, *Leptinotarsa decemlineata* Say. Comptes rendus de l'Academie des Sciences (Paris) 234: 1092-1094.

42. Lopez, R., D.N. Ferro and R.G. Van Driesche. 1992. Overwintering biology of *Myiopharus aberrans* (Townsend) and *Myiopharus doryphorae* (Riley) (Diptera: Tachinidae). Entomophaga 37: 311-315.

43. Martel, P. 1987. Chemical control and resistance development in potato pests. Pp. 173-183 in Potato Pest Management in Canada, ed. by G. Boiteau, R.P. Singh and R.H. Parry. Proceedings of a symposium on improving potato pest protection, Fredericton, New Brunswick, 27-29 January 1987.

44. Mateeva-Radeva, A. 1985. Colorado potato beetle in Bulgaria: geographical variation in population dynamics and considerations for its control. Pp. 139-144 in Proceedings of the symposium on the Colorado potato beetle, XVIIth International Congress of Entomology, ed. D.N. Ferro and R.H. Voss. Res. Bull. 704, Mass. Agric. Expt. Sta., Amherst, Mass.

45. Milner, M., K.-J. S. Kung, J.A. Wyman, J. Feldman and E. Nordheim. 1992. Enhancing overwintering mortality of Colorado potato beetle (Coleoptera: Chrysomelidae) by manipulating the temperature of its diapause habitat. J. Econ. Entomol. 85, *in press.*

46. Nalbandyan, A.V. 1987. Prediction of survival of the Colorado beetle. Zashchita Rastenii 1987. 9: 45.

47. Ng, Y.-S., and J.H. Lashomb. 1983. Orientation by the Colorado potato beetle (*Leptinotarsa decemlineata* [Say]). Anim. Behav. 31: 617-618.

48. Peferoen, M., R. Huybrechts and A. de Loof. 1981. Longevity and fecundity in the Colorado potato beetle, *Leptinotarsa decemlineata*. Entom. Exp. Appl. 29: 321-329.

49. Roush, R.T., C.W. Hoy, D.N. Ferro, and W.M. Tingey. 1990. Insecticide resistance in the Colorado potato beetle (Coleoptera: Chrysomelidae): influence of crop rotation and insecticide use. J. Econ. Entomol. 83: 315-319.

50. Roush, R., and W. Tingey. Strategies for the management of insect resistance to synthetic and microbial insecticides. This volume.

51. Salt, R.W. 1933. Some experiments on the freezing and hardening of adults of the Colorado potato beetle, *Leptinotarsa decemlineata* Say. MS Thesis, Montana State Univ., Bozeman.

52. Solbreck, C. 1978. Migration, diapause, and direct development as alternative life histories in a seed bug, *Neacoryphus bicrucis*. Pp. 195-217 in Evolution of insect migration and diapause, ed. H. Dingle. Springer, New York.

53. Szabó, L. 1988. Status of resistance to insecticides of the Colorado potato beetle (*Leptinotarsa decemlineata* Say) in Hungary (abstract). Növényvédelem 24: 219.

54. Szentesi, Á. 1985. Behavioral aspects of female guarding and inter-male conflict in the Colorado potato beetle. Pp. 117-126 in Proceedings of the symposium on the Colorado potato beetle, XVIIth International Congress of Entomology, ed. D.N. Ferro and R.H. Voss. Res. Bull. 704, Mass. Agric. Expt. Sta., Amherst, Mass..

55. Tauber, C.A., M.J. Tauber, B. Gollands, R.J. Wright and J.J. Obrycki. 1988. Preimaginal development and reproductive responses to temperature in two populations of the Colorado potato beetle (Coleoptera: Chrysomelidae). Ann. Entomol. Soc. Am. 81: 755-763.

56. Tauber, M.J., C.A. Tauber, J.J. Obrycki, B. Gollands, and R.J. Wright. 1988. Voltinism and the induction of aestival diapause in the Colorado potato beetle, *Leptinotarsa decemlineata* (Coleoptera: Chrysomelidae). Ann. Entomol. Soc. Am. 81: 748-754.

57. Tauber, M.J., C.A. Tauber, J.J. Obrycki, B. Gollands, and R.J. Wright. 1988. Geographical variation in responses to photoperiod and temperature by *Leptinotarsa decemlineata* (Coleoptera: Chrysomelidae) during and after dormancy. Ann. Entomol. Soc. Am. 81: 764-773.

58. Thiery, D., and J.H. Visser. 1987. Misleading the Colorado potato beetle with an odor blend. J. Chem. Ecol. 13: 1139-1146.

59. Tingey, W.M. and D.C. Yencho. Insect resistance in potato: a decade of progress. This volume.

60. Tisler, A.M., and G.W. Zehnder. 1990. Insecticide resistance in the Colorado potato beetle (Coleoptera: Chrysomelidae) on the Eastern Shore of Virginia. J. Econ. Entomol. 83: 666-671.

61. Tower, W.L. 1906. An Investigation of evolution in Chrysomelid Beetles of the Genus Leptinotarsa. Carnegie Institute, Washington, D.C.

62. Ushatinskaya, R.S. 1978. Season migration of adult *Leptinotarsa decemlineata* (Insecta: Coleoptera) in different types of soil and physiological variations of individuals in hibernating populations. Pedobiologia 18: 120-126.

63. Verenini, M. 1985. The Colorado potato beetle *Leptinotarsa decemlineata* Say. Informatore Fitopatologico 35: 31-33.

64. Visser, J.H. 1988. Host-plant finding by insects: orientation, sensory input and search patterns. J. Insect Physiol. 34: 259-268.

65. Vlasova, V.A. 1978. A prediction of the distribution of Colorado beetle in the Asiatic territory of the USSR. Zashchita Rastenii 1978 (6): 44-45.

66. Voss, R.H., and D.N. Ferro. 1990. Phenology of flight and walking by Colorado potato beetle (Coleoptera: Chrysomelidae) adults in western Massachusetts. Environ. Entomol. 19: 117-122.

67. Voss, R.H., and D.N. Ferro. 1990. Ecology of migrating Colorado potato beetles (Coleoptera: Chrysomelidae) in western Massachusetts. Environ. Entomol. 19: 123-129.

68. Voss, R.H., D.N. Ferro and J.A. Logan. 1988. Role of reproductive diapause in the population dynamics of the Colorado potato beetle (Coleoptera: Chrysomelidae) in western Massachusetts. Environ. Entomol. 17: 863-871.

69. Weber, D.C. 1992. Dispersal and Diet of Colorado Potato Beetle, *Leptinotarsa decemlineata*. Ph.D. Thesis. Univ. of Massachusetts, Amherst.

70. Weber, D.C., and D.N. Ferro. Distribution of overwintering Colorado potato beetle (*Leptinotarsa decemlineata*) (Coleoptera: Chrysomelidae) in and near Massachusetts potato fields. Entomol. Exp. Appl., 66: 191-196.

70a. Weber, D.C., D.N. Ferro and J.G. Stoffolano, Jr. 1993. Quantifying flight of Colorado potato beetle with a microcomputer-based flight mill system. Ann. Entomol. Soc. Am. 86: (In press).

71. Wegorek, W. 1959. The Colorado potato beetle (*Leptinotarsa decemlineata* Say). Prace Naukowe Instytutu Ochrony Roslin 1: 1-105.

72. Wiktelius, S. 1981. Wind dispersal of insects. Grana 20: 205-207.

73. Worner, S.P. 1988. Ecoclimatic assessment of potential establishment of exotic pests. J. Econ. Entomol. 81: 973-983.

74. Wright, R.J. 1984. Evaluation of crop rotation for control of Colorado potato beetles (Coleoptera: Chrysomelidae) in commercial potato fields on Long Island. J. Econ. Entomol. 77:1254-1259.

75. Wyman, J., J. Feldman and S.K. Kung. Cultural control Colorado potato beetle: off-crop management. This volume.

76. Zabel, A., and M. Kostić. 1988. Efficacy and persistance of some new insecticides in control of the Colorado potato beetle (*Leptinotarsa decemlineata* Say) (abstract only). Zastita Bilja 39: 171-182.

77. Zehnder, G.W., and G.K. Evanylo. 1989. Influence of extent and timing of Colorado potato beetle (Coleoptera:Chrysomelidae) defoliation on potato tuber production in eastern Virginia. J. Econ. Entomol. 82: 948-953.

BIOLOGY AND MANAGEMENT OF LEAFHOPPERS ON POTATO

Edward B. Radcliffe
Department of Entomology, University of
Minnesota, St. Paul, MN 55108

Kenneth B. Johnson
Department of Botany and Plant Pathology,
Oregon State University, Corvallis, OR 97331

Leafhoppers (Homoptera: Cicadellidae [= Jassidae]) are mostly crop pests of the tropics and subtropics. The leafhopper of greatest importance on potato, however, is a North American species, potato leafhopper, *Empoasca fabae* (Harris) (34,36).

In the midwestern and northeastern United States, potato leafhopper is so destructive on potato that insecticides must be applied routinely to prevent unacceptable yield losses. Potato leafhopper also occurs throughout most of the western United States, but there it is of minor importance. In Canada, potato leafhopper is the most important insect pest of potato in Ontario, but is rare in the Maritimes and west of Manitoba.

Potato leafhopper is not the only empoascan attacking potato in the United States. There are at least four closely related species: southern garden leafhopper, *E. solana* DeLong, a minor potato pest in the humid South-East; "intermountain leafhopper", *E. filamenta* DeLong, a pest in high arid regions between the Rocky Mountains and the Sierra Nevada; and western potato leafhopper, *E. abrupta* DeLong; and "arid potato leafhopper", *E. arida* DeLong, both potato pests along the Pacific Slope (6, 35).

Potato leafhopper is particularly destructive, perhaps because it feeds on phloem (28,32), whereas other empoascans are exclusively mesophyll feeders. All empoascans damage potato by direct feeding; no species has been implicated in transmission of potato pathogens.

Other leafhopper pests of potato in North America are: aster (sixspotted) leafhopper, *Macrosteles quadrilineatus* Forbes (=*fascifrons* Stål); beet leafhopper, *Circulifer tenellus* (Baker); and clover leafhopper, *Aceratagallia sanguinolenta* (Provancher) (35). Aster leafhopper and clover leafhopper occur throughout most of North America. Beet leafhopper occurs primarily in the arid west. These leafhoppers cause only minor direct injury to potato, but aster leafhopper is the principal vector of the aster yellows mycoplasma-like organism (AY-MLO), causal agent of potato purple top (2). Clover leafhopper transmits potato yellow dwarf virus and beet leafhopper transmits beet curly top virus (35).

Potato Leafhopper

In the United States, potato leafhopper overwinter in a permanent breeding area in the Mississippi Delta region and along the Gulf Coast to northern Florida (5). In spring, flying adults can be caught in updrafts and transported on upper level air streams to locations throughout the central and eastern United States and southern Canada.

Weather conditions associated with transport of potato leafhopper into the Mid-West are high atmospheric pressure over the East Coast, a low over the Great Plains, a north-south front moving east, and an east-west front in the fallout area (31). Influxes of potato leafhoppers from the Gulf generally are associated with southerly winds of at least 36 h duration and precipitation in the fallout area (13).

The first migrant potato leafhoppers in the spring often arrive in northern regions before potatoes have emerged. These early arrivals primarily colonize and reproduce on hosts other than potato, such as deciduous trees, soybean, or alfalfa. Invasion of potato can be reliably predicted by heat unit accumulations from the first consequential influx of long distance migrants (9). We found that invasion of potato is correlated with the accumulation of sufficient heat units (approximately 350-450 CDD, base 8.8°C) for development of the first post-immigration generation. It has been suggested that potato is invaded as a consequence of alfalfa harvest, but this is generally not true if harvest is timely and the crop is cut clean (40).

In Minnesota, the first arrival of potato leafhopper migrants can occur from late April to mid-June (30). Initial arrival is most often directly from overwintering sites, but transport may occur in stages. Later in the season, short duration southerly wind flows may transport potato leafhoppers from less distant points of origin, e.g., potato leafhoppers are often not found in northern Minnesota until some weeks after their arrival in southern Minnesota. Similarly, potato leafhopper invasion of the northeastern United States is often accomplished in stages.

Potato leafhopper can cause yield loss in potato even before visual symptoms become obvious. Large increases in respiration occur in plants subjected to potato leafhopper feeding, depleting reserves available for growth and tuber development (22). Effects on respiration are temporary if potato leafhoppers are controlled before leaf tissue is destroyed. However, feeding by potato leafhopper also impairs photosynthetic efficiency of the plant and this effect is irreversible.

The first visual symptom of potato leafhopper feeding is subtle paling of veins and curling of the leaflet. Necrosis occurs in tissues distal to the feeding site and is associated with accumulation of photosynthate due to occlusion of the phloem. In potato, this marginal necrosis of leaves distal to feeding sites is termed "hopperburn" (1). Hopperburn usually begins as a triangular lesion at the tip of infested leaflets. Lesions spread progressively back and inward from the margins finally destroying the leaves; plants may senesce and die prematurely (8). Water transport also is disrupted (48), resulting in wilting. Salivary secretions of potato leafhopper are rich in amylase and invertase, and are toxicogenic to phloem sieve cells (11). Controversy remains as to the relative importance of direct injury by mechanical occlusion of phloem cells (28,32), indirect injury by toxicogenic secretions (8), or induction of abnormal growth of tissues surrounding the phloem (25); however, economic injury occurs at extremely low potato leafhopper densities indicating that the effect is not merely mechanical.

Potato leafhopper has been described as a stylet-sheath feeder (28,32), but Backus and her co-workers find evidence for this unconvincing. Kabrick and Backus (21) believe that what earlier workers saw as sheaths actually are intra-cellular accumulations of coagulated watery saliva, not solid sheath saliva. Also contrary to earlier workers, Hunter and Backus (12) concluded that potato leafhopper is primarily a mesophyll feeder and only occasionally a phloem feeder. These studies were with alfalfa and broad bean and should be repeated with potato. It is evident that potato leafhopper shows great plasticity in its feeding behavior and that feeding responses may be host specific.

Potato leafhopper has long been recognized as a pest of potatoes, but its destructiveness was only fully appreciated with the introduction of modern synthetic insecticides. In Minnesota, annual losses to potato (including control costs) have been estimated at $7 million, roughly 10% of production value (27). Early investigators reported a strongly negative curvilinear yield response with increasing densities of potato leafhopper (29,47). However, because it takes so few potato leafhoppers to cause economic damage, the relationship between yield loss and potato leafhopper numbers can be considered directly linear (20).

Sampling midplant leaves has proven a practical aid for determining need to apply insecticides for potato leafhopper control

(3,18,19,20,44,46). In 1979, we proposed action thresholds (economic thresholds) of 10 nymphs per 105 leaves (three samples of 35 leaves) for application of insecticidal sprays to control potato leafhopper on nonirrigated potatoes in Minnesota (3). Spraying when potato leafhopper numbers reached this threshold was optimal in terms of preventing yield loss and avoiding unnecessary applications of insecticide. In Wisconsin, a "dynamic threshold" was proposed which takes into account presence of adults (44). Spraying is recommended at the first appearance of nymphs unless adults are fewer than one per sweep in which case spraying can be delayed until nymphs reach 10 per 25 leaves. Action thresholds in the range of 1-4 nymphs per 10 leaves are now recommended in Minnesota, North Dakota, Wisconsin, Michigan, Pennsylvania, New York, Massachusetts, and perhaps elsewhere.

In Minnesota, economic injury levels (EIL) for potato leafhopper nymphs on potato were determined by regressing tuber yields on cumulative daily populations of potato leafhopper nymphs on midplant leaves (PLH-days) (15,16,20,23). Resulting EILs were usually in the range of 40-250 PLH-days/100 leaves, where EIL = a graded-yield loss of 0.4 t/ha with a $0.075/kg value and control costs of $30/ha. If action thresholds are set at 1/7 of the EIL (on the assumption it would be practical to scout a field once a week) this was equivalent to 6-35 potato leafhopper nymphs/100 leaves.

Potato leafhopper infestations commonly occur on potato concurrently with other insect pests and diseases that reduce yield. Past research on pest-induced yield reductions has focused primarily on losses caused by single pest species. In several multi-year studies, we quantified interacting effects of varying levels of potato leafhopper, early blight (caused by *Alternaria solani* (Ell. & Mart.)) and Verticillium wilt (caused by *Verticillium dahliae*) Kleb.) on foliage and tuber production for three cultivars (15,16). All significant pest x pest interactions were less than additive in their combined effects on yield (negative coefficient). This is important in pest management because expected benefit of control of one pest is reduced by damaging levels of the other(s). This result was largely a consequence of competition among pests damaging green leaf tissue.

It has been suggested that early maturing potato cultivars generally are more susceptible to both hopperburn and early blight. In our experiments, the early maturing 'Norland' sustained much greater foliage loss than did late-season cultivars 'Red Pontiac' or 'Russet Burbank' (15,16) . However, tuber yield reductions were proportionately less in 'Norland' than in the other two cultivars, presumably because the early and rapid tuber-bulking of that cultivar reduced the effective duration of pest exposure.

We also examined interacting effects of potato leafhopper and water stress on 'Russet Burbank' tuber yields (23). Slopes of the negative linear relationship between yield and cumulative numbers of potato leafhopper-days were either not significantly different (two experiments) or were less negative in the low water treatment (four experiments). This was contrary to an often expressed opinion that combined effects of water stress and potato leafhopper are more than additive.

Because action thresholds for potato leafhopper on potato are very low, it is experimentally difficult to establish the dynamics of the yield loss function. Consequently, most thresholds that have been proposed either do not take into account growth stage-specific changes in plant susceptibility or use empirically established threshold ranges. As an alternative to field experiments, we coupled effects of potato leafhopper feeding to a potato growth model developed specifically for pest management problems (17). Our goal in this research was to develop a better understanding of the dynamics of the potato leafhopper/yield loss function.

The potato growth model used (14) accumulates and partitions dry matter into leaves, stems, roots and tubers based on inputs of solar radiation, temperature, and soil water potential. Potato leafhopper affected biomass accumulation by reducing the efficiency of use of captured solar radiation and by reducing green leaf area to hopperburn. Intensity of potato leafhopper effects on potato growth were logarithmically related to the density of nymphs on midplant leaves. Removal of the nymph population, e.g., by insecticides, allowed efficiency of use of solar radiation to return to normal after about three days. Overall, the model reasonably explained yield reductions observed in three seasons of field trials. Given the same economic assumptions used in our previous experiments, the model predicted that 7 potato leafhopper nymphs/30 midplant leaves feeding for one week would cause economic loss.

Within our initial model, potato leafhopper feeding intensity (i.e., ratio of nymph density to relative leaf size) was estimated for different age classes of leaves by assuming that potato leafhoppers feed most intensely on midplant leaves and least intensely on the oldest and youngest leaves. We made this assumption because it is known that potato leafhopper prefers to oviposit midplant (26). We have since verified that nymphs are concentrated on leaves of intermediate age (19), but that the ratio of overall density of nymphs per leaf to density of nymphs per midplant leaf showed linear increase with crop age. In addition, we found that relative vertical distributions of nymphs within the plant canopy were not influenced by potato leafhopper population size.

We have since modified our model to implement a response function that accurately estimates feeding intensity of nymphs within leaf age classes (Fig. 1) (18). This response function included both linear and quadratic terms for leaf and crop physiological age as well as an interaction term. Inclusion of the response function resulted in improved predictions of tuber yields and hopperburn development. The most important conclusions from simulation experiments with the new model were that potato shows a relatively constant sensitivity to potato leafhopper damage from about full bloom to 2 weeks before harvest, but is relatively insensitive to damage for the first month after plant emergence (Fig. 2). Walgenbach and Wyman (45) demonstrated a similar period of sensitivity to potato leafhopper by measuring photosynthesis within caged potato plants. We also found that maximum yield loss sensitivity to potato leafhopper occurs at a later stage of growth and for a longer period of time than yield reductions caused by defoliation.

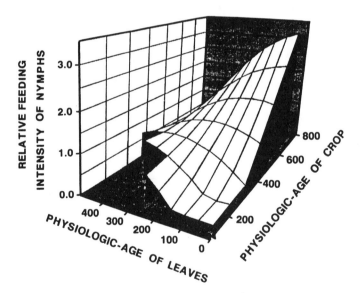

Fig. 1. Estimated multiple regression response function describing effects of leaf and crop physiological age on the distribution of relative feeding intensity of potato leafhopper nymphs on potato cv. Russet Burbank. (Reprinted from Johnson and Radcliffe 1991 (18) by permission of the publishers, 'Butterworth-Heinemann Ltd.©'

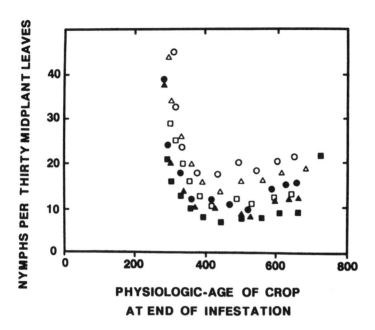

Fig. 2. Numbers of potato leafhopper nymphs per 30 midplant leaves that trigger action thresholds at various stages of simulated potato growth, cv. Russet Burbank. Open symbols = yield losses of 1% (EIL for irrigated potatoes), closed symbols = yield losses of 2% (EIL for dryland potatoes). Potato leafhopper numbers increased daily by one (□, ■), two (△, ▲), or three (○, ●) nymphs. (Reprinted from Johnson and Radcliffe 1991 (18) by permission of the publishers, 'Butterworth-Heinemann Ltd.©'

Simulation results with the model also showed reduced sensitivity of potato to yield loss during periods of moisture stress and increased sensitivity immediately before or after moisture stress; i.e., potato was most sensitive to potato leafhopper when conditions were otherwise optimal for photosynthesis and tuber-bulking. Simulation analysis using yield loss criteria of 2% yield reductions for dryland potatoes and 1% on irrigated potatoes yielded action thresholds generally in the range of those previously published (3,15,16,20,44).

Aster leafhopper

Aster leafhopper overwinter primarily in northern Texas, eastern Oklahoma, Arkansas, and western Missouri (4,7). Grasses are the preferred hosts of aster leafhopper and enormous populations can build up in small grains, particularly oats and wheat. As these cereals mature, hugh influxes of aster leafhopper can be transported into the North Central States on upper air streams. Populations of immigrant origin can reach damaging levels 5-6 weeks before damaging populations from locally overwintered aster leafhoppers can develop. As local cereals ripen, aster leafhopper move to other hosts, including potato.

Purple top symptoms develop only when aster leafhopper pressure is severe, but AY-MLO is of concern to processors because infected tubers can yield discolored chips (2). Aster leafhopper cannot acquire the pathogen from potato, but becomes infected feeding on other susceptible host plants during migration from ripening small grains to potato.

Management of Leafhoppers

Potato leafhopper can cause very substantial yield loss so insecticidal control is essential whenever populations exceed threshold densities. Since symptoms of plant injury may not be apparent until after yield loss has already occurred, the temptation is to apply sprays on a calendar-based schedule. This strategy is not recommended because of control costs and the potential that other insect pests on the crop may be flared or needlessly selected for insecticide resistance. AY-MLO infection is usually only of concern if the crop is intended for chipping or seed (infected tubers do not germinate). Since these two leafhopper species are so different in their potential for damage it is essential that management decisions be based on correct identification.

Adult leafhoppers (potato leafhopper or aster leafhopper) are most readily sampled by sweep net. Twenty-five sweeps across two rows of potato is a commonly recommended sample unit and should be taken at 3-5 locations within a field (46). Potato leafhopper nymphs can be sampled on 25-35 midplant leaves; again 3-5 locations per field is recommended (39). Density estimates obtained by these methods should be an adequate basis for management decisions. However, since even low densities of potato leafhopper nymphs can cause substantial yield loss, it is important that fields be scouted frequently, preferably weekly.

Presently, insecticides provide the only effective means of controlling leafhoppers on potato. Systemics applied in-furrow at planting or side-dressed at plant emergence give 6-8 weeks of control. However, for reasons of cost there is little use of systemic insecticides specifically for leafhopper control. Insecticide resistance is not a problem in leafhoppers and almost any registered material will give excellent control.

Leafhoppers have few effective natural enemies. A fungal pathogen, *Erynia radicans* (Brefeld) Batko (Entomophthorales: Entomophthoraceae)(syn *Zoophthora radicans*), has recently appeared in the Mid-West and sometimes provides substantial control of potato leafhopper (24). Environmental specificity and ineffectiveness at low host densities will probably limit usefulness of *E. radicans* against potato leafhopper on potato.

No present commercial potato cultivar has useful resistance to potato leafhopper. However, potentially useful sources of resistance to potato leafhopper have been identified in several wild potato species (10,38,42). Glycoalkaloids, especially tomatine, impart potato leafhopper resistance (10,37,43). *Solanum berthaultii* Hawkes, a wild potato with glandular trichomes that impart insect resistance, has been used as a parent in breeding for resistance to Colorado potato beetle. This species is also highly resistant to potato leafhopper and apparently to most other potato insect pests.

Empirically determined action thresholds have proven reasonably reliable and highly practical tools for making pest management decisions relative to potato leafhopper. By coupling effects of potato leafhopper feeding to a plant growth model, we have been able to better understand the dynamics of the leafhopper/yield loss function. In particular, we have explored the influence of stage-specific changes in plant susceptibility, effects of moisture stress, and distribution of feeding intensity within the plant canopy. Future research should consider such variables as leafhopper life stage (i.e., adults vs. nymphs), influence of plant cultivar, plant nutritional status, and interactions with other pest agents and causes of plant stress. Factors requiring further study include improved sampling methods, possibilities of integrating biological control agents such as the entomopathogenic fungus *E. radicans* and cultivar resistance, as exemplified by the so-called "Hairy Potato" developed collaboratively by The International Potato Center (CIP) and Cornell University (33).

Mismanagement of potato leafhopper has contributed to the development of insecticide resistance problems in Colorado potato beetle and green peach aphid throughout the Mid-West. Within the past three years, multiple insecticide resistance has transformed Colorado potato beetle from minor pest status to that of being the most important potato insect pest in the irrigated sand plains of east central Minnesota. Improved pest management strategies need to be developed from a holistic perspective, integrating multiple pests as sub-components of the overall crop management system. Prototypes of such models exist, e.g., the Potato Crop Management (PCM) software developed in Wisconsin which includes modules for entering weather and crop data, recording field activities, predicting emergence, managing two foliar diseases (early blight and late blight), managing insect problems, and scheduling irrigation (39,41). Ideally, such computer-aides will evolve into true knowledge-based decision support systems ("expert systems").

Literature Cited

1.   Ball, E. D. 1919. The potato leafhopper and its relation to the hopperburn. J. Econ. Entomol. 12: 149-154.

2.   Banttari, E. E., P. J. Ellis, and S. M. P. Khurana. 1993. Management of diseases caused by viruses and virus-like pathogens, pp. 127-133, *In* APS Plant Health Management in Potato Production, R. C. Rowe, ed. Amer. Phytopath. Soc.

3.   Cancelado, R. E. and E. B. Radcliffe. 1979. Action thresholds for potato leafhopper on potatoes in Minnesota. J. Econ. Entomol. 72: 566-569.

4.   Chiykowski, L. N. and R. K. Chapman. 1965. Part 2. Migration of the six-spotted leafhopper in central North America, pp. 21-45, *In* Migration of the Six-Spotted Leafhopper *Macrosteles fasicrons* (Stål). Univ. Wisconsin Res. Bull. 261.

5.   Decker, G. C. and H. B. Cunningham. 1968. Winter survival and overwintering area of the potato leafhopper. J. Econ. Entomol. 61: 154-161.

6.   DeLong, D. M. 1931. Distribution of the potato leafhopper (*Empoasca fabae* Harris) and its close relatives of *Empoasca*. J. Econ. Entomol. 24: 475-479.

7.   Drake, D. C. and R. K. Chapman. 1965. Part 1. Evidence for long distance migration of the six-spotted leafhopper into Wisconsin, pp. 3-20, *In*: Migration of the Six-Spotted Leafhopper *Macrosteles fasicrons* (Stål). Univ. Wisconsin Res. Bull. 261.

8.   Fenton, F. A. and I. L. Ressler. 1922. Artificial production of hopperburn. J. Econ. Entomol. 15: 288-295.

9.   Flanders, K. L. and E. B. Radcliffe. 1989. Origins of potato leafhoppers (Homoptera: Cicadellidae) invading potato and snap bean in Minnesota. Environ. Entomol. 18: 1015-1024.

10. Flanders, K. L., J. G. Hawkes, E. B. Radcliffe, and F. I. Lauer. 1992. Insect resistance in potatoes: sources, evolutionary relationships, morphological and chemical defenses, and ecogeographical associations. Euphytica 61: 83-111.

11. Hibbs, E. T., D. L. Dahlman, and R. L. Rice. 1964. Potato foliage sugar concentration in relation to infestation by the potato leafhopper, *Empoasca fabae* (Homoptera: Cicadellidae). Ann. Entomol. Soc. Am. 57: 517-521.

12. Hunter, W. B. and E. A. Backus. 1989. Mesophyll-feeding by the potato leafhopper, Empoasca fabae (Homoptera: Cicadellidae): results from electronic monitoring and thin layer-chromatography. Environ. Entomol. 18: 465-472.

13. Huff, F. A. 1963. Relation between leafhopper influxes and synoptic weather conditions. J. Appl. Meterol. 2: 39-43.

14. Johnson, K. B., S. B. Johnson, and P. S. Teng. 1986. Development of a simple potato growth model for use in crop-pest management. Agric. Sys. 19: 189-209.

15. Johnson, K. B., E. B. Radcliffe, and P. S. Teng. 1986. Effects of interacting populations of *Alternaria solani, Verticillium dahliae,* and the potato leafhopper *(Empoasca fabae)* on potato yield. Phytopathology 76: 1046-1052.

16. Johnson, K. B., P. S. Teng, and E. B. Radcliffe. 1987. Analysis of potato foliage losses caused by interacting populations of early blight, Verticillium wilt, and potato leafhopper and the relationship to yield. Z. Pflanzenkr. Pflanzenschutz 94: 22-33.

17. Johnson, K. B., P. S. Teng, and E. B. Radcliffe. 1987. Coupling feeding effects of potato leafhopper, *Empoasca fabae* (Homoptera: Cicadellidae), nymphs to a model of potato growth. Environ. Entomol. 16: 250-258.

18. Johnson, K. B. and E. B. Radcliffe. 1991. Validation of a model simulating the feeding effects of the potato leafhopper *(Empoasca fabae)* on potato growth. Crop Prot. 10: 416-422.

19. Johnson, K. B., C. G. Watrin, and E. B. Radcliffe. 1988. Vertical distributions of potato leafhopper nymphs (Homoptera: Cicadellidae) on potatoes relative to leaf position, plant age, and population size. J. Econ. Entomol. 81: 304-309.

20. Johnston, R. L. 1984. Determination of economic thresholds for potato leafhopper, *Empoasca fabae* (Harris), and action thresholds for Colorado potato beetle, *Leptinotarsa decemlineata* (Say), on potato in Minnesota. Ph.D. dissertation, University of Minnesota, St. Paul, Minn.

21. Kabrick, L. R. and E. A. Backus. 1990. Salivary deposits and plant damage associated with specific probing behaviors of the potato leafhopper, *Empoasca fabae,* on alfalfa stems. Entomol. exp. appl. 56: 287-304.

22. Ladd, T. L. and W. A. Rawlins. 1965. The effects of the feeding of the potato leafhopper on photosynthesis and respiration in the potato plant. J. Econ. Entomol. 58: 623-628.

23. Lagnaoui, A. 1991. Multiple pest, water, and nitrogen interactions with potato yield and quality. Ph. D. dissertation, Univ. Minnesota, St. Paul, MN.

24. McGuire, M. R., M. J. Morris, E. J. Armbrust, and J. V. Maddox. 1987. An epizootic caused by *Erynia radicans* (Zygomycetes: Entomophthoraceae) in an Illinois *Empoasca fabae* (Homoptera: Cicadellidae) population. J. Inver. Pathol. 50: 78-80.

25. Medler, J. T. 1941. The nature of injury to alfalfa caused by *Empoasca fabae* (Harris). Ann. Entomol. Soc. Am. 34: 439-450.

26. Miller, R. L. and E. T. Hibbs. 1963. Distribution of eggs of the potato leafhopper, *Empoasca fabae,* on *Solanum* plants. Ann. Ent. Soc. Am. 56: 737-740.

27. Noetzel, D. M., L. K. Cutkomp, and P. K. Harein (eds.). 1985. Estimated Annual Losses Due to Insects in Minnesota 1981-1983. Univ. Minnesota, Minnesota Instit. Agr., AES. AG-BU-2541.

28. Peterson, A. G. and A. A. Granovsky. 1950. Feeding effects of *Empoasca fabae* on a resistant and susceptible variety of potato. Am. Potato J. 27: 366-371.

29. Peterson, A. G. and A. A. Granovsky. 1950. Relation of *Empoasca fabae* to hopperburn and yields of potatoes. J. Econ. Entomol. 43: 434-487.

30. Peterson, A. G., J. D. Bates, and R. S. Sani. 1969. Spring dispersal of some leafhoppers and aphids. Minn. Acad. Sci. 35: 98-102.

31. Pienkowski, R. L. and J. T. Medler. 1964. Synoptic weather conditions associated with long-range movement of the potato leafhopper, *Empoasca fabae,* into Wisconsin. Ann. Entomol. Soc. Amer. 57: 588-591.

32.   Poos, F. W. and F. F. Smith. 1931. A comparison of oviposition and nymphal development of *Empoasca fabae* (Harris) on different host plants. J. Econ. Entomol. 24: 361-371.

33.   Plaisted, R.L., W.M. Tingey, and J.C. Steffens. 1992. The germplasm release of NYL235-4, a clone with resistance to the Colorado potato beetle. Am. Potato J. 69: 843-846.

34.   Radcliffe, E. B, K. L. Flanders, D. W. Ragsdale, and D. M. Noetzel. 1991. Pest management systems for potato insects, pp. 587-621, *In* CRC Handbook of Pest Management, second edition, Vol. III, D. Pimentel, (ed.) CRC Press, Boca Raton, Florida.

35.   Radcliffe, E. B., D. W. Ragsdale, and K. L. Flanders. 1993. Management of aphids and leafhoppers, pp. 117-126, *In* APS Plant Health Management in Potato Production, R. C. Rowe, (ed.) Amer. Phytopath. Soc.

36.   Raman, K. V. and E. B. Radcliffe. 1991. Pest Aspects of potato production, Part 2. Insect pests, pp. 476-506, *In* The Potato Crop, the scientific basis for improvement, second edition, P. Harris, ed. Chapman and Hall, London.

37.   Raman, K. V., W. M. Tingey, and P. Gregory. 1979. Potato glycoalkaloids: Effect on survival and feeding behavior of the potato leafhopper. J. Econ. Entomol. 72: 337-341.

38.   Sanford, L. L. and J. P. Sleesman. 1970. Genetic variation in a population of tetraploid potatoes: Response to the potato leafhopper and the potato flea beetle. Am. Potato J. 47: 19-34.

39.   Shields, E. J., J. R, Hygnstrom, D. Curwen, W. R. Stevenson, J. A. Wyman, and L. K. Binning. 1984. Pest management for potatoes in Wisconsin - - a pilot program. Am. Potato J. 61: 508-516.

40.   Simonet, D. E. and R. L. Pienkowski. 1979. Impact of alfalfa harvest on potato leafhopper populations with emphasis on nymphal survival. J. Econ. Entomol. 72: 428-431.

41.   Stevenson, W. R., D. Curwen, L. K. Binning, J. P. Koenig, G. J. Rice, R. Schmidt, and J. Zajda. 1989. Managment of potato production using integrated computer software. Am. Potato J. 66:547.

42.   Tingey, W. M. and S. L. Sinden. 1982. Glandular pubescence, glycoalkaloid composition, and resistance to the green peach aphid, potato leafhopper, and potato flea beetle in *Solanum berthaultii*. Am. Potato J. 59: 95-106.

43.   Tingey, W. M., J. D. MacKenzie, and P. Gregory. 1978. Total foliar glycoalkaloids and resistance of wild potato species to *Empoasca fabae* (Harris). Am. Potato J. 55: 577-585.

44.   Walgenbach, J. F. and J. A. Wyman. 1984. Dynamic action threshold levels for the potato leafhopper (Homoptera: Cicadellidae) on potatoes in Wisconsin. J. Econ. Entomol. 77: 1335-1340.

45.   Walgenbach, J.F. and J. A. Wyman. 1985. Potato leafhopper (Homoptera: Cicadellidae) feeding damage at various potato growth stages. J. Econ. Entomol. 78: 671-675.

46.   Walgenbach, J. F., J. A. Wyman, and D. B. Hogg. 1985. Evaluation of sampling methods and development of sequential sampling plan for potato leafhopper (Homoptera: Cicadellidae) on potatoes. Environ. Entomol. 14: 231-236.

47.   Wolfenbarger, D. O. and J. W. Heuberger. 1946. Potato yields from different potato leafhopper densities. Am. Potato J. 23: 389-395.

48.   Womack, C. L. 1984. Reduction in photosynthetic and transpiration rates of alfalfa caused by potato leafhopper (Homoptera: Cicadellidae) infestations. J. Econ. Entomol. 77: 508-513.

THE POTATO (TOMATO) PSYLLID, *PARATRIOZA COCKERELLI* (SULC), AS A PEST OF POTATOES

Whitney S. Cranshaw, Department of
Entomology, Colorado State University,
Ft. Collins, Colorado 80523

The potato (tomato) psyllid, *Paratrioza cockerelli* (Sulc), is a key insect pest of potato in many of the growing areas of western North America. Originally described by Sulc (52), from a sample collected on peppers in Boulder, Colorado, it has been recognized as a plant pest since it was found damaging to *Solanum capsicastrum* Link in Golden Gate Park (7).

Attention to potato psyllid as a threat to the regional potato crop followed a period of widespread outbreaks in the late 1920's. Although it was later recognized to have caused similar outbreaks of uncertain diagnosis during several earlier seasons, Richards (42) described it as "a new disease of potato which appeared suddenly in 1927 and purports to become the outstanding disease problem of the intermountain states. In its rate of spread and its degree of destruction it would seem that nothing has been more startling in American agriculture." Once its association with the potato psyllid was recognized, the term "psyllid yellows" was suggested for a description of the disorder induced by the feeding activities of the insect (41).

Distribution of the potato psyllid was recorded by Pletsch (40) as including Minnesota, North and South Dakota, Nebraska, Kansas, Oklahoma, Texas and all states west except for Oregon and Washington. Canadian records included Alberta and Saskatchewan and it was reported from as far south as Mexico City and Rio Frio, Puebla. In recent years, damage to potatoes has been most consistent in Colorado, Wyoming, and Nebraska, although severe crop injury has also been reported from Montana, Texas, New Mexico, Arizona, Utah, and California. Significant injury to tomatoes, the other economically important crop damaged by this insect, has also occurred recently in more southern regions, including both the central and Baja regions of Mexico.

Nature of Psyllid Yellows

The association of psyllid yellows with the potato psyllid was first established by the studies of Richards (43) and Richards and Blood (44). Psyllid yellows is induced by systemic and pathological disturbances to potato plant growth following feeding by nymphal stages of the insect. In his reviews of the disorder, Carter (5,6) classified it as type of systemic phytotoxemia and it appears to have a relationship to growth promoting hormones of the plant (10).

Symptomatology of psyllid yellows. Daniels (10) and others have reviewed the symptomatology of psyllid yellows. Primary symptoms in potatoes include: retarded growth; erectness of new foliage; mild chlorosis in new foliage with basal cupping of leaves; and a progression of red coloration in new leaves. As infestations progress, secondary foliar symptoms develop including: upward rolling of leaves throughout the plant; shortened and thickened terminal internodes resulting in rosetting; enlarged nodes, aerial tubers, or axillary branches; chlorosis increasing in intensity; growth at a standstill for weeks up to a month; and premature senescence and death of plants. The basal cupping of the leaflets accompanied by a reddish coloration is a primary and important diagnostic character of the disease in potatoes (10).

Aside from a reduction in tuber size and yield, a variety of other effects on tubers result from psyllid yellows. Plants often set an excessive number of tiny, misshapen tubers close to the main stem. Skin set is usually rough. Perhaps most notable is that dormancy is thoroughly disrupted, resulting in premature sprouting and/or production of chain tubers (4,6,10).

Internal necrosis and spindling sprout disorder is associated with infestation of psyllid. However, there are other cases where spindling sprout occurs without internal necrosis. This is perhaps a symptom of psyllid yellows that is associated with how tubers are subsequently stored (46,48,49).

In tomatoes, foliar symptoms are generally similar to those of potatoes. Fruit set can be affected variably, sometimes increasing, with adverse effects on fruit size, texture, and overall yield (1).

Peppers are commonly infested but show few if any symptoms of psyllid yellows (10) and significant yield effects from psyllid infestation generally do not occur on this crop (3). However, among four cultivars evaluated in a recent study, one showed a small decrease in yield from psyllid infestation, one showed no yield effect and two had higher yields when infested with psyllids (1,8).

On potato, the effects of psyllid yellows are reversible, at least in part. Richards (43) reported that if the progress of the disease is interrupted by removing nymphs 5 to 10 days after the appearance of the first symptoms, the plant apparently can assume a normal character. Full expression of psyllid yellows symptoms requires continuous feeding by the nymphs on the plant (44). Arslan et al. (2) found that when insecticides are applied after yellowing, recovery of plants is not complete.

Normal plants can be obtained from tubers grown from infested plants (43), although a variety of disorders are associated (12,44). Seed from psyllid-infested plots sprouted much earlier in storage than did seed from psyllid-controlled plots. The rest period appeared to be broken entirely. Sprouts were rather weak. Tubers grown from infected plants often produce spindling (hair) sprouts (12, 49). Once shoots begin to grow in soil, growth is fairly normal (49), although plants may be smaller and significantly lower stand may result from tubers harvested from plots showing greatest vine injury. Yields decrease with increasing severity of vine injury of the plants from which they were harvested (12), although yields from second generation progeny are normal (49). The threat of psyllid damage to seed has long been recognized (37).

Psyllids and psyllid yellows. The ability to produce psyllid yellows is generally reported to be limited to the nymphal stages of the potato psyllid. In repeated tests, Richards (43) found that adults, even when tested at densities of 1,000 per plant, failed to produce symptoms. However, nymphs from these adults uniformly were capable of producing psyllid yellows. Similar results have also been reported by Carter (4) who found that toxicity was lost at the final molt. A contrary finding was reported by Daniels (10) who found that some adults were able to produce a toxic reaction in tomato seedlings.

The ability to produce toxic effects is inherent. As originally reported by Richards (43), and subsequently repeated by many researchers, all efforts to rear young nymphs on healthy plants have failed to eliminate their ability to produce the psyllid yellows disorder. In fact, nymphs hatched on healthy plants are capable of producing more vigorous symptoms than those reared on psyllid yellows infected plants (44). However, the ability to produce a toxic reaction is irregular. Some nymphs are never toxic, whereas others may be able to cause disease for a short time and then become non-toxic (4). Tests of individual nymphs produced a range of symptoms on tomato seedlings from mild to severe (10). Ability to produce a toxic reaction appears to be heritable (4).

Interestingly, psyllids fed on potato plants infected with Nebraska haywire virus (= tomato big bud virus) were unable to subsequently produce psyllid yellows symptoms. The potato/tomato psyllid is not a vector of the virus (50). Attempts to have potato psyllids transmit potato leafroll (10,40) or aster yellows (10) have also been unsuccessful.

The systemic nature of the toxin which produces psyllid yellows has also been demonstrated by its ability to be transmitted through a graft. Subsequent grafts show a gradual recovery in the form of a reversible reaction (10). Symptoms could not be induced by injection of macerated psyllids into tomato or potato (4) nor could topically applied solutions of macerated psyllids or salivary extracts collected in membrane feeding systems (1) cause consistent symptoms. However, Schaal (47) reported that extracts of psyllid nymphs introduced into healthy plants could produce symptoms similar to those in the field. Symptoms only developed in plants after stolons were formed.

Psyllid feeding and psyllid yellows. The potato psyllid feeds on plant sap and the majority of feeding takes place in the border parenchyma immediately surrounding the vascular bundles (14). Late instars and adults produce thick, well-defined feeding tracks which are primarily intercellular. Penetration to the phloem can take about one hour (4).

Potato psyllid nymphs are quiescent and tend to move only during molting (10). As they feed they produce a distinctive sugary pelleted excrement resembling granulated sugar or salt. Some unusual properties of this material were explored by Pletsch (40) who found that this excrement fluoresced strongly under ultraviolet light with a peak wave length of 3,660 Angstroms. Attempts to induce symptoms with extracts of psyllid excrement have been unsuccessful (1).

Histological and biochemical changes within leaves at the feeding site have been studied. In addition to the mechanical rupturing of cells and withdrawal of carbohydrates, cell proteins are broken down and their disintegration products are detectable. Psyllid yellows infected plants are markedly deficient in nitrates. Chloroplasts are distorted, smaller, more lightly pigmented, and have reduced percentages of chlorophyll and carotin. Injury to the border parenchyma extends laterally with necrosis of the phloem (13) and as the vascular system is broken down the internal phloem appears as a dark mass. A large quantity of starch is present in the stem of affected plants, indicating that transfer of sugar from leaves is disrupted (9). Pseudocallouses form in the sieve tubes and sieve plugs increase in number. There are also a number of observable nuclear changes. The histological changes noted from psyllid yellows are very similar to those previously described with sugarbeet seedlings affected by curly top virus (15).

Symptoms following psyllid feeding can be expressed rapidly. When large numbers of psyllid nymphs are placed on potato plants, psyllid yellows symptoms may appear within 4 to 6 days (43). Under field conditions, the average length of time for symptoms to appear was reported to be 18 days with a maximum of 48 days (10). Arslan et al. (2) reported that onset of shoot yellowing and growth reductions can occur within two weeks. As a bioassay technique, Carter (4) found that symptoms could be obtained on tomato seedlings in as little as two hours, and within six hours with a single nymph.

Influence of environment on psyllid yellows. Expression of psyllid yellows symptoms has been associated with several environmental factors. In addition to being correlated with the number of nymphs feeding and the length of feeding period, intensity and duration of light exposure has long been recognized as a factor in symptom expression (43,47). Symptoms of psyllid yellows under unmodified sunlight may include: yellowing; basal leaf rolling and purpling of the younger leaves; yellowing and rolling of upper leaves; nodal enlargement; increased axillary angle; aerial tubers and shoots; frequent rosetting; various apical growths and distortion; excess tuberization; and inhibition of the rest period. Under decreased exposure and intensity of light, basal, marginal, and interveinal yellowing are a constant feature of the disease (44). The high light intensity and low temperatures common to the mountain valleys are conducive to extreme forms of psyllid yellows (10).

Suboptimal growing conditions may also increase symptom expression. Potato plants growing on highly alkaline soil, those infected with fungal diseases, and plants with injured stems and/or root systems developed psyllid yellows symptoms when fed on at relatively lower insect densities (47). Excessive irrigation stimulates symptom expression (10). Symptoms are also milder on older potatoes, which apparently can dissipate or tolerate some of the effects of psyllid feeding damage (10).

Biology of the Potato Psyllid

Aspects of the biology of the potato psyllid have been the subject of numerous studies. Davis (11) reported that 29 to 34 days were required to complete the life cycle, which averaged 31.2 days. However, the host plant may affect the life cycle of the potato psyllid. Pletsch (40) found that the first adults emerged after 20 days on pepper; 22 days on spiny buffalobur and cultivated ground cherry; 23 days on matrimony vine and tomato; 26 days on common nightshade; and 37 days on field bindweed.

There is little or no difference in developmental times between the sexes (11). The sex ratio is equal and mating obligatory; unfertilized eggs do not hatch (40). Mating usually occurred the second or third day after emergence and the average pre-oviposition period is six days (11).

Eggs are laid on both surfaces of the leaves, but especially on young apical leaves (30). Pletsch (40) noted that under greenhouse conditions most of the eggs were laid on leaf margins while in the field most oviposition occurred on the lower leaf surface. Nymphs appear to prefer the lower surface of the leaf (3,32), but are also found on the upper surface of shaded leaves.

The species is highly sensitive to adverse temperature. The optimum temperature was shown to be about 27^0C. Oviposition, hatching, and survival were reduced at 32^0 and ceased at 35^0C. Temperatures of 38^0C for two hours were lethal to eggs and nymphs (36).

The potato psyllid has a very wide host range, although most plants are members of Solanaceae (31). Several plants may be preferred over potato or tomato for egg laying, such as Chinese lattern (*Physalis francheti* Mast.), husk tomato (*P. pruinosa* L.) and horsenettle (*S. carolinense* L.) (56). However, psyllids will lay eggs on plants on which they cannot develop (31).

Furthermore, psyllids can survive for considerable time periods on plants on which they have not been found to develop. Survival varied from 17 days on honeysuckle to 96 days on Douglas-fir. These plants may be important in allowing survival during periods when host plants are not available (26). Adults can survive for long periods of time in the absence of food, in which case survival is related to relative humidity. For example, Pletsch (40) observed that some starved psyllids survived 92 days at 4^0C and 100% humidity.

Several wild host plants are important in the life history of the potato psyllid. Much of the overwintering populations that move into potato growing areas in the United states occur along the border region with Mexico. In southwest Texas, where potato psyllid has been reported as a pest on winter crops of tomato and potato, three important native host plants were observed, including *Lycium carolinianum* var. *quadrifidum* (Dunal) C. Hitchcock, *P. mollis* (Nutt. Waterfall), and *S. triquetrum* Cav. Psyllids were particularly abundant on the former, which occurs on cultivated land and land covered with native brush (20). In southern Arizona, potato psyllid normally breeds abundantly on *L. andersonii* Gray and to some extent on *L. macrodon* Gray. *Lycium andersonii* occurs commonly along washes in the semidesert areas of southern Arizona (45).

Breeding on the winter host plants occurs from January to May, with peak populations usually occurring in late April or early May. The adults move completely from these breeding sites by the middle of June (45). Migrations of psyllids that affect the potato growing areas of eastern Colorado, Nebraska, and Wyoming typically begin in late May and early June, and peak around July 1 (54). Psyllids are not found again in the overwintering areas until an influx occurs late in October or early

November. The source of psyllids affecting summer and fall potato crops may be different east and west of the Continental Divide (45).

Within the potato production areas, several non-crop hosts have been identified. Daniels (10) noted that matrimony vine (*L. halmifolium* Mill.), buffalobur (*S. rostratum* Dunal) and cull potatoes were important wild host plants and groundcherries (*Physalis* spp.) were of secondary importance. List (34) felt that the most important wild food-plants were *Quincula lobata* (Torr.) Raf., buffalobur, and *P. lanceolata* Michx. Wallis (57) disagreed, stating that potatoes growing in cull piles and matrimony vine were by far the most important non-economic host plants of the potato psyllid in the North Platte Valley. These hosts collected the greater part of the initial population of adult psyllids in the spring and served as a source of infestation for other hosts. He felt that buffalobur and groundcherry were not important host plants because they were not attractive to psyllids until after potato plants were already available.

Epidemiology of Potato Psyllid Outbreaks

Principal factors affecting psyllid populations after July 1 are the size of spring infestations, the size of host plants during psyllid migrations, and ambient temperature when plants are small (54). The sensitivity of potato psyllid to high temperatures (36) appears to be a critical feature in the epidemiology of outbreaks with several reports (39) ascribing high temperatures as being important in retarding incipient outbreaks. During outbreaks in the Rocky Mountain region, psyllids are usually more abundant in the mountainous area than the prairie area (12). At altitudes of 1,800 m or more, the summer temperatures are seldom detrimental and allow uninterrupted increase of psyllid populations (36).

Cool weather, or at least the absence of extreme heat, in late June and July has been associated with several psyllid outbreaks (19,39,53). The absence of excessively high temperatures during this period allows the psyllids to establish on the late crop during a period when the foliage affords little protection from the heat. Later in the growing season, when the crop canopy provides sufficient shading of the lower parts of the plant, optimum conditions for the psyllid can be maintained even under high temperatures (19). Some areas that experience lethal summer temperatures may have population build-up after mid-season, resulting in injury to tomato and late-planted potato (36).

Host plant factors are also important in development of outbreaks. Several researchers indicated that early-planted crops tend to be most severely damaged by potato psyllid (47,55). These plants are larger and provide more shade during periods when psyllid migration occurs. The presence of important early season host plants, such as matrimony vine or cull potatoes, is also an important factor in the development of local populations of potato psyllid (57). Hill (19) suggested that elimination of early potato plantings and volunteer growth on cull dumps should help to curtail psyllid populations considerably, a belief that concurred with Wallis (57).

Control of Potato Psyllid

Host plant resistance. There are several reports that partial resistance to psyllid yellows exists among potato cultivars (47,51). However, Starr (51) reported that no cultivar showed enough resistance to be of any commercial importance. More recently, an evaluation of eight cultivars showed yield decreases of between 19-65% from potato psyllid feeding injury (8). Psyllid populations on the various cultivars differed by only about a two-fold range, suggesting that there was little difference in antixenosis or antibiosis mechanisms affecting psyllid populations on these cultivars. However, there is evidence that tolerance to the effects of the psyllid toxin exists because relative susceptibility to psyllids was poorly correlated with yield. The cultivar showing the least response to psyllid control, 'Norland', is a very early maturing cultivar and the minimal effect from the insect is probably due more to escape than tolerance.

Biological control. Potato psyllids are attacked by several natural enemies. General insect predators recorded to feed on various stages of potato psyllid include chrysopid larvae, various coccinellids, and a variety of predatory Hemiptera, including *Nabis ferus* (L.), *Geocoris decoratus* Uhler, *Orius tristicolor* (White), *Anthocoris melanocerus* Reut., and *Deraeocoris brevis* (Uhler) (24,25,27,28,29,40). Although these predators feed on psyllids in the field, their effects on population regulation are considered modest, and considerably less important than abiotic factors, such as weather. Of the general predators, Pletsch (40) felt that only the chrysopids warranted detailed investigation.
Potato psyllid is also commonly attacked by a parasitic wasp, *Tetrastichus triozae* Burks. The female wasp paralyzes late instars, and lays eggs on the ventral surface. The developing wasp remains outside the body wall but cuts an emergence hole through the shell of the parasitized potato psyllid nymph (21,40). *Tetrastichus triozae* has also been reared from at least nine additional species of psyllids (21). Under field conditions, these wasps were not well synchronized with potato psyllid populations and offered little promise as a factor in natural control (23,40).

Chemical control. The first means identified to effectively control potato psyllid was lime sulfur (33). The toxicity of the treatment was largely due to the power of calcium pentasulphide and calcium tetrasulphide to take up large amounts of oxygen and to give off sulfur in finely divided particles. Control was obtained by the lethal effect of direct contact with the adults at application, by repelling ovipositing females, and by a residual effect on the nymphs (35).

Lime sulfur was widely used during the 1930's and 1940's. However, the treatment was potentially phytotoxic, with a small margin between the minimum amount that is toxic to psyllids and the maximum that potatoes and tomatoes can tolerate (35). Subsequently it was found that sulfur dusts could provide good control without apparent injury to the plants (35). Sulfur deposits affected egg deposition and killed recently emerged nymphs that tried to establish on sprayed/dusted surfaces for over two weeks after treatment (53).

Several additional controls have been identified. The soil applied systemic organophosphate insecticides, phorate (17) and disulfoton, are efficacious for controlling psyllids (18) and continue to be used for potato psyllid management (8). Gerhardt (16) also achieved good control with aldicarb, although poor and unacceptable control with this product and other carbamate insecticides has occurred in recent trials in Colorado (W. Cranshaw, unpublished data).

Alternatively, several synthetic insecticides, including most pyrethroid and organophosphate insecticides, as well as endosulfan, applied as foliar sprays also provide acceptable control. However, thorough coverage is needed to contact psyllid nymphs feeding on the underside of leaves.

Psyllid surveys. Outbreaks of potato psyllid are extremely sporadic but can occur suddenly over a vast area in any one season (44). As a result, efforts to predict or successfully detect incipient outbreaks have long been a stated goal of researchers (27,40,57).

Surveys of psyllids have typically involved sweep net sampling of psyllid host plants. For example, a psyllid index based on 100 sweeps during late June or early July was correlated with the amount of psyllid yellows observed (40). It should be pointed out that psyllid populations may not be uniformly distributed throughout the field. Potato psyllid damage typically appears first on plants at the edge of fields and then progresses towards the center at least two fold (22,57). Sweep-net sampling of fields in Colorado showed that adult captures were higher along field edges compared with the interior. Also, the southern edge of fields is often the most heavily infested (W. Cranshaw, unpublished data).

Wallis (57) suggested that a preseason survey of adult psyllid populations on non-economic host plants will help to predict the expected population and could be of great value to growers. Matrimony-vine was used in such surveys, but this plant is no longer abundant, in part due to its eradication for potato psyllid management. Pepper plants are currently recommended as an alternate trap plant in Colorado. Psyllids are commonly found in high numbers on pepper transplants early in the season, and the flat, smooth leaves of pepper simplify detection of nymphs on this plant.

Traps are also used to detect psyllid populations. Suction traps, widely used in much of western North America for detection of aphids affecting small grains, capture few potato psyllids even when local populations are high (W. Cranshaw, unpublished data). However, colored traps are useful for capturing alate potato psyllids. For example, in the San Luis Valley yellow pan traps are currently used to monitor flights of green peach aphid, *Myzus persicae* Sulzer. However, an important secondary benefit has been their use to detect psyllid migrations. The effectiveness of these traps could be improved further by studing the color responses of potato psyllid. Recent studies using sticky panels in infested greenhouses found neon lime-green and neon orange to be over seven times more attractive to alate potato psyllids than yellow (W. Cranshaw, unpublished data).

Epilogue

Potato psyllid historically has been a sporadic pest restricted to certain western United States potato growing areas. Because of its dependence on specific overwintering host plants it is unlikely to substantially spread its range to new production regions. Furthermore, because only a small fraction of the psyllid population occurs on potato or other cultivated crops, selective pressure to develop insecticide resistant strains is likely to be minimal.

One of the most productive research lines with this pest species appears to be related to development of improved means to detect incipient outbreaks. This includes the development of improved sampling systems as well as refinement of action thresholds. Because there appears to be a range in tolerance to potato psyllid feeding injury among exisiting cultivars, action thresholds will likely need to be cultivar-specific.

The unusual nature of feeding damage by this insect, i.e., systemic effects on growth apparently due to toxic saliva, further suggests that this insect may also be useful in studies related to potato physiology.

Acknowledgments

I would like to thank D. Patrick and R. Abernathy for their assistance in preparing the literature review for this paper. Development of this paper was supported, in part, by Colorado Agricultural Experiment Station Project 396.

Literature Cited

1. Abernathy, R. L. 1991. Investigations into the nature of the potato psyllid toxin. M.S. Thesis. Colorado State University, Ft. Collins, CO. 54 pp.

2. Arslan, A., Bessey, P. M., Matsuda, K., and Oebker, N. F. 1985. Physiological effects of psyllid (*Paratrioza cockerelli*) on potato. Amer. Potato J. 62:9-22.

3. Binkley, A. M. 1929. Transmission studies with the new psyllid-yellows disease of solanaceous plants. Science. 70:615.

4. Carter, R. D. 1950. Toxicity of *Paratrioza cockerelli* (Sulc) to certain solanaceous plants. Ph.D. Dissertation. University of California. 128 pp.

5. Carter, W. 1939. Injuries to plants caused by insect toxins. Bot. Rev. 5:273-326.

6. Carter, W. 1962. Insects in Relation to Plant Disease. Interscience Pub. New York. 705 pp.

7. Compere, H. 1915. *Paratrioza cockerelli* (Sulc). Monthly Bull. Calif. State Comm. Hort. 4:574.

8. Cranshaw, W.S. 1989. The potato/tomato psyllid as a vegetable insect pest. Proc., 18th Ann. Crop Prot. Inst., Colo. St. Univ. pp 69-76.

9. Daniels, L. B. 1934. The tomato psyllid and the control of psyllid yellows of potatoes. Colo. Agr. Exp. Stn. Bull. no. 410, 18 pp.

10. Daniels, L. B. 1954. The nature of the toxicogenic condition resulting from the feeding of the tomato psyllid *Paratrioza cockerelli* (Sulc). Ph.D. Dissertation. Univ. Minnesota. 119 pp.

11. Davis, A. C. 1937. Observations on the life history of *Paratrioza cockerelli* (Sulc) in southern California. J. Econ. Entomol. 30:377-378.

12. Edmundson, W. C. 1940. The effect of psyllid injury on the vigor of seed potatoes. Am. Potato J. 17:315-317.

13. Eyer, J. R. 1937. Physiology of psyllid yellows of potatoes. J. Econ. Entomol. 30:891-898.

14. Eyer, J. R., and Crawford, R. F. 1933. Observations on the feeding habits of the potato psyllid (*Paratrioza cockerelli* Sulc.) and the pathological history of the "psyllid yellows" which it produces. J. Econ. Entomol. 26:846-850.

15. Eyer, J. R., and Miller, M. 1938. A study of the pathological anatomy of psyllid yellows with special reference to similar changes in sugar beets affected with curly top. Phytopathology. 28:669.

16. Gerhardt, P. D. 1966. Potato psyllid and green peach aphid control on Kennebec potatoes with Temik and other insecticides. J. Econ. Entomol. 59:9-11.

17. Gerhardt, P. D., and Turley, D. L. 1961. Control of certain potato insects in Arizona with soil applications of granulated phorate. J. Econ. Entomol. 54:1217-1221.

18. Harding, J. A. 1962. Tests with systemic insecticides for control of insects and certain diseases on potatoes. J. Econ. Entomol. 55:62-64.

19.   Hill, R. E. 1947. An unusual weather sequence accompanying the severe potato psyllid outbreak of 1938 in Nebraska. J. Kans. Entomol. Soc. 20:88-92.

20.   Janes, M. J. 1939. Observations on the potato psyllid in southwest Texas. J. Econ. Entomol. 32:468.

21.   Jensen, D. D. 1957. Parasites of the Psyllidae. Hilgardia. 27:71-98.

22.   Jensen, J. H. 1939. Psyllid yellows in Nebraska - 1938. Plant Disease Reporter. 23:35-36.

23.   Johnson, T. E. 1971. The effectiveness of *Tetrastichus triozae* Burks (Hymenoptera: Eulophidae) as a biological control agent of *Paratrioza cockerelli* (Sulc.) (Homoptera: Psyllidae) in north central Colorado. M.S. Thesis. 45 pp.

24.   Knowlton, G. F. 1933. Aphis lion predators of the potato psyllid. J. Econ. Entomol. 26:977.

25.   Knowlton, G. F. 1933. Ladybird beetles as predators of the potato psyllid. Canadian Entomologist. 65:241-243.

26.   Knowlton, G. F. 1933. Length of adult life of *Paratrioza cockerelli* (Sulc). J. Econ. Entomol. 26:730.

27.   Knowlton, G. F. 1933. Notes on injurious Utah insects: Potato psyllid. Proc. Utah Acad. of Sciences. 10:153.

28.   Knowlton, G. F. 1934. A big-eyed bug predator of the potato psyllid. Florida Entomol. 18:40-43.

29.   Knowlton, G. F., and Allen, M. 1936. Three hemipterous predators of the potato psyllid. Proc. Utah Acad. Sci. 13:293-294.

30.   Knowlton, G. F., and Janes, M. J. 1931. Studies on the biology of *Paratrioza cockerelli* (Sulc). Annals Entomol. Soc. Am. 24:283-291.

31.   Knowlton, G. F., and Thomas, W.L. 1934. Host plants of the potato psyllid. J. Econ. Entomol. 27:547.

32.   Lehman, R. S. 1930. Some observations on the life-history of the tomato psyllid (*Paratrioza cockerelli* Sulc) (Homoptera). J. N. Y. Entomol. Soc. 38:307-312.

33.   List, G. M. 1917. A test of lime-sulphur and nicotine sulfate for the control of the tomato psyllid and effect of these materials upon plant growth. Colo. State Entomol. Ann. Rep. 9:40-41.

34.   List, G. M. 1932. Relation of the potato psyllid *Paratrioza cockerelli* (Sulc) to the potato disease known as "psyllid yellows." Forty-fifth Ann. Rept. of the State Entomologist, Colo. Agr. Expt. Stn. 1931-32:42-47. (Ref.)

35.   List, G. M. 1935. Psyllid yellows of tomatoes and control of the psyllid, *Paratrioza cockerelli* (Sulc), by the use of sulfur. J. Econ. Entomol. 28:431-436.

36.   List, G. M. 1939. The effect of temperature upon egg deposition, egg hatch, and nymphal development of *Paratrioza cockerelli* (Sulc.). J. Econ. Entomol. 32:30-36.

37.   Metzger, G. H. 1936. Some preliminary notes on the effect of psyllid yellows on seed stock from infected plants. Am. Potato J. 13:277-285.

38.   Meyer, W. 1991. Department of Entomology, Colorado State University, Ft. Collins, CO. Personal communication.

39.   Mills, H. B. 1942. Montana insect pests, 1941 and 1942. Twenty-ninth report of the State Entomologist. Bull. Mont. Agr. Exp. Stn. no. 408, 36 pp.

40. Pletsch, D. J. 1947. The potato psyllid *Paratrioza cockerelli* (Sulc), its biology and control. Montana Agr. Expt. Stn. Bull. 446. 95 pp.

41. Richards, B. L. 1928. A new and destructive disease of the potato in Utah and its relation to potato psylla. (Abstract) Phytopathology. 18:140-141.

42. Richards, B. L. 1929. Project 92--Psyllid yellows of potatoes. Biennial Rpt. of Director, July 1, 1926-June 30, 1928. Utah Agr. Expt. Stn. Bull. 209:50-51.

43. Richards, B. L. 1931. Further studies with psyllid yellows of the potato. (Abstract) Phytopathology. 21:103.

44. Richards, B. L., and Blood, H. L. 1933. Psyllid yellows of the potato. J. Agr. Res. 46:189-216.

45. Romney, V. E. 1939. Breeding areas of the tomato psyllid, *Paratrioza cockerelli* (Sulc). J. Econ. Entomol. 32:150-151.

46. Sanford, G. B. 1952. Phloem necrosis of potato tubers associated with infestation of vines by *Paratrioza cockerelli* Sulc. Sci. Agr. 32:433-439.

47. Schaal, L. A. 1938. Some factors affecting the symptoms of the psyllid yellows disease of potatoes. Am. Potato J. 15:193-212.

48. Snyder, W. C., Thomas, H. E., and Fairchild, S. J. 1946. A type of internal necrosis of the potato tuber caused by psyllids. Phytopathology. 36:480-481.

49. Snyder, W. C., Thomas, H. E., and Fairchild, S. J. 1946. Spindling or hair sprout of potato. Phytopathology. 36:897-904.

50. Staples, R. 1968. Cross protection between a plant virus and potato psyllid yellows. J. Econ. Entomol. 61:1378-1380.

51. Starr, G. H. 1939. Psyllid yellows unusually severe in Wyoming. Plant Disease Reporter. 23:2-3.

52. Sulc, K. 1909. *Trioza cockerelli* n.sp. Acta. Soc. Ent. Bohemiae. 6:102-108.

53. Tate, H. D., and Hill, R. E. 1944. Residual toxicity of sulphur to the potato psyllid in greenhouses. J. Econ. Entomol. 37:557-558.

54. Wallis, R. L. 1946. Seasonal occurrence of the potato psyllid in the North Platte Valley. J. Econ. Entomol. 39:689-694.

55. Wallis, R. L. 1948. Time of planting potatoes as a factor in prevention of potato psyllid attack. J. Econ. Entomol. 41:4-5.

56. Wallis, R. L. 1951. Potato psyllid selection of host plants. J. Econ. Entomol. 44:815-817.

57. Wallis, R. L. 1955. Ecological studies on the potato psyllid as a pest of potatoes. USDA Tech. Bull. 1107. 25 pp.

PART III

Advances in Potato Pest Biology and Management: Viruses and Associated Insect Vectors

ACTION THRESHOLDS FOR AN APHID VECTOR OF POTATO LEAFROLL VIRUS

David W. Ragsdale,
Edward B. Radcliffe,
Christina D. DiFonzo, and
Michael S. Connelly

University of Minnesota
Department of Entomology
St. Paul, Minnesota 55108

The concept of seed certification originated in the potato industry and has been implemented more extensively for this crop than for any other. Before the existence of viruses was known, it was recognized that asexually propagated potato seed degenerated or "ran out". When virus infected tubers are planted, yield can be reduced by as much as 50% (11). Historically, new seed was introduced by producing it in wind-swept isolated areas or by periodically producing seed from sexually propagated plants. Seed potato production now involves elaborate seed certification programs. A primary objective of seed certification is to supply producers with seed that is virtually free of tuber-borne pathogens. The fact that seed certification exists in every region where table stock potatoes are a major commodity testifies to the importance of certification programs. Indeed, one factor limiting potato production in underdeveloped countries is the lack of locally produced, virus-free seed (16).

The disease cycle in insect-vectored pathosystems is extraordinarily complex. Added to the disease triad of a susceptible host, viable inoculum, and environmental conditions is a fourth variable, a vector, that must disseminate and inoculate the pathogen (Fig. 1). The two most important aphid-vectored viruses in terms of yield and quality reduction are potato leafroll virus (PLRV) and potato virus Y (PVY). In North America, four aphid species commonly colonize potato: green peach aphid, *Myzus persicae* Sulzer; potato aphid, *Macrosiphum euphorbiae* (Thomas); buckthorn aphid, *Aphis nasturtii* Kaltenbach; and foxglove aphid, *Aulacorthum solani* (Kaltenbach) (17). Although each colonizing species can transmit both viruses, transmission efficiency varies (13). Of these four species, the green peach aphid is recognized as the most important aphid vector in potato and control is specifically targeted toward this species. Reasons for this include its high efficiency in transmitting these viruses (usually in excess of 50% of individuals transmit), abundance in the crop, and its propensity to develop insecticide resistance. However, for PVY the principle vectors may be non-colonizing species because few studies have demonstrated a correlation between densities of colonizing aphids and PVY spread.

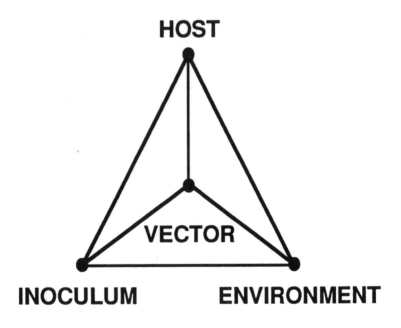

HOST

VECTOR

INOCULUM   **ENVIRONMENT**

Figure 1. The typical plant disease triad becomes more complicated when an insect vector is required for inoculation.

Aphids transmit potato viruses in either a persistent or nonpersistent fashion. In nonpersistent transmission, the virus is associated with the mouthparts or the lining of the foregut and no viral replication occurs within the vector (10). Both acquisition and inoculation occur after feeding only a few seconds in epidermal tissue (= sap sampling). Immediately after acquisition, aphids are able to transmit virus. Nonpersistent viruses are not retained after a molt and after a few brief probes on a healthy plant, aphids lose their charge of virus and must again feed on a diseased host to become infective. Nonpersistent viruses are usually high titered viruses which can be mechanically transmitted through seed cutting, cultivation, or other means. Nonpersistent transmission by aphids is a complex biological process and not simply a mechanical process associated with insect feeding. Transmission by aphids of a nonpersistent virus like PVY is an exception rather than a rule; most aphid species are not vectors. Even among vector species, there are large differences in transmission efficiency (8). Often proteinaceous (helper) factors that recognize binding sites on the virus and in the vector are required for successful transmission (15).

A persistent virus has a more intimate association with its vector. Before virus can be transmitted, it must circulate throughout the vector and it may need to replicate in the vector as well (6). Persistent viruses are often phloem-limited and require several minutes to hours of feeding for acquisition or inoculation to occur (10). A persistent virus, *e.g.*, PLRV, which is picked up only after feeding on phloem implies that the plant is an acceptable host because it takes a relatively long time for an aphid to reach phloem (10-30 minutes) (12). Contrast this with "sap sampling" which takes only seconds to complete. Following acquisition of a persistent virus, there is a latent period ranging from several hours to a few days before a vector can transmit. However, once virus is acquired, an individual aphid retains virus even after it molts and generally remains infective for life.

PLRV in Minnesota - the Problem

All aphid-vectored virus diseases of potato are transmitted nonpersistently except for PLRV. PLRV is a luteovirus containing single stranded RNA with replication confined to phloem tissue of a few species in the Solanaceae. It was not until 1906 that PLRV was recognized as a disease of potato and it was not discovered until 1920 that the green peach aphid transmits PLRV from diseased to healthy plants (21). In controlled studies with other colonizing species, generally less than 10% of the individuals are capable of transmitting PLRV (19).

In Minnesota, around 22,500 acres of certified seed potatoes are produced annually with an on-farm value of $23-29 million. Serious, unpredictable losses to seed quality by aphid vectored viral pathogens have occurred. Over 3,674 acres entered for certification from 1979 to 1990 have been rejected because of these viruses (R. Zink, personal communication). Nearly one-third of these rejections were due to PLRV. A review of the literature shows that each potato producing area has unique problems with aphid vectored viral diseases (18). Variables such as weed hosts for pathogens, overwintering hosts for aphid vectors, vector species complexes, varied production practices, and many different environmental and climatic factors all affect viral epidemics. Consequently, each growing region must understand the dynamics of the pathosystem and target controls accordingly. For example, attempted eradication of Canada plum (*Prunus nigra* L.) in Maine and management of peach (*P. persica* L.) and apricot (*P. armeniaca* L.) orchard pruning in the Pacific Northwest are valid attempts to reduce overwintering green peach aphid in their respective regions, but are of limited use in Minnesota because commercial production of peach and apricot is not possible. From 1985 to 1990 we focused on PLRV, and demonstrated that virus spread can be significantly reduced by controlling green peach aphid apterae. However, recommending insecticidal sprays based on density of green peach aphid apterae to control PLRV spread is a strategy uniquely suited to the Red River Valley of Minnesota and North Dakota.

It appears that the green peach aphid does not overwinter in Minnesota, but is a long distance migrant which usually arrives in potato fields in early to mid-July. More importantly, immigrating green peach aphids rarely arrive viruliferous for PLRV (5, 7). Their arrival is too early to successfully use yellow pan trap thresholds developed in Europe and New Brunswick, Canada (2) where vine kill is recommended when a cumulative number of 5 green peach aphids are collected in any one trap. In Minnesota, such thresholds are nearly always exceeded before tubers reach marketable size. Additionally, overwintering hosts for PLRV do not exist in our region; volunteer potatoes are rare and susceptible weed species are not perennial. Inoculum may come from home gardens or infected bedding plants and flowers (Mowry, this volume), but it seems unlikely these are major sources in Minnesota. The most likely source is the potato crop itself. Given these unique features of the PLRV pathosystem in the Midwest, we hypothesized that application of the threshold concept might be applied by sampling vector density (apterae) on potato. We suggest that adoption of such a concept is a more sound strategy than trying to maintain the crop free of green peach aphid apterae.

In Minnesota, one method that controls aphid vectors of PLRV and was formerly the standard control practice in the seed industry was to apply aldicarb (Temik 15G, at 2.24 kg AI/ha, Rhone-Poulanc Ag Co., Research Triangle Park, NC) at planting followed by foliar sprays of methamidophos (Monitor 4E, at 1.12 kg AI/ha, Miles Chemical Corp., Indianapolis, IN) applied on a calendar based schedule. Aldicarb was the insecticide most commonly found in groundwater and this led to its withdrawal from the Wisconsin market in 1988. Because of aldicarb residues in the crop, Temik was voluntarily withdrawn from the U.S.

potato market by the manufacturer in April 1990. Seed producers must now rely solely on foliar sprays for aphid control. It is important to apply foliar insecticides only as necessary because repeated applications not only increase production costs, but almost invariably trigger aphid resurgence which in turn could induce a viral epidemic. Moreover, frequent application of foliar sprays only exacerbates resistance problems and we might lose the few insecticides that currently give reliable aphid control.

PLRV - Green Peach Aphid Action Thresholds

Several pieces of this puzzle have come together since we began our research. First, we demonstrated that PLRV spread was not correlated with alatae captures in either yellow pan traps or nonattractive green tile traps (r^2 = 0.05 to 0.11) (7). The best relationship between green peach aphid density and PLRV infection was with in-field apterae counts (r^2 = 0.55 to 0.80) (5, 7). Also, PLRV spread more readily down rows than across rows, implicating apterae that walk from plant to plant, but not across bare ground (7). Spread to adjacent rows apparently does not occur until the canopy closes (Fig. 2). These findings contradict most published reports from Europe where alatae, not apterae, are highly correlated with PLRV spread and not with apterae (3). Clearly, different climatic and environmental conditions are driving the pathosystems at each location.

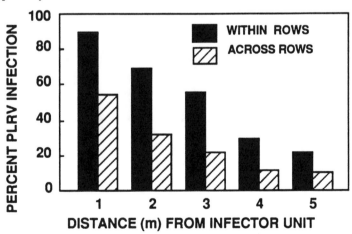

Figure 2. Percent PLRV infection across treatments in relation to distance (m) of plants (within and across rows) from infector unit, in 'Russet Burbank' potatoes at Rosemount, Minnesota, in 1986. (Reprinted with permission from the *Journal of Economic Entomology*)

A previous study tested various action thresholds and found this approach to be a practical means of aphid management (4). We began to study if action thresholds could be used to determine the time when foliar sprays should be applied to prevent PLRV spread. First, using high aphid densities, we demonstrated that weekly sprays of methamidophos alone were as effective as applications of aldicarb at planting in combination with weekly sprays of methamidophos (the industry standard for seed potato production) in preventing PLRV spread (Table 1). Next, we experimented with PLRV spread under low aphid densities using a PLRV susceptible cultivar, Russet Burbank, and began to test the feasibility of using action thresholds to control an aphid-vectored decease. We tested action thresholds of 0, 3, 10, 30 and 100 apterae per 100 leaves. We found cumulative aphid-days (apterae) and PLRV levels to be highly correlated ($r^2 = 0.79$) (5) and the pattern of virus spread was clumped, indicating spread by apterae. No significant differences in PLRV spread were obtained from the three lowest thresholds (5) (Fig. 3). We now recommend using an action threshold of 10 green peach aphid apterae per 100 leaves as an action threshold in seed fields to control PLRV.

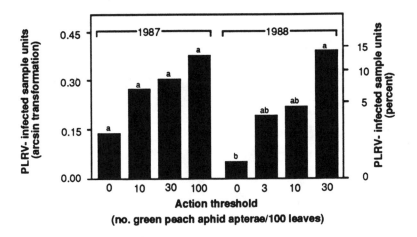

Figure 3. Mean percent leafroll infection in each apterae action threshold treatment, Rosemount, Minn. 1987-1988. Treatments with different letters were significantly different. (Tukey's HSD, P<0.05). (Reprinted with permission from the *Journal of Economic Entomology*)

Table 1. Cumulative apterae-days for green peach aphids and PLRV infection in 'Russet Burbank' potatoes at Rosemount, Minnesota. (Reprinted with permission from the *Journal of Economic Entomology*)

Treatment	AI/ha (kg)	Cumulative apterae-days per 100 leaves [a]		Percent PLRV infection [b]	
		1985	1986	1985[c]	1986[d]
Aldicarb + Methamidophos (7-day schedule)	3.4	48 a	69 a	23.7 a	12.3 a
Methamidophos (7-day schedule)	0.8	28 a	138 a	26.3 a	14.0 a
Methamidophos (14-day schedule)	0.8	55 a	236 a	38.7 ab	28.5 b
Untreated check	-	197 a	1139 a	47.5 b	43.5 c
Methoxychlor (14-day schedule)	0.2	896 b	4499 b	62.2 c	64.3 d
Methoxychlor (14-day schedule)	0.5	3223 c	9558 c	74.0 c	77.2 e

[a]Samples were taken from 216 leaves per treatment and converted to number per 100 leaves.
[b] Numbers within column followed by the same letter are not significantly different (P < 0.05; Duncan's multiple range test).
[c] 108 plants per treatment tested, 6 replications.
[d]240 sample units per treatment, 6 replications.

The initial threshold studies on PLRV in Minnesota used the cultivar Russet Burbank, a PLRV-susceptible cultivar. The next question we asked was could action thresholds be elevated in resistant cultivars. We conducted a field study using three cultivars that varied widely in PLRV susceptibility (1) but did not differ in aphid susceptibility (DiFonzo *et al.*, unpublished data). A highly resistant cultivar, Cascade, a moderately resistant cultivar, Kennebec, along with our standard susceptible cultivar, Russet Burbank, were used. As expected, PLRV resistance was highest in 'Cascade' and intermediate in 'Kennebec' and far more spread was observed for a given number of aphid-days in 'Russet Burbank'. These preliminary data (Table 2), demonstrate that action thresholds can be elevated for resistant cultivars.

Table 2. Comparison of potato leafroll virus spread when using action thresholds based on green peach aphid apterae per 100 leaves in potato leafroll sensitive, moderately resistant and resistant cultivars, Russet Burbank, Kennebec and Cascade, respectively. Data are reported as cumulative mean aphid-days and percent potato leafroll virus.

	Variety					
Treatment	Russet Burbank		Kennebec		Cascade	
or						
Target Threshold	Aphid-days	%PLRV	Aphid-days	%PLRV	Aphid-days	%PLRV
Temik/Monitor	9	4.6	9	2.7	5	0.0
Temik/Monitor - 0[a] + PLRV[b]	51	11.6	2	5.5	3	3.6
Threshold - 3 + PLRV	101	15.1	na	-	na	-
Threshold - 10 + PLRV	205	24.2	308	18.2	na	-
Threshold - 30 + PLRV	712	39.2	502	9.1	918	9.4
Threshold - 100 + PLRV	2,664	65.5	2,903	28.8	1,762	8.9
Threshold - 300 + PLRV	na	-	4,095	14.8	6,239	9.1
Threshold - 1000 + PLRV	na	-	na	-	19,988	30.9

[a] 0, 3, 10, 30, 100, 300, & 1000 = the target densities based on the number of green peach aphid apterae per 100 mid- to lower plant leaves. Once target densities were reached, methamidophos (Monitor, 1.12 kg AI/has) was applied.
[b] + PLRV = two center plants per plot were inoculated with PLRV.

PLRV Action Thresholds and PVY

As we develop action thresholds to control PLRV we must determine if using thresholds based on green peach aphid apterae density will adversely affect PVY spread. Specifically, would a PVY epidemic occur if seed producers allowed some low level aphid population to exist before applying controls? For nonpersistently transmitted viruses such as PVY, inoculation only needs seconds to occur and no conventional insecticide can kill an aphid quickly enough to prevent transmission. Indeed, only rarely has a study been published where insecticides have stopped nonpersistent virus spread (14).

We investigated the effect of various apterae target densities on PVY spread. The source of PVY was three adjacent plants in the center of the plot. We maintained certain plots near our proposed thresholds, but also included plots where aphid densities were allowed to reach much higher levels. The conclusion we drew from this experiment was that even in plots with relatively high aphid density (see Table 3, treatments: Asana 7-day schedule, Thimet, and Karate 7-day schedule), PVY did not spread significantly more than in plots where aphid densities per 100 leaves were kept as low as possible (see Table 3, treatments Thimet/Monitor and Temik/Monitor). Also, none of the treatments were entirely effective at preventing PVY spread. Based on these preliminary data, we concluded that if action thresholds were used for timing sprays for green peach aphid to control PLRV spread, the risk of PVY spread would not increase. Only when apterae-days greatly exceeded our threshold (see Thimet + PVY treatment in Table 3) was there any appreciable increase in PVY spread attributed to green peach aphid apterae.

Table 3. Evaluation of potato virus Y spread when action thresholds developed for control of potato leafroll virus are used. Data are reported as cumulative mean aphid-days and percent potato virus Y.

Treatment or Target Threshold	Aphid-days	%PVY
Thimet/Monitor - No PVY source	34 ac	1.4 a
Temik/Monitor - No PVY source	42 a	3.2 ab
Temik/Monitor - 0ª + PVYᵇ	747 a	1.8 ab
Action Threshold - 3 + PVY	96 a	2.2 ab
Action Threshold - 10 + PVY	338 a	3.2 ab
Action Threshold - 30 + PVY	1,590 a	2.9 ab
Action Threshold - 100 + PVY	1,820 a	3.5 ab
Asana 7-day schedule + PVY	4,240 ab	4.7 ab
Thimet alone + PVY	9,511 b	7.1 b
Karate 7-day schedule + PVY	10,420 b	6.3 ab

ª 0, 3, 10, 30, & 100 = the target densities or action thresholds based on the number of green peach aphid apterae per 100 middle to lower plant leaves. Once action thresholds were reached, methamidophos (1.12 kg Al/ha) was applied weekly until harvest.
ᵇ + PVY = two center plants per plot were inoculated with PVY.
ᶜ Means followed by the same letter are not significantly different ($P = 0.05$) using the LSD.

PVY Problem

PVY is one of the most devastating diseases of potato and is proving to be extraordinarily difficult to control with the current seed certification program. PVY is an increasingly common cause for rejection of potato acreage entered in seed certification programs. In Minnesota, over 4,000 acres were rejected in 1991 and for some cultivars no certified seed may be available for the 1992 crop, depending upon results of the winter test of seed lots entered for recertification. Although the green peach aphid, *M. persicae*, is the most efficient vector, at least 30 other species can transmit PVY even though most are incapable of colonizing the crop (9, 13). Reasons for the sustained increase in prevalence of PVY are unclear. Hypotheses proposed include: some cultivars, *e.g.*, Russet Norkotah are essentially symptomless and infected seed lots go undetected by seed certification personnel; that some insecticides widely used for control of other potato pests (*e.g.*, esfenvalerate) enhance aphid population build-up; that aphids transported on air-currents arrive viruliferous; that virus may be spread mechanically by seed cutters or field machinery; or that because of a prolonged drought, summer alatae are coming from weeds and other crops much earlier than normal and infecting plants at a more susceptible stage.

Clearly, appropriate management strategies for PVY in potato cannot be designed until we understand the key factors governing PVY epidemics in Minnesota. Specifically, we are determining what vector species are involved, when is virus being transmitted, what is (are) the principle virus source(s), and what impact spread would there be on PVY spread if action thresholds developed for PLRV (a persistent virus/vector pathosystem) were used.

Epilogue

Control of virus diseases in seed potato production presents a paradox. Seed certification has proven remarkably effective in minimizing the incidence of aphid-transmitted virus diseases including PVY and PLRV, but epidemics still occur. Many of the assumptions which underlie the virus/vector management strategies employed by certification programs are unproven. Particularly deficient is the belief that seed producers must control aphids to prevent PVY spread. Early season control is considered to be especially important because young plants are more susceptible and may in-turn become the source of further current-season spread (20). The standard practice in the potato seed industry is to apply frequent foliar sprays on a routine basis. Benefits of insecticidal therapies for control of non-persistent viruses such as PVY are quite uncertain. Unfortunately, variability in the composition of the pathosystems from one region to another necessitates site specific research programs. Growers rely heavily on insecticides because of their conviction that equivalent effective control alternatives are not available. This is disturbing, if for no other reason than because it makes the industry extremely vulnerable. Insecticides can and will be lost, insects can develop resistance, present uses can be restricted or canceled, and products can be withdrawn from the market. Indeed, the potato seed industry now has only one insecticide available, methamidophos, that is effective against green peach aphid. Unfortunately, present knowledge of the epidemiology of PVY is insufficient to permit informed modification of vector management programs.

The incorporation of genetic resistance to viruses, vectors, or both whether using conventional breeding techniques or by application of genetic engineering via transgenic plants offers great hope. Clearly, vector control is only a single component in a highly complex pathosystem. Currently no therapeutic control tactic can prevent PVY spread. If plants were engineered to be immune to virus infection then aphids would be only minor pests rather than one of the three major insect pests found on the crop (18).

References Cited

1. Bagnall, R. H., and G. C. C. Tai. 1986. PLRV: evaluation of resistance in potato cultivars. Plant Dis. 70: 621-623.
2. Boiteau, G. 1982. Potato pest management in New Brunswick. Proc. Ontario Hort. Conf. pp. 101-106.
3. Broadbent, L. 1950. The correlation of aphid numbers with spread of leafroll and rugose mosaic in potato crops. Ann. Appl. Biol. 37: 58-65.
4. Cancelado, R. E., and E. B. Radcliffe. 1979. Action thresholds for green peach aphid on potatoes in Minnesota. J. Econ. Entomol. 72: 606-609.
5. Flanders, K. L., E. B. Radcliffe, and D. W. Ragsdale. 1991. Potato leafroll virus spread in relation to densities of green peach aphid (Homoptera: Aphididae): implications for management thresholds for Minnesota seed potatoes. J. Econ. Entomol. 84:1026-1036.
6. Gibbs, A. and B. Harrison. 1976. Plant virology the principles. Edward Arnold Ltd. London.
7. Hanafi, A., E. B. Radcliffe, and D. W. Ragsdale. 1989. Spread and control of potato leafroll virus in Minnesota. J. Econ. Entomol. 82: 1201-1206.
8. Harrington, R., and R. W. Gibson. 1989. Transmission of potato virus Y by aphids trapped in potato crops in southern England. Potato Res. 32: 167-174.
9. Harrington, R., N. Katis, and R. W. Gibson. 1986. Field assessment of the relative importance of different aphid species in the transmission of potato virus Y. Potato Res. 29: 67-76.
10. Harris, K. F. 1977. An ingestion-egestion hypothesis of noncirculative virus transmission, pp. 165-220. In: K. F. Harris, and K. Maramorosch [eds.], Aphids as virus vectors. Academic Press, New York.
11. Killick, R. J. 1979. The effect of infection with potato leafroll virus (PLRV) on yield and some of its components in a variety of potato (Solanum tuberosum). Ann. Appl. Biol. 91: 67-74.
12. Leonard, S. H. and F. R. Holbrook. 1978. Minimum acquisition and transmission times for potato leaf roll virus by the green peach aphid. Ann. Entomol. Soc. Am. 71: 493-495.
13. MacGillivary, M. E. 1981. Aphids, pp. 101-103. In: W. J. Hooker [ed.], Compendium of potato diseases. American Phytopathological Society, St. Paul.
14. Perrin, R. M., and R. W. Gibson. 1985. Control of some insect-borne plant viruses with the pyrethroid PP321 (Karate). International Pest Control. Nov./Dec: 142-143, 145.
15. Pirone, T. P. 1977. Accessory factors in nonpersistent virus transmission, pp. 221-236. In: K. F. Harris, and K. Maramorosch [eds.], Aphids as virus vectors. Academic Press, New York.
16. Radcliffe, E. B. 1982. Insect pests of potato. Ann. Rev. Entomol. 27: 173-204.

17. Radcliffe, E. B., D. W. Ragsdale, and K. F. Flanders. 1988. Aphids and leafhoppers: economic importance, biology and control. *In:* American Phytopathology Society, Plant Health Management in Potato Production. American Phytopathology Society, St. Paul. (In Press)

18. Radcliffe, E. B., K. F. Flanders, D. W. Ragsdale, and D. M. Noetzel. 1989. Potato insects: pest management systems for potato insects, pp. 586-621, *In:* D. Pimentel [ed.], CRC Handbook of Pest Management in Agriculture. CRC Press, Boca Raton.

19. Robert, Y. 1971. Epidemiologie de l'enroulement de la pomme de terre: capacite vectrice de stades et de formes des pucerons *Aulacorthum solani* Kltb. *Macrosiphum euphorbiae* Thomas et *Myzus persicae* Sulz. Potato Res. 14: 130-139.

20. Sigvald, R. 1986. Forecasting the incidence of PVY, pp. 419-441. *In:* G. D. McLean, R. G. Garrett and W. G. Ruesink [eds.] Plant Virus Epidemics: Monitoring, Modeling and Predicting Outbreaks. Academic Press, New York.

21. van der Want, J. H. P. 1972. Introduction to plant virology, pp. 19-25. *In:* J. A. de Bokx [ed.] Viruses of potatoes and seed-potato production. Centre for Agricultural Publishing and Documentation, Wageningen.

POTATO LEAFROLL VIRUS MANAGEMENT IN THE PACIFIC NORTHWEST (USA)

Thomas M. Mowry
University of Idaho, Division of
Entomology, Parma Research
and Extension Center,
Parma, Idaho 83660

Potato leafroll virus (PLRV) is a luteovirus that infects a limited range of host plants, mostly in the Solanaceae, of which potato, *Solanum tuberosum* L., is most important economically. PLRV is transmitted by grafting, aphid vectors in a circulative, nonpropagative manner (11,20), and infected seed. Primary symptoms, including slight chlorosis and upright, rolled leaves, result from aphid transmission and are often not visible if infection occurs late in the season, making in-field diagnosis of potato leafroll impossible. Secondary symptoms result from PLRV-infected tubers and include chlorosis, stunting, dry or leathery leaves, and severe leaf rolling. PLRV infection is usually accompanied by yield reductions, sometimes reaching 40-70% (17,21). In addition to foliage symptoms and subsequent yield reductions, PLRV causes a diffuse net necrosis in infected tubers, rendering them nonmarketable. Of all potato cultivars, 'Russet Burbank' is the most susceptible to net necrosis (12).

In 1990, the Pacific Northwest (PNW; Idaho, Oregon, Washington) produced almost 60% of all potatoes grown on fall harvested hectares in the United States (Fig. 1) with a combined value of more than $1 billion (1,2). There were several cultivars grown, but 'Russet Burbank' accounted for 91.6%, 73.8%, and 72.7% of total potato production in Idaho, Oregon, and Washington, respectively (2). This large production and the overwhelming dominance of 'Russet Burbank' make PLRV control of paramount importance to PNW potato growers.

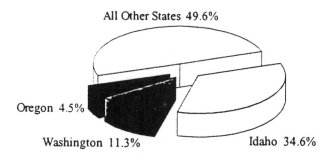

HECTARES HARVESTED

All Other States 49.6%

Oregon 4.5%

Washington 11.3%

Idaho 34.6%

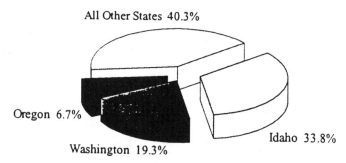

FALL PRODUCTION

All Other States 40.3%

Oregon 6.7%

Washington 19.3%

Idaho 33.8%

Fig. 1. Harvested hectares and production of potatoes (all cultivars) in the Pacific Northwest as percentages of the United States total fall harvest in 1990.

Geographical heterogeneity dictates the distribution of potato production in the PNW and probably indirectly influences the regional relationships of viral diseases. There are four main regions of potato production generally separated by mountains and/or deserts where potatoes are not grown (Fig. 2). Local geography also contributes to suppression of potato viral disease, e.g., the mountain valleys of eastern Idaho effectively separates several potato production areas and their aphid and virus populations. On a more local scale, most seed potatoes in the PNW are isolated from commercial potatoes, at least by certain minimum distances required for certification (see below).

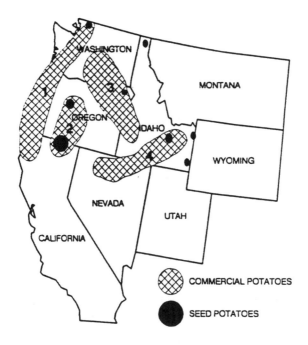

Fig. 2. Geographical distribution of commercial and seed potato production in the Pacific Northwest.

Potato Leafroll Virus Management System

Viral diseases pose a particularly difficult problem for potato production because there is no cure for viral infection. Therefore, control of these diseases, particularly potato leafroll, is oriented towards prevention by implementing several essentially unrelated and expensive measures meant to produce resistance to viral infection in breeding programs, eliminate virus inoculum through cultural practices, provide virus-free seed by certification, and reduce virus spread with vector control. Taken together, these practices have undoubtedly reduced PLRV problems in potato, but it is difficult, if not impossible, to quantify their overall impact, either individually or collectively. Even with these and other relatively expensive preventative measures, PLRV remains a significant threat to potato production in the PNW. Several other factors, such as climate (4), insecticide resistance (15), and variable transmission efficiencies by aphid vectors (19), are important in PLRV epidemiology and will require more research for future control of potato leafroll in the PNW.

Breeding Program

In the United States, 'Russet Burbank' is by far the most important potato cultivar for both processing and fresh market (18) which accounts for its dominance in the PNW. Therefore, acceptance of any new cultivar will depend upon its ability to duplicate the agronomic qualities of 'Russet Burbank' as well as expressing resistance to PLRV. Combining these two disparate characteristics in one cultivar has not been achieved. Moreover, potato producers do not favor tolerant cultivars that show no symptoms of PLRV infection, because asymptomatic plants cannot be identified for roguing (5). Producers fear that fields with these tolerant cultivars will be virus inoculum sources that might threaten nearby nontolerant potatoes.

No potato cultivar has significant resistance to PLRV infection, but several (e.g., 'Norgold Russet' [16,18]) are resistant to tuber net necrosis. Unfortunately, most of these are fresh market cultivars and do not process or store well, limiting their usefulness in PNW potato production. Overall, breeding for resistance has had minimal impact on PLRV management.

Cultural Practices

Crop rotation is an important and widely practiced component of PNW potato production. Many growers are on three or four year rotations with crops such as wheat, sugar beets, and onions. In general, farms are large enough to allow for significant distances between rotations, rather than rotating to adjacent fields. Because infected potato is the most significant source of PLRV (8,9,23), the wide rotational separation in time and space minimizes the effect of PLRV inoculum from volunteers infected the previous season.

In seed potato production, roguing is practiced rigorously to reduce within-field PLRV inoculum and its subsequent spread. The plants must be removed and destroyed because, as with many viruses, aphids easily acquire PLRV from excised plant parts. Normally, workers are able to identify secondary leafroll symptoms and, occasionally, primary symptoms in plants infected early in the season. However, due to climatic conditions that limit spring aphid populations in most areas, early season primary infection is rare. In the PNW, plants originating from infected seed are the most important PLRV inoculum sources and aphids transmit the virus from these to adjacent plants (8,14). Therefore, the roguing plan (Fig. 3), based on the difficulty of detecting primary leafroll symptoms and the pattern of within-field spread, involves destroying twelve additional plants around the symptomatic source (8,12). Roguing is seldom practiced in commercial potato fields.

Fig. 3. Roguing plan for removal of potato leafroll virus-infected and nearby noninfected plants. Plants must be removed from the field and destroyed.

Certified Seed

Production of virus-free seed through certification programs is probably the most effective means of controlling PLRV in the PNW primarily because established tolerance levels for certification translates into low in-field inoculum. While specific standards may vary slightly, the certification program in Idaho, conducted by the Idaho Crop Improvement Association, is representative of the region. Seven classes of seed are recognized for certification (3), including Nuclear (N) and Generations (G) 1-6, with G5 being the last generation accepted for recertification resulting in certified seed not being older than G6. To be eligible for entry into the program, seed potato fields must be a minimum of 6.1 m (20 ft.) from potatoes not entered for certification and have no more than 5% volunteers, except in N, G1 and G2 fields where no volunteers are allowed (3).

The program consists of seasonal field inspections and subsequent winter tests (plant-outs) of tuber samples for all acreage entered for certification. Field inspections for visible PLRV symptoms are done at least twice during the season (three times for N and G1 seed) and involve inspecting a minimum of 494 plants per ha (200/acre). The number of plants inspected varies somewhat with harvest class and field size. For example, in N fields, which tend to be small, all plants might be inspected. Disease tolerances are based on generation (Table 1) and are the basis for rejection of a given seed lot, so inspections are not designed to allow growers to rogue fields exceeding tolerance levels. However, as seen in Table 1, growers must maintain tolerance levels between inspections and, in some cases, reduce PLRV incidence, e.g., 0.07% PLRV would be acceptable in the first inspection of a G4 field, but not in the second. Seed stocks from fields showing 0.1% or more leafroll from any inspection are not eligible for recertification.

Table 1. Potato leafroll virus field inspection tolerances for certified potato seed in Idaho[a].

Inspection	Seed Generation[b]						
	N[c]	1[c]	2	3	4	5[d]	6
1st	0.00	0.00	0.01	0.03	0.08	0.20	0.20
2nd	0.00	0.00	0.01	0.01	0.05	0.20	0.20

[a]ICIA Idaho Rules for Certification (3).
[b]Percent infection based on minimum 494 plants/ha (200/acre).
[c]Nuclear and G1 fields are inspected 3 times per season.
[d]Last generation accepted for recertification.

Only potatoes from fields passing final inspection are eligible for winter testing, which is the planting out of tuber samples in southern states where climate allows winter potato growing. For PLRV, the winter test permits disease assessment, via secondary symptomology, that might not be evident in the field because of the difficulty in detecting primary symptoms. In general, the sample size for the winter test is 400 tubers per the first 49.4 ha (20 acres) of a field entered in the program. As with field inspections, sample size varies with harvest class and is not a constant function of acreage, e.g., in later generation seed, an 800 tuber sample might not be taken until 271.6 ha (110 acres) is reached (3). For recertification, additional winter test samples for each 12.3, 24.7 and 98.8 ha (5, 10 and 20 acres) are required for G1, G2 and G3 seed, respectively (3). Seed stocks showing 0.8% or more visible leafroll cannot be entered for recertification and those showing more than 2.0% cannot be certified for commercial production (3).

Vector Control

The green peach aphid, *Myzus persicae* (Sulzer), is the principle vector of PLRV (10,22) because it is the most efficient transmitter and generally the most abundant aphid colonizing potatoes (6). Other

116

potato colonizing aphids, such as the potato aphid, *Macrosiphum euphorbiae* (Thomas), transmit the virus much less efficiently. Consequently, management of PLRV vectors is aimed exclusively at controlling the green peach aphid through insecticides, elimination or treatment of overwintering hosts and aphid-free commercially available bedding plants.

Action Thresholds. The only insecticide treatment thresholds in the PNW for controlling the green peach aphid to reduce spread of PLRV were established for commercial potato production in southwestern and southcentral Idaho by Byrne and Bishop (10). These thresholds are based on leaf counts and apply only when PLRV infection within the field is less than 0.2%, the maximum tolerance for certified seed fields. The thresholds are 40 green peach aphids/50 leaves and 10 green peach aphids/50 leaves in two consecutive weeks prior to August 1 for southwestern and southcentral Idaho, respectively. In practice, these thresholds are often used regardless of PLRV inoculum levels. No treatment thresholds exist for eastern Idaho, primarily because green peach aphid numbers and PLRV inoculum are so low in this seed production area that correlations or good fits to linear models cannot be calculated (10). Consequently, seed potato growers currently practice zero-tolerance for the green peach aphid. Not only is this goal unattainable, this intensive insecticide use may contribute to resistance problems in the future.

Monitoring. For a number of years, various agencies in the PNW have conducted annual pan trap surveys, usually in conjunction with field sampling, for monitoring green peach aphid activity. Several of these surveys continue and serve to alert growers to increasing aphid infestations. In 1989, the Idaho pan trap survey and field sampling program operated by University of Idaho entomologists was terminated because of several years of exceedingly low aphid numbers. The 1989 survey for southwestern Idaho included 10 fields monitored weekly. The seasonal data (Fig. 4) showed that at no time did the leaf counts approach the southcentral Idaho threshold nor the southwestern threshold.

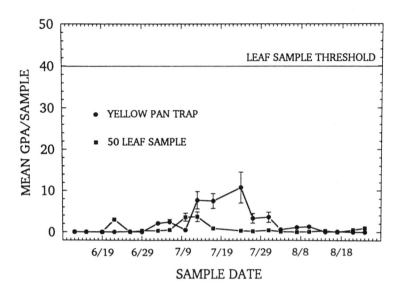

Fig. 4. Results of the 1989 pan trap and 50 leaf sample survey in southwestern Idaho. Each point is the mean ± SE for 10 fields sampled every 3-4 days throughout the season.

The Idaho Aphid Suction Trap Network, established in 1985 primarily to monitor cereal aphids for barley yellow dwarf control in wheat, provide green peach aphid flight data for several areas throughout the state. Green peach aphid suction trap data from Parma (southwestern), Kimberly (southcentral) and Tetonia (eastern) for the years 1987-1991 (Fig. 5) help explain the low PLRV incidence during this time (Mowry et al., unpublished data). In Parma and Kimberly, there was no significant spring flight activity and most flight occurred after the August 1 cutoff date for insecticide treatment (10). In addition, green peach aphid numbers were not particularly high, especially in Tetonia, where only 8 green peach aphids were collected in 5 years. It is reasonable to hypothesize that PLRV epidemiology is at least as dependent upon green peach aphid population dynamics as on rigorous management practices.

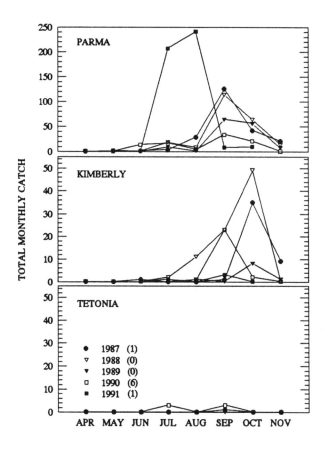

Fig 5. Green peach aphid seasonal flight activity detected by southwestern (Parma), southcentral (Kimberly) and eastern (Tetonia) Idaho aerial suction traps. The legend is for all three graphs. Numbers in parentheses are the total annual trap catches for Tetonia only.

Cultural Control. Because of severe winters in most areas of the PNW, the green peach aphid often overwinters holocyclically in the relatively hardy egg stage. Peach (*Prunus persica* L.) and apricot (*P. armeniaca* L.) are the most important primary hosts where green peach aphid oviparae lay eggs in leaf and bud axils. Removal of unwanted peach and apricot trees and early spring insecticide treatment of others is recommended for controlling the green peach aphid (7,12). This has apparently had a significant impact on green peach aphid populations in certain areas, especially eastern Idaho where aphid numbers have been very low in recent years (Fig. 5).

Home gardens have been identified as a source of both green peach aphid and PLRV (9) which threaten surrounding potato fields (Fig. 6). The problem begins by purchasing green peach aphid infested bedding plants from local commercial outlets and planting them in the home garden. Potatoes in the garden become infested with green peach aphids that can acquire PLRV if the plants are infected, which occurs frequently when gardeners save potatoes from previous years for seed. As aphid populations increase and alatae are formed, they migrate to nearby potato fields. These immigrating aphids can initiate severe infestations and, if viruliferous, are an immediate threat to the crop, especially in seed potatoes. Home gardeners have been asked to exercise care when buying and planting bedding plants and, in seed production areas, potato growers offer home gardeners free certified seed to eliminate PLRV inoculum in their gardens.

Fig. 6. Potential source of green peach aphid infestation of potato fields. Aphids originate from bedding plants for sale in local towns and cities.

A survey done in 1990 found that commercially available bedding plants continue to be significant sources of potential green peach aphid infestation (13; Table 2). Infested plants were found in every city or town surveyed, but not in every outlet. Data from the survey have been used to request that regulatory agencies police suppliers and retailers to maintain pest-free material. However, pressure to provide pest-free plants will likely mean greater insecticide use by producers and increased potential for resistant green peach aphids that might lead to resistance in field populations.

Table 2. Survey of green peach aphid infestations of bedding plants for sale in various eastern Idaho commercial outlets.

Plant[a]	Infested SU/n[b]	% SU Infested
Cole Crops (Brassica spp.)	45/245	18.4
Eggplant (Solanum melongena L.)	79/150	52.7
Forget-Me-Not (Myosotis sylvatica Hoffm.)	8/22	36.4
Green Pepper (Capsicum annuum L.)	204/490	41.6
Petunia (Petunia hybrida Vilm.)	13/32	40.6

[a]Mixed cultivars.
[b]Survey of salable units (SU), not individual plants. n = no. SU examined.

Epilogue

For at least the next decade, PLRV management in the PNW will depend on adherence to the various preventative measures described above. Because infected potato is the most important source of PLRV inoculum, strict seed certification programs will have the greatest impact on future disease control. Spread of PLRV is a function, inter alia, of vector population size and amount of in-field inoculum. Aphid vectors are often controlled by prophylactic insecticide applications, but, with changing insecticide registrations and more stringent controls on their use, minimizing in-field PLRV inoculum through certified seed will allow for more rational vector control strategies. Such strategies must include management of insecticide resistance as an important part of future PLRV control. Green peach aphid populations sampled in 1991 throughout Idaho all exhibited slight to moderate resistance levels (Mowry, unpublished data). Even with low in-field inoculum levels, PLRV epidemics may result from outbreaks of insecticide resistant vector populations. In addition, further research is needed to determine if, as mentioned above, highly resistant green peach aphids entering on commercially available bedding plants might exacerbate resistance in the field.

Genetic engineering of potato for virus disease resistance may offer another means of PLRV control. Several agencies have successfully transformed lines of 'Russet Burbank' to potentially express sense or antisense coat protein-mediated resistance to PLRV and/or other potato viruses. Field testing is now underway and identification of lines showing effective resistance, as well as maintaining the agronomic qualities of 'Russet Burbank', will provide an important means of managing PLRV. However, the practical usefulness of genetically transformed material will depend on whether or not it exhibits qualities that may enhance disease incidence in nontransformed potatoes. For example, transformed potatoes expressing PLRV coat protein may enhance aphid performance leading to larger vector populations. Also, if resistance is interpreted in terms of maintaining yield or reducing tuber net necrosis, i.e., tolerance, then transgenic material may act as asymptomatic inoculum reservoirs. Both of these possibilities present a threat to surrounding nontransformed potatoes and, therefore, to the industry in general. Research to determine the effects of genetically transformed plants on the overall potato-virus-vector system will be crucial to their widespread acceptance in PNW potato production.

Literature Cited

1. Anonymous. 1991a. Idaho Agricultural Statistics. Idaho Agric. Stat. Serv., Idaho Dept. Agric., Boise, ID. 72 pp.
2. Anonymous. 1991b. Potato Statistical Yearbook. National Potato Council, Englewood, CO. 69 pp.
3. Anonymous. 1991c. Idaho Rules for Certification. Idaho Crop Improvement Association, Inc., Boise, ID. 24 pp.
4. Bagnall, R.H. 1991. Cyclic epidemics of aphid-borne potato viruses in Northern seed-potato-growing areas. Adv. Dis. Vector Res. 7: 53-71.
5. Beekman, A.G.B. 1987. Breeding for resistance. Pp. 162-170 In: J.A. de Bokx and J.P.H. van der Want (eds.), Viruses of Potatoes and Seed-Potato Production. Pudoc, Wageningen. 259 pp.
6. Bishop, G.W. 1965. Green peach aphid distribution and potato leafroll virus occurrence in the seed-potato producing areas of Idaho. J. Econ. Entomol. 58: 150-153.
7. Bishop, G.W. 1967. A leaf roll virus control program in Idaho's seed potato areas. Am. Potato J. 44: 305-308.
8. Bishop, G.W. 1968. Potato leaf roll virus transmission as affected by plant locality. Am. Potato J. 45: 366-372.
9. Bishop, G.W. and J.W. Guthrie. 1964. Home gardens as a source of the green peach aphid and virus diseases in Idaho. Am. Potato J. 41: 28-34.
10. Byrne, D.N. and G.W. Bishop. 1979. Relationship of green peach aphid numbers to spread of potato leaf roll virus in southern Idaho. J. Econ. Entomol. 72: 809-811.
11. Eskandari, F., E.S. Sylvester and J. Richardson. 1979. Evidence for lack of propagation of potato leafroll virus in its aphid vector, Myzus persicae. Phytopathology 69: 45-47.
12. Flint, M.L., L.L Strand, P.A. Rude and J.K. Clark. 1986. Integrated Pest Management for Potatoes in the Western States. Univ. of Calif., Div. Agric. Nat. Res. Pub. No. 3316, West. Reg. Res. Pub. 011. 146 pp.

13.   Halbert, S.E. and T.M. Mowry. 1992. Survey of green peach aphid infestations on bedding plants for sale in eastern Idaho. Pan-Pacific Entomol. 68: 8-11.

14.   Hanafi, A., E.B. Radcliffe and D.W. Ragsdale. 1989. Spread and control of potato leafroll virus in Minnesota. J. Econ. Entomol. 82: 1201-1206.

15.   Harrington, R., E. Bartlet, D.K. Riley, R.H. ffrench-Constant and S.J. Clark. 1989. Resurgence of insecticide-resistant *Myzus persicae* on potatoes treated repeatedly with cypermethrin and mineral oil. Crop Prot. 8: 340-348.

16.   Johansen, R.H. 1965. Norgold Russet, a new early maturing potato variety with good type and scab resistance. Am. Potato J. 42: 201-204.

17.   Killick, R.J. 1979. The effect of infection with potato leafroll virus (PLRV) on yield and some of its components in a variety of potato (*Solanum tuberosum*). Ann. Appl. Biol. 91: 67-74.

18.   Pavek, J.J., D.L. Corsini, S.L. Love, D.C Hane, D.G Holm, W.M. Iritani, S.R. James, M.W. Martin, A.R. Mosley, J.C. Ojala, C.E. Stanger and R.E. Thornton. 1991. Frontier Russet: A new potato variety for early fresh and processing use with resistance to Fusarium dry rot. Am. Potato J. 68: 525-532.

19.   Peters, D. 1987. Spread of viruses in potato crops. pp. 126-145 *In*: J.A. de Bokx and J.P.H. van der Want (eds.), Viruses of Potatoes and Seed-Potato Production. Pudoc, Wageningen. 259 pp.

20.   Peters, D. and R.A.C. Jones. 1986. Potato Leafroll Virus. Pp. 68-70 *In*: W.J. Hooker (ed.), Compendium of Potato Diseases. APS Press, St. Paul, MN. 125 pp.

21.   van der Zaag, D.E. 1987. Yield reduction in relation to virus infection. pp. 146-150 *In*: J.A. de Bokx and J.P.H. van der Want (eds.), Viruses of Potatoes and Seed-Potato Production. Pudoc, Wageningen. 259 pp.

22.   van Emden, H.F., V.F. Eastop, R.D. Hughes and M.J. Way. 1969. The ecology of *Myzus persicae*. Annu. Rev. Entomol. 14: 197-270.

23.   Wright, G.C. and G.W. Bishop. 1981. Volunteer potatoes as a source of potato leafroll virus and potato virus X. Am. Potato J. 58: 603-609.

PART IV

Advances in Potato Pest Biology and Management: Bacteria and Fungi

MANAGEMENT OF BACTERIAL RING ROT OF POTATO

Neil C. Gudmestad
Department of Plant Pathology
North Dakota State University
Fargo, ND 58105

Bacterial ring rot of potato, caused by *Clavibacter michiganensis* ssp. *sepedonicus* (Spieck. & Kotth.) Davis et al., is a disease that has plagued the potato industry in North America only during the last half century. During this time significant improvement has been realized in the technology surrounding the detection of the disease and its pathogen and in the development of management strategies. The purpose of the discussion to follow is to outline the base of knowledge that has been developed for bacterial ring rot and how this has been used to develop disease management tactics in both seed and commercial potato production systems.

Pathogen and Disease Relationships

Symptomatology. Symptoms of bacterial ring rot in potato can develop anytime after mid-season. Initially, the lower leaves of infected plants will wilt during hot periods of the day with recovery at night. As foliage symptoms continue to develop, a larger proportion of the above ground plant will wilt. Areas between leaf veins become chlorotic and leaf margins also appear necrotic. Later, wilting, interveinal chlorosis and necrosis of leaves becomes more pronounced followed by the upward rolling of the leaves. A unique feature of ring rot is that some stems of a potato hill may appear healthy whereas other stems of the same hill are in advanced stages of disease development. If the stem of a plant showing advanced stages of the disease is cut across the base and squeezed, a creamy exudate can be expelled from the vascular tissue.

Ring rot derives its name from the characteristic breakdown of the vascular ring of infected tubers. The vascular ring at the stem end of infected tubers will show a cheesy rot which is creamy yellow or light brown in color. In advanced cases, the vascular ring will separate and a creamy exudate can be expelled if pressure is applied. Severely affected tubers may exhibit extensive periderm cracking and eventually be infected by secondary rot organisms. It is this stage of tuber infection that may lead to large losses in the field and in storage.

Pathogen. *C. m. sepedonicus* is a tuberborne bacterium that is spread primarily during seed cutting and planting operations. Wounds made during these operations are excellent infection courts for the ring rot bacterium. An infected seed tuber can act as the initial inoculum source from which the bacterium can be spread by a mechanical knife to the next 30-100 cut tubers. The ring rot bacterium has no protracted soil phase but is capable of surviving short periods of time in infected potato debris (20,21). Infected volunteer potato plants also can act as inoculum sources if a potato crop is planted in the same field on successive growing seasons. Ring rot bacteria can spread from these sources during all cultivation and harvesting operations. Ring rot infected volunteer potato plants are important sources of the bacterium primarily in seed potato fields.

Inoculum of *C. m. sepedonicus* can also originate from contaminated production equipment. Tubers can become infected by coming in contact with production surfaces; i.e., storage walls, sorting and piling equipment, trucks, etc. on which the bacterium has persisted as dried slime. The bacterium can survive in an infectious state for up to 5 yr under ideal conditions of cool temperatures and low relative humidity (21). Under less than ideal conditions, the bacterium can persist outside its host from one production season to the next (19).

Additional information has been generated recently concerning aspects of the biology and ecology of *C. m. sepedonicus* that may affect the persistence and spread of the bacterium. Potato has been regarded as the only natural host of the ring rot bacterium. Recent research has demonstrated that this bacterium is capable of establishing an endophytic relationship in sugar beet roots (2). Furthermore, the bacterium can be seedborne in sugar beet and hence distributed long distances (3).

Potato insect pests have been implicated in the spread of the ring rot bacterium. Colorado potato beetle, tarnished plant bug, potato flea beetle, and green peach aphid were demonstrated to be capable of transmitting *C. m. sepedonicus* under greenhouse conditions by Duncan and Genereux (10). Recently, the Colorado potato beetle, green peach aphid (4) and the potato flea beetle (Christie, Schulz and Gudmestad, unpublished data) were confirmed as vectors of the ring rot bacterium under field conditions. Because the role these insects play in the epidemiology of bacterial ring rot is not known, further research is warranted. Most certified seed fields in the United States must be isolated from noncertified fields only by distances of approximately 30.5 m, therefore insect dissemination of *C. m. sepedonicus* is possible.

A primary factor contributing to the persistence of ring rot in the potato industry is that this disease can exist as symptomless (latent) infections. A number of variables can influence whether or not a ring rot infection will be asymptomatic. Inoculum dosage at the time of infection (1,22), potato cultivar (13,14), strain of *C. m. sepedonicus* (1) and environmental conditions (1,14,23) can affect expression of disease symptoms. Additionally, the frequency of disease expression in a field may be so low that its visual detection in seed fields during field inspections is extremely difficult (5), if not improbable.

Control of bacterial ring rot of potato has been centered around the use of certified seed potatoes. A field inspection, performed by trained field inspectors, is conducted during the latter part of the growing season primarily to visually detect bacterial ring rot symptoms (25). Because a number of plant pathogens can cause wilting in potato, a plant visually suspected of being infected with *C. m. sepedonicus* is confirmed in the laboratory. The difficulty of the inspection process can be increased by the presence of confounding factors such as normal plant senescence, Verticillium wilt, Fusarium wilt, and other diseases and pests that destroy plant foliage.

Detection of the Pathogen

The first widespread use of a laboratory technique by the potato industry to detect a disease pathogen came about as a result of the introduction of bacterial ring rot into North America in the 1930s (11). The Gram stain was initially used to detect *C. m. sepedonicus*. It was recommended by the Potato Association of America that this technique be used to verify the presence of ring rot bacteria in cases where a creamy exudate could not be expelled from vines or tubers exhibiting typical symptoms. This technique takes advantage of the fact that the ring rot bacterium stains blue and most other plant pathogenic bacteria stain red. However, care had to be exercised by the diagnostician in confirming that properly stained bacteria also conformed to the proper size and morphology of *C. m. sepedonicus*.

In the case of a disputed or questionable diagnosis, it was recommended that the diagnostician resolve the issue by choosing among Gram stain, isolation and laboratory identification or indicator hosts such as tomato or eggplant (11). While the Gram stain is still widely used to confirm routine bacterial ring rot infections, it has been largely replaced by sensitive serological assays such as latex agglutination (26), enzyme-linked immunosorbent assay (9,12) and immunofluorescence (7,12). Widespread use of serological procedures was made feasible by the development of highly specific monoclonal antibodies (8,9) which virtually eliminated troublesome cross-reactions that plagued earlier serological techniques employing polyclonal antibodies (6,16,18). DNA-hybridization assays will undoubtedly become common place and increase detection sensitivity of this pathogen (17).

Current pathogen detection technologies have a number of applications other then disease confirmation as previously discussed. Serological techniques are widely used to screen and index pathogen-free seed stock that has been passed through laboratory tissue culture programs (27). A number of commercial and university laboratories offer testing services for seed potatoes to screen seed lots for ring rot bacteria when destined for commercial potato production. These techniques also have been used in ring rot eradication programs in Canada in which certified seed lots are specifically tested to detect symptomless infections (15). Serological techniques also can be used to determine ring rot infection levels in commercial potato fields to help determine their storability and marketability.

Disease Management

Seed potato industry. Bacterial ring rot has been managed quite successfully by the employment of the disease management principle of exclusion. *C. m. sepedonicus* is excluded from certified seed lots by use of the 'zero tolerance' regulation. This regulation was adopted by all states and Canadian provinces that certify seed potatoes. It means that no level of the disease is tolerable and a seed field or seed lot is rejected for certification if any plant or plant parts infected with the bacterium are found during the inspection process. Historically, this disease management practice has been accomplished by visual detection of symptomatic plants during field inspections.

Many states have either enacted or will soon enact regulations requiring the mandatory flushing of all seed lots on a farm where ring rot has been detected. Since ring rot can remain in a seed lot in an undetectable state, it is reasonable to assume that any seed lot retained on the seed farm where ring rot was found has been exposed to the pathogen. A 12 yr study performed in North Dakota supports this assumption (Gudmestad, unpublished data). Ninety percent of the seed farms where ring rot had been found remained free of any subsequent ring rot infestation if all seed on the farm had been discarded. Conversely, two thirds of the farms that did not replace all of their seed had a recurrence of the disease within the next 2 yr. Obviously, successful management of bacterial ring rot on a seed farm includes the disposal of any seed lots exposed to the pathogen.

For exclusion to be a successful disease management strategy, seed must first be free of the ring rot pathogen. This can be and has been done using a variety of seed production techniques. Most recently, pre-nuclear, pathogen-free seed stock has been developed using in vitro tissue culture techniques. Extensive pathogen testing is performed during several stages to insure that the plant materials are free from potato pathogens, including *C. m. sepedonicus*. Tissue culture technology has the advantage in that pathogen-free seed stock can be rapidly multiplied so that large quantities of pre-nuclear material, in the form of laboratory-produced microtubers, plantlets or greenhouse-produced minitubers, can be provided.

During potato production, seed or commercial, the plant is constantly exposed to sources of contamination by pathogens. The probability of a seed tuber or seed lot becoming contaminated with pathogenic organisms increases every year the seed lot is in production. To minimize this, pathogen-free seed stock technology is usually coupled with a limited generation system. In this type of system, seed lots are limited in the number of years that they can be produced in the field after the pre-nuclear material has left the greenhouse or laboratory. Pathogen-free seed stock technology and limited generation systems have probably done more to minimize the economic effects of ring rot in the potato industry than other factor.

Proper sanitation practices are also extremely important in the management of bacterial ring rot. Good sanitation on a seed farm can prevent the introduction of the ring rot pathogen and minimize its spread. Proper sanitation practices include: a) scraping all production surfaces to remove large amounts of debris and removing and discarding all debris; b) thoroughly washing all surfaces with hot water and detergent solution to remove organic debris which is best accomplished using a power washer; c) rinsing all surfaces with clean water; and d) applying a recommended disinfectant and maintaining a wet surface for a minimum of 10 min.

Proper use of a disinfectant is important in any sanitation program and not all of the chemicals are of equal efficacy (24). For example, formaldehyde was once considered the industry standard but at recommended concentrations (2% solution v/v), it was found to be quite ineffective. Steam, although widely used, also is ineffective unless temperatures are in excess of 80 C and the surface to be steamed is exposed to that temperature for a minimum of 5 min. Recommended disinfectants include quaternary ammonium, potentiated iodine, polyphenol and hypochlorite solutions (24). Care must be taken to evaluate the pH of the final solution, eliminate organic matter which can inactivate many disinfectants and to the length of time a surface is exposed to the chemical.

Attention must be given to any open-celled sponge rollers on mechanical seed cutters that are known to have cut a seed lot infected with ring rot. These types of rollers tend to absorb moisture from tubers during the seed cutting process. Under these conditions, ring rot bacteria can infiltrate to depths of 3-5 cm in the sponge roller and be extremely difficult to kill during sanitation procedures (Gudmestad, unpublished data).

Commercial potato industry. The management strategy for ring rot in a commercial potato operation is very similar to that previously discussed, with a few contrasting differences. The most important aspect of ring rot management for the commercial grower is to use certified seed. Although there can be no guarantee that certified seed potatoes will be free of ring rot, the probability of ring rot freedom is much greater in certified seed than if the commercial grower replants cull potatoes, pick-outs or noncertified potatoes.

Additional assurances of ring rot freedom can be obtained if a commercial grower has a post-harvest test to detect ring rot on a sample of a seed lot prior to its purchase. Sanitation, as previously discussed, is also extremely important in a commercial potato operation to minimize spread of the pathogen if it is present and to limit the potential economic impact of the disease.

For the commercial potato operation, the only other aspect of disease management that must be considered is to insure the proper identification of the pathogen involved if ring rot is suspected. Because a number of biotic and abiotic causal agents can cause symptoms in both the foliage and in the tuber that resemble bacterial ring rot, proper identification of the disease is imperative.

If the disease present is identified as ring rot, then the severity and extent of the infection on the farm must be determined. This involves careful monitoring of fields and sampling to determine disease incidence and severity. A trained individual with expertise in dealing with ring rot should be considered for these determinations. Levels of disease incidence also can be determined serologically in the laboratory. A number of state and privately run laboratories across the United States have this type of testing service available. This involves randomly sampling potato tubers from fields that are destined for storage. If infection levels are 5% or less, then long-term storage of the potato crop is feasible. The facility also must be capable of monitoring and implementing proper storage conditions. Potatoes must be kept as cool as possible with constant fresh air ventilation to prevent carbon dioxide build up. Care must be taken to avoid hot spots and to detect them when they occur so that the potato crop can be quickly marketed in the event that significant decay problems develop.

In extremely severe cases, it may be wise to delay the harvest of fields. This will accomplish two things. First, because the periderm of severely infected tubers will crack, these tubers will rot in the field if given sufficient time and will not be brought into storage. Second, by limiting the amount of ring rot infected tubers going into storage, the grower can limit the severity of other rots that may be incited by the presence of these infected tubers. Also, when ring rot infected fields are harvested last, contaminated equipment will not be used subsequently on fields without a ring rot problem.

Future management strategies. To this point there has been no discussion concerning the use of host resistance in the management of bacterial ring rot. Although resistant cultivars have been developed, such as Merrimack, Teton and Belrus (13), they have not been met with commercial acceptance by the potato industry. Fear within the industry that such cultivars will serve as "symptomless carriers" of *C. m. sepedonicus* has generally precluded their widespread production. Whether these fears are founded in scientific principle has not been determined. Recent developments in host resistance have occurred that may alter the present disease management strategies. Apparent immunity to ring rot has been identified in *Solanum acaule* (Jansky and Gudmestad, unpublished data).

Epilogue

Ring rot has been effectively managed through the use of certified seed potatoes. A sophisticated system involving pathogen-free, tissue culture derived seed potatoes has evolved which has drastically reduced the incidence and severity with which this seedborne disease occurs. Rigid sanitation of all production surfaces is also an effective means of reducing exposure and occurrence of this disease. Cultivar resistance is being intensively studied and may be a viable management strategy in the future.

Literature Cited

1. Bishop, A.L., and Slack, S.A. 1987. Effect of cultivar, inoculum dose, and strain of *Clavibacter michiganense* subsp. *sepedonicum* on symptom development in potatoes. Phytopathology 77:1085-1089.
2. Bugbee, W.M., Gudmestad, N.C., Secor, G.A., and Nolte, P. 1987. Sugar beet as a symptomless host for *Corynebacterium sepedonicum*. Phytopathology 77:765-770.
3. Bugbee, W.M., and Gudmestad, N.C. 1988. The recovery of *Corynebacterium sepedonicum* from sugar beet seed. Phytopathology 78:205-208.
4. Christie, R.D., Sumalde, A.C., Schulz, J.T., and Gudmestad, N.C. 1991. Insect transmission of the bacterial ring rot pathogen. Am. Potato J. 68:363-372.
5. Clayton, M.K., and Slack, S.A. 1988. Sample size determination in zero tolerance circumstances and the implications of stepwise sampling: Bacterial ring rot as a special case. Am. Potato J. 65:711-723.

6.   Crowley, C.F., and De Boer, S.H. 1982. Nonpathogenic bacteria associated with potato stems cross-react with *Corynebacterium sepedonicum* antisera in immunofluorescence. Am. Potato J. 59:1-8.

7.   De Boer, S.H., and McNaughton, M.E. 1986. Evaluation of immunofluorescence with monoclonal antibodies for detecting latent bacterial ring rot infections. Am. Potato J. 63:533-543.

8.   De Boer, S.H., and Wieczorek, A. 1984. Production of monoclonal antibodies to *Corynebacterium sepedonicum*. Phytopathology 74:1431-1434.

9.   De Boer, S.H., Wieczorek, A., and Kummer, A. 1988. An ELISA test for bacterial ring rot of potato with a new monoclonal antibody. Plant Dis. 72:874-878.

10.   Duncan, J., and Genereux, H. 1960. La transmission par les insectes de *Corynebacterium sepedonicum* (Spieck. & Kott.) Skapt. & Burkh. Can. J. Pl. Sci. 40:110-116.

11.   Gudmestad, N.C. 1991. A historical perspective to pathogen testing in seed potato certification. Am. Potato J. 68:99-102.

12.   Gudmestad, N.C., Baer, D., and Kurowski, C.J. 1991. Validating immunoassay test performance in the detection of *Corynebacterium sepedonicum* during the growing season. Phytopathology 81:475-480.

13.   Manzer, F.E. 1981. Reaction of the potato variety Belrus to bacterial ring rot infections. Maine Agric. Exp. Stn. Misc. Rep. No. 256. 2 pp.

14.   Manzer, F.E., Gudmestad, N.C., and Nelson, G.A. 1987. Factors affecting infection, disease development and symptom expression of bacterial ring rot. Am. Potato J. 64:671-675.

15.   McDonald, J., and Borrel, B. 1991. Development of post harvest testing in Canada. Am. Potato J. 68:115-122.

16.   Miller, H.J. 1984. Cross-reactions of *Corynebacterium sepedonicum* antisera with soil bacteria associated with potato tubers. Neth. J. Pl. Path. 90:23-28.

17.   Mogen, B.D., Oleson, A.E., and Gudmestad, N.C. 1987. Dot-blot detection of the ring rot pathogen: Evaluation of cloned *Corynebacterium sepedonicum* DNA sequences as potential hybridization probes. (Abstr.) Am. Potato J. 64:701.

18.   Naumann, K., Zielke, R., Pistrick, E., Schmidt, A., and Tegtmeier, H. 1984. Studies on the accuracy and reliability of the diagnosis of *Corynebacterium sepedonicum* by microscopical-cytological observations and serological assay. Zb. Mikrobiol. 139:173-194.

19.   Nelson, G.A. 1978. Survival of *Corynebacterium sepedonicum* on contaminated surfaces. Am. Potato J. 55:449-452.

20.   Nelson, G.A. 1979. Persistence of *Corynebacterium sepedonicum* in soil and in buried potato stems. Am. Potato J. 56:71-77.

21.   Nelson, G.A. 1980. Long-term survival of *Corynebacterium sepedonicum* on contaminated surfaces and in infected potato stems. Am. Potato J. 57:595-600.

22.   Nelson, G.A. 1982. *Corynebacterium sepedonicum* in potato: Effect of inoculum concentration on ring rot symptoms and latent infection. Can. J. Plant Pathol. 4:129-133.

23.   Nelson, G.A., and Kozub, G.C. 1983. Effect of total light energy on symptoms and growth of ring rot-infected Red Pontiac potato plants. Am. Potato J. 60:461-468.

24. Secor, G.A., DeBuhr, L., and Gudmestad, N.C. 1988. Susceptibility of *Corynebacterium sepedonicum* to disinfectants *in vitro*. Plant Dis. 72:585-588.
25. Shepard, J.F., and Claflin, L.E. 1975. Critical analyses of the principles of seed potato certification. Annu. Rev. Phytopathol. 13:271-293.
26. Slack, S.A., Kelman, A., and Perry, J.B. 1979. Comparison of three serodiagnostic assays for detection of *Corynebacterium sepedonicum*. Phytopathology 69:186-189.
27. Zink, R.T. 1991. Pathogen detection in seed potatoes. Am. Potato J. 68:103-106.

PROSPECTS FOR CONTROL OF POTATO DISEASES CAUSED BY PECTOLYTIC ERWINIAS

S. H. De Boer[*]
Agriculture Canada Research Station
Vancouver, British Columbia, V6T 1X2

Pectolytic erwinias are among the most common and ubiquitous pathogens on potato. Direct and indirect crop losses due to these bacteria have not been estimated but are known to be considerable.

The potato disease complex caused by the pectolytic erwinias is complicated by the involvement of different species and subspecies of bacteria, by the different host tissues that may be attacked, and by the various sources of primary inoculum from which infections emanate. Some control strategies address the entire soft rot complex caused by erwinias whereas other strategies are directed only towards control of a specific disorder caused by a single subspecies. To discuss the prospects for control, therefore, it is necessary to have a clear concept of the group of pathogenic bacteria that are involved and the disease manifestations they incur.

The Pectolytic Erwinias

The predominant species involved in the erwinia disease complex is *Erwinia carotovora* (Jones) Bergey et al. It is divided into several subspecies, two of which are important on potato. The subspecies *atroseptica* (van Hall) Dye and *carotovora* (Jones) Bergey et al are the important potato pathogens and possess an array of pectolytic enzymes as pathogenicity factors. *E. chrysanthemi* Burkholder et al also produces pectolytic enzymes but differs significantly from *E. carotovora* and warrants status as a separate species. Important characteristics of the three groups of pectolytic erwinias are as follows:

Erwinia carotovora **subsp.** *atroseptica*. *E. c. atroseptica* can be differentiated from *E. c. carotovora* on the basis of biochemical and physiological properties, serological specificity, DNA probe hybridization, and cellular fatty acid composition. Serologically, *E. c.*

---

*For the Department of Agriculture, Government of Canada. Used by permission.

atroseptica forms a relatively homogeneous group of bacteria. In many geographic areas over 90% of strains isolated from potato are serogroup I. Additional serogroups detected in some of these regions occur at low frequencies (15). Exceptions do occur, however, as in Finland where only 65% of the *E. c. atroseptica* strains from potato are serogroup I.

***Erwinia carotovora* subsp. *carotovora.* E. c. carotovora** is phenotypically and serologically far more heterogenous than *E. c. atroseptica.* In practice *E. carotovora* strains that are biochemically different from the subspecies *atroseptica, betavasculorum,* or *wasabiae* are considered to belong to the *carotovora* subspecies. More than 36 serogroups of *E. c. carotovora* have been established but these account for only about 70% of the strains isolated from potato. Further taxonomic studies will probably reveal that *E. c. carotovora* can be divided into several additional subspecies. Host specificity of subgroups within *E. c. carotovora* has not been established although serogroups III and XXIX occur most frequently on potato (8,14,32).

Erwinia chrysanthemi. *E. chrysanthemi* exhibits pectic enzyme activity similar to *E. carotovora,* but the major pectic enzymes of the two species differ in electrophoretic mobility, isoelectric point, and serological specificity. Biochemical and physiological properties also differentiate *E. chrysanthemi* from other erwinias. *E. chrysanthemi* can be divided into subgroups on the basis of serological reactivity, biochemical reactions, physiological properties, pectolytic enzyme profiles, and restriction fragment length polymorphisms (6). Some groups of strains appear to show host specificity while other strains cause soft rot in a wide range of host plants (24).

   E. chrysanthemi has been reported on potatoes in Peru, Australia, Japan, the Netherlands, and France but different biovars of *E. chrysanthemi* are involved in some of the different geographic regions. For example, biovar 3 occurs in Australia while biovars 1 and 7 are found on potato in France (43). Strains from potato in the Netherlands were classified among *E. chrysanthemi* from hosts that normally grow in temperate zones in contrast to strains found on hosts that grow in warmer areas (23). *E. chrysanthemi* on potato in Australia is chiefly a disease of seed pieces (13) whereas strains in Japan and the Netherlands chiefly cause disease in potato vines (16,46).

Ecology

   Survival of the pectolytic erwinias in the environment and in association with potato tubers is an important aspect of their ecology that has a direct bearing on the success of control strategies based on the disease management principle of avoidance of the pathogen. The ubiquity of *E. c. carotovora* in the environment has been well established. It appears to survive particularly well in aquatic environments (21) and may spread long distances in moist air currents and be deposited by precipitation. It also survives in soil and in weed and nonhost rhizospheres.

E. c. atroseptica favors cool, temperate climates. In northern potato growing regions such as Sweden, *E. c. atroseptica* is the predominant pectolytic erwinia on potato (5). Both *E. c. atroseptica* and *E. c. carotovora* survive on seed tubers which serve as an important source of inoculum (34).

Whether observations on survival characteristics of *E. c. carotovora* can be applied to *E. c. atroseptica* is questionable. Although *E. c. atroseptica* also has been detected in water, soil, and rhizospheres, its incidence is low in comparison to *E. c. carotovora*. The large difference in frequency of detection may result from isolation procedures being more favorable for *E. c. carotovora* than *E. c. atroseptica*. On the other hand, the observations may reflect the fact that *E. c. atroseptica* does, in fact, not survive well in the environment. In many instances when *E. c. atroseptica* was detected in water or soil it was detected in only one location or on only one occasion. *E. c. atroseptica* has been detected with greater relative frequency from sources closely associated with potatoes, particularly in areas with intensive potato culture, or from potato stems and tubers themselves. Comparison of serological and pathogenicity characteristics of strains from the environment with those from potato have generally not been done.

Seed potatoes contaminated with *E. chrysanthemi* are considered the major source of inoculum in the Netherlands (16) whereas in Australia, river water and soil are important sources (11,12). Ecology of *E. chrysanthemi* in relation to potato requires further study.

Symptom Expression

The pectolytic erwinias incite a range of symptoms on potato vines and tubers. Different types of symptoms have sometimes been regarded as different diseases but terminology has not been consistent (35). Naming diseases according to symptom expression is advantageous for recognition of the condition in the field. Basing disease nomenclature on the pathogen inciting the symptoms, however, has the advantage of relating disease to ecology of the incitant and hence to economic significance of the outbreak, particularly with respect to seed potato certification. Impact of disease occurrence and control measures are sometimes more dependent on the identity of the pathogen than on the type of symptom expressed. Thus merely identifying the disease by symptom type could be confusing or even meaningless unless the pathogen is known. In other instances the identity of the pathogen is of only minor importance. In this chapter, commonly used terminology is selected that best represents the symptom/pathogen combination and distinguishes among conditions that may call for differences in control strategies. The following conditions are identified.

Blackleg is the classical disease condition caused by *E. c. atroseptica*. The disease is characterized by blackening of the basal portion of the stem and symptoms invariably originate at the seed piece. Blackleg that occurs early in the growing season results in weak, upright, chlorotic plants which succumb to decay. Plants that become diseased later in the season develop the typical black tissue which often extends midway or even higher into the stem. Affected stems may or may not turn chlorotic but eventually they usually wilt and decay. Potato plants are particularly susceptible to blackleg under cool, moist conditions. The bacterium also may enter tubers via the stolons and cause black-colored decay inside the tuber leaving a hollow shell. This tuber condition is also often referred to as blackleg since it is closely associated with stem symptoms. Under high field temperatures (ave max. 30-35 C), blackleg can be caused by strains of *E. c. carotovora* (33). In Japan, *E. c. carotovora*-induced blackleg appeared to be caused by a distinct serotype (44). Because *E. c. carotovora* appears to be a far more prevalent bacterium than *E. c. atroseptica*, distinction between *E. c. atroseptica*-blackleg and *E. c. carotovora*-blackleg is significant.

Aerial stem rot is usually caused by *E. c. carotovora* and affects damaged or injured vines. In Sweden it has been reported to be caused by *E. c. atroseptica* in addition to *E. c. carotovora* (37). Symptoms do not originate at the seed piece as with blackleg but can be traced to damaged tissue or leaf scars that permitted entry of the bacterium. *E. c. carotovora* causing aerial stem rot may originate from soil, irrigation water, or insects (8,40). The decay is usually brown in color and may be either dry or mushy depending on field conditions. Aerial stem rot has increased in importance since the advent of center pivot irrigation. In irrigated circles aerial stem rot symptoms initially develop in stems lying on the ground but later develop in the upper foliage (39). Under these conditions aerial stem rot is not always associated with injury but is affected by microclimate in the potato canopy (7). The dense, succulent foliage and prolonged periods of foliage wetness that develop under frequent irrigation favor aerial stem rot.

The term **stem wet rot** is used here specifically to denote vine symptoms incited by *E. chrysanthemi* and is a translation of "stengelnatrot" widely used in the Netherlands for this condition (16). Stem wet rot symptoms occur primarily under warm field conditions. Although the disease is usually of minor consequence in temperate potato growing regions, it can be a major problem when contaminated seed potatoes from temperate regions are exported to warmer zones. The symptoms of stem wet rot originate at the seed piece just like blackleg and are characterized by brown to black discoloration of the lower stem and decay of the pith. Infected plants can sometimes be recognized by yellow discoloration in the apical stem region but often symptoms of stem wet rot are difficult to distinguish from blackleg symptoms in regions where both pathogens occur. In the early stages of disease development, stem wet rot tends to exhibit less blackening and more extensive pith decay than blackleg. In the later stages of disease, the entire stem succumbs to a mushy wet rot. When field temperatures become moderate after initiation of stem wet rot symptoms, plants may recover entirely.

Early dying is a syndrome involving several pathogens including *Verticillium* spp. and nematodes (42). However, pectolytic erwinias (mainly *E. c. carotovora*) are often also associated with affected plants and cause decay. The pectolytic erwinias may directly cause early dying symptoms in some situations or may play an important role in disease epidemics by enhancing symptoms caused by the other pathogens inciting this syndrome. This condition is a problem particularly in fields receiving overhead irrigation. High humidity and succulent foliage probably predispose the plants to infection by the erwinia.

Reduced vigor and **decreased yields** in plants grown from tubers inoculated with erwinia in the absence of overt disease symptoms has been noted by various authors (e.g. ref. 18). In Scotland, yields of symptomless plants grown from seed inoculated with *E. c. atroseptica* were reduced by as much as 25% compared with noninoculated plants (3). Yet it has not generally been regarded as an important problem from a commercial perspective. Recent work has shown that pectolytic erwinias inhibited potato root development in tissue culture and greenhouse-grown plants (Lan and De Boer, unpublished data). Perhaps erwinia metabolites leaching from decaying seed pieces inhibit root development and function thereby reducing vigor and yield. Further research may prove this phenomenon to be an important factor affecting potato production.

All pectolytic erwinias but particularly *E. c. carotovora*, cause **seed piece decay** resulting in reduced plant stand. In at least one geographic area, Valencia, Spain, seed piece decay was primarily associated with *E. c. atroseptica* (36), whereas in another, western Australia, it was caused by *E. chrysanthemi* (11). Seed piece decay in temperate zones is favored by cool, wet conditions at planting and may be exacerbated by cutting the seed.

Decay of tubers in storage which is caused by all of the pectolytic erwinias has classically been called **bacterial soft rot**. When tubers enter storage facilities most are externally contaminated with *E. c. carotovora* and to a lesser extent with *E. c. atroseptica*. Under optimal storage conditions these bacteria remain passive but if the tubers are wet and air movement around tubers is restricted, or if tuber surfaces are damaged, the bacteria proliferate and cause decay. The extent of decay can be very severe.

During the growing season, *E. c. atroseptica* may invade developing lenticels of progeny tubers. In low humidity storage environments these bacteria cause slightly sunken, brownish-black, dry, necrotic local pockets of decay. This condition results in typical **lenticel hard rot** (26). Washed tubers are particularly susceptible.

Management Strategies

Control of potato diseases caused by pectolytic erwinias has been notably difficult. Some of the bacterial strains involved in some of the diseases are quite ubiquitous. Others are less so, but potatoes, being a vegetatively propagated crop, maintain the bacteria from one season to another via the seed tubers. Furthermore, it is only quite recently that survival and spread of the erwinias is beginning to be understood and that tools are becoming available for rapid and accurate identification of the causal organisms. Most of the approaches to control recommended in the past remain valid but more focused tactics are now possible with a better understanding of the causal organisms. Control strategies can be classified under several general approaches.

Cultural practices. The traditional approach to the control of blackleg and seed piece decay was by good cultural practices. The underlying notion that good growing conditions and that undamaged tubers were most resistant to disease was sound and is still true today. A major source of inoculum for *E. c. carotovora* and in some regions *E. c. atroseptica* is cull piles and refuse dumps (20). Since insects transmit bacteria from these sources to growing plants, sanitation is of utmost importance. In Scotland 3-5% of the insects collected from potato cull piles were contaminated with either *E. c. carotovora* or *E. c. atroseptica* (22).

Since *E. c. carotovora*, and perhaps also *E. c. atroseptica*, may be present in water used for irrigation, treatment of the water to destroy the erwinias has been recommended. Contamination of tubers with erwinia also occurs during harvesting and grading of the tubers. A single rotting tuber contaminated 100 kg of potatoes during mechanical grading (17). Chemical disinfection of the grader with sodium hypochlorite immediately before use, and of tubers immediately after grading, reduced contamination. Identification of seed lots particularly susceptible to bacterial soft rot might help if those lots can be processed first, lessening their time in storage. Lund and Kelman (28) developed a method whereby the soft rot potential could be determined.

Planting of whole seed tubers is also beneficial but if seed cutting is an operational requirement, suberization of cut surfaces must be allowed to occur. Since fungal infections promote bacterial growth, application of fungicides also is recommended. Aerial stem rot can usually be controlled by avoiding mechanical and insect damage to the vines and by reducing long periods of leaf wetness in the foliage.

Bacterial soft rot can be controlled by minimizing tuber damage during harvesting and transport to storage. Harvesting only at temperatures below 20 C and avoiding solar irradiation and desiccation further helps prevent decay in storage. Advances in temperature and humidity monitoring and control technologies for potato storages have reduced bacterial soft rot and lenticel hard rot in storage.

Clean seed. The use of pathogen-free seed tubers is an important strategy for controlling some of the diseases caused by the erwinias. Clean seed is particularly important for the control of blackleg and stem wet rot. The causal organisms, *E. c. atroseptica* and *E. chrysanthemi*, respectively, may infect plants from environmental sources, but disease almost invariably originates from a contaminated seed piece. Population of bacteria in the field is probably too low to cause disease directly. Only when the bacterial populations have multiplied during one or more generations of potato culture will disease ensue.

Diseases caused by *E. c. carotovora* are less likely to be controlled by planting clean seed alone because of its widespread presence in the environment. Plants and progeny tubers are readily recontaminated with *E. c. carotovora* (19). Furthermore, there is no strong evidence that inocula for diseases such as aerial stem rot, early dying, and bacterial soft rot of tubers originate exclusively from the seed piece.

Tissue culture has provided a means of breaking the cycle of pathogen spread to successive generations of potatoes. Tissue culture in itself does not ensure freedom from bacterial contamination but there is a greater likelihood of them being free of pathogens, and plants can be tested readily. Once in the field, however, potatoes can be reinfected with the pathogens.

Maintenance of disease free seed potatoes for several field generations is dependent on quality control that ensures each succeeding generation of progeny tubers is free from the pathogen. Field inspection for blackleg has been traditionally carried out to certify crops for use as seed that have a zero or only low incidence of blackleg. The usefulness of field inspection is uncertain since it is now known that the level of tuber contamination with *E. c. atroseptica* may be quite independent of blackleg expression in the field. Indexing tubers for the bacterium would be a better measure of tuber contamination with *E. c. atroseptica*. Serological tests for *E. c. atroseptica* and *E. chrysanthemi* such as immunofluorescence, ELISA, and immunofluorescence colony staining are available. Although some of these procedures have been used on a routine basis, none has been entirely satisfactory. A DNA probe specific for *E. c. atroseptica* has now been constructed but its usefulness in indexing of seed potatoes needs to be confirmed (Ward and De Boer, unpublished data).

Heat (31) and chemical treatment with sodium hypochlorite or formaldehyde (41) also have been reported to be effective in obtaining erwinia-free potatoes. Whether these approaches are effective at the farm level must still be shown. Application of the antibacterial compound, dichlorophen, failed to control bacterial soft rot when applied to tuber surfaces (29).

Because recontamination of pathogen-free potatoes unavoidably occurs under field conditions, limiting the number of generations seed potatoes are multiplied is important. Build-up of inoculum is avoided if contaminated stock is flushed out of seed production systems on a continuous basis.

Biological control. Various ideas have been considered for biological control of diseases caused by the pectolytic erwinia. The use of bacteriocins has been particularly attractive but has not yet been shown to be effective. Axelrood et al (2) showed that an antibiotic substance produced by *E. c. betavasculorum* was effective against *E. c. carotovora*. In mixed tuber infections populations of *E. c. carotovora* were a million-fold lower than in corresponding infections with *E. c. carotovora* alone.

The use of antagonistic bacteria unrelated to the erwinias appeared to hold promise in early studies but has not given consistent results in field experiments. Several investigators, however, achieved significant control with antagonistic pseudomonads for a number of diseases incited by pectolytic erwinias in at least some experiments. Of particular interest is the apparent growth promotion of potato by some of the bacterial strains which were antagonistic towards erwinia. Perhaps growth promotion is related to control of erwinia-induced reduction in vigor and yield. Further investigation into biocontrol seems warranted on the basis of the various successful experimental results. Use of multiple antagonists in biocontrol inoculants should be considered for controlling the erwinias under diverse growing conditions. Multiple antagonists also would be beneficial in curtailing development of resistance in erwinia to antagonists, a phenomenon already detected under experimental conditions (10).

Resistance. Genetic resistance to disease is an attractive approach to control since it requires no action by growers. Natural resistance may involve calcium and complex polymers such as cutin, lignin and suberin in cell walls, constitutive phenolic compounds, and induced low molecular weight phytoalexins such as rishitin and phytuberin (30). However, the biochemical and genetic basis of resistance of potato vines and tubers to the erwinias is not well understood. Furthermore, it has been difficult to identify resistant material because of the difficulty in measuring and rating resistance and susceptibility to soft rot diseases. Cultivar susceptibility to blackleg, seed piece decay, and bacterial soft rot varies with inoculation technique and growing conditions (e.g. ref. 4 and 18). Screening of protoplast-derived callus tissue identified clones with enhanced resistance to decay by *E. c. carotovora* but correlation with plant resistance was inadequately tested (45). Recently, resistance to erwinia tuber and stem rot has been found in wild potato selections (27), and transferred from one of these, *Solanum brevidens* L., to *S. tuberosum* L. by protoplast fusion (1).

Incorporation of insect genes coding for antibacterial proteins into the potato genome is also an alternative provided by technological advancements. Cecropins from the hemolymph of the giant silk moth pupae, *Hyalophora cecropia* L. (25) and apidaecins from larval and adult honey bees, *Apis mellifera* L. (9) have been identified as potential useful antibacterial peptides. Several research groups have initiated work using a cecropin or apidaecin gene to construct bacteria-resistant transgenic potato plants. Although preliminary results suggest that transgenic plants are resistant, environmental and human health concerns may limit their immediate commercial production.

The insertion of genes coding for specific inhibitors of bacterial pathogenicity determinants also may be possible. One avenue is to incorporate into the potato genome a gene which codes for a monoclonal antibody that is specific and inhibitory to pectate lyase. Pectate lyase produced by erwinia in the plant would, then, immediately be inactivated by the antibody molecule. However, several pectic enzymes may need to be inhibited to totally prevent decay. By using transposon mutagenesis it was shown that bacterial motility was also essential for *E. c. carotovora* to initiate infection and spread of decay inside the plant tissue (38). Again inhibition of motility with the product of an appropriately constructed monoclonal antibody gene inserted into the potato genome may provide resistance. Genes for specific antibiotic agents such as bacteriocins or anti-erwinia metabolites from antagonistic pseudomonads or other bacteria also could be considered for construction of erwinia-resistant transgenic plants. Prior to construction of transgenic plants, however, consideration must be given to such potential impediments as naturally occurring and evolving recalcitrant strains, environmental impact, and food safety.

Epilogue

Potato growers, themselves, can do much to control diseases caused by pectolytic erwinias. The current trend of initiating seed stocks from tissue culture grown plantlets and flushing out such stocks after several field generations will also contribute significantly to decreasing disease incidence. In the long term, development of biocontrol schemes and exploitation of genes for resistance will likely provide even better means of minimizing losses due to the pectolytic erwinias.

Literature Cited

1. Austin, S., Lojkowska, E., Ehlenfeldt, M.K., Kelman, A., and Helgeson, J.P. 1988. Fertile interspecific somatic hybrids of *Solanum*: A novel source of resistance to *Erwinia* soft rot. Phytopathology 78:1216-1220.
2. Axelrood, P.E., Rella, M., and Schroth, M.N. 1988. Role of antibiosis in competition of *Erwinia* strains in potato infection courts. Appl. Environ. Microbiol. 54:1222-1229.
3. Bain, R.A., Perombelon, M.C.M., Tsror, L., and Nachmias, A. 1990. Blackleg development and tuber yield in relation to numbers of *Erwinia carotovora* subsp. *atroseptica* on seed potatoes. Plant Pathol. 39:125-133.
4. Bain, R.A., and Perombelon, M.C.M. 1988. Methods of testing potato cultivars for resistance to soft rot of tubers caused by *Erwinia carotovora* subsp. *atroseptica*. Plant Pathol. 37:431-437.

5. Bang, H. 1989. Prevalence of *Erwinia*-species in basic seed lots of potatoes grown in northern Sweden. Acta Agric. Scand. 39:373-379.

6. Boccara, M., Vedel, R., Lalo, D., Lebrun, M.-H., and Lafay, J.F. 1991. Genetic diversity and host range in strains of *Erwinia chrysanthemi*. Mol. Plant-Microbe Interact. 4:293-299.

7. Cappaert, M.R., and Powelson, M.L. 1990. Canopy density and microclimate effects on the development of aerial stem rot of potatoes. Phytopathology 80:350-356.

8. Cappaert, M.R., Powelson, M.L., Franc, G.D., and Harrison, M.D. 1988. Irrigation water as a source of inoculum of soft rot erwinias for aerial stem rot of potatoes. Phytopathology 78:1668-1672.

9. Casteels, P., Ampe, C., Jacobs, F., Vaeck, M., and Tempst, P. 1989. Apidaecins: antibacterial peptides from honeybees. EMBO J. 8:2387-2391.

10. Colyer, P.D., and Mount, M.S. 1984. Bacterization of potatoes with *Pseudomonas putida* and its influence on postharvest soft rot diseases. Plant Dis. 68:703-706.

11. Cother, E.J. 1980. Bacterial seed tuber decay in irrigated sandy soils of New South Wales *Erwinia carotovora carotovora* and *Erwinia chrysanthemi*. Potato Res. 23:75-84.

12. Cother, E.J., and Gilbert, R.L. 1990. Presence of *Erwinia chrysanthemi* in two major river systems and their alpine sources in Australia. J. Appl. Bacteriol. 69:729-738.

13. Cother, E.J., and Powell, V. 1983. Physiological and pathological characteristics of *Erwinia chrysanthemi* isolates from potato tubers. J. Appl. Bacteriol. 54:37-43.

14. De Boer, S.H. 1983. Frequency and distribution of *Erwinia carotovora* serogroups associated with potato in the Pemberton Valley of British Columbia. Can. J. Plant Pathol. 5:279-284.

15. De Boer, S.H., Verdonck, L., Vruggink, H., Harju, P., Bang, H.O., and De Ley, J. 1987. Serological and biochemical variation among potato strains of *Erwinia carotovora* subsp. *atroseptica* and their taxonomic relationship to other *E. carotovora* strains. J. Appl. Bacteriol. 63:487-495.

16. de Vries, P.M. 1990. Stengelnatrot-symptomen in aardappelplanten. Aardappelwereld Oktober 1990 (4):15-18.

17. Elphinstone, J.G., and Perombelon, M.C.M. 1986. Contamination of potatoes by *Erwinia carotovora* during grading. Plant Pathol. 35:25-33.

18. Gans, P.T., Jellis, G., Little, J.G., Logan, C., and Wastie, R.L. 1991. A comparison of methods to evaluate the susceptibility of potato cultivars to blackleg in the field at different sites. Plant Pathol. 40:238-248.

19. Graham, D.C., Quinn, C.E., and Harrison, M.D. 1976. Recurrence of soft rot coliform bacterial infections in potato stem cuttings: an epidemiological study on the central nuclear stock production farm in Scotland 1967-74. Potato Res. 19:3-20.

20. Harrison, M.D., and Brewer, J.W. 1982. Field dispersal of soft rot bacteria. Pages 31-53 in: Phytopathogenic Prokaryotes, Vol. 2. M. S. Mount and G. H. Lacy, eds. Academic Press, New York.

21. Harrison, M.D., Franc, G.D., Maddox, D.A., Michaud, J.E., and McCarter-Zorner, N.J. 1987. Presence of *Erwinia carotovora* in surface water in North America. J. Appl. Bacteriol. 62:565-570.

22.   Harrison, M.D., Quinn, C.E., Sells, I.A., and Graham, D.C. 1977. Waste potato dumps as sources of insects contaminated with soft rot coliform bacteria in relation to recontamination of pathogen free potato stocks. Potato Res. 20:37-52.

23.   Janse, J.D., and Scheepens, T. 1990. Further biochemical and serological classification of *Erwinia chrysanthemi* strains. Pages 779-787 in: Plant Pathogenic Bacteria, Vol. Part B. Z. Klement, eds. Akademiai Kiado, Budapest.

24.   Janse, J., and Ruissen, M. 1988. Characterization and classification of *Erwinia chrysanthemi* strains from several hosts in the Netherlands. Phytopathology 78:800-808.

25.   Jaynes, J.M., Xanthopoulos, K., Destefano-Beltran, G.L., and Dodds, J.H. 1987. Increasing bacterial disease resistance in plants utilizing antibacterial genes from insects. BioEssays 6:263-270.

26.   Logan, C. 1964. Bacterial hard rot of potato. Eur. Potato. J. 7:45-56.

27.   Lojkowska, E., and Kelman, A. 1989. Screening of seedlings of wild *Solanum* species for resistance to bacterial stem rot caused by soft rot erwinias. Am. Potato J. 66:379-390.

28.   Lund, B.M., and Kelman, A. 1977. Determination of the potential for development of bacterial soft rot of potatoes. Am. Potato J. 54:211-225.

29.   Lund, B.M., and Wyatt, G.M. 1979. A method of testing the effect of antibacterial compounds on bacterial soft rot of potatoes, and results for preparations of dichlorophen and sodium hypochlorite. Potato Res. 22:191-202.

30.   Lyon, G.D. 1989. The biochemical basis of resistance of potatoes to soft rot *Erwinia* spp. - a review. Plant Pathol. 38:313-339.

31.   Mackay, J.M., and Shipton, P.J. 1983. Heat treatment of seed tubers for control of potato blackleg (*Erwinia carotovora* subsp. *atroseptica*) and other diseases. Plant Pathol. 32:385-393.

32.   Maher, E.A., De Boer, S.H., and Kelman, A. 1986. Serogroups of *Erwinia carotovora* involved in systemic infection of potato plants and infestation of progeny tubers. Am. Potato J. 63:1-11.

33.   Molina, J.J., and Harrison, M.D. 1977. The role of *Erwinia carotovora* in the epidemiology of potato blackleg. I. Relationship of *Erwinia carotorora* var. *carotovora* and *Erwinia carotovora* var. *atroseptica* to potato blackleg in Colorado. Am. Potato J. 54:587-591.

34.   Perombelon, M.C.M., and Kelman, A. 1980. Ecology of the soft rot erwinias. Annu. Rev. Phytopathol. 18:361-387.

35.   Perombelon, M., and Kelman, A. 1987. Blackleg and other potato diseases caused by soft rot erwinias: proposal for revision of terminology. Plant Dis. 71:283-285.

36.   Perombelon, M., Lopez, M., Carbonell, J., and Hyman, L. 1988. Effects of contamination by *Erwinia carotovora* subsp. *carotovora* and *E. carotovora* subsp. *atroseptica* of potato seed tubers and of cultivar resistance on blanking or nonemergence and blackleg development in Valencia, Spain. Potato Res. 31:591-599.

37.   Persson, P. 1988. Blackleg and stem rot of potatoes in Sweden. Acta Agri. Scand. 38:177-182.

38.   Pirhonen, M., Saarilahti, H., Karlsson, M.-B., and Palva, E.T. 1991. Identification of pathogenicity determinants of *Erwinia carotovora* subsp. *carotovora* by transposon mutagenesis. Mol. Plant-Microbe Interact. 4:276-283.

39.   Powelson, M.L. 1980. Seasonal incidence and cause of blackleg and a stem soft rot of potatoes in Oregon Am. Potato J. 57:301-306.

40.   Powelson, M.L., and Apple, J.D. 1984. Soil and seed tubers as sources of inoculum of *Erwinia carotovora* pv. *carotovora* for stem soft rot of potatoes. Phytopathology 74:429-432.

41.   Robertson, K.J., Wale, S.J., Markos, F., and Foster, G. 1987. The use of heat treatment and bacteriocides to reduce *Erwinia* contamination on seed potatoes. Tests Agrochem. Cult. 8:74-75.

42.   Rowe, R.C., Davis, J.R., Powelson, M.L., and Rouse, D.I. 1987. Potato early dying: causal agents and management strategies. Plant Dis. 71:482-489.

43.   Samson, R., Poutier, F., Sailly, M., and Jouan, B. 1987. Caracterisation des *Erwinia chrysanthemi* isolees de *Solanum tuberosum* et d'autres plantes-hotes selon les biovars et serogroupes. EPPO Bul. 17:11-16.

44.   Tanii, A., and Akai, J. 1975. Blackleg of potato plant caused by a serologically specific strain of *Erwinia carotovora* var. *carotovora* (Jones) Dye. Ann. Phytopathol. Soc. Jap. 41:513-517.

45.   Taylor, R.J., and Secor, G.A. 1990. Potato protoplast-derived callus tissue challenged with *Erwinia carotovora* subsp. *carotovora*: survival, growth and identification of resistant callus lines. J. Phytopathol. 129:228-236.

46.   Tominaga, T., and Ogasawara, K. 1979. Bacterial stem rot of potato caused by *Erwinia chrysanthemi*. Ann. Phytopathol. Soc. Jap. 45:474-477.

COMMON AND ACID SCAB OF POTATO: MANAGEMENT, ETIOLOGY AND POTENTIAL USES FOR THE PHYTOTOXINS PRODUCED BY *STREPTOMYCES* SPECIES

Rosemary Loria
Department of Plant Pathology
Cornell University
Ithaca, NY 14853-5908

Potato scab, caused by species of *Streptomyces*, occurs in production areas throughout the world. Infection takes place through the lenticels of immature tubers, and lesions expand as the tubers grow. Scab lesions may be superficial, erumpent, or pitted, and cause direct losses to growers by reducing tuber quality, and therefore marketability. There are several management strategies for potato scab. Unfortunately, these strategies are not effective in all situations because of environmental and soil-type differences; some scab management practices may result in indirect economic losses. Soil moisture management during, and for several weeks after, tuber initiation can reduce disease severity, since some types of scab are suppressed in soils with a moisture level greater than -0.04 MPa (17). A large proportion of production acreage in the United States is not irrigated, or irrigation is inadequate to significantly suppress scab. Over-irrigation can lead to increased losses from other diseases, such as pink rot (9), and to excessive leaching of plant nutrients from the soil. In some areas, increased salinity of the soil also can be a problem. Another effective strategy is the maintenance of low soil pH, because potato scab often is not severe below   pH 5.4. Some types of scab, however, are not controlled by low pH, and indirect losses are associated with potato production in acidic soils. Most plant nutrients are utilized inefficiently at low pH, resulting in excessive fertilizer costs and yield reductions. Rotations of three to four years with nonhost crops can control populations of pathogenic *Streptomyces*. Such rotation systems often are not implemented, because many growers lack the land needed for lengthy rotations. In addition, many desirable nonhost crops, such as corn and alfalfa, do not grow well in acidic soils, thereby discouraging the use of crop rotation, a valuable pest management practice. Chemical control of potato scab is limited. Some fungicidal seed treatments, specifically mancozeb and captan, control scab by reducing seedborne inoculum. Seedborne inoculum is not eliminated, and the treatments are ineffective against existing soil inoculum. Scab-resistant potato cultivars can provide a significant degree of control, although immunity has not been identified in adapted germplasm. Unfortunately, there are relatively few resistant cultivars, and these still may develop scab if pathogenic population densities are high and soil conditions favor disease. Most potato breeding programs emphasize scab resistance, but market requirements often override such considerations. As a result, many newly-released cultivars lack scab resistance.

Several *Streptomyces* species cause scab of potato and other root crops. *Streptomyces scabies* (Thaxt.) Lambert and Loria is the predominant and most economically important causal agent of potato scab. In surveys conducted by our laboratory, *S. scabies* has been identified in most major production areas in the United States (19,20), and the populations appear to be relatively homogeneous in physiological and morphological characteristics. The species is characterized by smooth gray spores borne in spiral chains, production of melanin, utilization of all International *Streptomyces* Project (ISP) sugars, and a pH minimum of 5.0 for growth in culture media (13). *Streptomyces scabies* can cause a range of symptoms on potato tubers. Some lesions are superficial, limited to a russetting of the tuber surface, while other lesions are raised and extremely corky or deeply-pitted. A combination of lesion types often can be found on the same tuber. *Streptomyces scabies* can be seedborne or soilborne. Though this pathogen is well-established in most soils used for potato production, strains of the pathogen vary in their virulence. Growers should avoid planting seed contaminated with *S. scabies* because of the possibility of introducing an aggressive strain. This pathogen survives well in the absence of host crops, and is difficult to eliminate once established.

Streptomyces acidiscabies Lambert and Loria, although not found as commonly as *S. scabies*, also is an important cause of potato scab. This species can be differentiated from *S. scabies* on the basis of morphological and physiological characteristics: flexuous spore chains, white to red spore mass color (dependent on growth medium), a red/yellow pH-sensitive diffusible pigment, ability to utilize all ISP sugars except raffinose, and a pH minimum of 4.0 for growth in culture (14). Tolerance of low pH by *S. acidiscabies* allows it to cause scab in acidic soils, which justifies the species designation and the description "acid scab" for the disease which it incites. Unlike *S. scabies*, this pathogen does not survive for long periods in soil (21). Because seed tubers are the primary source of inoculum, seed treatments provide more effective control of *S. acidiscabies* than *S. scabies* (21,22). Some soil-applied insecticides also provide control of acid scab (22), implicating soil arthropods in the epidemiology of this disease. The symptoms caused by *S. acidiscabies* are indistinguishable from those caused by *S. scabies*. Resistance of potato cultivars to the two pathogens is the same (Loria, *unpublished data*), and Lambert (16) recently has shown that the two species have a common host range. The similarities in symptomatology and host range suggest that *S. scabies* and *S. acidiscabies* share determinants for pathogenicity on potato.

Other *Streptomyces* species have been reported to cause scab-like symptoms on potato tubers (2,6,10,23). Many of these isolates are less virulent than *S. scabies*, and produce only superficial lesions on potato tubers (1,7,24). Most strains in this "atypical" group have not been well-characterized, but those that have are much less homogenous than strains of either *S. scabies* or *S. acidiscabies* (13,15). Many of these species have some characteristics in common with either *S. scabies* or *S. acidiscabies*, including gray, smooth spores or flexuous spore chains, but often lack pigment production, have a pH minimum of 5.5, and have incomplete ISP sugar utilization patterns (13). None of these species have been studied thoroughly enough to completely determine their occurrence, host range, and the environmental conditions under which they cause potato scab. However, russet scab (7) and netted scab (24), presumably caused by atypical strains, are more severe at high rather than low soil moisture.

Lambert and Loria (13,14), Healy and Lambert (8), and Doering et al (5) demonstrated the great diversity among the three categories of scab-causing *Streptomyces* species. Fifty morphological and physiological characteristics of *S. scabies*, *S. acidiscabies* and the atypical category were scored and used to calculate similarity coefficients (13,14,15). Similarity among strains of *S. scabies* was high (96%); among *S. acidiscabies* strains, the similarity coefficient was 99%. Similarity among selected strains in the atypical category was 85%. However, there was much less similarity in comparisons of the three categories of *Streptomyces*. The similarity coefficient of *S. scabies* to *S. acidiscabies* was 65%, providing additional support that these are distinct species. In comparisons between *S. scabies* strains and those of the atypical category, similarity was 63%, while the similarity of *S. acidiscabies* to the atypical strains was 73%. *Streptomyces acidiscabies* and the atypical pathogens were more closely related to nonpathogenic strains of *S. griseus* than to *S. scabies*, based upon these studies. DNA-DNA hybridization studies conducted by Healy and Lambert (8) also indicated that the three categories of pathogenic *Streptomyces* are genetically diverse. Most of the *S. scabies* strains were very similar to the type strain, although the DNA relatedness ranged from 21% to greater than 70%. Since 70% is the minimum level of DNA relatedness which generally delimits a species, there was more diversity among strains classified as *S. scabies* than would be expected. In contrast, the strains of *S. acidiscabies* were closely related to the type strain (83-111%). Representative strains of the atypical category were not very similar at the DNA level. Comparisons between pairs of strains causing potato scab in the three categories indicated that these species were not closely related. Pairwise hybridizations did not exceed 20% in any comparison, which supports the phenotypic data and suggests that pathogens in the three categories are unrelated. In addition, restriction fragment length polymorphism (RFLP) analyses by Doering et al (5) showed a high degree of polymorphism among scab-causing *Streptomyces* in Israel; the RFLP analyses supported the phenotypic data indicating diversity. It appears that *S. scabies* is not the predominant scab pathogen in Israel (5).

Among these diverse *Streptomyces* species, is there a common factor which allows them to be potato pathogens? Recent publications (11,12,18) described two phytotoxins, produced by strains of *S. scabies* and *S. acidiscabies*, which may play a role in the pathogenicity of these species on potato. The toxins, thaxtomin A and B, are modified dipeptides composed of tryptophan and either phenylalanine or tyrosine. Thaxtomin A is more abundant in tuber tissue than thaxtomin B, but both compounds produce tissue necrosis when applied to potato tubers produced in vitro (18). These symptoms are similar to the initial necrotic, water-soaked lesions caused by the pathogens on tubers. The thaxtomins can be extracted from scab lesions on tubers, or from tuber slices colonized by pathogenic *Streptomyces* strains (12); the toxins are not found in healthy tuber tissue (18). Research done by King et al (12) and by Delserone et al. (3) indicated that thaxtomin A is produced by pathogenic strains of *S. scabies, S. acidiscabies*, but not by nonpathogenic strains. Ability to produce thaxtomins may be the common pathogenicity determinant among the diverse *Streptomyces* genotypes that cause potato scab.

Further study is needed before the thaxtomins are proven to be pathogenicity determinants, but exciting areas for future research can be identified now. Techniques for detection and quantification of pathogenic *Streptomyces* populations are needed for use in ecological and disease management research. If the thaxtomins are pathogenicity determinants in *Streptomyces*, the cloned biosynthetic genes may be useful in detection and quantification of the potato pathogens, either via DNA/DNA hybridizations or the polymerase chain reaction. This would be a great improvement over the current labor-intensive methods of dilution-plating and pathogenicity testing. Biological control of pathogenic *Streptomyces* may develop from confirmation that the thaxtomins are pathogenicity factors. Pathogenic, toxin-producing (Tox+) strains could be altered, perhaps by transposon mutagenesis, to create nonpathogenic, Tox- strains. The engineered strains might compete sucessfully with wild-type strains for infection sites in the tuber lenticels, thereby decreasing scab severity.

Another possible application for the thaxtomins is in the identification of scab-resistant potato germplasm. We developed an assay in which thaxtomin A was applied to immature tuber periderm, and tubers were rated for the rate and extent of periderm necrosis. A strong correlation between thaxtomin sensitivity and the susceptibility of nine cultivars to *S. scabies* and *S. acidiscabies* was obtained (4). Additional evaluations of established cultivars and advanced germplasm are underway. If thaxtomin sensitivity is directly related to susceptibility to *S. scabies* and *S. acidiscabies*, the phytotoxins may be useful in the identification and mapping of scab-resistance genes. Of course, if thaxtomins are to be integrated into potato breeding programs, a reliable source of thaxtomin A is critical. Recent research in our laboratory (3) has shown that thaxtomin A is produced by *S. scabies* and *S. acidiscabies* in several liquid culture media. Thin-layer chromatographic, UV absorbance and bioassay data were used to confirm the presence of thaxtomin A in culture filtrates. Optimization of production in liquid culture is in progress.

The discovery and characterization of the thaxtomins appears to be a major breakthrough in our understanding of the mechanism of disease development in the *Streptomyces* - potato system. Current research will determine whether thaxtomins are indeed pathogenicity determinants. Many useful developments may be based on knowledge of the role of the phytotoxins in the *Streptomyces*-potato interaction.

Literature Cited

1. Bång, H.O. 1979. Studies on potato russet scab. I. A characterization of different isolates from northern Sweden. Acta Agric. Scand. 29:145-150.
2. Corbaz, R. 1964. Etude des Streptomycetes provoquant la gale commune de la pomme de terre. Phytopathol. Z. 51:351-360.
3. Delserone, L.M., Bukhalid, R.A., and Loria, R. 1992. *In vitro* production of the phytotoxin thaxtomin A by *Streptomyces scabies* and *S. acidiscabies*. (Abstr.) Phytopathology 82:242.
4. Delserone, L.M., Loria, R., and Arias, I. 1991. Correlation between susceptibility of potato cultivars to *Streptomyces scabies* and sensitivity to thaxtomin (Abstr.) Phytopathology 81:1193.

5. Doering, C.O., Kampfer, P., Manulis, S., Kritzman, G., Schrempf, H., and Barash, I. 1991. Diversity of *Streptomyces* strains pathogenic on potato (Abstr.) Phytopathology 81:1171.
6. Gordon, R.E. and Horan, C. 1968. A piecemeal description of *Streptomyces griseus* (Krainsky) Waksman and Henrici. J. Gen. Microbiol. 50:223-233.
7. Harrison, M.D. 1962. Potato russet scab, its cause and factors affecting its development. Am. Potato J. 39:368-387.
8. Healy, F.G., and Lambert, D.H. 1991. Relationships among *Streptomyces* spp. causing potato scab. Int. J. Syst. Bacteriol. 41:479-482.
9. Hooker, W.J. 1981. Compendium of potato diseases. Am. Phytopath. Soc., St. Paul, MN, 125 pp.
10. Hütter, R. 1967. Systematic der Streptomyceten. Karger, Basel.
11. King, R.R., Lawrence, C.H., Clark, M.C., and Calhoun, L.A. 1989. Isolation and characterization of phytotoxins associated with *Streptomyces scabies*. J. Chem. Soc. Chem. Commun. 13:849-850.
12. King, R.R., Lawrence, C.H., and Clark, M.C. 1991. Correlation of phytotoxin production with pathogenicity of *Streptomyces scabies* isolates from scab infected potato tubers. Am. Potato J. 68:675-680.
13. Lambert, D.H., and Loria, R. 1989. *Streptomyces scabies* sp. nov. nom. rev. Int. J. Syst. Bacteriol. 39:387-392.
14. Lambert, D.H., and Loria, R. 1989. *Streptomyces acidiscabies* sp. nov. Int. J. Syst. Bacteriol. 39:393-396.
15. Lambert, D.H., and Loria, R. 1990. Taxonomy of Streptomycetes causing potato scab (Abstr.) Phytopathology 80:120-121.
16. Lambert, D.H. 1991. First report of additional hosts for the acid scab pathogen *Streptomyces acidiscabies*. Plant Dis. 75:750.
17. Lapwood, D.H. 1966. The effects of soil moisture at the time potato tubers are forming on the incidence of common scab (*Streptomyces scabies*). Ann. Appl. Biol. 58:447-456.
18. Lawrence, C.H., Clark, M.C., and King, R.R. 1990. Induction of common scab symptoms in aseptically cultured potato tubers by the vivotoxin, thaxtomin. Phytopathology 80:606-608.
19. Loria, R., Kempter, B.A., and Jamieson, A.A. 1986. Characterization of *Streptomyces*-like isolates from potato tubers with symptoms of common scab (Abstr.) Phytopathology 76:1078-1079.
20. Loria, R., Wilde, J.R., and Slack, S.A. 1988. Etiology of potato scab in Wisconsin (Abstr.) Phytopathology 78:1509.
21. Manzer, F.E., McIntyre, G.A., and Merriam, D.C. 1977. A new potato scab problem in Maine. Univ. Maine Tech. Bull. 85. 24 pp.
22. Manzer, F., Storch, R., Sewell, G., and Lambert, D. 1989. Control of acid scab with seed and soil treatments, 1989. Fung. Nemat. Tests 45:121.
23. Millard, W.A., and Burr, S. 1926. A study of twenty-four strains of *Actinomyces* and their relation to types of common scab of potato. Ann. Appl. Biol. 13:580-644.
24. Scholte, K., and Labruyère, R.E. 1985. Netted scab: A new name for an old disease in Europe. Potato Res. 28:443-448.

MANAGEMENT STRATEGIES FOR FUNGAL DISEASES OF TUBERS

Gary A. Secor
Department of Plant Pathology
North Dakota State University
Fargo, ND 58105

Three distinctly different diseases were selected as examples to illustrate the importance of multicomponent management strategies for reducing diseases in storage. These fungal diseases, silver scurf caused by *Helminthosporium solani*, dry rot caused by *Fusarium sambucinum*, and pink rot caused by *Phytophthora erythroseptica*, are common and of economic importance in North America. References pertaining to these diseases are listed (by disease) in the Literature Cited section.

Silver Scurf

This is a superficial disease of the periderm that is first seen at harvest. Symptoms are metallic patches of bronze or gold discoloration limited to the outermost layers of the periderm. No vine symptoms have been reported. Symptoms are most noticeable on red-skinned potatoes, but also occur on white- and russet-skinned cultivars. The disease distracts from the appearance of the tuber and processing quality, but does not cause a reduction in yield. It is, therefore, most important to fresh market, tablestock potatoes. It is especially severe after storage where it may lead to rejection of stocks. The disease has increased in economic importance within the last 5 yr.

Cultivar resistance. Nineteen cultivars and advanced selections from the North Dakota State University potato breeding program were evaluated for resistance to silver scurf. The six cultivars were red-skinned, and included Bison, Reddale, Red Norland, Redsen, Red Pontiac, and LaRouge. All advanced selections also were red-skinned. Potatoes were planted at the Potato Research Farm located near Grand Forks, ND in soil naturally infested with *H. solani*. Potatoes were stored for 6 mo before disease assessments were made. The most resistant cultivars were LaRouge and Red Pontiac. Although significant differences in resistance were found, no entry was identified with a high level of resistance. This is consistent with findings in Europe that high levels of resistance to silver scurf have not been identified.

Seed treatment. Whether the source of inoculum for silver scurf is primarily seedborne or soilborne in North America is unknown at this time. In Europe, most investigators consider silver scurf to be a seedborne disease; however, in the United States silver scurf has occurred on progeny of tissue culture-derived minitubers planted in soil which had never been cropped to potatoes (Secor, unpublished data).

Preliminary observations from annual seed treatment trials indicated that some treatments resulted in a reduction in disease. Following this observation, a trial was designed to evaluate the efficacy of seed treatments for control of silver scurf. In general, seed treatment reduced severity of silver scurf at harvest time. The best treatments were captan and thiophanate-methyl.

In another study, tubers were treated with various fungicides at planting, at post-harvest, or at both times. Seed treatment reduced silver scurf at harvest, but post-harvest treatments did not reduce silver scurf during storage. In fact, disease severity increased during storage regardless of treatment.

Resistance of *H. solani* to fungicides. Isolates of *H. solani* were recovered from silver scurf lesions on tubers obtained from Alaska, British Columbia, Maine, Minnesota, Nebraska, North Dakota, Oregon, and Washington. Single spore isolates were tested for sensitivity in vitro to the fungicides thiobendazole, thiophanate-methyl, iprodione, captan and imazalil. Sensitivity was measured by calculation of an ED50, defined as the concentration (mg/L) at which colony growth was reduced by 50%. Resistance was found in isolates from all locations to all fungicides except imazalil. The range of sensitivity was TBZ: 1.2 - 50; thiophanate-methyl: 0.5 - >1000; iprodione: 71 - >1000; captan: 25 - 794; imazalil: <0.1 - 0.5 mg/L. Clearly, resistance to commonly used fungicides exists in the *H. solani* population throughout the potato growing areas of North America.

Conclusions and future directions. No effective strategy for control of silver scurf, especially during storage, is available. No highly resistant germplasm has been identified, and seed treatment and/or post-harvest fungicide treatment have limited value. Seed treatment does result in a reduction in disease at harvest, however, its effect does not extend into storage. No post-harvest treatment was effective. In addition, resistance to fungicides commonly used in potato production is widespread in the pathogen population, which may contribute to the lack of control.

Four areas where additional research and further work are warranted include: 1) relative importance of seedborne and soilborne inoculum in epidemiology of this disease; 2) possible alternate hosts for *H. solani*; 3) identification of germplasm and cultivars with high levels of resistance; and 4) storage management practices that reduce disease development.

Fusarium Dry Rot

Fusarium is a persistent cause of disease throughout the entire life of the potato plant. It causes seed decay, wilt, and vascular discoloration and dry rot of tubers in storage. Consistently it is one of the most important pathogens, and diseases caused by this pathogen frequently result in economic losses. Many species of *Fusarium* are important in potatoes, including F. *roseum*, F. *sambucinum,* F. *sulphureum,* F. *solani,* F. *coeruleum* and F. *oxysporum*. Some cause wilt, some cause dry rot and some cause both. *Fusarium* spp. can produce three spore types: microconidia, macroconidia and chlamydospores. *Fusarium* is both soil- and seedborne and spores are abundant and ubiquitous. All spore types can infect potato, but each has a different survival time. Survival time of micro- and macroconidia can be measured in days whereas chlamydospores are long-lived and can persist in the soil for years.

A major factor in the disease cycle of *Fusarium* is that a wound is required for infection. Infection occurs primarily at harvest and seed cutting. Both operations cause cuts and bruises, many of which are too small to see.

Disease management has relied primarily on three strategies: avoidance of wounds, proper wound healing conditions, and chemicals. Prevention of bruising and wounds at harvest and during seed handling prevents infection. Wound healing of newly harvested potatoes in storage or of cut seed allows the potato to wall off infections. Proper conditions include moderate temperatures (10-13 C), high humidity, and plenty of oxygen (fresh air) for 10-14 days. For cut seed in the ground, it is important to avoid cold, hot, soggy or dry soils. Application of chemicals will prevent new infections but will not cure old infections. Seed treatments reduce dry rot of cut seed. The best chemicals are thiophanate-methyl, thiabendazole (TBZ), and the EBDC's. A standard and effective recommendation for the past 10 yr for dry rot control in storage has been post-harvest use of TBZ applied in an ultra-low volume of water. Although resistance to *Fusarium* is rare in the widely grown cultivars; resistant germplasm has been identified.

Current research. Despite these relatively effective control methods, Fusarium decay has become a serious problem in recent years.

Two incidents in particular prompted a re-examination of this old disease. One was the high frequency of dry rot in the north-central potato producing areas due to the prolonged drought of 1988-1990. Dry rot increased due to the higher specific gravities, increased bruising because of more clods and a later harvest, which meant colder potatoes and subsequently more bruising at harvest. There is a 2% tolerance for dry rot at shipping time, but dry rot is difficult to see because it is internal and dirt often hides the external injury and decay.

The second incident, which occurred primarily in Idaho, was the high incidence of decay of pre-cut seed that had been cut and stored. In these cases, seed was cut, treated with a fungicide, and stored for 4-6 wk prior to planting. Several of these seed lots had Fusarium decay of up to 100%. Seed of the same lot planted soon after cutting and seed treatment had little if any decay in the field.

In order to study these problems, we began to collect infected tubers and seed pieces to identify the cause of the decay. Over 200 isolates were collected by us or by colleagues from all over North America. Single spore isolates were grown on PDA amended with TBZ to determine if the isolates were resistant to this fungicide. TBZ is the main fungicide used for control of Fusarium dry rot, and resistance to TBZ could explain the increase in dry rot. An ED50, defined as the estimated concentration (mg/L) of TBZ causing a 50% reduction in colony diameter after 7 days growth on PDA, was calculated for each isolate. Almost all the isolates were *F. sambucinum* (synonym = *F. sulphureum*), regardless of geographic origin, and resistance was found in isolates from most areas (Table 1). A total of 72% of the TBZ isolates were resistant, and the ED50 ranged from 10 to 53 mg/L. Isolates resistant to TBZ were also resistant to thiophanate-methyl.

Once we established that resistance in *F. sambucinum* to TBZ was widespread, we wanted to know the biological implications of this resistance. Does resistance result in more dry rot? Batches of bruised Norchip potatoes were inoculated with spores from isolates that varied in their sensitivity to TBZ: fully sensitive (no growth at 1.0 mg/L), low resistance (ED50 = 15-20 mg/L), medium resistance (ED50 = 25-30 mg/L), and high resistance (ED50 = 40-50 mg/L). Inoculated potatoes were treated with TBZ and stored at 10 C. Resistance to TBZ resulted in a significant increase in incidence and severity of dry rot compared to TBZ sensitive isolates regardless of resistance level.

Fitness and genetics of inheritance of resistance to TBZ also was studied by Anne Desjardins, USDA-ARS, NCAUL, Peoria, IL. She found that these isolates were fertile, retained their pathogenicity, suffered no loss in mycotoxin production, were primarily in vegetative compatibility group 1, and were all mating type 1. This indicated that no obvious changes in other characters had occurred which may have affected fitness. She also found that the TBZ resistance was inherited as a single character, and no intermediate phenotypes occurred after crossing sensitive and resistant isolates. This means that the resistance genes will not be spread by sexual recombination, but still can spread easily in the population by heterokaryosis.

TABLE 1. Frequency of resistance to TBZ in *Fusarium* isolates recovered from potatoes with dry rot.

State/Province	Number of isolates	Resistant %	ED50[2]
North Dakota	74	84	30
Minnesota	17	82	30
South Dakota	2	0	<10
Idaho	67	85	35
Wisconsin	2	100	25
Maine	3	0	<10
Texas	1	0	<10
Washington	7	0	<10
Alaska	3	33	53
Prince Edward Island	3	0	<10
Colorado	15	7	21
New York	2	100	27
Michigan	7	100	32
Nebraska	12	75	32
TOTAL	215	22	--

[1]Almost exclusively *F. sambucinum*.
[2]Estimated concentration (mg/L) of TBZ causing a 50% reduction in colony diameter after 7 days.

Management implications and future directions. The most obvious implication of this knowledge is that we cannot rely on post-harvest application of TBZ as a sole control measure for dry rot. Instead we need to use a multitarget management program with TBZ as a component of this program. Its use should not be discontinued because many isolates are sensitive. Other management practices, most of which are grower practices, must be done to prevent bruising and hence suppress dry rot development. These suggestions are given on Tables 3 and 4.

Chemicals with modes of action different than benzimidazole fungicides need to be developed. Imazalil, at low concentrations, stops growth of all *Fusarium* isolates listed, including the TBZ resistant strains. It is extremely doubtful if any new chemicals will be approved for post-harvest application on potatoes, as TBZ is now, because of food safety concerns. However, a number of aromatic, naturally occurring GRAS (generally regarded as safe) compounds are being tested. If they are effective they may be available as post-harvest treatments in the future.

Fusarium dry rot, because of its complexity, constant association with the potato, and now resistance of the pathogen to TBZ, is a perfect candidate for in integrated management program. Successful economic control will depend on integration of multiple control practices.

TABLE 2. Checklist for reduced bruising of potato tubers.

1. See that all unnecessary drops are eliminated and all drops are kept to less than 15 cm.
2. At harvest time, place primary emphasis on keeping bruising at a minimum.
3. Make no modifications on the harvester without first considering the effect on injury.
4. Use either a tractor with a hydromatic transmission or a harvester that has a 3-speed transmission to provide the flexibility to adapt to varying soil conditions.
5. Minimize tangling and plugging problems caused by wet, tough vines by cutting the vines lying in the furrows with two disc blades or coulters mounted beside each other on a tool bar and angled to form a "V".
6. Adjust the digger blade or bridge the gap between the blade and the primary chain with metal plates so the potatoes do not bump into the front of the chain.
7. Replace the digger chain as often as the manufacturer recommends to minimize flexing of the links that may increase pinching.
8. Minimize link pinching by not using a one-up, one-down link pattern.
9. Use chain with a wider pitch to help minimize soil elimination problems.
10. Use rubber-covered chain throughout the harvester.
11. Keep the chains tight to minimize bouncing of tubers and rocks on the chain and to reduce whipping.
12. Run digger chain speed 1.2 to 1.5 times faster than forward speed.
13. Where hard clods are a problem, do not use severe shakers in a futile attempt to break up the clods.
14. Remember to lower or remove shakers when digging conditions are good.
15. Run the rear cross, elevator and boom chains at a speed which is 0.4 to 0.6 times ground speed in order to keep the chains full.
16. Install belting to divert potatoes away from link hooks and bare link ends.

TABLE 2. Checklist for reduced bruising of potato tubers (continued).

17. Adjust tilt of the rear crossover and elevator to give a uniform distribution of potatoes over the width of the chains.
18. Carefully regulate boom height to minimize the drop onto the pile in the truck.
19. Stop or slow down the chains whenever stopped or slow down the tractor.
20. If the harvester is PTO driven, increase forward speed by shifting gears rather than by opening the throttle.
21. If windrowing, allow the potatoes to lie for at least 20 min before picking them up.
22. Harvest during the hours of the day when the soil temperature is above 45 F.
23. Use bruise detector kits, available from extension service staff, to determine actual damage levels at harvest.
24. Have the proper number of trucks to keep the harvester going without hurrying.
25. Tarp every load to avoid the sun and wind damage that can prevent suberization.

TABLE 3. Checklist for dry rot reduction in storage.

1. See that bin filling equipment has adequate capacity to allow removal of dirt, debris, and undergrade product and to handle the crop without excessive speeds.
2. See that storage filling personnel are well trained in proper procedures to reduce tuber damage.
3. See that all potato handling surfaces are rubberized or padded on every piece of equipment used for handling potatoes into storage.
4. Insist on step-piling when placing the crop in the bins.
5. Good skin maturation helps prevent injuries at harvest time that could act as *Fusarium* entry sites.
6. Avoid cold harvest; cold tubers are more susceptible to bruise and injury.
7. *Fusarium* can only enter through a wound. By preventing injury, *Fusarium* infection is prevented.
8. TBZ is the only post-harvest chemical registered on potatoes for dry rot control. Application rate is 0.42 fl. oz./ton.
9. Use a TBZ application method that gives maximum coverage of the tubers. Best coverage occurs if chemical is applied under pressure to cause its swirling.
10. After tubers are harvested and in storage, provide conditions favorable for rapid wound healing; plenty of air, humidity and warm temperatures (55-65 F) for 10-14 days, then lower temperature about 0.5 F per day until desired temperature for long term storage.
11. Prevent any conditions, such as accumulation of soil or debris that would block air circulation around tubers. Rot can develop in areas of poor circulation.
12. Avoid free moisture on surface of tubers.

Pink Rot

Pink rot is a storage disease that, under favorable conditions, can result in serious losses. It is often called water rot. Widespread confusion exists over whether water rot is pink rot caused by *Phytophthora erythroseptica* or leak caused by *Pythium* sp. Weather is probably the most important factor affecting disease development. By the time disease occurs, it is generally too late to respond. Consequently, control has been difficult.

Potential control. Better water management, particularly late in the season, harvest temperatures less than 22 C, and prevention of bruising reduces leak and pink rot. However, the first two tactics are not always possible because of unfavorable weather. Therefore, alternative control measures are necessary. This led to investigation of metalaxyl as a tool in the control program for pink rot.

There is evidence for control of other diseases caused by other pythiacious fungi, namely late blight and leak, with metalaxyl. The label is restrictive, however, in timing of application and lacks specific information on pink rot control. Preliminary grower field studies indicated that metalaxyl reduced pink rot and there was an economic advantage under center-pivot-irrigated conditions. Based on these results, we began an in-depth study with the objectives: 1) to determine cause of "water rot," i.e., *Phytophthora* or *Pythium*; 2) compare application methods (air vs ground), number of applications, and timing of applications (early vs late) of metalaxyl for disease suppression; 3) to determine effect of metalaxyl on soil populations of pythiacious fungi; 4) to determine efficacy of metalaxyl for control of disease in storage; and 5) to develop methods to identify fields with potential pink rot problems in storage. One goal was to develop recommendations for judicious, therapeutic rather than routine, preventive applications of metalaxyl, in order to delay the buildup of resistance in the pathogen population.

Results of a survey of water rot tubers selected from storages in several states indicated that most of the disease was caused by *Phytophthora* and *Pythium*. This has management implications because pink rot infection occurs in the field under cool, wet conditions whereas leak occurs at or after harvest under hot temperatures.

Total pythiacious fungi in the soil was reduced following metalaxyl application; however, saprophytes were not distinguished from pathogens. We are continuing to work on soil populations of pythiacious fungi in order to correlate soil populations with disease losses. Fields with potential for pink rot decay based on populations of *P. erythroseptica* would be likely candidates for metalaxyl application.

We have compared pink rot in storages containing tubers from center pivot-irrigated-fields in which one half was treated with metalaxyl and the other half was not treated. Data indicate a significant reduction in pink rot in stored potatoes from metalaxyl-treated plots compared to the stored potatoes from nontreated plots. Metalaxyl application also may have a positive impact on yield and grade.

Future research and applications. The thrust of our research is to evaluate the efficacy of metalaxyl for pink rot control, provide information on application to ensure grower flexibility, and prolong the life of the chemical by judicious application to prevent or delay development of metalaxyl resistant strains of *P. erythroseptica*. Other management factors such as proper identity of the disease and water management, especially late in the season, must be considered in addition to chemicals for disease control. Metalaxyl appears to be effective in reducing pink rot in storage. Additional work needs to be done to allow maximum flexibility for its incorporation into disease management programs.

Acknowledgements

The research reported here is the result of the work of many of my colleagues, technicians and students. They deserve credit and recognition for their contributions. The silver scurf work was the thesis research of Dorian Rodriguez at NDSU. The dry rot research was funded by Merck Inc. in cooperation of Duane Preston, Extension Potato Specialist, NDSU/U of MN, and much of the lab work was done by Jane Rodriguez. The genetic and biochemical work on *Fusarium* was done by Anne Desjardins, USDA-ARS, NRRL, Peoria, IL. The pink rot research was done in collaboration with two fellow faculty members at NDSU, Robert Stack and Neil Gudmestad, and was funded by Offutt Farms and Universal Foods.

Literature Cited

Silver Scurf

Cayley, G.R., Hide, G., Read, P, and Dunne, Y. 1983. Treatment of potato seed and ware tubers with imazalil and thiabendazole for control of silver scurf and other storage diseases. Potato Res. 26:163-173.

Frisullo, S., Cicarese, F, and Cirulli, M. 1988. Chemical control trials against silver scurf of potato (Abstr). Rev. Plant Pathol. p. 935.

Hide, G., and Adams, M. 1980. Relationship between disease levels on seed tubers, on crops during growth and in stored potatoes. 2. Silver Scurf. Potato Res. 23:229-240.

Hide, G.A., Hall, S., and Boorer, K. 1988. Resistance to thiabendazole in isolates of *Helminthosporium solani*, the cause of silver scurf disease of potatoes. Plant Pathol. 37:377-380.

Jellis, G.J., and Taylor, G. 1977. The development of silver scurf *(Helminthosporium solani)* disease of potato. Ann. Appl. Biol. 86:19-28.

Jellis, G.J., and Taylor, G. 1977. Control of silver scurf *(Helminthosporium solani)* disease of potato with benomyl and thiabendazole. Ann. Appl. Biol. 86:59-67.

Lennard, J.H. 1980. Factors affecting the development of silver scurf *(Helminthosporium solani)* on potato tubers. Plant Pathol. 29:87-92.

Merida, C.L., and Loria, R. 1990. First report of resistance of *Helminthosporium solani* to thiabendazole in United States (Abstr). Phytopathology 80:557.

Rodriguez, D., Secor, G., and Nolte, P. 1990. Resistance of *Helminthosporium solani* isolates to benzimidazole fungicides. (Abstr.) Am. Potato J. 67:574-575.

Wright, N.S. 1981. Silver scurf, *Helminthosporium solani* Dur. and Mont. control by chemical treatment of seed tubers. Pesticide Research Report. Res. Stn. Agric. Canada, Vancouver, 247 pp.

Zimmerman-Gries, S., and Blodgett, E. 1974. Incidence and tuber transmission of silver scurf on potatoes in Israel. Potato Res. 17:97-112.

Fusarium Dry Rot

Adams, M.J., and Lapwood, D. 1983. Transmission of *Fusarium solani* var. *coeruleum* and *F. sulphureum* from seed potatoes to progeny tubers in the field. Ann. Appl. Biol. 103:411-417.

Desjardins, A., Christ, E., McCormick, S., and Secor, G. 1992. Heritability and other characteristics of thiabendazole-resistance in *Gibberella pulicaris (Fusarium sambucinum)* from dry rotted potato tubers. Phytopathology. 83:164-170.

Iritani, W.M., and Sparks, W. 1975. Potatoes: Storage and Quality Maintenance in the Pacific Northwest. Pacific Northwest Corp. Ext. Bull. 257 pp.

Langerfield, E. 1986. Thiabendazol - Resistenz bei *Fusarium sulphureum*. Nachrichtenbl. Deut. Pflanzenschutzd (Braunschweig) 38:165-168.

Leach, S.S. 1985. Contamination of soil and transmission of seed borne potato dry rot fungi *(Fusarium spp.)* to progeny tubers. Am. Potato J. 62:129-136.

Leach, S.S., and Webb, R. 1981. Resistance of selected potato cultivars and clones to *Fusarium* dry rot. Phytopathology. 71:623-629.

Nelson, P.E., Toussoun, T.A., and Marasas, W. 1983. *Fusarium* species: An Illustrated Manual for Identification. The Pennsylvania State Univ. Press, University Park. 193 pp.

Secor, G.A., Preston, D., Gudmestad, N., and Lamey, H.A. 1992. Fusarium Dry Rot. North Dakota State Univ. Ext. Publ. 1039. 4 pp.

Staub, T. 1991. Fungicide resistance: practical experience with antiresistance strategies and the role of integrated use. Ann. Rev. Phytopathol. 29:421-442.

Theron, D.J., and Holz. G. 1991. Prediction of potato dry rot based on the presence of *Fusarium* in soil adhering to tubers at harvest. Plant Dis. 75:126-130.

Water Rot

Barak, E., Edgington, L., and Ripley, B.D. 1984. Bioactivity of the fungicide metalaxyl in potato tubers against some species of *Phytophthora, Fusarium,* and *Alternaria,* related to polyphenol-oxidase activity. Can. J. Plant Pathol. 5:38-42.

Lennard, J.H. 1980. Factors influencing the development of potato pink rot *(Phytophthora erythroseptica)*. Plant Pathol. 29:80-86.

Lonsdale, D., Cunliffe, C., and Epton, H.A.S. 1980. Possible routes of entry of *Phytophthora erythroseptica* Pethyb. and its growth within potato plants. Phytopathology Z. 97:109-117.

Mulrooney, R.P. 1982. Evaluation of Ridomil for pink rot control. Fung. Nema. Tests 28:105.

Rowe, R.C., and Schmitthenner, A.F. 1977. Potato pink rot in Ohio caused by *Phytophthora erythroseptica* and *P. cryptogea*. Plant Dis. Reptr. 61: 807-810.

ROLE OF EARLY AND LATE BLIGHT SUPPRESSION IN POTATO PEST MANAGEMENT

W. E. Fry
Plant Pathology Department
Cornell University, Ithaca, NY 14853

Potato early blight, caused by *Alternaria solani* [Sorauer] and late blight, caused by *Phytophthora infestans* [Mont.] de Bary, have especially important roles in potato pest management. Suppression of each disease depends in part on the application of fungicides to the plants in the field because each disease can limit production dramatically. The very visible and frequent applications of fungicides focus grower and environmentalist attention to these two diseases. Only rarely are fungicides applied to potato plants for the suppression of other diseases.

Both diseases limit the quantity of production and reduce the quality. Disease caused by either pathogen reduces the amount of photosynthate available to support tuber growth. Because late blight can affect potatoes at any stage of growth, early epidemics can lead to 100% loss. In contrast, early infections by *A. solani* are typically unimportant, and the disease does not become important until the plants approach senescence. Thus, maximum documented yield reductions are usually 20-30% (26,33).

Tuber infections are possible with both pathogens, but are particularly problematic with *P. infestans*. Infection of tubers typically happens when sporangia or zoospores are washed from foliage through the soil to developing tubers. If infected tubers are stored at moderate temperatures (10-15 C) bacterial soft rot can become established and can lead to severe losses in storage. Thus, tuber infections are probably much more important than are foliage infections. Although *A. solani* also infects tubers, such infections are not associated with subsequent breakdown in storage. It is because late blight can effect such drastic reductions in yield quantity, as well as quality of product, that this disease is considered to be the most important disease of potatoes on a world wide basis (24). The dramatic distructive potential of *P. infestans* has caused growers around the world to use large amounts of fungicide to prevent foliage (and therefore tuber) infections.

Changes in the physiology of potato plants affect *A. solani* and *P. infestans* differently. Stressed plants are much more susceptible to *A. solani* than are vigorously growing plants. In contrast, stressed plants seem less susceptible to *P. infestans* than do vigorously growing plants. Susceptibility to *A. solani* increases dramatically with maturity of the potato plant. Young plants are quite resistant, but mature and senescent plants are very much more susceptible (34,35). Potato plants in all stages of growth are susceptible to *P. infestans*, but there is a slight increase in susceptibility as the plants age (17).

The pathogens are very different from each other in terms of their between-season survival. *Phytophthora infestans* survives from one season to the next as living mycelium in a nutritionally-dependent association with host tissue. Because tubers are the only plant parts that survive from one season to the next, survival of the fungus is dependent upon survival of infected tubers. This is an especially effective survival mechanism when infected tubers are used to plant the next season's crop. Sometimes infected tubers left in the field after harvest may survive the interval between seasons, and plants produced from such infected tubers may be a source of initial inoculum. Although *A. solani* also may survive the between season interval as infected tubers, the fungus also survives in the field in plant debris. It appears that *A. solani* can survive for some years in the soil. Thus, inoculum in soil becomes the most important source of initial inoculum for potato early blight.

During the 1980's potato late blight had been relatively rare in those portions of the country where it historically has been more troublesome -- the eastern and midwestern production areas -- but early blight appears to be increasing in importance in those areas. In western production areas, late blight has appeared only sporadically, and early blight remains a chronic production factor. The reasons for the enhanced importance of early blight in eastern and midwestern production are not known with certainty, but may include: a) increased use of the late blight-specific fungicide, metalaxyl, and lessened use of broad spectrum protectant fungicides effective against both early blight and late blight, b) increased use of early blight susceptible cultivars, c) decreased use of rotations, and d) occurrence of environments less favorable to late blight and relatively more favorable to early blight.

Many factors contribute to the effective suppression of early blight and late blight. Some of the most effective and some especially promising approaches are described next. These are grouped under the general headings of cultural practices, resistant cultivars, and fungicides. Additionally, the implications of probable population shifts are described.

Cultural Practices

Rotation. Because *A. solani* persists in plant debris in the field from one season to the next, rotation with non-host crops reduces the amount of initial inoculum. Early blight is typically not a severe problem in fields in which potatoes are the first solanaceous crop in many years. In an effort to quantify the impact of rotation, the influence of various rotations on the first appearance of early blight lesions was assessed in field experiments (42). In relation to lesion appearance in fields cropped continuously to potatoes or tomatoes, rotations which included either potatoes or tomatoes in only 1 out of 3 or 4 yr delayed the appearance of the initial early blight lesions by only a few days. The impact of rotations on yields or on the amounts of initial inoculum have not yet been quantified. However, it seems safe to conclude that *A. solani* can survive for long periods of time in soil.

Rotations would influence late blight only if infected tubers survived from one year to the next in the field. In climates with mild winters, such survival might be common, and a 1-yr rotation could effectively eliminate this source of initial inoculum.

Pathogen-free seed tubers. Because *P. infestans* does not survive in soil in production areas of the United States and Canada, a major source of inoculum and mechanism for distribution of inoculum has been via seed tubers, and therefore use of pathogen-free seed tubers has contributed significantly to overall late blight suppression. Infected seed tubers are important in the epidemiology of late blight, even though the proportion of infected tubers that gives rise to infected plants is very small (12). In contrast, the survival of *A. solani* in soil makes negligible the impact of using pathogen-free tubers to suppress early blight.

Elimination of infected volunteers or plants from culled tubers. When late blight infected tubers were culled during the grading of stored potatoes in the spring and then dumped near production fields, sprouts from these potatoes frequently became infected with *P. infestans* and served as a source of inoculum for production fields (4). The elimination of piles of culled potato tubers has contributed to late blight suppression. Practices which suppress between-season survival of *P. infestans* will be most noticeable when late blight is rare. The effective aerial dispersal of *P. infestans* sporangia from an explosive late blight epidemic will easily overwhelm the benefits of various cultural practices aimed at reducing the amount of initial inoculum.

Fertilization practices. Because early blight is associated with mature and senescing plants, there have been many investigations concerning the effects of fertilizers which prolong the active growth phase of the potato plant. Large amounts of nitrogenous fertilizer have been repeatedly shown to suppress early blight (1,30,44). Unfortunately, extreme amounts of nitrogenous fertilizer produce undesirable tuber characteristics (decreased specific gravity and impaired chip color), and have adverse effects on the environment. There appears to be too large a difference between the fertilizer rate for maximum disease suppression and that required for optimal yield (1,30). Therefore, plant pathologists have investigated the possibility of applying nitrogenous fertilizers via foliar sprays (foliar feeding). In some tests "foliar" feeding appears to have significant promise, but the inconsistency of positive results (for tomatoes and potatoes) indicates that we have not yet optimized the use of foliar fertilizers (47,48,52,53).

Resistant Cultivars

Plant resistance is a highly desired component in any pest management scheme, and certainly in potato IPM. For both early blight and late blight, there are differences among cultivars in terms of resistance. For both diseases, resistance is partially effective, but even partial resistance can contribute to overall disease suppression. (Vertical resistance, sensu VanderPlank [49], which is controlled by single genes in potato to *P. infestans*, is excluded from this discussion because it characteristically lacks durability.) Partially resistant plants require less fungicide for adequate disease suppression than do susceptible plants (8,15,16). Guidelines have been established for adjusting fungicide dosage based on cultivar resistance, and these have been transmitted to growers and plant protection specialists (22). Unfortunately, most cultivars, including the most popular cultivars, are quite susceptible to both diseases. Thus, widespread utilization of resistant cultivars awaits the development of a greater number of resistant cultivars acceptable to the market, or a change in market requirements.

A recent study using simulation models of early blight (33) and late blight (5,11) identified the relative contributions of currently available fungicides and currently available resistant cultivars to the suppression of early blight and late blight (43). This study confirmed the opinion of potato pathologists that protectant fungicides can be quite effective against late blight, but less effective against early blight. On the other hand, levels of resistance to early blight available in commercial cultivars had up to a three-fold greater effect in suppressing disease than did levels of late blight resistance (43). Conversely, a protectant fungicide (chlorothalonil) was about half as effective in suppressing early blight as in suppressing late blight (43). These studies indicate that near-term pest management programs should emphasize host resistance for early blight suppression and fungicide for late blight suppression. The studies also suggest that there should be increased efforts to develop cultivars resistant to late blight, and that there is a significant opportunity for improvements in efficacy of fungicides for suppression of early blight.

Fungicides

Future strategies for the suppression of early blight and late blight are likely to utilize new fungicides, old and new fungicides in novel ways (with more effective forecasts), and place greater reliance on plant resistance. Currently available protectant fungicides are effective against both early blight and late blight. One systemic fungicide is particularly effective against late blight, but ineffective against early blight.

Forecasts. Disease forecasts may be expected to assume an increasingly important role in early blight and late blight suppression. Many forecasts have been developed for late blight (3,18,21,25,29,50), and a few have been developed for early blight on potato (14,23,36,37), and on tomato (31). The most common late blight forecast in the United States is BLITECAST (29), which is based on the earlier forecasts of Hyre (25) and Wallin (50). The most commonly used portion of BLITECAST is that portion which specifies when the initial fungicide application of a season should be applied (12,46).

Unfortunately, the component of BLITECAST which schedules sprays during the season has been less successful (13). It may be that the failure of BLITECAST to schedule fungicide applications more effectively than a weekly conventional schedule is due to the use of past weather conditions for BLITECAST (13). BLITECAST schedules protectant fungicide sprays using previous weather, but protectant fungicides are ineffective against established infections. Thus, incorporation of weather forecasts should increase the efficacy of potato late blight forecasts utilizing protectant fungicides.

Development of a model relating forecasts of temperature and dewpoint to temperature and relative humidity periods in the subsequent 23 hr (51) provides the technology for developing a method of incorporating weather forecasts into disease forecasts. Availability of computer simulation models of early blight and late blight provides opportunity for predicting the potential benefit of incorporating these weather forecasts into disease forecasts (5-7,11,33,40). An initial simulation analysis has given limited encouragement that incorporation of future weather into a disease forecast can achieve efficiences in disease suppression (38). The model of Wilks

170

and Shen (51) was used to generate typical moist period duration and temperature forecasts consistent with particular historical weather observations. These forecasts (23 hr into the future) were used as the "seventh" day in the component of BLITECAST which determines the frequency of fungicide sprays. Fifty years of historical weather data were then used to run the simulator, and within each of the 50 yr, there were 50 sets of weather forecasts, so that 2,500 simulations were accomplished. Table 1 indicates that incorporation of future weather into BLITECAST achieved slightly better disease suppression without increasing fungicide use. The next steps are to investigate the utility of such weather forecasts with different decision rules.

TABLE 1. Effect of incorporating weather forecasts into BLITECAST to control late blight using protectant fungicide in simulation experiments with 50 yr of weather data.[a]

Weather	AUDPC[b]	Fungicide Applications ($\pm$ SE)
Previous	4.01 a[c]	10.6 ($\pm$1.13)
Previous + Forecast[d]	3.79 b	10.8 ($\pm$1.08)

[a] Data of R. Raposo, 1992.
[b] Mean of area under disease progress curve in proportion-days.
[c] Numbers within the column for each type of weather followed by the same letter are not significantly different at 5% level, as determined by Fisher's protected LSD test.
[d] Mean of 50 runs per year of stochastically generated daily weather forecasts.

Programmed Uses. Recent investigations at the University of Wisconsin and at Cornell University have led to programmed uses of protectant fungicide which promise significant reductions in fungicide use while maintaining effective suppression of both diseases (40,46). Both approaches utilize the observation that early applications of fungicide for suppression of early blight are essentially ineffectual (20,40,41). Thus, if there is no threat from late blight, there is no need to spray potato plants early in the season. The need for late blight sprays is determined from an estimate of initial inoculum availability as well as an estimate (provided by BLITECAST) of the weather effects on the establishment of initial late blight infections. Early blight forecasts are more closely related to host plant maturity than to any other factor (14,23,33-35,40). Stevenson has further suggested that the first early blight sprays should be at a lower fungicide dosage than later early blight sprays. If late blight is thought to be a factor, then fungicide sprays should be adjusted to complement the late blight resistance of the cultivar in question (40,41). Additionally, Shtienberg et al (40,41) suggested that sprays made late in the season have little influence on yield quantity. However, late season sprays had previously been thought to be important in preventing tuber infections. These expectations were not confirmed in field experiments in which late season sprays were eliminated (41). Thus it appears that employment of either of these programs (Cornell, Wisconsin) can contribute significantly to early blight and late blight suppression with reduced amounts of fungicide.

Resistance management. Management of fungicide resistance is likely to become a major consideration in late blight suppression in the near term future. Resistance in *P. infestans* populations to the specific, systemic fungicide, metalaxyl, has been reported from Europe and Mexico (9, Matuszak and Fry, unpublished data). Reports of metalaxyl resistance in *P. infestans* populations in the United States and Canada were nonexistent until 1990, when isolates resistant to metalaxyl were detected in the Pacific northwest (Inglis, Deahl, Matuszak, Goodwin, and Fry, unpublished data). and Florida in 1991 (Matuszak, Goodwin, Fry, unpublished data).

The dual goals of fungicide resistance management are: a) maintaining a low frequency of resistant individuals in a pathogen population; and b) maintaining a small pathogen population. These two goals are sometimes in conflict and may result in conflicting recommendations (19). On the basis of theoretical and simulation analyses, the strategies for managing fungicide resistance are to reduce growth rates of both sensitive and resistant biotypes, and to reduce the growth rate of the resistant biotype relative to that of the sensitive biotype (19,32). These recommendations translate to very limited use of the "at risk" fungicide. If metalaxyl is to be used only once or twice each season, then it becomes important to determine the timing of application. From analyses based on separate criteria, the middle part of the season is the best time to apply metalaxyl. On the assumption that inoculum is available early in the season, it turns out that applications mid-season are most effective using the criterion of best overall disease suppression (11). Furthermore, mid-season applications are also most effective using the criterion of protecting tubers from infection (39).

Population Shifts

Analyses of *P. infestans* populations from different continents stimulated Spielman and colleagues to hypothesize that there had been a recent world-wide migration and shift in the composition of the European population of *P. infestans* (45). Certain genotypes (termed "new" genotypes, defined on the basis of allozyme and nuclear DNA RFLP's) were displacing other genotypes (termed "old"). Displacement has been rapid (just a few years), The mechanisms of displacement have not yet been determined, but it seems likely that "new" genotypes may have more rapid growth rates and/or more effective survival mechanisms than the "old" genotypes.

Recent collections of isolates from countries outside western Europe indicate that representatives of the "old" genotype are present in most of the rest of the world (including the United States and Canada). "New" genotypes have already been detected in Russia, Rwanda, Brazil, Colombia, and Ecuador (Fry, unpublished data). To our knowledge, only "old" genotypes have been detected in the Philippines, Peru, and the United States and Canada. However, the recent report of A2 isolates from the United States and Canada (10), may indicate that the "new" genotypes also have been introduced here. If A2 mating types become widely distributed, then oospores may be produced -- an event that could lead to a major change in the ecology of the fungus. Wide-scale production of oospores could speed evolutionary change in the fungus and, if oospores survive in soil, could cause the soil to become an important source of initial inoculum.

Although it is not yet known whether "new" genotypes will be more difficult to suppress than "old" genotypes, such may be the case. Comparisons of metalaxyl-resistant isolates of *P. infestans* in Israel with metalaxyl-sensitive isolates indicated that the metalaxyl resistant isolates were more aggressive than the metalaxyl-sensitive isolates (2,27,28). It turns out that the metalaxyl-resistant isolates were "new" genotypes (Fry, unpublished data), but it is not known whether the metalaxyl-sensitive isolates were "old" genotypes; if so, this suggests that the "old" genotypes are less aggressive than the "new" genotypes. Thus, if the "new" genotypes are introduced into the United States and Canada, late blight suppression could be more difficult.

Epilogue

It seems very clear that potato early blight and potato late blight will figure prominently in potato IPM for the foreseeable future. The increasing pressure to restrict fungicide use should stimulate adoption of techniques that might otherwise not be accepted. With increasing restrictions on fungicide use, there should be greater acceptance of disease resistant cultivars. Perhaps early blight and late blight resistances will receive higher priority in potato breeding programs. Development of fungicides that are more effective for *A. solani* would be welcomed, particularly if they enable reductions in the total amount of fungicide used. The incorporation of weather forecasts into early and late blight disease forecasts is likely to occur in the near term future. Adoption of such forecasts will depend partially on the availability of fungicides. Unproven techniques such as "foliar feeding" need to be investigated more fully and incorporated into a management system where appropriate. Management techniques for fungicide resistance need to be incorporated into late blight management throughout the United States and Canada. *Phytophthora infestans* populations should be monitored to detect both metalaxyl resistance and the appearance of "new" genotypes (imported from other continents).

Optimization of all management strategies needs to be accomplished, with the overall goals of environmental safety, economically feasible production, and efficiency of resource utilization. It seems probable that such efficiencies can be determined and implemented via expert systems, in which the various components are interactive. In this way, conflicting recommendations will be resolved. A major challenge will be to identify the common denominator which will enable development of a management system that is internally consistent.

Literature Cited

1. Barclay, G.M., Murphy, H.J, Manzer, F.E., and Hutchinson, F.E. 1973. Effects of different rates of nitrogen and phosphorus on early blight in potatoes. Am. Potato J. 50:42-48.

2. Bashan, B., Kadish, D., Levy, Y., and Cohen, Y. 1989. Infectivity to potato, sporangial germination, and respiration of isolates of *Phytophthora infestans* from metalaxyl-sensitive and metalaxyl-resistant populations. Phytopathology 79:832-836.

3. Beaumont, A. 1947. The dependence on the weather of the dates of outbreak of potato blight epidemics. Trans. Br. Mycol. Soc. 31:45-53.

4. Bonde, R., and Schultz, E.S. 1943. Potato refuse piles as a factor in the dissemination of late blight. Maine Agr. Exp. Stn. Bull 416: 229-246.

5. Bruhn, J.A., and Fry, W.E. 1981. Analysis of potato late blight epidemiology via simulation modeling. Phytopathology 71:612-616.

6. Bruhn, J.A., and Fry, W.E. 1982. A mathematical model of the spatial and temporal dynamics of chlorothalonil residues in a potato canopy. Phytopathology 71:1306-1312.

7. Bruhn, J.A., and Fry, W.E. 1982. A statistical model of fungicide deposition in a potato canopy. Phytopathology 72:1301-1305.

8. Christ, B.J. 1990. Influence of potato cultivars on the effectiveness of fungicide control of early blight. Am. Potato. J. 67: 419-426.

9. Davidse, L.C. 1985. Resistance to acylalanines in *Phytophtora infestans* in the Netherlands. EPPO Bull. 15-403-409.

10. Deahl, K.L., Goth, R.W., Young, R., Sinden, S.L., and Gallegly, M.E. 1991. Occurrence of the A2 mating type of *Phytophthora infestans* in potato fields in the United States and Canada. Am. Potato J. 68:717-726.

11. Doster, M.A., Milgroom, M.G., and Fry, W.E. 1990. Quantification of factors influencing potato late blight suppression and selection for metalaxyl resistance in *Phytophthora infestans*: A simulation approach. Phytopathology 81:1190-1198.

12. Doster, M.A., Sweigard, J.A., and Fry, W.E. 1989. The influence of host resistance and climate on the initial appearance on foliar late blight of potato from infected seed tubers. Am. Potato J. 66:227-233.

13. Fohner, G.R., Fry, W.E., and White, G.B. 1984. Computer simulation raises question about timing protectant fungicide application frequency according to a potato late blight forecast. Phytopathology 74:1145-1147.

14. Franc, G.D., Harrison, M.D., and Lahman, L.K. 1988. A simple day-degree model for initiating chemical control of potato early blight in Colorado. Plant Dis. 72:851-854.

15. Fry, W.E. 1975. Integrated effects of polygenic resistance and a protective fungicide on development of potato late blight. Phytopathology 65:908-911.

16. Fry, W.E. 1978. Quantification of general resistance of potato cultivars and fungicide effects for integrated control of potato late blight. Phytopathology 68:1650-1655.

17. Fry, W.E., and Apple, A.E. 1986. Disease management implications of age-related changes in susceptibility of potato foliage to *Phytophthora infestans*. Am. Potato J. 63:47-56.

18. Fry, W.E., Apple, A.E., and Bruhn, J.A. 1983. Evaluation of potato late blight forecasts modified to incorporate host resistance and fungicide weathering. Phytopathology 73:1054-1059.

19. Fry, W.E., and Milgroom, M.G. 1990. Population biology and management of fungicide resistance. Pages 275-285 In: Managing Resistance to Agrochemicals, M.B. Green, H.M. LeBaron, and W.E. Moberg, eds. Am. Chem. Soc. Symposium Series 431.

20. Fry, W.E., and Shtienberg, D. 1990. Integration of host resistance and fungicide to manage potato diseases. Can. J. Plant Pathol. 12:111-116.

21. Grainger, J. 1953. Potato late blight forecasting and its mechanization. Nature. 171: 1012-1014.

22. Halseth, D.E., Sieczka, J.B., Tingey, W.M., and Zitter, T.A., 1987. Cornell Recommendations for commercial potato production. Cornell University. Ithaca, NY.

23. Harrison, M.D., Livingston, C.H., and Oshima. N. 1965. Control of early blight in Colorado. Fungicidal spray schedules in relation to the epidemiology of the disease. Am. Potato J. 42:319-327.

24. Hooker, W.J. (ed.) 1981. Compendium of Potato Diseases. Amer. Phytopathol. Soc., St. Paul, MN.

25. Hyre, R.A. 1954. Progress in forecasting late blight of potato and tomato. Plant Dis. Rep. 38:245-253.

26. Johnson, K.B., Radcliffe, E.B., and Teng, P.S., 1986. Effects of interacting populations of *Alternaria solani, Verticillium dahliae,* and potato leafhopper (*Empoasca fabae*) on potato yield. Phytopathology 76: 1046-1052.

27. Kadish, D., and Cohen, Y. 1988. Fitness of *Phytophthora infestans* isolates from metalaxyl-sensitive and resistant populations. Phytopathology 78:912-915.

28. Kadish, D., Grinberger, M., and Cohen, Y. 1990. Fitness of metalaxyl-sensitive and metalaxyl-resistant isolates of *Phytophthora infestans* on susceptible and resistant potato cultivars. Phytopathology 80:200-205.

29. Krause, R.A., Massie, L.B., and Hyre, R.A. 1975. Blitecast: A computerized forecast of potato late blight. Plant Dis. Rep. 59:95-98.

30. MacKenzie, D.R. 1981. Association of potato early blight, nitrogen fertilizer rate, and potato yield. Plant Dis. 65:575-577.

31. Madden, L.V., Pennypacker. S.P., and MacNab, A.A. 1978. FAST, a forecasting system for *Alternaria solani* on tomato. Phytopathology 68:1354-1358.

32. Milgroom, M.G., and Fry, W.E. 1988. A simulation analysis of the epidemiological principles for fungicide resistance management in pathogen populations. Phytopathology 78:565-570.

33. Pelletier, J.R. 1988. Computer simulation of cultivar resistance and fungicide effects on epidemics of potato early blight. Ph.D. Thesis, Cornell University, Ithaca, NY. 127 p.

34. Pelletier, J.R., and Fry, W.E. 1989. Characterization of resistance to early blight in three potato cultivars: incubation period, lesion expansion rate, and spore production. Phytopathology 79:511-517.

35. Pelletier, J.R., and Fry, W.E. 1990. Characterization of resistance to early blight in three potato cultivars: Receptivity. Phytopathology 80:361-366.

36. Pscheidt, J.W., and Stevenson, W.R. 1986. Comparison of forecasting methods for control of potato early blight in Wisconsin. Plant Dis. 70: 915-920.

37. Pscheidt, J.W., and Stevenson, W.R. 1988. The critical period for control of early blight (*Alternaria solani*) of potato. Am. Potato J. 65:425-438.

38. Raposo, R. 1992. Incorporation of weather forecasts into potato late blight forecasts. MS Thesis. Cornell University, Ithaca NY.

39. Schwinn, F.J. and Margot, P. 1991. Control with chemicals. Pages 225-265 in Advances in Plant Pathology, Vol. 7, D.S. Ingram, and P.H. Williams, eds. Academic Press, San Diego, CA.

40. Shtienberg, D., Doster, M.A., Pelletier, J.R., and Fry, W.E. 1989. Use of simulation models to develop a low risk strategy to suppress early and late blight in potato foliage. Phytopathology 79:590-595.

41. Shtienberg, D., and Fry, W.E. 1990. Field and computer simulation evaluation of spray-scheduling methods of control of early and late blight of potato. Phytopathology 80:772-777.

42. Shtienberg, D., and Fry, W.E. 1990. Influence of host resistance and crop rotation on initial appearance of potato early blight. Plant Dis. 74:849-852.

43. Shtienberg, D., and Fry, W.E. 1990. Quantitative analysis of host resistance, fungicide, and weather effects on potato early and late blight using computer simulation models. Am. Potato J. 67:277-286.

44. Soltanpour, P.N., and Harrison, M.D. 1974. Interrelations between nitrogen and phosphorus fertilization and early blight control of potatoes. Am. Potato J. 51:1-7.

45. Spielman, L.J., Drenth, A., Davidse, L.C., Sujkowski, L.J., Gu, W.-K., Tooley, P.W., and Fry, W.E. 1991. A second world-wide migration (and population displacement) of the potato late blight fungus? Plant Pathol. 40:422-430.

46. Stevenson, W.R., Pscheidt, J.W., Thielman, D.G., and Shields, E.J. 1987. PDM (Potato Disease Management): A computer tool for potato disease management. University of Wisconsin-Madison. Version 1.1. April 1986, IPM Program, 39 pp.

47. Stevenson, W.R., and Stewart, J. 1988. Evaluation of control of early blight, 1987. Fungicide & Nematicide Tests 43:137.

48. Stevenson, W.R., Stewart, J.S., and James, R.V. 1989. Evaluation of early blight control with fungicides, 1988. Fungicide and Nematicide Tests 44:122.
49. Van der Plank, J.E. 1968. Disease Resistance in Plants. Academic Press, New York, 206 pp.
50. Wallin, J.R. 1962. Summary of recent progress in predicting late blight epidemics in the United States and Canada. Am. Potato J. 39:306-312.
51. Wilks, D.S., and Shen, K.W. 1991. Threshold relative humidity duration forecasts for plant disease prediction. J. Appl. Meteorol. 30:463-477.
52. Zitter, T.A., and Wolfe, D.W., 1989. Effects of nitrogen rates, foliar urea, fungicide application and varietal susceptibility on early blight and tomato yields. 1988. Biological and Cultural Tests 4:30.
53. Zitter, T.A., and Wolfe, D.W. 1990. Effects of nitrogen rates, foliar urea, fungicide application and varietal susceptibility on early blight and tomato yield, 1989. Biological and Cultural Tests 5:38.

POTATO EARLY DYING:
CAUSES AND MANAGEMENT TACTICS
IN THE EASTERN AND WESTERN
UNITED STATES

Mary L. Powelson
Department of Botany and Plant Pathology
Oregon State University
Corvallis OR 97331-2902

Randall C. Rowe
Department of Plant Pathology
The Ohio State University
Ohio Agricultural Research and Development Center
Wooster OH 44691

Premature vine death and declining yields are a long-standing problem wherever potatoes have been in production for several years. This syndrome, called potato early dying (PED), occurs in both nonirrigated and irrigated production areas of the United States. It is especially important in irrigated areas of the central, southern and western states (23,26,32,34,36). Common synonyms for this disease include early maturity wilt, early die, and Verticillium wilt.

To assess critical needs of the U.S. potato industry, the Potato Association of America conducted a survey of growers and research personnel in 1984. Both groups rated PED as the most important disease affecting commercial potato production (1). In a more recent survey, PED was ranked as the most important disease of both seed or commercial potatoes and as the second most important field production constraint in North America (40).

Symptoms

Symptoms of PED are difficult to distinguish from normal senescence and initially may involve only slower plant growth. Foliar chlorosis and necrosis usually begin at the base of the plant and then extend into the upper foliage, often occurring on one side of the plant or on individual leaves. The affected portion of the plant may eventually die. Vascular browning is often prominent in the bases of affected stems, and necrosis of the vascular ring is seen in tubers of some cultivars. Advanced symptoms usually do not occur until the tuber bulking stage and may consist of decline of isolated plants or, in severe cases, early maturity of an entire crop (7,22,38).

Pathogens and Disease Interactions

The soilborne fungus *Verticillium* is recognized as the primary cause of PED in North America. Two species are involved, *Verticillium dahliae* Kleb and *V. albo-atrum* Reinke and Berthold. In some regions root-lesion nematodes, primarily *Pratylenchus penetrans* (Cobb) Filipjev & Schuur. Stekh., have been shown to interact with *V. dahliae* as a critical component of this disease. Although numerous other biotic and abiotic factors may cause potato plants to die prematurely, only *Verticillium* alone or in combination with *Pratylenchus* can cause premature death associated with the symptoms described above. Thus, this paper will focus on the soilborne fungus, *Verticillium* and the root-lesion nematode, *Pratylenchus*.

PED is a monocyclic disease, i.e., there is only one cycle of infection, pathogen growth, and reproduction each season. The two species of *Verticillium* differ in the survival structures they form within infected tissues of dying vines: *V. dahliae* forms true microsclerotia whereas *V. albo-atrum* forms melanized hyphae. Once established in a field, *both* fungi can survive in soil for several years in a dormant state (32). Dormant microsclerotia or melanized hyphae germinate in proximity to growing roots of susceptible host plants and penetrate the outer root cells. Infection soon proceeds to the vascular system where the fungus establishes itself in the xylem. Conidia are formed within xylem vessels, transported with the transpiration stream, and then germinate at remote locations. Systemic colonization of the entire plant results, and symptoms develop. As the plant dies, the fungus colonizes all the tissues saprophytically and forms either microsclerotia or melanized hyphae, which are released into the soil as the tissues decay.

Verticillium dahliae is the more widespread of the two species and predominates in the north central states and the Pacific Northwest where average summer temperatures frequently exceed 25 C. Both *V. albo-atrum* and *V. dahliae* are involved in PED in more northern production areas, such as Maine and the Red River Valley, and in the winter production areas of Florida, where average temperatures are cooler during the growing season.

These species of *Verticillium* have an extensive host range which includes trees, ground covers, shrubs, vines, vegetable and field crops, herbaceous ornamentals and many weeds (Table 1) (22,27). Plants regarded as resistant or immune include ferns, gymnosperms, many monocots (including grasses, lilies, irises, orchids, and palms) and one group of dicots, the cactus family. In addition to susceptible plants on which these fungi can infect and reproduce, they also can maintain themselves at low populations on the roots of many symptomless crop and weed species (22).

TABLE 1. Some common hosts of *Verticillium dahliae* and/or *albo-atrum*.

Agronomic Crops	Fruits and Vegetables	Shade Trees	Weeds
alfalfa	eggplant	ash	lambsquarter
clover	grape	catalpa	nightshade
hops	olive	magnolia	pigweed
mint	pepper	maple	sagebrush
peanut	potato	redbud	shepherd's purse
rape	raspberry	tulip poplar	velvet leaf
sunflower	tomato		
tobacco	watermelon		

Root-lesion nematodes are migratory endoparasites, i.e., they enter root tissues, but move freely between roots and soil. All stages persist in soil in the absence of host plants, but fourth-stage juveniles and adults are the primary overwintering forms. Nematodes hatch as second-stage juveniles and molt three times before becoming adults and reproducing. Juvenile and adult nematodes feed on root surfaces and burrow into the root cortex. When plant cells die in response to feeding, root-lesion nematodes move in search of new feeding sites.

Although many species of *Pratylenchus* have been described, only four are commonly found on potato in North America (Table 2) (2,20,42). These nematodes have wide host ranges, including vegetable, forage and fruit crops, and many weed species. Some hosts favor large increases in nematode populations, while others support only limited reproduction.

TABLE 2. Root-lesion nematodes commonly found on potato in North America.

Species	Other Important Host Crops	U.S. Distribution
Pratylenchus crenatus	wheat	northern
Pratylenchus neglectus	alfalfa	widespread
Pratylenchus penetrans	alfalfa, wheat	widespread
Pratylenchus scribneri	corn, soybeans	widespread

Although different species of *Pratylenchus* (especially *P. penetrans*) can affect potato directly in some cases if soil populations are high, their importance in PED is related to their ability to interact with *Verticillium*. Synergistic interactions between wilt fungi and nematodes in several crops have been well documented (24,31). Detailed field microplot studies on PED conducted in Ohio (26,33,38), and Wisconsin (21,23) have conclusively demonstrated the involvement of root-lesion nematodes in PED. Data from Ohio studies over the past 10 yr have followed consistent patterns in which *V. dahliae* and *P. penetrans* interact synergistically. Together they cause severe symptom development and significant yield losses at population densities that have little or no effect with each pathogen individually.

The mechanism of the *Pratylenchus-Verticillium* interaction in PED is unknown. A general assumption has been that root wounding as a result of nematode feeding provides entry into the root for fungal pathogens, thus bypassing host defenses to disease (24,31). This assumption initially seemed reasonable, especially with nematodes such as *Pratylenchus* that physically injure roots while feeding, penetrating, and moving through root tissues. However, the fact that the interaction occurs with some species of *Pratylenchus* and not others, despite the fact they all feed and reproduce on potato roots, casts doubt on the root-wounding theory. It is probable that interactions between these two pathogens are more complex and involve modification of host plant physiology. Split-root studies have demonstrated the interaction in mint (13) and potato (Rowe, unpublished data) even when fungal and nematode pathogens were physically separated on halves of the same root system. Current histological studies using an immunostaining technique indicate that infection of potato by *V. dahliae* occurs primarily through root tips and is not spatially associated with root wounds caused by nematode feeding (Bowers and Rowe, unpublished data).

Overall evidence from several pathosystems indicates that fungal-nematode interactions are most likely biological or physiological rather than physical in nature. One theory is that various *Pratylenchus* species in their feeding elicit different physiological changes in the potato plant, some of which then favor infection and/or colonization by *V. dahliae*.

Environmental Influences

Severity of PED and associated yield loss varies greatly from field to field and year to year. Although differences in soil texture do not account for this variability (16), seasonal environmental differences do play a key role. Temperature appears to be the most significant factor because it relates to the geographical distribution of the pathogens, disease development, severity, and effects on yield.

Potatoes grow optimally within a temperature range of 18-20°C. The optimum range for growth of *V. dahliae*, however, is 21-27°C (22). Reflecting these temperature optima, disease severity in potatoes infected with this pathogen tend to increase as the mean air temperature increases from 20 to 28°C (30). In this study (30), symptom development in potatoes infected with *V. dahliae* was arrested by reducing the temperature from 20 to 13°C. In the field, interactions between temperature, symptom development and yield have been demonstrated by comparing seasons or locations. In a season where the average July-August temperature was 24° C, a multilocation study in Ohio (38) demonstrated yield reductions ranging from 24 to 37% in potatoes grown in fumigated microplots infested with *V. dahliae*. This same treatment, however, had little effect on tuber yield in a season when the average July-August temperature was 20°C. Using correlation analysis on 8 years' data from Ohio microplot studies, Francl and co-workers (15) showed that periods of high temperature (average > 24° C) during early emergence and early tuber bulking were correlated with lower yields from infected plants as compared with noninfected controls. In two warm production areas of Colorado, a negative relationship was observed between yield and population densities of *V. dahliae* in soil, but a similar relationship could not be demonstrated in a cool growing region, though the crops were infected (30).

Influence of soil moisture on development of *Verticillium* diseases on potato is less clear than that of temperature. Some studies have shown that the disease is enhanced by drought, while others indicate it is more severe in wet soils. McLean (28) reported that Verticillium wilt in Idaho occurred earlier and symptoms were more severe in moderately resistant potatoes during a growing season with wet soil conditions than in a dry season. Davis et al (12) showed disease incidence was greater when wilting-point stress on the crop was delayed until mid-August than when moisture stress was applied in late June. In field microplot studies in Oregon, severity of PED increased with an increase in soil moisture content under both a long-season and short-season environment (4). In a later field microplot study, irrigation treatments were applied either early or mid-season to determine effect of soil moisture status on severity of PED. Disease severity was greater in plots with excessive compared to moderate or deficit early season moisture treatments. Mid-season soil moisture status had no effect on symptom expression (5).

Management Strategies

Severity of PED that develops in a given crop is a function of the populations of *V. dahliae* and associated pathogens such as *P. penetrans* in the soil at planting, susceptibility of the host plant, and favorability of the environment. Management tactics for this disease thus are aimed at reducing the populations of these pathogens in soil, altering the efficacy of these inocula, or changing the susceptibility of the host.

Because no single practice will provide complete control, effective management strategies for PED must emphasize integrated crop management systems in which decisions are implemented throughout multiple-year, rotational cropping programs. Most management decisions must be made before potatoes are planted. Potential components of integrated systems include cultural methods (crop rotation, green manures, fertility, irrigation, vine removal), host resistance, pesticides (primarily fumigation), and biological controls. Appropriate strategies will vary from region to region and will be dictated by climate, soil characteristics, availability of irrigation, market requirements of cultivars grown, and overall economics of production.

Soil fumigation. Soil fumigation has been used effectively for many years to control Verticillium wilt in several crops including potato, strawberry, tomato, eggplant, melon, and mint. The soil fumigant, chloropicrin and the water-soluble fungicide, metham-sodium are effective in controlling PED (8,11,36). To a limited degree, nonfumigant nematicides such as aldicarb and ethoprop also have been shown to suppress PED (37,39), although these products have no direct effect on *Verticillium*.

Soil fumigation is accomplished in two ways. Some fumigant materials are injected into the soil using a shank injection applicator, plow-sole applicator, or blade applicator. On coarse-textured soils where water infiltration rates are high, metham-sodium products are applied in water directly through sprinkler irrigation systems. Due to effectiveness and ease of application, this technique became a very common practice during the last decade for the suppression of PED in the Pacific Northwest and several production areas of Wisconsin and Michigan.

If done correctly, soil fumigation is highly effective in suppressing populations of nematodes and soilborne fungal pathogens, controlling weeds and soilborne insects and, thereby, improving market quality of harvested tubers. These biocidal effects may carry over into other crops and thus provide benefits for several seasons. In spite of these advantages, soil fumigation is becoming an increasingly unacceptable option due to financial, applicator and food safety, and environmental concerns. Specific problems include potential contamination of ground water, drift of sprinkler-applied products, non-target effects such as destruction of beneficial soil microorganisms, and incompatibility with some cultural and biocontrol practices. In addition, many fumigants are being removed from the market by governmental regulations. Use of fumigants as part of future management programs for PED is questionable, and more emphasis must be placed on host resistance and cultural manipulations.

Crop rotation. Crop rotation is practiced in most potato production areas for improvement in soil structure and fertility and for disease and pest management. Several crops that are grown in rotation with potatoes do not serve as hosts of *Verticillium*, including cereals, corn, grasses, onion, carrot, bean, pea, and asparagus. Although watermelon and mint, which are highly susceptible, are grown in potato production areas, they are seldom if ever grown in rotation with potatoes. Unfortunately, root-lesion nematodes also have a wide but different host range among potential rotational crops. Alfalfa, corn, soybeans, and wheat will host large populations of certain species of *Pratylenchus* (Table 2).

The effectiveness of short-term (2-4 yr) rotations in potato production as a strategy for managing PED is limited by the fact that microsclerotia of *V. dahliae* can survive in soil for as long as 8 yr in the absence of susceptible hosts (22). The population of microsclerotia in soil may decline each year due to microbial activity, but whenever a susceptible crop is produced, additional microsclerotia are formed on dying plant tissues at the end of the season. A 4-yr study in Ohio of 15 fields in an alternate-year, wheat-potato rotation showed a general pattern of a 30-60% increase in soil populations of *V. dahliae* the year following cropping to potato (when wheat was grown). A similar decline was noted the following year when potatoes were planted (18).

There is considerable disagreement concerning the value of crop rotation as a management tool for *Verticillium*. The inconsistent effect of rotation may be due to the fact that soil populations of *V. dahliae* vary widely among production areas. Although rotation away from a susceptible crop will lead to reduced populations of viable microsclerotia, short-term rotations in areas with high populations may not reduce populations of the fungus sufficiently to drop them below thresholds necessary to prevent crop loss.

In addition to rotational crops, green-manure crops grown just prior to potatoes may play a useful role in PED management programs. Studies in Idaho (10) have shown disease suppression following green-manure treatments which included rye, oats, corn, sudangrass, rape, and peas.

Irrigation. Where potatoes are grown under irrigation, the amount and timing of water application can be managed to suppress the severity of PED. Although available soil water must be kept at 80-90% following tuber initiation to optimize growth and prevent tuber disorders, there is some flexibility for water management during early vegetative growth of a potato crop. In field studies conducted in Oregon and Wisconsin with the moderately resistant cultivar Russet Burbank, disease severity was two to four-fold less with irrigation treatments that supplied 75 or 100% compared to 125% of estimated consumptive use by the plant from planting to tuber initiation. In Oregon, tuber yield of the 125% estimated consumptive use treatment was 19% less compared to the 100% treatment. In Wisconsin, the 100% estimated consumptive use treatment had slightly less yield (8%) compared to the 125% treatment (6). Soil moisture prior to tuber initiation does affect disease onset, and irrigation management may be effective as a component of an integrated disease management program.

Biological control. Little is known about biological control of PED or any disease caused by *Verticillium*. In reality, the effectiveness of most cultural practices is probably rooted in some effects on the community of soil microorganisms, the host, and interactions between the two. Microbial antagonists of *Verticillium* have been tested for potential use as biocontrol agents with varying success (17, 25). To date, effectiveness of these as soil or at-planting amendments for control of PED has not been encouraging (41), but future research may lead to useful products.

Host resistance. Planting resistant cultivars will ultimately be the most practical method for management of PED. Although a few of the most widely grown potato cultivars have some resistance to *Verticillium* (Atlantic, Monona, Norchip, Russet Burbank), most are susceptible (Table 3). Efforts are now underway in several USDA and state breeding programs to develop commercial potato cultivars with resistance to *Verticillium*. Although market acceptance of those currently available cultivars has not yet been widespread, horticultural characteristics of resistant cultivar releases are continuing to improve.

In developing PED-resistant potato cultivars, a logical question is whether resistance to *Pratylenchus* is needed as well as resistance to *Verticillium*. Microplot studies in Ohio have shown that the host-resistance response to *Verticillium* may be altered in the presence of *Pratylenchus penetrans*, although this varies from year to year (35, Wheeler and Rowe, unpublished data). When conducting breeding programs for PED resistance, it seems prudent to screen against both pathogens together when evaluating germplasm. Several isolates of both organisms should be used to ensure selection of germplasm that will remain resistant in many areas.

Development of IPM Systems for Potato Early Dying

Improved control of PED will require the use of a totally integrated management program, most elements of which must be implemented before the crop is planted. Development and use of high-quality cultivars with resistance to both PED pathogens will be the foundation of this program. Multiyear rotational cropping schemes and/or the use of appropriate cover/green-manure crops will play a significant role in limiting populations of *Verticillium* and *Pratylenchus* in soil, and possibly manipulating *Pratylenchus* species. Use of fumigants and pesticides may continue to play a role in some situations. Increasing public concern about these methods may limit their future use, however, as would the development of microbial biocontrol agents that might be developed to replace them.

Cultural management will be an important IPM component. Planting and harvest dates can be timed to minimize losses in some situations, especially with early-market cultivars. Careful irrigation and fertility management also will be significant. Vine removal or burning may be appropriate to minimize incorporation of new *Verticillium* inoculum into soil, although this is likely to be limited by legal and practical considerations.

Timely implementation of management practices for PED requires that some estimate of potential disease losses be available before the crop is planted. Traditionally this has been done by considering the disease and crop history of a given planting site and then basing control measures on past experience. To allow growers to approach management options from

TABLE 3. Susceptibility of some potato cultivars to *Verticillium**.

Susceptible	Moderately Resistant or Moderately Susceptible	Resistant
BelRus	Allegany	Abnaki
Butte	Atlantic	Century Russet
Hilite Russet	Centennial Russet	Desiree
Irish Cobbler	Frontier Russet	Elba
Kanona	Hampton	Gemchip
Kennebec	Katahdin	Ranger Russet
Lemhi Russet	Monona	Reddale
Norgold Russet	Norchip	Rideau
Onaway	Russet Burbank	Russette
Russet Norkotah	Russet Nugget	Targhee
Sangre		
Shepody		
Superior		
Viking		
White Rose		

*Responses of potato cultivars to *Verticillium* are related to maturity type and vary somewhat both regionally and seasonally. Placement of cultivars in the above categories is based on several published sources as well as opinions of several authorities.

a more informed basis, various yield-loss risk-assessment systems have been developed to serve as decision aids. These are based on the fact that incidence and severity of PED is related to preplant population densities of *Verticillium* and *Pratylenchus* (14,29,30) and to various environmental factors (9,14,16,19).

Several action thresholds have been developed that would alert growers to implement control measures if analysis of soil samples indicate pathogen populations are above these amounts (14,29,30,43). Although there is some variability in published values, they fall in the range of 5-30 cfu/cm^3 air-dried soil for *V. dahliae* alone. In the presence of sufficient populations of *P. penetrans* to cause an interaction (10-20 vermiforms/100 cm^3 soil), the threshold for *V. dahliae* drops to 2-13 cfu/cm^3. Various yield-loss risk-assessment models also have been developed that quantitatively relate preplant populations of one or both pathogens directly to projected yield losses or yield-loss categories (14,43).

A problem with using either action thresholds or risk-assessment models is that they rely on accurate estimates of the pre-plant populations of both pathogens. These estimates can be compromised by sampling errors during collection of soil samples and by the assay method used to evaluate population densities. Spatial patterns of both organisms in soil are typically clustered or aggregated (3) and considerable work is still needed to ascertain sample numbers, collection technique, and timing necessary to develop reliable population estimates. Current indirect assay techniques for *Verticillium* rely on propagules of the fungus growing on plates of a selective medium. Accuracy of these techniques depends on the method of placing the soil on the plates (wet sieving, dilution plating, Anderson sampler) and on potential microbial interactions on the agar surface. Development of quantitative direct assays for *Verticillium* in soil based on serological tests or use of DNA probes may, in the future, improve population estimates.

PED is a complex disease that is managed now by fumigation, planting of cultivars with moderate resistance, and managing fertility and irrigation. Our understanding of PED is steadily improving and with continued research directed towards the above goals, implementation of viable IPM systems using improved management techniques should become a reality.

Literature Cited

1. Anon. 1987. National Potato Research Proposal. The National Potato Council, Englewood, CO. 24 pp.
2. Brown, M.J., Riedel, R.M., and Rowe, R.C. 1980. Species of *Pratylenchus* associated with *Solanum tuberosum* cv Superior in Ohio. J. Nematol. 12: 189-192.

3. Campbell, L., and Noe, J. 1985. The spatial analysis of soilborne pathogens and root diseases. Ann. Rev. Phytopathol. 23:129-148.

4. Cappaert, M.R., Powelson, M.L., Christensen, N.W., and Crowe, F.J. 1992. Influence of irrigation on severity of potato early dying and associated yield loss. Phytopathology 82:1448-1453.

5. Cappaert, M.R., Powelson, M.L., and Christensen, N.W. 1992. Effect of soil moisture status on symptom expression of potato early dying. (Abstr.) Phytopathology 82:1138.

6. Cappaert, M.R., Powelson, M.L. Christensen, N.W., Stevenson, W.R., and Rouse, D.I. 1992. Irrigation management of potato early dying. (Abstr.) Phytopathology 82:1075.

7. Davis, J.R. 1981. Verticillium wilt of potato in southeastern Idaho. University of Idaho Curr. Inf. Ser. No. 564.

8. Davis, J.R. 1985. Approaches to control of potato early dying caused by *Verticillium dahliae*. Am. Potato J. 62:177-185.

9. Davis, J.R., and Everson, D.O. 1986. Relation of *Verticillium dahliae* in soil and potato tissue, irrigation method, and N-fertility to Verticillium wilt of potato. Phytopathology 76:730-736.

10. Davis, J.R., Huisman, O.C., Sorensen, L.H., and Schneider, A.T. 1991. *Verticillium* and *Rhizoctonia* control with cover crops. (Abstr.) Am. Potato J. 68:604

11. Davis, J.R., and Sorensen, L.H. 1986. Controlling soilborne pathogens: Effects of vapam and other options for the present and future. Proceedings of University of Idaho Winter Commodity Schools 12:121-126.

12. Davis, J.R., Sorensen, L.H., Stark, J.C., and Westermann, D.T. 1990. Fertility and management practices to control Verticillium wilt of the Russet Burbank potato. Am. Potato J. 67:55-65.

13. Faulkner, L.R., Bolander, W.J., and Skotland, C.B. 1970. Interaction of *Verticillium dahliae* and *Pratylenchus minyus* in Verticillium wilt of peppermint: Influence of the nematode as determined by a double root technique. Phytopathology 60:100-103.

14. Francl, L.J., Madden, L.V., Rowe, R.C., and Riedel, R.M. 1987. Potato yield loss prediction and discrimination using preplant population densities of *Verticillium dahliae* and *Pratylenchus penetrans*. Phytopathology 77:579-584.

15. Francl, L.J., Madden, L.V., Rowe, R.C., and Riedel, R.M. 1990. Correlation of growing season environmental variables and the effect of early dying on potato yield. Phytopathology 80:425-432.

16. Francl, L.J., Rowe, R.C., Riedel, R.M., and Madden, L.V. 1988. Effects of three soil types on potato early dying disease and associated yield reduction. Phytopathology 78:159-166.

17. Fravel, D.R., Davis, J.R., and Sorensen, L.H. 1986. Effect of *Talaromyces flavus* and metham sodium on Verticillium wilt incidence and potato yield, 1984-1985. Biol. Cult. Tests 1:17.

18. Joaquim, T.R., Smith, V.L., and Rowe, R.C. 1988. Seasonal variation and effects of wheat rotation on populations of *Verticillium dahliae* Kleb. in Ohio potato field soils. Am. Potato J. 65:439-447.

19. Johnson, K.B., Radcliffe, E.B., and Teng, P.S. 1986. Effect of interacting populations of *Alternaria solani, Verticillium dahliae*, and potato leafhopper *(Empoasca fabae)* on potato yield. Phytopathology 76:1046-1052.

20. Kimpinski, J. 1979. Root lesion nematodes in potatoes. Am. Potato J. 56:79-86.

21. Kotcon, J.B., Rouse, D.I., and Mitchell, J.E. 1985. Interactions of *Verticillium dahliae, Colletotrichum coccodes, Rhizoctonia solani,* and *Pratylenchus penetrans* in the early dying syndrome of Russet Burbank potatoes. Phytopathology 75:68-74.

22. Mace, M.E., Bell, A.A., and Beckman, C.H. 1981. Fungal Wilt Diseases of Plants. Academic Press, New York. 640 pp.

23. MacGuidwin, A.E., and Rouse, D.I. 1990. Role of *Pratylenchus penetrans* in the potato early dying disease of Russet Burbank potato. Phytopathology 80:1077-1082.

24. Mai, W.F., and Abawi, G.S. 1987. Interactions among root-knot nematodes and Fusarium wilt fungi on host plants. Ann. Rev. Phytopathol. 25:317-338.

25. Marois, J.J., Johnston, S.A., Dunn, M.T., and Papavizas, G.C. 1982. Biological control of Verticillium wilt of eggplant in the field. Plant Dis. 66:1166-1168.

26. Martin, M.J., Riedel, R.M., and Rowe, R.C. 1982. *Verticillium dahliae* and *Pratylenchus penetrans:* Interactions in the early dying complex of potato in Ohio. Phytopathology 72:640-644.

27. McCain, A.H., Rabbi, R.D., and Wilhelm, S. 1981. Plants resistant or susceptible to Verticillium wilt. University of California Leaflet 2703.

28. McLean, J.G. 1955. Selecting and breeding potatoes for field resistance to Verticillium wilt in Idaho. Idaho Agric. Exp. Stn. Bull No. 30. pp. 36-51.

29. Nicot, P.C., and Rouse, D.I. 1987. Relationship between soil inoculum density of *Verticillium dahliae* and systemic colonization of potato stems in commercial fields over time. Phytopathology 77:1346-1355.

30. Nnodu, E.C., and Harrison, M.D. 1979. The relationship between *Verticillium albo-atrum* inoculum density and potato yield. Am. Potato J. 56:11-25.

31. Powell, N.T. 1971. Interactions between nematodes and fungi in disease complexes. Ann. Rev. Phytopathol. 9:253-274.

32. Powelson, M.L. 1979. Verticillium wilt of potatoes in irrigated sands: The Oregon experience. Ore. Agric. Exp. Stn. Tech. Bull, 5106. 6 pp.

33. Riedel, R.M., Rowe, R.C., and Martin, M.J. 1985. Differential interactions of *Pratylenchus crenatus, P. penetrans,* and *P. scribneri* with *Verticillium dahliae* in potato early dying disease. Phytopathology 75:419-422.

34. Rowe, R.C. 1985. Potato early dying - A serious threat to the potato industry. Am. Potato J. 62:157-161.

35. Rowe, R.C. 1989. Alteration in potato cultivar response to *Verticillium dahliae* by co-inoculation with *Pratylenchus penetrans.* (Abstr.) Am. Potato J. 66:542.

36. Rowe, R.C., Davis, J.R., Powelson, M.L., and Rouse, D.I. 1987. Potato early dying: Causal agents and management strategies. Plant Dis. 71:482-489.

37. Rowe, R.C., and Riedel, R.M. 1976. Association of *Pratylenchus penetrans* with the "early dying" disease complex of potatoes. Fungic. Nematic. Tests 31:218.

38. Rowe, R.C., Riedel, R.M., and Martin, M.J. 1985. Synergistic interactions between *Verticillium dahliae* and *Pratylenchus penetrans* in potato early dying disease. Phytopathology 75:412-418.

39. Schultz, O.E., and Cetas, R.C. 1977. Evaluation of granular nematicides for control of "early maturity wilt" of potatoes in New York State. Proc. 1977 Br. Crop Prot. Conf. Pests Dis. 2:491-498.

40. Slack, S.A. 1991. A look at potato leafroll virus and potato virus Y: Past present and future. The Badger Common Tater 43:16-21.

41. Spink, D.S., and Rowe, R.C. 1989. Evaluation of *Talaromyces flavus* as a biological control agent against *Verticillium dahliae*. Plant Dis. 73:230-236.
42. Townshend, J.L., Potter, J.W., and Willis, C.B. 1978. Ranges of distribution of species of Pratylenchus in northeastern North America. Can. Plant Dis. Surv. 58:80-82.
43. Wheeler, T.A., Madden, L.V., Rowe, R.C., and Riedel, R.M. 1992. Modeling of yield loss in potato early dying caused by *Pratylenchus penetrans* and *Verticillium dahliae*. J. Nematol. 24:99-102.

PART V

Advances in Potato Pest Biology and Management: Nematodes

BIOLOGY AND MANAGEMENT OF ROOT-KNOT NEMATODES ON POTATO IN THE PACIFIC NORTHWEST

G. S. Santo
Department of Plant Pathology
Irrigated Agriculture Research & Extension Center
Washington State University
Prosser, WA 99350

The Columbia *(Meloidogyne chitwoodi* Golden, et al., 1980) and northern *(M. hapla* Chitwood 1949) root-knot nematodes are serious pests to potato production. *M. chitwoodi* and *M. hapla* blemish tubers and render them unmarketable (22). Root-knot nematode infection seriously affects the cooking quality of processed potato products, such as French fries and potato chips. A potato crop with 10% or more of the tubers infected with nematodes may be rejected or downgraded by the processor. Also, tubers exhibiting internal and/or external symptoms are unacceptable for fresh market. Of the potato acreage grown in Washington, 70-80% receive nematicide treatments to control these nematodes at an estimated annual cost of $20 million. The loss without chemical treatments may be as high as $40 million. Despite these costly chemical control practices, root-knot nematodes remain a serious problem, and appear to have increased over the past several years. This is due, in part, to inadequate fumigation practices, and the build-up of nematode population densities resulting from mild winters, unusually warm growing seasons, and poor cropping sequences.

Geographical Distribution

Root-knot nematodes were first observed in the Columbia Basin near Quincy, WA in 1960. *M. chitwoodi* was first recognized as a new species in 1978 (23). These nematodes have been found widely distributed throughout the western United States (6,13,14). The principle means of spread appears to be through recycling of irrigation water and infected seed potato tubers (3,13). *M. chitwoodi* also has been reported in the United States from Virginia (1), and from Argentina, Holland and Mexico (2). Two races of *M. chitwoodi* were discovered in 1984 (25), and both races are widely distributed in the major potato growing regions of the Pacific Northwest (17).

Symptoms and Damage

External symptom produced by *M. chitwoodi* on Russet Burbank potato is quite distinct compared to *M. hapla*. *M. chitwoodi* like other *Meloidogyne* species produces distinct pimple-like bumps (galls) on the surface of the tuber (28), whereas *M. hapla* usually produces more of a general swelling. It is difficult to differentiate between a tuber infected with *M. hapla* and a healthy tuber by external symptoms alone. However, internal symptoms produced by *M. chitwoodi* and *M. hapla* are similar. Both species produce typical brown spots within 6 mm of the tuber surface (28). Within each brown spot, a female nematode may be observed. She is capable of producing 200-1,000 eggs that are deposited in a gelatinous egg sac at the posterior end of her body. Brown spots become evident only when the females begin egg production. Symptoms produced on potato roots are also distinct between the two species. *M. hapla* causes small galls and lateral root proliferation, whereas *M. chitwoodi* does not (28). Root-knot nematode infection rarely causes above ground symptoms in potatoes.

Importance of *M. chitwoodi* and *M. hapla*

Before the discovery of *M. chitwoodi*, *M. hapla* was considered the most important nematode problem on potato. Subsequent research has shown that most of the damage of potato tubers attributed to *M. hapla* was caused by *M. chitwoodi*. *M. chitwoodi* is of greater importance on potato than *M. hapla*, causing more severe tuber damage. Damage threshold studies show that less than one *M. chitwoodi* per 250 cm^3 of soil can cause economic damage (24). The principal reason is the ability of *M. chitwoodi* to reproduce at lower soil temperatures than required by *M. hapla* (22). This is significant because potatoes in the northwestern United States are planted in the spring when soil temperatures range between 4.4 and 12.8 C at the 15 cm depth. Therefore, *M. chitwoodi* is able to penetrate and reproduce on potato roots earlier in the season than *M. hapla*. Consequently, *M. chitwoodi* will have more generations during the growing season than *M. hapla* which results in earlier tuber infection and more severe damage.

The number of generations is dependent upon the number of degree days (heat units) accumulated during the growing season. Both *M. chitwoodi* and *M. hapla* require about 1000-1100 degree days from the time of planting to complete the first generation and 500-600 degree days for the subsequent generations (18). However, the minimum or base temperature for activity differs significantly between the two species: 5°C for *M. chitwoodi* and 10 C for *M. hapla* (7). Thus, depending on the soil temperature during the growing season and the length of the growing season

M. chitwoodi may complete 3-5 generations and *M. hapla* 1-3 generations. An extra generation, especially late in the season, will result in a tremendous increase in nematode population densities. The first generation is completed in the roots and the subsequent generations in roots or within tubers.

Host Range

Both *M. chitwoodi* and *M. hapla* have very wide host ranges (4,12,14). The principal difference between these species is that many gramineae are hosts for both races of *M. chitwoodi* but are not hosts for *M. hapla*. The differences between the two races of *M. chitwoodi* lay in their differential reproduction on alfalfa (*Medicago sativa* 'Thor') and carrot (*Daucus carota* 'Red Cored Chantenay'). Race 1 reproduces on carrot but poorly or not at all on alfalfa, whereas alfalfa is a suitable host and carrot a nonhost to race 2 (12).

Vertical Migration

More than 80% of the root-knot nematode population occurs in the upper 60 cm of soil where feeder roots are abundant. However, populations of *M. chitwoodi* have been observed as deep as 180 cm (26). Deep nematode populations are usually associated with deep rooted crops such as alfalfa. Root-knot nematodes by themselves do not move downwards long distances (8). Vertical migration studies using soil columns under laboratory conditions have shown that *M. chitwoodi* is able to migrate upwards faster and farther than *M. hapla* (16). In columns buried in the field, *M. chitwoodi* was able to migrate upwards from depths of 60, 120 and 180 cm to infect tomato roots (8). In 1988 and 1989 the importance of deep-placed *M. chitwoodi* populations in causing potato tuber damage was investigated under field conditions at Prosser, WA and Hermiston, OR (8). At Prosser, *M. chitwoodi* placed at 0, 30 and 60 cm deep was able to migrate upwards during the season and cause significant tuber damage. Nematodes at 90 and 120 cm were not able to infect tubers. At the Hermiston site, *M. chitwoodi* from all depths was able to infect tubers. Thus, it appears that the ability of *M. chitwoodi* to migrate and cause tuber damage is influenced by soil texture. The Prosser soil contained a much higher silt content (44-55%) than the Hermiston soil (16-17%). This effect of soil type on migration was confirmed in the laboratory using soil columns (8). The sandier Hermiston soil used in these studies is more typical of soil in which potatoes are grown in Washington and Oregon. Thus, if *M. chitwoodi* is not adequately controlled to at least the 90 cm depth significant tuber damage could occur. Once the nematodes have infected roots, the degree of tuber damage will be influenced by the accumulation of degree days during the growing season and the length of the growing season. Increase in degree days and longer the tubers remain in the ground will result in more nematode generations, and increased tuber infection.

Management Strategies

There are several strategies that may be used to manage root-knot nematode population densities before planting potatoes. Management strategies may include prevention of spread, crop rotation, early harvest, green manure cover crops, and nematicides. The best means to suppress nematode populations would be to employ a combination of these management practices.

Prevention of spread. Nematodes under their own power move very short distances. Spread of nematodes from infested to noninfested areas is by means of soil carried on sampling tools, boots, hoofs of animals, and farm equipment, infected plant material, and in reused irrigation water. Boots, tools and equipment should be cleaned between nematode infested and noninfested fields to prevent the movement of contaminated soil. When irrigating with reused irrigation water, the use of settling ponds will minimize the spread of nematodes. Nematodes in the settling ponds will settle to the bottom and eventually die.

A common means of spreading root-knot nematodes is by infected seed potato tubers. *M. chitwoodi* and/or *M. hapla* have been reported from most of the seed potato growing areas in the western United States and Canada. However, it is very difficult to detect root-knot nematode infection in seed potato tubers. Seed potatoes are usually not as severely damaged by root-knot nematodes as are potatoes grown for processing and fresh market. The environmental conditions in seed production areas are generally not optimal for root-knot nematode development. These areas usually have cooler soil temperatures, finer textured soils, and a shorter growing season resulting in 1-2 generations compared to two or more in commercial production areas. Consequently, symptoms and damage by root-knot nematodes on seed potato are not evident. Although external symptoms of *M. chitwoodi* may be evident, it is often very difficult to detect any internal tuber damage because the females are immature and brown spots have not yet developed. Probably the best means to determine if a seedlot is infested with root-knot nematodes is to obtain soil samples from the field in question or to sample the tare soil.

Crop rotation. Crops most commonly grown in rotation with potato in the Pacific Northwest are alfalfa (*Medicago sativa*), corn (*Zea* *mays)* and wheat *(Triticum aestivum)*. Corn and wheat are hosts for *M. chitwoodi*, but not for *M. hapla* (4,14). Thus, corn and wheat (and other cereals) would be excellent crops to rotate with potato to suppress *M. hapla* populations. Although both field corn and wheat are suitable hosts for *M. chitwoodi*, field corn is a longer season crop than wheat and *M. chitwoodi* is able to complete more generations on field corn than wheat. Thus, wheat would be a better rotational crop than field corn to minimize *M. chitwoodi* populations. Sweet corn is preferred as a rotational crop to field corn because it is a less suitable host to *M. chitwoodi*. Several super sweet corn cultivars have been demonstrated to be resistant to both races of *M. chitwoodi* (12). Alfalfa is an excellent crop to suppress *M. chitwoodi* race 1 populations (23). However, race 2 of *M. chitwoodi* and *M. hapla* populations will increase to high population densities on alfalfa (9). Studies indicate that alfalfa germplasms Nevada Synthetic XX and W12SR2W1 exhibit a high degree of resistance to *M. chitwoodi* race 2 and *M. hapla* (9). An important factor in a crop rotation program is proper weed control in the rotational crop. Many weeds are suitable hosts for both the nematode species (4,14).

Crops that are not suitable hosts to both *M. chitwoodi* races include asparagus *(Asparagus officinalis)*, cowpea *(Vigna unguiculata)*, fodder radish *(Raphanus sativus)*, lima bean *(Phaseolus limensis)*, Scotch spearmint *(Mentha cardiaca)*, and several cultivars of sudangrass *(Sorghum bicolor* var. *sudanense)*, popcorn *(Zea mays)* and super sweet corn (12,14). Asparagus, lima bean, sudangrass and sweet corn are also unsuitable hosts for *M. hapla* (4). Use of appropriate potato rotational crops to reduce nematode populations will greatly aid in the performance of a nematicide.

Early harvest. Severity of tuber damage to *M. chitwoodi* and *M. hapla* is greatly increased the longer the tubers remain in the ground. Thus, by harvesting tubers as early as possible damage may be lessened. Early maturing potato varieties, which are harvested by early August usually escape damage by root-knot nematodes. Early harvest is especially beneficial for fields infested with *M. hapla*, because severe tuber damage is usually not observed until late September to early October (28). On the other hand, severe tuber infection by *M. chitwoodi* may be evident by mid-August. Even if nematicide treatments were made for *M. chitwoodi*, tubers should be harvested as soon as possible. This is because nematicide treatments do not kill 100% of the nematodes in the soil. Tubers infected with *M. chitwoodi* should be processed immediately and not stored. At storage temperatures of 7.8-8.9°C, *M. chitwoodi* continues to develop and tuber damage becomes more pronounced. *M. hapla* is not known to increase tuber damage at these storage temperatures.

Green manure. Control of root-knot nematodes on potatoes in the northwestern United States is heavily dependent on soil fumigation. How long these nematicides remain available is of major concern to potato growers. Thus, the search for alternative measures to manage root-knot nematodes on potatoes and other vegetable crops has become increasingly important. Rapeseed *(Brassica napus* and *B. campestris)* and sudangrass may provide an alternative method for managing nematodes. Rapeseed and sudangrass contain glucosinolate and cyanogenic glycoside compounds, respectively, which have pesticidal effects when the plants are incorporated into the soil as green manure (5). Following incorporation, enzymic hydrolysis produces isothiocyanate from glucosinolates and hydrogen cyanide from cyanogenic glycosides. These compounds are toxic to certain insects, fungi, nematodes, and weeds (5). Within the potato rotational scheme rapeseed and sudangrass can be planted in early August after harvest of wheat or sweet corn rotation crops and incorporated as green manure either in the fall (rapeseed or sudangrass) or following spring (rapeseed).

Greenhouse and field studies show that rapeseed and sudangrass are toxic to *M. chitwoodi* (10,20). In field plots winter rapeseed cv. Jupiter incorporated in the spring and sudangrass cv. Piper incorporated in the fall reduced potato tuber infection comparable to ethoprop at 13.4 kg a.i./ha with about 20% cullage (20). Studies are in progress to determine the best time to incorporate green manure crops, depth of their incorporation to achieve, and use of green manure crops in rotation with nematode resistant crops and in combination with nematicides to better manage *M. chitwoodi* populations.

Nematicides. The most common method used to control root-knot nematodes on potatoes in the northwestern United States is by soil fumigation with 1,3-dichloropropene (1,3D) or metham sodium (19,21). 1,3D has been more consistent in controlling *M. chitwoodi* than metham sodium (21). Metham sodium is an excellent nematicide; however, in certain soils the desired depth of control is not achieved. Metham sodium is applied in water with sprinklers and is dependent on water for movement into the soil profile.

In fields with high and deep populations of *M. chitwoodi* soil fumigation alone may not be adequate. Laboratory and greenhouse studies have demonstrated the excellent nematicidal properties of ethoprop in controlling *M. chitwoodi* and *M. hapla* (11). Because ethoprop does not move readily with water, its effectiveness in the field is limited to the depth of mechanical incorporation. Ethoprop is most effective when applied as a broadcast and incorporated 10-15 cm by disking or rototilling just before planting (21). Ethoprop is registered for control of *M. hapla* on potatoes, but only for suppression of *M. chitwoodi*. The best treatment for controlling *M. chitwoodi* has been the combination of 1,3D with ethoprop applied as a broadcast-incorporated treatment just before planting (19). Excellent control of *M. chitwoodi* also has been achieved with the combination of lower rates of 1,3D and metham sodium (27). 1,3D is injected 46 cm deep followed by metham sodium in 1.25 cm of water instead of the normal 2.5 cm of water. 1,3D provides control of the deeper placed nematodes, and metham sodium controls nematodes and certain fungal pathogens near the surface.

Epilogue

M. chitwoodi is one of the most important problems to potato production in the Pacific Northwest. *M. chitwoodi* is of greater importance than *M. hapla* because it causes more severe tuber damage. The principal reason is the ability of *M. chitwoodi* to reproduce at lower soil temperatures than required by *M. hapla*. Management strategies most commonly used for control of *M. chitwoodi* includes prevention of spread, crop rotation, early harvest, green manure cover crops, and menaticides. The best means to suppress nematode populations would be to integrate all or a combination of these management practices.

Literature Cited

1.   Eisenback, J.D., Stromberg, E.L., and McCoy, M.S. 1986. First report of Columbia root-knot nematode *(Meloidogyne chitwoodi)* in Virginia. Plant Dis. 70:801.

2.   Esbenshade, P.R., and Triantaphyllou, A.C. 1985. Use of enzyme phenotype for identification of *Meloidogyne* species. J. Nematol. 17:6-20.

3.   Faulkner, L.R., and Bolander, W.J. 1970. Agriculturally polluted irrigation water as a source of plant-parasitic nematode infection. J. Nematol. 2:368-374.

4.   Faulkner, L.R., and McElroy, F.D. 1964. Host range of northern root-knot nematode on irrigated crop plants and weeds in Washington. Plant Dis. Reptr. 48:190-193.

5.   Grainge, M., and Ahmed, S. 1988. Handbook of plants with pest-control properties. John Wiley & Sons, New York, NY. 470 pp.

6.   Griffin, G.D. 1988. The Columbia root-knot nematode, *Meloidogyne chitwoodi* discovered in the state of Utah. Plant Dis. 72:363.

7.   Inserra, R.N., Griffin, G.D., and Sisson, D.V. 1983. Effect of temperature and root leachates on embryonic development and hatching of *Meloidogyne chitwoodi* and *M. hapla*. J. Nematol. 15:123-127.

8.   Mojtahedi, H., Ingham, R.E., Santo, G.S., Pinkerton, J.N., Reed, G.L., and Wilson, J.H. 1991. Seasonal migration of *Meloidogyne chitwoodi* and its role in potato production. J. Nematol. 23:162-169.

9. Mojtahedi, H., Pinkerton, J.N., Santo, G.S., and Peaden, R.N. 1989. Host status of alfalfa cultivars and germ plasms to *Meloidogyne chitwoodi* race 2 and reactions of selected cultivars to *M. chitwoodi* and *M. hapla* infection. Plant Dis. 73:391-394.

10. Mojtahedi, H., Santo, G.S., Hang, A.N., and Wilson, J.H. 1991. Suppression of root-knot nematode populations with selected rapeseed cultivars as green manure. J. Nematol. 23:170-174.

11. Mojtahedi, H., Santo, G.S., Pinkerton, J.N., and Wilson, J.H. 1988. Effect of ethoprop on *Meloidogyne chitwoodi* and *M. hapla*. J. Nematol. 20:649.

12. Mojtahedi, H., Santo, G.S., and Wilson, J.H. 1988. Host test to differentiate *Meloidogyne chitwoodi* race 1 and 2 and *M. hapla*. J. Nematol. 20:468-473.

13. Nyczepir, A.P., O'Bannon, J.H., Santo, G.S., and Finley, A.M. 1982. Incidence and distinguishing characteristics of *Meloidogyne chitwoodi* and *M. hapla* in potato from the northwestern United States. J. Nematol. 14:347-353.

14. O'Bannon, J.H., Santo, G.S., and Nyczepir, A.P. 1982. Host range of the Columbia root-knot nematode *(Meloidogyne chitwoodi)*. Plant Dis. 66:1045-1048.

15. Pinkerton, J.N., and McIntyre, G.A. 1987. The occurrence of *Meloidogyne chitwoodi* in potato fields in Colorado. Plant Dis. 71:192.

16. Pinkerton, J.N., Mojtahedi, H., Santo, G.S., and O'Bannon, J.N. 1987. Vertical migration of *Meloidogyne chitwoodi* and *M. hapla* under controlled temperature. J. Nematol. 19:152-157.

17. Pinkerton, J.N., Santo, G.S., and Mojtahedi, H. 1987. Reproductive efficiency of Pacific Northwest populations of *Meloidogyne chitwoodi* on alfalfa. Plant Dis. 71:345-348.

18. Pinkerton, J.N., Santo, G.S., and Mojtahedi, H. 1991. Population dynamics of *Meloidogyne chitwoodi* on Russet Burbank potatoes, *Solanum tuberosum*, in relation to degree-day accumulation. J. Nematol. 23:283-290.

19. Pinkerton, J.N., Santo, G.S., Ponti, R.P., and Wilson, J.H. 1986. Control of *Meloidogyne chitwoodi* in commercially grown Russet Burbank potatoes. Plant Dis. 70:860-863.

20. Santo, G.S., Mojtahedi, H., Hang, A.N., and Wilson, J.H. 1991. Control of the Columbia root-knot nematode using rapeseed and sudangrass green manure. Pages 41-46 in Proceedings of the 30th annual Washington State Potato Conference, Moses Lake, WA.

21. Santo, G.S., Mojtahedi, H., and Wilson, J.H. 1988. Biology and control of root-knot nematodes on potatoes, 1987. Pages 67-70 in Proceedings of the 27th annual Washington State Potato Conference, Moses Lake, WA.

22. Santo, G.S., and O'Bannon, J.H. 1981. Effect of soil temperature on the pathogenicity and reproduction of *Meloidogyne chitwoodi* and *M. hapla* on Russet Burbank potato. J. Nematol. 13:483-486.

23. Santo, G.S., O'Bannon, J.H., Finley, A.M., and Golden, A.M. 1980. Occurrence and host range of a new root-knot nematode *(Meloidogyne chitwoodi)* in the Pacific Northwest. Plant Dis. 64:951-952.

24. Santo, G.S., O'Bannon, J.H., Nyczepir, A.P., and Ponti, R.P. 1981. Ecology and control of root-knot nematodes on potato. Pages 135-139 in Proceedings of the 20th annual Washington Potato Conference, Moses Lake, WA.

25. Santo, G.S., and Pinkerton, J.N. 1985. A second race of *Meloidogyne chitwoodi* discovered in Washington State. Plant Dis. 69:361.

26. Santo, G.S., Ponti, R.P., and Wilson, J.H. 1985. Control of *Meloidogyne chitwoodi* on potato with DD, 1983. American Phytopathological Society Nematicide and Fungicide Tests 40:106-107.

27. Santo, G.S., Wilson, J.H., and Mojtahedi, H. 1991. Control of *Meloidogyne chitwoodi* on potato with 1,3-dichloropropene and metham sodium alone and in combinations. Am. Potato J. 68:632.

28. Western Regional IPM Project. 1986. Integrated management for potatoes in the Western United States. Univ. Calif. Div. Agr. and Nat. Res., Oakland, CA.

MANAGEMENT OF NEMATODES AND SOIL-BORNE PATHOGENS IN SUBTROPICAL POTATO PRODUCTION

D. P. Weingartner
University of Florida, IFAS
Agricultural Research and Education Center,
P. O. Box 728, Hastings, FL 32145

R. McSorley
University of Florida, IFAS
Department of Entomology and Nematology,
P. O. Box 110630, Gainesville, FL 32611

Potato (*Solanum tuberosum* L.) is an important vegetable crop in Florida. During 1987-1989 an average of 354.8 X 10^3 mt of potatoes valued at 96 million dollars were produced on 15.4 X 10^3 ha in the state. The importance of the potato industry in Florida, however, is determined not so much by the quantity of potatoes produced but by the availability of fresh potatoes when other potato regions are not in production. Although Florida's potato crop during 1987-1989 was only 2.1% of total U.S. potato production during this period, it provided 35.2% of all fresh potatoes sold during the winter-spring production seasons of the three years. As a result, Florida's potato crop usually commands premium prices and is often valued greater than the crop in other states. Average value of Florida potatoes in 1987-1989 was $6158/harvested ha and $274/mt compared, respectively, to U.S. average values of $3866/harvested ha and $119/mt (7,8). The relatively high value of Florida potatoes enables farm managers to utilize disease and pest management strategies which may be cost prohibitive in other potato production systems.

Potatoes are grown in northeast, southeast, and southwest Florida. Nematodes and soilborne pathogens and management of the diseases they cause in the two most important areas (northeast and southeast Florida) are the subjects of this review (Fig. 1).

Florida Agricultural Experiment Station, Journal Series N-00633

Northeast Florida

Production is concentrated in St. Johns, Putnam, and Flagler counties. Soils are sandy flatwoods series and are typically composed of 90-95% sand, <2.5% clay, and <5% silt. Fields are sublayered at a depth of 60 to 120 ± cm with a zone of impervious clay. The clay layer facilitates seepage irrigation which is accomplished through a series of water furrows placed at 18.3 m intervals coupled with ridged rows to grow the crop. The crop is planted from the last week in December until early March and is lifted during mid April to mid June. Approximately 85% of the crop is sold to potato chip processors through preseason contracts. The chipping cultivar Atlantic is planted on 65±% of the hectarage with the remainder planted to Sebago, Superior, LaChipper, and several red-skinned varieties. A summer cover crop is planted after potatoes are harvested. During the past 15 yr the most widely planted cover crop has been a sorghum X sudangrass hybrid (*Sorghum bicolor X S. arundinaceum* var *sudanense*). Most northeast Florida potato fields have been monocultured to a spring potato crop and a summer cover crop for over 85 yr.

Figure 1. Shaded counties indicate locations of the two major potato production areas of Florida.

Southeast Florida

Most of the production in this area occurs in Dade County in Perrine marl soil (Typic Fluvaquent). This soil type is unusual, originates from oolitic limestone, and is characterized by a pH of 7-8 (2). Land is limited, and so the same sites may be used for production each year. Potatoes are planted during November and December and harvested in March and April. Usually a small red cultivar such as LaRouge is grown for the specialty market. Sites are planted to cover crops such as sorghum (*Sorghum bicolor*) or corn (*Zea mays*) during the summer, or they are either fallowed or permitted to grow a cover of weeds.

Nematodes and Soilborne Pathogens

Northeast Florida. A polyspecific community of at least 12 genera of phytoparasitic nematodes exists in northeast Florida potato fields (13-20). The most important of these are *Meloidogyne incognita, Belonolaimus longicaudatus*, and the trichodorids *Paratrichodorus minor, Trichodorus viruliferous*, and *T. proximus*. Heavy losses in tuber yields result from root damage due to *M. incognita* and *B. longicaudatus* whereas trichodorids are mainly important as vectors of tobacco rattle virus, the cause of corky ringspot disease (15, 20). Corky ringspot occurs on ~3200 ha in northeast Florida. The disease causes severe internal tuber necrosis which renders many tubers unmarketable. Bacterial wilt, caused by *Pseudomonas solanacearum*, has existed in northeast potato production since the start of the industry in the early 1900's (14). Severity of bacterial wilt has been reported to be enhanced by *Meloidogyne* spp. (14, 16).

Southeast Florida. Plant-parasitic nematodes commonly found in the marl soils include *M. incognita, Rotylenchulus reniformis, Helicotylenchus dihystera, Criconemella onoensis, Quinisulcius acutus*, and *Tylenchorhynchus martini* (4, 6, 9). *Belonolaimus longicaudatus* and *P. minor*, both serious pests of potatoes in northeast Florida, have not been found in the Perrine marl soils in the southeastern part of the state. The root-knot nematode *M. incognita*, however, is the most damaging nematode in this region. Root-knot galling of tubers is not tolerated by the local market, and results in a substantial down grading in tuber quality and grower profits. The reniform nematode, *R. reniformis*, is a known pathogen of potatoes (10) and can be common locally if favorable weed hosts are grown in production sites (6). No pathogenic effects of *H. dihystera, Q. acutus*, or *T. martini* on potato have been reported.

The ring nematode, *C. onoensis*, can increase to high levels (several hundred to > 1000/100 cm³ of soil) following cover crops of sorghum (5). In greenhouse pathogenicity tests, *C. onoensis* failed to significantly ($P \leq 0.10$) affect plant top weight, root weight, number of tubers, or weight of tubers (5). In a field test with initial densities of approximately 1100 *C. onoensis*/100 cm³ of soil, fumigation with metam-sodium reduced densities to <5% of the initial level, but yields were not increased in fumigated plots (5).

In surveys of the nematode community of marl soils, plant-parasitic species were found to comprise 38.4% of the total nematode community. *C. onoensis* comprised 16.7%, but the serious plant parasites *R. reniformis* and *M. incognita* accounted for only 0.7 and 0.6%, respectively, of total nematode numbers. Bacterial-feeding genera (*Rhabditis, Acrobeloides, Panagrolaimus, Cephalobus, Eucephalobus, Alaimus*) accounted for 38.2% of the soil nematode community, with *Rhabditis* the most abundant nematode genus (29.2% of total nematodes). Fungivores (*Aphelenchoides, Aphelenchus, Psilenchus,* and *Tylenchus*) accounted for 21.4% of the nematode community. Predators and omnivores were rare (4).

Management of Nematode and Soil-borne Pathogens in Northeast Florida

Nematodes. Chemicals have been the mainstay of nematode control in this area. Dramatic increases in tuber yields following soil fumigation in research plots prompted rapid grower acceptance in the late 1960s of preplant soil fumigants such as DD, EDB, and 1,3-D. Later, in the 1970s, the development and high degree of success of certain nonvolatile nematicides, especially aldicarb, resulted in use of these both alone and in combination with soil fumigation by all northeastern Florida commercial potato growers (13, 18-20). For example, in field tests conducted from 1977-1985, average tuber yields following treatment with 1,3-D + aldicarb (26.4 mt/ha) were superior ($P=0.05$) to treatment with either 1,3-D (23.2 mt/ha) or aldicarb (22.7 mt/ha) alone, both of which produced higher yields ($P=0.05$) than the nontreated plots (16.8 mt/ha). Population densities of *B. longicaudatus* typically remained stable or increased during the season in nontreated plots, but decreased following fumigation with 1,3-D or treatment with aldicarb. Lowest nematode densities have resulted after using a combination of 1,3-D plus aldicarb (13, 18-20). In this production system soil fumigants tend to be more effective in relatively dry soil (i.e.,

<10% by weight) and nonvolatile nematicides are better when soil is more moist (i.e., >10% by weight).

Another management option has been the planting of different summer cover crops. Relative to sorghum-sudangrass, a crop of the tropical legume hairy indigo *(Indigofera hirsuta)* resulted in reduced densities of *B. longicaudatus*, and 7.2 and 15.2% improvements, respectively, in tuber yield and appearance (12). Several constraints, however, limit the utility of hairy indigo as a cover crop. The crop is highly sensitive to metribuzin, the standard potato herbicide used in northeast Florida; hairy indigo seed must be hot-water treated and dried, a cumbersome process for growers; the crop is open pollinated, so that resistance to nematodes can vary widely in a given plant population (1) thereby reducing its maximum effectiveness for nematode suppression; and potatoes are harvested 6-8 wk beyond the optimum April planting period for hairy indigo.

Corky ringspot. Disease resistance and chemicals are available for managing corky ringspot. Although soil fumigation has been ineffective for controlling this disease, certain nonvolatile nematicides including aldicarb, oxamyl, and carbofuran have provided economical control (13). Fenamiphos, ethoprop, fensulfothion, and phorate (each applied at 3.36 kg ai/ha) have failed to control corky ringspot. The fumigants, DD, 1,3-D, DD MENCS, metam-sodium, EDB, and methyl bromide also have been ineffective. Additionally, broadcast equivalent rates of 1,3-D, EDB, and metam-sodium applied with multiple chisels per row (15-18, Weingartner, unpublished data) and deep injection of methyl bromide or methyl bromide under plastic have been met with failure (Weingartner, unpublished data).

Resistance to corky ringspot exists in Pungo, Superior, New Superior, Oceania, BelRus and Hudson. Green Mountain is moderately resistant (Table 1). It is not known whether resistance is due to escape from infection or to true genetic resistance to either the nematode vector or the virus.

From a disease management standpoint it is unfortunate that each of the above cultivars have one or more shortcomings which limit their use in northeastern Florida. Pungo, Superior, and New Superior are highly susceptible to bacterial wilt (Table 1). Early and late blight also are severe in the latter two cultivars. Oceania is highly susceptible to blackleg. None of the above cultivars yields as well as Atlantic nor do they have the high specific gravity of Atlantic which is desired by potato chip processors. Additionally, Pungo and Green Mountain tend to produce dark-colored potato chips (Weingartner, unpublished data).

Bacterial wilt. This disease has increased in importance in recent years apparently due to widespread use of Atlantic, a susceptible cultivar (14). The disease can be more severe when the root-knot nematode (*M. incognita*) occurs concomitantly (16). Four disease management practices aimed at reducing commercial losses due to bacterial wilt have been studied. These include placement position of liquid fertilizer, harvest date, cultivar resistance (Table 1), and soil fumigation. Bacterial wilt was reduced by widening spacing between liquid fertilizer chisels to minimize root damage (Weingartner, unpublished data).

TABLE 1. Relative field susceptibility of selected potato cultivars to corky ringspot and bacterial wilt[a].

Potato	Relative susceptibility	
cultivar	Corky ringspot[b]	Bacterial wilt[c]
Atlantic	3-4	4
BelRus	1	3
Green Mountain	2	2-3
Hudson	1	3
Katahdin	3	3
Kennebec	3	?
LaChipper	3	3
LaRouge	5	5
New Superior	1	5
Oceania	1	3
Ontario	4	1
Pungo	1	5
Red LaSoda	5	5
Red Pontiac	5	5
Sebago	5	2
Superior	1	5

[a] Based on observations made in research plots and northeast Florida commercial potato fields.

[b] Corky ringspot: 1=rarely affected, occasional superficial lesions and/or internal necrosis; 2=highly tolerant, some lesions and internal necrosis, easily controlled with carbamate nematicides; 3=moderately susceptible, surface lesions and/or necrosis common, controlled with carbamate nematicides; 4=very susceptible, surface lesions and/or necrosis very common, control with nematicides good to fair; 5=highly susceptible, lesions/necrosis severe, some crop loss occurs even with most effective nematicides.

[c] Bacterial wilt/tuber brown rot: 1=highly tolerant, susceptible but rarely affected in field; 2=moderately tolerant, disease occurs in heavily infested fields, soil fumigation effective; 3=moderately susceptible, wilt and tuber rot develop slowly, soil fumigation moderately effective; 4=very susceptible, wilt develops rapidly, broadcast rates of soil fumigants needed to control; 5=highly susceptible, wilt develops rapidly, plants collapse and tubers rot extensively in field. Controlled poorly with broadcast fumigation.

Economic losses due to bacterial wilt can be serious if the disease escapes detection in infected tubers because the crop can be rejected by the buyer and then the producer loses both the crop and the cost of shipping. Delaying harvest and allowing infected tubers to rot in the field before lifting may be one way of reducing this type of loss. Effect of delaying harvest on percent tubers with undetected brown rot symptoms varied with cultivar (Fig. 2). As harvest date was extended, undetected brown rot progressively decreased in Superior from 22.5 to approximately 5% whereas the amount decreased during the first week in Red LaSoda and LaChipper and then leveled off. Delaying harvest 2-3 wk in most cultivars seems to decrease the amount of undetected brown rot at harvest.

Soil fumigation significantly reduces the incidence and severity of bacterial wilt. Also, using broadcast equivalent dosages of soil fumigants applied with multiple chisels per row reduced the incidence of bacterial wilt in the susceptible cultivar Atlantic to that of the more resistant cultivar Sebago fumigated with the standard single chisel/row and nematicide rate (16). Nematode and soilborne pathogen management options available to northeast Florida potato growers are summarized in a management matrix (Table 2).

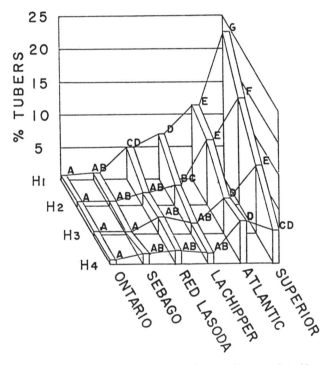

Figure 2. Relationship of brown rot incidence to cultivar and harvest date. Harvest dates H1, 2, 3, and 4 are respectively, 93, 100, 107 and 113 days from planting. The vertical axis is percent tubers having brown rot which escaped culling during grading. Percent tuber values for the harvest date x cultivar interactions having common letters do not differ significantly (P=0.05) according to Duncan's multiple range test.

TABLE 2. Management matrix for northeast Florida nematodes and soilborne pathogens.[a]

| Problem | Table stock | | Chip stock | |
| | Soil moisture | | Soil Moisture | |
	<10%	>10%	<10%	>10%
Nematodes	Fum or Fum+V[b] or M	V[b] or M	Fum	V[b] or M
Nematodes + CRS	Fum + ResC or Fum+V[b]	V[b] or ResC+V[b] Ms?+V Ms?+ResC Ms?+V+ ResC	Fum + ResC	ResC + M or V[b]
Nematodes + B. Wilt[a]	Fum + ResW or Fum 3X	ResW + M or V[b] or Ms?	Fum + ResW Fum 3X	ResW + M or V[b] or Ms?
Nematodes + CRS + B. Wilt[a]	Fum + ResW + V[b] or Fum 3X + ResC	ResW + V[b] or Ms? or Ms 3X?	ResW+V[b] Fum 3X+ ResC	ResW+V[b] or Ms 3X?

[a] Abbreviations used in matrix: Fum=fumigate with 1,3-D or metam sodium (Ms=metam sodium); Fum or Ms 3X=fumigate with broadcast equivalent rates applied with multiple chisels per row; Ms?=insufficient data, however soil moisture restrictions may not apply to metam-sodium; V=oxamyl; M=ethoprop; ResW=resistance to bacterial wilt; ResC=resistance to corky ringspot; CRS=corky ringspot; B. wilt=bacterial wilt.

[b] Registration of soil applied chemicals is changing. The carbamate nematicides aldicarb, carbofuran, and oxamyl control CRS, whereas the organophosphatic compounds ethoprop, phorate, and phenamiphos do not. Consult labels and use restrictions before selecting a nematicide.

Management of Nematodes in Southeast Florida

Nematode management in southern Florida is much less complex than that in northeast Florida. Management strategies have been and continue to be directed against *M. incognita*. Until the suspension of EDB in 1983, potato fields in southeast Florida were routinely fumigated with this material. Since that time, management with nematicides has not been widely attempted; in addition, performance of systemic nematicides (organophosphates and carbamates) has been poor in the alkaline soils (McSorley, unpublished data). Suspension of EDB did not cause a resurgence of *M. incognita* in southeast Florida. Its distribution is sporadic, and it is a problem only in some fields.

Early detection of *M. incognita* in potato fields is important, and sampling plans have been developed based on Taylor's power law statistics (11) for fields ranging in size from 0.2 to 1.2 ha (4). It was not possible to devise reliable sampling plans for areas greater than 1.2 ha, because the distribution of *M. incognita* is so clumped that Taylor's power law statistics are not reliable (b > 2). Numbers of cores needed to estimate specified densities of *M. incognita* in a 0.4 ha area with a 25% level of precision decreased from 100 to 24 as nematode density increased from 1 to $104/100$ cm^3 soil (4). Therefore, to conservatively detect *M. incognita*, an initial density of $1.0/100$ cm^3 soil should be assumed and 100 soil cores per 0.4 ha should be taken, a very intense sampling load. This sampling strategy applies to fallow fields sampled 1-2 mo prior to potato planting, the most difficult situation in which to detect *M. incognita*. Densities are generally higher, and hence fewer soil cores would be required near the end of the previous potato crop (April).

One reason why root-knot nematode densities have remained low or absent may be the practice of fallow (chemical or mechanical) or cover cropping (sorghum or weeds). Populations of *M. incognita* may build up on weed hosts (e.g., *Acalypha ostryifolia, A. alopecuroides, Chenopodium* spp.) which grow on these sites during the summer months. In contrast, densities of *C. onoensis* were little affected by fallow or weed growth, but increased following a sorghum-sudangrass cover crop (Table 3). *Rotylenchulus reniformis* densities were lower following a chemical or mechanical fallow than with sorghum or weeds (Table 3). The similarity in *R. reniformis* densities in plots with weeds and sorghum is surprising because sorghum is a nonhost (3). However, it should be pointed out that morning glory (*Ipomoea* spp.), an excellent host of *R. reniformis*, encroached into the sorghum plots in this study (6).

Total gross weights of potatoes harvested from these plots did not differ ($P \leq 0.05$) with fallow or cover crop. However, wireworm damage was greatest ($P \leq 0.001$) with sorghum compared to weeds or fallow (6). The level of wireworm damage following sorghum was unacceptable and represented a substantial number of culls. In other experiments, wireworm damage in a subsequent potato crop was related to the number of days sorghum had been grown the previous summer (6). In general, substantial wireworm damage ($\geq 5\%$ of tubers) can be anticipated if the sorghum cover crop is maintained for ≥ 35 days.

TABLE 3. Nematode populations on selected sampling dates following four summer management treatments, 1984-85.

Summer management treatment	Nematodes per 100 cm³ soil[a]				
	19 Apr	9 Oct	23 Oct	10 Dec	12 Mar
		Criconemella onoensis			
Weeds	698	1099	901	692	512
Sorghum	808	1994	1561	1190	841
Mechanical fallow	810	911	1002	795	551
Chemical fallow	819	1137	859	648	486
Contrasts:[b]	n.s.	n.s.	n.s.	SxW	n.s.
		Rotylenchulus reniformis			
Weeds	21	289	576	301	35
Sorghum	22	192	216	172	20
Mechanical fallow	80	1	92	89	2
Chemical fallow	45	96	41	44	0
Contrasts:[b]	n.s.	FxNF	FxNF	FxNF	FxNF

[a] Dates correspond to start of summer management treatment (19 Apr), first discing (9 Oct), second discing (23 Oct), shortly after potato.planting (10 Dec), and potato harvest (12 Mar).

[b] Significant ($P < 0.05$) contrasts: SxW=sorghum vs. weeds; FxNF=fallow vs. non-fallow; n.s.=not significant at ($P \leq 0.05$).

Epilogue

In Northeast Florida the management system is heavily dependent upon chemicals. The recent withdrawal of aldicarb from use in potatoes has both increased the cost and reduced the effective number of options for soilborne pathogen and nematode control. The wide host range of the principal nematodes and pathogens (i.e., tobacco rattle virus and *P. solanacearum*) present major challenges in developing alternative management strategies. Efforts to find resistance to corky ringspot and bacterial wilt have received and will continue to receive major research effort. In addition, use of different cover crops and green manuring methods to suppress the vector of corky ringspot and the bacterial wilt pathogen also are being studied. Additional data on economic thresholds of *B. longicaudatus, M. incognita,* and trichodorids in different soil types are needed.

In Southeast Florida, problems with *M. incognita* are sporadic. When problem fields are identified, management by summer fallow or by means of a summer cover crop of sorghum may be helpful provided the sorghum planting is timed judiciously to avoid peak wireworm flights.

In both locations, it appears that planting date and temperature may determine the level of *M. incognita* galling on tubers. In Southeast Florida for example, early planting (Nov) and harvest (Mar) may result in a lower incidence of disease. Potatoes harvested in late April are more often damaged, probably because the warmer soil temperatures permit more rapid development of visual disease symptoms and tuber infection by a later generation of root-knot nematodes (McSorley, unpublished data). Additional research is needed to determine the relationship between planting date and tuber damage before planting date could be used as a reliable management tool. The severity and complexity of nematode problems on potatoes in Florida present a continual challenge to growers and pest managers in the state.

Literature Cited

1. Dominguez, H.E., Baltensperger, D.D., Reith, P.E., and Dunn, R.A. Genotypic variation in *Indigofera hirsuta* L. reaction to *Meloidogyne* spp. Soil Crop Sci. Soc. Fla. Proc. 45:189-192.
2. Gallatin, M.H., Ballard, J.K., Evans, C.B., Galberry, H.S., Hinton, J.J., Powell, D.P., Truett, E., Watts, W.L., Wilson Jr., G.C., and Leighty, R.G. 1958. Soil survey (detailed-reconnaissance) of Dade County, Florida. U.S. Government Printing Office, Washington, DC. 56 pp.
3. MacGowan, J.B. 1977. The reniform nematode. Nematology Circular No. 32., Florida Dept. Agric. and Consumer Serv., Div. Plant Ind., Gainesville. 2 pp.
4. McSorley, R., Dankers, W.H., Parrado, J.L., and Reynolds, J.S. 1985. Spatial distribution of the nematode community on Perrine marl soils. Nematropica 15:77-92.
5. McSorley, R., Parrado, J.L., Tyson, R.V., and Reynolds, J.S. 1987. Effect of *Criconemella onoensis* on potato. J. Nematol. 19:228-232.
6. McSorley, R., Parrado, J.L., Tyson, R.V., Waddill, V.H., Lamberts, M.L., and Reynolds, J.S. 1987. Effect of sorghum cropping practices on winter potato production. Nematropica 17:45-60.
7. National Potato Council. 1990. Potato Statistical Yearbook. National Potato Council. Englewood, CO. 69 pp.
8. National Potato Council. 1991. Potato Statistical Yearbook. National Potato Council. Englewood, CO. 69 pp.
9. Overman, A.J., Bryan, H.H., and Harkness, R.W. 1970. Effect of off-season culture on weeds, nematodes, and potato yields on marl soils. Proc. Florida State Hort. Soc. 84:135-139.
10. Rebois, R.V., Eldridge, B.J., and Webb, R.E. 1978. *Rotylenchulus reniformis* parasitism of potatoes and its effect on yields. Plant Dis. Rept. 62:520-523.
11. Taylor, L.R. 1961. Aggregation, variance and the mean. Nature (London) 189:732-735.
12. Weingartner, D.P., Meldrum, Jill, Shumaker, J. R., and Wallis III, Louis. 1991. Influence of *Indigofera hirsuta* and *sorghum bicolor* X *arundinaceum* var sudanense on nematodes, corky ringspot disease, and potato yields in Florida. (Abstr) Nematropica 21:135.
13. Weingartner, D.P., and Shumaker, J.R. 1983. Nematicide options for northeast Florida potato growers. Proc. Florida State Hort. Soc. 96:122-127.

14. Weingartner, D.P., and Shumaker, J.R. 1984. Bacterial wilt and tuber brown rot as a potential threat to potato production in northeast Florida. Proc. Florida State Hort. Soc. 97:198-200.

15. Weingartner, D.P., and Shumaker, J.R. 1990. Effects of soil fumigants and aldicarb on corky ringspot disease and trichodorid nematodes in potato. Suppl. to J. Nematol. 22:665-671.

16. Weingartner, D.P., and Shumaker, J.R. 1990. Effects of soil fumigants and aldicarb on bacterial wilt and root-knot nematodes in potato. Suppl. to J. Nematol. 22:681-688.

17. Weingartner, D.P., and Shumaker, J.R. 1990. Effects of soil fumigants and aldicarb on nematodes, tuber quality and yield in potato. Suppl. to J. Nematol. 22:767-774.

18. Weingartner, D.P., and Shumaker, J.R. 1990. Control of nematodes and soil-borne diseases in Florida potatoes with aldicarb and 1,3-D. Suppl. to J. Nematol. 22:775-778.

19. Weingartner, D.P., Shumaker, J.R., and Smart Jr., G.C. 1978. Nematode and soil-borne disease control. Hastings ARC Research Report PR78-1. 4 pp.

20. Weingartner, D.P., Shumaker, J.R., and Smart Jr., G.C. 1983. Why soil fumigation fails to control potato corky ringspot disease in Florida. Plant Dis. 67:130-134.

BIOLOGY AND MANAGEMENT OF
NEMATODE PARASITES OF POTATO
IN DEVELOPING COUNTRIES

P. Jatala
Department of Nematology and Entomology
International Potato Center, P.O. Box 5969
Lima, Peru

Potato, *Solanum tuberosum L.*, is a major food crop in many countries and occupies fourth place among the crops of major importance, in terms of dry matter production per ha. It ranks first and third in edible energy and protein production per ha per day, respectively (10). Potatoes are grown in more countries than any other crop, with the exception of maize, and it is the only tuber crop produced in significant amounts in developed countries. Its range of production extends over 5.7 million ha in over 90 developing countries with an annual production of over 75 million mt. The importance and popularity of this crop in developing counties is primarily due to its high yielding capacity, high market value and adaptability in the cereal-based cropping system which predominates in these countries (36).

In recent years, in subtropical and tropical countries, potato production has gradually extended out of its traditional cool environmental conditions at higher altitudes into hotter and generally drier zones which are optimum for the development of many pathogens and pests, including nematodes (16). Of the biotic factors which adversely influence the production of potato from seed tubers or true potato seed, nematodes are among the most important pest constraints. While nematode infestations and damage to potato in some countries and production areas may be regarded as minor, in other areas high infestations cause severe yield losses in addition to affecting the quality of the crop. Although there are over 60 nematode species known to be associated with potato, only a few are of major economic concern.

In general, it is well known that nematode damage is more severe in lighter sandy soils than in heavier soils. Similarly, the damage due to nematodes is usually more severe in the areas where plants are under environmental stress because the tolerance or resistance is lowered (31,32,42). Additionally, much of the yield loss attributed to nematodes may be due to the fact that they predispose plants to pathogenic fungi or bacteria, and may aid in the dissemination of viruses (33,39).

This chapter provides information on the biology and distribution of the most important nematode pests affecting potato in developing countries and reviews the control measures practiced by farmers in those countries. It also updates the significant advances made in the development of IPM components and strategies, which will be useful to the national agricultural research systems of developing countries and to many institutions in the developed world studying these important pests.

Potato Cyst Nematodes

Potato cyst nematodes, *Globodera pallida* (Stone 1972) Beherens 1975 and *G. rostochiensis* (Wollen. 1923) Beherens 1975 are the most important nematode pests of potatoes and consequently, they have been studied most extensively (25). These nematodes are primarily distributed in cooler areas of tropical and subtropical regions, as well as in the temperate regions of the world where potatoes are cultivated. Losses as high as 80% are not uncommon in some potato-growing areas of the tropics where infestation levels are high and continuous potato cultivation is practiced.

Apparently, these nematodes have evolved along with their principal host, potato, in the highlands of Peru and Bolivia (16). They were introduced to Europe around the mid or late 19th century on potatoes imported for breeding purposes (43). They have since spread into most of the potato growing areas of Europe and South America, and into some potato-growing areas of North America (USA, Canada, and Mexico), Pakistan, India, Morocco, Sri Lanka, the Philippines, and Japan.

There are no specific above-ground diagnostic symptoms associated with the infection by these nematodes. However, the early senescence and proliferation of lateral roots or the presence of small spherical females of white or yellow stages on the roots (Fig. 1) at flowering and sometimes on the surface of the young tubers are diagnostic signs of the infection by these nematodes (2,7). The visual differentiation of the two species is based on the presence of the yellow stage in females of *G. rostochiensis* prior to the development of cyst stage, whereas in *G. pallida* this yellow stage is absent.

Eggs of these nematodes remain viable in the cysts for over 20 years in the soil and withstand temperature extremes of cold (-15°C) and soil desiccation for long periods. A large portion of eggs will hatch only if they are stimulated by potato root exudates.

Juveniles become active at about 10°C and maximum root invasion takes place at about 16°C (6). After penetration of the roots, the juveniles move inter- and intracellularly in the cortex and alongside the vascular system in search of an appropriate feeding site. Once feeding site is located, the nematode becomes sedentary and passes through three molts before mature females are formed.

The mature, enlarged females rupture the root tissue and extend their bodies out to the root surface (Fig.1). They attach their heads and protruding necks to the roots. Fertilization occurs and females become gravid and spherical. They undergo a series of color changes from white to cream and yellow before dying and forming cysts. They generally complete one generation per growing season.

These nematodes are principally disseminated as cysts on infected seed tubers or in the adherent soil on the tubers and by the movement of infested soil by farm implements. They can also be disseminated in the irrigation water.

Potato cyst nematodes are host specific and have a limited host range. Eggplant, tomato, and a few solanaceous weeds are considered to be nonefficient hosts, although they do harbor these nematodes. Populations of both species behave differently on resistant cultivars. Several years of potato monoculture may lead to the development of a new race which may reproduce on resistant cultivars (4).

Using various host differentials, Kort, et al. (26) introduced a standard system of race identification to differentiate races of the two species occurring in Europe. This classification scheme differentiates five races (Ro 1-5) in *G. rostochiensis* and three races (Pa 1-3) in *G. pallida* from the United Kingdom, the Netherlands, and Germany. Canto-Saenz and Mayer de Scurrah (3) determined that the European system of race classification was unsuitable for differentiating the races of these nematodes from the Andean regions of South America. They used four differential plants that separated four races of *G. rostochiensis* and three races of *G. pallida* in addition to three races from the Andes (Table 1). Recently, Llontop (25) determined the presence of a new race in *G. pallida* (P6A) in Peru and suggested the addition of two potato clones in the scheme for differentiating this race. Canto (unpublished data), however, suggested the inclusion of only clone *Solanum tuberosum* ssp. *andigena* 280090.10 in the previous scheme of classification, thus increasing the number of differentials to 5 clones. This scheme recognizes 6 groups of races in *G. pallida* consisting of two variants each of races 1 and 4, three variants of race 2, and races 3, 5, and 6 with no variants (Table 2).

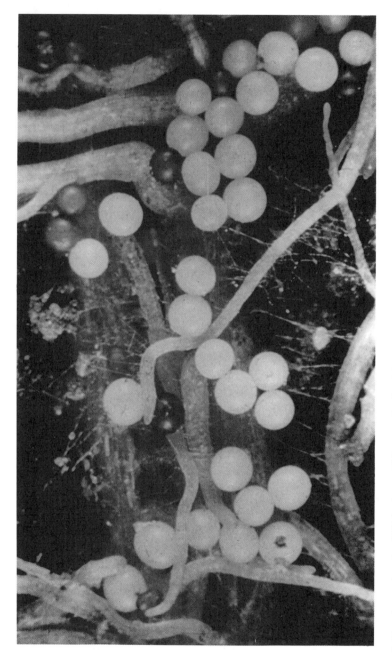

Fig. 1. Females and cysts of *Globodera pallida* on roots of potato.

TABLE 1. Differential hosts used for separating races of *Globodera rostochiensis* and *G. pallida* as proposed in European and S. American schemes.

S. American Scheme / European Scheme	Globodera rostochiensis				Globodera pallida					
	R₁A Ro1	R₁B Ro4	R₂A Ro2	R₃A Ro3	P₁A Pa1	P₁B	P₂A	P₃A	P₄A Pa2	P₅A Pa3
Differential host										
Solanum tuberosum ssp. *tuberosum*	+	+	+	+	+	+	+	+	+	+
Solanum tuberosum ssp. *andigena* CPC 1673 hybr.	-	-	-	+	+	+	?	?	?	+
Solanum kurtzianum hybr. 60.21.19	-	+	-	+	+	+	-	+	+	+
Solanum vernei hybr. 58.1642/4	-	+	-	-	+	+	+	-	+	+
Solanum vernei hybr. 62.33.3	-	-	-	-	-	+	-	-	-	+
Solanum multidissectum hybr. P55/7	+	+	+	+	-	-	+	+	+	+

[1]After Kort et al. (26) and Canto and De Scurrah (3).

TABLE 2. Differential hosts used for separating races of *Globodera pallida* as proposed by M. Canto, 1992. (Unpublished data)

Differential Plants	No. Desig. to Diff. Plants	RACES									
		P_1A	P_1B	P_2A	P_2B	P_2C	P_3A	P_4A	P_4B	P_5A	P_6A
Solanum tuberosum ssp. *tuberosum*	0	+	+	+	+	+	+	+	+	+	+
Solanum multidissectum p55/7	1	-	-	+	+	+	+	+	+	+	+
Solanum kurtzianum KTT 60.21.19	2	+	+	-	-	-	+	+	+	+	+
Solanum vernei GLKS 58.1642.4	3	+	+	+	+	+	-	+	+	+	+
Solanum vernei (VT) 63.33.3	4	-	+	+	+	+	-	-	-	+	+
Solanum tuberosum ssp. *andigena* 280090.10	5	NT	NT	+	+	-	NT	-	+	-	+

+ = Pf/Pi >1
- = Pf/Pi <1
NT = not tested

Potato cyst nematodes are known to interact with other plant pathogenic organisms in the development of disease complexes. Such interactions include the association of *G. pallida* with *Pseudomonas solanacearum* (E.F. Smith) E.F. Smith (19) and *Verticillium dahliae* Kleb. (8,9).

Root-knot Nematodes

Root-knot nematodes, *Meloidogyne* spp., are cosmopolitan in distribution, attacking almost all the major crops and many weed species. Although many root-knot nematode species are known to be associated with potato, only five species, *M. incognita* (Kofoid and White, 1919) Chitwood, 1949, *M. javanica* (Treub, 1885) Chitwood, 1949, *M. arenaria* (Neal, 1889) Chitwood, 1949, *M. hapla* Chitwood, 1949, and *M. chitwoodi* Golden, O'Bannon, Santo and Finley, 1980, are of economic concern.

The first two species occur principally in the warm temperate, tropical, and subtropical regions of the world, while the last two species are found primarily in the cool temperate and the cool tropical regions. *M. arenaria* occurs in most locations (40).

Losses due to these nematodes may reach 25% or more and vary depending on cultivar resistance, environmental conditions, and nematode species (28). These nematodes not only reduce yield by infecting the roots and limiting plant growth, but also by affecting crop quality.

These nematodes are not considered to be a major economic concern globally because the potato is grown predominantly in the cooler climates. However, the extension of potato cultivation into the warm tropics could drastically change this situation. Perhaps the most important aspect of these nematodes in disease etiology is their interaction with other pathogenic organisms in the development of disease complexes. The most important interaction involving these nematodes on potato is their association with the bacterial wilt organism. *Solanacearum*, in which the resistance of plants to the bacterial wilt organism is broken when *Meloidogyne* is present (18,23). Recently, Jatala and coworkers (17) demonstrated the implication of *M. incognita* in the dissemination of spindle tuber viroid. Apparently, the egg masses formed by this nematode while feeding on a viroid infected plant contained viroid particles. Upon hatching, juveniles carried the particles on their cuticle and disseminated them to other plants.

There are no diagnostic above-ground symptoms associated with the infection by these nematodes. Infected roots, however, have galls or knots of different shapes and sizes (Fig. 2). The incidence and size of galls depends upon plant susceptibility, nematode density and species, and environmental conditions, particularly temperature. Galls caused by *M. hapla* and *M. chitwoodi* are usually smaller than those caused other species and have extensive lateral root formation. Infected tubers are not marketable and may serve as the source of inoculum (12). Under favorable environmental conditions tubers of all shapes and sizes can become infected. The infected tubers are warty in appearance and can become completely deformed, particularly if they became infected at the early stages of development (Fig. 3). Although the depth of penetration in tubers varies depending on the size of tubers and the time of infection, adult females are usually found at about 1-2 cm below the skin, feeding on vascular tissues (12). Up to 6 generations may occur within one growing season, and this depends upon the species of the nematode, the environmental conditions and the host susceptibility. The first generation occurs mainly on the roots, while the succeeding generations attack tubers. There are physiological races in some of the *Meloidogyne* species and all these races attack potato in varying degrees.

Because *Meloidogyne* attack a rather large number of plant species, their population can be maintained on weeds and volunteer crops. However, their population will be drastically reduced in the absence of suitable hosts. They usually overwinter as eggs in gelatinous matrix, although some species have the ability to go through anhydrobiosis as a means of survival. These nematodes are usually disseminated through the movement of the infected tubers, roots or planting material. Movement of infested soil by farm machinery and through irrigation water are other modes of disseminating *Meloidogyne* species (16).

False Root-knot Nematode

The false root-knot nematode, *Nacobbus aberrans*, Thorne and Allen, 1944, is primarily found in the cool tropical regions of Argentina, northern Chile, Peru, Bolivia, and Ecuador, as well as in Mexico, USA, and Russia (15,28). The presence of this nematode has also been reported in glasshouses in England and the Netherlands (15,16). There is also a suspect report on its occurrence in India. While this nematode is considered to be one of the most important nematode pests of potato in Northern Argentina, Bolivia, and the southern, central, and northern highlands of Peru, it is a nematode pest of sugarbeets primarily in the USA (11,15,28,41). It is the most important pest constraint of potato production in Bolivia (16). Under favorable conditions for nematode development, yield losses as high as 90% have been observed in Bolivia and southern Peru.

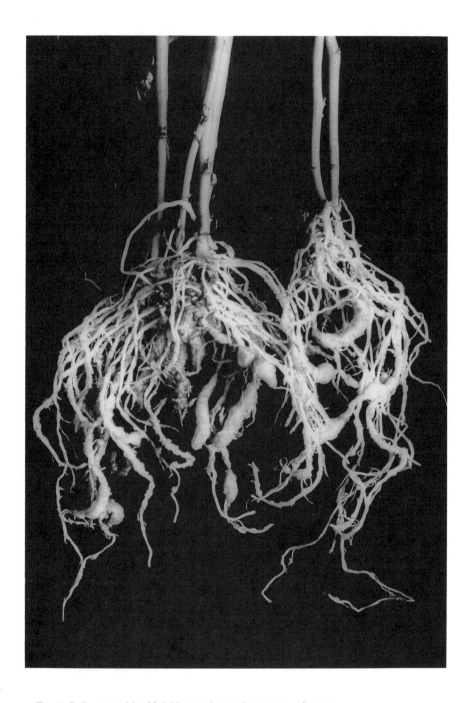

Fig. 2. Galls caused by *Meloidogyne incognita* on roots of potato.

Fig. 3. Swelling or galls caused by *Meloidogyne incognita* on potato tubers.

Although there are no above-ground symptoms associated with the presence of this nematode, the infected plants are usually stunted and wilt under moisture stress. Root symptomatology is very similar to that caused by root-knot nematodes. However, galls are usually formed laterally on roots in a rosary bead-like pattern and often with the formation of rootlets on the galls (Fig. 4). Hence, the common name of rosary nematode is given to this nematode in Argentina, Bolivia and Peru. Although this nematode does not cause recognizable symptoms on tubers, it penetrates the tubers to a depth of 1-2 mm below the skin (24,28). Infected tubers serve as a good source for disseminating this nematode. For this reason, strict quarantine regulations are imposed in northern Argentina for movement of seed tubers from infested fields (16).

This nematode can withstand adverse environmental stresses, such as low temperature (-15°C), and can survive in desiccated soil (20). Therefore, it can also be disseminated in infested soil that adheres to tubers and farm implements. Irrigation water is another source of disseminating this nematode from infested fields.

False root-knot nematode has a rather wide host range and, therefore, can survive on a series of weeds and alternate hosts. There are variations in the severity of attack by different populations of this nematode on various crops. Inserra (11) reported the presence of three races of *N. aberrans*. Boluarte and Jatala (1), however, reported the presence of six races and one variant each of two races in *N. aberrans* populations from different countries. They proposed an international scheme for differentiating the races of this nematode. They have since modified the scheme which now recognizes six races and two variants in race 2 and three variants in race 3 (Nematropica 23: in press).

Nacobbus aberrans is often associated with *Meloidogyne* species. In the Andean mountains of Peru and Bolivia, this nematode is often associated with *Meloidogyne* and *Globodera* species and *Spongospora subterranea*. The nature and consequences of such associations on potato cultivation has not been well documented.

Nacobbus aberrans is adapted to a wide range of temperatures. Although it survives and reproduces most rapidly at temperatures between 20 and 28°C, in the Andes this nematode is associated with potato at temperatures between 15 to 18°C, and is not limited by soil type. Apparently, periods of soil cooling (even freezing) and desiccation aid in stimulation of nematode activity during spring, causing immediate root infection after planting tubers (16,20).

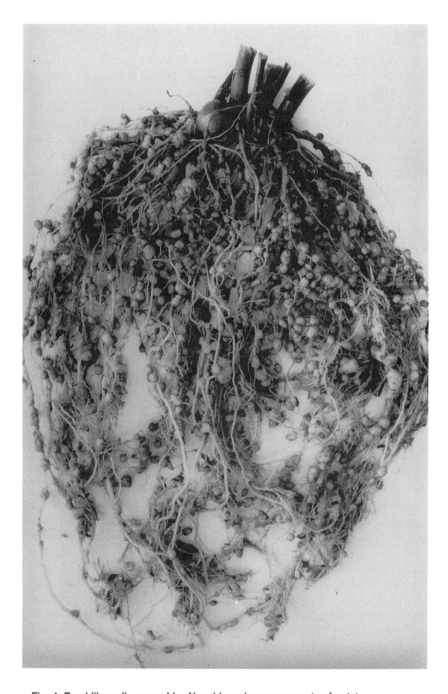

Fig. 4. Bead-like galls caused by *Nacobbus aberrans* on roots of potato.

Other Nematodes of Potatoes

Although the list of nematodes attacking potatoes is rather extensive, few of these nematodes are of global economic concern. However, several of these nematodes may limit potato production in some areas. In some temperate, tropical and subtropical regions, nematode species, including several *Pratylenchus* spp., *Thecavermiculatus andinus* Golden, Franco, Jatala and Aztocaza, 1983, *Belanolaimus longicaudatus* (Steiner, 1949) Rau, 1958, *Radopholus similis* (Cobb, 1983) Thorne, 1949, *Rotylenchulus reniformis* Linford and Oliveira, 1940, *Ditylenchus destructor* Thorne, 1945, and *D. dipsaci* (Kuhn, 1857) Filipjev, 1936, *Tylenchorhynchus* spp., and *Helicotylenchus* spp., are known to cause severe damage to this crop and reduce the yield significantly (14,16,28). However, the incidence of these species is usually localized with the exception of the damage caused by infection of *Pratylenchus* spp. (Fig. 5). These nematodes are rather widely distributed in many agroecological zones and have a wide host range. Additionally, these nematodes interact with many plant pathogenic organisms and aid in the development of disease complexes. In many instances, these nematodes have been reported to be of major economic concern.

Xiphinema spp., *Trichodorus* spp., and *Paratrichodorus* spp. are also associated with potato. Although they can cause direct damage to the crop, they are most important because they can disseminate some important potato viruses (25).

Management of Potato Nematodes

To combat the damage and yield loss caused by infection of nematodes, farmers in many developing and developed countries have depended upon the use of chemical pesticides. In the past, the use of chemical pesticides increased rapidly, particularly in areas where there is economic pressure on land use (which limits the use of crop rotation and other cultural methods) and a lack of cultivars (13). However, the use of pesticides is a short-term solution to nematode problems because nematode populations tend to increase to levels higher than the initial population several months after the use of nematicides and/or new races of nematodes can develop due to selection pressure caused by the continuous use of resistant cultivars. This has caused farmers to be led onto the "pesticide treadmill" (13).

Excessive and indiscriminate use of nematicides has its drawbacks. It increases production costs, and is a serious health hazard, particularly for the farmers in the developing countries who generally do

Fig. 5. Lesions caused by *Pratylenchus* sp. on potato tubers.

not take precautionary measures when handling and applying these pesticides. Many of the most commonly used nematicides are expensive in developing countries, highly toxic compounds, some with known carcinogenic activities, have harmful effects on humans and animals, as well as pose a major threat in environmental contamination, such as their persistence in the soil or their contamination of ground water. For these reasons, they are gradually being taken off the market in many developed countries. However, regardless of such drawbacks, many of these pesticides continue to be used in developing countries.

In general, farmers in developing countries fall into three groups: high, medium, and low economic capability. Those with the high economic capability are usually large landholders and depend upon the use of nematicides, regardless of the cost, to offset the losses due to nematodes. Farmers with medium economic capability use nematicides frequently. Their use, however, depends upon the nematode species, severity and extent of the damage, and the demand for the crop. However, price increases of nematicides have made the use of these products often prohibitive for this group of farmers. Farmers with low economic capability, who constitute the majority of the farmers in the developing world, rarely or never use nematicides for control of nematodes. However, they often use certain insecticides which may provide them additional protection against nematodes.

One of the oldest, most effective and widely used, and most important approaches for controlling plant-parasitic nematodes in the world is crop rotation. The aim of rotation is to provide a sufficient time interval between susceptible host crops, by growing a less favored or resistant plant, to reduce nematode population build up. The cropping systems approach and crop rotation are similar concepts. Crop rotation is the fixed yearly sequence and spatial arrangement of crops or the alteration of crops and fallow in a given area. The cropping systems concept incorporates crop rotation over several years and involves long-term planning of planting patterns of various crops in different sequences, including monoculture, in a given area. In the past, farmers in the Andean region practiced a seven-year rotation scheme for the control of potato cyst nematodes. However, because of increasing population pressure and the subsequent demand for food, intensive land use has accelerated to levels whereby many farmers in the developing world have been forced to modify the old practices. Nevertheless, almost all the farmers in the developing world practice a one-year rotation with a nonhost crop in an attempt to reduce the nematode populations below damaging thresholds. While such practices may still be effective for reducing the populations of host-specific nematodes, such as *Globodera* spp., they are of limited value for controlling polyphagous nematodes, such as *Meloidogyne, Nacobbus,* and *Pratylenchus* species. Members of the *Gramineae* and *Leguminosae* are widely used in crop rotations to control *Globodera* spp. and *N. aberrans.* The use of resistant cultivars and rotation with non-host crops is the most economic means of controlling *Meloidogyne* spp. This requires knowledge of the species of *Meloidogyne* before recommending a non-host crop (e.g., although peanut is susceptible to *M. hapla* and race 1 of *M. arenaria,* it is a non-host for *M. incognita*).

Another common practice for controlling nematodes is the addition of animal or organic manure to the field. Such practices may markedly reduce populations of plant parasitic nematodes. Organic amendments containing high levels of ammoniacal N, or that result in the liberation of NH_3 upon application to the soil, are very effective at reducing nematode populations (29,30,34,37). Additionally, organic matter stimulates microbial activity in the soil and may increase populations of microorganisms that are antagonists of plant-parasitic nematodes (35). Application of chicken manure to the field is a common practice in the Philippines (R. Davide, personal communication) and many countries in Africa, Asia, and in Central and South America. This practice seems to be effective at controlling *Globodera* and *Meloidogyne* species on potato.

Use of resistant cultivars has aided in the control of *G. rostochiensis* in some developing countries. Stegemann and Schnick (38) have provided a list of such cultivars resistant to the European races of *Globodera* species. Recently, a potato cultivar, Maria Huanca, developed by the International Potato Center (CIP), was released in Peru. This cultivar is resistant to races P4A and P5A of *G. pallida* and is adapted for cultivation in the Andean region.

There are no known potato cultivars with a high degree of resistance to different species and races of *Meloidogyne.* However, resistance has been identified in some wild tuber-bearing *Solanum* species. Breeders at CIP have transferred this resistance to tetraploid potato germplasm adapted to the warm tropics. Use of these sources constitutes the most practical means of controlling these nematodes. One such example is the planned release of a potato clone by the National Potato Program of Burundi which is highly resistant to different *Meloidogyne* species. Limited work has been done on the development of potato cultivars with resistance to *N. aberrans.* However, there are some primitive clones with a high degree of resistance to this nematode and attempts are being made to transfer the resistance to cultivars adapted to the high altitudes of the Andes.

There are apparently some potato cultivars that are tolerant to some of the nematodes mentioned above. However, their use is rather limited and studies are warranted to identify cultivars with high degrees of tolerance which can be used by the farmers in developing countries.

Recent advances in the field of biological control and the use of biorational methods as alternatives for controlling nematodes have provided some hope for the farmers in developing countries. Results of several studies indicate the fungus *Paecilomyces lilacinus* can be used to control nematodes on potatoes (5,13,21,22). This organism is now being produced commercially in the Philippines and Peru under the names of Bioact and Biocon, respectively. It is also being studied by the scientists in many developing countries for its recommendation as an effective alternative measure for controlling nematodes.

Use of various nematode control strategies within the concept of modern integrated pest management is the current trend which is an important aspect of the sustainable agriculture. The application of sustainable agriculture in developing countries is welcome because it provides an improvement in the pest control tactics within the context of a productive and wholesome environment.

Literature Cited

1.   Boluarte, T., and P. Jatala. 1992. Development of an international race classification scheme for determination of physiological races of *Nacobbus aberrans*. Nematropica 22: 119.

2.   Brown, E.B. 1969. Assessment of damage caused to potatoes by potato cyst eelworm, *Heterodera rostochiensis* Woll. Ann. App. Bio. 63:493-502.

3.   Canto-Saenz, M., and M. Mayer de Scurrah. 1977. Races of potato cyst nematode in the Andean region and a new system of classification. Nematologica 23:340-349.

4.   Cole, C.S., and H.W. Howard. 1966. The effects on a population of potato root eelworm *Heterodera rostochiensis* of growing potato resistant to pathotype B. Ann. App. Bio. 58:487-495.

5.   Davide, R.G., and R.A. Zorilla. 1983. Evaluation of a fungus *Paecilomyces lilacinus* (Thom.) Samson for the biological control of the potato cyst nematode, *Globodera rostochiensis* Woll., as compared with some nematicides. Philippine Agriculture 66:397-404.

6.   Franco, J. 1979. Effect of temperature on hatching and multiplication of potato cyst nematode. Nematologica 25:237-244.

7.   Franco, J. 1981. Potato cyst nematodes, *Globodera* spp. Technical Information Bulletin 9. International Potato Center, Lima, Peru. 21 p.

8.   Franco, J., and E. Bendezu. 1985. Estudio del complejo *Verticillium dahliae* Kleb. y *Globodera pallida* Stone y su efecto en el comportamiento de algunos cultivares Peruanos de papa. Fitopatologia 20:21-27.

9.   Harrison, J.A.C. 1971. Association between the potato cyst nematode, *Heterodera rostochiensis* Woll. and *Verticillium adhliae* Kleb. in the early-dying disease of potatoes. Ann. App. Bio. 67:185-193.

10. Horton, D., J. Lynam, and H. Knipscheer. 1984. Root crops in developing countries - an economic appraisal, Proceeding of Sixth Symposium of the International Society for Tropical Root Crops. International Potato Center, Lima, Peru.

11. Inserra, R.N. 1983. Development and pathogenicity of the false root-knot nematode *Nacobbus aberrans* and its relationships with *Heterodera schachtii* and *Meloidogyne hapla* on sugarbeet. Ph.D. Dissertation, Utah State University, Logan, Utah.

12. Jatala, P. 1975. Root-knot nematodes (*Meloidogyne* species) and their effect on potato quality in Proceedings of the 6th Triennial Conference of the EAPR. Wageningen, Netherlands. 194 p.

13. Jatala, P. 1986. Biological control of plant parasitic nematodes. Annu. Rev. Phytopathol. 24:453-489.

14. Jatala, P. 1987. Nematodes in tuber and root crops and their management, pages 110-114 in Proceedings of the 11th International Congress of Plant Protection. International Plant Protection: Focus on the Developing World. Manila, Philippines.

15. Jatala, P. 1991. Reniform and false root-knot nematodes, *Rotylenchulus* and *Nacobbus* spp., pages 502-528 in Manual of Agricultural Nematology, R. Nickle, Marcel Dekker, New York.

16. Jatala, P., and J. Bridge. 1990. Nematode parasites of root and tuber crops, pages 137-180 in Plant Parasitic Nematodes in Subtropical and Tropical Agriculture, M. Luc, R.A. Sikora and J. Bridge (eds.), CAB International.

17. Jatala, P., R. Delgado de la Flor, M. Querci, and L. Salazar. 1991. Possible implication of *Meloidogyne incognita* in the dissemination of potato spindle tuber viroid. Nematropica 21: pp.

18. Jatala, P., E.R. French, and L. Gutarra. 1975. Interrelationships of *Meloidogyne incognita acrita* and *Pseudomonas solanacearum* on potatoes. J. Nematol. 7:324-325.

19. Jatala, P., L. Gutarra, E.R. French, and J. Arango. 1976. Interaction of *Heterodera pallida* and *Pseudomonas solanacearum* on potatoes. J. Nematol. 8:289-290.

20. Jatala, P., R. Kaltenbach. 1979. Survival of *Nacobbus aberrans* in adverse conditions. J. Nematol. 11:303.

21. Jatala, P., R. Kaltenbach, and M. Bocangel. 1979. Biological control of *Meloidogyne incognita acrita* and *Globodera pallida* on potatoes. J. Nematol. 11:303.

22. Jatala, P., R. kaltenbach, M. Bocangel, A.J. Devaux, and R. Campos. 1980. Field application of *Paecilomyces lilacinus* for controlling *Meloidogyne incognita* on potatoes. J. Nematol. 12:226-227.

23. Jatala, P., and C. Martin. 1977. Interaction of *Meloidogyne incognita acrita* and *Pseudomonas solanacearum* on *Solanum acoense* and *S. sparsipilum*. Proceeding of the American Phytopathological Society 4:178.

24. Jatala, P., and M.M. de Scurrah. 1975. Mode of dissemination of *Nacobbus* spp. in certain potato growing areas of Peru and Bolivia. J. Nematol. 7:324-325.

25. Jensen, H.J., J. Armstrong, and P. Jatala. 1979. Annotated Bibliography of Nematode Pests of Potato. Joint publication of the International Potato Center, Lima, Peru, and Oregon State University Agricultural Experiment Station, Corvallis, Oregon 315 p.

26.   Kort, J., H. Ross, H.J. Rumpenhorst, and A.R. Stone. 1977. An International scheme for identifying and classifying pathotypes of potato cyst nematodes *Globodera rostochiensis* and *G. pallida*. Nematologica 23:333-339.

27.   Llontop, J.A. 1988. Variabilidad del nematodo quiste de la papa (*Globodera* spp.) en la zona Andina del departamento de la Libertad, Peru. M.S. thesis, Universidad Nacional Agraria, La Molina, Peru. 119 p.

28.   Mai, W.F., B.B. Brodie, M.B. Harrison, and P. Jatala. 1981. Nematodes, pages 93-101. Compendium of Potato Diseases, [W.J. Hooker (ed.)] American Phytopathological Society, St. Paul, Minnesota.

29.   Mian, I.H., and R. Rodriguez-Kabana. 1982. Soil ammendments with oil cakes and chicken litter for control of *Meloidogyne arenaria*. Nematropica 12:205-220.

30.   Mian, I.H., and R. Rodriguez-Kabana. 1982. Organic ammendments with high tannin and phenolic contents for control of *Meloidogyne arenaria* in infested soil. Nematropica 12:221-234.

31.   Olthof, T.H.A., and J.W. Potter. 1972. Relationship between population densities of *Meloidogyne hapla* and crop losses in summer-maturing vegetables in Ontario. Phytopathology 62:981-86.

32.   Oteifa, B.A., and K.A. Diab. 1961. Significance of potassium fertilization in nematode infested cotton fields. Plant Dis. Reptr. 45:932.

33.   Powell, N.T. 1971. Interaction between nematodes and fungi in disease complexes. Ann. Rev. Phytopathol. 9:253-74.

34.   Rodriguez-Kabana, R., and P.S. King. 1980. Use of mixtures of urea and blackstrap molasses for control of root-knot nematodes in soil. Nematropica 10:38-44.

35.   Rodriguez-Kabana, R.G. Morgan-Jones, and I. Chet. 1987. Biological control of nematodes; soil ammendments and microbial antagonists. Plant and Soil 100:237-247.

36.   Scott, G., S. Wiersema, and P.I. Ferguson (eds.). 1992. Product development for root and tuber crops. Vol.I-Asia. Proceeding of the International Workshop, Sponsored by the International Potato Center (CIP), the Centro Internacional de Agricultura Tropical (CIAT), and the International Institute for Tropical Agriculture (IITA). CIP, Lima, Peru, 384 p.

37.   Spiegel, Y., I. Chet, and E. Cohn. 1985. Use of chitin for controlling plant parasitic nematodes. II. Mode of action. Plant and Soil 98:337-345.

38.   Stegemann, H., and D. Schinck. 1985. Index 1985 of European potato varieties. National registers, characteristics, genetic data. Mitteilungen aus Biologischen Bundesanstalt fur Land-und Forstwirtschaft. Berlin-Dahlem. 227 p.

39.   Taylor, C.E. 1971. Nematodes as vectors of plant viruses, pages 185-211 in Plant Parasitic Nematodes. B.M. Zuckerman, W.F. Mai, and R.A. Rohde (eds.), V. Academic, New York, 345 p.

40.   Taylor, C.E., and J.N. Sasser. 1978. Biology, identification and control of root-knot nematodes (*Meloidogyne* species) International Meloidogyne Project. North Carolina State University Graphics, Raleigh, 111 p.

41.   Thorne, G., and M.L. Schuster. 1956. *Nacobbus batatiformis* n. sp.(Nematoda: Tylenchida), producing galls on the root of sugar beets and other plants. Proc. Helminthol. Soc. Washington 23:128-134.

42.   Wallace, H.R. 1973. Nematode ecology and plant disease. Edward Arnold, London. 228 p.

43.	Winslow, R.D. 1978. An overview of the important nematode pests of potato. Development in control of nematode pests of potato, pages 16-30 in Report of the 2nd Nematode Planning Conference. International Potato Center, Lima, Peru.

PART VI

Pesticide Resistance and Resistance Management

STRATEGIES FOR THE MANAGEMENT OF INSECT RESISTANCE TO SYNTHETIC AND MICROBIAL INSECTICIDES

Richard T. Roush and Ward M. Tingey
Department of Entomology, Comstock Hall,
Cornell University, Ithaca, NY 14853-0999 USA

Potato insect pests feature prominently in the insecticide resistance literature (5,6). Resistance in the peach-potato aphid, *Myzus persicae*, has played a major role in our understanding of insecticide resistance mechanisms (3), whereas the Colorado potato beetle (CPB) is frequently cited as a stunning example of the speed and extent to which resistance can evolve. Recently on Long Island, New York, for example, where all registered classical insecticides have failed, the principal methods for control of CPB are the use of propane flame machines against adults and an inorganic insecticide (cryolite, or sodium fluoaluminate) against the larvae. The propane flamers have proven to be cost effective compared to insecticides, but can only be used against overwintering adults and their eggs until the plants are about 12-15 cm tall (15). Among the major insect pests of potatoes in the United States, only the polyphagous and highly migratory potato leafhopper, *Empoasca fabae* (Harris), remains susceptible to all insecticides.

The purpose of this paper is to suggest ways to avoid worsening the resistance problems in insect pests of potato. For the sake of brevity, we will concentrate on the CPB with only a few remarks about the peach-potato aphid, but the principles discussed here should prove useful for the management of other potato pests that have shown resistance.

The causes of high selection pressure for resistance in the CPB appear to include: (a) capacity for rapid population growth which, if unchecked by other means, requires frequent pesticide applications; (b) high fraction of the population being treated each generation (due to the relative scarcity of populations on untreated alternative host plants) ; (c) selection across all active life stages; (d) the existence of a single mechanism capable of causing broad cross-resistance; and (e) the use of soil insecticides, which are relatively more persistent than foliar insecticides, therefore selecting for resistance for a relatively longer time, and show cross-resistance with foliar insecticides (23). Similar features appear to accelerate selection for resistance in the peach-potato aphid.

Clearly, any plan to manage resistance in these pests must reduce the impact of these factors. Fortunately, there are several options for both potato beetles and aphids that can integrate resistance management with good crop management and also meet societal goals for reduced pesticide use. As discussed in the rest of this chapter, these include: (a) crop rotation and flame technology to reduce early season population densities of CPB without insecticide use; (b) use of border sprays, especially in concert with a host plant "trap", that can allow a portion of the CPB population to escape exposure; (c) scouting and rigorous use of economic thresholds to avoid insecticide applications that will not increase profits; (d) alternation of insecticides to reduce dependence on any one chemistry and to avoid selection for any one resistance gene across several life stages of the CPB; (e) replacement of soil insecticides that can select for resistance on CPB with non-selecting soil or foliar insecticides or other alternative controls; (f) use of insecticides that confer only low levels of resistance; and (g) coordination of pesticide use patterns to preserve beneficial predators, parasites, and insect pathogens.

Non-Insecticidal Control of Colorado Potato Beetle: Crop Rotation and Flame Technology

One of the most effective resistance management strategies for any pest is to reduce the number of insecticide applications used (20). For pests with potential for very rapid population growth, like CPB, this generally requires alternative non-pesticidal controls to keep populations below damaging levels. In the case of the CPB, a readily applied and very effective control tactic is crop rotation, perhaps the most important single feature of any attempt to manage resistance in the CPB. The CPB tends to disperse relatively slowly, at least in the spring. Thus, rotation of potatoes with non-solanaceous crops delays colonization by CPB adults, which allows the crop to grow to a less sensitive stage, and reduces the total density of overwintered adults that find the crop (13, 35). Where rotation is practiced rigorously, the number of insecticide applications and frequencies of insecticide-resistant individuals are less than where rotation is not used or used only on a small scale (24). In rotations where potatoes are planted at least 2 km from the previous years crop, insecticide applications are often not needed for CPB (unpublished observations). Rotations with maize seem especially useful for enhancing the abundance of natural enemies in potatoes, as discussed later in this chapter.

Another non-insecticidal control for the CPB is the use of heat, in the form of tractor-mounted propane flame burners, to kill overwintered adult beetles when they first come to the field in the spring (15). Normally constructed for 4 rows, these devices can kill 90% of adult CPB under ideal weather and crop conditions (usually between 10 AM and 3 PM on warm days such that the adult beetles are up on the plants rather than in cracks in the soil, with relatively little wind to blow the heat away from the rows, and when the plants are less than 15 cm tall), at application speeds of 10 kilometers per hour (kph; 6 miles per hour [mph]), at a cost of about $17 per hectare ($7 per acre). This is less expensive than most insecticides, especially where insecticide resistance is present.

The use of propane flamers is enhanced by crop rotation. Even where crop rotation is only between adjacent fields, the heaviest CPB infestations are generally closest to previous year's potato fields and surrounding hedge rows. In the first few weeks after crop emergence, CPB densities tend to be highest within the first 10 rows (roughly 10 meters) along the edge of the potato field (Fig. 1). Especially as weather conditions are not always ideal and flamers cannot cover as much area as rapidly as commercial insecticide spray rigs (often as many as 30 rows per pass at speeds of 20 kph [12 mph]), concentrating the beetles by crop rotation greatly diminishes the area across which control must be applied.

Creating Untreated Rafuges for Susceptible CPB: Border Sprays and Trap Crops

The relatively limited early season dispersal of CPB also encourages the use of border sprays, which allow the remaining area of the field to become a refuge for susceptible CPB. Even though most overwintered CPB appear to be arrested by the first potato plants encountered during their dispersal into a field, at least 10% of the population disperses beyond the first 10-15 meters targeted in border sprays (Fig. 1). Border sprays are readily practiced and widely adopted by growers. Although it has not yet been directly demonstrated that border sprays help to manage resistance, the availability of untreated refuges appears to be a major factor for delaying resistance in many pest species (21).

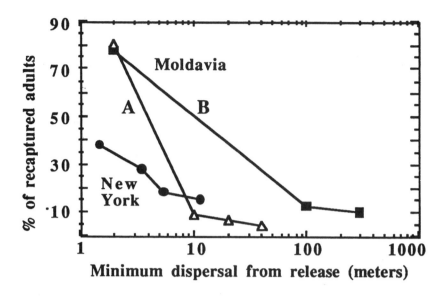

Fig. 1. Minimum distance between release and recapture of adult CPB in mark-release studies in Moldavia (previously Soviet Union, from [1]), and New York (23). For Moldavia, "A" and "B" refer to dispersal after and before oviposition started to occur, respectively.

The border approach may be made even more effective by planting a "trap crop" of early emerging potatoes along the edge of the field. In a trial in 1991, pre-sprouted potatoes were planted by hand, and emerged approximately 7 days earlier than the crop field (Fig. 2). Even though the trap consisted of only a small area compared to the total field, adult CPB were concentrated in the trap, where they were controlled by insecticide applications (Fig. 3). Although this approach limited the total amount of insecticide applied, its greatest potential for resistance management is that it can facilitate the use of flame technology as a non-insecticidal control. The limiting factor for the adoption of this technique is equipment to plant "no till" potatoes. Nevertheless, a number of growers have shown interest in exploiting this tactic in New York, and, according to a trade journal report, it has been applied in Michigan.

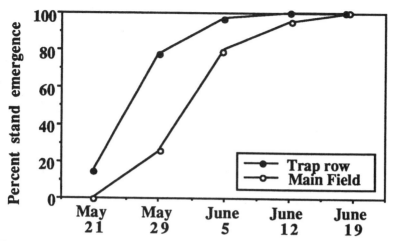

Fig. 2. Emergence of early-planted trap potatoes in contrast with plants in an adjacent, commercially planted field.

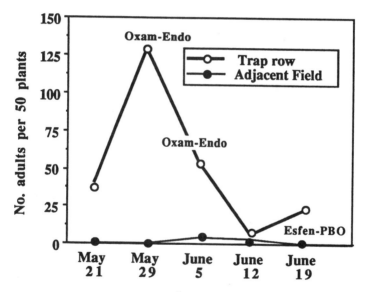

Fig. 3. Efficacy of a one row "trap strip" of early planted potatoes (Fig. 2) in arresting dispersal of CPB adults. The trap row was planted in the spring of 1991 along the edge of the field planted to potatoes 1990 and 10 m from the edge of the 1991 field. CPB densities are given for the trap strip and the adjacent three rows of the 4 ha 1991 potato field. Pesticide applications (a mixture of oxamyl and endosulfan or esfenvalerate and piperonyl butoxide) were applied to the trap row on the dates indicated.

Field Scouting and Use of Economic Thresholds

Another obvious way to reduce the number of insecticide applications is to use them only when absolutely needed. With a relatively high value crop such as potatoes, growers often look upon pesticide applications as relatively cheap insurance because the cost of any single application is only a few percent of the value of the crop. However, this simple calculation does not account for all of the costs of the application. When a pesticide is applied against pest densities lower than the economic threshold, the grower is actually buying pesticide resistance while obtaining no economic benefit, not even over the short term. Further, as insecticides used for one pest can select for resistance in others that were not targeted, as discussed below, it is important to follow thresholds for all pests in the complex, even those that do not currently show resistance such as leafhoppers. Thus, careful application of economic thresholds for all insect pests of potatoes is a key to effective resistance management and is consistent with public demands for reduced pesticide use.

Insecticide Alternation

Given two insecticides that do not show cross-resistance, one could use them in mixtures, or could alternate them in different weeks or across different generations. Simple computer simulation models demonstrate that alternation across generations is never worse than and is often much better than alternation within generations or use of mixtures (20). Field and laboratory experiments are either ambiguous or support alternation (12, 34). The fundamental problem with either mixtures or alternation within a generation is that both approaches may expose the same individuals to selection with both compounds at doses that do not necessarily kill all individuals susceptible to either one alone, thus selecting for resistance to both compounds simultaneously. In choosing the optimal alternation scheme, we considered several factors, including the effects on beneficial predators and the patterns of cross-resistance between the candidate insecticides. To evaluate cross-resistance, we used the procedure of repeated backcrossing to isolate individual resistance genes (reviewed in 22). Separate family lines were selected with carbofuran, phosmet, or endosulfan every second generation at a dose that was just sufficient to kill about 95% of the susceptible beetles. In addition to the patterns of cross-resistance that would have been predicted from studies of resistance mechanisms (reviewed by Clark and Argentine in this volume), a single gene, apparently controlling a microsomal oxidase (as indicated by [at least 4-

fold] synergism with piperonyl butoxide), confers broad cross-resistance to a wide range of compounds (Table 1). It is one of two genes that contribute to resistance to endosulfan (the other being one that confers resistance to dieldrin and appears to be due to cyclodiene insensitivity). This major gene even confers about 3X resistance to pyrethroids, but apparently not to oxamyl. Although resistance to oxamyl is widespread, the mechanism(s) of resistance is unknown, although an altered acetylcholinesterase(33) is suspected. Thus, there are really only two groups of classical insecticides that consistently show little within-group cross-resistance in the CPB: (I) the pyrethroids, especially when applied in a mixture with the synergist piperonyl butoxide, and (II) organophosphates, carbamates, and endosulfan. Of these, only the pyrethroids and a mixture of oxamyl and endosulfan are generally effective in those areas of New York where classical insecticides are even marginally effective (24). In addition, novel insecticidal endotoxins produced by *Bacillus thuringiensis tenebrionis* (*Bt*) are effective against small (first and second instar) CPB larvae (4, 36) and the inorganic stomach poison cryolite (sodium fluoaluminate) is effective against both early and later larval instars. Both are very selective in the potato ecosystem, apparently suppressing only the CPB. Although we have not detected any resistance against cryolite in recent monitoring efforts, resistance to *Bt* has been reported from an intensively-selected laboratory population of the CPB (Whalon, et al., this volume).

Table 1. Resistance ratios (LD_{50} for the resistant strain divided by the LD_{50} of the susceptible strain, as measured by topical assays on adults) in strains repeatedly backcrossed to a North Carolina susceptible strain and selected only with the insecticide indicated (Carbo=carbofuran, Endo=Endosulfan, Phos=phosmet).

Insecticide tested	Insecticide used in strain selection		
	Carbo	**Endo**	**Phos**
Carbofuran	505	94	45
Parathion	208	199	---
Azinphosmethyl	40	27	---
Endosulfan	15	59	---
DDT	21	5	---
Phosmet	8	7	6
Fenvalerate	2.5	3	---

Perhaps the most important goal for any resistance management program on potatoes is to preserve the effectiveness of insecticides for control of adult CPB when all other control tactics have failed. Even where there is severe resistance to classical insecticides, the stomach poisons *Bt* and cryolite can be used against larvae, but neither are useful for control of adults, which can be severely damaging to the crop. Selection against the larvae is probably even stronger than against the adults because selection against the larvae occurs before mating. At least with adults, mated females provide a refuge for susceptible genes in any sperm they carry from matings previous to the pesticide spray. Thus, it is important to avoid selection with insecticides that are effective against the adults when there are other options for the control of the larvae.

The most practical way to achieve this is to use *Bt* and cryolite whenever possible. Further, as *Bt* resistance has already been described from CPB, it is also important to avoid its overuse by alternating with cryolite, a compound for which we have been unable to find resistance, and which, as a stomach poison, appears to be very selective. As the currently registered *Bt*'s are most effective only against small larvae (36), and even then under conditions of warm, dry weather (which encourage consumption of foliage by the larvae without wash off of the residues), the best time to use *Bt* is when there is a uniform cohort of hatching larvae, which usually only occurs at the beginning of the season (37). The obvious role for cryolite, which can control larger larvae, is to manage larval populations that escaped adequate control by *Bt*. We recognize that there may still be occasions when a chemical insecticide is needed. In greenhouse tests, we have found endosulfan to be effective against CPB larvae (especially small larvae), even when used alone on resistant strains; coupled with its selectivity in favor of the beneficial species found in potatoes (as discussed below), this may make endosulfan the compound of choice where both cryolite and *Bt* are inadequate (due to heavy CPB densities or poor weather) for control of larvae.

This leaves the question of optimal use of the classical insecticides, which we reserve primarily as adulticides. Pyrethroids are somewhat more effective under cooler than warmer temperatures (8), which would predispose them toward use at the beginning of the season. A preference for early season use of the pyrethroids is also consistent with avoiding mortality of beneficial predators and parasites of potato pests and avoiding resistance in aphids, as discussed later in this chapter. Thus, where two generations of adult CPB must be controlled in the same season in New York, we recommend the use of pyrethroids (applied with piperonyl butoxide) in the early season and all other insecticides in the late season. Where only one generation per year must be treated, these two groups of insecticides should be used in alternate years. As noted above, pesticide mixtures should be avoided unless absolutely necessary for control. Therefore, in areas where CPB is more susceptible to insecticides than in New York, all effective insecticides should be alternated by categories of potential resistance mechanisms (Table 2) rather than mixed.

Table 2. Provisional grouping of some insecticides used for CPB control on the basis of actual or potential cross-resistance. Headings indicate documented or presumed resistance mechanisms (mfo: microsomal oxidases; AChE: acetylcholinesterase). Compounds are listed in approximately decreasing order of preference on the basis of resistance management, efficacy, and minimal impacts on beneficials. Not all compounds available for use in all jurisdictions; consult local regulatory authorities.

MFO/, Altered AChE/ esterases	Altered Na channel ("kdr")	Cyclodiene receptor
oxamyl	esfenvalerate	endosulfan
endosulfan	fenvalerate	
azinphosmethyl	permethrin	
phosmet		
phorate		
parathion		
carbofuran		

A different approach to achieve alternation might be that the grower could determine which pesticide was likely to be most effective through a simple bioassay technique (11, Kennedy and French, this volume) and use only that pesticide for the next CPB generation or season. However, many growers cannot seem to find time to monitor for resistance; we therefore recommend an alternation program that will work in most fields.

Insecticide alternation can be most effective in managing resistance when there are fitness disadvantages to the resistance genes (20). Although such disadvantages have not been specifically identified for CPB, they have been described for kdr-type and cyclodiene resistances in other pest species (18, 25). In our laboratory strains, resistance to carbofuran and azinphosmethyl (due to the presumed microsomal oxidase) appears to decline in the absence of continued selection.

Soil Insecticides

It has long been recognized in the pesticide resistance management literature that persistent pesticides and formulations generally select for resistance more strongly than less persistent ones because selection continues for a longer period of time, and generally long after the pest population has been suppressed below an economically damaging level (20). In a sense, persistent formulations continue to select for resistance even though there is no longer any significant economic benefit. Even though soil-applied formulations of carbofuran are no longer registered for potatoes in the United States, carbofuran provides an excellent example for comparing soil and foliar insecticide formulations because both were previously available. When susceptible first and second instar larvae were placed on plants treated with carbofuran granules (at planting) or sprays, the soil insecticide caused significant mortality for up to three weeks, compared to only one week for the foliar application (Fig. 4). Carbofuran also shows strong cross-resistance with several other insecticides (Table 1); therefore, the effectiveness of foliar insecticides can be dramatically reduced by the use of soil insecticides. Another soil insecticide, phorate, also shows cross-resistance to several foliar insecticides in the CPB (larvae of the strains shown in Table 1 suffer less than 50% mortality when placed on treated plants, compared to 100% mortality of larvae from the susceptible strain) and a similar duration of selection. In contrast, a third soil insecticide, disulfoton, caused little or no mortality of even susceptible CPB larvae, and thus probably does not select for resistance in the CPB.

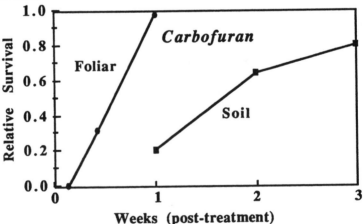

Fig. 4. Effect of carbofuran in soil and foliar formulations on the survival (corrected for control mortality) of North Carolina susceptible first instar CPB larvae.

At least in New York, neither carbofuran nor phorate are effective in control of CPB because insecticide resistance (presumably due to the major microsomal oxidase gene) is so widespread. However, some growers have used phorate for control of leafhoppers and aphids, even though it is not always effective, and thus continued to select for resistance in the CPB, counteracting any fitness disadvantages that might otherwise cause the resistance gene(s) to decline in frequency. Given the implications for resistance management (and continuing environmental concerns about ground water contamination from soil insecticides), we compared three foliar insecticides (dimethoate, parathion, and methamidophos; the latter used at half the maximum labeled rate) with three soil insecticides (phorate, disulfoton, and carbofuran) on seven farms in 1990 and one farm in 1991. Phorate usually provided excellent control of leafhoppers, although disulfoton appeared to be more effective for aphids. However, all of the foliar insecticides proved to be as effective and less costly, when applications were based on careful scouting, than soil insecticides for the control of leafhoppers. In addition, methamidophos provided excellent control of aphids.

Cross-resistance to methamidophos in the CPB is weak. Methamidophos is not effective for control of CPB in the field and, in greenhouse trials on sprayed foliage, methamidophos killed only early instar larvae of a fully susceptible strain. In contrast, methamidophos is the most effective foliar insecticide available against aphids and leafhoppers in New York. Further, because leafhoppers generally disperse into fields near the end of the first larval generation, small CPB larvae are generally not present in the fields at the time leafhopper applications must be made; thus, methamidophos is not likely to select strongly for resistance in CPB when used for leafhopper or aphid control. The soil insecticide disulfoton appears to cause little or no mortality even of susceptible CPB; thus, where a soil insecticide is needed, disulfoton may be preferred to phorate, which can kill susceptible CPB larvae and select for cross-resistance to other insecticides. However, even the use of disulfoton should be considered carefully. Although it may not select for resistance in the CPB, it may still select for resistance in aphids, against which it was once highly effective.

In the long term, a more desirable solution for the control of CPB, aphids and especially leafhoppers, for which there appear to be no other non-insecticidal controls, is the development of resistant potato varieties, which are nearing commercial feasibility (Tingey and Yencho, this volume).

Use of Insecticides that Confer Only
Low Levels of Resistance

Within any given group of insecticides that demonstrates cross-resistance, there are generally some compounds that confer very high levels of resistance, and thereby select for resistance quite strongly, and others that confer only low levels of resistance. In the CPB for example, carbofuran and parathion show very high levels of resistance compared with azinphosmethyl (Table 1), which suggests that azinphosmethyl should be preferred for resistance management purposes (Table 2).

Although most of our management program has been designed around CPB, resistance management in aphids is also a concern, especially in seed potato production due to virus transmission. Although we have not studied resistance in aphids, the mechanism of resistance in British populations seems relevant. In those aphids, levels of resistance from the amplified esterase mechanism are very high for dimethoate and pyrethroids (and probably for parathion), but low (2 fold) for acephate (26, 27). In at least some insects, acephate is metabolized to methamidophos (19). Based on the fact that methamidophos is the only registered compound that continues to provide consistent control of *Myzus persicae* in New York, we suspect that the British and New York aphids possess a similar resistance mechanism. Thus, methamidophos appears to be the preferred option for combined leafhopper and aphid control.

Preserving Beneficial Predators, Parasites,
and Insect Pathogens

As noted above, one of the most effective resistance management strategies for any pest is to reduce the number of insecticide applications through the use of alternative non-pesticidal controls, which include predators, parasites, and insect pathogens. Before deciding how to preserve these natural enemies, it is necessary to determine which ones are most important and why.

In the case of aphids, susceptibility to natural enemies is a significant weakness. The usefulness of parasitoids for control of aphids has not been as well documented in potatoes as in other crops but predators appear to be very important (17). However, in Maine, entomophagous fungi, not predators and parasites, appeared to be an important source of mortality (28-32). On the seven New York commercial farms studied in 1990, processing potatoes that did not receive mid- to late-season applications of foliar insecticides had abundant populations of at least three species of parasitic Hymenoptera and two species of lady beetles, especially *Coleomegilla maculata* DeGeer, and sub-economic populations of aphids. In contrast, plots that received foliar applications of insecticides (other than methamidophos, which is very effective in suppressing *Myzus persicae* (Sulzer) independent of natural enemies, as discussed above), suffered significantly larger populations of aphids (predominately *Myzus*). Under moist weather conditions, entomophagous fungi also caused significant mortality. Similar conditions may exist in other potato producing areas. Thus, with the exception of fields grown for seed potatoes, natural enemies may be sufficient to keep aphid populations below economic thresholds under some conditions.

In contrast, the practical significance of natural enemies for the control of the CPB is likely to remain a matter of controversy. There are many such enemies, including the predators *Podisus maculiventris* (Say), *Perillus bioculatus* F., *Lebia grandis* Hentz, and *C. maculata* and the tachinid parasites *Myiopharus aberrans* (Townsend) and *M. doryphorae* (Riley) (7,9,10, Ferro, this volume). At least in New York, only *C. maculata* appears to be present in potato fields in sufficient densities at the beginning of the season to make any significant contribution to control of CPB. Further, we suspect that the relative ineffectiveness of *P. maculiventris*, *P. bioculatus*, and *L. grandis* is not limited to New York; all three species were established in Europe during the 1930's with no apparent benefits for control of CPB (2).

Even *C. maculata* seems to be of limited effectiveness against CPB in New York. We have not found any case where *C. maculata* saved even a single insecticide application against CPB. This predator will eat a large number of egg masses, but does not seem to consume enough to keep CPB larvae below damaging densities. At least one of the problems in western New York seems to be that *C. maculata* prefers aphids in oats, which are an important rotational crop with potatoes. *C. maculata* is common in oats throughout May and June, often at densities of one per square meter, generally higher than in potatoes. A preference for aphids in oats was also demonstrated in laboratory tests. In one meter cubic cages in the greenhouse, we introduced 15 cm tall oat seedlings and 15 cm tall potatoes in pots. The oats were lightly infested with oat bird-cherry aphids (*Rhopalosiphum padi* L., about ten per six inch diameter pot). The potatoes were infested heavily with potato beetle egg masses (5-10 per pot as laid on the plants by adults). In eight replicates of five lady beetles each, the densities of *C. maculata* on the oats always exceeded those on potatoes by an average of an eight to one margin. We speculate that in the field, *C. maculata* wanders by flight in search of food and is arrested in oats by its preference for aphids. *C. maculata* may be more effective against CPB in maize-potato rotations, because there are few aphids in maize in May and June to draw *C. maculata* from potatoes and because the predators seem to reproduce very effectively on maize in late summer, feeding on both aphids and pollen.

C. maculata by itself seems unlikely to suppress CPB densities sufficiently that pesticide applications can be avoided under our conditions. However, it appears to be a more significant predator of aphids on potatoes in the latter part of the season. Thus, the optimal way to use *C. maculata* is to avoid the late season application of the insecticides that are most toxic to it.

We have tested the toxicity to *C. maculata* of nearly all of the insecticides used on potatoes in New York by caging the adults (the life stage most commonly found in potatoes) on sprayed plants in the greenhouse (Figs. 5A, 5B). Endosulfan, oxamyl, endosulfan-oxamyl and even methamidophos allowed significant survival of the beetles, especially when the residues were more than a day or two old. In contrast, the pyrethroid esfenvalerate, especially when mixed with piperonyl butoxide, was the most toxic insecticide tested against *C. maculata*. Thus, both for reasons of efficacy and effects on beneficials, the optimal time for pyrethroid use when thresholds have been exceeded is in the early season, which reserves endosulfan-oxamyl for control of adults in the second (summer) generation. Endosulfan also appears relatively non-toxic to aphid parasites (28). Consistent with a preference for efficacious control of aphids and leafhoppers, methamidophos is the least toxic to lady beetles of the foliar insecticides targeted against aphids and leafhoppers, described above. Finally, the use of selective rather than broad spectrum fungicides for management of disease in potatoes may enhance entomophagous fungi antagonisitic to aphids and the Colorado potato beetle (14,16).

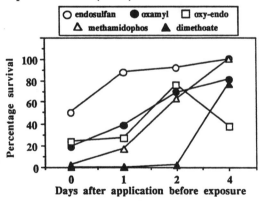

Figure 5A.

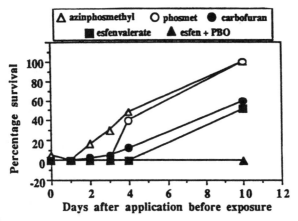

Figure 5B.

Figures 5A & 5B. Toxicity of insecticide residues over time to *C. maculata* when caged on treated plants in the greenhouse. Pesticides sprayed on the plants at minimum labeled rates; "oxy-endo" and "esfen+PBO" are mixtures of oxamyl with endosulfan and esfenvalerate with piperonyl butoxide, respectively.

Epilogue

Recommendations for pest management and resistance management may be integrated for the Colorado potato beetle, aphids and leafhoppers in a way that is consistent with public concerns for reduced pesticide use. Working with Cooperative Extension, we are currently implementing the program summarized here. Our next goal is to integrate resistant plant varieties which will further reduce the need for chemical insecticides for control of CPB, aphids and leafhoppers.

Acknowledgment

We thank Nada Carruthers and Patti Beckley for technical assistance with most of the work described here, Dr. George Kennedy of North Carolina State University for providing the North Carolina susceptible strain of CPB, and Dr. Don Vacek, USDA Mission Biological Control Laboratory, Mission, Texas for supplying most of the *Coleomegilla maculata* used in our bioassays, and M. J. Tauber, C.A. Tauber, and J. G. Scott for advice. This research was supported in part by the USDA Northeast Regional IPM program, the National Potato Council Research Initiative, and the Cornell IPM program, a part of the Cornell University Agricultural Experiment Station, New York State College of Agricultural and Life Sciences.

Literature Cited

1. Chigarev, G. A., and V. A. Molchanova. 1967. Application of radio-active labeling method in studying the efficiency of spring potato survey and spreading of over-wintered Colorado beetles. Trudy Vsesoyuznogo Instit. Zashchity Rastenil 27: 75-81.

2. Clausen, C. P. (ed.). 1978. Introduced Parasites and Predators of Arthropod Pests and Weeds: A World Review. Agricultural Handbook No. 480. ARS, USDA.

3. Devonshire, A. L., and L. M. Field. 1991. Gene amplification and insecticide resistance. Annu. Rev. Entomol. 36:1-23.

4. Ferro, D. N., and W. D. Gelernter. 1989. Toxicity of a new strain of *Bacillus thuringiensis* to Colorado potato beetle (Coleoptera: Chrysomelidae). J. Econ. Entomol. 82: 750-755.

5. Forgash, A. J. 1984. History, evolution, and consequences of insecticide resistance. Pestic. Biochem. Physiol. 22: 178-186.

6. Georghiou, G. P. 1986. The magnitude of the resistance problem, pp.14-43. *In* National Academy of Sciences (ed.), Pesticide resistance: strategies and tactics for management. National Academy Press: Washington, D.C.

7. Gollands, B., M. J. Tauber, and C. A. Tauber. 1991. Seasonal cycles of *Myiopharus aberrans* and *M. doryphorae* (Diptera: Tachinididae) parasitizing Colorado potato beetles in upstate New York. Biol. Con. 1: 153-163.

8. Grafius, E. 1986. Effects of temperature on pyrethroid toxicity to Colorado potato beetle (Coleoptera: Chrysomelidae). J. Econ. Entomol. 79: 588-591.

9. Groden, E., F. A. Drummond, R. A. Casagrande, and D. L. Haynes. 1990. *Coleomegilla maculata* (Coleoptera: Coccinellidae): its predation upon the Colorado potato beetle (Coleoptera: Chrysomelidae) and its incidence in potatoes and surrounding crops.. J. Econ. Entomol. 83: 1306-1315.

10. Hazard, R. V., D. N. Ferro, R. G. van Driesche, and A. F. Tuttle. 1991. Mortality of eggs of the Colorado potato beetle (Coleoptera: Chrysomelidae) from predation by *Coleomegilla maculata* (Coleoptera: Coccinellidae). Environ. Entomol. 20: 841-848.

11. Heim, D. C., G. G. Kennedy, and J. W. van Duyn. 1990. Survey of insecticide resistance among North Carolina Colorado potato beetle (Coleoptera: Chrysomelidae) populations. J. Econ. Entomol. 83: 698-705.

12. Immaraju, J. A., J. G. Morse, and R.F. Hobza. 1989. Field evaluation of insecticide rotation and mixtures using formetanate and fluvalinate as strategies for citrus thrips (Thysanoptera: Thripidae) resistance management in California. J. Econ. Entomol. 83: 698-704.

13. Lashomb, J. H., and Y. S. Ng. 1984. Colonization by Colorado potato beetle, *Leptinotarsa decemlineata* (Say) (Coleoptera: Chrysomelidae), in rotated and non-rotated potato fields. Environ. Entomol. 13: 1352-1356.

14. Loria, R., S. Galaini, and D. W. Roberts. 1983. Survival of inoculum of the entomopathogenic fungus *Beauveria bassiana* as influenced by fungicides. Environ. Entomol. 12:1724-1726.

15. Moyer, D., R. Kujawski, R. Derksen, R. Moeller, J. B. Sieczka, and W. M. Tingey. 1991. Development of a propane flamer for Colorado potato beetle control. Mimeo (also on videotape), Cornell Cooperative Extension, Suffolk County. Riverhead, New York .

16. Nanne, H. W. and E. B. Radcliffe. 1971. Green peach aphid population on potatoes enchanced by fungicides. J. Econ. Entomol. 64: 1569-1570.

17. Obrycki, J. J., M. J. Tauber, and W. M. Tingey. 1983. Predator and parasitoid interaction with aphid-resistant potatoes to reduce aphid densities: a two-year field study, J. Econ. Entomol. 76: 456-462.

18. Plapp, Frederick W., Jr., C. Campanhola, R. D. Bagwell, and B. F. McCutcheon. 1990.   Management of pyethroid-resistant tobacco budworms on cotton in the United States   237-260 In Pesticide Resistance in Arthropods, Roush, R. T., and Tabashnik, B. E., (eds.), Chapman and Hall, New York.

19. Rose, R. L., and T. C. Sparks. 1984. Acephate toxicity, metabolism, and anticholinesterase activity in *Heliothis virescens* (F.) and *Anthonomous grandis* Boheman. Pest. Biochem. Physiol. 22: 69-77.

20. Roush, R. T. 1989. Designing resistance management programs: How can you choose ? Pest. Sci.26: 423-441.

21. Roush, R.T., and B.A. Croft. 1986. Experimental population genetics and ecological studies of pesticide resistance in insects and mites, pp. 257-270. In Pesticide Resistance: Strategies and Tactics for Management, National Research Council, ed. National Academy Press, Washington, D.C.

22. Roush, R. T., and Daly, J. C. 1990. The role of population genetics in resistance research and management, pp. 97-152 In Pesticide resistance in arthropods, Roush, R. T., and Tabashnik, B. E. (eds.), Chapman and Hall, New York.

23. Roush, R. T., and W. M. Tingey. In press. Evolution and management of resistance in the Colorado potato beetle, *Leptinotarsa decemlineata*. In Resistance '91, I. Denholm and T. Dennehy, (eds.), Elsevier, Essex, England.

24. Roush, R. T., C.W. Hoy, D. N. Ferro, and W.M. Tingey. 1990. Insecticide resistance in Colorado potato beetles (Coleoptera:Chrysomelidae): Influence of crop rotation and insecticide use. J. Econ. Entomol. 83 :315-319.

25. Rowland, M. 1991. Activity and mating competitiveness of HCH/dieldrin resistant and susceptible male and virgin female *Anopheles gambiae* and *An. stephensi* mosquitoes, with assessment of an insecticide-rotation strategy. Med. Vet. Entomol. 5: 207-222.

26. Sawicki, R. M., and A.D. Rice. 1978. Response of susceptible and resistant peach-potato aphids *Myzus persicae* (Sulz.) to insecticides in leaf dip bioassays. Pestic. Sci.: 9: 513-516.

27. Sawicki, R. M., A. L. Devonshire, A. D. Rice, G. D. Moores, S. M. Petzing, and A. Cameron. 1978. The detection and distribution of organophosphorous and carbamate insecticide-resistant *Myzus persicae* (Sulz.) in Britain in 1976. Pestic. Sci. 9: 189-201.

28. Shands, W.A., G.W. Simpson, C. F. W. Muesebeck, and H. E. Wave. 1965. Parasites of potato-infesting aphids in northeastern Maine. Maine Agricultural Experiment Station Tech. Bull. T 19, 77 pp.

29. Shands, W.A., G.W. Simpson, and B.A. Simpson. 1975. Evaluation of field introductions of two insect parasites (Hymenoptera: Braconidae) for controlling potato-infesting aphids. Environ. Entomol.: 4: 499-503.

30. Shands, W.A., G. W. Simpson, and C. C. Gordon. 1972. Survey of internal parasites of potato-infesting aphids in northeastern Maine, 1963 through 1969. Maine Agricultural Experiment Station Tech. Bull. No. 60, 16 pp.

31. Shands, W.A., G. W. Simpson, and M. H. Brunson. 1972. Insect predators for controlling aphids on potatoes in small plots. J. Econ. Entomol. 65: 511 - 514.

32. Shands, W.A., W. S. Geddes, H. E. Wave, and C. C. Gordon. 1972. Importance of arthropod predators in controlling aphids on potatoes in northeastern Maine. Maine Agricultural Experimental Station Technical Bulletin, 54, 40 pp.

33. Soderlund, D. M., and Bloomquist, J. R. 1990. Molecular mechanisms of insecticide resistance, pp. 58-96 *In* Pesticide resistance in arthropods, R.T. Roush and B.E. Tabashnik (eds.), Chapman and Hall, New York.

34. Tabashnik, B.E. 1989. Managing resistance with multiple pesticide tactics. J. Econ. Entomol. 82: 1263-1269.

35. Wright, R. J. 1984. Evaluation of crop rotation for control of Colorado potato beetles (Coleoptera: Chrysomelidae) in commercial potato fields on Long Island. J. Econ. Entomol. 77: 1254-1259.

36. Zehnder, G. W., and W. D. Gelernter. 1989. Activity of the M-ONE formulation of a new strain of *Bacillus thuringiensis* against Colorado potato beetle (Coleoptera: Chrysomelidae): relationship between susceptibility and insect life stage. J. Econ. Entomol. 82: 756-761.

37. Zehnder, G. W., G. M. Ghidiu, and J. Speese III. 1992. Use of the occurrence of peak Colorado potato (Coleoptera:Chrysomelidae) egg hatch for timing of *Bacillus thuringiensis* spray applications in potatoes . J. Econ. Entomol. 85: 281-288.

RESISTANCE MANAGEMENT STRATEGIES FOR TRANSGENIC POTATO PLANTS

F. Gould, P. Follett, B. Nault
and G.G. Kennedy
Department of Entomology
North Carolina State University
Raleigh, North Carolina 27695

Rapid progress is being made towards the commercialization of transgenic crop plants expressing foreign genes that confer resistance to important insect pests. As these plants approach commercialization, it is important to develop strategies for deploying them in a manner that minimizes selection for pest adaptations that mitigate the benefits of host-plant resistance. For a variety of reasons that include technical and market considerations, insect-resistant potato is likely to become one of the first transgenic crops to be commercialized. Resistance to insects in these plants is likely to involve expression of a gene from the bacterium *Bacillus thuringiensis* (*Bt*) that codes for a protein that is toxic to major insect pests of potato.

Naturally occurring *Bt* strains possess genes which code for a number of distinct toxic proteins (delta endotoxins) having different spectra of activity against insects. In terms of genetically engineering potato, two classes of toxin genes are important: those coding for toxins active against the Colorado potato beetle (CPB), *Leptinotarsa decemlineata* (Say) (Coleoptera: Chrysomelidae), and those coding for toxins active against lepidopterous pests, such as the potato tuberworm (PTW), *Phthorimaea operculella* (Zeller) (Lepidoptera: Gelechiidae). To date, no single *Bt* toxin has been identified that is effective against both of these pests.

From an economic perspective, the CPB and the PTW are important targets because they are widespread pests of potato and are difficult to control with conventional chemical insecticides. CPB is problematic in many areas because it is resistant to most available insecticides (11, Roush [this volume], Kennedy and French [this volume]), while the potato tuberworm is difficult to control because of its feeding habits (i.e., protected in leaf mines, tubers, and stems) (1,29,30).

The widespread occurrence of insecticide resistance in CPB and the successful selection of CPB for adaptation to a Bt-toxin in the laboratory (Whalon et al., this volume) indicate the very real potential for CPB to adapt to Bt-toxin in the field following widespread commercialization of transgenic potato plants expressing Bt-toxin. We will therefore use this chapter to explore resistance management strategies for CPB. While it is impossible to precisely predict evolutionary events, we will use basic population ecology and population genetics theory to examine approaches to the engineering and deployment of Bt-toxin expressing potato plants that have been suggested to slow the rate of adaptation by CPB and still provide economically acceptable levels of yield protection.

Options in Design and Deployment
of CPB-Resistant Potato

Basic population genetic models that have been adapted for studying the evolution of pesticide resistance (32 and references within) are also useful in designing strategies for development and deployment of genetically engineered crops that express insect-toxin genes.

Five basic strategies have been proposed for the design and deployment of such genetically engineered crops (13,14,27). They are as follows: (1) high level of expression of a single toxin; (2) high expression of multiple toxins; (3) mixtures containing plants expressing toxin(s) and toxin-free plants; (4) low levels of toxin expression coupled with effects of natural enemies; and (5) targeted expression of the toxin gene(s) (including time, tissue, and environmentally restricted expression).

For the purpose of briefly discussing advantages and disadvantages of each strategy, we assume that resistance to each insect toxin is controlled by a single gene with two alleles, one of which (R) confers resistance to that toxin. The goal of strategies (1) and (2) is to minimize survival in individuals carrying single alleles for resistance by making resistance functionally recessive i.e., the toxin is lethal to RS heterozygotes. Strategy (3) attempts to slow resistance by allowing survival of susceptible beetles, thereby reducing the probability of mating between resistant (RR) beetles, while strategies (4) and (5) attempt to decrease the overall selection on the insect pest population.

The theoretical underpinning of all of these strategies is Fisher's fundamental theorem which demonstrates that the rate of change of a trait under direct natural selection is proportional to the population's additive genetic variance for that trait. The greater the additive genetic variance, the faster the trait will change. It is important to note that the rate of increase of resistance alleles due to selection is therefore frequency dependent. When these alleles are at low frequency, they produce relatively little additive genetic variance and evolutionary change is slow (7). It is only at relatively high frequencies of the R allele that a significant fraction of the population of insects have two R alleles for each toxin. Therefore, strategies that succeed in similarly decreasing fitness of all individuals that are not carrying two R alleles for each toxin (i.e., RS and SS individuals) depress the initial additive genetic variance for resistance expression in an insect population and further slow the rate at which the entire population becomes resistant.

In this chapter we do not delve into details of population genetics. Instead, we focus on the predicted utility and farm-level feasibility of various strategies for engineering potato to decrease the rate of beetle evolution (i.e., *Bt* resistance management). We define a strategy for *Bt* resistance management as an approach to the development and/or use of a *Bt*-toxin-containing product that is likely to slow resistance development relative to other approaches. We will confine our discussion to a single type of *Bt* product, engineered plants. For comparison sake we will measure the predicted long term efficacy of each resistance management strategy relative to the case of homogeneous plantings of potato with "moderate" expression of a single Bt toxin that kills 99% of the susceptible beetles, 0% of the totally resistant beetles, and an intermediate percentage of partially resistant heterozygous beetles (Fig. 1 shows the durability of this reference approach).

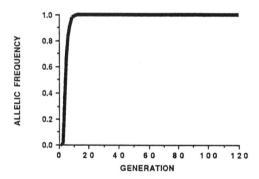

Fig. 1. Rate of resistance development when the initial frequency of resistance alleles is 10^{-5} and the relative fitness of totally susceptible beetles, heterozygous-, and homozygous-resistant beetles are 0.01, 0.505, and 1.0, respectively. This is the case by which other strategies are judged in terms of how much they decrease the rate of resistance development.

Strategy 1: High Levels of Expression
of a Single Toxin

For the purposes of this discussion, we define high expression as a concentration 25 times higher than a concentration that kills 99% of the most vulnerable stage of totally susceptible beetles. We have chosen this concentration because examination of dose response curves for many hybrids between pesticide-resistant and susceptible strains of insects indicates that this relative concentration is likely to kill all or most F_1 hybrids. The tools for attaining high levels of toxin expression throughout the plant are already available, as evidenced by other chapters in this volume. If the only way that beetles can adapt to a single Bt-toxin involves biochemical adaptation based on a functionally recessive, single gene trait (Fig. 2A) or a polygenically inherited trait, this strategy has promise. The planting of homogeneous varieties with high levels of Bt-toxin would certainly be feasible to implement at the farm level and, given the genetic conditions stated above, it could lead to fairly long term utility of the engineered potatoes (Fig. 2A).

The weakness of this strategy is in the genetic assumption of complete functional recessiveness of the resistance trait, i.e., all SS and RS beetles have equal fitness, or, for a multigenic case, all susceptible and "partially" resistant beetles have equal fitness on the Bt plants. Even slight differential mortality among genotypes will compromise the high dose tactic. If 1 in 1000 totally susceptible beetles survive on these plants, while 2 in 1000 beetles with one allele for resistance survive, there would be a severe decrease in the number of generations required for beetle populations to adapt to the toxin (Fig. 2B). Differential mortality might occur if some plants produced a few leaves with lower titers of Bt-toxin at certain times of the year, or, as a result of stressful environmental conditions that decreased the plant's ability to produce high Bt-toxin concentrations.

If a mutant beetle arose with a biochemical change that conferred a high level of resistance (more than 25x) in heterozygous individuals, this high expression strategy would offer even less utility than seen in Fig. 2B. Fortunately, most Bt resistance that has been documented to date is inherited in a fully or partially recessive fashion (8, 19, 25, 31, 33). This evidence decreases concern about the potential for resistance traits with dominant expression. However, it is hard to predict whether or not such a mutation could appear in field populations of CPB which are very large compared to laboratory populations, and therefore would offer more opportunities for rare mutants to arise (also see Whalon et al., in prep.).

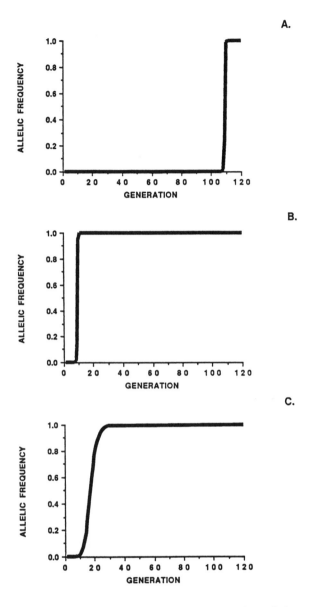

Fig. 2. Effectiveness of high dose and low dose strategies when all plants have a single *Bt* gene. (A) High dose when there is complete recessiveness and fitnesses are as follows: SS, 0.0001; RS, 0.0001; RR, 1.0. (B) High dose when fitnesses are SS, 0.0001; RS, 0.0002; RR, 1.0. (C) Low dose when fitnesses are SS, 0.40; RS, 0.70; RR, 1.0).

The above discussion assumes that the only time beetles encounter *Bt* is in high expression plants. If some companies produce high expression plants and others produce low or moderate expression plants, this strategy is of minimal utility. The same applies if a large number of farmers use normal potatoes and foliar *Bt* sprays.

Strategy 2: High Expression of Multiple Toxins

Until recently there was only one basic type of *Bt*-toxin identified that was active against CPB. However, there are now reports establishing the existence of five or more toxins in the CryIII grouping (M. Adang, Univ. Georgia, personal communication) that have CPB activity. There are some potential non-Bt toxins for CPB such as protease inhibitors and toxic peptides, but their efficacy is as yet unconfirmed.

A number of studies on conventional insecticides (32, for review) indicate that simultaneous use of two insecticides is unlikely to significantly slow resistance under typical field conditions. A major problem brought to light by these studies is that even if high pesticide doses were applied to plants, the pesticide residues would decay over time to intermediate levels. Engineered crops with high constitutive levels of expression may overcome this problem.

If two toxins with distinct modes of action could each be engineered into the same potato plants at high levels relative to CPB tolerance, the rate of beetle adaptation could be decreased considerably. As with high levels of expression of a single toxin, it must be assumed that beetles with a single allele for resistance to one of the two toxins would have survival equal or similar to totally susceptible beetles. Furthermore, even if a beetle had 2 alleles for resistance to one toxin, it is assumed that its survival would be about equal to that of a totally susceptible beetle due to the high toxicity of the second toxin. As long as the initial frequencies of alleles for toxin resistance were low (e.g., 10^{-3}), the fraction of beetles totally resistant to both toxins ($R_1R_1 R_2R_2$) would be incredibly low (10^{-12}). This would result in low additive genetic variance and a slow rate of population level adaptation (see 13).

As with strategy 1, the use of homogeneous cultivars with multiple toxins are useful as long as all of the assumptions are met. If there was complete cross adaptation to the two toxins, the toxins would act as if they were one toxin in terms of resistance development. If each of the single toxin concentrations alone was not high enough to kill most of the beetles, then beetles with incomplete resistance to one toxin would have heightened survival compared to totally susceptible beetles (13). This would increase the rate of adaptation by the beetle population.

Strategy 3: Mixtures of Resistant
and Susceptible Plants

Planting mixtures of two or more isolines or two or more distinct varieties of a crop is not a common practice in most mechanized agricultural systems, but there are exceptions in the U.S. (e.g., corn with drought tolerance in the Midwest, grains with fungus resistance in Oregon), and this practice is more widespread in less mechanized agriculture systems of developing countries. There are a number of problems associated with growing mixtures of potato varieties. Problems include differences in time to harvest and differences in processing qualities of varieties used in the mixture. Isolines that differ in only one or a few specific genetic traits are more amenable to use in mixtures, but these isolines have not been available in potatoes, at least in part because of the nature of the potato breeding process.

The entry of genetic engineering into potato breeding will make development of certain types of potato isolines easier. At least during the initial phases of potato engineering, new plant types will be developed that differ from their parent stock in only one or a few traits, such as the production of Bt-toxin. Therefore, in the near future it will be possible to plant a field with a mixture of seed pieces that differ only in whether or not they carry the *Bt*-toxin gene. Unfortunately, "possible" does not necessarily translate to "feasible" at the farm level. Cutting and mixing seed pieces would be time-consuming and the extra handling prior to planting could increase the incidence of disease. Mixing different potato lines before bagging for shipment to the farmer might be more efficient, but could also pose logistic and certification problems for the seed potato producers.

Another approach for establishing a mixture of resistant and susceptible potato plants is to plant fields with border rows of resistant plants and center rows of susceptible plants. This would require planning by the farmer and would add significant time to the planting operation. On a larger scale, farmers could plant some fields with *Bt*- potatoes and other fields with normal potatoes. This would be the easiest approach for making the general habitat a mixture, but it also has a number of potential drawbacks, as is pointed out in the discussion of spatial scale below.

Another factor in the development of mixtures is the type and strength of resistance in the engineered portion of the mixture. The use of high levels of two or more toxins in the resistant component of the mixture is optimal in many cases, but as with strategies 1 and 2, details regarding the genetics and biology of the beetle will have a strong impact on expectations. Fig. 3 from Gould (15) shows that mixtures with two toxins in one set of plants and no toxins in the other part of the mixture should be less sensitive to a lack of perfect recessiveness than use of pure lines with all plants having two toxins.

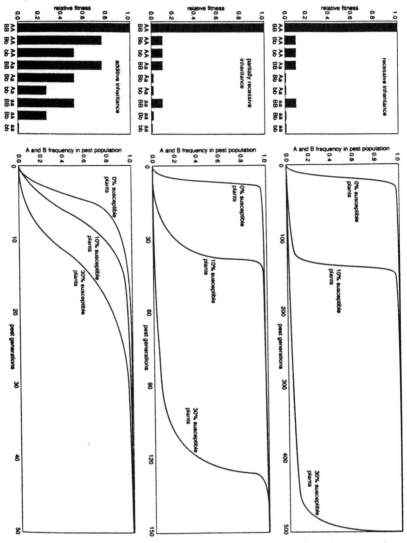

Fig. 3. Simulations examined a pest species with two genetic loci for resistance to plant-produced toxins; the A and B alleles confer resistance, whereas the a and b alleles do not. The effect of selection pressure is most dramatic when resistance is inherited as a recessive trait (top). In this case, only the AABB genotype has high fitness when the pest must live on a host plant that produces both toxins. (All the genotypes are equally fit when the host plant has no defensive toxins.) If the simulated pests are exposed exclusively to toxin-producing plants, resistance emerges quickly; within about 30 pest generations the frequency of the A and B alleles goes from near 0 to near 1. Adding just 10 percent susceptible plants delays the development of resistance for almost 150

generations, and with 30 percent susceptible plants the resistant pests do not dominate the population until after 500 generations. The benefits of reduced selection pressure are smaller but still significant when resistance in the pest is inherited as a partially recessive trait (middle). In this case, when individuals with a single A or a single B allele feed on plants expressing both toxins, their fitness is slightly higher than the fitness of aabb individuals (0.02 versus 0.01). If the pests feed exclusively on toxin-producing plants, the population becomes resistant in fewer than 10 generations. A 30-percent admixture of susceptible plants delays the onset of resistance until about generation 120. If resistance to the toxins is an additive trait, so that each A or B allele contributes incrementally to fitness on toxin-producing plants, the advantage of adding susceptible plants decreases further but is not completely lost (bottom). Note that the three graphs have different horizontal scales. In all cases the initial frequencies of alleles A and B are set at 0.01. The effects would be more dramatic at lower initial frequencies, but the true initial frequencies are as yet unknown (from Gould [15]).

The spatial scale of mixtures. The scale at which a mixture is planted could have important implications for resistance management and warrants detailed discussion. A major issue with the use of seed piece mixtures is that beetle adults and larvae could move between resistant and susceptible plants. If beetles moved specifically to avoid *Bt* toxicity, interplant movement could in some cases decrease the rate of resistance development (16, 19). However, evidence to date does not support the hypothesis that CPB larvae or adults are more likely to leave a resistant than a susceptible plant (see discussion below).

The natural movement of CPB between adjacent plants in a mixture could increase the rate of resistance development if high doses of one or more toxins were used in the resistant component of the mixture. As pointed out by R. Roush and J. Mallett (personal communication), if a partially resistant larva developed to third instar on a susceptible plant, then wandered over to a Bt plant when it was developmentally more tolerant of Bt (10), the larva's fitness might be much higher than that of a totally susceptible beetle that made the transfer at the same age. Similarly, a partially resistant adult which after feeding on a *Bt* plant moved to a susceptible plant, might have a better chance of reproducing than a totally susceptible beetle that made the same move if the sublethal effects of feeding on a toxic plant were more severe for the susceptible genotype. In contrast, neither of these types of beetles would produce any surviving off-spring in a field of only highly toxic plants.

Unfortunately, we lack rigorous field data on the extent of interplant movement. Precise information on the proportion of larvae and adults that move between plants is critical if we are to assess the impact of mixtures on development of resistance. In a preliminary study (Gould, Kennedy and Follett unpublished data), alternate potato plants in two experimental plots were sprayed with Foil®, a commercial formulation of *Bt* (Ecogen Inc., Langhorn, PA). We then placed 15 adult CPB on each of the sprayed and unsprayed plants. Beetles placed on the sprayed and unsprayed plants were coated with different colors of fluorescent powder (Sirchie Finger Print Laboratories Inc., Research Triangle Park, NC) to make them distinguishable. In plot #1, after 6 hrs, we counted the number of beetles that had moved to unsprayed plants from sprayed plants within the same row, and visa versa. In plot #2 we took similar counts after 20 hrs. This experiment was repeated 9 days later in a different area of the same field. In this second replicate of the experiment, we used 4 small plots instead of 2 plots.

Data from these experiments are presented in Table 1. In the first replicate of this experiment, there was significantly more movement from treated to untreated plants within a row, while in the second test there was no effect of treatment on movement. Our only explanation for the difference between tests was that the cohort of beetles in the first test were mostly newly emerged individuals, while beetles in the second test were older.

Data from our field tests indicate that there was a high rate of beetle movement between plants within the same rows. For example, after 6 hrs. in test #1, approximately one-third of the beetles placed on treated plants had moved to untreated plants. This could have been due to our handling of the beetles, but our observations indicated that most beetles resumed normal feeding after placement on plants.

Table 1. Experiment to determine if marked adult CPB were more prone to move to untreated plants from treated plants than they were to move from untreated to treated plants. In test no. 1, significantly more beetles moved to untreated plants ($\underline{P} < 0.001$). In test no. 2, there were no significant differences $\underline{P} > 0.50$).

Mean no. beetles that moved to each type of plant

	N	Mean	S.E.
Test no. 1 - 6 hours after placement			
Untreated	9	5.22	0.795
Treated	9	1.78	0.641
Test no. 2 - 6 hours after placement			
Untreated	11	5.18	0.730
Treated	11	6.27	1.760
Test no. 1 - 20 hours after placement			
Untreated	10	7.20	1.540
Treated	10	3.20	0.590
Test no. 2 - 20 hours after placement			
Untreated	11	7.09	0.900
Treated	11	6.09	0.560

In parallel with the first replicate of the experiment which examined within-row movement, we examined the beetles' potential for moving across rows that did not have a full canopy. This was done by spraying all of the plants in one of two rows. Beetles with one color of fluorescent marker were placed on plants in the treated rows and beetles with another color of fluorescent mark were placed in untreated rows. A total of 200 beetles were placed in the untreated and treated rows. Beetles were counted after 20 hrs.

Results from these preliminary studies are useful in describing the relative amount of movement within and between rows. In the first replicate of the experiment on within-row movement, 48% of the beetles placed on treated plants were found on untreated plants after 20 hrs, whereas in the replicate for between-row movement, none of the 100 beetles placed on treated rows were found in untreated rows.

The most important point from our preliminary study may be that beetles are less prone to move across rows when the foliage does not overlap across rows. If a farmer planted a fraction of the rows in a field with non-*Bt* potatoes, the amount of movement might be low enough to ensure the death of susceptible and partially resistant beetles that started feeding on rows with high Bt-toxin expression. There is a possibility that this lower rate of movement might not be sufficient to ensure adequate mating between beetles that developed on *Bt* and non-*Bt* plants, which is one of the goals of planting mixtures. The strategy of planting border rows around a field with high expression *Bt* potatoes might have a similar impact in terms of movement. Our study is only preliminary and only measured movement over a single day. Longer term studies will be needed to assess the true level of full generation beetle movement and gene flow at varying spatial scales.

At a conceptual level, one difficulty in determining the optimal level of movement is that this parameter has two very different effects on resistance depending on the life stage that is moving and the inheritance of resistance to *Bt*. When mixtures of potatoes with high *Bt*-toxin expression and no *Bt*-expression are used, we would want little movement of larvae and of fertilized females for reasons discussed above, but we want as much movement as possible from adult males and pre-mating females to achieve approximately random mating. If, in the extreme case, adult beetles never moved between *Bt* and non-*Bt* plants, we would in effect have two separate beetle populations and we would lose the benefits of mating between unselected beetles that developed on the refuge of non-*Bt* plants, and selected individuals that survived on Bt plants. Assuming that we cannot decouple factors that influence movement of different stages and sexes of beetles during a single season, we are unlikely to find a perfect spatial scale of plant mixing. However, models could be developed that explore which of two or three scales of mixture would be best.

It has been proposed that the simplest type of mixture from the farmer/business perspective would involve planting some fields to normal potatoes and others to *Bt* potatoes. This strategy would have two technical problems. One is the issue of limited mating between beetles from different fields during a season. The second is the fact that a farmer is not going to leave a field unprotected from beetle damage. We often talk about the ratio of resistant to susceptible plants, but the real issue involves measuring the relative numbers of beetles that successfully develop on *Bt* versus non-*Bt* plants. For example, if a farmer plants 50% of his/her fields to non-*Bt* "refuge" potatoes but then sprays them with conventional insecticides, leaving only 2% of the CPB alive, that 50.0% refuge acreage is converted to a 1.0% population refuge. If the "insecticide" used is a *Bt* spray, the situation would be even worse because this would further select for resistance.

Another practical option for a farmer who plants half of his/her fields in *Bt*-potatoes is to alternate which of the fields are planted to Bt potatoes. The *Bt* plants would be used to lower the population in a field the first year. If this field was not close to other potato fields, *Bt* potatoes might not be needed in that field in the second year because there would only be a small, lingering CPB population at the beginning of the season. If this population increased by the end of the season, the farmer could plant that field to *Bt* potatoes in the third year. This approach sounds appealing at first glance, but a model of adaptation to resistant wheat by an organism (Hessian fly) with movement similar to that of CPB adults indicates that this approach could promote the rapid development of Bt resistance because of limited gene flow (Gould (13) reproduced in Fig. 4).

If a farmer combined the approach of planting half of his/her potato fields to *Bt* potatoes with a crop rotation plan, the problem of limited gene flow could be partially overcome. If each year potatoes were planted on land that had been used for another crop in the preceding year, all beetles in the area would be forced to relocate each year. This mass movement could cause an increase in mating between beetles that originated in fields with Bt-potatoes and those from fields with normal potatoes. A theoretical drawback to this approach is that beetles mate *in situ* before diapause, and use sperm from this mating in the spring. This peculiar aspect of CPB biology curtails random mating, even with rotations. Detailed simulation models will be needed to determine how much this pre-diapause mating interferes with the usefulness of this approach. From a practical perspective farmers would have to minimize use of insecticides (especially Bt-sprays) in normal potato fields.

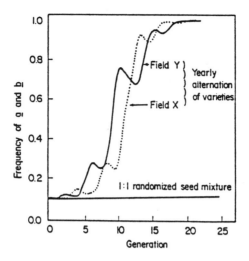

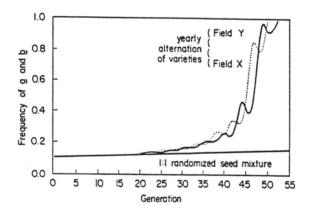

Fig. 4. Two-field model with alternate planting of a pyramided two-factor resistant cultivar and susceptible cultivar in the fields compared with a 1:1 random mixture of resistant-susceptible plants in both fields (W = fitness). Top: Initial frequency of a and b is 0.10; W_{aaBb} and W_{Aabb} on resistant plants are 0.28; bottom line depicts the slow change in allelic frequencies when a 1:1 random seed mixture is used. With 1:1 mixture, 92 generations are required before W reaches 0.80. Bottom: Same as A, except that W_{aaBb} and W_{Aabb} are equal to W_{AABB} = 0.04. With a 1:1 mixture, 435 generations are required before W reaches 0.80 (from 13).

The general issue for the farmer is how to raise the largest number of useful, susceptible beetles on non-*Bt* potatoes while incurring the least damage to his/her fields. The discussion above indicates that the issue of how useful each beetle is depends on the spatial scale of the refuge. The next question is whether the scale of the refuge can influence how much yield loss the feeding of a single beetle causes? This would be a simple question to answer if there was a linear relationship between beetle numbers and yield. However, as pointed out by E.E. Ewing, et al. (this volume), the CPB-damage/potato-yield equation can be complex.

Most of the data available on the damage/yield relationship in potatoes have been generated based on uniform plantings of potatoes with varied temporal patterns of CPB damage. These damage/yield relationships are useful when dealing with refuges at the larger spatial scale of a row or field, but might not be fully applicable to seed piece mixtures. One major question that arises with seed piece mixtures is whether *Bt* plants that are adjacent to partially or fully defoliated non-*Bt* plants will grow more vigorously due to decreased competition, and thereby compensate for some of the yield lost from damaged non-*Bt* plants. If this is the case, damage/yield relationships taken on uniform plots will overestimate yield loss in seed piece mixtures.

A rough approximation of the ability of potatoes to compensate for damaged plants in a stand can be garnered from the literature on how changes in planting density affect yield, and from work on how variance in planting density affects yield. There are many studies of this relationship in potato (e.g., 2, 3, 20, 26). We will use two of them to illustrate the general findings.

Rex et al. (28) examined the effect of a range of in-row plant spacing (22 cm to 46 cm) on potato yield, marketability, the number of over- sized tubers, specific gravity of tubers, and net crop value. Their study encompassed a three-year period and results of the study were complex. In general, yield did decrease at the larger plant spacing, but the total yield lost due to more than a doubling of spacing between plants was only ca. 20%. Interestingly, the net crop value was sometimes higher at the lower plant density because of the decrease in total cost of seed potatoes per acre. This result should be kept in mind because the farmer who plants a mixture will only pay the premium price for engineered potato seed pieces for that portion of the field planted to *Bt*-plants.

A study by Entz and LaCroix (6) examined the effect of irregular in-row spacing on yield. They varied the coefficient of variation in distance between seed pieces from 0% to 75%. Other variables in the study were seed piece size and type, mean distance between seed pieces, location and year. Results of the study showed no consistent effect of variance in spacing on yield. Entz and LaCroix (6) found that plants produced twice as many branches per plant-mainstem when the distance between plants was doubled, and proposed this as one mechanism of compensatory growth that maintained similar yields. They concluded that environmental stresses had a strong effect on the outcome of their experiments and that it would be hard to establish a single recommendation for mean and variance in seed-piece spacing.

Results of the above studies indicate that potatoes generally have a substantial capacity for compensatory growth. Thus, in a seed piece mixture of *Bt* and non-*Bt* potatoes, there could be compensa- tion for defoliated non-Bt plants. Unfortunately, all of the studies referred to consider only differences in densities that are initiated at planting, while important CPB damage in Bt and non-Bt mixtures that could reduce stand density, occurs in both early- and mid-season. In order to more rigorously determine if *Bt*-plants in the same rows as defoliated non-*Bt* plants could compensate, we conducted a preliminary experiment that mimicked fields planted to random seed-piece mixtures of *Bt* and non-*Bt* plants at differing ratios (Nault et al., unpublished data).

Normal potato seed pieces, var. 'Atlantic', were planted uniformly at one per 0.3 m with 25 plants per row in a 3-row plot. After plants began to grow, plants in the middle row of the plot were randomly assigned as Bt-toxin producing "mimics" or normal plants. We varied the ratio of *Bt*-plant mimics to normal plants as follows: 25:0, 22:3, 19:6, 13:12, and 0:25. Each treatment was replicated five times in a Latin square design to account for two potential sources of nonrandom error effects: soil type and the unidirectional invasion typically observed by colonizing, overwintered CPB. Each non-*Bt* plant had one 30-cm stake placed to its left and right in the row. Twice a week, during periods of high CPB densities, and once a week when CPB densities were low, large paper grocery bags were placed over each non-*Bt* plant (using the stakes as supports) and *Bt*- plant mimics were sprayed with either Foil® or Trident II® at a rate of 9.4 and 4.7 liters per ha, respectively. Sprays were applied using a CO_2-powered back-pack sprayer equipped with three nozzles (D-3/25 cone) and calibrated to deliver 317.9 liters of spray per ha at 40 psi. Damage estimates were taken as percent defoliation from a pretransformed rating scale developed by Little and Hills (24). Spraying was very effective, with the highest mean percent defoliation per plot to *Bt*-plant mimics being 3% and 0% during bloom and post-bloom, respectively, while the highest mean percent defoliation in non-*Bt* plots was 65% and 98%. Defoliation in non-*Bt* plots was well above action thresholds determined for bloom (30%) and post-bloom (50%) stages of potatoes in the southeastern U.S. (G.W. Zehnder, personal communication). At harvest, the middle row of each plot was assessed for total yield and yield of U.S. #1 grade potatoes. Unfortunately, beetle densities within the experimental field varied so greatly that even with a

Latin square design, the variance in yield due to variation in beetle density made testing of treatment effects difficult. However, yield results from these tests (Fig. 5) suggest that there was plant compensation as indicated by the lack of linearity between proportion of *Bt*-plant mimics and yield.

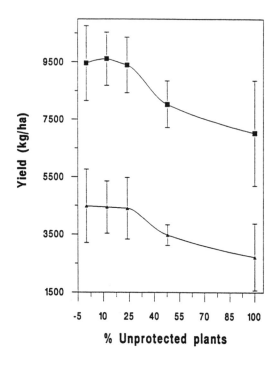

Fig. 5. Mean yield (± SE) of varying mixtures of protected and unprotected potato, var. Atlantic, after defoliation by *Leptinotarsa decemlineata* during bloom. Total yield (■) and U.S. no. 1 yield (▲) represented in kg/ha were extrapolated from a single row (7.62 m, 25 plants).

These results are only preliminary and require replication (Nault et al. in prep.), as well as studies in different potato-growing areas with a number of potato varieties. However, if there is a reasonable amount of compensation for loss of non-*Bt* plants, a seed piece mixture would have this advantage over other approaches. One problem with the seed piece mixture strategy, pointed out by Ferro (9), is that under high beetle pressure all of the non-*Bt* plants could be consumed. The beetles would then move to the *Bt* plants as larger larvae where they would be subjected to selection for adaptation to the *Bt*-endotoxin. The intensity of selection would be affected by the level of toxin expression relative to the susceptibility of these larger larvae. Further, when a second generation of beetles emerged, non-*Bt* plants which had been extensively fed upon by first generation beetles would no longer be available for the existing beetles to feed upon unless the plants had refoliated.

Ferro's insight is important. If one were to adopt such a seed piece mixture strategy, it would be important to start in a rotated field where the initial beetle population was low, and the potential for complete defoliation of non-*Bt* plants was low. In subsequent seasons, the overall population of beetles would be expected to be even lower, so defoliation of non-*Bt* plants would be of less concern, assuming beetles did not oviposit preferentially on non-*Bt* plants.

Strategy 4: Low Levels of Toxin Expression
Plus Biological Control

In terms of insect pest mortality and rates of larval development, engineered plants with low levels of toxin expression are similar to what is often called "partial resistance" in the classical host-plant resistance literature. (This is not to say they are completely equivalent because partial resistance may be due to a variety of physical, nutritional, and toxicological effects, while the engineered plant's resistance is due to one factor.) Partial resistance can protect crop yield by allowing plants to "outgrow" their insect pests and by decreasing the reproductive rate of insect pests that reside in the crop for a number of generations (22). Conventional wisdom among scientists working on plant resistance to insects and pathogens has held that pests are likely to adapt more slowly to partial resistance than to strong resistance, in part due to the decreased mortality experienced by a pest population exposed to partial resistance. However, this may not always translate to reduced selective pressure. For example, if a type of partial resistance is deployed that does not kill any developing larvae but these larvae take so long to grow that the adults are never able to enter successful diapause, there is still strong selection to adapt to the partial resistance. On the other hand, if selection slows insect growth in a way that allows a plant to outgrow a pest but the pest becomes a fully successful adult, there may be no selection pressure (12).

Partial resistance has sometimes been shown to interact synergistically with natural enemies in decreasing pest populations (21 and references within). This means that adding up the negative effect of partial resistance alone, and the negative effect of natural enemies alone, gives a sum negative effect on the pest of lesser magnitude than the actual combined effect of these two agents (i.e., the whole is greater than the sum of its parts). Although partial plant resistance and parasites of pests cause very different types of pest mortality, theoretical studies have shown that it is possible for natural enemies to increase or decrease the rate at which pests adapt to partial host plant resistance (18).

In examining the effects of low *Bt* expression on CPB, it has been shown (9) that slowing the developmental rate of CPB larvae in the Northeast could delay emergence of F1 generation adults until daylengths drop below the critical photoperiod for diapause induction (this occurs in early August in western Massachusetts). Adult CPB emerging when the daylengths are shorter than the critical photoperiod produce few progeny and enter diapause (34). Thus, the prolonged development of the F1 generation CPB larvae on transgenic potato plants expressing low levels of endotoxin could delay emergence of a significant proportion of the F1 generation adults until after daylengths drop below the critical length. Because these adults would produce few, if any, offspring before entering diapause, the size of the F2 generation would be reduced. The proportion of F1 adults entering diapause could be increased further by using the transgenic plants in conjunction with crop rotation to delay invasion of the crop by overwintered CPB (23,34,35).

Although this approach could greatly reduce the size of the F2 larval generation without much added mortality, this lack of mortality is not equivalent to a lack of selection for adaptation. The level of selection imposed would depend upon the difference between *Bt*-toxin resistant and susceptible CPB females in the average number of offspring contributed to the next season's population. If, for example, *Bt*-adapted F1 generation females emerge prior to the critical photoperiod and produce an average of 10 female offspring which survive to the following season, while unadapted females emerge after the critical photoperiod for diapause, and would therefore add a maximum of one female to the population in the following season, the selection differential would be 0.9. This is the equivalent of 90% difference in mortality.

The selection for adaptation to the Bt-toxin imposed by transgenic plants that express low levels of the toxin and act primarily by slowing the development rate of unadapted CPB could be affected significantly by the action of natural enemies which cause age or stage-specific mortality. The effect of these natural enemies on selection may be neutral or it may increase or decrease the level of selection. The interactions involved can be complex and would be determined by the specific nature of the behavioral and physiological effects of the transgenic resistant plants on the CPB, as well as the behavior of the natural enemy, and the population dynamics of the natural enemy/CPB system in which the interaction occurs (see Gould et al. (18) for a detailed discussion).

Strategy 5: Targeted Toxin-gene Expression

To date, potatoes engineered for commercial use, express *Bt*-toxin genes all season long throughout their above ground parts. When grown in the field, such plants would expose beetles to the toxin no matter where on the plant they fed and no matter what time of the season they fed. Published reports on the quantity of Bt found in different parts of the plants at different times of the season are not available, but the general indication is that the levels are always very high.

Experiments with the genetic engineering of tobacco and some other plants have demonstrated that it is possible to insert genes into plants in ways that result in the genes being expressed only in certain parts of the plant or only under certain environmental conditions. It is even possible to engineer tobacco plants to express *Bt*-toxin genes only when the plants are sprayed with an inducing compound (John Ryals, Ciba-Geigy, personal communication).

Reports on the relationship between beetle feeding and yield loss indicate that potatoes are more sensitive to feeding damage at certain times in their growth cycle (4,5, 35), so it could be useful to have Bt genes expressed only at times when they were needed. Furthermore, Cranshaw and Radcliffe (4) found that damage to young leaves at the top of the potato plant has more impact on yield than damage to leaves from the middle and lower parts of the plant. This offers some support for the possible utility of expressing *Bt*-toxins only in young potato leaves with the assumption that the toxin will degrade or will be diluted by the time a leaf grows to full size and ages.

One problem with time- or tissue-specific expression is that during the phase when genes are being turned on or off, beetles are likely to be exposed to intermediate concentrations of *Bt* toxins. Under certain assumptions regarding the genetics of *Bt* resistance, this could increase the rate of resistance development. The effect on resistance of turning Bt genes on and off in different tissues would depend in part on the rate at which levels of Bt rose and fell. It would also depend on whether or not the beetles moved between plant parts with and without *Bt*-toxin. Only more field experiments will give us solid answers to these questions, but observations of larval and adult movement on normal plants indicates that we should expect some problems (P. Follett, personal observation).

Research Outlook

In outlining five general approaches for *Bt*-resistance management, the most important missing component seems to be information on how the beetles will interact with *Bt* potatoes in the field. Companies have been distributing small numbers of engineered potatoes to some academic researchers; however, there is a need for public access to large lots of engineered seed pieces if we are to answer critical questions. Although there are many legitimate short term business concerns that have led to a lack of such seed piece supplies, there are no insurmountable technical limitations impeding the distribution of such seed pieces.

Current genetic engineering processes have led to the production of many lines of potatoes that have valuable levels of *Bt* expression, but are not used in breeding programs because of minor problems with agronomic characteristics. The seed pieces from such potato lines could easily be transferred to academic laboratories that could increase the seed lots and use them in large-scale field experiments. While such potatoes would not be quite as good as the commercial *Bt*-producing lines, the differences would be minor. Academic and government research scientists could do large scale tests with these potato lines before transgenic potatoes were commercially available. The information gained from such tests could indicate what kinds of mixtures would work best, and what the initial frequencies of *Bt*-resistance genes were. Most importantly, these large-scale experiments would tell us how potatoes with varying levels of *Bt* toxins and mixtures of *Bt* potatoes would be expected to influence the long-term population dynamics of the CPB. Without such knowledge, it is difficult to develop robust strategies.

Epilogue

Entomologists and genetic engineers have only begun to explore the options available for designing and deploying crop plants that produce their own toxins. At this point, there are many ideas being examined, but the in-field testing of these ideas has barely started. As can be seen from the discussion above, a detailed knowledge of CPB ecology, behavior, and genetics will be required before we are able to make informed statements about the utility and feasibility of various strategies for using engineered plants. After examining many strategies for slowing the development of Bt-resistance in CPB, we feel that if farmers replaced Bt sprays with transgenic plants, then 1) seed piece mixtures or 2) rotating potatoes and other crops, combined with use of field level mixtures of high expression Bt potatoes, might offer effective and feasible approaches. However, we cannot offer a strong argument for using these approaches without empirical data from on-farm tests.

It must be noted that even with the best research, the critical issue will be implementing research findings. Resistance management strategies will have to be feasible at the farm level and good educational programs will have to reach farm managers.

Work concerning CPB and plants expressing *Bt* toxins may serve as a model for many other plant/pest systems for which insect-toxic, engineered plants may soon be available. There are many potential advantages of using engineered plants instead of broad spectrum pesticides for insect control. If the first cases where engineered plants are used for crop protection fail because of insect resistance, this entire approach for pest control could be negatively impacted. We hope that engineered potatoes will reach the market place, but only after adequate research and outreach programs have improved the potential for long-term utility of this technology.

Acknowledgments

We appreciate the invitation by the symposium organizers and editors to participate in this work. We are thankful for insightful comments on this topic and manuscript by Mike Caprio, Rick Jansson, Tracy Johnson, Rick Roush, and Bruce Tabashnik, This work was supported by a cooperative agreement between NCSU and the USDA. We thank William Cantelo for fostering this cooperative research program.

Literature Cited

1. Bacon, O. C. 1960. Control of the potato tuberworm in potatoes. J. Econ. Entomol. 53: 868-871.
2. Bishop, J. C. and D. N. Wright. 1959. The effect of size and spacing of seed pieces on the yield and grade of White Rose potatoes in Kern County, California. Am. Potato J. 36: 235-240.
3. Bleasdale, J.K.A. and R. Thompson. 1969. Some effect of plant spacing on potato quality. Eur. Potato J. 12:173-187.
4. Cranshaw, W.S and E.F. Radcliffe 1980. Effects of defoliation on yield of potatoes. J. Econ. Entomol. 73:131-134.
5. Dripps, J. E. and Z. Smilowitz 1989. Growth analysis of potato plants damaged by Colorado potato beetle (Coleoptera: Chrysomelidae) in rotated and nonrotated potato fields. Environ. Entomol. 12:1352-1356.
6. Entz, M. H. and L. J. LaCroix. 1984. The effect of in-row spacing and seedtype on the yield and quality of potato cultivar. Am. Potato J. 61:93-105.
7. Falconer, D. S. 1981. Introduction to quantitative genetics, 2nd edition. Longmans Green, NY. 340 pp.

8.   Ferre, J., M. D. Real, J. Van Rie, S. Jansens and M. Peferoen. 1991. Resistance to the *Bacillus thuringiensis* in a field population of *Plutella xylastella* is due to a change in a midgut membrane receptor. Proc. Nat. Acad. Sci. 88:5119-5123.

9.   Ferro, D. N. 1993. Potential for resistance to *Bacillus thuringiensis*: Colorado potato beetle (Coleoptera: Chrysomelidae) -- a model system. Am. Entomol. 39:38-44.

10.   Ferro, D. N. and S. M. Lyon. 1991. Colorado potato beetle (Coleoptera: Chrysomelidae) larval mortality: operative effects of *Bacillus thuringiensis* subsp. *san diego*. J. Econ. Entomol. 84:806-809.

11.   Forgash, A. J. 1981. Insecticide resistance of the Colorado potato beetle, *Leptinotarsa decemlineata* (Say), pp. 34-37. In J. H. Lashomb and R. Casagrande [eds.], Advances in potato pest management. Hutchinson & Ross, Stroundsburg, PA.

12.   Gould, F. 1983. Genetics of plant-herbivore systems: interactions between applied and basic study, pp. 599-653. In R. Denno and B. McClure [eds.], Variable plants and herbivores in natural and managed systems. Academic Press, New York.

13.   Gould, F. 1986. Simulation models for predicting durability of insect-resistant germ plasm: Hessian fly (Diptera: Cecidomyiidae)-resistant winter wheat. Environ. Entomol. 15:11-23.

14.   Gould, F. 1988. Evolutionary biology and genetically engineered crops. BioScience 38: 26-33.

15.   Gould, F. 1991. The evolutionary potential of crop pests. Amer. Sci. 79:496-507.

16.   Gould, F. and A. Anderson. 1991. Effects of *Bacillus thuringiensis* and HD-73 delta-endotoxin on growth, behavior, and fitness of susceptible and toxin-adapted *Heliothis virescens* (Lepidoptera: Noctuidae) strains. Environ. Entomol. 20:30-38.

17.   Gould, F., A. Anderson, D. Landis and H. Van Mellaert. 1991a. Feeding behavior and growth of *Heliothis virescens* larvae (Lepidoptera: Noctuidae) on diets containing *Bacillus thuringiensis* formulations or endotoxins. Entomol. exp. appl. 58:199-210.

18.   Gould, F., G. G. Kennedy and M. T. Johnson. 1991b. Effects of natural enemies on the rate of herbivore adaptation to resistant host plants. Entomol. exp. appl. 58:1-14.

19.   Gould, F., A. Martinez-Ramirez, A. Anderson, J. Ferre, F. J. Silva, and W. J. Moar. 1992. Broad-spectrum resistance to *Bacillus thuringiensis* toxins in *Heliothis virescens*. Proc. Natl. Acad. Sci. 89:7986-7990.

20.   Iritani, W. M., R. Thornton, L. Weller and G. O'Leary. 1972. Relationships of seed size, spacing, and stem numbers to yield of Russet Burbank potatoes. Am. Potato J. 49:463-469.

21.   Johnson, M. T. and F. Gould. 1992. Interactions of genetically engineered host-plant resistance and natural enemies of *Heliothis virescens* (Lepidoptera: Noctuidae) in tobacco. Environ. Entomol. 21:586-597.

22.   Kennedy, G. G., F. Gould, O. M. B. dePonti and R. E. Stinner. 1987. Ecological, agricultural, genetic, and commercial considerations in the deployment of insect-resistant germ plasm. Environ. Entomol. 16: 327-338.

23.   Lashomb, J. and Y.S. Ng. 1984. Colonization by Colorado potato beetles, *Leptinotarsa decemlineata* (Say) (Coleoptera: Chrysomelidae) in rotated and nonrotated potato fields. Environ. Entomol. 12:1352-1356.

24.   Little, T. M. and F. J. Hills. 1978. Agricultural Experimentation: Design and Analysis. Wiley & Sons, NY.

25.   McGaughey, W. and R. W. Beeman. 1988. Resistance to *Bacillus thuringiensis* in colonies of Indiameal moth and almond moth (Lepidoptera: Pyralidae). J. Econ. Entomol. 81:28-33.

26.   Nelson, D. C., D. A. Jones and M. C. Thoreson. 1979. Relationships between weather, plant spacing and the incidence of hollow heart in Norgold Russet potatoes. Am. Potato J. 56:581-586.

27.   Raffa, K. F. 1989. Genetic engineering of trees to enhance resistance to insects. BioScience 39:524-534.

28.   Rex, B. L., W. A. Russell and H. R. Wolfe. 1987. The effect of spacing of seedpieces on yield, quality and economic value for processing of shepody potatoes in Manitoba. Am. Potato J. 64:177-189.

29.   Shelton, A. M. and J. A. Wyman. 1979. Potato tuberworm damage to potatoes under different irrigation and cultural practices. J. Econ. Entomol. 72:261-264.

30.   Shelton, A. M., J. A. Wyman and A. J. Moyer. 1981. Effects of ommonly used insecticides on the potato tuberworm and its associated parasites and predators in potatoes. J. Econ. Entomol. 74:303-308.

31.   Stone, T. B., S. R. Sims and P. G. Marrone. 1989. Selection of tobacco budworm for resistance to a genetically engineered *Pseudomonas fluorescens* containing the delta-endotoxin of *Bacillus thuringiensis* subsp. *kurstaki*. J. Invert. Pathol. 53:228-234.

32.   Tabashnik, B. E. 1990. Modeling and evaluation of resistance management tactics, pp. 153-182. *In* R. T. Roush and B. E. Tabashnik [eds.], Pesticide resistance in arthropods. Chapman and Hall, NY.

33.   Van Rie, J., W. H. McGaughy, D. E. Johnson, B. D. Barnett and H. Van Mellaert. 1990. Mechanism of insect resistance to the microbial insecticide *Bacillus thuringiensis*. Science 247:72-74.

34.   Voss, R. H., D. N. Ferro and J. A. Logan. 1988. Role of reproductive diapause in the population dynamics of the Colorado potato beetle (Coleoptera: Chrysomelidae) in western Massachusetts. Environ. Entomol. 17:863-871.

35.   Wright, R. J. 1984. Evaluation of crop rotation for control of Colorado potato beetles (Coleoptera: Chrysomelidae) in commercial fields in Long Island. J. Econ. Entomol. 77:1254-1259.

MONITORING RESISTANCE IN
COLORADO POTATO BEETLE POPULATIONS

George G. Kennedy and Ned M. French II
Department of Entomology
North Carolina State University
Raleigh, North Carolina 27695-7630

Insecticide resistance in the Colorado potato beetle, *Leptinotarsa decemlineata* (Say), has been a severe problem in the northeastern and middle Atlantic regions of the United States for a number of years (6,9,10). More recently, the problem has become serious in other areas of the US (1, 11). The threat posed by this resistance to the commercial viability of potato production has focused attention on the development of Colorado potato beetle management methods that are not singularly reliant on conventional insecticides. Indeed, insecticide resistance in the potato beetle has proven to be a major force leading to advances in insect pest management on potato. The resistance problem has also provided a market for *Bacillus thuringiensis* Berliner based products for use in managing the Colorado potato beetle.

The dynamic and widespread nature of resistance has created a need for resistance monitoring to facilitate both potato beetle management in the short term and resistance management in the long term. This chapter describes a procedure for monitoring resistance in Colorado potato beetle populations in a pest management context. More general discussions of resistance monitoring are provided by Brent (2) and ffrench-Constant and Roush (8).

Resistance Monitoring Objectives for Colorado Potato Beetle

There are at least seven different objectives for resistance detection and monitoring efforts (2,8). These are: 1) to document the contribution of resistance to control failures; 2) to provide early warning of impending resistance problems; 3) to accurately measure the frequency of resistant genotypes in a population; 4) to document changes in the spectrum or level of resistance in a population; 5) to aid in selection of insecticides that are least affected by resistance; 6) to evaluate the effectiveness of resistance management efforts; and 7) to measure biological characteristics of resistant and susceptible populations in the field.

In the case of the Colorado potato beetle, the widespread occurrence of insecticide resistance clearly demonstrates the potential for resistance to evolve wherever significant selection pressure is applied. Consequently, in a pest or resistance management context, we can assume that low frequencies of resistant genotypes are present in most, if not all, populations where resistance is not a recognized problem. Thus, resistance monitoring need not be directed toward detecting low frequencies of resistance in a population. This is fortunate because monitoring to achieve such an objective requires extensive sampling and is both time consuming and expensive (14). Resistance monitoring, however, should be focused on detecting major shifts in the spectrum or level of resistance in local potato beetle populations before control failures occur. A monitoring procedure with this as a primary objective would provide information of value in the selection of control measures that avoid control failures due to resistance. The information generated would also be of value in assessing the effectiveness of resistance management efforts and in documenting, after the fact, the contribution of resistance to control failures.

Requirements for a Resistance Monitoring Protocol

Research in North Carolina (11), Maryland (Dively, Ellis and Linduska unpublished), Virginia (15) and Michigan (1), (Grafius unpublished) has documented extensive variation among local Colorado potato beetle populations in both the spectrum of insecticides resisted and the general levels of resistance. This widespread variation, in conjunction with the relatively small size of commercial potato fields in North Carolina and much of the eastern U.S., dictates that a resistance monitoring protocol be simple, rapid and inexpensive so that an individual can monitor a large number of local populations in a timely fashion.

A key component of a monitoring protocol involves the specific assay used to characterize a sample of the test insect as resistant or susceptible. Both biochemical assays and bioassays have been used to monitor insecticide resistance in various insects (4,5,7,12,13). Biochemical assays, suitable for use in resistance monitoring, that measure levels of enzyme activity or the occurrence of specific nucleic acid sequences are not currently available for Colorado potato beetle (for discussions of these types of assays see 3,5,8). Because of the involvement of multiple mechanisms for resistance of the Colorado potato beetle to each of several different insecticides, it is unlikely that any single biochemical assay will be suitable for resistance monitoring in a pest or resistance monitoring context.

In the absence of biochemical assays, efforts to monitor resistance in Colorado potato beetle have used bioassays. Several have been proposed as suitable for routine use in a pest management context. All involve exposing beetles to a concentration of insecticide that distinguishes between resistant and susceptible individuals. Techniques include immersion of adults or larvae in appropriate concentrations of insecticide solutions, or confinement of neonates or adults on insecticide treated filter paper (1,11), and recording subsequent mortality. Mortality in these bioassays can be compared to the expected mortality for a population known to be susceptible, the mortality in previous bioassays of the same population, or a critical level of mortality in the bioassay below which efficacy of the insecticide in the field is reduced. The resulting information can be used in making management decisions.

A Resistance Monitoring Protocol for Colorado Potato Beetle

The resistance monitoring protocol to be described was developed as part of an effort to manage Colorado potato beetle populations and insecticide resistance during a period when insecticide resistance was becoming widespread in North Carolina. The protocol was developed specifically for use by county extension agents, pest management consultants, and potato growers to predict loss of insecticide efficacy due to resistance before control failures were experienced, and to detect major shifts in the resistance status of local potato beetle populations over time. For purposes of protocol development, we defined a control failure to be a population reduction of less than 90% following application of the insecticide. This level was chosen because, when populations are high, even a 90% reduction leaves sufficient beetles to severely damage the crop.

Bioassay procedure. The bioassay procedure involves measuring mortality of neonate potato beetles confined for 24 h on filter paper treated with a diagnostic concentration of the insecticide being tested (11). In practice, egg masses are collected in the field, and excess foliage is trimmed from around the egg mass. Each egg mass is placed on insecticide-treated filter paper (Fisher Brand P-5) in a Petri dish (1 egg mass per dish). The eggs are observed for hatch twice daily. At approximately 50% eclosion, 4 drops of water are added to the filter paper and the Petri dish is covered and sealed with Parafilm. After 24 h at room temperature, mortality is recorded in each bioassay unit (bioassay unit = all neonates from a single egg mass).

Diagnostic concentrations were developed from concentration/ mortality data for known susceptible and resistant Colorado potato beetle populations for each registered insecticide. When possible, concentrations were selected which killed greater than 95% of susceptible neonates and less than 5% of resistant neonates. When a population resistant to a particular insecticide was unavailable, the LC_{95} for the standard susceptible population was used as the diagnostic concentration.

To relate mortality in the bioassay to the level of control achieved in the field with each insecticide, a series of field experiments was conducted in which numerous potato beetle populations, varying in their level of resistance, were subjected to bioassay and to field insecticide efficacy trials. Although we have data for most of the insecticides commonly used on potato to control the Colorado potato beetle, we report here only the results for the insecticide carbofuran. These results illustrate the important relationships that form the foundation for the resistance monitoring protocol.

The relationship that exists for carbofuran between mean mortality of neonates in the bioassay (diagnostic concentration = 0.2 $\mu g/cm^2$ treated filter paper) and the level of control achieved in the field (Figure 1A) reveals that the bioassay is more sensitive to small changes in the level of resistance than is the level of control. In fact, as mean mortality in the bioassay decreases, there is little decline in the level of control until mortality in the bioassay drops below approximately 25%. At lower mortality levels, control in the field declines precipitously. The bioassay mortality level below which potato beetle control in the field declines rapidly represents a critical mortality level or threshold for predicting control failures due to resistance. Similar relationships are observed for the other insecticides we have studied, although the critical mortality level in the bioassay may differ (Figure 1B).

These results clearly demonstrate that the bioassay can be used to identify resistance in a Colorado potato beetle population before a control failure is experienced. However, if the bioassay is to be useful in a pest and resistance management context, it must be used in conjunction with a statistically valid sampling plan.

Sampling constraints. If mean mortality in the bioassay is to be used as the basis for predicting whether a population will be controllable in the field, it is necessary to determine, with an acceptable degree of confidence, whether the true mean response of the beetle population in the bioassay is greater or less than the critical mortality

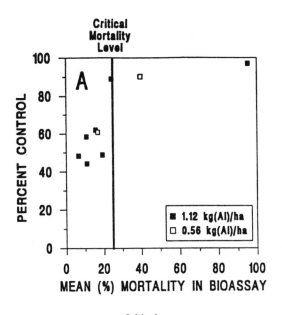

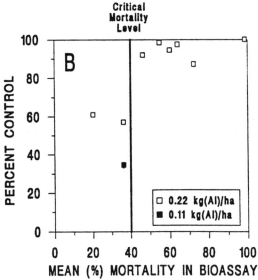

Fig. 1. Relationship between mean % mortality of Colorado potato beetle neonates in the bioassay and % control (relative to untreated) of the populations in field efficacy trials. Each data point represents a different potato beetle population. Studies conducted in eastern North Carolina potato fields in 1989 and 1990. A: Carbofuran, diagnostic concentration in bioassay=0.2 μg/cm^2. B: Permethrin, diagnostic concentration=0.16 μg/cm^2. Note higher critical mortality level for permethrin.

level. In the case of carbofuran, one needs to know if the true mean mortality for the population being tested is greater or less than 25%. For carbofuran the relationship between mean mortality and variance in the bioassay is such that beetle populations having mean mortalities between 20 and 80% are characterized by high variances in bioassay mortality (Figure 2). This is not surprising since such populations represent various mixtures of homozygous resistant, homozygous susceptible and heterozygous beetle genotypes. In contrast, the variances of populations that are clearly resistant (low mortality) or clearly susceptible (high mortality) in the bioassay are relatively low, reflecting the greater homozygosity of such populations.

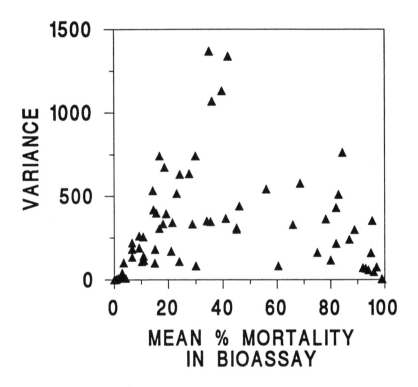

Fig. 2. Variance (s^2) associated with mean percent mortality of Colorado potato beetle neonates in the bioassay in response to the diagnostic concentration of carbofuran (0.2 μg/cm^2). Each data point represents a different potato beetle population.

A consequence of this pattern of variation is that highly resistant or highly susceptible populations can be accurately characterized as controllable or uncontrollable (i.e. true mean bioassay response of greater than or less than 25% mortality) by testing neonates from a modest number of egg masses (n≤5). In contrast, because of the high variances associated with intermediate levels of mortality, impractically large sample sizes (n>30) are needed to reliably classify populations of intermediate resistance as having true mean responses in the bioassay of greater or less than 25%. Consequently, without inordinately large sample sizes, it is possible to reliably classify as resistant (uncontrollable) or susceptible (controllable) only those populations that have very high or very low mean mortality responses in the bioassay. The response of populations with intermediate mean mortality responses cannot be reliable classified.

The practical limitations on sample size are severe. Our experiences over 2 years with potato growers, IPM consultants and county extension agents who have used this bioassay indicate that the maximum sample size likely to be used in practice is 5 units (egg masses) per insecticide. This assumes that, in areas where resistance is known to be a problem, each population will be bioassayed with three different insecticides to ensure that at least one effective material can be identified. We also found that most end-users took very limited care in quantifying mortality in each bioassay unit. Rather than counting living and dead neonates, most users merely classified their populations as resistant or susceptible based on whether most of the neonates were dead or alive.

To address these constraints, we developed a protocol for rapidly classifying populations as controllable or uncontrollable based on the proportion of egg masses in a sample that are classified as resistant.

Classification scheme. Under our classification scheme, each bioassay unit (cohort of neonates from a single egg mass) is classified as resistant or susceptible. The beetle population is then classified as controllable or uncontrollable based on the proportion of bioassay units, in a sample of 5 units per population, that are resistant.

Individual bioassay units are classified as resistant if mortality is 50% or less. Conversely, units with mortality exceeding 50% are classified as susceptible. Using these criteria, we found that for each of 5 different resistant potato beetle populations a mean of at least 95% of the bioassay units were classified as resistant. In addition, this criterion allows most sampled units to be rapidly classified without actually counting living and dead neonates. Only those units in which mortality is close to 50% require counting.

Predicting control failures. The proportion of bioassay units classified as resistant (mortality $\leq$ 50%) is an excellent predictor of mean mortality in the bioassay ($R^2=0.94$, df=21, $P\leq0.0001$, Figure 3). Consequently, the proportion of units classified as resistant in a sample also predicts control failures in the field (Figure 4). Based on bioassays with carbofuran and on field evaluations of carbofuran efficacy involving seven different potato beetle populations, control failures (i.e. population reduction of less than 90% following application of insecticide) occurred when the proportion of resistant units in the bioassay sample exceeded approximately 0.8. In a sample of five bioassay units, this would be when all units are classified as resistant.

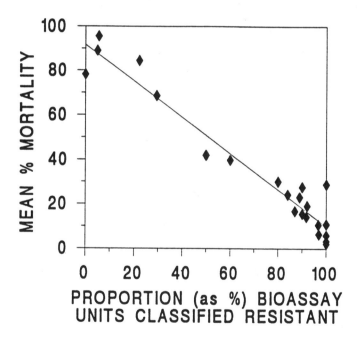

Fig. 3. Relationship between mean % mortality of potato beetle neonates in the bioassay in response to the diagnostic concentration of carbofuran (0.2 μg/cm^2) and the proportion of those bioassay units classified as resistant (mortality$\leq$ 50%). Linear regression based on samples of 22 potato beetle populations from eastern North Carolina in 1989 and 1990. Each sample consisted of 9 to 33 bioassay units ($r^2=0.94$, df=21, P<0.0001).

Taking sample variation into account, in populations for which field control was less than 90%, the proportion of resistant bioassay units minus 2 standard deviations never fell below 0.75 resistant units (Figure 4). In a sample of 5, the proportion of resistant units will be 0, 0.2, 0.4, 0.6, 0.8, or 1.0. To provide an added degree of protection against erroneously classifying a resistant population as controllable and to preclude the possibility of a sample outcome equal to the critical proportion, we set the critical proportion of resistant units at 0.75. Thus, only populations giving rise to 4 or 5 resistant units in a sample of 5 are classified as uncontrollable.

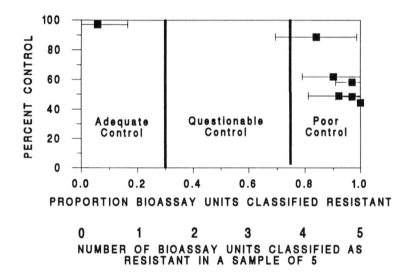

Fig. 4   Relationship between % control of Colorado potato beetle populations in field efficacy trials with carbofuran applied at 1.12 kg(AI)/ha and proportion of bioassay units in a sample from each population classified as resistant. 25-33 egg masses from each population were subjected to bioassay. Error bars represent $\pm$ 2 SD about the mean proportion resistant for each population. Poor control of potato beetle populations can be expected when the proportion of resistant bioassay units in a sample exceeds a critical level of 0.75. Adequate control can be expected when the proportion of resistant bioassay units in a sample falls below 0.3. When the proportion of resistant units in the sample falls between 0.3 and 0.75 the controllability of the population cannot be reliably predicted.

The decision scheme. There are two classification errors that are inherent in using a monitoring scheme to predict insect control failures. The first involves predicting that a population is controllable when it is not. The second involves predicting that a population is not controllable with a particular insecticide when it is. While both errors should be avoided to the extent possible, the practical consequence of the latter error is that an alternative control would be employed. In contrast, the consequence of the former is far more serious and involves the potential for crop failure. Thus, the decision scheme must be structured to minimize the probability of misclassifying a resistant population as controllable.

The probability of misclassifying resistant populations as controllable can be calculated using the binomial expansion $(p+q)^n$; where p is the true proportion of resistant units in the population; q is the true proportion of susceptible units in the population; $p+q=1$; and n is sample size. For this scheme, sample size (n) is fixed at 5 bioassay units. A thorough analysis of the probabilities of misclassification indicates that, given a sample size of 5, the resistance status or controllability of a population yielding a sample containing 2 or 3 resistant units (proportion= 0.4 or 0.6) cannot be reliably predicted.

Thus, to minimize the probability of misclassifying an uncontrollable population as controllable, we established a classification scheme in which only populations yielding a sample of 5 containing 0 or 1 resistant units (proportions=0.0 or 0.2) are classified as controllable (Figure 4). Populations yielding samples of 5 containing 4 or 5 resistant units (proportions=0.8 or 1.0) are classified as uncontrollable. Because of the high probability of misclassifying populations yielding samples containing 2 or 3 resistant units (proportions=0.4 or 0.6), the controllability of such populations is classified as questionable. In practice, we recommend treating questionable populations as uncontrollable. To minimize further selection for resistance in a population that already has a detectable level of resistance to the insecticide in question, we further advise that growers avoid using an insecticide if any of the egg masses in a sample are classified as resistant.

The decision scheme is highly conservative and biased against misclassifying uncontrollable populations as controllable. The probability of classifying a population as controllable decreases in a nonlinear fashion as the true proportion of resistant egg masses in the population increases (Figure 5).

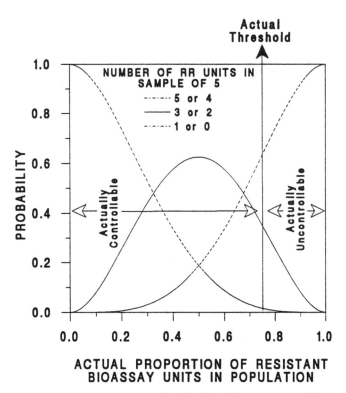

Fig. 5. Relationship between the true proportion of resistant egg masses in a population and the probability of a sample of 5 containing 0 or 1 resistant units and classifying the population as controllable, 2 or 3 resistant units and being able to classify the population, or 4 or 5 resistant units and classifying the population as uncontrollable. Indeed, the probability of obtaining a sample of 5 containing 0 or 1 resistant units from an uncontrollable population (i.e. with a true proportion of resistant egg masses >0.75) is very low ($P<0.01$).

In contrast, the probability of classifying a population as uncontrollable (i.e. obtaining a sample of 5 containing 4 or 5 resistant units) increases nonlinearly as the true proportion of resistant egg masses in the population increases (Figure 5). For controllable populations with a true proportion of resistant egg masses of <0.25, the probability of obtaining a sample of 5 containing 4 or 5 resistant egg masses and classifying the population as uncontrollable is very small ($P<0.01$). However, the probability of classifying controllable populations as uncontrollable reaches rather high levels as the true proportion of resistant egg masses in the population approaches the threshold value of 0.75.

The probability of obtaining a sample of 5 containing 2 or 3 resistant units (proportion=0.4 or 0.6) and classifying the population as resistant egg masses in the population increases (Figure 5). A significant limitation of this decision scheme is that the probability of classifying uncontrollable populations (true proportion of resistant units >0.75) as questionable can be rather high for populations with a true proportion of resistant egg masses close to the threshold. Similarly, the probability of classifying controllable populations (true proportion of resistant egg masses <0.75) as questionable can be very high, especially for populations with intermediate proportions of resistant egg masses (Figure 5). These probabilities can be reduced somewhat by increasing the sample size from 5 to 10 or even 15 egg masses when possible.

The limitations of this decision scheme result from practical constraints on sample size and the desire to minimize the probability of misclassifying uncontrollable populations as controllable. The constraints imposed by these limitations are less severe than they may seem at first because, for at least some insecticides (e.g., carbofuran), most populations are either predominantly resistant or susceptible (French & Kennedy, unpublished), (1). Further, the occurrence of any resistant units in a sample of 5 clearly indicates that there is a significant frequency of resistant phenotypes in the population. When the insecticide in question is used to control such a population, the resulting selection can cause a dramatic increase in the frequency of resistant phenotypes. This is illustrated by the increase in resistance that was observed in a potato beetle population following a single aerial application of carbofuran (Figure 6). Pretreatment bioassays of this population in a commercial potato field showed that fewer than 20% of the sample units (n=25) had less than 50% mortality. The reduction of this population following application of carbofuran at 1.12 kg (AI)/ha was 97%. Bioassays of the next generation of potato beetles in this field revealed that 98% of the sample units (n=46) had mortality levels of less than 50%. This population would no longer be controllable using carbofuran. Because of situations like this, we advise against using an insecticide if any of the egg masses in a sample are classified as resistant.

Validation of the monitoring protocol. To obtain data to validate the protocol, 7 populations were bioassayed for resistance to carbofuran and then treated with carbofuran at 1.12 kg (AI)/ha in small plot field trials to evaluate efficacy (Table 1). Six of these populations were classified as resistant based on both small (5 egg masses) and large (22 to 25 egg masses) samples. Control in the field was poor in 5 of these populations (Tony II, MDJR, Murray, Pump, and New Ground)

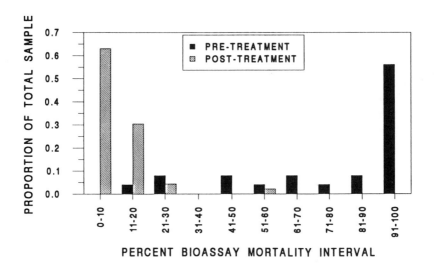

PERCENT BIOASSAY MORTALITY INTERVAL

Fig. 6. Response of a Colorado potato beetle population (HOT SPOT) from Washington County, North Carolina to a single aerial application of carbofuran at 1.12 kg(Al)/ha. Bioassays with the diagnostic concentration of carbofuran (0.2 μg/cm^2) were conducted in May and June 1991, approximately one week before treatment (n=25 bioassay units) and one month after treatment (n=49).

TABLE 1. Relationship between bioassay mortality and field control in field trials to validate the resistance monitoring scheme - 1991.

Field	Proportion resistant n=22-25	n=5[a]	Classification of population	% Control[b]
Tony II	1.0	1.0	R	5.7
MDJR	1.0	1.0	R	33.3
Murray	1.0	1.0	R	33.8
Pump	.96	1.0	R	53.0
New ground	.78	1.0	R	59.5
Geo II	.91	1.0	R	97.7
Hot Spot	.20	.40	?	97.0

[a]Bioassay sample size.
[b]Mean % control with field spray of carbofuran (1.12 kg[Al]ha).

290

and satisfactory in one (Geo II). One of the populations (Hot Spot) was classified as questionable; control of that population was satisfactory. None of the populations in which control was unsatisfactory were classified as controllable.

The only classification error made was in misclassifying the controllable population in Geo II as uncontrollable, and this is not surprising given the probabilities of such misclassifications (Figure 4).

Two concentration bioassay strategy. The frequency of misclassification errors may be reduced by including two diagnostic concentrations in the monitoring protocol: a low concentration (i.e., LC_{95} for a susceptible population) for detecting shifts in resistance before they result in control failures, and a higher concentration for predicting control failures. In Geo II, 91% of 23 bioassay units were classified as resistant at the standard lower carbofuran concentration ($0.20\,\mu g\,[AI]/cm^2$); but at a higher concentration ($8.50\,\mu g[AI]/cm^2$), only 25% of 20 units were classified as resistant. Using the higher concentration and a classification scheme similar to the one described for the lower concentration, the Geo II population would have been correctly judged as controllable. The higher concentration is well suited for predicting control failures in populations where resistance has previously been detected or is at least suspected. It is, however, relatively insensitive to changes in resistance levels below those that affect field control. In a two concentration bioassay scheme, the lower diagnostic concentration would be used for a given population until a shift in resistance was detected. Subsequent bioassays of that population would use the higher diagnostic concentration and be directed at predicting control failure with greater reliability.

Epilogue

Because the history of insecticide resistance in the Colorado potato beetle clearly demonstrates the potential of this insect to evolve resistance whenever significant selection pressure is applied, it can be assumed that low frequencies of resistant genotypes are present in most potato beetle populations. Consequently, resistance monitoring in a pest and resistance management context is most appropriately directed at detecting significant changes in the frequency of resistant phenotypes and predicting control failures before they occur. The described resistance monitoring protocol meets these objectives and is suitable for use by pest management consultants, potato growers and county extension agents. The procedure is safe, rapid, and easy to use. It reliably detects resistance in a population before control failures result, and it can be used as an aid in insecticide selection.

Because of constraints on sample size, the scheme is not suitable for detection of low frequencies of resistant individuals in a population. The bioassay technique, however, is suitable for detecting low frequencies if the sample sizes are appropriate. The resistance monitoring protocol has its greatest utility in those areas where resistance varies greatly among beetle populations or where resistance levels change rapidly over time.

Although we have presented only supporting data for carbofuran, similar research with other insecticides (French and Kennedy unpublished, Dively, Linduska and Everich unpublished) indicates the scheme will work for most, if not all, insecticides that have contact toxicity, provided an appropriate diagnostic concentration is used.

Literature Cited

1.   Bishop, B. A. & E. Grafius. 1991. An on-farm insecticide resistance monitoring test kit for Colorado potato beetle (Coleoptera: Chrysomelidae). Amer. Potato J. 68: 53-64.

2.   Brent, K. J. 1986. Detection and monitoring of resistant forms: an overview, pp. 298-312. *In* National Academy of Sciences (Board on Agriculture), Pesticide resistance: strategies and tactics for management. National Academy of Sciences, Washington, D.C.

3.   Brown, T. M. & W. G. Brodgon. 1987. Improved detection of insecticide resistance through conventional and molecular techniques. Annu. Rev. Entomol. 32: 145-162.

4.   Dennehy, T. J., J. Granett, T. F. Leigh & A. Calvin. 1987. Laboratory and field investigations of spider mite (Acari: Tetranychidae) resistance to the selective acaricide propargite. J. Econ. Entomol. 80: 565-574.

5.   Devonshire, A. L., G. D. Moores & R. H. ffrench-Constant. 1986. Detection of insecticide resistance by immunological estimation of carboxylase activity in *Myzus persicae* (Sulzer) and cross-reaction of the antiserum with *Phorodon humuli* (Schrank) (Hemiptera: Aphididae). Bull. Ent. Res. 76: 97-107.

6.   Ferro, D. N. 1985. Pest status and control strategies of the Colorado potato beetle, pp. 1-8. *In* D. N. Ferro & R. H. Voss [eds.], Proceedings of the Symposium on the Colorado Potato Beetle, XVII International Congress of Entomology. Mass. Agr. Exp. Stn. Bull. 704, Amherst, Mass.

7.   ffrench-Constant, R. H., A. L. Devonshire & S. J. Clark. 1987. Differential rate of selection for resistance by carbamate, organophosphorus and combined pyrethroid and organophosphorus insecticides in *Myzus persicae* (Sulzer) (Hemiptera: Aphididae). Bull. Ent. Res. 77: 227-238.

8.   ffrench-Constant, R. H. & R. T. Roush. 1990. Resistance detection and documentation: the relative roles of pesticidal and biochemical assays, pp. 4-38. *In* R. T. Roush & B. E. Tabashnik [eds.], Pesticide Resistance in Arthropods. Chapman and Hall, New York.

9. Forgash, A. J. 1981. Insecticide resistance of the Colorado potato beetle *Leptinotarsa decemlineata* (Say), pp. 34-46. *In* J. H. Lashomb & R. Casagrande [eds.], Advances in Potato Pest Management. Hutchinson & Ross Publ. Co., Stroudsburg, PA.

10. Gauthier, N. L., R. H. Hofmaster & M. Semel. 1981. History of Colorado potato beetle control, pp. 13-33. *In* J. H. Lashomb and R. Casagrande [eds.], Advances in potato pest management. Hutchinson and Ross Publ. Co., Stroudsburg, Pa.

11. Heim, D. C., G. G. Kennedy & J. W. Van Duyn. 1990. Survey of insecticide resistance among North Carolina potato beetle (Coleoptera: Chrysomelidae) populations. J. Econ. Entomol. 83: 1229-1235.

12. Hemingway, J., C. Smith, K. G. I. Jayawardena & P. R. J. Herath. 1986. Field and lab detection of the altered acetylchlionesterase resistance genes which confer organophosphate and carbamate resistance for mosquitoes (Diptera: Culicidae). Bull. Ent. Res. 76: 559-565.

13. Pasteur, N. & G. P. Georghiou. 1989. Improved filter paper test for detection and quantifying increased esterase activity in organophosphate-resistant mosquitoes (Diptera: Culicidae). J. Econ. Entomol. 82: 347-353.

14. Roush, R. T. & G. L. Miller. 1986. Considerations for design of insecticide resistance monitoring programs. J. Econ. Entomol. 79: 293-298.

15. Tisler, A. M. & G. W. Zehnder. 1990. Insecticide resistance in the Colorado potato beetle (Coleoptera: Chrysomelidae) on the eastern shore of Virginia. J. Econ. Entomol. 83: 666-671.

BIOCHEMICAL MECHANISMS
OF INSECTICIDE RESISTANCE IN
THE COLORADO POTATO BEETLE

J. Marshall Clark and Joseph A. Argentine
Department of Entomology
Fernald Hall
University of Massachusetts
Amherst, MA 01003

In this chapter, we will briefly summarize the most salient biochemical features of resistance elicited by the Colorado potato beetle (CPB) to three insecticides. Each of these compounds represent a separate major class of insecticides (i.e., an organophosphate, azinphosmethyl; a pyrethroid, permethrin and an avermectin, abamectin).   Resistance to azinphosmethyl and permethrin by CPB has been widely reported, especially in northeastern United States. In view of this, neither insecticide is likely to be used again to any great extent in the control of this pest. However, information on the genetics, biochemistry and molecular biology of resistance to abamectin, prior to its use commercially, would allow the development of management strategies to prolong the usefulness of this very important and novel insecticide.

For this purpose, we have prepared isogenic strains of CPB using a laboratory susceptible strain from North Carolina (SS) and a multiply-resistant field strain from Massachusetts (MA-R) by classical backcrossing and mutational schemes. These isogenic strains are specifically resistant to azinphosmethyl (AZ-R strain), permethrin (PE-R strain) and abamectin (AB-F from the field strain and AB-L from the laboratory strain). Experimental details and background genetic information of these strains can be found in a series of previously published papers (2,3,4,7). Such an approach is certainly tedious, time consuming, and expensive but absolutely necessary if the biochemical and molecular changes that have resulted in resistance are to be examined with any degree of accuracy (5).

Using similar approaches, insects such as *Drosophila melanogaster, Musca domestica* and *Tribolium castaneum* have set the standards by which genetic and molecular animal models are judged (5). Unfortunately, CPB has not proved to be a good genetic model (because of its long generational time, complex dietary needs, etc). Preliminary data also indicate that CPB is not likely to be a good molecular model because of its large genome size (approximately 13-times larger than *Drosophila*), which is organized into 17 pairs of autosomes with short period interspersions of repetitive DNA (J.M. Clark, unpublished data). Nevertheless, genetic, biochemical and molecular investigations with CPB are justified due to its stature as perhaps the most insecticide-resistant insect available to date. CPB is certainly one of the most notorious examples of pest control failure due to insecticide resistance. It is multiply and cross-resistant to all five major groups of insecticides (9), resistant to *Bacillus thuringiensis* (see Whalon, et al., this volume), and abamectin (2) and is consistently one of the first target pest insects to develop resistance to any insecticide used to control it. In a single genomic compliment, CPB has demonstrated all resistance mechanisms identified to cause insecticide resistances (e.g., pharmacokinetic resistances, metabolic resistances, pharmacodynamic/site-insensitivity resistances, physiological/behavioral resistances) (1-4). Although some insects are more easily studied, the development of CPB as a resistance model is not only meritorious in its own right but most necessary due to the virtual lack of available effective control means.

Biochemical Mechanisms of
Azinphosmethyl Resistance

Resistance to azinphosmethyl in the AZ-R and MA-R strains appears to be complex, involving at least 3 mechanisms and possible a fourth. Evidence indicates that oxidative metabolism is a contributing factor. The azinphosmethyl-resistant strains (AZ-R & MA-R) produced substantially higher levels of metabolites under both *in vivo* and *in vitro* conditions compared with the SS strain (Tables 1 & 2, respectively). The increase in the levels of metabolites ranged from 2.0-fold to 4.0-fold in these experiments. Metabolite formation was greatly attenuated by the addition of piperonyl butoxide (PBO) to both systems (data not shown). Since cytochrome P_{450} levels and overall oxidase activities using general substitutes were not significantly different between the SS and the AZ-R strains (1), a different isozyme of cytochrome P_{450} most likely has been produced in the AZ-R and MA-R strains.

Table 1. *In vivo* metabolism of [^{14}C]azinphosmethyl in susceptible (SS) and azinphosmethyl-resistant (AZ-R & MA-R) strains of fourth-instar CPB larvae.

	% metabolite formed from applied dose ± S.D.		
Metabolite	SS	AZ-R	MA-R
Desmethyl-oxon Excrement			
2 hr	0.87 ± 0.12	1.89 ± 0.44[a]	3.11 ± 0.79[a]
6 hr	1.32 ± 0.81	3.67 ± 1.20[a]	5.71 ± 1.40[a]
Benzazimide Excrement			
2 hr	3.00 ± 0.48	5.53 ± 1.03[a]	6.90 ± 0.92[a]
6 hr	5.28 ± 0.84	9.84 ± 1.93[a]	11.62 ± 1.62[a]

[a] Significantly different from SS strain, *t*-test, $P < 0.05$, n = 3.

Table 2. In vitro metabolism of [^{14}C]azinphosmethyl in susceptible (SS) and azinphosmethyl-resistant (AZ-R & MA-R) strains of fourth-instar CPB larvae.

	(pmole/min/mg protein ± S.D.)		
Subcellular fractions and metabolites	SS	AZ-R	MA-R
105,000g Supernatant (GSH)			
Desmethyl-oxon	0.44 ± 0.03	0.42 ± 0.07	0.37 ± 0.07
Microsomes (NADPH)			
Azin-oxon	10.9 ± 1.6	14.9 ± 2.4	16.6 ± 0.4[a]
Methyl benzazimide	2.1 ± 1.6	14.9 ± 2.4	5.5 ± 1.8[b]
Benzazimide	12.7 ± 2.2	28.6 ± 6.2[b]	37.3 ± 8.0[a]
Desmethyl-azin	1.8 ± 0.3	4.0 ± 0.1[a]	3.2 ± 0.8[b]
Desmethyl-oxon	1.9 ± 0.5	3.3 ± 1.4	2.7 ± 0.2
Unknown	1.5 ± 0.1	4.0 ± 1.1[b]	4.8 ± 1.0[a]
Microsomes + 105,000g Supernatant (GSH + NADPH)			
Azin-oxon	8.7 ± 0.6	9.8 ± 1.4[c]	18.9 ± 4.5
Benzazimide	22.6 ± 4.6	38.5 ± 13.3	50.2 ± 8.2

[a]Significantly different from SS strain, *t*-test, $P < 0.01$, n = 3.
[b]Significantly different from SS strain, t-test, $P < 0.05$, n = 3.
[c]Significantly different from azin-oxon activity of AZ-R with microsomes alone (t-test, $P < 0.05$, n = 3).

The role of glutathione-S-transferase activity (GST) in azinphosmethyl resistance is not as clear as the role of monoxygenases. However, the GST-dependant conjugation of dichloronitrobenzene was significantly higher in the AZ-R strain (1) and metabolites produced *in vivo* [i.e., desmethyl-azinphosmethyl oxon (desmethyl-oxon) and benzazimide] could have been formed by GST activity (Table 1). Nevertheless, only a low level of the desmethyl-oxon metabolite was identified from metabolism which occurred in the 105,000g supernatant fortified with GSH and the levels of this metabolite in the azinphomethyl-resistant strains were not significantly different from the SS strain (Table 2).

The activity of GST on monooxygenase metabolites, particularly azinphosmethyl oxon (azin-oxon), was studied by incubating the microsomal suspension with the 105,000g supernatant fortified with NADPH and GSH (bottom, Table 2). Only benzazimide was produced at a higher total level compared with microsomes alone. After subtraction of the monooxygenase component, it was determined that there was no significant difference between strains in benzazimide formation, indicating GST may not be directly involved in azinphosmethyl resistance. However, the increased levels of benzazimide in this preparation indicate that GST is active against an oxidative metabolite, which is probably azin-oxon. Thus, GST could be important in the detoxification of excess azin-oxon produced by the AZ-R and MA-R strains (1), even if GST activity is similar in the SS and azinphosmethyl-resistant strains.

The MA-R strain appears to have a reduced penetration factor involved in overall azinphosmethyl resistance. The MA-R strain had significantly more azinphosmethyl (approx. 2-fold) remaining on the cuticle surface 2 hr after topical-application of [^{14}C]azinphosmethyl compared with either the SS or AZ-R strain (Figure 1). It is likely that this mechanism exhibits cross-resistance to a number of other insecticides and, because of this, was lost during the backcrossing procedure to establish the AZ-R strain. It is expected that the reduced penetration mechanism will potentiate the oxidative metabolic factors involved in azinphosmethyl resistance. Additionally, a reduced penetration factor may be important in azinphosmethyl resistance in CPB because of the rapid excretion of radiolabeled compound (1). Reduced penetration coupled with rapid excretion could prevent internal levels of azinphosmethyl from reaching toxic levels.

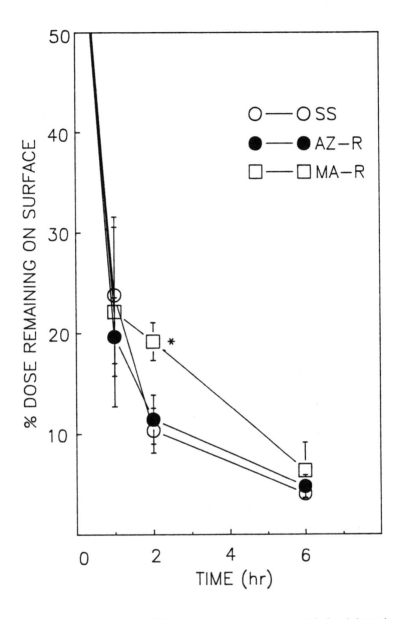

Figure 1. Penetration rate of [^{14}C]azinphosmethyl (60ng/larvae) in fourth-instar larvae of the susceptible (SS) and azinphosmethyl-resistant (AZ-R & MA-R) strains of CPB. Asterisk (*) indicates significant difference from the susceptible (SS) strain *t*-test, $P < 0.05$ (n=5).

The AZ-R strain also appears to have an altered cholinesterase component in its resistance. Although there was no difference between the SS and AZ-R strains in V_{max} of cholinesterase activity towards acetylthiocholine, there was a significant difference in K_m values between the two strains (Table 3). This indicates that an altered cholinesterase is present in the AZ-R strain with a lower affinity for acetylthiocholine. Enzyme inhibition (10) studies revealed a significant difference in the bimolecular rate constant (k_i) between the SS and AZ-R strains to azin-oxin (Table 3). The effect of an altered acetylcholinesterase would be greatly potentiated when combined with the reduced penetration and increased oxidative metabolism mechanisms found in the azinphosmethyl-resistant strains.

Table 3. Kinetic analysis of acetylcholinesterase activity (Ellman reaction) for fourth-instar larvae of the susceptible (SS) and azinphosmethyl-resistant (AZ-R) strains of CPB.

Kinetic Constants	SS	AZ-R
$K_m (\mu M)$	8.45 ± 1.09[a]	20.28 ± 4.08[b]
V_{max} (nmoles/min/mg protein)	18.77 ± 2.81	22.33 ± 1.74
Azinphosmethyl oxon		
$k_i \ 10^{-4} \times k_i (M^{-1}min^{-1})$	15.70 ± 0.63	8.63 ± 3.34[b]
$k_p \ (min^{-1})$	0.25 ± 0.10	0.20 ± 0.08
$K_d \ (\mu M)$	1.61 ± 0.36	2.32 ± 0.41

[a]Mean value ± standard deviation for 3 separate experiments.
[b]Significantly different from SS strain, t-test, $P < 0.05$, $n = 3$.

Biochemical Mechanisms of Permethrin Resistance

Permethrin resistance in the PE-R strain of CPB appears to be due principly to increased carboxylesterase activity (i.e., permethrin carboxylesterase) and possibly site-insensitivity (e.g., cross-resistance to DDT).

General esterase activity as determined by α-naphthyl butyrate hydrolysis was only slightly enhanced in the PE-R strain above the level of the SS strain, while carboxylesterase activity was found to be significantly higher in the PE-R strain (Table 4).

Table 4. *In vitro* esteratic activities of fourth-instar larvae of susceptible (SS) and permethrin-resistant (PE-R) strains of CPB.

	nmole/min/mg protein ± S.D.	
Assays[a]	SS	PE-R
General Esterases		
α-Naphthyl acetate	650.7 ± 55.4	800.2 ± 237.0
α-Naphthyl butyrate	906.9 ± 153.4	1102.1 ± 328.3
Carboxylesterases[b]		
α-Naphthyl acetate	115.1 ± 24.4	131.3 ± 50.1
α-Naphthyl butyrate	75.3 ± 21.2	107.4 ± 16.8[c]

[a]Six replicates used in each assay.
[b]Carboxylesterase activity determined in the presence of eserine (0.1mM) and PHMB (0.1mM).
[c]Significantly different from SS strain, (*t*-test, $P < 0.05$).

A Lineweaver-Burk double reciprocal plot was constructed to determine the kinetic constants of the carboxylesterase activity associated with both the SS and the PE-R strains. No significant difference in K_m values between the two strains was found indicating no change in affinity, but V_{max} was significantly increased in the PE-R strain (Table 5). This result indicates that the PE-R strain has higher levels of carboxylesterase or a carboxylesterase with higher activity compared with the SS strain.

Table 5. Kinetic analysis of carboxylesterase activity associated with α-naphthyl butyrate hydrolysis in fourth-instar of the susceptible (SS) and permethrin-resistant (PE-R) strains of CPB.

Kinetic Constants	SS	PE-R
$K_m (\mu M)$	145.1 ± 11.1	167.5 ± 13.7
V_{max}(nmoles/min/mg protein)	122.2 ± 5.1	182.8 ± 13.6[a]

[a] Significantly different from SS strain, *t*-test, $P < 0.05$, n = 3.

Studies on the *in vivo* and *in vitro* metabolism of [^{14}C]permethrin substantiates the above general enzyme activity results. Phenoxybenzyl alcohol (PBA) was the only metabolite identified during the *in vivo* metabolism of topically-applied [^{14}C] permethrin by the CPB strains. Both PE-R and MA-R strains produced significantly higher levels of PBA as determined by radioactivity in internal solvent extracts at 6 hr compared to SS strain (Table 6). This difference was even more pronounced in the excrement where both resistant strains had levels of PBA over 2-fold higher compared with the SS strain at 2 hr post-application. Thus, both resistant strains produced more PBA than the SS strain, indicating either hydrolytic or oxidative metabolism as a mechanism in permethrin resistance.

Table 6. Levels of [^{14}C]phenoxybenzyl alcohol (PBA) formed *in vivo* by fourth-instar larvae of the susceptible (SS) and permethrin-resistant (PE-R & MA-R) strains of CPB.

| Time Interval | % PBA formed from applied dose ± S.D. | | |
	SS	PE-R	MA-R
Internal			
2 hr	2.60 ± 0.96	3.76 ± 2.11	3.00 ± 1.24
6 hr	2.51 ± 0.52	3.93 ± 0.82[a]	3.71 ± 1.16[b]
Excrement			
2 hr	3.36 ± 1.77	7.00 ± 1.52[a]	6.73 ± 1.89[a]
6 hr	3.02 ± 1.02	4.29 ± 1.65	3.54 ± 1.30

[a]Significantly different from SS strain, *t*-test, $P < 0.05$, n = 4.
[b]Significantly different from SS strain, *t*-test, $P < 0.10$, n = 4.

There was no evidence of any difference in the hydrolysis rate of [^{14}C]permethrin in the three strains using an *in vitro*, PBO-treated, 13,000g supernatant enzyme preparation (Table 7). This indicates that a soluble esterase is not significantly involved in permethrin resistance. Also the principle metabolite isolated was not PBA, as was the case *in vivo*, but phenoxybenzoic acid (PBacid). In contrast, a microsomal preparation which also included PBO had significantly higher levels of permethrin hydrolysis in both permethrin-resistant strains compared with the SS strain (Table 7). This demonstrates that a membrane-associated esterase is involved in permethrin resistance and is responsible for increased hydrolytic cleavage of permethrin, thus detoxifying it.

Oxidative metabolism appears to be involved in the detoxification of permethrin, but the role of monoxygenases in resistance in the permethrin-resistant strains is less certain. Ester cleavage products were formed oxidatively (microsomes plus NADPH/DFP), but at a slightly reduced level compared to hydrolytic cleavage of permethrin by the microsomal preparation (microsomes plus PBO) (Table 7). Also, there was no difference between the level of oxidative ester cleavage products formed by the SS and MA-R strains, and only a slight increase was apparent with the PE-R strain. Since there was no highly significant difference in the oxidative metabolism of permethrin between the susceptible and resistant strains, it is doubtful that monooxygenases function as permethrin resistance mechanisms in these strains.

Table 7. *In vitro* metabolism of [^{14}C] permethrin by various subcellular fraction from larvae of the susceptible (SS) and permethrin-resistant (PE-R & MA-R) strains of CPB.

Subcellular Fractions	pmole/hr/mg protein ± S.D.		
	SS	PE-R	MA-R
13,000g			
Supernatant (+PBO)			
Hydrolytic ester cleavage			
PBA	10.9 ± 1.1	8.9 ± 3.7	7.7 ± 1.2
PBacid	19.8 ± 5.6	20.9 ± 6.0	18.1 ± 8.9
Microsomes (+PBO)			
Hydrolytic ester cleavage			
PBA	13.0 ± 5.1	10.2 ± 1.3	10.3 ± 1.2
PBacid	57.2 ± 14.7	91.3 ± 11.0[a]	74.9 ± 5.8[b]
Microsomes (+NADPH/DFP)			
Oxidative ester cleavage			
PBA	8.0 ± 5.1	7.1 ± 1.3	5.8 ± 1.2
PBacid	45.5 ± 8.7	70.6 ± 19.0[b]	57.9 ± 13.6
HO-per	47.2 ± 4.7	65.4 ± 12.8[a]	52.1 ± 12.0

[a]Significantly different from the SS strain, *t*-test, $P<0.05$, n=4.
[b]Significantly different from the SS strain, *t*-test, $P<0.10$, n=4.

An additional metabolite was formed by oxidative metabolism *in vitro* in the NADPH/DFP-treated microsomal fraction; the hydroxylated gem-methyl moiety of [^{14}C]permethrin (HO-per). The HO-per metabolite was produced in all of the strains under *in vitro* conditions, yet was not isolated *in vivo*. A plausible explanation is that HO-per metabolite is rapidly conjugated and excreted *in vivo*. The conjugated product could be the principle component of the unextractable radioactivity found in the excrement at 6 hr post-topical application (1). If ester cleavage occurred soon after hydroxylation *in vivo*, the only metabolite that would be detectable would be PBA, since [^{14}C]permethrin was labeled at the methylene carbon of PBA.

The multiply-resistant MA-R field strain was found to be highly resistant to DDT (1). This cross-resistance could be due to a number of different resistance mechanisms. However, the PE-R strain, which has a genome approximately 96% that of the SS strain (3), was also cross-resistant to DDT (Table 8). It is doubtful that metabolic factors are involved in this cross-resistance because DDT and permethrin have very different structures and metabolic requirements. Because of the backcrossing and selection procedures used, most factors from the MA-R strain not associated with permethrin resistance would not be present in the isogenic PE-R strain. This indicates a possibility of a site-insensitivity mechanism in the nervous system similar to that associated with DDT and other pyrethroid-resistant insects. Although cross-resistance to DDT in the MA-R and more importantly the PE-R strain provides strong evidence that a site-insensitivity mechanism may also play a role in permethrin resistance in these strains, electrophysiological and knockdown data is necessary to prove conclusively that nerve site insensitivity is a mechanism in permethrin resistance found in CPB.

Table 8. Log-dose versus logit mortality regressions of DDT and permethrin to fourth-instar larvae of the susceptible (SS) and permethrin-resistant (PE-R & MA-R) strains of CPB.

Strains	N	LD$_{50}$(CL)[a]	Slope[b]	RR[c]
		DDT(μg)/larvae		
SS	246	4.47(1.60-9.89)	1.83(0.25)	-
PE-R	430	38.92(19.18-208.1)	1.51(0.22)	9
MA-R	183	>124.62	1.24(0.46)	29
		Permethrin(μg)/larvae		
SS	187	0.06(0.053-0.083)	2.25(0.74)	-
PE-R	448	1.13(0.743-1.535)	0.96(0.119)	19
MA-R	547	3.33(2.564-4.686)	1.36(0.22)	55

[a]95% confidence interval limit (CL) in parentheses.
[b]Standard error of mean (SE) in parentheses.
[c]Resistance ratio = LD$_{50}$(Resistant strain)/LD$_{50}$ (Susceptible strain).

Biochemical Mechanisms of Abamectin Resistance

Resistance to abamectin in both abamectin-resistant strains (AB-F and AB-L) appears to be oxidative and may possibly involve esterases. Cytochrome P_{450} levels were significantly elevated (i.e., 60-90%) in the two abamectin-resistant strains compared to the SS strain (bottom, Table 9). However, overall oxidative activities (i.e., oxidases) were not increased for any of the general oxidative substrates tested and there was no concurrent increase in cytochrome c reductase activity (1) or cytochrome b_5 levels (Table 9).

Table 9. *In vitro* metabolic activities of fourth-instar larvae of the susceptible (SS) and abamectin-resistant (AB-F & AB-L) strains of CPB.

Assays	SS	AB-F	AB-L
	(nmole/min/mg protein ± S.D.)		
General Esterases(4)[a]			
α-Naphthyl acetate	356.5 ± 39.9	516.6 ± 11.5[b]	505.7 ± 37.4[b]
α-Naphthyl butyrate	450.0 ± 72.3	689.4 ± 63.5[b]	711.0 ± 0.3[b]
Carboxylesterases(4)[c]			
α-Naphthyl acetate	77.7 ± 6.7	97.6 ± 12.6[d]	117.2 ± 8.1[b]
α-Naphthyl butyrate	73.3 ± 17.2	150.7 ± 43.8[b]	193.7 ± 20.3[b]
	(pmole/mg protein ± S.D.)		
Cytochromes(6)			
P420	139.2 ± 79.7	108.8 ± 32.3	116.4 ± 28.8
P450	240.2 ± 35.1	457.5 ± 140.3[d]	388.8 ± 113.9[d]
b_5	264.3 ± 35.1	221.2 ± 31.8	205.1 ± 63.4

[a]Number of replicates in parentheses (n).
[b]Significantly different from SS strain, *t*-test, $P<0.01$. n=4.
[c]Carboxylesterase activity measured in the presence of eserine (0.1mM) and PHMB (0.1mM).
[d]Significantly different from SS strain, *t*-test, $P<0.05$.

General esterase and carboxylesterase activities in the abamectin-resistant strains were also significantly enhanced compared to the SS strain (Table 9). This was most apparent in the carboxylesterase assay where there was over a 2-fold increase in carboxylesterase activity to α-naphthyl butyrate in both abamectin-resistant strains compared with the SS strain. The overall increases in esterase activities indicates that either higher levels of esterases are being produced or esterases with enhanced activities (e.g., turn over rate, etc.) or substrate affinities have been selected in the resistant strains. A Lineweaver-Burk double reciprocal plot of carboxylesterase activity (Figure 2) indicates that there is no apparent change in substrate affinities since the K_m values are approximately equal in the SS and abamectin-resistant strains (150uM vs. 144uM, respectively) but the V_{max} values are 2.4-fold higher (297 vs. 118 nmoles/min/mg protein) in the abamectin-resistant strains. Using native polyacrylamide gel electrophoresis to separate the proteins of the 105,000g supernatant and determining carboxylesterase activity as above, it was possible to detect strain differences in their ability to hydrolyze α-naphthyl butyrate by dianisidine staining (12). Total hydrolytic activity in the major staining band of the gel (i.e., largest peak identified by scanning desitometry) increased 1.3-fold in the AB-L strain. These results further indicate that abamectin resistance may be in part attributable to increased levels of carboxylesterase(s) (7).

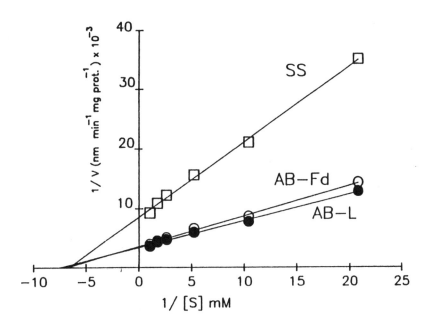

Figure 2. Lineweaver-Burk double reciprocal plot of carboxylesterase activity (α-naphthyl butyrate hydrolysis in the presence of eserine and PHMB) in the susceptible (SS) and abamectin-resistant (AB-F & AB-L) strains of CPB.

In Vivo metabolism of [³H]avermectin B1a by reverse-phase (C_{18}) HPLC analysis with radiometric detection (7) of the excrement at 6 hr post topical-application revealed no significant difference in [³H]avermectin B1a levels in any of the strains (Table 10). However, significantly higher levels of 3"desmethyl avermectin B1a (3"desmethyl), 24-hydroxylmethyl avermectin B1a (24-OH), and an unidentified metabolite which eluted off the reverse-phase column at 14-15 min (i.e., Fraction 14) were associated with the abamectin-resistant strains compared with the SS strains. The AB-F strain had slightly elevated levels of all metabolites, which may explain why the AB-F had a slightly higher level of resistance to abamectin compared with the AB-L strain (2). The AB-L strain had significantly higher 24-OH and Fraction 14 metabolite levels but did not have a significantly higher level of 3"desmethyl. The increased levels of more polar, oxidative metabolites strongly indicate a monooxygenase-based form of resistance in the AB-F and AB-L strains. Interestingly, the major metabolite formed in all strains was 3"desmethyl and is similar to the findings in rat (11).

Table 10. *In vivo* and *in vitro* metabolism of [^{3}H]Avermectin B1a by susceptible (SS) and abamectin-resistant (AB-F & AB-L) strains of CPB.

Assay and Metabolites	% of applied dose in sample ± S.D.		
	SS	AB-F	AB-L
In Vivo[a]			
Avermectin B1a	32.71 ± 3.61	35.80 ± 5.50	33.35 ± 4.45
3" Desmethyl	1.26 ± 0.18	2.30 ± 0.28[b]	1.51 ± 0.19
24-OH	0.45 ± 0.01	1.16 ± 0.21[b]	0.87 ± 0.21[c]
Fraction 14	140.58 ± 0.03	1.83 ± 0.69[c]	1.50 ± 0.50[c]
In Vitro			
Microsomes (+ NADPH)			
Avermectin B1a	77.00 ± 5.03	64.30 ± 11.07	72.19 ± 8.40
3" Desmethyl	2.72 ± 0.21	6.37 ± 0.01[b]	5.21 ± 0.72[b]
24-OH	N.D.	1.50 ± 0.75[b]	0.72 ± 0.27[b]
Fraction 14	N.D.	3.33 ± 1.00[b]	1.34 ± 0.74[b]

[a]Extraction from excrement collected from CPB at 6 hr, (n = 3).
[^{3}H]Avermectin B1a was applied at 0.46ng/larva.
[b]Significant difference from the SS strain, (*t*-test, $P < 0.01$, n = 3).
[c]Significant difference from the SS strain, (*t*-test, $P < 0.05$, n = 3).
[d]N.D., Not detected.

However, unlike rat, the novel metabolite, Fraction 14, was detected at the same or greater levels as 24-OH regardless of the strain but was particularly evident in the abamectin-resistant strains (Table 10). Apparently, Fraction

14 has a water solubility intermediate between 24-OH and 3"desmethyl, since these two metabolites eluted off the reversed-phase HPLC column at 6 and 19 min, respectively.

In vitro metabolism of [^{3}H]avermectin B1a produced similar results as in the *in vivo* studies (Table 10). The 3"desmethyl metabolite formation was elevated 2.3-fold and 2.0-fold in the AB-F and AB-L strains, respectively. The Fraction 14 and 24-OH metabolites were not detectable in the SS strain, while both abamectin-resistant strains had detectable levels of these metabolites. These metabolites are apparently formed by monooxygenases, since PBO-treated microsomes produced no metabolites in any strain, including Fraction 14 (1,7).

Based on synergism studies (1,7), *in vivo* and *in vitro* metabolism, and cytochrome P_{450} data, abamectin resistance is at least partly due to oxidative metabolism. This is not surprising since abamectin metabolism in mammals is principally oxidative (6,10). In all CPB strains, the major metabolite detected was 3"desmethyl avermectin B1a. The level of this oxidative metabolite was significantly elevated in both abamectin-resistant strains under *in vivo* and *in vitro* assay conditions. Interestingly, a new but unidentified metabolite (Fraction 14) was found and its formation was enhanced principally in the abamectin-resistant strains.

Evidence also suggests that a carboxylesterase(s) may be involved in abamectin resistance. Synergism to DEF was not as high as with PBO, but was significantly higher in the abamectin-resistant strains compared with the SS strain (7). Carboxylesterase activity as judged by α-naphthyl butyrate hydrolysis was much higher in the abamectin-resistant strains than in the SS strain and this difference was due to an elevated V_{max} rather than to a change in affinity (K_m) of the enzyme activity. Because no radiolabeled hydrolysis products of abamectin were observed, it is unclear if hydrolytic degradation of abamectin is a resistance mechanism. Alternatively, carboxylesterase(s) may be acting as sequestering agents against abamectin. A carboxylesterase in *Myzus persicae* has been shown to act as a sequestering agent against a variety of insecticides (8). Preliminary evidence from this laboratory indicates that abamectin is a competitive inhibitor of carboxylesterase activity but has a very low affinity for the enzyme(s)(H. Lin, unpublished data).

Acknowledgment

This work was supported by research grant USDA-TPSU-UM-2977-40 and MAES (Hatch Project #617).

Literature Cited

1. Argentine, J.A. 1991. Ph.D. Dissertation, Biochemistry and genetics of insecticide resistance in the Colorado potato beetle. Dept. of Entomol., U. Massachusetts, pp.113.

2. Argentine, J.A. and Clark, J.M. 1990. Selection for abamectin resistance in Colorado potato beetle (Coleoptera: Chrysomelidae). Pestic. Sci. 28:17-24.

3. Argentine, J.A., Clark, J.M. and Ferro, D.N. 1989. Genetics and synergism of azinphosmethyl and permethrin resistance in the Colorado potato beetle (Coleoptera: Chrysomelidae). J. Econ. Entomol. 82:698-705.

4. Argentine, J.A., Clark, J.M. and Ferro, D.N. 1989. Relative fitness of insecticide-resistant Colorado potato beetle strains (Coleoptera: Chrysomelidae). Environ. Entomol. 18:705-710.

5. Beeman, R.W., Stuart, J.J., Denell, R.E., McGaughey, W.H. and Dover, B.A. 1992. *Tribolium* as a model insect for study of resistance mechanisms, in "Molecular Mechanisms of Resistance in Herbivorous Pests to Natural Synthetic and Bioengineered Control Agents." C.A.Mullin and J.G.Scott, (eds.), ACS Symposium Series, Amer. Chem. Soc. Washington, D.C. 505:205-212.

6. Chiu, S.L., Sestokas, E., Taub, R., Smith, J.L., Arison, B. and Lu, A.Y. 1984. The metabolism of avermectin $-H_2b_{1a}$ and $-H_2B_{1b}$ by pig liver microsomes. Drug Metab. Dispos. 12:464-469.

7. Clark, J.M., Argentine, J.A., Lin, H., and Gao, X.-Y. 1992. "Mechanisms of abamectin resistance in the Colorado potato beetle" Molecular Mechanisms of Resistance in Herbivorous Pests to Natural, Synthetic and Bioengineered Control Agents. Amer. Chem. Soc. Symposium Series, 505:251-268.

8. Devonshire, A.L. and G.D. Moores. 1982. A carboxylesterase with broad substrate specificity causes organophosphorus, carbamate and pyrethroid resistance in peach-potato aphids (*Myzus persicae*). Pestic. Biochem. Physiol. 18:235-246.

9. Forgash, A.J. 1981. Insecticide resistance of the Colorado potato beetle, *Leptinotarsa decemlineata* (Say): Advances in Potato Pest Management, J.H. Lashomb and R.A. Casagrande (eds.). Hutchinson Ross, Stroudsburg, PA pp.34-45.

10. Hart, G.J. and O'Brien, R.D. 1973. Recording spectrophotometric method for determination of dissociation and phosphorylation constants for the inhibition of acetylcholinesterase by organophosphates in the presence of substrate. Biochem. 12:2940-2945.

11. Maynard, M.S., Halley, B.A., Green-Erwin, M., Alvaro, R., Gruber, V.F., Hwang, S.C., Bennett, B.W., and Wislocki, P. G. 1990. Fate of avermectin B_{1a} in rats. J. Agric. Food Chem. 38:864-870.

12. Sparks, T.C. and Hammock, B.D. 1979. A comparison of induced and naturally occurring juvenile hormone esterases from last instar larvae of *Trichoplosia Ni*. Insect Biochem. 9:411-421.

SELECTION AND MANAGEMENT OF
BACILLUS THURINGIENSIS-RESISTANT
COLORADO POTATO BEETLE

Mark E. Whalon, Utami Rahardja and
Patchara Verakalasa
Department of Entomology
Pesticide Research Center
Michigan State University
East Lansing, MI 48824

The microevolutionary process of insect pest adaptation leading to the failure of many broad spectrum insecticides has become a formidable problem in agriculture and human health protection today. Certainly Colorado potato beetle (CPB), *Leptinotarsa decemlineata* (Say), is one of the premier species exhibiting the ability to develop resistance to virtually every organic insecticide deployed against it.

The recent discovery that several species of insects could adapt to *Bacillus thuringiensis* (Bt) δ-endotoxins (1,15,16,27,28,29,30,35,39)put to rest the assertion that insects would not likely develop resistance to bacterial insecticides (2,3,6). These developments have also raised considerable alarm among theoretical and applied entomologists who continue to advocate the development of sound resistance management programs within the context of integrated pest management (IPM) systems (8,34,40,43).

The development and impending commercialization of successful genetic engineering methodologies to produce transgenic plants (13, 4, 5) that express the δ-endotoxins of Bt for control of insects has heightened the need for resistance management programs (31). The question of the durability of these newly developed cultivars given the mixed success of conventional host plant resistance breeding programs (12, 22) has been raised in Washington at the Office of Technology Assessment for the US Congress (21). Certainly the advantages of transgenic plants over conventionally applied organic insecticides are compelling and include: 1) limiting the use of broad spectrum, environmentally expensive insecticides, 2) reducing the impact of conventionally applied insecticides on nontarget organisms, 3) enhancing biological control in most agricultural settings, 4) targeting only plant damaging species, and 5) protecting plant parts that are difficult to reach (3). Considerable public debate and scientific and policy scrutiny remain before transgenics are widely used in commercial agriculture, but their development certainly advocates a strong understanding of insecticide resistance.

The purpose of this chapter is to report the recent field and laboratory selection of CPB resistance to the CryIIIA coleopteran specific δ-endotoxin of Bt subsp. *tenebrionis*. We review data on the partial behavioral, genetic, and physiological characterization of the Bt-resistant CPB strain, and we advocate the development of a sound resistance management program for deployment of both conventionally applied and transgenic Bt.

Strategy for Selection of the Bt-resistant CPB Strain

For more than 20 years various Bts have been used commercially to control various insect pests. However, so far only *Plutella xylostella* has developed resistance in a field crop environment (39). It is not clear why researchers did not detect field resistance to Bt before the 1980s. We believe that Bt may not have been applied frequently enough, nor were they formulated in such a way that long residual activity could be achieved. Another factor could have been the mixture of multiple toxins and spores in early and currently available Bt formulations.

Based on extensive field and laboratory experience in selecting resistance in several different species (7,9,23), our strategy for selecting CPB resistance was to maximize the initial variability in the gene pool and to select with the highest selection pressure that we could practically achieve. We began our resistance selection experiments in six Michigan field sites representing different insecticide use histories. The density of CPB larvae in these fields was estimated between 2-6 million. A range of 6-10 applications of coleopteran-specific Bt insecticides were targeted against two CPB generation per year in 1987 and 1988 (maximum label rates of the toxin were used). At the end of the last year's selection, approximately 25,000 surviving beetles were collected and transported to our greenhouse at Michigan State University. The beetles were placed randomly on potted potato plants (cv. Atlantic) and allowed to mate and mature normally.

The resulting first generation larvae were selected in the second instar using a Bt (M-One Insecticide, Mycogen Corp., San Diego, Calif., USA) concentration that produced 95% mortality. All subsequent generations were selected using a 5X concentration to yield 98%

mortality in 2-3 days. Survivors were then transferred to untreated foliage to complete development; at least every other generation was bioassayed to determined resistance status. Conventional dosage mortality experiments were conducted on second instars using 5-6 concentrations of M-One Insecticide on potato leaflets. Between 25-30 larvae were tested per concentration and the experiment was replicated at least three times. Data were analyzed using standard probit analysis (43).

The selection experiments demonstrated that resistance to Bt in the bioassays increased with increasing CPB generation (Table 1). We have now achieved 200+ fold resistance in 17 generations. The resistance ratio (RR) is calculated as the LC_{50} of the selected strain divided by the LC_{50} of the unselected (original) field collected strain. RR values increased dramatically in the 4th, 8th, 12th and 17th generations.

Table 1. Selection for *Bacillus thuringiensis* resistance in 17 generations of Colorado Potato Beetle

| A | B | C | Probit Analysis[a] | | b | LC_{50} | RR |
			D	N			
F1	34,933	0.9	22-53	1,185	1.8	1.6	
F2	7,909	0.4	35	75	1.1	3	2
F3	14,125	1.4	35	NA	NA	NA	NA
F5	18,186	1.1	35-54	705	1.5	35	22
F6	13,664	1.9	35-72	330	1.3	35	15
F7	14,974	2.1	37-49	420	1.8	35	14
F8	9,329	2.6	37-49	1,122	1.5	64	38
F9	8,137	2.3	49-62	633	1.5	50	30
F10	5,921	0.5	790	594	1.9	45	27
F11	2,879	1.7	790	270	1.6	84	50
F12	2,034	2.2	790	270	1.2	100	59
F13	4,210	2.5	790	750	1.3	133	81
F14	3,321	2.1	790	NA	NA	NA	NA
F15	2,096	2.5	790	450	1.0	162	98
F16	2,231	2.6	790	450	1.9	241	146
F17	912	6.4	790	450	0.8	330	200

[a] N: Number of second instars used for bioassay; b: slope of the probit line; LC_{50}: Concentration of *Bacillus thuringiensis* that kill 50% of Colorado potato beetle colonies (mg/L).
NA: Data not available
A: Generations.
B: Number of larvae selected each generation
C: % adults emerged.
D: Concentration of *Bacillus thuringiensis* formulation used for selection (mg/L).
RR: Resistance ratio (LC_{50} Fx/ LC_{50} NS; where x is generation and NS is original, field-collected strain).

Table 2 presents data on the stability of resistance from a cohort of the 8th generation (58 fold resistant) after which selection was discontinued. RR decreased to approximately 3 after 5 generations and has since remained constant. The reversion of resistance in the absence of exposure to toxic agent may be due to selection against the resistance gene, the introduction of susceptible alleles, or a combination of the two (8, 41). In our case, the reversion could have resulted from selection against the Bt resistance gene(s). Reduced fecundity of resistant *Spodoptera frugiperda* (J.E. Smith) females was suspected as a result of selection against the nuclear polyhedrosis virus-resistance gene (11). Genetic variation may also increase when the selection pressure is removed due to the increase of susceptible alleles remaining in the resistance-selected colony.

Table 2. Stability of *Bacillus thuringiensis* resistance in Colorado Potato Beetle after selection was discontinued for six generations.

Generation	N	Slope	LC_{50} mg/L	RR
F8	1122	1.5	64	38
F9	450	1.1	16	10
F10	450	0.9	12	7
F11	450	1.3	14	8
F12	450	1.1	9	5
F13	450	1.0	5	3

N,   Number of second instars used for bioassay.
RR,   Resistance ratio (LC_{50} Fx/ LC_{50} NS; where x is generation)

Characterization of The Bt-Resistant CPB Strain

Adult feeding and oviposition behaviors of selected (F8, 38-fold resistance) and unselected beetles were evaluated in a paired comparison test on simulated transgenic and untreated plants. Two Bt concentrations, a standard field rate of 12 mg/L and a 4X rate (49 mg/L) and water-only check were tested. Treated and untreated plants were placed in a screened cage along with five pairs of mated 2-week-old male and female beetles. The study was replicated three times using a total of 180 beetles. The beetles were allowed free movement and the plants were positioned so that Bt-treated and untreated plants were in contact. The experiment was continued for several weeks by replacing the Bt-treated plants every 3 days (43).

We observed that the movement of unselected beetles was arrested on Bt-treated plants, but movement of selected beetles was not inhibited. Selected beetles also oviposited on the Bt-treated (simulated transgenic) plants while the unselected beetles were essentially oostatic. Most significantly, we observed a leaf clipping behavior (nonleaf feeding) in both strains following ingestion of simulated transgenic plant material.

Since these experiments were conducted on a population of beetles expressing relatively low Bt resistance (F8 = 38 fold), we do not know at this time whether these results will be accentuated with subsequent selection for increased resistance (to be determined in future experiments). However, this work raises important questions regarding developmental and behavioral differences between selected and unselected CPB in response to transgenic and conventially-deployed Bts.

Synergism and Antagonism of Bt.

In 1990 a series of standard bioassays were carried out utilizing different materials that had been reported (33) or suspected to synergize or antagonize Bt products. We evaluated several proteinase inhibitors, surfactants and insect growth regulators, Serine (Kunitz) and cystein (E-64 and chymopapain) inhibitors, DMSO, amitraz, cyromazine, abermectin, dimilin, Neem (*Azadirachta indica* A. Juss) extracts and 3 numbered compounds. Our standard procedure was to determine a range of concentrations of the test compound that had little or no effect on the Bt-selected and unselected CPB strains. We then combined an LC_{20} dose of Bt (Bt-unselected = 2.3 μg/ml and Bt-selected = 135.3 μg/ml) with this range of target compound concentrations and observed the mortality effects. The bioassays were carried out in the same manner as those previously described except that in several situations the larvae were pretreated with either the LC_{20} concentration of Bt or the compound under test. We observed synergism of Bt with chymopapain and antagonism with dimilin and neem extracts. We are continuing these studies to determine the specific effects of these materials on the mode of action of Bt and the development of CPB resistance.

Bt-resistant Strain Detection: Minisatellite DNA Fingerprinting

A significant proportion of most eukaryotic genomes consist of repetitive DNA, called satellite DNA, which form short sequences that are repeated in identical or slightly variant copies. Repetitious DNA sequences are thought to arise from sudden replications followed by a mutational event (37), or an unequal crossover which could lead to deletion and/or a tandem duplication (36). The number of repetitions of these sequences can vary dramatically, resulting in extensive genetic polymorphism (24).

Genetic polymorphism as detected by minisatellite DNA has been used to develop unique fingerprints of individuals, but it is more commonly used to analyze genetic population diversity (14). Genetic analysis may be accomplished by the development of minisatellite DNA probes for hypervariable regions in an organism's DNA which show multiallelic variation and correspond to or segregate with a target trait. This technique holds promise for the development of genetic markers for identification of polymorphic insect populations.

In Figure 1 we show that the human minisatellite 33.15 probe (supplied by Cellmark Diagnostic, U.K.) detects a highly variable region creating complex DNA fingerprints in all strains of CPB tested. Comparison of the banding patterns of CPB Bt-resistant (R) and susceptible (S) individuals showed that one band at 1745 basepairs (Figure 1, see arrow) is present in resistant CPB but not in susceptible individuals. This band may have potential use as a marker for detection of Bt resistance. Further experimentation with additional individuals is needed to confirm this result. It is likely that linkage analysis using genetic markers will be the foundation for further study of the molecular basis of Bt resistance in CPB.

A recent technique known as random amplified polymorphic DNA (RAPD) is also useful in studies of genetic variation in insect populations (44). RAPD polymorphisms, detected as DNA segments which may amplify in one individual (or population) but not the other, are inherited in a Mendelian fashion. Figure 2 shows CPB RAPD fragment patterns amplified using a 10 nucleotide primer (Operon Inc.). A diagnostic band of 1 kb was amplified in all Bt-resistant (R) CPB tested, but was not in Bt-susceptible (S) individuals except at a very low frequency (see Figure 2, lane 9). Since the susceptible strain is of the same genetic stock as the resistant strain, it may be expected that an unknown frequency of susceptible beetles would have the 'R' genotype. We are currently investigating patterns of inheritance for this band among individual CPB.

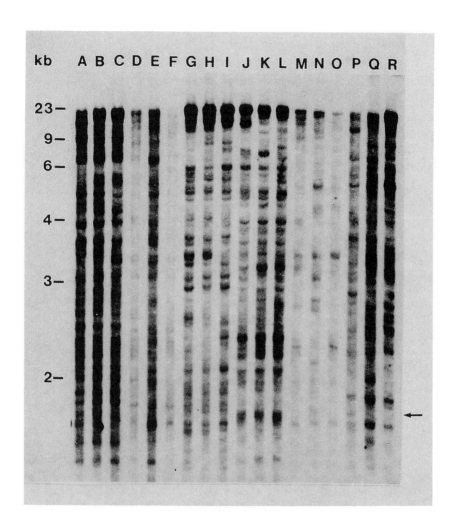

Figure 1. DNA fingerprints of Colorado potato beetles. Lanes A-C, the Arizona strain, lanes D-F, the Baker strain; lanes G-I, the Long Island strain; lanes J-L, the Vesteburg strain; lanes M-O and P-R, the *Bacillus thuringiensis* d-endotoxin susceptible and resistant strain, respectively. Each lane contains DNA from one insect.

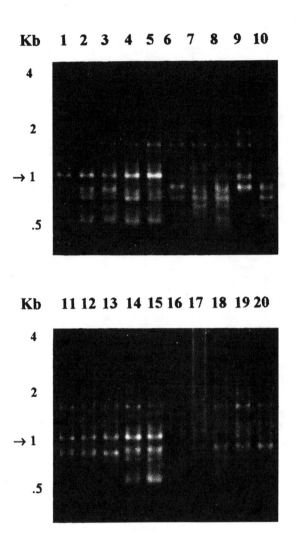

Figure 2. RAPD DNA fingerprints of Colorado potato beetle. Lanes 1-5 and 11-15 contain individuals of the Bt-resistant strain. Lanes 6-10 and 16-20 contain individuals of the Bt-susceptible strain. Each lane contains DNA from one insect. The arrow indicates a potential diagnostic marker for Bt-resistant gene(s).

Resistance Management of Conventionally-Deployed
and Transgenic Bt

Bts in general have a much narrower spectrum of biological activity and a much shorter residual period than synthetic organic insecticides. Therefore, Bt resistance should theoretically be slower to develop and easier to manage than resistance to synthetic organic pesticides. Unfortunately, there is very little known about managing Bt resistance. Tabashnik et al. (40) reported that Bt resistance in diamondback moth larvae did not abate rapidly when Bt sprays were halted. They concluded that much higher diamondback moth resistance than has been reported to date (>800 fold) is possible. Most importantly, field populations were capable of evolving resistance to mixtures of Bt toxins. If these trends hold for other systems, Bt may be a short-lived pest suppression tool in the absence of resistance delaying strategies and tactics.

There is a general euphoria among plant genetic engineers associated with the tremendous potential to engineer plant resistance to pests (32). Yet pests may adapt to transgenic Bt plants just as they have to conventionally-deployed Bt. Several authors, most notably Gould (19, 20, and in this volume), have warned of the risk of insects developing resistance to genetically engineered plants. Certainly, many other insect and disease pests have adapted to conventionally-selected resistant cultivars. Probably one of the best examples of this phenomenon in the United States is the wheat resistance programs which have identified at least 13 genes that confer resistance to the Hessian fly, *Mayetiola destructor* (Say) (22). However, resistance has been short lived due to the evolution of resistant Hessian fly biotypes (12). Another example is the development of distinct races of plant pathogens in response to resistant cultivars (25).

Although host-plant resistance programs have been successful in many instances, they are not without controversy, particularly concerning resistant cultivar deployment strategies and tactics. Gould (17, 18) has developed models to simulate the development of host-plant resistance. He compared some of the gene-deployment strategies and tactics including: (1) sequential release of two single-gene factors (seed rotation or alteration), (2) random spatial mixtures of two single-gene factors (mosaics or multilines), (3) two pyramided single-genes (stacked), and (4) adding susceptible refugia to each of the above. The stability of host resistance apparently varied depending upon the number of resistant pest alleles, the manner of inheritance (dominant or recessive), and the epistasis involved. Pyramided cultivars were often better than mixtures or sequences, particularly if susceptible cultivars were added (pyramided mixture). These transgenic deployment strategies have been tested theoretically, but much remains to be done both in transgenic plant development and in the actual evaluation of these and other deployment strategies.

There are basically three types of Bt transgenetic cultivars that can be developed: single, multiple, and chimeric (mutated or changed). Some transgenic engineers assert that they will be able to replace (substitute) or add different resistance genes ad infinitum to effectively "out run" pest evolution. This is reminiscent of the attitude of chemical engineers in the synthetic organic pesticide industry in the mid-1960s and early 1970s when pesticide resistant pests were becoming an increasing problem. Certainly many applied ecologists and field entomologists are concerned about the biological, ecological, evolutionary, operational, and economic costs of this assertion in the short and long term.

Expression and dosage of gene products are functions of the various genetic promoters and transcriptional and translational factors associated with each resistance gene. Considerable controversy exists about how transgenic genes can and/or should be expressed and tactically deployed to delay resistance development. The high dose, constitutively-expressed gene tactic may be particularly vulnerable to resistance development since it could lead to selection of all plant feeding life-stages of a pest on all parts of the transgenic plant throughout the entire growing season. However, some feel that the high dose tactic is a compelling advantage of transgenics and would effectively result in plants that are immune to insects and disease pests. Their argument is that pests with both heterozygous and homozygous resistance genes will be killed and no attenuation of the gene product will occur in the living plant. However, this approach is essentially based on the gamble that all allelic variants of the pest will be killed by the insecticidal plant through a single-gene defense.

Expression of low dosages of gene products presumably would have many of the same advantages that resistance managers have utilized with synthetic organic pesticides, primarily that of reduced selection pressure. Combinations of high and low expression are essentially pyramided genes with additional expression which may delay pest resistance development. Unfortunately, the economic, social and regulatory environment for the development, registration and marketing of transgenic plants in the United States may initially preclude all strategies except cultivars constitutively-expressing high dosages of a single Bt protein. None of the transgenic deployment strategies offer clear advantages in all environments with all pests (see the simulation models by Gould discussed above) except perhaps, plant mixtures with susceptible phenotypes. In addition, many of the operational tactics for transgenics may require more market-end investment, restricted seed handling processes, and a change in producer philosophy. The realization of these changes will likely be slowed by the same implementation challenges that have occurred with other pest management innovations (26).

Epilogue

Certainly the preservation of the effectiveness of Bt genes is of critical importance to pest suppression strategies of the future. As of this writing, transgenic plants have not been tested in the field to determine the potential for insect resistance development. We believe these studies are critical for the successful deployment of Bt transgenic plants in commercial crop production.

Literature Cited

1. Brewer, G.J. 1991. Resistance to *Bacillus thuringiensis* subsp. *kurstaki* in the sunflower moth (Lepidoptera: Pyralidae). Environ. Entomol. 20: 316-322.
2. Briese, D. T. 1981. Resistance of Insect Species to Microbial Pathogens, pp. 511-545. In Davidson, E. W. [ed.], Pathogenesis of Invertebrate Microbial Diseases. Allanheld Osmun, Totowa, N.J.
3. Boman, H. G. 1981. Insect responses to microbial infection, pp. 769-784. In Burges, H. D. [ed.], Microbial Control of Pests and Plant Diseases 1970-1980. Academic Press, New York.
4. Boulter, D., J. A. Gatehouse, A. M. R. Gatehouse, and V. A. Hilder. 1990. Genetic engineering of plants for insect resistance. Endeavor, New Series 14: 185-190.
5. Brunke, K. J., and R. L. Meeusen. 1991. Insect control with genetically engineered crops. Tibtech 9: 197- 200.
6. Burges, H. D. 1971. Possibilities for pest resistance to microbial control agents, pp. 445-457. In Burges, H. D. and Hussey, N. W. [eds.], Microbial Control of Insects and Mites. Academic Press, New York.
7. Chang, C.K. and M.E. Whalon. 1986. Hydrolysis of permethrin by pyrethroid esterases from resistant and susceptible strains of *Amblyseius fallacis* (Acari: Phytoseiidae). Pestic. Biochem. Physiol. 25:446-452.
8. Croft, B.A. 1990. Developing a philosophy and program of pesticide resistance management, pp. 277-296. In: R.T. Roush and B.E. Tabashnik [eds.], Pesticide resistance in arthropods. Chapman and Hall, NY.
9. Croft, B.A and M.E. Whalon. 1982. Selective toxicity of pyrethroid insecticides to arthropod natural enemies and pests of agricultural crops. Entomophaga 27:3-21.
10. Curtis, C.F., L.M. Cook, and R.J. Wood. 1978. Selection for and against insecticide resistance and possible method of inhibiting the evolution of resistance in mosquitoes. Ecol. Entomol. 3:273-287.

11. Fuxa, J.R. and A.R. Ritcher. 1989 . Reversion of resistance by *Spodoptera frugiperda* to nuclear polyhedrossis virus. J. Invertebr. Pathol. 53:52-56.

12. Gallun, R. L. 1977. Genetic basis of Hessian fly epidemics. Ann. N. Y. Acad. Sci. 287: 223-229.

13. Gasser, C. S., and R. T. Fraley. 1989. Genetically engineering plants for crop improvement. Science 244: 1293-1299.

14. Georges, M., A. Lequarre, M. Castelli, R. Hanset and G. Vassart. 1988. DNA fingerprinting in domestic animals using four different minisatelites probes. Cytogenet. Cell Genet. 47:127-131.

15. Georghiou, G.P., and M.G. Vasquez. 1982. Assessing the potential for development of resistance to *Bacillus thuringiensis* var. *israelensis* toxin (BTI) by mosquitoes. Mosquito Control Research: Annual Report. Pg. 80-81.

16. Goldman, I.F., J. Arnold, and B.C. Carlton. 1986 Selection for resistance to *Bacillus thuringiensis* subspecies *israelensis* in field and laboratory populations of the mosquito *Aedes aegypti*. J. Invertebr. Pathol. 47: 317-324.

17. Gould, F. 1986a. Simulation models for predicting durability of insect-resistant germ plasm: Hessian fly (Diptera: Cecidomyiidae) resistant winter wheat. Environ. Entomol. 15: 11-23.

18. Gould, F. 1986b. Simulation models for predicting durability of insect-resistant germ plasm: a deterministic diploid, two-locus model. Environ. Entomol. 15: 1-10.

19. Gould, F. 1988a. Evolutionary biology and genetically engineered crops: Consideration of evolutionary theory can aid in crop design. BioScience 38: 26-33.

20. Gould, F. 1988b. Genetic engineering, integrated pest management and the evolution of pests, pp. 15-18. In: Planned Release of Genetically Engineered Organisms. Elsevier Publications, Cambridge (UK).

21. Gould, F. 1991. Evolution of resistance to toxic compounds by arthropods, weeds and pathogens. Office of Technol. Assess., US Congress.

22. Hatchett, J.H., T.J. Marin and R.W. Livers. 1981. Expression and inheritance of resistance to Hession Fly in synthetic hexaploid wheat derived from *Triticum tauschii* (Coss) Schmal. Crop Sci. 21: 731-734.

23. Ioannidis, P. I., E. J. Grafius & M. E. Whalon. 1992. Patterns of insecticide resistance to azinphosmethyl, carbofuran, and permethrin in the Colorado potato beetle (Coleoptera: Chrysomelidae). J. Econ. Entomol. In Press.

24. Jeffreys, A.J., V. Wilson and S.L. Thein. 1985. Hypervariable minisatellite regions in human DNA. Nature 314:67-73.

25. Kiyosawa, S. 1982. Genetics and epidemiological modeling of breakdown of plant disease resistance. Ann. Rev. Phytopathology 20: 93-117.

26. Lamber, M.T., M.E. Whalon, and F.A. Fear. 1985. Diffusion theory and integrated pest management: illustration from the Michigan fruit IPM program. Bull. Entomol. Soc. Amer. 40: 40-45.

27. McGaughey, W. H. 1985a. Insect resistance to the biological insecticide *Bacillus thuringiensis*. Science 229: 193-195.

28. McGaughey, W. H. 1985b. Evaluation of *Bacillus thuringiensis* for controlling Indianmeal moths (Lepidoptera: Pyralidae) in farm grain bins and elevator silos. J. Econ. Entomol. 78: 1089-1094.

29. McGaughey, W. H., and R. W. Beeman. 1988. Resistance to *Bacillus thuringiensis* in colonies of Indianmeal moth and almond moth (Lepidoptera: Pyralidae). J. Econ. Entomol. 81: 28-33.

30. McGaughey, W. H., and D. E. Johnson. 1987. Toxicity of different serotypes and toxins of *Bacillus thuringiensis* to resistant and susceptible Indianmeal moths (Lepidoptera: Pyralidae). J. Econ. Entomol. 80: 1122-1126.

31. McGaughey, W. H., and M.E. Whalon. 1992. Managing insect resistance to *Bacillus thuringiensis* toxins. Science 258: 1451-1455.

32. Meeusen, R.L., and G. Warren. 1989. Insect control with genetically engineered crops. Ann. Rev. Entomol. 34: 373-381.

33. Novotny, J., M. Svetska, and P. Kanecka. The efficacy of mixtures of *Bacillus thuringiensis* Berl. and insect growth regulators. LESNICTVI (PRAGUE) 36(3):229-240 (in Slovak).

34. Roush, R.T. 1989. Designing resistance management programs: How can you choose? Pestic. Sci. 26: 423-441.

35. Stone, T. B., S. R. Sims, and P. G. Marrone. 1989. Selection of tobacco budworm for resistance to a genetically engineered *Pseudomonas fluorescens* containing the δ-endotoxin of *Bacillus thuringiensis* subsp. *kurstaki*. J. Invertebr. Pathol. 53: 228-234.

36. Smith, G.P. 1976. Evolution of repeated DNA sequences by unequal crossover. Science 191:528-535.

37. Southern, E.M. 1975. Long range periodicities in mouse satellite DNA. J. Mol. Biol. 94:51-69.

38. Tabashnik, B.E. 1990. Modeling and evaluation of resistance management tactics, pp. 153-182. In: R.T. Roush and B.E. Tabashnik [eds.], Pesticide resistance in arthropods. Chapman and Hall, NY

39. Tabashnik, B. E., N. L. Cushing, N. Finson, and M. W. Johnson. 1990. Field development of resistance to *Bacillus thuringiensis* in diamondback moth (Lepidoptera: Plutellidae). J. Econ. Entomol. 83: 1671-1676.

40. Tabashnik, B. E., N. Finson, and M. W. Johnson. 1991. Managing resistance to *Bacillus thuringiensis*: Lessons from the diamondback moth (Lepidoptera: Plutellidae). J. Econ. Entomol. 84: 49-55.

41. Uyenoyama, M. K. 1987. Pleotrophy and the evolution of genetic systems conferring resistance to pesticides. pp. 207-221. In Pesticide resistance: strategies and tactics for management. National Research Council (U.S). Committee on strategies for the management of pesticide resistance pest populations. National Academy Press. Washington, D.C.

42. Whalon, M.E. and R.L. Hollingworth. (eds.) Newsletter. 1989-91. Pesticide Res. Center, MI State Univ., E. Lansing, MI Vol 1-3.

43. Whalon, M.E., D.L. Miller, R.M. Hollingworth. E.J. Grafius, and J.R. Miller. 1993. Selection of a Colorado potato beetle (Coleoptera: Chrysomelidae) strain resistant to *Bacillus thuringiensis*. J. Econ. Entomol. 86: 226-233.

44. William, C.B., N.M. DuTeau, G.J. Puterka,, J.R. Nechols, and J.M. Pettorini. 1992. Use of the random amplified polymorphic DNA polymerase chain reaction (RAPD-PCR) to detect DNA polymorphisms in aphids (Homoptera: Aphididae). Bulletin of Entomol. Res. 82:151-159.

PART VII

Alternative Management Strategies for Potato Pests: Cultural and Biological Control

CONTROL OF BLACK SCURF AND OTHER DISEASES OF POTATO TUBERS WITH GREEN-CROP-HARVESTING AND ANTAGONISTIC ORGANISMS

L.J. Turkensteen[1], A. Mulder[2] and A. Bouman[3]
[1]Research Institute for Plant Protection,
[2]H.L. Hilbrands Laboratory for Soilborne Pests
and Diseases, Assen,
[3]Institute for Agricultural Engineering,
Wageningen, The Netherlands

In the Netherlands vine killing is a common practice to prevent late season virus transmission. A main problem with this method is the increased incidence of black scurf caused by *Rhizoctonia solani* Kuhn (10,19,24, 25). Rapid killing of vines leaves the roots undamaged, therefore, the root system continues to serve as a water pump (8,9). Because evaporation through the foliage is reduced, tubers serve as a sink for the water surplus, which results in an increase in weight and a release of exudates. These exudates plus volatile compounds released by disintegrating under-ground plant parts promote sclerotium initiation and maturation. To prevent leaking of tubers, the method of green-crop-harvesting was developed (4). This method involves removing the vines, digging potatoes with a lifter, placing them on a soil bed, and covering them with soil. As existing equipment caused too much damage with this method, diggers have been adjusted to meet the requirements for safe lifting of immature tubers (3).

Green-crop-harvesting is an alternative mechanical vine killing method, and it is being adopted by seed potato growers on sandy soils in The Netherlands. As regrowth does not occur, it is the only vine killing method which prevents late season virus transmission. An interesting feature of green-crop-harvesting is that tubers on the lifter can be treated to prevent disease (20,28). For example, the risk of increased tuber blight by *Phytophthora infestans* (Mont.) de Bary, which is regarded as a critical factor with green-crop-harvesting, can be reduced by application of fungicides at lifting. In addition, a specific inhibitor of oomycetes (cymoxanil, 200 g ai/ha) accelerated rotting of affected tubers, which led to reduced tuber blight at harvest (21).

Biological Control

Vine killing creates a huge amount of slowly dying plant tissues, and hence creates a favorable substrate for weakly pathogenic organisms such as *Erwinia* spp. (22) and *Phoma exigua* var. *foveata* (1,26). With green-crop-harvesting a considerable amount of this substrate is removed and as a result inoculum build-up with such organisms is expected to be less.

Antagonistic organisms have been reported for *R. solani* (2,11,12,13,14), *Erwinia* spp. (17,23), and *P. e. foveata* (27). Dressing of seed tubers with *Verticillium biguttatum, Trichoderma harzianum* or fluorescent pseudomonads before planting led to reduced incidence of black scurf (15), soft rot (6,7), and gangrene (27), respectively. However, the effects were too small to rely on for control. The principal problem is that the period between the application of the antagonist and the moment of desired action is too long to insure its success. In addition, there is no guarantee that daughter tubers will be colonized by the antagonist. For effective control, adequate amounts of the antagonist should be present when needed. For pathogens developing in the relatively short time frame between vine killing and harvest, such requirement may be fulfilled when antagonists are applied with the first lifting of green-crop-harvesting.

Black Scurf and *Verticillium biguttatum*

Initially, green-crop-harvesting trials were harvested by hand and tubers were separated from other plant parts before covering them with soil. With this procedure black scurf was not aggravated. With mechanical harvesting, however, tubers and plant parts were not completely separated and black scurf was a problem (Table 1).

Four antagonistic fungi recovered from soils suppressive to black scurf (2,11,12) were screened for their ability to suppress this disease in storage. Of the four evaluated, *V. biguttatum* was the most effective (13). However, it was only effective if applied after harvest and not as a seed dressing. If applied as a seed dressing it was not efficacious if soil temperatures at planting were 10°C or less. If applied after harvesting, it was effective if the relative humidity was 99% or higher and temperatures were above 15°C for 6-8 wk (14,29). Under bulk storage conditions, these requirements were not met (16). In addition, such treatment is not compatible with long term storage of cultivars with a short dormancy period.

TABLE 1. Effect of green-crop-harvesting, haulm pulling and chemical vine killing on severity of black scurf.

Treatment	Disease Severity			
	1987	1988	1989	1990
Green-crop-harvesting[a]	34[a]	4[a]	37[b]	10[a]
Haulm pulling	31[a]	5[a]	19[a]	16[ab]
Chemical vine killing	41[b]	18[b]	34[b]	24[b]

[a]Numbers in the same column followed by different letters were significantly different according to the studentized range test.

Temperature and relative humidity in the ridges met these requirements. Application of spores of *V. biguttatum* (40 ml/m^2 with 10^8 spores/ml) at the first lifting with green-crop-harvesting resulted in a suppression of black scurf. Control was as good as or better than with pencycuron (Monceren, ai 25%; 20 l/ha, Table 2). In addition, sclerotia were killed which resulted in approximately 100% control of black scurf on the tuber.

Gangrene

The fungus that causes gangrene (a type of dry rot), *Phoma exigua* var. *foveata*, develops on dying sub-soil plant parts which are available for colonization after chemical vine killing and haulm pulling. Consequently, after vine killing, there is a strong increase of soilborne inoculum of this pathogen (26). This disease was used for a case study on integrated control by green-crop-harvesting plus antagonists. Incidence of gangrene differed considerably for the three successive years of testing. Averaged over years, green-crop-harvesting reduced tuber infection by 80%. When coupled with a fungicide application a 98% reduction in disease incidence resulted (28).

Silver Scurf

Silver scurf, caused by *Helminthosporium solani*, is primarily a tuberborne disease. Spores are formed on mother tubers and are spread to daughter tubers (5,18). With green-crop-harvesting, mother tubers and daughter tubers are mixed and incorporated together in the newly formed ridges.

TABLE 2. Average disease incidence of black scurf, gangrene, and silver scurf as influenced by vine killing method and application of a fungicide or an antagonist.[1]

Treatments	Percent		
	Black scurf	Gangrene	Silver scurf
Chemical vine killing	42.3 c[2]	4.90 c	40.2 a
Green-crop-harvesting (GCH)	28.8 b	0.91 b	43.4 ab
GCH + antagonist	15.6 a[3]	0.61 b[4]	49.2 b[3]
GCH + fungicide	17.8 a[5]	0.11 a[6]	48.2 b[5]
Studentized range at p<0.05	4.5	0.38	6.2

[1] Results of replicated field experiments over several years.
[2] Numbers in the same column followed by different letters are significant different according to the studentized range test.
[3] *Verticillium biguttatum*
[4] *Trichoderma harzianum*
[5] Pencycuron
[6] Thiabenzimidazole

Consequently, this practice may lead to a higher incidence of silver scurf. The effect of green-crop-harvesting alone and in combination with fungicides and biocontrol agents were compared with chemical vine killing. Compared to chemical vine killing, green-crop-harvesting had no effect on disease. In contrast, application of *V. biguttatum* or the fungicide pencycuron with green-crop-harvesting increased the incidence of silver scurf compared to chemical vine killing (Table 2).

Bacterial Soft Rot

Digging immature tubers may carry a risk of increased tuber infection with pathogenic bacteria. Research on risks of increased infection with soft rot erwinias was initiated in 1990. Results obtained with heavily inoculated field trials indicate a small, but insignificant increase in tuber infestation by *Erwinia chrysanthemi*. Considerable reduction of soft rot was experienced after the application of the antagonistic organisms *Gliocladium roseum* or *T. harzianum* in a crop severely affected by *E. chrysanthemi* (21). The effect of *T. harzianum* on suppression of diseases caused by soft rot erwinias has been reported earlier (17).

Epilogue

Green-crop-harvesting is a tactic that interferes with the development of black scurf and gangrene. Similar effects may exist with other pathogens such as soft rot erwinias and *Fusarium* spp. Wounding should be avoided which may not be possible in soils containing too many rocks or flints. Soil temperatures of 10 to 20°C and RH > 95% are favorable for wound healing (30). If there is a need for late blight control, fungicides can be applied, some of which are compatible with the application of antagonistic organisms for control of other diseases.

Although some antagonistic organisms have potential to control one or more diseases, it is unlikely that a single organism will control all diseases. To control several diseases, more than one antagonistic organism may be needed. It remains to be determined, however, if they will be compatible with one another. For an integrated approach to control more than one disease, choices of compatible combinations of antagonistic organisms and specific fungicides will be dictated, in part, by the nature and importance of the diseases.

Literature Cited

1. Bång, U. 1989. Effect of haulm treatment and harvest time on incidence of tuber rots of potato (*Solanum tuberosum* L.) after standard wounding and on frequency of stem lesions caused by *Phoma foveata*. Potato Res. 32:101-112.
2. Boogert van den, P.H.J.F., and Jager, G. 1984. Biological control on potatoes by antagonists. 3. Inoculation of seed potatoes with different fungi. Neth. J. Pl. Path. 90:117-126.
3. Bouman, A. 1991. Groenrooien van aardappelen. Landbouwmechanisatie 42:11-13.
4. Bouman, A., Mulder, A., and Turkensteen, L.J. 1990. A green-crop-lifting method as a new system for lifting potatoes. Pages 386-387 in: Proc. 11th Triennial Conf. EAPR, Edinburgh, Scotland.
5. Boyd, A.E.W. 1972. Potato storage diseases. Rev. Phytopathol. 51:297-321.
6. Chard, J., 1991. Problems and progress with biological control of *Erwinia* diseases of potato. Page 13 in: EFPP/IOBC Workshop on New Approaches in Biological Control of Soilborne Diseases, Copenhagen, Denmark.
7. Colyer, P.D., and Mount, M.S. 1984. Bacterization of potatoes with *Pseudomonas putida* and its influence on post-harvest soft rot diseases. Plant Dis. 68:703-706.
8. Dijst, G. 1985. Investigations on the effect of haulm destruction and additional root cutting on black scurf on potato tubers. Neth. J. Pl. Path. 91:153-162.
9. Dijst, G., Bouman, A., Mulder, A., and Roosjen J. 1986. Effect of haulm destruction supplemented by cutting off roots on the incidence of black scurf and skin damage, flexibility of harvest period and yield of seed potatoes in field experiments. Neth. J. Pl. Path. 92:287-303.

10. Dijst, G., Mulder, A., Roosjen, J., Loon, C. van, and Bouman, A. 1984. The effect of root cutting on the development of sclerotia by *Rhizoctonia solani* and on the harvest period of seed potatoes. Page 111 in: Proc. 9th Triennial Conf. EAPR, Interlaken, Switzerland.

11. Jager, G., Ten Hoopen, A., and Velvis, H. 1979. Hyperparasites of *Rhizoctonia solani* in Dutch potato fields. Neth. J. Pl. Path. 85:253-268.

12. Jager, G., and Velvis, H. 1980. Onderzoek naar het voorkomen van Rhizoctonia-werende aardappelpercelen in Noord Nederland. Instituut voor Bodemvruchtbaarheid, Rapport 1-80, 62 pp.

13. Jager, G., and Velvis, H. 1985. Biological control of *Rhizoctonia solani* in potato by antagonists. 4. Inoculation of seed tubers with *Verticillium biguttatum* and other antagonists in field experiments. Neth. J. Pl. Path. 91:49-63.

14. Jager, G., and Velvis, H. 1988. Inactivation of sclerotia of *Rhizoctonia solani* on potato tubers by *Verticillium biguttatum*, a soilborne mycoparasite. Neth. J. Plant Path. 94:225-231.

15. Jager, G., Velvis, H., Lamers, J.G., Mulder, A., and Roosjen, J. 1991. Control of *Rhizoctonia solani* by biological, chemical and integrated measures. Potato Res. 34: 269-284.

16. Lamers, J. 1991. Biologische bestrijding van *Rhizoctonia solani* in aardappelen. OBS-publikatie 7: Verslag over 1986. Lelystad, PAGV.

17. Lugauskas, A. 1961. Fungi of the genus *Trichoderma* from the rhizosphere of fodderplants from some soils of Lithuania and their antagonistic properties. Darb. Liet. moks Akad., Ser. C. 1:11-21.

18. Mooi, J.C. 1968. The silver scurf disease of the potato. Verslagen Landbouwkundig Onderzoek 716. 62 pp.

19. Mulder, A., and Bouman, A. 1984. The effects of harvest time and method of haulm destroying on the tendencies of skinning and on the rate of infection of seed potatoes by *Rhizoctonia solani*. Pages 112-113 in: Proc. 9th Triennial Conf. EAPR, Interlaken, Switzerland.

20. Mulder, A., Bouman, A., Turkensteen, L.J., and Jager, G. 1990. A green-crop-harvesting method: Effects and possibilities of biological and chemical control of black scurf caused by *Rhizoctonia solani*. Pages 101-102 in: Proc. 11th Triennial Conf. EAPR, Edinburgh, Scotland.

21. Mulder, A., Turkensteen, L.J., and Bouman, A. 1992. Perspectives of green-crop-harvesting to control soilborne and storage diseases of seed potatoes. Proc. Internat. Symposium Adv. Pot. Crop Protect. Supplement 2 of the Neth. J. Pl. Path. 98:103-114.

22. Pérombelon, M.C.M., and Kelman, A. 1980. Ecology of the soft rot erwinias. Ann. Rev. Phytopath. 18:361-260.

23. Rhodes, D.J., and Logan, C. 1986. Effects of fluorescent pseudomonads on the potato black leg syndrome. Ann. App. Biol. 108:511-518.

24. Spencer, Dorothy and Fox R.A. 1978. The distribution of sclerotia of *Rhizoctonia solani* Kühn on the surface of the potato tuber. Potato Res. 21:291-300.

25. Spencer, D., and Fox, R.A. 1979. The development of *Rhizoctonia solani* Kühn on the underground parts of the potato plant. Potato Res. 22:29-39.

26. Turkensteen, L.J. 1986. *Phoma exigua* var. *foveata* en de teelt van aardappelen in Nederland. Gewasbescherming 17:179-187.

27. Turkensteen, L.J., Looijen, D., and Veenbaas-Rijks, J.W. 1990. Application of antagonistic fungi at planting and with green-crop-harvesting to control gangrene. Proc. 1st Conf. European Found. Plant Path., Wageningen.

28. Turkensteen, L.J., Mulder, A., and Bouman, A. 1990. Control of gangrene and late blight on seed potatoes by a green-crop-harvesting method and application of fungicides and antagonists. Pages 86-87 in: Proc. 11th Triennial Conf. EAPR, Edinburgh, Scotland.

29. Velvis, H., and Jager, G. 1983. Biological control of *Rhizoctonia solani* on potatoes by antagonists. 1. Preliminary experiments with *Verticillium biguttatum*, a sclerotium-inhabiting fungus. Neth. J. Pl. Path. 89:113-125.

30. Wigginton, M.I. 1974. Effects of temperature, oxygen tension and relative humidity on the wound-healing process in the potato tuber. Potato Res. 17:200-214.

THE INFLUENCE OF COVER CROPS ON THE SUPPRESSION OF VERTICILLIUM WILT OF POTATO

J.R. Davis[1], O.C. Huisman[2], D.T. Westermann[3], L.H. Sorensen[1], A.T. Schneider[1], and J.C. Stark[1]

[1]University of Idaho Research and Extension Center, Aberdeen, ID 83210

[2]Department of Plant Pathology, University of California, Berkeley, CA 94720

[3]USDA-Agricultural Research Service, Kimberly, ID 83341

In Idaho and other arid regions of the world, Verticillium wilt of potato is caused by the soilborne fungus, *Verticillium dahliae* Kleb. Field studies involving soil fumigation, solarization (4,5,8,14), and cropping practices (e.g., fallow vs continuous potato cropping) that result in different soil inoculum levels demonstrate the importance of this disease. Research in Idaho has consistently demonstrated that yield losses due to Verticillium wilt commonly exceed 5 to 12 metric T/ha (4,5). When the inoculum concentration in the soil is high, size and quality of potato tubers also may be affected. Thus, the impact of this disease is of economic importance and the need for control persists.

Commonly used rotations of 5 yr or less are not effective for the suppression of Verticillium wilt (4). There are currently only two methods for reducing the amount of soilborne inoculum: application of soil fungicides (e.g., chloropicrin, metam-sodium) and solarization (14). Of these approaches, only fungicides applied either as fumigants (e.g., chloropicrin) or water-soluble pesticides (e.g., metam-sodium) are widely used, and these products are commonly restricted by both cost and concerns for the environment. Although solarization offers potential, its use also is limited by both cost and lack of biodegradable plastics. Consequently, there is an urgent need for other approaches to manage this disease.

Since the beginnings of documented history, cultural practices have been used to suppress plant diseases. Earliest records include an account of Fan Shêng-Chih (10) advising, "If a field gives a poor crop in the second year, fallow it for one year." Long before the conquest by the Spanish in the 16th century, the Incas were utilizing corn and amaranth rotations to suppress diseases of potato (11). Prior to 1950, farmers commonly utilized green manures in their fields, and during more recent times, numerous papers have expounded upon the effects of a wide variety of green manures and soil amendments for the suppression of plant diseases (1-3,7,12,15-26,28-32). Among these accounts, however, we can find no reference to the effect of green manure crops on the suppression of Verticillium wilt of potato. Additionally, there exist relatively few published explanations on the biological mechanisms by which green manures suppress disease. Generally lacking is research on the effect of green manures on the ecology of plant-associated microorganisms, plant nutrition, and the resulting influence of plant nutrition on disease.

Our purpose for this presentation is to discuss some of the effects of green manures on soil-microbial ecology, suppression of Verticillium wilt, and plant nutrition in potato.

Disease Suppression and Yield Response

Initial studies were designed to screen green manures for their influence on potato diseases. These investigations were conducted in the field and, in each case, involved the planting of a crop for either two or three consecutive years within the same plot location. Depending on the experiment, green manures [sudangrass (*Sorghum vulgare* var. *sudanese*), pea (*Pisum sativum*), rape (*Brassica napus*), oats (*Avena sativa*), rye (*Secale cereale*), and corn (*Zea mays*)] were incorporated into the soil either by discing or rotovating during early August. All green manures were compared to a weed-free fallow. Russet Burbank was planted into plots following the second or third year of the green manure and fallow treatments.

Green-manures consistently suppressed Verticillium wilt more than the fallow. Following 2 yr of continuous cropping with green manures, incidence of Verticillium wilt with green manures ranged from 22 to 40% compared with 77% for fallow (Table 1). Similar relationships occurred after three years of continuous green-manure cropping (Table 2). Disease incidence was associated with number of root infections by *V. dahliae*(13): number of root infections were significantly lower with sudangrass, oats, corn, and rape compared to the fallow (Tables 1 and 2). However, none of the green manures except sudangrass significantly reduced soil populations of *V. dahliae* (Table 2).

Total yield and tuber quality responses from green manures were inconsistent depending on the particular green manures. Yields of tubers >280 g in size, however, were consistent and were increased by 2- to 4-fold over the fallow.

Soil and Root Microflora

Estimates of the total microbial activity in soil were made using the technique of Schnurer and Rosswall(27). Total soil microbial activity was significantly higher with green manures than with fallow. When correlated with the incidence of Verticillium wilt, a highly significant negative correlation was evident between total microbial activity and disease incidence (Fig. 1). This suggests that some aspect of biological control may be involved with the disease suppression associated with green manures.

Effects of green manures on soil and root microflora were both qualitative and quantitative. For example, colonization of potato roots by *Fusarium equiseti* was significantly higher among the green manures that had the greatest impact upon disease suppression (Tables 1 and 2). Sudangrass had both the highest soil populations and number of root infections of *F. equiseti*. In contrast, populations of *F. solani* and *F. oxysporum* in soil and on roots were not significantly affected by the green manures. Whether these differences are or are not related to the suppression of Verticillium wilt is yet to be determined, but the need exists to further investigate the effects of green manures.

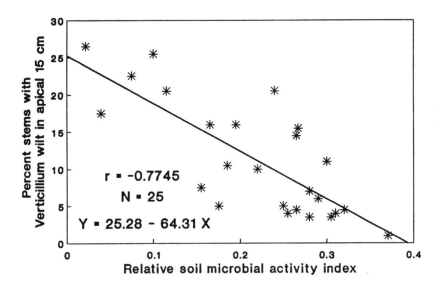

Fig. 1. Relationship between incidence of Verticillium wilt in Russet Burbank and index of soil microbial activity.

TABLE 1. Effects of a two-year continuous cropping of green manures on Verticillium wilt and yield of potato.

Treatments	Disease incidence[w] (%)	Soil populations Verticillium dahliae[x] (cfu/g)	Root colonization[y] Verticillium dahliae (cfu/100 cm root)	Fusarium equiseti (cfu/100 cm root)	Yield (T/ha) Total	U.S. #1	>280 g
Fallow	77 a[z]	58	76 a	41 a	26 a	14 a	2.5 a
Oats	31 bc	43	54 b	112 bc	30 b	17 ab	5.9 b
Rye	40 b	48	56 ab	100 b	30 b	18 ab	5.8 b
Sudangrass	17 d	40	35 b	137 c	36 c	24 c	11.3 d
Corn	22 cd	34	42 b	104 b	34 c	20 bc	9.1 c

[w] Disease readings were made on 27 August.

[x] Soil samples were collected on 23 May.

[y] Root colonization by V. dahliae and F. equiseti was determined from samples collected 1 August.

[z] Treatments followed by the same letter do not differ significantly according to Fischer's protected LSD test (P=0.05).

TABLE 2. Effects of a three-year continuous cropping of green manures on Verticillium wilt and yield of potato.

Treatments	Disease incidence[w] (%)	Soil populations Verticillium dahliae[x] (cfu/g)	Root colonization[y] Verticillium dahliae (cfu/100 cm root)	Root colonization[y] Fusarium equiseti (cfu/100 cm root)	Yield (T/ha) Total	Yield (T/ha) U.S. #1	Yield (T/ha) >280 g
Fallow	50 a[z]	52 a	63 a	34 a	30 a	20	6.1 a
Austrian pea	32 b	33 a	50 a	43 a	34 a	23	11.4 b
Sudangrass	7 c	15 b	18 b	107 c	39 b	27	17.4 c
Dwarf Essex rape	35 b	42 a	30 b	60 b	32 a	22	7.8 a
Bridger rape	35 b	37 a	30 b	76 b	32 a	21	8.8 ab

[w] Disease readings were made on 27 August.

[x] Soil samples were collected on 23 May.

[y] Root colonization by *V. dahliae* and *F. equiseti* was determined from samples collected 3 July and 1 August, respectively.

[z] Treatments followed by the same letter do not differ significantly according to Fischer's protected LSD test (P=0.05).

Nutritional Benefits

Effects of green manure cropping on plant nutrition were substantial. Preplant soil NO_3-N and extractable P concentrations were affected by the green manures in both studies (Table 3), however, the effect was not consistent. There were also green manure effects on petiole NO_3-N, P, Zn, Cu, and Mn concentrations in both studies for at least one sampling date. Petiole nutrient concentrations were generally lowest with fallow, and highest with sudangrass, particularly at the last sampling (data not shown). Petiole NO_3-N, K and Mn concentrations, in at least one sampling, was correlated with the preplant soil test.

Green manures significantly affected the total plant uptake of N, P, Zn, Cu, K, Ca, Mg, Cl and S in late-August in both studies (data not shown). Total plant dry matter production was affected by green manures in the 2-yr study. Nutrient uptake also was correlated with preplant soil tests for N, Mn, and Fe.

Green manures were shown to affect the availability of many nutrients. The causes for these differences in nutrient levels are not readily evident because there were very few consistent correlations between preplant soil nutrient and petiole nutrient concentrations. Differences may be explained by differences in nutrient cycling, kind of organisms infecting the root, or populations of microorganisms in the rhizosphere.

Nutrient responses of Russet Burbank also may have contributed to the reduced severity of Verticillium wilt. Recent studies (6,8,9) show the importance of optimal N and P concentration and uptake on the suppression of this disease.

Potential Problems

Green manures may inhibit tuberization early in the growing season. This inhibition was demonstrated in our study. As the season progressed, however, yield differences became less apparent and by mid-August, yields of potato among the green manure treatments did not differ from the fallow. By the third week of August, wilt symptoms were generally more severe in the fallow than with the green manures, and these differences were closely correlated with yield.

Specific gravities of tubers may be affected with some green manures. Specific gravities of Russet Burbank were reduced when preceded by green manures of either of the two rape varieties (Dwarf Essex and Bridger). Because the NO_3-N concentration was higher in petioles of potatoes grown in rape plots, lower specific gravities may have been related to a tuber-maturity effect.

TABLE 3. Probability levels associated with two or three consecutive years of green manures on preplant soil tests and potato petiole nutrient concentrations at three samplings.

| | 2 yr green manure | | | | 3 yr green manure | | | |
| | Preplant soil test | Petiole nutrient concentration | | | Preplant soil test | Petiole nutrient concentration | | |
Nutrient		1st	2nd	3rd		1st	2nd	3rd
NO_3-N	***[x]	NS	**	**	***	NS	*	**
N_{min}[w]	NS[y]	--[z]	---	---	NS	---	---	---
P	**	NS	*	**	*	NS	**	***
K	NS	NS	NS	NS	***	***	*	***
Zn	NS	***	*	*	NS	**	***	***
Cu	NS	NS	NS	NS	NS	NS	**	***
Mn	*	NS	NS	***	NS	NS	NS	***
Fe	NS	NS	NS	NS	NS	NS	NS	NS

[w] N_{min} = N mineralized in a 3-wk aerobic incubation at 30°C.
[x] *, **, *** = Probability levels of 0.05, 0.01 and 0.001, respectively.
[y] NS = Nonsignificant.
[z] --- = data not taken.

Carry-Over Benefits

To determine if there existed carry-over benefits for more than one season, plots were again re-cropped to potatoes in 1991. Among treatments cropped for three consecutive years with either sudangrass or rape, the incidence of Verticillium wilt continued to be suppressed by 63 to 70%. Thus, the effect of green manures on disease suppression persisted in the second crop of potatoes.

Epilogue

As pesticide and fumigant options are withdrawn, we shall become increasingly dependent upon the use of alternative methods for management of Verticillium wilt of potato. In addition to resistant cultivars and solarization, green manures may be a viable tool for the suppression of this disease. Not only does it provide an alternate approach for disease control, it offers potential for increasing the availability of plant nutrients to the potato, the possibility of reducing ground water contamination, and a positive shift in the soil environment toward beneficial microflora.

Literature Cited

1.   Adams, P.B., and Papavizas, G.C. 1969. Survival of root-infecting fungi in soil. X. Sensitivity of propagules of *Thielaviopsis basicola* to soil fungistasis in natural and alfalfa-amended soil. Phytopathology 59:135-138.

2.   Bhattacharyya, P., Dey, B.K., Nath, S., and Banik, S. 1986. Organic manures in relation to rhizosphere effect. III. Effect of organic manures on populations of ammonifying bacteria in mineralization of nitrogen in rice and succeeding wheat rhizosphere soils. Zentralbl. Mikrobiol. 141:267-277.

3.   Dath, A.P. 1982. Effect of soil amendment with some green manures on the survival of sclerotia of *Corticium sasaki*. Indian Phytopathol. 35:523-525.

4.   Davis, J.R. 1981. Verticillium wilt of potato in southeastern Idaho. Univ. of Idaho CIS Bull. No. 564.

5.   Davis, J.R. 1985. Approaches to control of potato early dying caused by *Verticillium dahliae*. Am. Potato J. 62:177-185.

6.   Davis, J.R., and D.O. Everson. 1986. Relation of *Verticillium dahliae* in soil and potato tissue, irrigation method, and N-fertility to Verticillium wilt of potato. Phytopathology 76:730-736.

7.   Davis, J.R., Sorensen, L.H., Schneider, A.T., Hafez, S.L., and Auld, D.L. 1990. The influence of rape meal upon the incidence of Verticillium wilt, root lesion nematode populations, yield and grade of potato, 1987-1988. Biological and Cultural Tests 5:29.

8.   Davis, J.R., Sorensen, L.H., Stark, J.C., and Westermann, D.T. 1990. Fertility and management practices to control Verticillium wilt of the Russet Burbank potato. Am. Potato J. 67:55-65.

9.   Davis, J.R., Stark, J.C., and Sorensen, L.H. 1988. Reduced *Verticillium dahliae* colonization in potato stems, wilt suppression, and reduction of *V. dahliae* cfu in soil with optimal N and P, 1986. Biological and Cultural Tests 3:22.

10.   Fan, Shêng-Chih. 1974. "Fan Shêng-Chih", an Agriculturist Book of China written by Fan Shêng-Chih in the First Century B.C. Science Press, Peking. 67 pp.

11.   Garcilasco de la Vega. 1966. Royal Commentaries of the Incas. Univ. of Texas Press, Austin. 1530 pp.

12.   Ghaffar, A., Zentmyer, G.A., and Erwin, D.C. 1969. Effect of organic amendments on severity of *Macrophomina* root rot of cotton. Phytopathology 59:1267-1269.

13.   Huisman, O.C. 1988. Colonization of field-grown cotton roots by pathogenic and saprophytic soilborne fungi. Phytopathology 78:716-722.

14.   Katan, J. 1981. Solar heating (solarization) of soil for control of soilborne pests. Ann. Rev. Phytopathol. 19:211-236.

15.   Kundu, E.K., and Mandi, B. 1984. Control of *Rhizoctonia* disease of cauliflower by competitive inhibition of the pathogen using organic amendments in soil. Plant and Soil 83:357-362.

16.   Lewis, J.A., and Papavizas, G.C. 1969. Effect of sulfur-containing volatiles present in cabbage on *Aphanomyces euteiches* (Abstr). Phytopathology 59:1558.

17.   Lewis, J.A., and Papavizas, G.C. 1971. Effect of sulfur-containing volatile compounds and vapors from cabbage decomposition on *Aphanomyces euteiches*. Phytopathology 61:208-214.

18.   Maier, C.R. 1961. Selective effects of barley residue on fungi of the pinto bean root-rot complex. Plant Dis. Rep. 45:808-811.

19.   Manning, W.J., and Crossan, D.F. 1969. Field and greenhouse studies on the effects of plant amendments on *Rhizoctonia* hypocotyl rot of snap bean. Plant Dis. Rep. 53:227-231.

20.   Pandey, R.K., and Pendleton, J.W. 1986. Soybeans as green manure in a main intercropping system. Exp. Agric. 22:179-185.

21.   Papavizas, G.C. 1966. Suppression of *Aphanomyces* root rot of peas by cruciferous soil amendments. Phytopathology 56:1071-1075.

22.   Papavizas, G.C. 1968. Survival of root-infecting fungi in soil. VI. Effect of amendments on bean root rot caused by *Thielaviopsis basicola* and on inoculum density of the causal organism. Phytopathology 58:421-428.

23.   Papavizas, G.C., Davey, C.E., and Woodard, R.E. 1962. Comparative effectiveness of some organic amendments and fungicides in reducing activity and survival of *Rhizoctonia solani* in soil. Can. J. Microbiol. 9:915-922.

24.   Papavizas, G.C., Lewis, J.A., and Adams, P.B. 1970. Survival of root-infecting fungi in soil. XIV. Effect of amendments and fungicides on bean root rot caused by *Thielaviopsis basicola*. Plant Dis. Rep. 54:114-118.

25.   Papavizas, G.C., Lewis, J.A., and Adams, P.B. 1968. Survival of root-infecting fungi in soil. II. Influence of amendment and soil carbon-to-nitrogen balance on *Fusarium* root rot of beans. Phytopathology 58:365-372.

26. Snyder, W.C., Schroth, M.N., and Christou, T. 1959. Effect of plant residues on root rot of bean. Phytopathology 49:755-756.

27. Schnurer, J., and Rosswall, T. 1982. Fluorescein diacetate hydrolysis as a measure of total microbial activity in soil and litter. Appl. Environ. Microbiol. 43:1256-1261.

28. Sun, S., and Huang, J. 1985. Formulated soil amendment for controlling Fusarium wilt and other soilborne diseases. Plant Dis. 69:917-920.

29. Verma, B., Narain, P., and Singhal, A.K. 1985. Effect of Crotalaria juncea green manuring on irrigated wheat. Indian J. Agron. 28:182-184.

30. Villapudua, J.R., and Munnecke, D.E. 1986. Solar heating and amendments control cabbage yellows. Calif. Agric. 40:11-13.

31. Weinhold, A.R., and Bowman, T. 1968. Selective inhibition of the potato scab pathogen by antagonistic bacteria and substrate influence on antibiotic production. Plant and Soil 27:12-24.

32. Weinhold, A.R., Oswald, J.W., Bowman, T., Bishop, J., and Wright, D. 1964. Influence of green manures and crop rotation on common scab of potato. Am. Potato J. 41:265-273.

DEPLOYMENT STRATEGIES FOR ANTIFEEDANTS IN MANAGEMENT OF COLORADO POTATO BEETLE

Randy Alford
Department of Entomology
University of Maine
Orono, Maine 04469

The use of allelochemicals as antifeedants in insect pest management is certainly not a novel approach. What began in the 1930s with a survey of hundreds of plant extracts for insect repellency (33) has developed into a major area of collaborative research by chemists, ecologists, physiologists, behaviorists, agronomists and pest management specialists. The multidisciplinary appeal lies in the chemicals' natural origin, apparent specificity and perceived negligible non-target effects. Numerous extensive reviews of antifeedant use and their potential have appeared in recent years, and in each, continued exploration and development is encouraged (6, 7, 18, 19, 38). As we face increasing concerns over environmental contamination by synthetic pesticides and their declining effectiveness, natural materials such as allelochemicals are likely to have an increasing role in agriculture.

Despite decades of study, attempts to protect plants with antifeedants in commercial operations have generally been viewed as unsuccessful. The factors behind these shortcomings are numerous, but a primary reason is that these substances have been evaluated in the same manner as synthetic insecticides, often in side-by-side trials. In traditional insecticide trials the parameters monitored center around a single variable, i.e., mortality, with rapid and persistent kill often being the most desired features. While there are certainly cases in which phytochemicals elicit mortality, such as with the pyrethrums, more often their effects are multiple, less dramatic and require longer periods of time before protective effects become measurable. Consequently, these comparative studies have resulted in their perceived failure.

Another explanation for the poor performances of antifeedants is the inherent variability of the insect response. There are no known universally-active feeding deterrents, so each antifeedant - insect - crop system must be evaluated in a variety of controlled laboratory and field situations before their real value can be determined (6, 39). With the past availability of inexpensive and effective synthetic insecticides and the large amount of time and money required to develop a comprehensive use strategy for each antifeedant, there have been few incentives for the adoption of antifeedants as a control measure.

Role of Insect Sensory Mechanisms in Antifeedant Activity

For the practitioner, the primary measurable and most obvious effect of an antifeedant is a reduction in the amount of food eaten by the insect, which would translate into reduced crop defoliation and increased yield. Although these principles and their relationships seem simple, the situation has proven to be quite complicated. Different insect species vary greatly with respect to their chemical senses and their ability to perceive certain chemicals, which has led to inconsistent antifeedant performances. In our current efforts to deploy antifeedants, a better understanding of the roles natural feeding deterrents play in insect-plant relationships is essential. In doing so, criteria for the efficient use of an antifeedant against a specific insect pest and in a particular crop management system can be established.

In the host selection process, phytophagous insects are able to select their food based on plant chemical characteristics through a two-dimensional chemosensory system (16, 39). Compounds present in their food may serve as attractants and phagostimulants which promote feeding. Conversely, the sensitivity of other chemoreceptors to some substances may inhibit feeding on suboptimal or toxic foods. Knowledge of this system has provided the sensory basis for the use of antifeedants in insect control (17).

Two primary limitations to the practical interpretation of the dual chemoreception system exist. First, phytophagous insects do not perceive only positive and negative chemical characteristics of the plant, they perceive complex sensory input. Dethier (8) postulated that insects have many receptor types, which are sensitive to a variety of primary and secondary plant compounds, and a central command system, through which appropriate behaviors are associated with specific sensory inputs. Secondly, the two-way receptor specificities and sensitivities are not equivalent since a primary phagostimulant occurring in the host plants can easily be masked by inhibitory substances. Also, an intense antifeedant effect cannot be counterbalanced even with optimal phagostimuli (17). Therefore, the search for antifeedants and their use should take into consideration the total biochemical complexity of the plants perceived by the insects.

Considerations for Deployment in the Field

In general, however, it is now widely recognized that the evolution of food specialization in phytophagous insects is due to the adaptation to both specific feeding stimulants and deterrents, and that host-plant selection is based to a large extent on the distribution of repellent and deterrent chemicals in the plant kingdom (6). In the coevolution of plants and insects, often referred to as their "arms race" (10), it is estimated that hundreds of thousands of plant allelochemicals have resulted, many of which have insecticidal and behavior-modifying activities. These plant-produced defense chemicals have been the subject of many ecological investigations of insect host range, and to a lesser extent, their use has been an objective in insect pest management. The incorporation of these allelochemical components and the elevation of their levels in plants have been and remain primary goals in crop resistance breeding and biotechnological crop improvement programs. Allelochemicals, including antifeedants, have been used in their natural state or as models for synthesis of crop protection chemicals (43).

Since many different plant substances may inhibit feeding by insects (and since certain plant species in every community are avoided by most insect species of the same community), antifeedants must be present in the plants of every ecosystem, both within and outside the host range of the insect species of interest. Kubo & Nakanishi (22) proposed that plant species of the tropics, which are constantly exposed to attack by numerous and different herbivores, have the highest levels of defensive substances. Tropical plants have certainly provided substances with considerable antifeedant activity (30), but similar assumptions may be made for plant species outside the tropics, where resources are more limited (20).

In natural systems, the effective defense mechanism of nonhost plants is most likely due to a number of different chemicals that exert a range of biological activities on multiple sites and act in concert as deterrents and toxins (18). The large number of secondary plant chemicals present are often found in groups within a single plant species (13). Therefore, it is reasonable to assume that the chemical defense systems of unacceptable, non-host plants consist of several secondary plant substances interacting in additive, antagonistic or synergistic ways on the behavioral and physiological systems of the insect. Adams & Bernays (1) found that combinations of feeding deterrents were additive in their effects on the feeding behavior of *Locusta migratoria* (F.). Jermy et al. (20) bioassayed extracts of three plant species from the sagebrush community for antifeedant effects on Colorado potato beetle,

Leptinotarsa decemlineata (Say). They also found that active materials were mixtures of compounds from different chemical classes.

Accepting the biochemical complexity of plants, crude plant materials may contain several phytochemicals and thus, may be more effective than single, purified compounds (20). Development and use of effective crude plant material may be more economical because quantities required for field use have been a limiting factor in the past. Related plant species that are available in large quantities should first be considered as sources of antifeedants, as should waste materials, because they too may contain significant proportions of the plant defense system. The search for effective compounds may be more profitable if attention is concentrated on particular chemical groups with proven success, such as the terpenoids (6), or plant taxonomic groups with a high frequency of active allelochemicals (42).

When biologically-active natural products are found, they may serve as leads for chemical synthesis of related models. The synthetic mimics may also have more favorable properties than the original natural products. The biorational design of chemicals forms the basis of the pharmaceutical industry which has successfully utilized the elucidation of drug structure-activity relationships in the development of new medicinals (44). There are numerous cases (including the pyrethroids [9], which are based on the natural phytochemical pyrethrum, and the farnesene-based insect growth regulators [14]) where a detailed analysis of natural product structure-activity relationships has led to the design and synthesis of potent insect control agents. In 1987, Ley et al. (24) reported the synthesis of the first model insect antifeedant based on the structure of azadirachtin.

Plants must be uniformly protected if an antifeedant or its synthetic mimic is to be used successfully for insect management. The chemical may not kill the pest directly, and the insect may also have the chemoreceptive ability to detect the presence of the antifeedant. Therefore, insects may aggregate on untreated parts or new growth areas, such as buds or leaves, that appear after application. In addition, chemicals that are applied to the surface of leaves will be washed off by rain unless effective stickers are included in the spray mixture. For these reasons, antifeedants with systemic properties are preferred. However, a systemic antifeedant has a greater chance of being phytotoxic or being exposed to biochemical alteration within the plant (6). The importance of systemic action in antifeedants has long been recognized (7, 17), but few have been evaluated for this quality (although Gill & Lewis [11] did report azadirachtin and neem seed extract to be systemic without phytotoxicity).

Other potential pitfalls to the development of effective antifeedants are also related to their field application requirements. Considering the often slow elicitation of antifeedant activities and the necessity for their even distribution on the plants, insects may be exposed to the chemical for long periods of time. With this requisite of prolonged exposure comes an increase in the potential of habituation and subsequent loss of effectiveness (36). It is also important that the material maintain persistent activity under field conditions (6). Many plant compounds are known to have short-lived chemical stability outside the plant, and improvements in this area will take concerted efforts by plant physiologists, organic and formulation chemists, and entomologists.

Antifeedants will rarely be effective enough as a sole control measure, as previous studies indicate (7, 17, 19, 42, 43), but will have greatest utility when used as a component of integrated control schemes. As has been learned in countless other insect control efforts, combined effects are more stable and consequential than are single measures. Through our understanding of natural insect-plant relationships, pests like the Colorado potato beetle may be managed successfully with antifeedant components when the materials are used as they are deployed by the plant. The approach should involve multiple inputs, using phytochemicals with different modes of action and with multiple effects. To effect any desired response, whether it be feeding deterrence, repellency or toxicity, with a single chemical or mode of action would most likely lead to resistance in the pest population. This has been the fate of many synthetic insecticides, and the deployment of allelochemicals in an integrated program would reduce the potential for resistance development (19).

As mentioned previously, antifeedant chemicals act at the behavioral level and do not necessarily kill the herbivore, and therefore require different criteria for their evaluation. There are numerous direct antifeedant effects which may impact insect populations and subsequent crop damage (Table 1). These include acute toxicity, feeding reduction, growth disruption, slowed development, oviposition suppression, and repellency. The composite of these effects will influence physiological and genetic fitness and may also represent a powerful stress on phytophagous insects. As a consequence, antifeedants could increase the susceptibility of the pests to pathogens and insecticides (35, 37). Antifeedants may also cause population asynchrony, which may influence mating, utilization of available food resources, and parasitoid and predator efficiencies. Therefore, antifeedants should be considered as both stress agents and conventional control agents in their deployment and assessment (42).

346

Table 1. Potential effects and benefits of antifeedants for crop protection.

Direct effects on insects	Insect management benefits
Repellency	Reduced colonization
Acute toxicity	Increased mortality
Feeding deterrence	Reduced defoliation
Slowed development	Population asynchrony
Growth disruption	Developmental abnormality
Egg development suppression	Reduced oviposition
Physiological stress	Increased vulnerability to natural and applied biological and chemical control agents

The Citrus Limonoid - Colorado Potato Beetle - Potato System

The use of antifeedants for Colorado potato beetle control has a long history (42), and many substances have been found to reduce its feeding significantly. Some of these (with examples) include inorganic compounds (copper sulfate [15]), organo-metallic compounds (organotin fungicides [12]), crude plant extracts (neem seed extract [40]), and many natural secondary products (the potato glycoalkaloids [23]).

At the University of Maine, we have been working during the past several years on antifeedant-based management programs against a range of insect species. Our greatest success to date has been with the citrus limonoid - Colorado potato beetle - potato system. The primary allelochemical on which we have focussed is limonin, a modified triterpene which is structurally related to the potent insect antifeedant azadirachtin. Limonin is the primary bitter component present in citrus tissues, is easily extracted from the seeds, and is available as a by-product of the citrus fruit processing industry (21).

347

Of the many substances screened for antifeedant activity in my laboratory, limonin is only moderate in its level of feeding reduction (2, 3, 25, 31). It is, however, limonin's diversity of biological activities that distinguishes it from other natural products, and these are summarized below. Application of pure limonin resulted in a 60% reduction in feeding when Colorado potato beetle larvae were exposed to dosages $\geq$ 10 μg per cm^2 leaf disk in a no-choice assay situation. The no-choice test was more sensitive than the choice assay. Almost 90% feeding depression was found with dosages $\geq$ 30 μg per disk in the no-choice tests, but a maximum feeding depression of only 67% occurred in the choice situation at 100 μg per disk (3).

Bernays (6) concluded that choice tests are not appropriate except for use with a mobile insect, although this is the most common bioassay method. With limonin and Colorado potato beetle, we found that conducting both no-choice and choice tests have provided insight into possible modes of action and utilization criteria. A closer examination of the data from our original study (3) explained the differences in the two test methods. If we assume uniform distribution of limonin on each treated disk and convert the amount of foliage consumed to the amount of limonin ingested, larvae in the choice tests ingested an almost equal amount of limonin (13-14 μg) in each treatment where a measurable feeding depression occurred. In no-choice tests, the amount of limonin ingested was greater than in choice tests but varied only from 23 to 26 μg for dosages $\geq$10 μg/disk. These data suggest that the higher levels of antifeedant activity demonstrated in the no-choice situation were directly related to the greater amounts of limonin ingested and to the resultant effects on the overall feeding activity of the exposed larvae. We therefore concluded that limonin acts primarily as a toxin against Colorado potato beetle larvae.

The structure of limonin is complex (Fig. 1), and this lends appeal as a subject for structure-activity studies. Limonin contains a number of polar functional groups which are potential sites for interaction with receptor proteins. We prepared ten structural analogs as synthetic modifications of limonin, and each was evaluated for antifeedant activity against Colorado potato beetle larvae in no-choice assays (4). We determined that the furan and epoxide groups on the C and D rings, respectively, were primary structures responsible for the antifeedant activity.

Limonin and two other naturally-occurring citrus limonoids, obacunone and nomilin, were compared in larval feeding assays. Results from choice and no-choice assays showed no significant differences in feeding reduction among the three limonoids, but as in

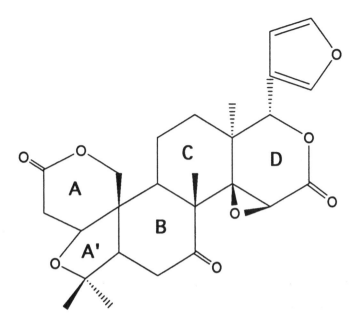

Fig. 1. Structure of limonin.

the earlier work, greater activity was found in the no-choice situation (32). Behavioral observations identified symptoms of acute toxicity in the assay arenas (e.g., regurgitation and loss of mobility and searching behavior), indicating a primary toxic mode of action for each limonoid. These compounds differ only in the structure of the A-ring. Therefore, the component is probably not critical to the types of biological activity measured in these tests.

To assess the impact of long-term exposure, limonin and five derivatives synthetically prepared from limonin were evaluated for disruption of growth and development of Colorado potato beetle larvae (29). Limonin, epilimonol, and limonin diosphenol significantly delayed larval development following a three-day exposure, but growth rate was not reduced. Adult emergence rate was reduced, which may be explained by a hormonal disruption of the pupal stage (mortality occurred in both prepupae and pupae). More detailed studies with epilimonol and limonin diosphenol indicated that these compounds, which differ from limonin in B-ring structure, act primarily as receptor-mediated feeding deterrents, not as toxins (27, 29).

The structure - activity relationships established in these studies provided a sound basis for the design of a model antifeedant. We prepared two synthetic compounds based on the C and D rings of limonin and the two essential functionalities (i.e., furan and epoxide groups), and both were shown to have antifeedant activity comparable to that of limonin (5). In other, unpublished studies, we found that the model compounds were equally active in both the choice and no-choice assay situations. These findings and behavioral observations indicated an important chemoreceptor-mediated behavioral mode of action for the synthetic models, which is different from the natural product. Additional model synthesis is underway to incorporate other features of the allelochemical which are potentially responsible for the different biological effects and associated modes of action. It is the ultimate goal of these endeavors to characterize a generalized, multi-component and multi-modal antifeedant for the Colorado potato beetle which can be efficiently synthesized.

Epilimonol was tested in short and long term bioassays against Colorado potato beetle adults for feeding reduction and oviposition suppression (26). Feeding was reduced by 65% at a dosage of 30 $\mu g/cm^2$ in the short-term no-choice assays. However, overall feeding was even more greatly reduced in the choice tests, where there was no evidence of preference for untreated foliage. In the long-term tests, 10 $\mu g/cm^2$ of epilimonol evoked significant mortality and completely suppressed oviposition for up to 25 days. Even with females which had begun to lay eggs, oviposition was terminated after four days of epilimonol exposure. Examination of egg follicles demonstrated that egg maturation did not occur in epilimonol-exposed females, but this symptom was not distinguishable from starvation-induced oviposition suppression. Importantly, epilimonol's effectiveness as an antifeedant and oviposition suppressant was maintained for 9 and 25 days, respectively, indicating no habituation by the adults.

Recent laboratory, greenhouse and field experiments with the crude limonoid extract have elicited larval feeding reduction and adult oviposition suppression activities comparable to those found with the pure chemicals (34). The extract has not shown any phytotoxicity when applied to potato foliage at levels as high as 100 $\mu g/cm^2$, and we have seen no habituation to the crude material by adults or larvae. The crude limonoid extract contains > 95% limonin and related limonoids. With an estimated annual availability of 300 metric tons in the U. S. (21), crude limonoid extract from citrus seeds should be a readily available source of antifeedants for Colorado potato beetle management programs.

We have field-tested the citrus limonoids over the past three growing seasons in Maine (34, unpublished data). In field cages and small plots, the crude extract was applied at rates approximating 40 $\mu g/cm^2$ foliage in an acetone solution with a commercial spreader-sticker. Both in the cages, where adult beetles were introduced, and in the field plots, where naturally-occurring beetles colonized, seasonal densities were measured for adults, eggs, egg masses, small larvae (first and second instars) and large larvae (third and fourth instars). Stability of the crude extract activity was also determined under field conditions.

The results of the field tests indicated that the greatest direct impacts of the limonoids were on oviposition rates inside the cages and on adult densities in the natural, small-plot populations (Fig. 2). Adult survival was not affected by the antifeedant treatment, but comparisons of field cage and small plot data provide important information for the interpretation of our findings. Inside the cages, where adults were introduced and confined, oviposition was suppressed, which is consistent with laboratory studies (26). Outside the cages, reduction in the numbers of colonizing adults and subsequent egg density in treated plots indicated a repellency effect. This is substantiated further by the characterization of egg masses deposited in all treatments, because numbers of eggs per egg mass were not different from controls. Only numbers of egg masses were different between treatments. Unpublished behavioral observations of adults in laboratory, greenhouse, and field situations verify the repellent activity of high dosages of limonoids. Exposed adults demonstrated high levels of erratic locomotor activity, which resulted in their departure from treated plants. These findings are in contrast with studies on Bordeaux mixture, which indicated increased Colorado potato beetle oviposition on plants treated with this antifeedant (41).

In both field cages and plots, the development and numerical growth of small larval populations were delayed. Delayed development was maintained through the fourth instar in the cage studies, but there were no differences in seasonal population densities of large larvae in the small plots. We conclude that the major effects on larvae in the field will likely be a direct consequence of adult oviposition suppression through repellency. Nearly half of the larval feeding depression activity was lost after three days of field exposure, and therefore, in order to maintain biological activity for the required period, UV protection, encapsulation or repeated application will be necessary.

Essential to the adoption and effectiveness of the limonoids is compatibility with other pest management tools. We are interested in utilization strategies which might optimize the performance of antifeedants and other methods when used together. *Bacillus thuringiensis* (BT) is a biological insecticide which has proven to be quite useful in Colorado potato beetle management. Therefore, we examined the interactive effects of the citrus limonoids and BT (34). In

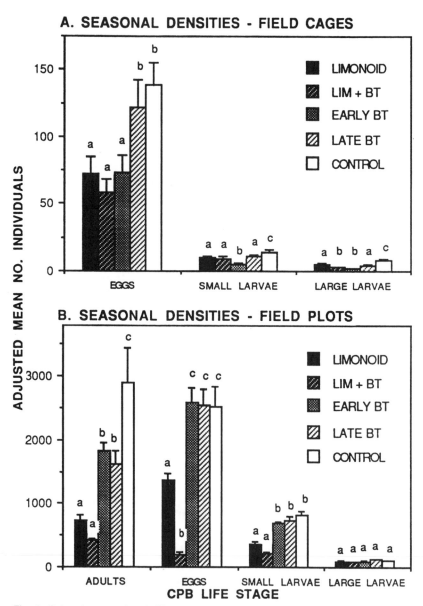

Fig. 2. Colorado potato beetle life-stage densities in limonoid - BT field trials. Density estimates are means of seasonal numbers of individuals per plot adjusted for treatment differences in developmental time (34).

laboratory and field experiments we have shown that pre-exposure to the limonoids did not interfere with BT-induced larval mortality, nor did the BT-treatment inhibit the limonoid-induced delays in larval development or adult oviposition (Fig. 2). Rather, pre-exposure to limonoids resulted in lower adult colonization rates, reduced oviposition and fewer numbers of first and second instars in potato fields compared with either material used alone (Fig. 2b).

From these studies we became interested in limonoid compatibility and deployment with synthetic insecticides. In preliminary tests (unpublished data), we found that three days of prior exposure to the antifeedant increased the susceptibility of third instars to the insecticides azinphosmethyl, esfenvalerate and oxamyl. As seen in earlier studies (35, 37), each antifeedant-insecticide combination will have to be tested because no generalizations can be made about the compatibility of the two chemical approaches. We are focussing much of our attention in this area to examine a whole array of antifeedant-insecticide application scenarios. Included in these studies is an assessment of the effects of synergists, such as piperonyl butoxide (shown to enhance the effects of neem extract on Colorado potato beetle larvae and adults [45]), on the activity of the limonoids. We realize that any incompatibility of a pest management tool with other practices will not likely meet with grower acceptance. During times of emergencies, such as excessive Colorado potato beetle populations, insecticides will have to be used, and inhibitory effects of antifeedants on subsequent insecticide application will be unacceptable. Optimally, antifeedants will serve to enhance insecticidal activity, which could result in fewer applications and lower rates of insecticides used over the season.

In the field trials the crude extract was dissolved in acetone because initial attempts to formulate with commercially available carriers have failed. We are currently exploring other approaches, including different formulations and microencapsulation. We determined that the double salt derivative of limonin (i.e., with A and D rings opened) was taken up through leaf petioles and transported in potato leaves resulting in a reduction in larval feeding activity and growth disruption (28). Interestingly, the double salt applied to the leaf surface was not active, indicating the salt was converted back to limonin within the leaf tissue under its low pH conditions. At high dosages, the material taken up by the leaf proved to be phytotoxic. Feasibility studies for the use of the salt forms of limonin and its models as systemic antifeedants are ongoing.

Epilogue

The citrus limonoid-Colorado potato beetle-potato system has met the general criteria for potential success set forth by previous authors (6, 19, 39, 42). It has been the composite effects that distinguish this system from others studied. The advantages of limonoids are: the limonoid phytochemicals are in the terpene class and detailed structure activity relationships are described; a synthetic model of limonin's partial structure is effective; the material is available in large amounts as an industry waste product from several localities around the globe; limonoids are not phytotoxic at biologically active application levels; there is no evidence of insect habituation; limonoids are compatible with other management tools, including insecticides; and they are effective under field conditions. The development of specific limonoid deployment strategies which utilize these characteristics is henceforth under way for the management of Colorado potato beetle on potatoes.

Literature Cited

1.   Adams, C. M., & E. A. Bernays. 1978. The effect of combinations of deterrents on the feeding behavior of *Locusta migratoria*. Entomol. Exp. Appl. 23: 101-109.
2.   Alford, A. R., & M. D. Bentley. 1986. Citrus limonoids as potential antifeedants for the spruce budworm (Lepidoptera: Tortricidae). J. Econ. Entomol. 79: 35-38.
3.   Alford, A. R., J. A. Cullen, R. H. Storch & M. D. Bentley. 1987. Antifeedant activity of limonin against the Colorado potato beetle (Coleoptera: Chrysomelidae). J. Econ. Entomol. 80: 575-578.
4.   Bentley, M. D., M. S. Rajab, A. R. Alford, M. J. Mendel & A. Hassanali. 1988. Structure-activity studies of modified citrus limonoids as antifeedants for Colorado potato beetle larvae, *Leptinotarsa decemlineata*. Entomol. Exp. Appl. 49: 189-193.
5.   Bentley, M. D., M . S. Rajab, M. J. Mendel & A. R. Alford. 1990. Limonin model antifeedants. J. Agric. Food Chem. 38: 1400-1403.
6.   Bernays, E. A. 1983. Antifeedants in crop management, pp. 259-271. *In* D. L. Whitehead & W. S. Bowers (eds.), Natural products for innovative pest management. Pergamon, Oxford.
7.   Chapman, R. F. 1974. The chemical inhibition of feeding by phytophagous insects: a review. Bull. Entomol. Res. 64: 339-363.
8.   Dethier, V. G. 1980. Evolution of receptor specificity to secondary plant substances with special reference to deterrents. Am. Nat. 115: 45-66.
9.   Elliot, M. 1977. Synthetic pyrethroids, pp. 1-28. *In* M. Elliot (ed.), Synthetic pyrethroids. American Chemical Society Symposium Series No. 42. American Chemical Society, Washington, D.C.
10.   Feeny, P. 1983. Coevolution of plants and insects, pp. 167-186. *In* D. L. Whitehead & W. S. Bowers (eds.), Natural products for innovative pest management. Pergamon, Oxford.

11.   Gill, J. S., & C. T. Lewis. 1971. Systemic action of an insect feeding deterrent. Nature 232: 402-403.

12.   Hare, J. D., P. A. Logan & R. J. Wright. 1983. Suppression of Colorado potato beetle, Leptinotarsa decemlineata (Say) (Col., Chrysomelidae), populations with antifeedant fungicides. Environ. Entomol. 12: 1470-1477.

13.   Hegnauer, R. 1966. Chemotaxonomie der Pflanzen, Vol. 4. Birkhauser Berlag, Basel.

14.   Hendrick, C. A., G. B. Stall & J. B. Sidall. 1973. Alkyl 3,7,11-trimethyl-2-3-dodecadienoates, a new class of potent insect growth regulators with juvenile hormone activity. J. Agric. Food Chem. 21: 354-359.

15.   Jermy, T. 1961. The rejective effect of some inorganic salts on Colorado potato beetle (Leptinotarsa decemlineata Say) adults and larvae. Ann. Inst. Prot. Plant. 8: 121-130.

16.   Jermy, T. 1966. Feeding inhibitors and food preference in chewing phytophagous insects. Entomol. Exp. Appl. 9: 1-12.

17.   Jermy, T. 1971. Biological background and outlook of the antifeedant approach to insect control. Acta Phytopath. Acad. Sci. Hung. 6: 253-260.

18.   Jermy, T. 1983. Multiplicity of insect antifeedants in plants, pp. 223-236. In D. L. Whitehead & W. S. Bowers (eds.), Natural products for innovative pest management. Pergamon, Oxford.

19.   Jermy. T. 1990. Prospects of antifeedant approach to pest control - a critical review. J. Chem. Ecol. 16: 3151-3166.

20.   Jermy, T., B. A. Butt, L. M. McDonough, D. L. Dreyer & A. F. Rose. 1981. Antifeedants for the Colorado potato beetle - I. Antifeeding constituents of some plants from the sagebrush community. Insect Sci. Appl. 1: 237-242.

21.   Klocke, J. A., & I. Kubo. 1982. Citrus limonoid by- products as insect control agents. Entomol. Exp. Appl. 32: 299-301.

22.   Kubo, I., & K. Nakanishi. 1979. Some terpenoid insect antifeedants from tropical plants, pp. 284-294. In H. Geissbuhler (ed.), Advances in Pesticide Science, Part 2. Pergamon, Oxford.

23.   Kuhn, R., & I. Low. 1955. Resistance factors against Leptinotarsa decemlineata Say, isolated from the leaves of wild Solanum species, pp. 122-132. In M. G. Sevag, R. D. Reid & O. E. Reynolds (eds.), Origin of Resistance to Toxic Agents. Academic Press, New York.

24.   Ley, S. V., D. Santafianos, W. M. Blaney & M. S. J. Simmonds. 1987. Synthesis of a hydroxy dihydro-23B- methoxyazadirachtin. Tetrahedron Lett. 26: 6435-6438.

25.   Lugemwa, F. N., F. Y. Huang, M. D. Bentley, M. J. Mendel & A. R. Alford. 1990. A Heliothis zea antifeedant from the abundant birchbark triterpene betulin. J. Agric. Food Chem. 38: 493-496.

26.   Liu, Y.-B., A. R. Alford & M. D. Bentley. 1989. Effects of epilimonol and starvation on feeding and oviposition by Leptinotarsa decemlineata. Entomol. Exp. Appl. 53: 39-44.

27.   Liu, Y.-B., A. R. Alford & M. D. Bentley. 1991. A study on mode of antifeedant effects of epilimonol against Leptinotarsa decemlineata. Entomol. Exp. Appl. 60: 13-18.

28.   Liu, Y.-B., A. R. Alford & M. D. Bentley. 1991. Changes in antifeedant activity of limonin double salt in potato leaves. J. Econ. Entomol. 84: 1154-1157.

29.   Liu, Y.-B., A. R. Alford, M. S. Rajab & M. D. Bentley. 1990. Effects and modes of action of citrus limonoids against Leptinotarsa decemlineata. Physiol. Entomol. 15: 37-45.

30. Meinwald, J., G. D. Prestwich, K. Nakanishi & I. Kubo. 1978. Chemical ecology: studies from East Africa. Science 199: 1167-1173.

31. Mendel, M. J., A. R. Alford & M. D. Bentley. 1991. A comparison of the effects of limonin on Colorado potato beetle, *Leptinotarsa decemlineata*, and fall armyworm, *Spodoptera frugiperda*, larval feeding. Entomol. Exp. Appl. 58: 191-194.

32. Mendel, M. J., A. R. Alford, M. S. Rajab & M. D. Bentley. 1991. Antifeedant effects of citrus limonoids differing in A-ring structure on Colorado potato beetle (Coleoptera: Chrysomelidae) larvae. J. Econ. Entomol. 84: 1158-1162.

33. Metzger, F. W., & D. H. Grant. 1932. Repellency to the Japanese beetle of extracts made from plants immune to attack. USDA Tech. Bull. No. 299, 21pp.

34. Murray, K. D., A. R. Alford, E. Groden, F. Drummond, R. H. Storch, M. D. Bentley & P. M. Sugathapala. 1993. Interactive effects of an antifeedant used with *Bacillus thuringiensis* subsp. *san diego* on the Colorado potato beetle. J. Econ. Entomol. 86: In press.

35. Parmar, B. S., & S. Dutta. 1986. Neem oil as a synergist for insecticides. Neem Newsl. 3: 3-5.

36. Raffa, K. F., & J. L. Frazier. 1988. A generalized model for quantifying behavioral desensitization to antifeedants. Entomol. Exp. Appl. 46: 93-100.

37. Salama, H. S., & A. Sharby. 1988. Feeding deterrence induced by some plants in *Spodoptera littoralis* and their potentiating effect of *Bacillus thuringiensis* Berliner. Insect Sci. Appl. 9: 573-578.

38. Schoonhoven, L. M. 1982. Biological aspects of antifeedants. Entomol. Exp. Appl. 31: 57-69.

39. Schoonhoven, L. M., & T. Jermy. 1977. A behavioural and electro-physiological analysis of insect deterrents, pp. 133-146. *In* N. R. McFarlane (ed.), Crop protection agents - their biological evaluation. Academic Press, New York.

40. Steets, R. 1976. Zur Wirkung eines gereinigten Extraktes aus den Fruchten von *Azadirachta indica* A. Juss. auf *Leptinotarsa decemlineata* Say, Col., Chrysomelidae. Acta Phytopathol. Acad. Sci. Hung. 16: 203-209.

41. Szentesi, A. 1981. Antifeedant-treated potato plants as egg-laying traps for the Colorado potato (*Leptinotarsa decemlineata* Say, Col., Chrysomelidae). Acta Phytopath. Acad. Sci. Hung. 16: 203-209.

42. Szentesi, A., & T. Jermy. 1985. Antifeedants of the Colorado potato beetle: an overview and outlook, pp. 17-27. In D. N. Ferro and R. H. Voss (eds.), Proc. of the Symp. on the Colorado potato beetle, XVIIth Intl. Cong. Entomol., Res. Bull. No. 704, Univ. Mass., Amherst, Mass.

43. Whitehead, D. L., & W. S. Bowers (eds.). 1983. Natural products for innovative pest management. Pergamon, Oxford.

44. Wolff, M. (Ed.). 1981. Burger's Medicinal Chemistry, Parts II & III. John Wiley & Sons, New York.

45. Zehnder, G., & J. D. Warthen. 1988. Feeding inhibition and mortality effects of neem-seed extract on the Colorado potato beetle (Coleoptera: Chrysomelidae). J. Econ. Entomol. 81: 1040-1044.

BIOLOGICAL CONTROL
OF THE COLORADO POTATO BEETLE

David N. Ferro
Department of Entomology
University of Massachusetts
Amherst, MA 01003

The Colorado potato beetle (CPB), *Leptinotarsa decemlineata* (Say), is the most destructive insect pest of potato in North America (69), and has not been effectively managed in the 125 years since its host shift from endemic solanaceous weeds to cultivated potato (14).   In the northeastern region of the United States, the beetle has developed resistance to all currently registered insecticides (25,73), except for the recently introduced *Bacillus thuringiensis* subsp. *tenebrionis*-based bioinsecticides. Bio-insecticides can be used to effectively maintain CPB populations below economic injury levels, however these materials have some important drawbacks. They are only effective against early instars, have little residual activity and are only effective when applied at the right time and under the right conditions (23).   Also, there is evidence that CPB could become resistant to these materials if they are over-used (Whalon this volume).

In view of the key nature of CPB as a pest of potato and the poor prospects for developing chemical controls that are effective and environmentally safe, vigorous efforts are needed to develop biological controls for incorporation into CPB management programs.   Biological control agents cannot stand alone in combating this pest, and must be integrated with cultural practices (e.g. crop rotation, delayed planting or early harvest using short season cultivars), host plant resistance and selective insecticides. The use of cultural practices and biological control agents were proposed as early as the late 1800s by Riley (72). A year later Bethune (7) published a list of 22 arthropod natural enemies of the CPB.

The first thorough discussion of the biology of predators and parasites of the CPB, and the potential for these agents in controlling this important pest was in the 1930's (91).   The Europeans, however, were the first to embrace the use of biological control agents by importing natural enemies from North America (26,91).   These natural enemies failed to provide acceptable levels of control in Europe.   At the time of these introductions, little was known about the biology of the CPB and its natural enemies. A recent study has provided insight into the enemies of CPB in

Mexico, thought to be the area of origin of this pest (13). An understanding of the biology and ecology of species of natural enemies is necessary if we hope to effectively employ these agents for management of crop pests like CPB.

There are certain limitations that must be overcome for biological control agents to be successful. These include : 1) the inability of agents to control CPB at high population densities, 2) host plant resistance factors may not be compatible with natural enemy development, 3) foraging activity must be in synchrony with CPB behavior and development, 4) limited knowledge base exists on the biology of most agents, 5) limited agents are available due to the lack of foreign exploration, and 6) inundative releases of natural enemies is of questionable practical value because of costs associated with rearing. These limitations should be remembered when reading the following discussion on CPB biological control agents.

Bacillus thuringiensis and Other Selective Insecticides

Strains of *B. thuringiensis* (Berliner) have been isolated that are active against Colorado potato beetle larvae (37, 53, subsp. *tenebrionis*, subsp. *san diego*). These strains contain the Cry III A insecticidal crystal protein and are now marketed worldwide by several companies and have demonstrated effectiveness for control of CPB in the field (22,49a,98a). They are formulated and applied in a manner similar to synthetic insecticides; however, they are much more selective in their activity. Beneficial insects, including hymenopterous parasites, coccinellid predators, common green lacewing (*Chrysopa carnea* Stephens) and honey bees (*Apis mellifera* L.) are unaffected by contact or ingestion of *B. thuringiensis* subsp. *tenebrionis* (22). A new strain of *B. thuringiensis* has been isolated that contains a unique crystal protein designated Cry IIIB2. This toxin protein is as toxic to larvae and 20X more toxic to CPB adults than the Cry IIIA protein (49b). M-Trak, a new formulation of subsp. *tenebrionis*, demonstrated greater persistence in the field, compared to M-One, the first coleopteran-active formulation to be developed commercially (24b). Optimal timing of the initial *B. thuringiensis* application is critical for maximizing its effectiveness against CPB. The occurrence of peak CPB egg hatch has proven to be a reliable indicator for timing of the initial application (98b). The environmental compatibility of the *B. thuringiensis* delta-endotoxin, combined with its unusual mode of action, make these bioinsecticides an important tool in biointensive potato IPM programs. Other selective insecticides that are toxic to CPB (such as the chitin synthesis inhibitor teflubenzuron, 6,21), but innocuous to beneficial insects, could also play an important role in biointensive CPB management.

Coleoptera

Coccinellidae. C. V. Riley (71) reported *Coleomegilla maculata* DeGeer feeding on CPB, yet a more recent study (34) did not identify *C. maculata* as an important predator of CPB. Subsequent studies present evidence that *C. maculata* is an important predator of CPB eggs (32,36). Groden et al. (32) observed overwintered adult *C. maculata* present in Michigan and Rhode Island USA potato fields soon after CPB eggs were first laid, with peak densities of *C. maculata* occurring 7-10 days after peak CPB egg densities. Hazzard et al. (36) found *C. maculata* to migrate into potato fields shortly after plant emergence in June, with peak densities of *C. maculata* occurring 5-7 days prior to peak densities of CPB eggs. Observed mortality to first and second generation CPB eggs was 38% and 58%, respectively.

In a laboratory study, female *C. maculata* exhibited a Type II functional response when offered 10-70 CPB eggs per 24 h at 26° (35). *C. maculata* feeding on eggs at high densities was suppressed 30% when aphids were present as an alternate host. Although there would likely be a reduction in predation of CPB eggs when aphids are present in the field, the presence of aphids may encourage *C. maculata* adults to remain in potato fields in the absence of eggs.

C. maculata produces few offspring in potato which may be due to the lack of proper nutrition; however, they do reproduce well in other crops, particularly in corn (16). Large *C. maculata* populations develop on aphids and corn pollen in late-season corn, then move into undisturbed habitats adjacent to corn fields to overwinter. We have observed a large, early-season influx of *C. maculata* into potato fields if potatoes are rotated into fields planted in corn the previous season. In addition, because CPB adults would not have overwintered in the rotated field, these fields would be colonized later and generally at lower population levels than nonrotated fields, effectively providing a better ratio of *C. maculata* adults to CPB egg masses. In areas where crop rotation is an acceptable option, *C. maculata* may play an important role in the biological control of CPB.

Aiolocaria mirabilis (Motschulsky) is a coccinellid predator endemic to Siberia where it feeds on the chrysomelid *Gastrolina thoracica* Baly (52). Because it was capable of consuming large numbers of CPB eggs and larvae, it was introduced into the Ukraine as a potential biological control agent of CPB.

Carabidae. Little research has been done in North America on ground beetles (Carabidae) as predators of CPB, however several studies in Europe have demonstrated that ground beetles actively feed on different life stages of CPB. Obligatory and free choice feeding tests identified 10 species that commonly occur in potato fields in the former Soviet Union that feed on one or more life stages of CPB (86). In the same study, 10 carabid species collected from pitfall traps tested positive in serological tests for feeding on CPB; three of these species were in addition to those tested in the laboratory (86). Studies were also conducted on the seasonal population dynamics and movement of three of the carabid species (67,86).

In Massachusetts, USA, 6 different carabid species were collected from pitfall traps or from burlap traps placed in a commercial potato field (36). Specimens of all species were returned to the laboratory and provided with fresh CPB eggs and moistened dental wicking. Only *Lebia grandis* Hentz and *Pterostichus lucublandus* Say consumed all or most of the eggs provided. In large cage studies, where egg masses were placed at three levels in the potato foliage, only *L. grandis* actively searched for eggs.

L. grandis is endemic to North America where it is distributed in the USA from the Mississippi Valley to Virginia and from the Great Lakes east to Maine (91). Groden (30) has completed the most thorough studies to date on the biology and potential for *L. grandis* as a biological control agent of CPB. Her research was conducted in Michigan and Rhode Island, USA. She reported that adult *L. grandis* feed on CPB eggs and larvae, consume up to 47 eggs per day, and that *L. grandis* larvae develop as obligate ectoparasites on the prepupal stage of CPB. She regards *L. grandis* to be one of the most significant predators of CPB in North America; however more research in other areas is needed on this predator.

Hemiptera

Pentatomidae. There are several species of pentatomids that have been examined as potential biological control agents of the CPB. The spined soldier bug, *Podisus maculiventris* (Say), and the twospotted stinkbug, *Perillus bioculatus* (F.) have received the most attention. The biology of the Mexican race of another species, *Oplomus dichrous* (Herrich-Schaeffer), and its potential for controlling the CPB has recently been discussed (17). Because of the relatively slow population growth rate of *O. dichrous* in cool climates and its inability to overwinter in northern temperate areas, it is of doubtful value in controlling CPB in these areas, although it may be of importance in warmer climates.

P. bioculatus has received much attention and until recently most of the research conducted on this agent was done in Europe. A thorough review of European research efforts during the past several decades on *P. bioculatus* has been published elsewhere (48). *P. bioculatus* feeds on all life stages of CPB, but appears to prefer eggs (56). Various environmental factors affecting the performance of *P. bioculatus* have been studied, including: temperature preference (82), humidity and cold hardiness (84), temperature and humidity on embryonic development (80), fluctuating temperatures on nymphal development (92) and cold hardiness (85). It has been shown that eggs could survive supercooling to -28.8° C and that diapausing nymphs were also very cold tolerant, indicating that factors other than cold winters may limit spring abundance of this predator (85). Experiments involving photoperiodic response (83), diurnal activity (81), diapause physiology (46) and other diapause behavior (45,79) have been conducted which indicate *P. bioculatus* is well adapted for overwintering in harsh environments. The bionomics of *P. bioculatus* was studied in Czechoslovakia from 1964-1969 (47). The food requirements of this predator have been examined (62), and research has shown no adverse effects on *P. bioculatus* when fed CPB larvae infected with *B. thuringiensis* (11). Researchers in Washington state constructed an age-specific life table for this predator, and deduced that 1.5 fifth-instar nymphs per plant were required for control of CPB populations (87). These *P. bioculatus* population densities were much higher than are normally observed in the field. A four year life table study in Ontario, Canada, indicated that endemic CPB predators, including *P. bioculatus*, coccinellids, *Nabis* spp. and chrysopids, accounted for only 5.1% of CPB mortality (34).

Only recently has there been concerted efforts to study *P. bioculatus* and *P. maculiventris* as biological control agents of CPB in North America. In field cage tests, *P. bioculatus* was found to be more effective than *P. maculiventris* for CPB population reduction and plant protection (8). Field plot studies conducted by these researchers demonstrated that three *P. bioculatus* per plant provided over 60% reduction of a naturally-occurring population of CPB on potato. Large numbers of *P. bioculatus* can be reared on cabbage looper, *Trichoplusia ni* (Hübner), for inundative releases (8). Biever and Chauvin (unpublished data) also examined the interactive effects of delaying colonization by overwintered CPB with single or multiple releases of *P. bioculatus* in potato plots. Delayed colonization appeared to concentrate CPB egg laying during a shorter interval, resulting in an abundance of larvae during this time and an inability of the predator to effectively control the larval population. They also found that multiple releases of the predator were more effective than a single release because higher predator populations were maintained in the field. Results from a small field plot study in Delaware, USA demonstrated the effectiveness of *P. bioculatus* for control of CPB (40). Several insecticides and fungicides were identified that could be safely used with this predator (40). The chemical composition of a pheromone released by *P. bioculatus* males has been identified which potentially could be used for monitoring local populations to determine if augmentative predator releases are necessary (2).

Introductions of *P. maculiventris* into Europe for biological control of the CPB have been unsuccessful (9a). The reason for failure has been attributed to the predator's inability to overwinter, however it does overwinter in the northern temperate areas of North America. The rate of development and survival of *P. maculiventris* on several hosts including the CPB has been studied (20), and CPB was determined to be a suboptimal host. A simulation model that investigated developmental rates of *P. maculiventris* when fed CPB larvae indicated a large developmental advantage for CPB over this predator when using average spring field conditions in Rhode Island, USA. In a separate field study, *P. maculiventris* was observed to feed on potato foliage even in the presence of abundant prey (74). They found that when potato foliage was added in supplement with prey, survival of the predator increased by 27.5%, developmental time from second instar to adult eclosion was reduced by 2.4 days, and the preoviposition period was shortened by 1.4 days. A male *P. maculiventris* pheromone has been identified which may have potential for monitoring purposes (1).

Although there has been considerable research done on these Hemipteran predators, the reasons for their low abundance in study sites in Europe and in potato production areas of North America are not known.

Diptera

Tachinidae. *Myiopharus* species are the principal indigenous parasites of the CPB in North America. They are widely distributed throughout the continent and are capable of overwintering in temperate areas. Four *Myiopharus* species have been reared from CPB: *M.* (=*Doryphorophaga*) *aberrans* (Townsend), *M. australis* (Reinhard), *M. doryphorae* (Riley), and *M. macella* (Reinhard). Most of the research reported in the literature has been restricted to *M. doryphorae* and unless otherwise specified I will be referring to this species. *M. doryphorae* has been reported to cause 30-70% parasitism of second generation CPB in the field (38,50,88).

The biology of the spring-summer generations of *Myiopharus* spp. have been discussed in some detail (9,50,88). Only recently has the overwintering mechanism of this fly been discovered. Post-diapause CPB adults were collected from field soil in early spring before soil temperatures exceeded 10°C and were placed individually into separate rearing containers (58a). *M. aberrans* and *M. doryphorae* adults emerged from approximately 10% of the collected beetles. Dissections of additional post-diapause CPB adults revealed first instar *Myiopharus* spp. overwintering inside the beetles.

Research in Manitoba, Canada (51), and in Washington (88) and Massachusetts, USA (58b) found high levels of parasitism by *Myiopharus* species in second generation CPB larvae and low levels in first generation larvae. These studies were conducted in areas where CPB larval population densities are very high (10-30 4th instars/plant). In Colorado, USA, levels of *M. doryphorae* parasitism of CPB larvae collected from potato and *Solanum sarrachoides* Sendt. were examined (38). Percentages of parasitism were high, averaging 67, 58 and 45% during the 4 study years, in June, July and August, respectively when averaged for both plant hosts. However, on *S. sarrachoides*, densities of late instars rarely exceeded a mean of two to three per plant, and numbers were considerably lower on potato.

Lopez and Ferro (unpublished) have completed temperature-dependent developmental studies on overwintered parasites, from initial larviposition to fly emergence and preovipositional development. These studies demonstrate the biology of the fly to be in synchrony with CPB development. For this reason, and because of the high levels of parasitism observed in June by Horton and Capinera (38), the low levels of parasitism observed in first generation CPB is a result of the high host/parasite ratio present at this time. A laboratory study demonstrated that each fly can larviposit 215 times at the rate of 10.8 larvae per day (89). Post-diapause CPB collected from the field produce an average of 377 eggs (24a). Therefore, even if large numbers of fly parasites overwinter, it is impossible for high levels of parasitism to occur due to the disproportionately high numbers of CPB. In contrast, the summer generation beetles that emerge before the induction of diapause (93) produce an average of only 45 eggs; this shifts the numerical advantage to the fly.

It is doubtful that the *Myiopharus* parasite complex will be important in controlling first generation CPB in most potato producing areas. However, it may be important in control of second generation larvae and in reducing the number of post-diapause adults. Much work is still needed on the biology of this CPB parasite to develop methods to encourage even higher levels of late-season parasitism.

Hymenoptera

Eulophidae. *Edovum puttleri* Grissell (Eulophidae), an exotic egg parasite of *L. undecemlineata* (Stal.), was imported into the United States from Colombia, South America, in 1980 as a potential biological control agent of CPB (29,68). *E. puttleri* causes mortality by parasitizing CPB eggs and also by host feeding. Host specificity experiments demonstrated that *E. puttleri* successfully parasitized CPB eggs, but rejected eggs of 10 coccinellid species and 8 chrysomelid species, except for low levels of parasitism of *Labidomera clivicollis* (Kirby) (68).

To date, most early-season field releases of *E. puttleri* have not resulted in significant parasitism of CPB in potato in temperate regions of North America. However, a single study in Maryland achieved a seasonal average of 50% parasitism (77). Obrycki et al. (65) suggested that the early-season effectiveness of *E. puttleri* may be limited by temperatures that are, on average, about 4°C lower in late May and June than the corresponding seasonal mean temperature in the parasite's native habitat. (a conclusion supported by researchers in Canada [78]). However, cool temperatures may not be the major limiting factor in the parasite's ability to parasitize first generation CPB eggs.

Idoine and Ferro (42) suggested that the diurnal peak ovipositional activities (1100-1600 E.S.T.) of *E. puttleri* coincide with favorable temperatures that normally occur early in the potato-growing season in Massachusetts, USA. The mid-day (1100-1600) temperatures from late-May through mid-June exceeded 22°C on 17 and 20 of 26 days in 1985 and 1986, respectively. This is well above the threshold temperature of 17°C for *E. puttleri* ovipositional activity (54). Aphid honeydew was identified as the primary carbohydrate source for *E. puttleri* under field conditions (41), however honeydew-producing aphids generally do not colonize potato crops until early July in the northeastern USA. Therefore, the lack of honeydew may preclude early-season establishment of this parasite. In another field study, *E. puttleri* wasps spent more time foraging on plants with aphids and/or host eggs than on potato plants without either food source (43).

Various aspects of the biology of *E. puttleri* have been studied in detail, including temperature dependent growth (54,66,99), interaction with resistant potato cultivars (65,76), relationship between host density and levels of parasitism (75), effects of herbivore's host and parasite's previous host on parasite host conditioning (44) and the effects of parasite age and host quality on parasitism (55,61). Based on the information gained from the many (>30) studies published on *E. puttleri* within the past 10 years, it is doubtful whether this parasite will be of any value in controlling CPB on potato in the northern temperate areas of the beetle's distribution.

Neuroptera

Chrysopidae. Ridgeway and Murphy (70) reported that Chrysopid larvae have been released in the former Soviet Union into potato fields and have caused high levels of CPB mortality. Laboratory and field studies have been conducted to study the predation of *Chrysoperla rufilabris* (Burmeister) larvae on CPB (64). Under laboratory conditions, a 99% reduction of CPB was achieved when CPB eggs and young larvae were exposed to 5 *C. rufilabris* larvae per cage. In field cage experiments, an 84% population reduction of CPB was obtained with release rates of 81,000 *C. rufilabris* larvae per hectare. Most of the research to date on this predator has been conducted in the southern USA, therefore the potential use of this predator in the northern temperate areas is currently limited to periodic releases during the growing season.

Nematoda

Steinernematidae and Heterorhabditidae. *Steinernema feltiae* Filipjev (=*Neoaplectana carpocapsae*) was first tested by Welch and Briand (96) against the CPB. Infective juvenile stages are ingested with food by the host, then passed through the gut wall into the haemocoele. The symbiotic bacterium *Xenorhabdus nematophilus* (Poinar and Thomas) is then released whereupon the host dies by septicemic infection. The nematode feeds on the body contents of the dead host, passes through several generations, and eventually leaves the host as an infective larva. A recent greenhouse study found several strains of *S. carpocapsae* and *S. feltiae* to cause over 98% mortality of CPB prepupae at 82.3 nematodes/cm^2 (11a). In a field-cage study using moistened soil treated with *S. feltiae*, 71% mortality of fourth instars was achieved at the highest nematode release rate of 310 nematodes/cm^2 (90). The limiting factor affecting nematode survival appears to be desiccation following application. However, studies have demonstrated that various antidesiccant materials may be used to extend the infection period of nematodes sprayed on potato foliage (60). All formulations tested retarded nematode desiccation and increased retention of nematodes on leaf surfaces, yielding infection rates of 30 to 60%, while water alone produced infection rates of 10%.

In another study using field cages, three strains of *S. feltiae* and one of *Heterorhabditis heliothidis* (Khan, Brooks and Hirschmann) were tested for control of CPB (97). A single application of a nematode suspension in water was made to each cage after plants were full grown (nematodes were applied to the foliage as well as to the soil). An application rate of 155 *H. heliothidis*/cm^2 caused a 67% reduction in emergence of CPB adults compared with the control, and a rate of 155 *S. feltiae*/cm^2 caused a 79% reduction.

Breeding studies have been conducted to enhance the behavioral characteristics of *S. feltiae* (27). A hybridized "foundation" population of *S. feltiae* was selected for enhanced host-finding. The proportion of infectives initiating positive chemotaxis was increased from less than 33% to more than 80% through selective breeding. It is questionable whether nematodes can be sustained in the field from one season to the next, therefore their utility will probably be based on multiple applications each season.

Mermithidae. Nickle and Kaiser (63) report on a mermithid nematode *Hexamermis* sp. that was released into small field cages in Maryland, USA in early June and recovered from CPB larvae and adults the following summer. This nematode has been found in Austria, Poland and the former Soviet Union. However, additional studies have not been done to evaluate mermithid nematodes as biological control agents of CPB.

Fungi

Deuteromycetes. *Beauveria bassiana* (Balsamo) Vuillemin is a soil-borne pathogen of many insect pest species. Results from *B. bassiana* applications to foliage to control CPB have been mixed (33,4). In both studies, levels of control and tuber yields were significantly better in the insecticide-treated fields than in the *B. bassiana* treated fields. A number of studies have been conducted to examine the interaction between *B. bassiana* and insecticides and fungicides commonly used in potato production. No significant inhibition of *B. bassiana* colony growth was observed in *in vitro* tests with abamectin, triflumuron, thuringiensin ABG-6162A and carbaryl (5). Emulsifiable concentrate insecticide formulations using xylene-based, aromatic solvents were found to be more inhibitory to *B. bassiana* growth than wettable powder formulations (3). Clark et al. (15) observed a reduction in growth of *B. bassiana* in liquid culture when the insecticides carbofuran and azinphosmethyl were present and also when the fungicides chlorothalonil and mancozeb were present. However, in field tests the fungicides chlorothalonil and metalaxyl had no adverse effects on the survival of *B. bassiana* spores, while mancozeb was highly inhibitory (59).

Failure of foliar applications of *B. bassiana* to control CPB populations below economic levels have prompted studies where suspensions of conidia were applied to the soil surface or incorporated into the soil. Cantwell et al. (12) had limited success in applying a suspension of conidia in water to soil. In another study, separate suspensions of blastospores and conidia were applied to the soil using a hand-held sprayer (95). The conidial soil treatment resulted in a 74% reduction of first generation beetles emerging from the soil in July and a 77% reduction of the second generation in August, compared with the control. Conidia were superior to blastospores in reducing emergence. However, even though a 74% reduction in emergence of first generation CPB was achieved, the remaining population (>60 beetles emerging/m^2) far exceeded the economic injury level. Gaugler et al. (28) found tilling the conidia into the soil enhanced fungal persistence, compared with conidia applied to the soil surface. Based on this study it is doubtful whether *B. bassiana* should be targeted against overwintered adults in the field. However, applications of *B. bassiana* conidia to CPB overwintering sites in the fall prior to diapause and in the spring just prior to emergence may have merit. And, because of the high incidence of postemergence mycosis there may be potential utility against subsequent stages, as reported by Watt and LeBrun (95).

It has been shown that soil has a fungistatic effect on *B. bassiana* and that levels of fungistasis (spores of soil-borne fungi are not able to germinate, or germ tubes rapidly lyse) were found to increase exponentially with increases in soil pH (31). It has been suggested that the inhibitory effects of soil on *B. bassiana* germination could be counteracted by the presence of insect hosts (94). This may account for the increased levels of mycosis under conditions of high beetle density reported by Watt and LeBrun (95). *B. bassiana* may still have promise as a biological control agent of CPB. However, more studies on the soil ecology of this fungal pathogen are needed before these benefits are realized.

Arachnida

Acari. Drummond et al. (18) conducted a series of laboratory and field experiments on *Chrysomelobia labidomerae* Eickwort, a mite parasite of CPB adults. This mite was originally collected from Cuernavaca, Mexico, where it was found to infest populations of CPB. Mite infestations significantly reduced longevity of adult CPB, with greatest reduction in longevity resulting from high initial mite infestations. Caged beetles in Rhode Island, U.S.A. did not die from mite infestations and there was no reduction in beetle fecundity or overwintering survivorship. However, experiments conducted in Mexico indicated that infested beetles initiated flight less often and engaged in shorter flights than non-infested beetles. Research has not been conducted to study the interaction of this mite with other biological control agents.

Phalangidae. *Phalangium opilio* (L.) is a species of harvestman commonly associated with disturbed habitats such as fencerows, gardens, and cultivated crops. Laboratory and field studies on this species have been conducted in Michigan (19). Field cage studies suggest that *P. opilio* is not a major source of mortality to CPB. *P. opilio* populations are not well synchronized temporally with CPB prey, and predation in laboratory tests was restricted to eggs and first and second instars.

Microsporidia

Nosematidae. The first microsporidium to be isolated from CPB was *Nosema leptinotarsae* Lipa which was described from adult CPB collected in the Lvov region of the former Soviet Union (57). The microsporidia *Nosema gastroideae* Hostounsky & Weiser and *N. equestris* are reported to be highly pathogenic to CPB, and alternate chrysomelid hosts (*Gastrophysa polygoni* and *G. viridula*) have been used to produce spores of these pathogens (39).

Pleistophoridae. The microsporidium *Pleistophora fidelis* (Hostounsky and Weiser) has recently been placed in the newly created genus *Endoreticulatus* (10). *E. fidelis* (Hostounsky and Weiser) was originally observed in the midgut epithelial cells of *L. undecimlineata* collected in Cuba. It was later tested as a potential biological control agent of CPB, but did not cause high levels of mortality.

It is doubtful that microsporidia will be used in an inundative manner because infections exhibit chronic symptoms (such as reduced fecundity, slower rates of development, reduced feeding rates etc.) rather than acute mortality. However, inoculative releases could be made into CPB populations to serve as an additional stress on a population.

Epilogue

Biological control agents should play a vital role in the management of this key pest of potato. However, the development of biological control tactics cannot be accomplished in a vacuum. There are a number of cultural practices that should enhance the effectiveness of biological control agents by reducing the density of colonizing beetles. We must also recognize that there are other insect pests of potato to contend with, and controls for these pests may not be compatible with the preservation of natural enemies of CPB. Because the margin of profit on potato is not very high, it may not be cost-effective to use biological control agents in an inundative manner. The relative contribution of biological control agents in CPB management programs will be increased by a better understanding of CPB biology, ecology and natural enemies, and also from the identification of new, exotic agents. We cannot simply think in terms of managing CPB. We must also make efforts to develop farming practices that allow for better management and proliferation of CPB natural enemies.

Acknowledgments

I wish to thank Ted Andreadis, Jeff Aldrich, Ellie Groden, Frank Drummond and Duane Biever for providing me with information for this chapter.

Literature Cited

1.   Aldrich, J. R., J. P. Kochansky and C. B. Abrams. 1984. Attractant for a beneficial insect and its parasitoids: pheromone of the predatory spined soldier bug, *Podisus maculiventris*. Environ. Entomol. 13: 1031-1036.

2. Aldrich, J. R., J. E. Oliver, W. R. Lusby and J. P. Kochansky. 1986. Identification of male-specific exocrine secretions from predatory stink bugs (Hemiptera, Pentatomidae). Arch. Insect Biochem. Physiol. 3: 1-12.

3. Anderson, T. E. and D. W. Roberts. 1983. Compatibility of *Beauveria bassiana* isolates with insecticide formulations used in Colorado potato beetle (Coleoptera: Chrysomelidae) control. J. Econ. Entomol. 76: 1437-1441.

4. Anderson, T. E., D. W. Roberts and R. S. Soper. 1988. Use of *Beauveria bassiana* for suppression of Colorado potato beetle populations in New York state (Coleoptera: Chrysomelidae). Environ. Entomol. 17: 140-145.

5. Anderson, T. E., A. E. Hajek, D. W. Roberts, H. K. Preisler and J. L. Robertson. 1989. Colorado potato beetle (Coleoptera: Chrysomelidae): effects of combinations of *Beauveria bassiana* with insecticides. J. Econ. Entomol. 82: 83-89.

6. Becher, H. M., P. Becker, R. Prokie-Immel and W. Wirtz. 1983. CME-134, a new chitin synthesis inhibiting insecticide. Proc. 10th Intl. Congress Plant Prot. 1: 408-415.

7. Bethune, C. J. S. 1872. Report of the Entomological Society of Ontario for the year 1871. Hunter, Ross, Toronto.

8. Biever, K. D. and R. L. Chauvin. 1992. Suppression of the Colorado potato beetle (Coleoptera: Chrysomelidae) with augmentative releases of predaceous stinkbugs (Hemiptera: Pentatomidae). J. Econ. Entomol. 85: 720-726.

9. Bjegovic, P. 1968. Depressive role of some parasites of the Colorado potato beetle (*Leptinotarsa decemlineata* Say) in northwest Arkansas, 1967. Zastita Bilja 19: 119-124.

9a. Bjegovic, P. 1971. The natural enemies of the Colorado potato beetle (*Leptinotarsa decemlineata* Say) and an attempt of its biological control in Yugoslavia. Zast. Bilja 21: 97-111.

10. Brooks, W. M., J. J. Becnel and G. G. Kennedy. 1988. Establishment of *Endoreticulatus* N. G. for *Pleistophora fidelis* (Hostounsky & Weiser, 1975) (Microsporidia: Pleistophoridae) based on the ultrastructure of a microsporidium in the Colorado potato beetle, *Leptinotarsa decemlineata* (Say) (Coleoptera: Chrysomelidae). J. Protozool. 35: 481-488.

11. Burgerjon, J. and G. Biache. 1967. Laboratory feeding of *Perillus bioculatus* Fabr. with *Leptinotarsa decemlineata* Say larvae intoxicated by thermostable toxin of *Bacillus thuringiensis* Berliner. Entomophaga 11: 279-284.

11a. Cantelo, W. W. and W. R. Nickle. 1992. Susceptibility of prepupae of the Colorado potato beetle (Coleoptera: Chrysomelidae) to entomopathogenic nematodes (Rhabditida: Steinernematidae, Heterorhabditidae). J. Entomol. Sci. 27: 37-43.

12. Cantwell, F. E., W. W. Cantelo and R. F. W. Schroder. 1986. Effect of *Beauveria bassiana* on underground stages of the Colorado potato beetle, *Leptinotarsa decemlineata* (Coleoptera: Chrysomelidae). Great Lakes Entomol. 19: 81-84.

13. Cappaert, D. L., F. A. Drummond and P. A. Logan. 1991. Incidence of natural enemies of the Colorado potato beetle, *Leptinotarsa decemlineata* [Coleoptera: Chrysomelidae] on a native host in Mexico. Entomophaga 36: 369-378.

14. Casagrande, R. A. 1987. The Colorado potato beetle: 125 years of mismanagement. Bull. Entomol. Soc. Am. 18: 142-150.

15.   Clark, R. A., R. A. Casagrande and D. B. Wallace. 1982. Influence of pesticides on *Beauveria bassiana*, a pathogen of the Colorado potato beetle. Environ. Entomol. 11: 67-70.

16.   Conrad, M. S. 1959. The spotted lady beetle, *Coleomegilla maculata* (DeGeer), as a predator of European corn borer eggs. J. Econ. Entomol. 52: 843-847.

17.   Drummond, F. A., R. A. Casagrande and E. Groden. 1987. Biology of *Oplomus dichrous* (Heteroptera: Pentatomidae) and its potential to control Colorado potato beetle (Coleoptera: Chrysomelidae). Environ. Entomol. 16: 633-638.

18.   Drummond, F. A., R. A. Casagrande and P. A. Logan. Impact of the extoparasite, *Chrysomelobia labidomerae* Eickwort, on the Colorado potato beetle. Internat. J. Acarol. 18: 107-115.

19.   Drummond, F. A., Y. Suhaya and E. Groden. 1990. Predation on the Colorado potato beetle (Coleoptera: Chrysomelidae) by *Phalangium opilio* (Opiliones: Phalangidae). J. Econ. Entomol. 83: 772-778.

20.   Drummond, F. A., R. L. James, R. A. Casagrande and H. Faubert. 1984. Development and survival of *Podisus maculiventris* (Say) (Hemiptera: Pentatomidae), a predator of the Colorado potato beetle (Coleoptera: Chrysomelidae). Environ. Entomol. 13: 1283-1286.

21.   Ferro, D. N. 1990. Teflubenzuron: a novel benzoylphenyl urea for managing the Colorado potato beetle. pp. 411-416. *in* M. Hoshi and O. Yamashita (eds.), Advances in Invertebrate Reproduction 5. Elsevier Science Publ., New York.

22.   Ferro, D. N. and W. D. Gelernter. 1989. Toxicity of a new strain of *Bacillus thuringiensis* to Colorado potato beetle (Coleoptera: Chrysomelidae). J. Econ. Entomol. 82: 750-755.

23.   Ferro, D. N. and S. M. Lyon. 1991. Colorado potato beetle (Coleoptera: Chrysomelidae) larval mortality: operative effects of *Bacillus thuringiensis* subsp. *san diego*. J. Econ. Entomol. 84: 806-809.

24a.   Ferro, D. N., A. F. Tuttle and D. C. Weber. 1991. Ovipositional and flight behavior of overwintered Colorado potato beetle (Coleoptera: Chrysomelidae). Environ. Entomol. 20: 1309-1314.

24b.   Ferro, D. N., Q. C. Yuan, A. Slocombe and A. F. Tuttle. 1993. Residual activity of insecticides under field conditions for controlling the Colorado potato beetle (Coleoptera: Chrysomelidae). J. Econ. Entomol. 86: 511-516.

25.   Forgash, A. J. 1985. Insecticide resistance in the Colorado potato beetle. pp. 33-53. *in* D. N. Ferro and R. H. Voss (eds.), Proceedings of the symposium on the Colorado potato beetle. XVIIth International Congress of Entomology. Res. Bull. #704, Mass. Agric. Expt. Sta., Amherst.

26.   Franz, J. 1957. Beobachtungen uber die naturliche Sterblichkeit des Kartoffelkafers (*Leptinotarsa decemlineata* (Say)) in Kanada. Entomophaga 2: 197-212.

27.   Gaugler, R. and J. F. Campbell. 1989. Selection for host-finding in *Steinernema feltiae*. J. Invert. Path. 54: 363-372.

28.   Gaugler, R., S. D. Costa and J. Lashomb. 1989. Stability and efficacy of *Beauveria bassiana* soil inoculations. Envion. Entomol. 18: 412-417.

29.   Grissell, E. E. 1981. *Edovum puttleri* n.g., n. sp. (Hymenoptera: Eulophidae), an egg parasite of the Colorado potato beetle (Chrysomelidae). Proc. Entomol. Soc. Wash. 83: 790-796.

30.   Groden, E. 1989. Natural mortality of the Colorado potato beetle, *Leptinotarsa decemlineata* (Say). Ph.D. Thesis, Michigan State University, E. Lansing.

31.   Groden, E. and J. L. Lockwood. 1991. Effects of soil fungistasis on *Beauveria bassiana* and its relationship to disease incidence in the Colorado potato beetle, *Leptinotarsa decemlineata*, in Michigan and Rhode Island soils. J. Invert. Pathol. 57: 7-16.

32.   Groden, E., F. A. Drummond, R. A. Casagrande and D. L. Haynes. 1990. *Coleomegilla maculata* (Coleoptera: Coccinellidae): its predation upon the Colorado potato beetle (Coleoptera: Chrysomelidae) and its incidence in potatoes and surrounding crops. J. Econ. Entomol. 83: 1306-1315.

33.   Hajek, A. E., R. S. Soper, D. W. Roberts, T. E. Anderson, K. D. Biever, D. N. Ferro, R. A. LeBrun and R. H. Storch. 1987. Foliar applications of *Beauveria bassiana* (Balsamo) Vuillemin for control of the Colorado potato beetle, *Leptinotarsa decemlineata* (Say) (Coleoptera: Chrysomelidae): an overview of pilot test results from the northern United States. Can. Entomol. 119: 959-974.

34.   Harcourt, D. G. 1971. Population dynamics of *Leptinotarsa decemlineata* (Say) in eastern Ontario. III. Major population processes. Can. Entomol. 103: 1049-1061.

35.   Hazzard, R. V. and D. N. Ferro. 1991. Feeding responses of adult *Coleomegilla maculata* (Coleoptera: Coccinellidae) to eggs of Colorado potato beetle (Coleoptera: Chrysomelidae) and green peach aphids (Homoptera: Aphididae). Environ. Entomol. 20: 644-651.

36.   Hazzard, R. V., D. N. Ferro, R. G. Van Driesche and A. F. Tuttle. 1991. Mortality of eggs of Colorado potato beetle (Coleoptera: Chrysomelidae) from predation by *Coleomegilla maculata* (Coleoptera: Coccinellidae). Environ. Entomol. 20: 841-848.

37.   Herrnstadt, C., G. G. Soares, E. R. Wilcox and D. L. Edwards. 1986. A new strain of *Bacillus thuringiensis* with activity against coleopteran insects. Biotechnology 4: 305-308.

38.   Horton, D. R. and J. L. Capinera. 1987. Seasonal and host plant effects on parasitism of Colorado potato beetle by *Myiopharus doryphorae* (Riley) (Diptera: Tachinidae). Can. Entomol. 119: 729-734.

39.   Hostounsky, Z. 1984. Production of microsporidia pathogenic to the Colorado potato beetle (*Leptinotarsa decemlineata*) in alternate hosts. J. Invert. Pathol. 44: 166-171.

40.   Hough-Goldstein, J. and C. B. Keil. 1991. Prospects for integrated control of the Colorado potato beetle (Coleoptera: Chrysomelidae) using *Perillus bioculatus* (Hemiptera: Pentatomidae) and various pesticides. J. Econ. Entomol. 84: 1645-1651.

41.   Idoine, K. and D. N. Ferro. 1988. Aphid honeydew as a carbohydrate source for *Edovum puttleri* (Hymenoptera: Eulophidae). Enviorn. Entomol. 17: 941-944.

42.   Idoine, K. and D. N. Ferro. 1990. Diurnal timing of ovipositional activities of *Edovum puttleri* (Hymenoptera: Eulophidae), an egg parasitoid of *Leptinotarsa decemlineata* (Coleoptera: Chrysomelidae). Environ. Entomol. 19: 104-107.

43.   Idoine, K. and D. N. Ferro. 1990. Persistence of *Edovum puttleri* (Hymenoptera: Eulophidae) on potato plants and parasitism of *Leptinotarsa decemlineata* (Coleoptera: Chrysomelidae): effects of resource availability and weather. Envion. Entomol. 19: 1732-1737.

44.   Jansson, R. K. and J. H. Lashomb. 1988. Host-habitat conditioning in the eulophid egg parasitoid, *Edovum puttleri*: effects of herbivore's host and its food plant. Entomol. Exp. Appl. 46: 173-180.

45.   Jasic, J. 1967. A contribution to the knowledge of the diapause in *Perillus bioculatus* (Fabr.) (Heteroptera, Pentatomidae). Acta Entomol. Bohemoslov. 64: 333-334.

46.   Jasic, J. 1970. Water content and oxygen consumption in overwintered adults of *Perillus bioculatus* (Fabr.). Acta Entomol. Bohemoslov. 67: 6-8.

47.   Jasic, J. 1975. On the life cycle of *Perillus bioculatus* (Heteroptera, Pentatomidae) in Slovakia. Acta Entomol. Bohemoslov. 72: 383-390.

48.   Jermy, T. 1980. The introduction of *Perillus bioculatus* into Europe to control the Colorado potato beetle (*Leptinotarsa decemlineata*). Bull. Oepp. 10: 475-480.

49a.   Jaques, R. P. and D. R. Laing. 1989. Effectiveness of microbial and chemical insecticides in control of the Colorado potato beetle (Coleoptera: Chrysomelidae) on potatoes and tomatoes. Can. Entomol. 121: 1123-1131.

49b.   Johnson, T. B., A. C. Slaney, W. P. Donovan and M. J. Rupar. 1993. Insecticidal activity of EG4961, a novel strain of *Bacillus thuringiensis* toxic to larvae and adults of southern corn rootworm (Coleoptera: Chrysomelidae) and Colorado potato beetle (Coleoptera: Chrysomelidae). J. Econ. Entomol. 86: 330-333.

50.   Kelleher, J. S. 1960. Life history and ecology of *Doryphorophaga doryphorae* (Riley), a tachinid parasite of the Colorado potato beetle. Ph.D. thesis, University of Minnesota, Minneapolis.

51.   Kelleher, J. S. 1966. The parasite *Doryphorophaga doryphorae* (Diptera: Tachinidae) in relation to populations of the Colorado potato beetle in Manitoba. Ann. Entomol. Soc. Am. 59: 1059-61.

52.   Koval, Y. V. 1972. A predator of the Colorado potato beetle. Rev. Appl. Entomol. 60: 47-66.

53.   Kreig, A., A. M. Huger, G. A. Langenbruch and W. Schnetter. 1983. *Bacillus thuringiensis* var. *tenebrionis*: ein neuer gegenuber Larven von Coleopteren wirksamer. Pathotyp. Z. Ang. Entomol. 96: 500-508.

54.   Lashomb, J., Y. S. Ng, R. K. Jansson and R. Bullock. 1987. *Edovum puttleri* (Hymenoptera: Eulophidae), an egg parasitoid of Colorado potato beetle (Coleoptera: Chrysomelidae): development and parasitism on eggplant. J. Econ. Entomol. 80: 65-68.

55.   Lashomb, J., D. Krainacker, R. K. Jansson, Y. S. Ng and R. Chianese. Parasitism of *Leptinotarsa decemlineata* (Say) eggs by *Edovum puttleri* Grissell (Hymenoptera: Eulophidae): effects of host age, parasitoid age and temperature. Can. Entomol. 119: 75-82.

56.   LeBerre, J. R. and G. Portier. 1963. Utilisation d'un heteroptere Pentatomidae *Perillus bioculatus* (Fabr.) dans la lutte contre le doryphore*Leptinotarsa decemlineata* (Say): premiers resultats obtenus en France. Entomophaga 8: 183-190.

57.   Lipa, J. J. 1968. *Nosema leptinotarsae* sp. n., a microsporidian parasite of the Colorado potato beetle, *Leptinotarsa decemlineata* (Say). J. Invert. Pathol. 10: 111-115.

58a.   Lopez, R., D. N. Ferro and R. G. Van Driesche. Overwintering biology of *Myiopharus aberrans* (Townsend) and *Myiopharus doryphorae* (Riley) (Diptera: Tachinidae) larval parasitoids of the Colorado potato beetle (Coleoptera: Chrysomelidae). Entomophaga 37: 311-315.

58b.   Lopez, R., D. N. Ferro and R. G. Van Driesche. 1993. Direct measurement of host and parasitoid recruitment for assessment of total losses due to parasitism in the Colorado potato beetle, *Leptinotarsa decemlineata* (Coleoptera: Chrysomelidae), and *Myiopharus doryphorae* (Riley) (Diptera: Tachinidae). Biol. Contr. 3: (in press)

59.   Loria, R., S. Galaini and D. W. Roberts. 1983. Survival of inoculum of the Entomopathogenic fungus *Beauveria bassiana* as influenced by fungicides. Environ. Entomol. 12: 1724-1726.

60.   MacVean, C. M., J. W. Brewer and J. L. Capinera. 1982. Field tests of antidesiccants to extend the infection period of an entomogenous nematode, *Neoaplectana carpocapsae*, against the Colorado potato beetle. J. Econ. Entomol. 75: 97-101.

61.   Maini, S. and G. Nicoli. 1990. *Edovum puttleri* (Hym.: Eulophidae): biological activity and responses to normal and frozen eggs of *Leptinotarsa decemlineata* (Col.: Chrysomelidae). Entomophaga 35: 185-193.

62.   Moens, R. 1965. Observations on the food requirements of *Perillus bioculatus* Fabr. (hemiptera, Asopidae). Mendel Landbouw-Hoesch Opzoekings Sta. Staat. Gent. 30: 1504-1515.

63.   Nickle, W. R. and H. Kaiser. 1984. An Austrian mermithid nematode parasite offers biological control of the Colorado potato beetle, *Leptinotarsa decemlineata* (Say). Proc. Helminthol. Soc. Wash. 51: 340-341.

64.   Nordlund, D. A., D. C. Vacek and D. N. Ferro. 1991. Predation of Colorado potato beetle (Coleoptera: Chrysomelidae) eggs and larvae by *Chrysoperla rufilabris* (Neuroptera: Chrysopidae) larvae in the laboratory and field cages. J. Entomol. Sci. 26: 443-449.

65.   Obrycki, J. J., M. J. Tauber, C. A. Tauber and B. Gollands. 1985. *Edovum puttleri* (Hymenoptera: Eulophidae), an exotic egg parasitoid of the Colorado potato beetle (Coleoptera: Chrysomelidae): responses to temperate zone conditions and resistant potato plants. Envion. Entomol. 14: 48-54.

66.   Obrycki, J. J., M. J. Tauber, C. A. Tauber and B. Gollands. 1987. Developmental responses of the Mexican biotype of *Edovum puttleri* (Hymenoptera: Eulophidae) to temperature and photoperiod. Environ. Entomol. 16: 1319-1323.

67.   Prisnyy, A. S. 1987. Seasonal dynamics of migratory activity of some predatory Coleoptera. Entomol. Rev. 66: 181-186.

68.   Puttler, B. and S. H. Long. 1983. Host specificity tests of an egg parasite, *Edovum puttleri* (Hymenoptera: Eulophidae), of the Colorado potato beetle, *Leptinotarsa decemlineata* (Coleoptera: Chrysomelidae). Proc. Entomol. Soc. Wash. 85: 384-387.

69.   Radcliffe, E. B., K. L. Flander, D. W. Ragsdale and D. M. Noetzel. 1991. Potato insects - pest management systems for potato insects. pp. 587-621. *in* D. Pimentel (ed.), CRC Handbook of Pest Management (2nd edition). CRC Press, Boca Raton, Fl.

70.   Ridgeway, R. L. and W. L. Murphy. 1984. Biological control in the field. pp. 220-228. *in* M. Canard, Y. Semeria and T. R. New (eds.). Biology of Chrysopidae. Dr. W. Junk, The Hague.

71.   Riley, C. V. 1869. First annual report on the noxious, beneficial, and other insects of the state of Missouri. Ellwood Kirby, Jefferson City, Mo.

72.   Riley, C. V. 1871. Third annual report on the noxious, beneficial, and other insects of the state of Missouri. Horace Wilcox, Jefferson City, Mo.

73.   Roush, R. T., C. W. Hoy, D. N. Ferro and W. M. Tingey. 1990. Insecticide resistance in the Colorado potato beetle (Coleoptera: Chrysomelidae): influence of crop rotation and insecticide use. J. Econ. Entomol. 83: 315-319.

74.   Ruberson, J. R., M. J. Tauber and C. A. Tauber. 1986. Plant feeding by *Podisus maculiventris* (Heteroptera: Pentatomidae): effect on survival, development, and preoviposition period. Environ. Entomol. 15: 894-897.

75.   Ruberson, J. R., M. J. Tauber, C. A. Tauber and B. Gollands. 1991. Parasitization by *Edovum puttleri* (Hymenoptera: Eulophidae) in relation to host density in the field. Ecol. Entomol. 16: 81-89.

76.   Ruberson, J. R., M. J. Tauber, C. A. Tauber and W. M. Tingey. 1989. Interactions at three trophic levels: *Edovum puttleri* Grissell (Hymenoptera: Eulophidae), the Colorado potato beetle, and insect-resistant potatoes. Can. Entomol. 121: 841-851.

77.   Schroder, R. F. W. and M. M. Athanas. 1989. Potential for the biological control of *Leptinotarsa decemlineata* (Col.: Chrysomelidae) by the egg parasite, *Edovum puttleri* (Hym.: Eulophidae) in Maryland, 1981-1984. Entomophaga 34: 135-141.

78.   Sears, M. K. and G. Boiteau. 1989. Parasitism of Colorado potato beetle (Coleoptera: Chrysomelidae) eggs by *Edovum puttleri* (Hymenoptera: Eulophidae) on potato in eastern Canada. J. Econ. Entomol. 82: 803-810.

79.   Shagov, E. M. 1967a. Photoperiodic reaction of *Perillus bioculatus* (Heteroptera, Pentatomidae). Zool. ZH 46: 948-950.

80.   Shagov, E. M. 1967b. Effect of temperature and humidity on the embryonic development of *Perillus bioculatus* Fabr. (Heteroptera, Pentatomidae). Zool. ZH 46: 1260-1262.

81.   Shagov, E. M. 1976. Daily rhythmicity of some life processes in the two-spotted stink bug, *Perillus bioculatus* (Heteroptera, Pentatomidae). Zool. ZH 55: 721-726.

82.   Shagov, E. M. 1977a. Temperature preferences of the two-spotted stink bug, a parasite of the Colorado potato beetle. Ekologiya 1: 97-99.

83.   Shagov, E. M. 1977b. Photoperiodic reaction and variability in the twospotted stink bug, *Perillus bioculatus*. Ekologiya 4:96-97.

84.   Shagov, E. M. 1977c. The effect of air humidity on *Perillus bioculatus*. Ekologiya 6: 95-96.

85.   Shagov, E. M. and S. I. Chesnek. 1978. Resistance to cold in the predatory bug *Perillus bioculatus* (Heteroptera, Pentatomidae). Zool. ZH 57: 398-406.

86.   Sorokin, N. S. 1981. Ground beetles (Coleoptera: Carabidae) as natural enemies of the Colorado beetle *Leptinotarsa decemlineata* Say. Entomol. Rev. 60: 44-52.

87.   Tamaki, G. and B. A. Butt. 1978. Impact of *Perillus bioculatus* on the Colorado potato beetle and plant damage. USDA, Tech. Bull. 1581.

88.   Tamaki, G., R. L. Chauvin and A. K. Burditt, Jr. 1983. Field evaluation of *Doryphorophaga doryphorae* (Diptera: Tachinidae), a parasite, and its host the Colorado potato beetle (Coleoptera: Chrysomelidae). Environ. Entomol. 12: 386-389.

89.   Tamaki, G., R. L. Chauvin and A. K. Burditt, Jr. 1983. Laboratory evaluation of *Doryphorophaga doryphorae* (Diptera: Tachinidae), a parasite of the Colorado potato beetle (Coleoptera: Chrysomelidae). Environ. Entomol. 12: 390-392.

90.   Toba, H. H., J. E. Lindegren, J. E. Turner and P. V. Vail. 1983. Susceptibility of the Colorado potato beetle and the sugarbeet wireworm to *Steinernema feltiae* and *S. glaseri*. J. Nematol. 15: 597-601.

91.   Trouvelot, B. 1931. Recherches sur les parasites et predateurs attaquant le Doryphore en Amerique du Nord. Ann. des Epiphyt. 6: 408-445.

92.   Volkovitch, T. A., L. I. Kolechnichenko and A. Kh. Saulich. 1991. The role of thermal rhythms in the development of *Perillus bioculatus* (Hemiptera, Pentatomidae). Entomol. Rev. 70: 68-80.

93.   Voss, R. H., D. N. Ferro and J. A. Logan. 1988. Role of reproductive diapause in the population dynamics of the Colorado potato beetle (Coleoptera: Chrysomelidae) in western Massachusetts. Environ. Entomol. 17: 863-871.

94.   Wartenberg, H. and K. Freund. 1961. Der Konservierungseffekt antibiotscher Mikroorganismen an Konidien van *Beauveria bassiana* (Bals.) Vuill. Zentralbl. Bakteriol. 114: 718-724.

95.   Watt, B. A. and R. A. Briand. 1984. Soil effects of *Beauveria bassiana* on pupal populations of the Colorado potato beetle (Coleoptera: Chrysomelidae). Environ. Entomol. 13: 15-18.

96.   Welch, H. E. and L. J. Briand. 1961. Tests of the nematode DD 136 and an associated bacterium for control of the Colorado potato beetle, *Leptinotarsa decemlineata* (Say). Can. Entomol. 93: 759-763.

97.   Wright, R. J., F. Agudelo-Silva and R. Georgis. 1987. Soil applications of Steinernematid and Heterorhabditid nematodes for control of Colorado potato beetles, *Leptinotarsa decemlineata* (Say). J. Nematol. 19: 201-206.

98a.   Zehnder, G. and J. D. Gelernter. 1989. Activity of the M-One formulation of a new strain of *Bacillus thuringiensis* against the Colorado potato beetle (Coleoptera: Chrysomelidae): relationship between susceptibility and insect life stage. J. Econ. Entomol. 82: 756-761.

98b.   Zehnder, G. W., G. M. Ghidiu and J. Speese III. 1992. Use of the occurrence of peak Colorado potato beetle egg hatch for timing of *Bacillus thuringiensis* spray applications in potatoes. J. Econ. Entomol. 85: 281-288.

99.   Ziskind, L. A. and O. N. Mityakina. 1991. *Edovum puttleri* (Hymenoptera, Eulophidae) - an introduced entomophage of the Colorado potato beetle, *leptinotarsa decemlineata* (Coleoptera, Chrysomelidae). Entomol. Rev. 70: 142-148.

CULTURAL CONTROL OF COLORADO POTATO BEETLE: OFF-CROP MANAGEMENT

J. A. Wyman, J. Feldman and S. K. Kung
University of Wisconsin, Madison, WI 53706

In the past decade, Colorado potato beetle, *Leptinotarsa decemlineata* (Say), has emerged as the predominant insect pest of potatoes. Defoliation from overwintered adults, spring larvae, second-generation summer adults and occasionally second generation larvae can cause serious yield reduction and limit production in some areas. The Colorado potato beetle is a particularly severe pest in eastern and north central production areas of North America and is increasing in the north west.

Current control strategies are focused on maintaining adult and larval populations below damaging levels on the potato crop with systemic and foliar insecticides. Widespread resistance to conventional insecticides (3, 11) has greatly reduced the effectiveness of such therapeutic control strategies, however, and as a result, damage caused by the Colorado potato beetle has increased annually. Insecticide resistance management strategies can be effective in delaying the onset of resistance, particularly if initiated before resistance is established. Management programs which reduce selection pressure by avoiding adult treatment and precisely targeting early summer larvae (34) in combination with rotation of insecticidal classes and spot treatments of population aggregations have been successfully employed to hold resistance at low levels.

To achieve long term, economical control of the Colorado potato beetle, however, it will be necessary to implement multifaceted management programs which incorporate not only insecticides but also biological controls, cultural controls and host plant resistance.

Potential Utility of Cultural Controls

A significant portion of the Colorado potato beetle life cycle occurs in non-crop habitats. In northern growing areas approximately five months are actually spent on the current season crop, between infestation in the spring (May-June) and dispersal in the fall (August-September). For the remainder of the year the insect survives in the adult stage in the ecosystem surrounding the potato field. During this period the adult beetle must disperse from the potato crop following senescence or vine kill in the fall, locate a suitable overwintering habitat, survive severe winter conditions, and emerge from diapause, and disperse to locate and infest new potato crops in the spring. These complex ecological and behavioral patterns provide excellent opportunities to use cultural controls to increase levels of natural mortality outside of the potato crop, and thus reduce the need for management of subsequent populations on the crop (Fig.1). The potential utility of the various cultural strategies noted in Figure 1 will vary with local agronomic practices and climate. However, a combination of tactics may be selected to increase off-crop mortality under a wide range of growing conditions.

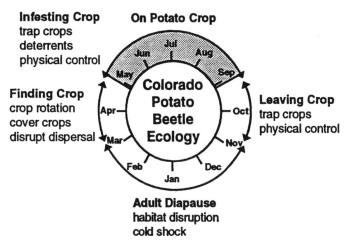

Fig. 1 Colorado potato beetle ecology in relation to off-crop management.

Fall Strategies

In late summer and fall, diapause is initiated in adult beetles resulting in a dispersal from senescing or vine-killed potato fields to new food resources or suitable overwintering habitats. Diapause is induced by photoperiod (5) but is also mediated by temperature and host plant quality (10). Senescing foliage can induce diapause under conditions which would otherwise promote reproduction, and a reduction on food quality can increase the percentage of diapausing beetles (4). Once diapause is induced, beetles burrow into the soil to optimize winter survival. The eventual site of overwintering may vary with location but most frequently a high proportion of beetles disperse from the crop to field margins and/or woodlots and wind breaks located in close proximity to the crop (29, 18, 30). The successful location of suitable overwintering sites is an important component of beetle survival. Cultural strategies which seek to reduce the number of adults reaching the overwintering habitat would be an effective means of population reduction.

A fall trap crop consisting of a strip of potatoes on the edge of the main crop, which remain attractive when the crop is killed or senesces, is an effective tactic to concentrate large numbers of dispersing beetles in a small area (18). Such areas may either be created outside of the crop with late plantings or within the crop by differential application of vine killer to preserve strips of foliage. When concentrated in the trap crop area, beetles can be controlled by targeted insecticidal treatments or, in areas where resistance is prevalent, removed by physical controls to reduce the number of adults reaching an overwintering habitat. Commercially available physical controls such as vacuum suction (1) or propane flaming (20) are most effective when used on highly aggregated beetle populations in limited areas.

Winter Strategies

Natural winter mortality of overwintering beetles is high, but is also extremely variable and dependent on a range of factors which include soil type, soil moisture and temperature. Snow and surface mulch moderate soil temperature fluctuations and may enhance adult survival, but natural mortality during this phase is a significant factor in regulating Colorado potato beetle populations. Greatest mortality occurs in late fall when beetles are unprepared physiologically to withstand extreme cold, and in spring when they are unable to restore adequate water balance (24). Mortality is highest in heavy soils where high moisture increases susceptibility to cold temperatures (19). Depth of burrowing and exposure to cold temperature are also related to soil type, with more shallow overwintering in heavy soils than in sandy soils (9, 31, 19). Lashomb et al. (16) found that a 10 cm increase in soil depth decreased mortality by 32%. A major factor in the overwintering survival of insect pests is their ability to cold-harden (17). Winter survival may involve several physiological and behavioral adaptations (17) and exploitation of these mechanisms holds considerable potential for increasing natural mortality in colder northern growing regions. Therefore, the overwintering habitat is critical to beetle survival and cultural manipulations which increase mortality in this habitat would be effective in reduction of subsequent populations.

Studies in Wisconsin (18) illustrate the potential for winter habitat disruption by exposing adults to low temperature thermal shocks to increase natural mortality. Since natural overwintering habitats are commonly permanent field margins or wooded wind breaks (30) which

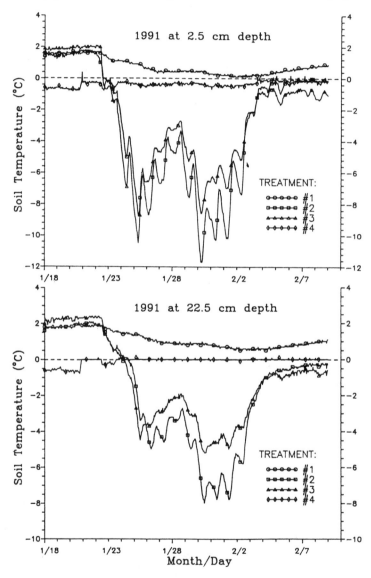

Fig. 2 Soil temperature fluctuations in Colorado potato beetle overwintering habitats, Hancock, WI 1991. 0 -plots mulched season long; ¤-mulched removed 1/22; ▲- mulch removed 1/22, replaced 1/26; ◇- plots mulched.

are not easily disrupted, adults were concentrated in fall trap crops of potatoes. These trap areas were then mulched in fall with wheat straw to simulate natural overwintering sites and to retain adults. Mulch was removed during passage of an Arctic cold front in mid-winter to expose adults to the sudden low temperature cold shock. In mulched and unmulched control areas, soil temperatures remained close to 0°C throughout the winter since both areas were covered by snow. Where snow and mulch were removed in mid-winter, soil temperature dropped to -8 to -10°C at 2.5 cm and -3 to -5°C at 22.5 cm within two days of habitat disruption (Fig. 2). The majority of beetles overwintered within 15 cm of the soil surface in all plots as a result of early winter snow cover, survival was significantly reduced from 0-15 cm by mulch removal and exposure of beetles to cold shock temperatures of -8 to -10°C (Table 1). Survival at 15-25 cm, where temperatures were -3 to -5°C following mulch removal, was also reduced.

TABLE 1. Survival rates of Colorado potato beetles following winter habitat disruption, Hancock, WI (1991)

Overwintering	Mean Percent Survival [y]	
Habitat Treatment	0-15 cm	15-25 cm
Season long mulch (with snow)	23.1 $\pm$ 5.6a	51.5 $\pm$ 6.3a
Mulch/snow removed 1/22	3.8 $\pm$ 2.5b	26.7 $\pm$ 16.5a
Mulch/snow removed 1/22, replaced 1/26	9.2 $\pm$ 3.8b	33.3 $\pm$ 20.2a
No mulch (with snow)	28.7 $\pm$ 7.2a	37.9 $\pm$ 20.8a

[y]Mean $\pm$ SD, 3 replicates, followed by the same letter are not significantly different (P>0.05) by LSD.

In experiments under controlled conditions to determine the magnitude of cold shock required to cause adult mortality, beetles were maintained for 180 days in a simulated fall, winter and spring temperature regime and exposed to cold shocks of -4,-6,-8,-10 and -12°C during the winter phase (14). Survival was not affected until cold shocks of -6°C were experienced, when mortality sharply increased (Table 2). Virtually no survival occurred following exposure to -8 to -12°C. Precise whole body supercooling points for Colorado potato beetle populations from several growing regions were measured by Vencill (25). Supercooling points of -5.92 ± 3.4°C, -4.5 ± 3.56°C and -5.36 ± 0.83°C for populations from Maine, Washington and Canada (Prince Edward Island), respectively, were in close agreement with the critical temperature for mortality determined for Wisconsin populations, indicating that similar cold tolerance mechanisms may exist in northern growing regions. A supercooling point of -10.53 ± 4.12°C for a Virginia population was significantly lower and suggests that other cold tolerance mechanisms may be implicated in survival in warmer climates.

Table 2. Survival rates of Wisconsin Colorado potato beetle adults following exposure to six cold shock temperatures during diapause.

Cold Shock Temperature (°C)	Percent Survival [y]
0	53.0 " 17.9a
-4	54.8 ± 16.3a
-6	6.2 ± 7.6b
-8	0.7 ± 2.4c
-10	0.0c
-12	0.0c

[y]Mean ± SD, 6 replicates, n = 123-126/treatment. Means followed by the same letter are not significantly different (P>0.05) by LSD.

The relatively mild critical temperatures (-5°C) required to cause mortality in adult Colorado potato beetles from northern growing regions demonstrated that cultural manipulations which expose beetles to cold shock can significantly increase mortality. Experiments are currently being conducted to determine the potential of ice nucleating bacteria in raising the supercooling point of overwintering beetles to further decrease survival under low temperature conditions (17)

Spring Strategies

Following diapause, adult Colorado potato beetles emerge from the soil as temperatures reach 10-14°C at the overwintering depth (31, 16).

Emergence can be predicted but varies between location and soil type (22). Emergence occurs close to the previous potato crop and the primary need following emergence is to locate food and suitable host plants for oviposition. This process is dependent upon the speed of dispersal and the ability of beetles to locate host plants.

In northern growing areas dispersal speed is relatively slow. Dispersal may be achieved through walking or flying and both are highly dependent on temperature. Johnson (13) reported a flight threshold of 18°C with maximum flight 25°C. Similar results were reported in Virginia (36) and Michigan (2). The temperature threshold for walking is lower than for flying (15). Although both dispersal mechanisms are possible in spring, the low temperatures prevalent in northern production areas tend to promote dispersal primarily by walking, thus slowing the dispersal process considerably.

The ability of overwintered adult Colorado potato beetles to locate host plants may also be limited. Several workers have reported that Colorado potato beetles are attracted to host odor (6, 26, 27, 23) but, in the field, adults exhibit a high degree of directionality in dispersal which does not appear to be host oriented (21, 32, 12).

The combination of slow dispersal, primarily by walking, and a relatively inefficient host finding ability enhances the potential for cultural manipulations which can be used to delay crop infestation in the spring.

Crop rotation is commonly practiced in potato production for disease control but can also be beneficial in reducing Colorado potato beetle infestation pressure (33, 15). Beetle populations overwinter close to the site of previous crops and the timing and severity of infestations in rotated fields are proportional to the distance between the previous crop and the new crop (28). In intensively cropped areas, rotation options may be limited by agronomic considerations but rotation significantly impacts spring beetle dispersal and should be included in management programs wherever practical.

Spatial separation achieved by rotation of crops may also be effected temporally by advancing or delaying planting dates, where economics permit. Early plantings may be well established and able to sustain damage resulting from infestation at less critical growth stages, whereas later plantings may not emerge until beetle dispersal is complete (28).

The difficulties encountered by adult beetles in dispersing by walking can be increased using cultural strategies which slow dispersal and delay infestation. Wheat (15), grass (21) and weeds (35) have been reported as natural barriers, along with physical landscape features such as streams or woods, in delaying field infestation. Artificially constructed barriers such as straw mulch (37) or plastic-lined trenches which are currently under investigation in Canada, may also be effective in areas of intensive beetle pressure.

When adult beetles have successfully located a host crop, the infestation process typically begins with aggregations on the field edges (7, 8). Cultural controls using trap crops consisting of early planted potatoes can be used to concentrate dispersing adult beetles in areas outside of commercial fields. Physical or chemical controls can then be applied to prevent main crop infestation. In situations where early plantings are not feasible outside the crop, the crop edge itself may be utilized as a trap. The narrow window of 1-2 weeks when adults remain close to the crop edge may be extended by application of repellents to the crop adjacent to the edge (7).

Epilogue

The successful long term management of Colorado potato beetle can only result from the integration of a wide range of control strategies. Management must be practiced not only on the crop, where host plant resistance and chemical controls which promote biological regulation and lessen the potential for resistance will continue to be important, but also in the ecosystem surrounding the crop. Off-crop cultural controls which may include fall and spring trap crops, crop rotations and habitat disruption serve to increase mortality and decrease populations infesting subsequent potato crops. Such cultural controls are compatible with existing on-crop management strategies and can be adopted using existing farm equipment with minimal disruption of normal agronomic practices. The effectiveness of individual tactics will differ between locations, and strategies must be designed to account for local variations in climate and farming practice.

Literature Cited

1. Boiteau, G., C. Misener, R. P. Singh and G. Bernard. 1992. Evaluation of a vacuum collector for insect pest control in potato. Am. Pot. J. 69: 157-166.
2. Caprio, M. A. and E. J. Grafius. 1990. Effects of light, temperature and feeding status on flight initiation in post-diapause Colorado potato beetles. Environ. Entomol. 19: 281-285.
3. Casagrande, R. A. 1987. The Colorado potato beetle: 125 years of mismanagement. Bull. Entomol. Soc. 33: 142-150.
4. deWild, J., J. W. Bongers and H. Schooneveld. 1969. Effects os host plant age on phytophagous insects. Entomol. Exp. Appl. 12: 714-720.
5. deWild, J., C. S. Duintjer, and L. Mook. 1967. Physiology of diapause in the adult Colorado potato beetle (Leptinotarsa decemlineata (Say)). I. The photoperiod as a controlling factor. J. Insect Physiol. 3: 75-85.

6. deWild, J. H. R. Lambers-Suverkr, and A. van Tol. 1969. Responses to air flow and air borne plant odour in the Colorado potato beetle. Neth. J. Pl. Path. 75: 53-57.

7. Feldman, J. 1990. Management of the Colorado potato beetle through thermal unit prediction of larval instars, and manipulation of adult behavior with feeding deterrents. M. S. Thesis, Univ. Wisconsin, 135p.

8. French, N. M., P. A. Follet, B. A. Nault and G. G. Kennedy. 1992. Colonization of potato fields in Eastern North Carolina by Colorado potato beetle. Entomol Exp. Appl. (in press).

9. Gibson, A., R. P. Gorham, H. F. Hudson, and J. A. Flock. 1925. The Colorado potato beetle *Leptinotarsa decemlineata* (Say) in Canada. Bulletin, Canada Dept. of Agriculture 52: 3-30.

10. Horton, D. R., and J. L. Capinera. 1988. Effects of host availability on diapause and voltinism in a non-agricultural population of Colorado potato beetle (Coleoptera: Chrysomelidae). J. Kan. Entomol. Soc. 61: 62-67.

11. Ioannidis, P. I., E. J. Grafius, and M. E. Whalen. 1991. Patterns of insecticide restance of azinphosmethyl, carbofuran, and pemethrin in the Colorado potato beetle (Coleoptera: Chrysomelidae). J. Econ. Entomol. 84: 1417-1423.

12. Jermy, T., A. Szentesi and J. Horvath. 1988. Host plant finiding in phytophagous insects: the case of the Colorado potato beetle. Entomol. Exp. Appl. 48: 83-98.

13. Johnson, C. G. 1969. The Migration and Dispersal of Insects by Flight. Methuen & Co. Ltd. London. 763p.

14. Kung, K-J. S., M. Milner, J. A. Wyman, J. Feldman and E. Nordheim. 1992. Survival of Colorado potato beetle after exposure to sub-zero thermal shocks during diapause. J. Econ. Entomol. 85: 1695-1700.

15. Lashomb, J. H. and Y. S. Ng. 1984. Colonization by Colorado potato beetles, *Leptinotarsa decemlineata* (Say) (Coleoptera: Chrysomelidae), in rotated and non-rotated potato fields. Environ. Entomol. 13: 1352-1356.

16. Lashomb, J. H., Y. S. Ng, G. Ghidiu and E. Green. 1984. Description of spring emergence by the Colorado potato beetle, *Leptinotarsa decemlineata* (Say) (Coleoptera: Chrysomelidae), in New Jersey. Environ. Entomol. 13: 907-910.

17. Lee R. E. 1991. Principles of insect low temperature tolerance. pp. 170-43 in Insects at Low Temperatures, R. E. Lee and D. L. Denlinger eds. Chapman and Hall, London.

18. Milner, M. K-J. S. Kung, J. A. Wyman, J. Feldman and E. Nordheim. 1992. Enhancing overwintering mortality of Colorado potato beetle by manipulating the temperature of its diapause habitat. J. Econ. Entomol. 85: 1701-1708.

19. Minder, I. F. 1966. Hibernation conditions and survival rate of the Colrado potato beetle in different types of soils. pp. 28-58. in Ecology and Physiology of Diapause in the Colorado Beetle, K. V. Arnodi ed. Indian Nat. Scientific Doc. Centre, New Delphi. (reprinted by U. S. Dept. of Agric.), .

20. Moyer, D. D. 1992. Fabrication and operation of a propane flamer for Colorado potato beetle control. Cornell Coop. Extension Bulletin, 7p.

21. Ng, Y. S. and J. Lashomb. 1983. Orientation by the Colorado potato beetle (*Leptinotarsa decemlineata* Say). Animal Behavior 31: 617-619.

22. Tauber, C. A., M. J. Tauber, B. Gollands, R. J. Wright, and J. J. Obrycki. 1988. Preimaginal development and reproductive responses to temperature in two populations of the Colorado potato beetle (Coleoptera: Chrysomelidae). Ann. Entomol. Soc. Am. 81: 755-763.

23. Thiery, D. and J. H. Visser. 1987. Misleading the Colorado potato beetle with an odor blend. J. Chem. Ecol. 13: 1139-1146.

24. Ushatinshaya, R. S. 1978. Seasonal migration of adult *Leptinotarsadecemlineata* in different soil and physiological variations of individuals in hibernating populations. Pedobiologia, Bd 18: 120-126.

25. Vencill, A. M. 1992. Investigations of Colorado potato beetle pest management including: sampling strategies for insecticide resistance detection, development of a knowledge based expert system and the physiology of cold tolerance. Ph. D. Thesis, Virginia Polytechnic Institute.

26. Visser, J. H. 1976. The design of a low-speed wind tunnel as an instrument for the study of olfactory orientation in the Colorado poato beetle (*Leptinotarsa decemlineata*). Entomol. Exp. Appl. 20: 275-268.

27. Visser, J. J. 1988. Host-plant finding by insects: Orientation, sensory input and search patterns. J. Insect Physiol. 34: 259-268.

28. Voss, J. H., D. N. Ferro and J. A. Logan. 1988. Role of reproductive diapause in the population dynamics of the Colorado potato beetle (Coleoptera: Chrysomelidae) in Western Massachusetts. Environ. Entomol. 17: 863-871.

29. Voss, J. H. and D. N Ferro. 1990. Phenology of flight and walking by Colorado potato beetle (Coleoptera: Chrysomelidae) adults in Western Massachusetts. Environ. Entomol. 19: 112-117.

30. Weber, D. C. and D. N. Ferro. 1992. Distribution of overwintering Colorado potato beetles in and near Massachusetts potato fields. Entom. Exp. Appl. 66: 191-196.

31. Wegorek, W. 1959. The Colorado potato beetle. Centralny Institut Informacji Nauk, 105p.

32. Williams, C. E. 1988. Movement, dispersion, and orientation of a population of the Colorado potato beetle, *Leptinotarsa decemlineata* (Coleoptera: Chrysomelidae), in eggplant. Great Lakes Entomol. 21: 31-38.

33. Wright, R. 1984. Evaluation of crop rotation for control of Colorado potato beetle in commercial potato fields on Long Island. J. Econ. Entomol. 77: 1254-1259.

34. Wyman, J., J. Feldman, J. Walgenbach and L. K. Binning. 1991. Timing management decisions for Colorado potato beetle control (abs.). Am. Pot. J. 68:842

35. Zehnder, G. W. and J. J. Linduska. 1987. Influence of conservation tillage practices on populations of Colorado potato beetle (Coleoptera: Chrysomelidae) in rotated and non-rotated tomato fields. Environ. Entomol. 16: 135-139.

36. Zehnder, G. W. and J. Speese III. 1987. Assessment of color response and flight activity of *Leptinotarsa decemlineata* (Say) (Coleoptera: Chrysomelidae) using window flight traps. Environ. Entomol. 16: 1199-1202.

37. Zehnder, G. W. and J. Hough-Goldstein. 1990. Colorado potato beetle (Coleoptera: Chrysomelidae) population development and effects on yield of potatoes with and without straw mulch. J. Econ. Entomol. 83: 1982-1987.

METHODS FOR OPTIMIZING FIELD PERFORMANCE OF *BACILLUS THURINGIENSIS* ENDOTOXINS AGAINST COLORADO POTATO BEETLE

Paul G. Bystrak and Steve Sanborn
Mycogen Corporation
4980 Carroll Canyon Road
San Diego, CA 92121

Geoffrey Zehnder
Department of Entomology
Auburn University
Auburn, AL 36849

Insecticides based on the naturally-occurring bacterium *Bacillus thuringiensis* (Bt) have been commercially available for many years, but not widely used. There has been a recent increase in the use of these products for reasons including: loss of chemical insecticides to regulatory action; insecticide resistance in pest populations to synthetic insecticides; increased concern about human and environmental safety; and improvement in efficacy of Bt products (6). In addition, the discovery of Bt strains active against Colorado potato beetle (CPB), *Leptinotarsa decemlineata* (Say), has extended the use of Bt into non-traditional markets. Because of the increased use of Bt products, there exists a need to develop methods to optimize performance of Bts under field conditions.

Before discussion of the strategies for improving Bt performance, it is first necessary to review some of the characteristics of Bt insecticides that may effect field performance. One consideration is that Bt toxins are fragile and rapidly degrade upon release into the environment (5). In addition, Bt insecticides must be ingested by the target insect because mortality results from damage to gut cells (6). Limited persistence and the specific mode of action of Bt insecticides require different field application strategies than those used for conventional insecticides.

Field Trials

Most of the information presented herein is based on field experiments done by the authors. Bt efficacy in the field must be evaluated differently than with synthetic insecticides. This is because many susceptible insect species, including CPB, are most susceptible to Bt toxins as early instars. Zehnder and Gelernter (13) determined that CPB first and second instars are very susceptible to Bt (M-One® Insecticide), but third instars are about one-half as susceptible as earlier instars, and fourth instars and adults are least susceptible. Probably the most important factor in the differential susceptibility among instars is the positive relationship between the amount of toxin needed to produce mortality and insect body weight (4). Connelly et al. (1) demonstrated increased susceptibility of early CPB instars, compared with older instars, to azadirachtin (neem extract active ingredient) and esfenvalerate (a pyrethroid), in addition to an encapsulated Bt formulation (M-Trak®). For practical purposes, it is convenient to separate CPB instars into two categories; "small" larvae are first and second instars, and "large" larvae are third and fourth instars. When evaluating Bt field performance, it is important to remember that even the susceptible small larvae may require several days to die (13).

Field counts of CPB small larvae generally are not representative of the effectiveness of Bt spray application. This is because first instars feed on egg mass material before moving onto the leaf surface, and a high percentage of first instars may not have ingested Bt toxin before counts are made. Numbers of large larvae are most representative of Bt efficacy because they are distributed throughout the plant, and surviving large larvae indicate escapes from Bt treatment (2). We have found that the "peak large larval count" is the best indicator for comparison of Bt treatment effectiveness (i.e., counts in all treatments taken on the day that the untreated control has the greatest density of large larvae). Adult counts are useful for following CPB population development, and we have found that summer generation adult counts correlate well with Bt treatment efficacy where effective barriers prevent adult movement between treatment plots (16).

Estimates of plant defoliation provide an excellent means to determine Bt treatment efficacy. We have evaluated a pre-transformed, weighted defoliation rating scheme based on dividing 90° into 13 defoliation categories corresponding to arcsin transformation values (16). After some experience, the method is easy to use and provides an accurate estimate of CPB feeding damage and treatment efficacy. Defoliation ratings most reflect Bt treatment effectiveness during the period before first generation (summer) adults emerge and begin movement between treatment plots. Potato tuber yield may be used as a measure of Bt treatment effectiveness, as it is negatively correlated with CPB defoliation (12). However, treatment yield should not be the only parameter considered because it may be influenced by many factors not related to CPB population density (e.g., weather, soil conditions, non-target pest species).

Our studies have demonstrated that there are four primary factors influencing the efficacy of Bt spray application. These are; timing of initial spray, spray interval, spray coverage, and rate of Bt formulation. We define timing of initial spray as the date on which the first Bt application is made. Spray interval is the number of days between subsequent spray applications. Spray coverage is the percentage of the plant contacted by spray droplets, which influences the amount of toxin that is available for ingestion by insects on the plant. Rate is the amount of Bt product used per unit area, usually expressed as quarts per acre or liters per hectare. The following four sections present the results of studies done to examine the independent and interactive effects of these factors on Bt efficacy against CPB.

Timing of Initial Spray

Because CPB small larvae are most susceptible to Bt insecticides, it was apparent that the initial spray must be made soon after egg hatch. This raised the question: how soon after egg hatch should the first spray be applied for maximum effectiveness? To test this, Zehnder et al. (16) established field experiment treatments in 1989 and 1990 in which the initial Bt applications were made either on the day of peak egg hatch, or on 3, 6, 9, 12, and 15 days after peak hatch (subsequent sprays were applied on 5 or 10 day intervals). The designation "peak egg hatch" was applied when approximately one-third of the first egg masses laid by overwintered adults had hatched (16). Percentage egg hatch following initial oviposition by overwintered females was determined by marking and daily monitoring of individual egg masses on potato plants in the field. Results in the 1989 test, when rain was not a factor affecting Bt persistence on foliage, indicated a positive relationship between density of large larvae and the number of days after peak egg hatch when the first spray was applied. On 15 June, when percentage defoliation was 90% in the untreated control, defoliation did not exceed 25% if the initial spray was applied within 9 days of peak hatch (Fig. 1). If the initial spray was delayed until 12 or 15 days after peak hatch, defoliation exceeded 60%. In 1990, 5.5 cm rainfall fell immediately after the 0 (peak hatch) and 3-day sprays, and additional rainfall (2.0 cm) fell after the 6-day spray. As a result, in

1990, spray interval was more important than timing of the initial spray (Fig. 2). This is because the initial Bt spray was diluted or washed off the foliage by rainfall, and surviving CPB larvae were able to mature into less-susceptible instars by the time the 10-day interval sprays were next applied. Based on these results, Zehnder et al. (16) recommended that the initial Bt application be applied no later than 6-9 days after estimated peak early egg hatch. Sprays should be immediately re-applied if rainfall occurs within 12-24 hours of spray application (as soon as field conditions permit).

There has been some confusion over the meaning of "peak egg hatch", and this warrants clarification. As used by Zehnder et al. (16), peak egg hatch is when there is a sudden increase in percentage egg hatch (above 30%) of the *first brood of egg masses laid by overwintered females.* Using this system, plants are examined for egg masses as soon as adult colonization of plants begins. A field scout attempting to apply the 30% hatch rule to later brood egg masses may make the initial Bt application much too late, because oviposition occurs throughout the spring. Studies were done to compare timing of the initial Bt application based on peak hatch of the "early" egg masses with timing based on peak hatch of later egg populations (9,10,11). Results indicated that application of the first spray would be delayed 3-5 days if later egg populations were sampled, and that timing of the inital Bt spray based on hatch of early egg masses resulted in superior control.

For most effective commercial use of Bt against CPB, potato growers must be able to determine the peak egg hatch event in a cost-effective manner. Zehnder et al. (16) indicated that 178-193 cumulative degree-days (base 10° C) (range in values from 1989, 1990 and 1991 field studies) were required from the date when eggs were first observed on potato plants until peak hatch (33-64%) of first brood egg masses. It is interesting to note that for all 3 years of the study, peak egg hatch occurred exactly 7 days after first oviposition (when approximately 10% of plants had egg masses). Providing that degree-day estimates were validated in each potato-growing region, the degree-day method would enable an estimate of peak CPB egg hatch without frequent sampling.

Other methods of egg hatch determination require varying amounts of field sampling. Mycogen Corporation has distributed over 20,000 plot flags to growers to use for marking egg masses in the field. Because most growers indicate that they do not have time to scout fields and to mark and monitor egg masses, the response to use of flags has been weak. To simplify the sampling process, Mycogen initiated studies to evaluate methods of holding egg masses for observation without repeated trips to the field. Results of lab and field tests in 1989 and 1990 demonstrated that egg masses taken from the field and held in a

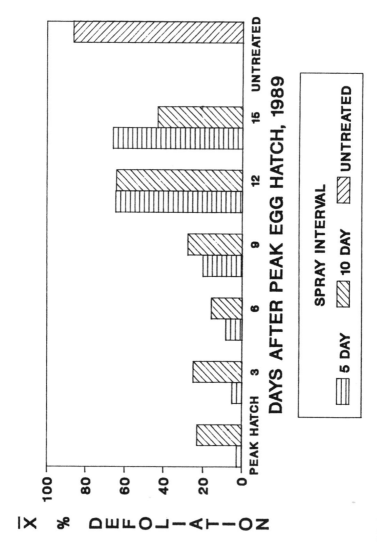

Fig. 1. Effect of Bt insecticide spray timing on mean percentage CPB defoliation, 15 June, 1989 (40 stem samples per treatment). From Zehnder et al. (16).

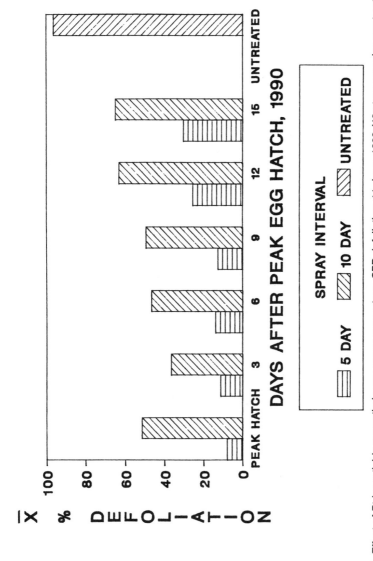

Fig. 2. Effect of Bt insecticide spray timing on mean percentage CPB defoliation, 11 June, 1990 (40 stem samples per treatment). From Zehnder et al. (16).

Petri dish at ambient temperature would hatch at approximately the same time as those on plants in the field (Bystrak and Sanborn, unpublished). Based on this work, several thousand Petri dishes with instructions were distributed to northeastern U.S. potato growers in 1991. Growers were instructed to collect 10-20 egg masses from each field and to apply the initial Bt spray when one-third or more of the egg masses hatched. Grower interest in this method has been stronger than for the flag method, and we plan to expand on the Petri dish program in the future.

Spray Interval

The optimal interval between successive Bt applications is highly dependent on weather conditions. Zehnder et al. (16) found that given typical warm, dry conditions in eastern Virginia during early summer, a 10-day interval between Bt sprays resulted in fair to moderate control (Fig. 1) (provided that the initial spray was made within 9 days of peak egg hatch). However, a 5-day spray schedule resulted in significantly better CPB control than the 10-day schedule. In 1990 when rainfall effected persistence of some initial spray treatments, the 10-day spray interval resulted in poor control, even if the initial spray was applied at peak hatch (Fig. 2).

In another experiment, Zehnder et al. (16) evaluated three spray intervals (4, 7 and 10 days) in a factorial experiment with two Mycogen Bt formulations, one with exposed toxin crystals (M-One®) and the other with bioencapsulated crystals (M-Trak®; previously designated MYX 1806). There was a significant, positive relationship between spray interval and large larval counts and defoliation ratings with both Bt products (Fig. 3). However, the bioencapsulated formulation provided significantly better control of CPB larvae, such that 10-day applications of M-Trak® resulted in superior control, compared with 7-day applications of M-One®.

Additional experiments were performed in Virginia and Michigan in 1991 to examine the influence of spray interval on the effectiveness of various rates of Bt product. In Virginia, two spray intervals (5 and 7 days) were combined with three rates of M-Trak® (2.50, 1.87, and 1.25 qts/acre). No significant differences ($P>0.05$) in mean CPB counts or percentage defoliation were observed among any of the treatments. However, treatments were applied using a three nozzle per row, drop-nozzle arrangement on the spray boom to provide maximum spray coverage. Therefore, it is possible that the high level of spray coverage masked any interval or rate treatment effects that may have been observed using less efficient spray coverage. The same rates

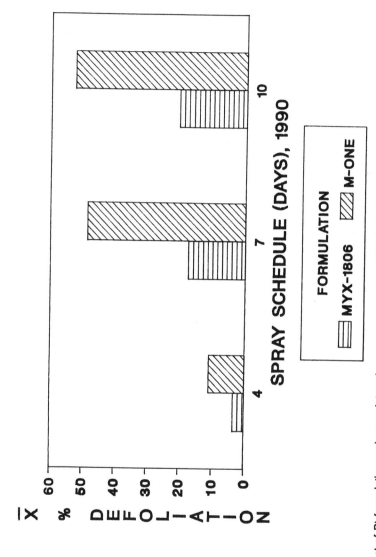

Fig. 3. Effect of Bt formulation and spray interval on mean percentage CPB defoliation, 20 June, 1990 (40 stem samples per treatment). From Zehnder et al (16).

and intervals were tested in the Michigan study, except that over-the-top boom-mounted nozzles were used. In this test, the 5-day interval provided significantly better CPB control than the 7-day interval in all three rate treatments. Analysis of variance indicated that interval effects were greater than rate effects, with the half-rate treatment on a 5-day interval providing equivalent control to the full rate applied on a 7-day interval.

Spray Coverage

The percentage of plant foliage covered with the treatment spray will, in large part, determine the amount of toxin made available to the target insect. Thorough spray coverage is particularly critical in the effectiveness of Bt insecticides because they degrade rapidly in the environment (6) and the target insect must ingest the toxin soon after application. In addition, CPB small larvae, the most susceptible CPB stage, are not highly mobile and may reside in the lower portions of the plant canopy. Therefore, the Bt spray applicator must be cognizant of the limitations of Bt insecticides, and adjust spray application methods accordingly.

Many factors may affect spray coverage, including crop architecture, application equipment, behavior of the target insect, and those inherent in the insecticide product. Although crop, product and insect factors are difficult or impossible to manipulate by the applicator, methods of spray application may be altered to achieve optimal spray coverage for each product and target insect combination. Some application factors that may be manipulated include spray volume per unit area, sprayer pressure, and nozzle type and placement.

Zehnder and Speese (14) tested different spray nozzle and volume combinations in a factorial experiment. Nozzles were hollow cone type, with the core and disc varied to produce 15, 30 or 60 gallons per acre (gpa) at 100 psi from a hydraulic sprayer. The two nozzle position treatments were: (1) nozzles mounted over the tops of the plants at 18 inch intervals on the spray boom ("top nozzles"); and (2) a three nozzle drop arrangement with one nozzle over the row center and the other two nozzles on drop pipes on each side of the row ("drop nozzles"). Nozzles on drop pipes were directed into the plant canopy at a 10° up-angle. Use of drop nozzles resulted in significantly ($P < 0.05$) lower numbers of CPB large larvae and percentage defoliation values, compared with the top nozzle arrangement (% defoliation data shown in Fig. 4). Significant F values for nozzle x volume interaction indicated that the effect of spray volume depended on nozzle position. This is shown in Fig. 4, where an increase in spray volume from 15 to 30 gpa

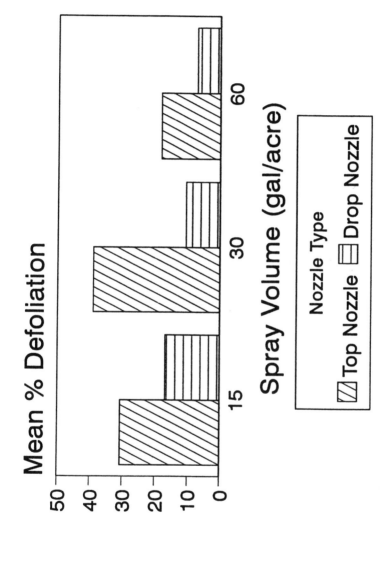

Fig. 4. Effect of Bt insecticide spray volume and nozzle type on mean percentage CPB defoliation, 27 June, 1990 (40 stem samples per treatment). From Zehnder and Speese (14).

resulted in reduced defoliation in the drop nozzle treatment, but not in the top nozzle treatment. However, in both nozzle treatments, CPB larval density and defoliation were significantly ($P=0.008$) reduced by increasing spray volume from 15 to 60 gpa. Based on these results, Zehnder and Speese (14) recommended that Bt insecticides for CPB control be applied using a three nozzle per row, drop nozzle system for superior spray coverage. In addition, increasing spray volume up to 60 gpa will enhance CPB control with Bt insecticides.

Bystrak and Sanborn (unpublished) studied the effects of nozzle position in 1991 with different rates of Bt product, but spray volume remained constant (30 gpa at 40 psi). These field experiments were done in northern potato-growing areas in Wisconsin, Michigan and Pennsylvania. The Mycogen M-One® and M-Trak® products were tested at the maximum label rate, and at 0.50 and 0.25 label rates (the amount of toxin in each treatment comparison was equivalent between the two products). Sprays made with drop nozzles resulted in significantly ($P<0.05$) lower CPB larval counts and defoliation than the top nozzle spray treatments. Nozzle position was more important than rate; the 0.50 label rate of both Bt products using drop nozzles gave significantly better control than the 1.0 label rate using top nozzles. When products were compared over all treatments, the bioencapsulated M-Trak® formulation was superior to M-One® for control of CPB larvae.

Aerial application of Bt is commonly used in potatoes. To our knowledge, the only study done to compare aerial application of Bt with ground application for CPB control was done by W.B. O'Neil (unpublished) of Sandoz Crop Protection Corporation. Potato test fields were divided into narrow strips, treated either with a hydraulic ground sprayer (top nozzles delivering 50 gpa at 100 psi), an airblast sprayer (50 gpa at 250 psi), or a fixed-wing aircraft (5 gpa at 30 psi). The Bt product tested was Trident™ (Sandoz Crop Protection, Des Plaines, IL), a formulation of *B. thuringiensis* var *tenebrionis*, applied at 4.0 quarts per acre. All three spray treatments resulted in commercially-acceptable control, but the air blast sprayer treatment resulted in the lowest CPB larval counts and defoliation ratings. The air blast spray creates a strong air blast resulting in violent leaf movement such that most of the plant canopy, including leaf undersides, are covered with spray. Aerial application of Bt resulted in the least effective CPB control of all treatments.

Although no formal studies have been done, commercial experience with controlled droplet applicators (CDA) has suggested that these do not provide satisfactory control of CPB with Bt insecticides. CDA equipment is designed to deliver spray volume in the range of 3-10 gpa from the height and spreed of a typical hydraulic boom sprayer. Similar problems have resulted with Bt application to potatoes using high-speed hydraulic sprayers which travel at relatively high speeds and deliver low spray volumes (5-20 gpa). Although not tested, the small particle size (resulting in greater drift and evaporation) and low spray volumes (resulting in poor spray coverage) may be factors in the poor to moderate levels of CPB control obtained with these sprayers and Bt insecticides.

Rate of Bt Formulation

While there may be a theoretical concentration, or rate, of the Bt delta endotoxin to result in acceptable CPB control, it is not clear what this specific rate should be, based on the amount of product per unit area. Bt manufacturers do not use the same system to express the active contents of their product. Even when terms are the same (e.g., grams toxin per gallon), the actual determination of the active ingredient is formulation-dependent; and formulations are trade secrets. This situation may be disconcerting to the scientist, but is not a serious concern of the grower, whose primary interest is whether the material is cost/effective.

Experience has indicated that there is not much variability in CPB control within the recommended range in rates of Bt products. Zehnder and Speese (15) found no significant differences in CPB control using different rates (43-96 fl. oz. per acre) of MYX 1806 (M-Trak®). It is usually necessary to evaluate several studies performed at different locations to detect rate treatment effects of Bt insecticides.

Based on calculations incorporating an approximate Bt LD_{50} for second instar CPB (4), the number of larvae in a typical CPB population on potato, and the amount of Bt product delivered in a field application, approximately 1000 fold more Bt toxin is usually applied than is needed to do the job. However, much is lost due to spray drift, environmental degradation, or poor spray coverage. This may explain why other factors (e.g., coverage, spray interval) are more important for effective CPB control with Bt products than the actual rate used (within the recommended range).

Spray Additives

Many additives are commercially available which advertise improved performance when mixed with Bt or other insecticides. These may be divided into the following categories: anionic and nonionic surfactants, film-forming stickers, synergists, feeding stimulants, crop oils, Bt spores, other Bt toxins. Hough-Goldstein et al (8) evaluated several feeding stimulants, and determined that, although CPB larval feeding increased, CPB mortality or field performance was not improved. Addition of the feeding stimulants Coax® (CCT Corp., Litchfield Park, AZ) and Entice® (Fermone Corp., Phoenix, AZ) to the Bt product M-One® actually resulted in less effective CPB control than M-One® alone, although the difference was not statistically significant ($P>0.05$). These feeding stimulants were developed for use with insecticides against lepidopterous larvae, so the results with CPB were not suprising.

Bystrak and Sanborn (unpublished) have tested representative products from all the above additive categories, and significant effects on Bt effectiveness have not been demonstrated, with a few exceptions. The anionic surfactant products based on potassium salts of fatty acids (Safer's Soap®, Ringer Corp., Minneapolis, MN; M-Pede®, Mycogen Corp., San Diego, CA) significantly reduce the effectiveness of Bt insecticides when added at $>1\%$ (v/v) (Fig. 5). High alkalinity of the surfactants was suspected as a factor effecting Bt activity, but another acidified surfactant (pH 7.4) demonstrated similar, negative effects in 1991 studies. These surfactants exert a negative effect on Bt products containing both exposed and bioencapsulated protein crystals.

Another exeption is the insecticide amitraz (Mitac^R; NorAm Corp., Wilmington, DE). When applied to potato at 0.25 lb active ingredient per acre with a low, label-recommended rate of Bt insecticide, the resulting CPB control is superior to either product alone (15). The mechanism of apparent synergy of the two toxins is not known.

Utilization of Bt in Potato Pest Management Programs

We have so far considered Bt insecticides without discussion of their use in a complete potato pest management program. The presence of arthropod potato pests other than CPB (e.g., flea beetles, aphids, leafhoppers) that are not affected by Bt may necessitate the use of other insecticides. Some of these insecticides may also control CPB. In the northeast U.S., for example, oxamyl used to control the potato leafhopper (PLH), *Empoasca fabae*, also gives varying levels of CPB control, depending on the resistance status of the CPB population. Alternation of synthetic insecticides with Bt may act to slow the development of CPB resistance to Bt. When an insecticide is needed for a pest other than CPB, and CPB control is not necessary, the selection of an insecticide with little or no effect on CPB is recommended.

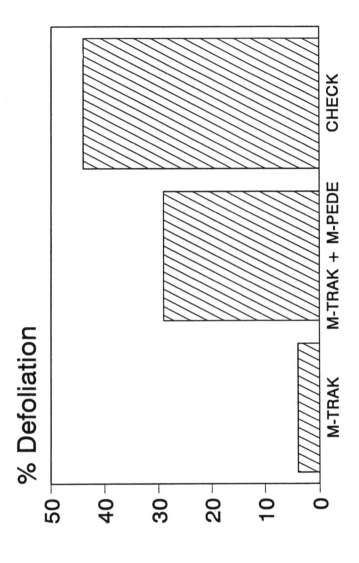

Fig. 5. Effect of the surfactant M-PEDE® on Bt insecticide (M-Track®) for control of CPB, 1990. From Bystrak (unpublished).

This may help to preserve the longevity of synthetic materials that do have activity against CPB.

Ferro (personal communication) has recommended one application of a synthetic pyrethroid insecticide in Massachusetts potato fields against early-season CPB larvae before Bt products are used. Bt applications follow at recommended intervals for control of newly hatched larvae. This approach obviates the need for growers to determine peak egg hatch for effective timing of the initial Bt spray. In addition, the temperature-activity relationships for each material are favorable because pyrethroid efficacy is negatively correlated with temperature (3), and Bt efficacy is positively correlated with temperature (early potato season conditions in Massachusetts are cool, with warm temperatures later in the season). Radcliffe et al. (11) evaluated this insecticide program in small potato plot experiments and determined that a pyrethroid applied as the first spray against CPB larvae (preceding Bt) resulted in better control than when the pyrethroid was applied following a series of Bt sprays.

Epilogue

At least four factors are important in the field efficacy of Bt endotoxin insecticides against Colorado potato beetle (CPB) in potato. These are spray timing, spray interval, spray coverage, and rate of the Bt formulation applied (concentration of the Bt toxin). Optimal control is obtained when the initial Bt application is made within a few days after peak CPB egg hatch (approximately one-third hatch of the early brood of eggs). The length of spray interval, or time between subsequent sprays, is inversely related to efficacy of the Bt application. However, weather conditions affect the spray frequency necessary for optimum control. Spray coverage is difficult to determine quantitatively, but application methods that result in maximum spray coverage of the plant also result in superior CPB control. Rate of Bt formulation has the least effect on CPB control.

The discovery of CPB-active Bt endotoxins is timely, given the high level of resistance to synthetic insecticides present in many eastern U.S. CPB populations. In addition, Bts are safe to the user and the environment, including natural enemies of CPB, and their use in potato pest management programs may serve to delay development of CPB resistance to synthetic insecticides. However, their specificity and short residual activity require application methods that differ from those used with conventional insecticides. Nonetheless, sufficient information on the factors influencing field efficacy of Bt is now available to ensure the successful use of CPB-active Bt products.

Literature Cited

1.   Connelly, M.S., A. Lagnaoui, & E.B. Radcliffe. 1991. Control of Colorado potato beetle with natural product insecticides, 1991. Insecticide and Acaricide Tests. 17: 125.
2.   Ferro, D.N. & W.D. Gelernter. 1989. Toxicity of a new strain of *Bacillus thuringiensis* to Colorado potato beetle (Coleoptera: Chrysomelidae). J. Econ. Entomol. 82: 750-755.
3.   Ferro, D.N., J.A. Logan, R.H. Voss, & J.S. Elkinton. 1985. Colorado potato beetle (Coleoptera: Chrysomelidae) temperature-dependent growth and feeding rates. Environ. Entomol. 14: 343-348.
4.   Ferro, D.N. & S.M. Lyon. 1991. Colorado potato beetle (Coleoptera: Chrysomelidae) larval mortality: operative effects of *Bacillus thuringiensis* subsp. *san diego*. J. Econ. Entomol. 84: 806-809.
5.   Gelernter, W.D. 1990. *Bacillus thuringiensis*, bioengineering and the future of bioinsecticides. Proceedings, Brighton Crop Protection Conference: Pests and Diseases. 617 pp.
6.   Gelernter, W.D. 1990. Targeting insecticide-resistant markets. pp. 105-117. *In* M.B. Green [ed.], Managing Resistance to Agrochemicals: From Fundamental Research to Practical Strategies. ACS Symposium Series No. 421.
7.   Hough-Goldstein, J., & C.B. Keil. 1991. Prospects for integrated control of the Colorado potato beetle (Coleoptera: Chrysomelidae) using *Perillus bioculatus* (Hemiptera: Pentatomidae) and various pesticides. J. Econ. Entomol. 84: 1645-1651.
8.   Hough-Goldstein, J., A.M. Tisler, G.W. Zehnder, & K.A. Uyeda. 1991. Colorado potato beetle (Coleoptera: Chrysomelidae) consumption of foliage treated with *Bacillus thuringiensis* var *san diego* and various feeding stimulants. J. Econ. Entomol. 84: 1645-1651.
9.   Lagnaoui, A., E.B. Radcliffe, J.R. Vaadeland, & A.E. Watland. 1991. Evaluation of a biological and a botanical insecticide for Colorado potato beetle, Rosemount, 1990. Insecticide and Acaricide Tests 16: 93-94.
10.   Radcliffe, E.B., A. Lagnaoui, J.R. Vaadeland, A.E. Watland, & K.L. Flanders. 1991. Control of Colorado potato beetle with natural product insecticides, Grand Forks, 1990. Insecticide and Acaricide Tests 16: 94-95.
11.   Radcliffe, E.B., A. Lagnaoui, J.R. Vaadeland, A.E. Watland, & K.L. Flanders. 1991. Control of Colorado potato beetle with natural product insecticides, Rosemount, 1990. Insecticide and Acaricide Tests 16: 96-97.
12.   Zehnder, G.W. & G.K. Evanylo. 1988. Influence of Colorado potato beetle sample counts and plant defoliation on potato tuber production. Am. Potato J. 65: 725-736.
13.   Zehnder, G.W. & W.D. Gelernter. 1989. Activity of the M-One formulation of a new strain of *Bacillus thuringiensis* against the Colorado potato beetle (Coleoptera: Chrysomelidae): Relationship between susceptibility and insect life stage. J. Econ. Entomol. 82: 756-751.

14.   Zehnder, G.W. & J. Speese III. 1991. Evaluation of various spray nozzle and volume combinations for control of Colorado potato beetle (Coleoptera: Chrysomelidae) with synthetic and biological insecticides. J. Econ. Entomol. 84: 1842-1849.

15.   Zehnder, G.W. & J. Speese III. 1991. Colorado potato beetle control on potato, 1990. Insecticide and Acaricide Tests. 16: 109-110.

16.   Zehnder, G.W., G.M. Ghidiu, & J. Speese III. 1992. Use of the occurrence of peak Colorado potato beetle (Coleoptera: Chrysomelidae) egg hatch for timing of *Bacillus thuringiensis* spray applications in potato. J. Econ. Entomol. 85: 281-288.

PART VIII

Alternative Management Strategies for Potato Pests: Host Plant Resistance

INSECT RESISTANCE IN POTATO: A DECADE OF PROGRESS

Ward M. Tingey and G. Craig Yencho
Department of Entomology, Comstock Hall, Cornell University, Ithaca, New York, USA 14853-0999

The conference held at Rutgers University in 1980 was a milestone in attracting scientists from around the world interested in potato pest management and resulted in the widely cited publication, *Advances in Potato Pest Management* (42). Our intent in this paper is to update significant advances made in the development of insect-resistant potato germplasm during the past decade and to describe our increasing understanding of plant mechanisms conferring resistance. For reviews of a more specialized nature and additional citations of the primary literature not referenced here, the reader is referred to the following papers (15, 28, 29, 73). Our remarks will focus on research efforts utilizing traditional plant breeding methodology because the developments in potato insect resistance associated with recombinant DNA technology such as *Bacillus thuringiensis*-transformed potatoes are considered elsewhere in this volume.

Resistant Mechanisms of Wild Species

Some of the most exciting findings over the past decade have come from studies of the biochemistry of wild potatoes and the mechanisms that impart resistance to insect attack and colonization. The best known insect resistance factors in potatoes, foliar glycoalkaloids and glandular trichomes, have been most extensively studied using the wild tuber-bearing South American species, *Solanum chacoense* and *S. berthaultii*, respectively.

Leptine Glycoalkaloids. Although the insect-defensive properties of the leptine glycoalkaloids had been described by the early 1960's (6, 39, 64, 65, 67, 72), the first intensive efforts to determine their inheritance and to utilize leptines in developing hybrid germplasm began in the early 1980's with a series of studies by Sinden and Sanford and their colleagues at the USDA Vegetable Breeding Laboratory in

Beltsville, Md (68-70). The leptines are extremely rare glycoalkaloids found only in a few   accessions of *S. chacoense* and differ from commonly occurring *Solanum* glycoalkaloids such as solanine and chaconine only in the substitution of an acetyl on carbon-23 of the steroid aglycone (Fig. 1). The leptines are potent antifeedants for both adults and larvae of the Colorado potato beetle, *Leptinotarsa decemlineata* (Say); typical responses on high leptine synthesizing plants include avoidance by adults and larvae, an extended larval development period, and nearly 100% preimaginal mortality (Table 1). Apart from their remarkable defensive activity, leptines are an attractive target for resistance breeding because unlike other glycoalkaloids, they are synthesized only in foliage and thus do not threaten tuber quality. Also, while the genes for the esterase synthetases that acetylate the aglycones of *S. chacoense* to produce leptines are exceedingly rare, they appear to be simply inherited, another advantage for breeding purposes. The research group at Beltsville has developed hybrids between *S. tuberosum* and high leptine-synthesizing clones of *S. chacoense* and their expression of resistance to the Colorado potato beetle is currently under study.

Table 1. Influence of leptine glycoalkaloids on larval growth, survival, and adult feeding of the Colorado potato beetle. [adapted from (69, 70)].

Clone	Glycoalkaloids[a]		Larvae[b]		Adult feeding (mg/hr)
	Lep	Sol+ Chac	Growth (mg/larva)	Survival (%)	
320287-2	0	167	20.1	53	5.6
320287-1	120	11	3.5	5	1.6
458310-3	51	253	6.9	35	1.8
458310-1	271	69	3.3	3	1.1
458313-4	0	704	14.8	48	2.3
45813-1	306	243	4.8	8	1.2
Kennebec	0	45	17.9	40	10.8

[a] Glycoalkaloids determined were leptine I and II (Lep), solanine (sol), and chaconine (chac).
[b] Larval weight after 5 days and percent larvae surviving to adult eclosion, respectively.

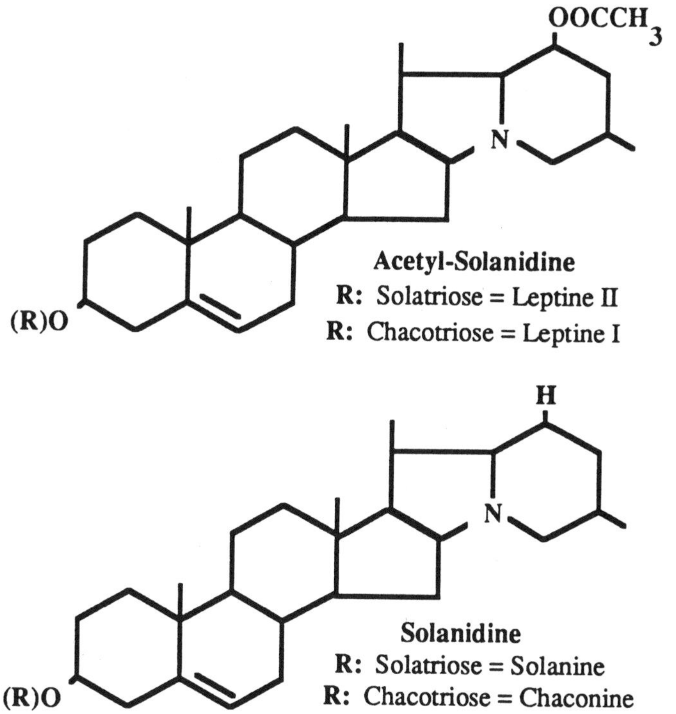

Fig. 1. Structures of the *Solanum* glycoalkaloids, leptine I and II, solanine, and chaconine.

Glandular trichomes. Much of our understanding of the role of glandular trichomes in insect resistance of potato has been derived from studies of *S. berthaultii, S. neocardenasii, S. polyadenium, S. tarijense*, and hybrids of *S. berthaultii* x *S. tarijense* over the past decade. Although the taxonomic status of *S. berthaultii* and *S. tarijense* is being questioned (71), we will refer to them as two species in this paper.

Aphids and leafhoppers. The biochemical basis for resistance to insects conferred by the type A and B glandular trichomes of *S. berthaultii* has been a particularly fruitful area of investigation. Type A and B trichomes (22) interact at a number of levels, resulting in a complex and complementary set of insect-defensive properties best illustrated by examining an encounter between the green peach aphid, *Myzus persicae* (Sulzer), and foliage of *S. berthaultii* [for a review, see Tingey, (73)] Upon arriving at the plant, the aphid first encounters the taller type B trichomes which continually secrete a viscous mixture of acyl sugars (36, 40) (Fig. 2). These compounds are powerful

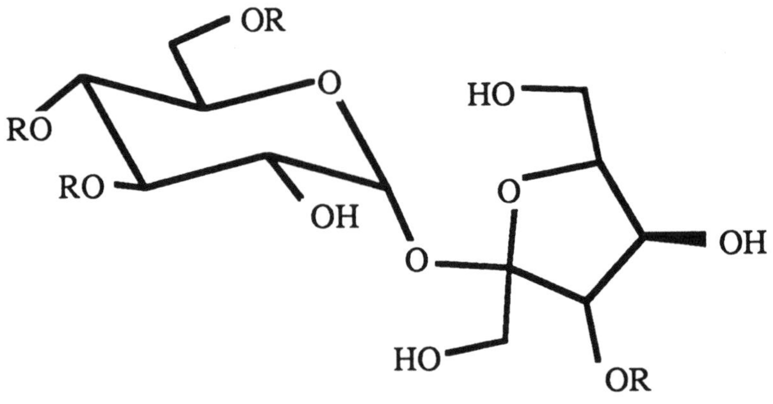

R = 2 - methylpropanoic (*i* C4; 45%)
     2 - methylbutyric (*i* C5; 28%)
     8 - methylnonanoic (*i* C10; 23%)
     n-decanoic (*n* C10; 2%)
     n-dodecanoic (*n* C12; 2%)

Fig. 2. Structure of the acylsucroses secreted by type B glandular trichomes of *Solanum berthaultii*, PI 473331.

antifeedants for a number of insect species (26) including the green peach aphid (46) and are most likely perceived by receptors on the tarsi, mouthparts, and/or antennae. As the aphid begins to walk and probe the plant surface for feeding, it comes into contact with the shorter, membrane enclosed type A trichomes (75). Rupture of the tetralobulate gland results in the release of a mixture of sesquiterpenes (2) and the enzyme, polyphenol oxidase (4, 37, 60), each of which play an interactive role in mediating resistance. One of the predominant constitutive sesquiterpenes is the well known aphid alarm pheromone, β-farnesene (25). The behavioral excitation and increased locomotion caused by the release of β-farnesene, coupled with tarsi that are already partially coated with the viscous type B exudate, increase aphid encounters with undisturbed type A trichomes. The resulting increased rate of rupture of type A trichomes results in release of yet more polyphenol oxidase which catalyzes a phenolic oxidation reaction, resulting in the entrapment, immobilization, and eventual death of the aphid (73). The combined impacts of trichome-mediated resistance on aphid performance, including the disabling influence of viscous exudate on locomotion, the mortality associated with entrapment, and the host avoidance conditioned by sesquiterpenes and acyl sugars reduce the vector efficiency of the green peach aphid for potato virus Y thus providing protection against a major worldwide pathogen of potato (31, 41).

Glandular trichomes of *S. berthaultii* also confer high levels of resistance (approaching immunity) to the potato leafhopper, *Empoasca fabae* (Harris), through entrapment-immobilization and occlusion of mouthparts by the phenolic oxidation products of type A trichomes (74, 75); type B trichomes are an important element in resistance by severely limiting feeding (76) probably through repellent activity of their constitutive acyl sugars similar to the defense posed against the green peach aphid. While precise identification of the phenolic substrate of the type A trichome has not been achieved, a trichome-specific polyphenol oxidase has been biochemically characterized and the inheritance of this 59 kD protein has been determined to involve a single nuclear gene (38).

Colorado potato beetle. Most of our knowledge regarding the role of glandular trichomes in resistance to the Colorado potato beetle was developed during the past decade beginning in 1982 with the discovery of resistance in *S. berthaultii* and an *S. tuberosum* x *S. berthaultii* hybrid (11). Subsequently, we have learned that resistance is far more subtle than the readily apparent entrapment experienced by aphids and leafhoppers, and that host acceptance behaviors and developmental physiology of *L. decemlineata* both appear to be altered by glandular trichomes and their biochemical products. For example, both adults and larvae (Fig. 3) are reluctant to accept *S. berthaultii* as food (17, 51). Neonates experience significant mortality within 72 h of confinement on *S. berthaultii* because of starvation (45). Egg mass size and lifetime fecundity on *S. berthaultii* are typically less than 1/2 that on commercial cultivars of potato (14, 15, 30). The reluctance of adults and larvae to accept *S. berthaultii* foliage for food can be largely eliminated by mechanical and/or solvent removal of glandular trichomes (Fig. 3) (45). The cumulative impacts of trichome-mediated resistance in *S. berthaultii* result in a net replacement rate (R_o) of 5-20 daughters per generation in contrast to over 100 on *S. tuberosum* cultivars (20). An as yet undefined characteristic of type A trichomes appears to form the basis of resistance in *S. berthaultii* (17, 45); however, type B trichomes and their constitutive acyl sugars also contribute to the expression of resistance by acting as antifeedants against adults (50, 51).

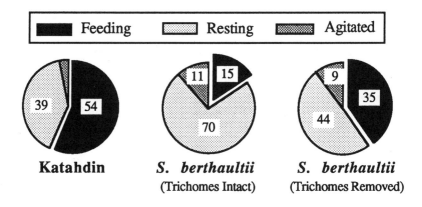

| Feeding | Resting | Agitated |

Katahdin | **S. berthaultii** (Trichomes Intact) | **S. berthaultii** (Trichomes Removed)

Fig. 3. Incease in host acceptance and feeding by 2nd instar larvae of the Colorado potato beetle after removing glandular trichomes on foliage of *Solanum berthaultii*, PI 310927. Ithaca, NY. 1985.

Recent research on the digestive and reproductive physiology of the Colorado potato beetle has shed light on another site impacted by the resistance of *S. berthaultii*. França (20) described a state of arrested ovarian development accompanied by grossly enlarged, discolored mid and hind guts filled with undigested plant material (including recognizable trichomes) in females given access only to foliage of *S. berthaultii*. Whether the resistance of *S. berthaultii* should be characterized as primarily behavioral or developmental in its expression can be debated, but the digestive and reproductive system abnormalities provide a possible explanation for the dramatic reduction in fecundity typically experienced by females on *S. berthaultii*.

In addition to the Colorado potato beetle, aphids and leafhoppers, glandular trichomes of *S. berthaultii* also confer resistance to tarsonemid mites, spider mites, flea beetles, thrips (21, 23, 24), leafminer flies (K. V. Raman, pers. comm.), and the late blight pathogen, *Phytophthora infestans* (34,) and have been implicated in resistance to the potato tuber moth (80).

New Sources of Reistance in Wild Species

Colorado potato beetle. Traditional (pre-1960) sources of resistance to the Colorado potato beetle included *S. demissum*, *S. chacoense*, *S. jamesii*, and *S. polyadenium* (58, 79). Beginning in 1966, Radcliffe and his associates in Minnesota embarked on a intensive effort to examine wild *Solanum* species for resistance to a number of pest species including the Colorado potato beetle (53, 54). Later in 1983, the Interregional Potato Introduction Project (USDA, Sturgeon Bay, WI, USA) sponsored a series of studies intended to identify new sources of resistance in its expanding wild germplasm collection. These and other studies (10, 18) have revealed significant levels of resistance in at least 15 additional species including *S. acroglossum, S. berthaultii, S. canasense, S. capsicibaccatum, S. chomatophilum, S. circaeifolium, S. immite, S. jalcae, S. lycopersicoides, S. megistacrolobum, S. pinnatisectum, S. spegazzinii, S. tarijense*, and *S. trifidum*. A recently described species, *S. neocardenasii* (32), can also be added to this list and its near immunity to the Colorado potato beetle (16) is probably associated with the presence of the newly discovered steroid alkaloid, solanocardinol (Fig. 4), in its foliage (49).

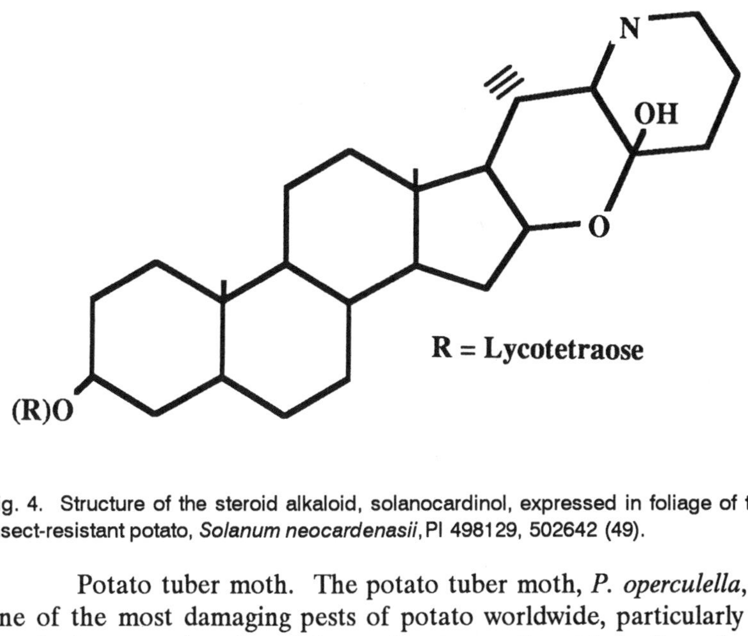

Fig. 4. Structure of the steroid alkaloid, solanocardinol, expressed in foliage of the insect-resistant potato, *Solanum neocardenasii*, PI 498129, 502642 (49).

Potato tuber moth. The potato tuber moth, *P. operculella*, is one of the most damaging pests of potato worldwide, particularly in developing countries where it is a major storage threat to both seed and consumer potatoes. Resistance to this pest has been identified in accessions of *S. berthaultii, S. commersonii, S. pinnatisectum, S. sparsipilum, S. sucrense* and *S. tarijense*. Interspecific crosses made using *S. berthaultii, S. commersonii, S. sparsipilum, S. sucrense*, and *S. tarijense* yielded resistant progenies in all cases except that involving the latter species (12). Resistance to the potato tuber moth has also been reported in primitive Andean cultivars (57) and in tetraploid hybrids of *S. tuberosum* x *S. berthaultii* bearing glandular trichomes (66, 80).

411

Aphids. The intensive efforts by Radcliffe and his associates at the University of Minnesota have identified many sources of resistance to aphids from the germplasm collection of the Interregional Potato Introduction Project (53, 54). Species with numerous accessions resistant to the green peach and/or potato aphid, *Macrosiphum euphorbiae* (Thomas), include *S. brachistotrichum, S. bukasovii, S. bulbocastanum, S. canasense, S. chomatophilum, S. etuberosum, S. hjertingii, S. hougasii, S. infundibuliforme, S. jamesii, S. lignicaule, S. marinasense, S. medians, S. multidissectum, S. sanctae-rosae, S. stoloniferum, S. tarijense, S. toralapanum, S. trifidum,* and *S. verrucosum* (18). Although aphid resistance has been reported in cultivated species such as *S. tuberosum ssp. andigena, phureja,* and *stenotomum,* its expression is much less than in the wild species listed above (43). Hybrids of *S. tuberosum* x *S. berthaultii* bearing type A and B glandular trichomes reduce aphid populations as much as 61% compared to susceptible cultivars (78, 84).

Potato leafhopper and potato flea beetle. Sanford and Ladd (62) produced high levels of resistance to the potato leafhopper in *S. tuberosum* populations exposed to seven generations of recurrent selection. Infestation densities of nymphs were reduced nearly 60% compared to the nonselected base population and were accompanied by a decrease in hopperburn, as well. The level of resistance increased with each generation of selection and was accompanied by an increase of the steroid alkaloid, solanidine, in foliage, thus implicating this compound or its glycosides, solanine and chaconine, as the factors responsible for resistance (63).

Interestingly, *S. tuberosum* clones susceptible to infestation by the potato leafhopper but tolerant to yield loss have also been reported (61). Despite similar infestation densities, the best of these clones suffered only 19% loss in tuber yield compared to 33% loss for the susceptible cultivar, Katahdin. The tolerance of these clones does not appear to result from protection against leafhopper feeding or replacement of damaged tissues (as tolerance is classically defined in the literature of plant resistance to insects), but rather because rapid and early tuber development enables the plant to escape some of the damaging effects of leafhopper infestation.

Wild tuber-bearing species with high levels of resistance to the potato leafhopper include *S. agrimonifolium, S. berthaultii, S. brachycarpum, S. demissum, S. etuberosum, S. polyadenium,* and natural hybrids of *S. berthaultii* x *S. tarijense;* those resistant to the potato flea beetle include *S. alandiae, S. berthaultii, S. bulbocastanum, S. lignicaule, S. marinasense, S. megistacrolobum, S. microdontum, S. mochiquense, S.*

pampasense, S. polyadenium, S. polytrichon, S. sanctae-rosae, S. stoloniferum, and *S. toralapanum* (18, 53, 77). Hybrids of *S. tuberosum* x *S. berthaultii* bearing type A and B glandular trichomes are highly resistant to the potato leafhopper and reduce populations by as much as 80% compared to susceptible cultivars (76).

Compatibility of Resistance
With Biological Control and Insecticides

The integration of insect resistant cultivars and biological control has a number of advantages over the use of either tactic alone. However, insect resistance and biological control can be antagonistic (3, 7) and it is important that such interactions be clearly understood before both management tactics are deployed. In the case of potato, studies involving *S. berthaultii*, the Colorado potato beetle and the egg parasitóid, *Edovum puttleri* Grissell, revealed that the host plant had several undesirable effects on the parasitoid (59). For example, type B trichomes entrapped a high proportion of parasitoids, thus reducing egg parasitism rates compared to those on *S. berthaultii* accessions lacking type B trichomes (Fig. 5). In addition, *S. berthaultii* exerted indirect effects on *E. puttleri* by reducing parasitoid feeding (and thus feeding-induced egg mortality) on eggs laid by female potato beetles which had been reared on the resistant host. The life span of female parasitoids emerging from these eggs was also reduced.

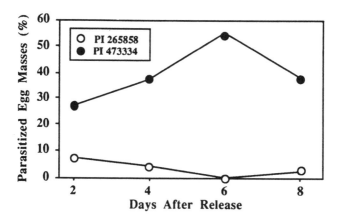

Fig. 5.   Field parasitization of Colorado potato beetle egg masses by the egg parasitoid, *Edovum puttleri*. PI 265858 and PI 473334 are *S. berthaultii* accessions with and without secretory type B trichomes, respectively. Adapted from (59).

While antagonistic interactions such as those involving *S. berthaultii* and *E. puttleri* demonstrate the importance of understanding tritrophic level relationships in the development of insect-resistant crop plants, other studies indicate that trichome-based resistance in potato is compatible with some species of natural enemies and that results obtained in the laboratory may not be indicative of what occurs in the field. In greenhouse studies, Obrycki and Tauber (48) observed a direct negative relationship between glandular trichome density and performance of several predators and parasitoids of aphids. However, under field conditions, the same species of predators and parasitoids contributed to a substantial reduction in aphid densities on trichome-bearing *S. tuberosum* x *S. berthaultii* hybrids, thus complementing plant resistance (47). From these studies it is clear that while greenhouse and laboratory studies can be useful in identifying possible incompatibility of natural enemies with plant defensive phenomena, they may not be a true indicator of the agricultural interactions.

Another potential antagonistic interaction between resistant potato germplasm and biocontrol agents involves resistance conditioned by foliar glycoalkaloids and *Beauveria bassiana* (Balsamo) Vuillemin, an entomopathogen (8) of the Colorado potato beetle. Solanine and tomatine both inhibit colony formation and growth of *B. bassiana* (13) and might interfere with the infection process in insects consuming tissue of plants resistant by means of foliar glycoalkaloids.

A frequently cited advantage of host resistance is its compatibility with other pest management tactics, but as with the case of biological control, the use of resistant cultivars and insecticides may be antagonistic (27). For example, a major insect resistance factor in tomato, the trichome-borne ketone, 2-tridecanone (81), increases the tolerance of *Helicoverpa zea* (Boddie) to carbaryl apparently by induction of cytochrome p-450 oxidases (35). In the case of potato, Raman (56) investigated the susceptibility of three geographically isolated populations of the green peach aphid to four major insecticides used worldwide on potatoes (azinphosmethyl, methamidophos, permethrin, pirimicarb) using an aphid-resistant *S. tuberosum* x *S. berthaultii* hybrid (D888-4) bearing both type A and B glandular trichomes. Although the aphid populations (from Minnesota, New York, and Puerto Rico) differed greatly in their insecticide susceptibility, the aphid resistant potato did not affect their level of susceptibility (Fig. 6).

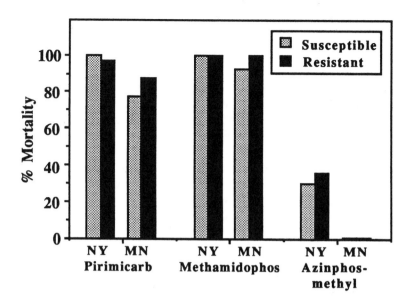

Fig. 6. Interaction of insecticides, aphid-susceptible (cv. Red Pontiac) and resistant (D888-4) potatoes, and two geographic strains of green peach aphid. Aphid strains were obtained from New York (NY), and Minnesota (MN). Adapted from (56).

Durability of Resistance

In a number of cases involving crops grown over large areas such as rice, alfalfa and small grains, the release of cultivars imposing high insect mortality has been accompanied by the development of resistance-breaking biotypes, thus rendering the cultivar susceptible to attack. Resistance-breaking biotypes have been reported for at least 13 species of insect pests in 12 different crop species and should be of concern to any program attempting to develop insect-resistant cultivars.

The durability of resistance in *S. berthaultii* to the Colorado potato beetle was questioned by Groden and Casagrande (30) who reported loss in expression of resistance after two generations. The rapid onset of an apparent resistance-breaking biotype was surprising given the moderate mortality imposed by *S. berthaultii* on *L. decemlineata*. Thus, our laboratory initiated a study involving 10 generations of consecutive rearing on *S. berthaultii* and on an *S. tuberosum* cultivar, and imposed directional selection on *S. berthaultii*-reared animals at each generation for improved performance including decreased developmental time, increased preimaginal survival, and increased reproductive output (20). A key finding of this study was that the net replacement rate [(R_o) = number of daughters produced per mother per generation] for cohorts reared on *S. berthaultii* was significantly less than that for cohorts reared on *S. tuberosum* in all generations. At the tenth generation, each *S. berthaultii* - reared female replaced herself with approximately 12 daughters, whereas females on *S. tuberosum* produced an average of 110 daughters. Furthermore, the slopes of the regression lines for net replacement rate for *S. tuberosum* and *S. berthaultii*-reared animals did not differ from zero indicating that adaptation did not occur despite our efforts to select for it (20).

Cantelo et al. (9) also examined the ability of the Colorado potato beetle to adapt to host resistance by utilizing leptine synthesizing clones of *S. chacoense*. After twelve months of continuous rearing on these clones, improvements in larval growth rate, preimaginal survival, and fecundity were observed indicating that adaptation to the feeding deterrency imposed by these foliar glycoalkaloids had occurred.

In both of these studies, 7 to 10 generations of continuous rearing in the laboratory is comparable to at least 4 to 5 years of selection pressure under extremely stringent and unlikely field conditions, including: (a) that all acreage is planted to resistant clones; (b) recruitment of susceptible animals from wild hosts and susceptible cultivars does not occur; and (c) natural field mortality from parasites, predators, pathogens, and abiotic phenomena and that imposed by management tactics other than host resistance does not occur. Thus, we anticipate that resistance to the Colorado potato beetle derived from either *S. berthaultii* or *S. chacoense* is likely to be durable, especially when combined with management practices that lessen selection pressure on host resistance such as the use of rotations to nonhosts (82), early emerging trap plots [especially in contiguous rotations (W.M.T., unpublished)], biological control agents (33), propane flaming (44), and vacuum removal (44). However, given the remarkable ability of the Colorado potato beetle to adapt to synthetic insecticides (19) and to plant toxins (5, 9), it is prudent to continue investigations of approaches that will maximize the durability of resistant germplasm after it is deployed.

In addition to the Colorado potato beetle, the durability of resistance to the green peach aphid has also been investigated. Radcliffe et al. (55) examined 42 wild potato species for resistance at five widely separated sites using aphids originating in England, Minnesota, New York, Puerto Rico, and Peru. The relative resistance of these species was remarkably consistent with regard to test location and aphid source indicating that resistance derived from these species could be widely used and would prove stable.

Combining Resistance and Horticultural Quality

As noted earlier, numerous genetic resources for insect resistance in potato have been described, but because nearly all major sources of resistance are found in wild species, introgressing this resistance into *S. tuberosum* backgrounds has resulted in the transfer of undesirable growth and tuber characters associated with the daylength sensitivity and growth characteristics of the wild species from which resistance was derived. Thus, perhaps the most daunting challenge posed over the past ten years has been the problem of incorporating economically useful insect resistance into genetic backgrounds possessing acceptable yield and quality attributes. This has been especially challenging given that some of the wild species used in breeding programs have the potential to introduce undesirable quality factors such as tuber glycoalkaloids, into hybrid populations.

The experience of the Cornell University program in introducing insect resistance into potato may be instructive in this regard. Since initiating a program with *S. berthaultii* twelve years ago, the senior author and R.L. Plaisted, our potato breeder colleague, have always been able to demonstrate high levels of resistance under field conditions and to recover insect-resistant progenies in segregating hybrid populations (83). Until recently, however, expression of adequate resistance in clones with acceptable yielding ability and tuber quality was difficult to achieve. Following improvements in screening and evaluation protocols and with expanded understanding of the impacts of resistant germplasm on target pests such as the Colorado potato beetle, we have been able to develop hybrid germplasm with much improved horticultural quality. A good example of this is the clone L 235-4, an F7 hybrid of an interspecific cross between *S. tuberosum* and *S. berthaultii*, bearing type A glandular trichomes (52). The field resistance of this clone to the Colorado potato beetle has been evaluated for several years on both research and commercial farms and typically results in at least 50% reduction in first generation densities of Colorado potato beetle larvae compared with commercial cultivars (Fig. 7). In comparison with plots protected against insect attack by use of insecticides, L 235-4 has experienced a 10-15% yield reduction, in contrast to a 50-70% yield reduction for standard commercial cultivars (Fig. 8). But more importantly from the standpoint of commercial quality, this clone and others like it currently in development, have the ability to produce commercial-scale yields in the absence of significant insecticide input. This resistance (during the period of exposure to overwintered adults and the first larval generation) has been nearly equivalent to a soil application of aldicarb (Fig. 9) or to at least 3 applications of foliar insecticide. While yielding ability is an important criterion, a multitude of other production (disease resistance, maturity, dormancy, storage quality) and consumer (appearance, cooking quality) factors are important in the fresh and processing market acceptance of new cultivars; thus, our challenge in this decade will be to maintain economic levels of insect resistance in hybrid populations while improving quality traits.

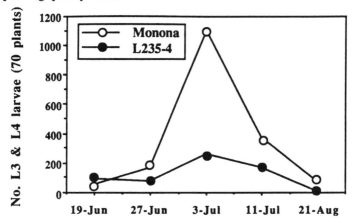

Fig. 7. Densities of 3rd and 4th instar larvae of the Colorado potato beetle on the insect-resistant hybrid potato, L235-4, in comparison to the susceptible commercial cv. Monona. Mahany Farms, Arkport, NY. 1991.

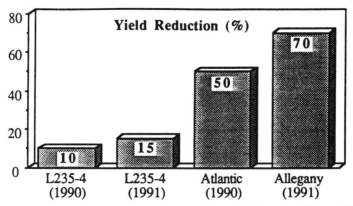

Fig. 8. Yield reduction by the Colorado potato beetle in control (insecticide-free) compared to insecticide-treated (Temik 15G) plots of the insect-resistant hybrid potato, L235-4, and the susceptible commercial cultivars, Atlantic and Allegany. Freeville, NY. 1990-91.

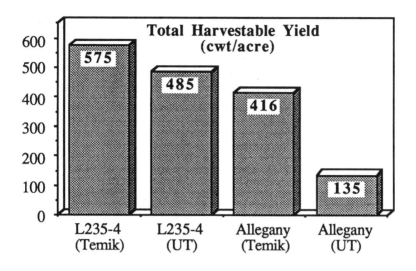

Fig. 9. Comparison of yields between the insect-resistant and susceptible potato clones, L235-4 and Allegany, respectively. Temik: Temik 15 G applied at planting @ 20 lbs/acre for control of the Colorado potato beetle and potato leafhopper. UT: Untreated control. Freeville, NY. 1991.

A View To the Future

We have made much progress since efforts to develop insect resistant potato cultivars began in the mid 1930's by French and German scientists, but the fact remains that commercially acceptable cultivars are still unavailable for growers and are probably five to ten years from release. However, because of the efforts of plant collectors and botanists from around the world, we now have large germplasm collections from which to search for sources of insect resistance. We must continue to maintain and enhance these collections. The challenge of the future will be to identify and introgress sources of insect resistance into commercial cultivars using these invaluable genetic resources. Programs with this goal will increasingly be multidisciplinary in nature with plant breeders, agronomists, entomologists, plant pathologists, biochemists, and molecular biologists, working in concert toward specific goals.

Advances in biotechnology, instrumentation and analytical techniques will undoubtedly speed the time between identification of useful sources of insect resistance and eventual deployment, but pest resistant plants must first be identified. The means by which we identify resistant germplasm over the next decade will largely continue to involve traditional screening methods. To this end, the development of rearing procedures and artificial diets for insect pests of potatoes is essential. Our screening protocols must be accurate, rapid and cost effective. When possible, we must strive to identify the specific attributes of a plant that impart resistance to a given pest or pests. This knowledge will enable the development of precise biochemical (1) and molecular screens for the presence of resistant genotypes in large populations of segregating progeny. Advances in this area will aid the commercial development of insect-resistant cultivars in three ways. First, they will enable us to more efficiently select and evaluate resistant genotypes because potentially resistant germplasm can be evaluated at early growth stages prior to evaluation by time and labor consuming field trials. Second, specific knowledge of the genetic products that mediate resistance can be put to immediate use by researchers as a basis for genetic engineering of resistant plants. Lastly, a clear understanding of the factors that impart resistance will contribute to the development of ecologically sound deployment strategies that maximize the durability of plants possessing resistance.

Literature Cited

1. Avé, D.A., Eannetta, N.T., and Tingey, W.M. 1986. A modified enzymic browning assay for potato glandular trichomes. Am. Potato J. 63: 553-558.
2. Avé, D.A., P. Gregory, and W.M. Tingey. 1987. Aphid repellent sesquiterpenes in glandular trichomes of *Solanum berthaultii* and *S. tuberosum*. Entomol. Exp. Appl. 44: 131-138.
3. Bergman, J.M. and W.M. Tingey. 1979. Aspects of interaction between plant genotypes and biological control. Bull. Entomol. Soc. Amer. 25: 275-279.
4. Bouthyette, P.Y., N.T. Eannetta, K.J. Hannigan, and P. Gregory. 1987. *Solanum berthaultii* trichomes contain unique polyphenoloxidases and a peroxidase. Phytochemistry 26: 2949-2954.
5. Brattsten, L.B. 1979. Biochemical defense mechanisms in herbivores against plant allelochemicals. pp. 199-270. In: G.A. Rosenthal and D.H. Janzen, (eds.). Herbivores: their interaction with secondary plant metabolites. Academic Press, NY. 718 pp.
6. Buhr, H., R. Toball, and K. Schreiber. 1958. The effect of several plant-derived compounds, particularly alkaloids, on the development of larvae of the Colorado potato beetle (*Leptinotarsa decemlineata* Say). Entomol. Exp. Appl. 1: 209-224. (in German).
7. Campbell, B.C. and S.S. Duffey. 1979. Tomatine and parasitic wasps: potential incompatibility of plant-antibiosis with biological control. Science 205: 700-702.

8.   Campbell, R.K., T.E. Anderson, M. Semel, and D.W. Roberts. 1985. Management of the Colorado potato beetle using the entomogenous fungus *Beauveria bassiana*. Am. Pot. J. 62: 29-37.

9.   Cantelo, W.W., L.L. Sanford, S.L. Sinden, and K.L. Deahl. 1987. Research to develop plants resistant to the Colorado potato beetle, *Leptinotarsa decemlineata* (Say). p. 380. In: Labeyrie, V., G. Fabres, and D. Lachaise, (eds.). Insects-plants: proceedings of the 6th international symposium on insect-plant relationships. Dr. W. Junk Publishing, Dordrecht. 459 pp.

10.   Carter, C.D. 1987. Screening *Solanum* germplasm for resistance to the Colorado potato beetle. Am. Pot. J. 64: 563-568.

11.   Casagrande, R. 1982. Colorado potato beetle resistance in a wild potato, *Solanum berthaultii*. J. Econ. Entomol. 75: 368-372.

12.   Chavez, R., P.E. Schmiediche, M.T. Jackson, and K.V. Raman. 1988. The breeding potential of wild potato species resistant to the potato tuber moth, *Phthorimaea operculella* (Zeller). Euphytica 39: 123-132.

13.   Costa, S. D. and R. Gaugler. 1989. Influence of *Solanum* host plants on Colorado potato beetle (Coleoptera:Chrysomelidae) susceptibility to the entomopathogen *Beauveria bassiana*. Environ. Entomol. 18: 531-536.

14.   Dimock, M.B. 1985. Studies on mechanisms of resistance in the wild potato *Solanum berthaultii* (Hawkes) to the Colorado potato beetle, *Leptinotarsa decemlineata* (Say) (Coleoptera:Chrysomelidae). Ph.D. Dissertation, Cornell University, Ithaca, NY. 93pp.

15.   Dimock, M.B. and W.M. Tingey. 1985. Resistance in *Solanum* species to the Colorado potato beetle: mechanisms, genetic resources, and potential. pp. 79-106. In: D.N. Ferro and R.H.Voss, (eds.). Proceedings of the symposium on the Colorado potato beetle, XVIIth International Congress of Entomology, Mass. Agric. Exp. Sta. Bull. No. 704. 144 pp.

16.   Dimock, M.B., S.L. Lapointe, and W.M. Tingey. 1986. *Solanum neocardenasii*: A new source of potato resistance to the Colorado potato beetle (Coleoptera: Chrysomelidae). J. Econ. Entomol. 79: 1269-1275.

17.   Dimock, M.B. and W.M. Tingey. 1988. Host acceptance behavior of Colorado potato beetle larvae influenced by potato glandular trichomes. Physiol. Entomol. 13: 399-406.

18.   Flanders, K.L., J.G. Hawkes, E.B. Radcliffe, and F.I. Lauer. 1992. Insect resistance in potatoes: sources, evolutionary relationships, morphological and chemical defenses, and ecogeographical associations. Euphytica 61: 83-111.

19.   Forgash, A.J. 1985. Insecticide resistance in the Colorado potato beetle. pp. 33-52. In: D.N. Ferro and R.H. Voss, (eds.). Proceedings of the symposium on the Colorado potato beetle, XVIIth International Congress of Entomology, Mass. Agric. Exp. Sta. Bull. No. 704. 144 pp.

20.   França, F. H. 1991. Stability and aspects of resistance of *Solanum berthaultii* Hawkes to populations of the Colorado potato beetle, *Leptinotarsa decemlineata* (Say) (Coleoptera: Chrysomelidae). Ph.D. Dissertation. Cornell University, Ithaca, NY. 316 pp.

21.   Gibson, R.W. 1978. Resistance in glandular haired wild potatoes to flea beetles. Am. Potato J. 55: 595-598.

22.   Gibson, R.W. 1979. The geographical distribution, inheritance and pest-resisting properties of sticky-tipped foliar hairs on potato species. Potato Res. 22: 223-236.

23.   Gibson, R.W. and R.H. Turner. 1977. Insect-trapping hairs on potato plants. PANS 23: 272-277.

24.   Gibson, R.W. and L. Valencia. 1978. A survey of potato species for resistance to the mite *Polyphagotarsonemus latus*, with particular reference to the protection of *Solanum berthaultii* and *S. tarijense* by glandular hairs. Potato Res. 21: 217-223.

25.   Gibson, R.W. and J.A. Pickett. 1983. Wild potato repels aphids by release of aphid alarm pheromone. Nature 302: 608-609.

26.   Goffreda, J.C., D.A. Avé, M.A. Mutschler, W.M. Tingey, and J.C. Steffens. 1989. Aphid deterrence by glucose esters in the glandular trichome exudate of the wild tomato, *Lycopersicon pennellii*. J. Chem. Ecol. 15: 2135-2147.

27.   Gould, F., C.R. Carroll, and D.J. Futuyma. 1982. Cross-resistance to pesticides and plant defenses: a study of the two-spotted spider mite. Entomol. Exp. Appl. 31: 175-180.

28.   Gregory, P., W. M. Tingey, D. A. Avé, and P. Y. Bouthyette. 1986. Potato glandular trichomes: A physicochemical defense mechanism against insects. pp. 160-167. In: M.B. Green and P.A. Hedin, (eds.). Natural resistance of plants to pests: roles of allelochemicals. ACS Symposium Series No. 296. 243 pp.

29.   Gregory, P., W.M. Tingey, D.A. Avé, and P.Y. Bouthyette. 1986. Insect-defensive chemistry of potato glandular trichomes. pp. 173-183. In: B.E. Juniper and T.R.E. Southwood, (eds.). The plant surface and insects. Blackwell Publishing, Oxford. 360 pp.

30.   Groden, E. and R. A. Casagrande. 1986. Population dynamics of the Colorado potato beetle, *Leptinotarsa decemlineata* (Coleoptera:Chrysomelidae), on *Solanum berthaultii*. J. Econ. Entomol. 79: 91-97.

31.   Gunenc, Y. and R.W. Gibson, 1980. Effects of glandular foliar hairs on the spread of potato virus Y. Potato Res. 23: 345-351.

32.   Hawkes, J.G., and J.P. Hjerting. 1983. New tuber-bearing *Solanum* taxa from Bolivia and northern Argentina. Bot. J. Linn. Soc. 86: 405-417.

33.   Hazzard, R. V. and D. N. Ferro. 1991. Feeding responses of adult *Coleomegilla maculata* (Coleoptera: Coccinellidae) to eggs of Colorado potato beetle (Coleoptera: Chrysomelidae) and green peach aphids (Homoptera: Aphididae). Environ. Entomol. 20: 644-651.

34.   Holley, J.D., R.R. King, and R.P. Singh. 1987. Glandular trichomes and the resistance of *Solanum berthaultii* (PI 473340) to infection from *Phytophthora infestans*. Can. J. Plant Pathol. 9: 291-294.

35.   Kennedy, G.G. 1984. 2-tridecanone, tomatoes, and *Heliothis zea*: potential incompatibility of plant antibiosis with insecticidal control. Entomol. Exp. Appl. 35: 305-311.

36.   King, R.R., Y. Pelletier, R.P. Singh, and L.A. Calhoun. 1986. 3, 4-O-isobutyryl-6-O-caprylsucrose: the major component of a novel sucrose ester complex from the type B glandular trichomes of *Solanum berthaultii* Hawkes (PI 473340). Chem. Comm. 14: 1078-1079.

37.   Kowalski, S.P. 1989. Insect resistance in potato: purification and characterization of a polyphenol oxidase from the type A glandular trichomes of *Solanum berthaultii* Hawkes. Ph.D. Dissertation. Cornell University, Ithaca, NY. 156 pp.

38.   Kowalski, S.P., J.B. Bamberg, W.M. Tingey, and J. C. Steffens. 1990. Inheritance of polyphenol oxidase in type A glandular trichomes of *Solanum berthaultii*. J. Heredity 81: 475-478.

39.   Kuhn, R. and I. Löw. 1955. Resistance factors against *Leptinotarsa decemlineata* Say, isolated from the leaves of wild *Solanum* species. pp. 122-132. In: M.G. Sevag, R.D. Reid, and D.E. Reynolds, (eds.). Origins of resistance to toxic agents. Academic Press, NY. 471 pp.

40.   Lapointe, S.L. and W.M. Tingey. 1984. Feeding response of the green peach aphid (Homoptera:Aphididae) to potato glandular trichomes. J. Econ. Entomol. 77: 386-389.

41.   Lapointe, S. L., W. M. Tingey, and T. A. Zitter. 1987. Glandular trichomes and potato virus Y transmission in an aphid resistant potato species. Phytopathol. 77: 819-822.

42.   Lashomb, J. and R.A. Casagrande (eds.). 1981. Advances in Potato Pest Management. Hutchinson Ross Publishing Co. Stroudsburg, PA. 288 pp.

43.   Mndolwa, D., G. Bishop, D. Corsini, and J. Pavek. 1984. Resistance of potato clones to the green peach aphid and potato leafroll virus. Am. Potato J. 61: 713-722.

44.   Moyer, D. D. 1991. Alternative controls for Colorado potato beetle: propane flaming, bug vacuums and *Bt*s, and managing equipment wear due to cryolite. pp. 65-66. In: Proc. 1991 New York State Veg. Conf. 162 pp.

45.   Neal, J.J., J.C. Steffens, and W.M. Tingey. 1989. Glandular trichomes of *Solanum berthaultii* and resistance to the Colorado potato beetle. Entomol. Exp. Appl. 51: 133-140.

46.   Neal, J.J., W.M. Tingey, and J.C. Steffens. 1990. Sucrose esters of carboxylic acids in glandular trichomes of *Solanum berthaultii* deter settling and feeding by the green peach aphid. J. Chem. Ecol. 16: 487-497.

47.   Obrycki, J.J., M.J. Tauber, and W.M. Tingey. 1983. Predator and parasitoid interaction with aphid-resistant potatoes to reduce aphid densities: a two-year field study. J. Econ. Entomol. 76: 456-462.

48.   Obrycki, J.M. and M. J. Tauber. 1984. Natural enemy activity on glandular pubescent potato plants in the greenhouse: an unreliable predictor of effects in the field. Environ. Entomol. 13: 679-683.

49.   Osman, S.F., S.L. Sinden, P. Irwin, K. Deahl, and W. M. Tingey. 1991. Solanocardinol: 16-iso-3-desamino-3b-hydroxysolanocapsine from *Solanum neocardenasii*. Phytochemistry. 30: 3161-3163.

50.   Pelletier, Y. and Z. Smilowitz. 1990. Effect of trichome B exudate of *Solanum berthaultii* Hawkes on consumption by the Colorado potato beetle, *Leptinotarsa decemlineata* [Say]. J. Chem. Ecol. 16: 1547-1555.

51.   Pelletier, Y. and Z. Smilowitz. 1991. Feeding behavior of the adult Colorado potato beetle, *Leptinotarsa decemlineata* (Say), on *Solanum berthaultii* Hawkes. Can. Ent. 123: 219-230.

52.   Plaisted, R. L., W. M. Tingey, and J. C. Steffens. 1992. The germplasm release of NYL 235-4, a clone with resistance to the Colorado potato beetle. Am. Potato J. 69: 843-846.

53.   Radcliffe, E. B. and F. I. Lauer. 1968. Resistance to *Myzus persicae* (Sulzer), *Macrosiphum euphorbiae* (Thomas), and *Empoasca fabae* (Harris) in the wild tuber-bearing *Solanum* (Tourn.) L. species. Minn. Agr. Exp. Stn. Tech. Bull. 259.

54.   Radcliffe, E. B., F. I. Lauer, M. H. Lee, and D. P. Robinson. 1981. Evaluation of the United States potato collection for resistance to green peach aphid and potato aphid. Minn. Agr. Exp. Stn. Tech. Bull. 331.

55.   Radcliffe, E.B., W.M. Tingey, R.W. Gibson, L. Valencia, and K.V. Raman. 1988. Stability of green peach aphid (Homoptera:Aphididae) resistance in wild potato species. J. Econ. Entomol. 81: 361-367.

56. Raman, K.V. 1988. Insecticide toxicity to three strains of green peach aphid (*Myzus persicae* Sulzer) reared on resistant and susceptible cultivars. Crop Protection 7: 62-65.

57. Raman, K. V. and M. Palacios. 1982. Screening potato for resistance to potato tuberworms. J. Econ. Entomol. 75:47-49.

58. Ross, H. 1966. The use of wild potato species in German potato breeding of the past and today. Am. Potato J. 43: 63-80.

59. Ruberson, J.R., M.J. Tauber. C.T. Tauber, and W.M. Tingey. 1989. Interactions at three trophic levels: *Edovum puttleri* Grissell (Hymenoptera:Eulophidae), the Colorado potato beetle, and insect-resistant potatoes. Can. Ent. 121: 841-851.

60. Ryan, J.D., P. Gregory, and W.M. Tingey. 1982. Phenolic oxidase activities in glandular trichomes of *Solanum berthaultii*. Phytochem. 21: 1885-1887.

61. Sanford, L.L. and T. L. Ladd, Jr. 1986. Tolerance of potato leafhopper in *Solanum tuberosum* L. Gp. Tuberosum clones. Am. Pot. J. 63: 39-46.

62. Sanford, L. L. and T.L. Ladd, Jr. 1987. Recurrent selection for potato leafhopper resistance in potato, *Solanum tuberosum* L. Gp. Tuberosum. Am. Pot. J. 64: 367-375.

63. Sanford, L.L., K.L. Deahl, S.L. Sinden, and T.L. Ladd, Jr. 1990. Foliar solanidine glycoside levels in *Solanum tuberosum* populations selected for potato leafhopper resistance. Am. Pot. J. 67: 461-466.

64. Schreiber, K. 1957. Natural plant resistance compounds against the Colorado potato beetle and their possible mode of action. Züchter 27: 289-299. (in German).

65. Schreiber, K. 1958. Concerning several chemical components of the Solanaceae and their importance in resistance to the Colorado potato beetle. Entomol Exp. Appl. 1: 28-37. (in German).

66. Scurrah, M. and K.V. Raman. 1984. Breeding for resistance to major potato pests. Report of the XXII Planning Conference on Integrated Pest Management, CIP. June 4-8, 1984, Lima, Peru. pp. 103-113.

67. Schwarze, P. 1963. Concerning the glycoalkaloid content and the composition of glycoalkaloid complexes in progeny of the interspecific cross *Solanum tuberosum* x *Solanum chacoense*. Züchter 33: 275-281. (in German).

68. Sinden, S.L., L.L. Sanford, and K.L. Deahl. 1986. Segregation of leptine glycoalkaloids in *Solanum chacoense* Bitter. J. Agric. and Food Chem. 34: 372-377.

69. Sinden, S.L., L.L. Sanford, W.W. Cantelo, and K.L. Deahl. 1986. Leptine glycoalkaloids and resistance to the Colorado potato beetle (Coleoptera:Chrysomelidae) in *Solanum chacoense*. Environ. Entomol. 15: 1057-1062.

70. Sinden, S.L., L.L. Sanford, W.W. Cantelo, and K.L. Deahl. 1988. Bioassays of segregating plants a strategy for studying chemical defenses. J. Chem. Ecol. 14: 1941-1950.

71. Spooner, D.M. and R.G. van den Berg. 1991. Species boundaries of *Solanum berthaultii* Hawkes and *S. tarijense* Hawkes. Am. Potato J. 68: 635 (abstract).

72. Strückow, B. and I. Löw. 1961. The effects of some *Solanum* glycoalkaloids on the Colorado potato beetle. Entomol. Exp. Appl. 4: 133-142. (in German).

73.   Tingey, W.M. 1991. Potato glandular trichomes defensive activity against insect attack. pp. 126-135. In: P. A. Hedin, (ed.). Naturally occurring pest bioregulators. ACS Symposium Series 449, ACS, Washington, DC. 456 pp.

74.   Tingey, W.M. and R.W. Gibson. 1978. Feeding and mobility of the potato leafhopper impaired by glandular trichomes of *Solanum berthaultii* and *Solanum polyadenium*. J. Econ. Entomol. 71: 856-858.

75.   Tingey, W.M. and J.E. Laubengayer. 1981. Defense against the green peach aphid and potato leafhopper by glandular trichomes of *Solanum berthaultii*. J. Econ. Entomol. 74: 721-725.

76.   Tingey, W.M. and J.E. Laubengayer. 1986. Glandular trichomes of a resistant hybrid potato alter feeding behavior of the potato leafhopper (Homoptera:Cicadellidae). J. Econ. Entomol. 79: 1230-1234.

77.   Tingey, W.M. and S.L. Sinden. 1982. Glandular pubescence, glycoalkaloid composition, and resistance to the green peach aphid, potato leafhopper, and potato fleabeetle in *Solanum berthaultii*. Amer. Potato J. 59: 95-106.

78.   Tingey, W.M., R.L. Plaisted, J.E. Laubengayer, and S.A. Mehlenbacher. 1982. Green peach aphid resistance by glandular trichomes in *Solanum tuberosum* x *S. berthaultii* hybrids. Am. Potato J. 59: 241-251.

79.   Torka, M. 1950. Breeding potatoes with resistance to the Colorado potato beetle. Am. Potato J. 27: 263-271.

80.   Valencia, V. 1991. Fitomejoramiento a insectos plagas de la papa en la region Andina. Conferencia presentada en el taller de trabajo advances en el mejoramiento genetico de la papa en los paises Andinos. Centro Internacional de la Papa (CIP) Lima, Peru. (in Spanish).

81.   Williams, W.G., G.G. Kennedy, R.T. Yamamoto, J.D. Thacker, and J. Bordner. 1980. 2-tridecanone: a naturally occurring insecticide from the wild tomato *Lycopersicon hirsutum* f. *glabratum*. Science 207: 888-889.

82.   Wright, R.J. 1984. Evaluation of crop rotation for control of Colorado potato beetle in commercial potato fields on Long Island. J. Econ. Entomol. 77: 1254-1259.

83.   Wright, R.J., M.B. Dimock, W.M. Tingey, and R.L. Plaisted. 1985. Colorado potato beetle (Coleoptera:Chrysomelidae): expression of resistance in *Solanum berthaultii* and interspecific potato hybrids. J. Econ. Entomol. 78: 576-582.

84.   Xia, J. and W.M. Tingey. 1986. Green peach aphid (Homoptera:Aphididae): developmental and reproductive biology on a resistant hybrid potato. J. Econ. Entomol. 79: 71-75.

ENHANCING RESISTANCE TO ROOT-KNOT NEMATODES DERIVED FROM WILD SOLANUM SPECIES IN POTATO GERMPLASM

C.R. Brown, U. S. Department of Agriculture,
Agricultural Research Service, Washington State
University-Irrigated Agriculture Research
and Extension Center (WSU-IAREC),
Prosser, Washington 99350,

H. Mojtahedi and G.S. Santo,
Washington State University-Irrigated Agriculture
Research and Extension Center (WSU-IAREC),
Prosser, Washington 99350,

and Sandra Austin-Phillips,
Plant Biotechnology Center, University
of Wisconsin, Madison, Wisconsin 53705

The potato (*Solanum tuberosum* L. ssp. *tuberosum*) originated in the Andean Cordillera of South America. Although in modern times the vast majority of world potato production takes place outside of South America, use of wild tuber-bearing potato from the center of origin in breeding has had a significant impact on resistance traits in potato varieties. Resistances to viruses, nematodes (*Globodera* spp.), and major fungal diseases have been retrieved from wild species and deployed in new varieties during the twentieth century (3,23). The following report describes the identification of resistance in several wild Solanum species to Columbia (*Meloidogyne chitwoodi* Golden et al.) and Northern (*M. hapla* Chitwood) root-knot nematodes. The former was discovered and described only recently (8).

The Columbia root-knot nematode is a serious pest of potato (1). Damage in potato (cv. Russet Burbank) is characterized by tuber gall formation visible on the outside of the tuber and necrotic spots in the flesh of peeled tubers, conditions which are unacceptable for processing and fresh markets (1). *Meloidogyne hapla* also causes necrotic spots in flesh without exterior pimpling blemishes. Control of these nematodes is heavily dependent on soil fumigation, but it is clear that new varieties with resistance would provide a better long-term solution. Infraspecific variation in host preference of certain isolates of *M. chitwoodi* on alfalfa (*Medicago sativa* L.) and carrot (*Daucus carota* L.) has led to division into two races (10,17,24). Alfalfa was thought to be a useful rotation crop to alternate with potato to reduce the impact of *M. chitwoodi*, but the discovery of a second race of *M. chitwoodi* for which alfalfa is a suitable host has placed this in doubt. Furthermore, the good host suitability of cereals for *M. chitwoodi* further detracts from the utility of crop rotation as an option to suppress the nematode.

Hoyman (12) reported on wild potato species resistant to root and tuber galling caused by *Meloidogyne hapla* in tests performed in infested fields. The plots were probably also infested with *M. chitwoodi*, which had not been taxonomically described yet. Resistance to galling caused by *M. incognita* (Kofold and White) Chitwood was reported by Nirula et al. (18) in a number of wild tuber-bearing *Solanum* species. A survey of breeding materials with wild species *S. sparsipilum* (Bitt.) Juz. et Buk. and *S. chacoense* Bitt. in their ancestry found resistance to root galling incited by races 1, 2, and 3 of *M. incognita*, races 1 and 2 of *M. arenaria* (Neal) Chitwood, and isolates of *M. javanica* (Treub) Chitwood, and *M. hapla*. Combined resistance to all nematode species and races was found in 5 percent of progeny examined. A strong correlation was found between index of reproduction (number of eggs on test plants compared to that produced on a susceptible control) and egg mass index (13). Potato with *S. sparsipilum* in the ancestry was reported resistant to *M. javanica*, *M. incognita*, and *M. arenaria* by Gomez et al. (9). Mendoza and Jatala (16) genetically analyzed resistance to root galling in diploid potato incited by *M. incognita* derived from several wild species. There was an apparent difference in reciprocal crosses attributable to maternal inheritance of resistance. Resistance to root galling induced by *M. incognita* was also reported in diploid and tetraploid breeding materials by Iwanaga et al. (15). Diploid parents that produced "2n" pollen were more efficient in the transmission of resistance to tetraploid progenies in 4x-2x crosses than tetraploid parents with normal "n" pollen in 4x-4x crosses. These workers failed to find a significant maternal component although the same sources of resistance were used. The wild species source of the resistance in common to reports by Hartman et al. (13), Gomez et al. (9), Mendoza and Jatala (16), and Iwanaga et al. (15) was *S. sparsipilum*. Screening of the above mentioned nematodes emphasized the scoring of the degree of root galling as a correlate of susceptibility to the nematode. The damage caused by *M. chitwoodi* is fundamentally different in that no galls are formed on the roots, and the primary economic damage is detectable on the tuber surface as bumps and on the surface of peeled potatoes as necrotic spots. As a consequence, the screening reported in this chapter emphasizes reproductive factor (R_f). Potato breeding lines with ancestry reported by Gomez et al. (9) were checked for resistance to *M. chitwoodi* and were found to be susceptible (Brown, unpublished). Surveys of potato germplasm for resistance to *M. chitwoodi* and *M. hapla* failed to identify resistance in cultivated potato, but preliminary indications of resistance were detected in several wild species by Sasser et al. (26), and this report served as a starting point for the studies described below.

Screening Methodology

Reproductive efficiency (R_f = final population/initial population) depends on the fecundity of a proportion of the primary inoculum and intermediate generations that successfully infest the host and reach reproductive maturity. R_f is one measure of resistance of a host crop species to *Meloidogyne* species (20,25). We chose to use this measurement as the resistance parameter in our search for resistance. Host status has been divided into three categories on the basis of R_f values as follows: R_f > 1.0, suitable host; $0.1 < R_f < 1.0$, poor host; $R_f < 0.1$, non-host (25).

Rooted cuttings of potato entries, approximately 7 cm tall, were transplanted into plastic pots (10 cm diam) containing loamy sand (84% sand, 10% silt, and 6% clay) fumigated with methyl bromide. The nematode populations used in these experiments were maintained in the Irrigated Agriculture Research and Extension Center (IAREC) collection (21). Those used were WAMc1 (*M. chitwoodi*, race 1), ORMc8 (*M. chitwoodi*, race 2), and WaMh2 (*M. hapla*). Inoculum was derived from single egg mass cultures, and prepared by collecting eggs after shaking infested roots of tomato (*Lycopersicon esculentum* Mill cv. Columbian) in 0.5% NaOCl (14). At transplanting, an aliquot containing 5000 eggs was pipetted onto the soil. Soil in five pots per clone was infested with each race of nematode. The pots were arranged in a completely randomized design on greenhouse tables. Potato (cv. Russet Burbank), tomato (cv. Columbian), alfalfa (cv. Thor), pepper (*Capsicum annuum* L., cv. California Wonder), wheat (*Triticum aestivum* L., cv. Nugaines), and carrot (*D. carota* L., cv. Chantenay) were included in all tests. Potato and tomato, suitable hosts for both races of *M. chitwoodi* and *M. hapla*, were used as standards. Alfalfa, a non-host for race 1 but a suitable host for race 2, and carrot, a non-host for race 2 but a suitable host for race 1, were included to detect cross contamination between the two races. In addition, pepper is a non-host for *M. chitwoodi* and a suitable host for *M. hapla*, while wheat is a non-host for *M. hapla* and suitable host for *M. chitwoodi*. Plants were grown with regular watering and fertilization at 24 $\pm$3° C for 55 days, and eggs were extracted and counted.

Resistance Among Diverse Wild Species

A preliminary screening was performed using race 1 on seedlings from true seed of PI accessions. Resistant seedlings were vegetatively multiplied and further tested for resistance to races 1 and 2. Table 1 shows the reproductive factor of *M. chitwoodi*, races 1 and 2, on clonal selections from wild tuber-bearing *Solanum* species selected from initial PI accession screenings.

Some of the clones tested had non-host or poor host reactions to one of the races, but with one exception there was no clear-cut resistance to both races. The exception is, however, noteworthy in that the four clonal selections of PI 161726 (*Solanum hougasii* Corr.) failed to support the reproduction of both races. Two clones were poor hosts for both races, while two were non-hosts for race 1 and poor hosts for race 2. The clone, 161726.2, which was successfully crossed to cultivated tetraploids, was a non-host to race 1 and a poor host to race 2.

Resistance to *Meloidogyne chitwoodi* from *Solanum hougasii*

The wild Mexican species, *S. hougasii,* is a hexaploid, 2n=6x=72, in the Series Demissa, and has an Endosperm Balance Number (EBN) of 4 (11). Another species in the series Demissa, *Solanum demissum* Lindl., which has been used extensively in breeding during this century as a source of late blight resistance, is directly crossable with cultivated tetraploid potato (22,23). The sharing of the same EBN is a predictor of crossability between cultivated tetraploid, 4x-4EBN *S. tuberosum* ssp. *tuberosum*, and 6x-4EBN *S. hougasii*. Over 600 seeds were produced from crosses, 64 seeds germinated, but only 14 seedlings grew normally and vigorously allowing clonal multiplication.

These 14 interspecific hybrids were evaluated for host response to both races of the nematode (Table 2). Three out of the 14 hybrids we evaluated were non-hosts for race 1 and poor hosts for race 2. Five hybrids were non-hosts to race 1 but suitable hosts for race 2. Three hybrids were

Table 1. Reproductive efficiency ($R_f = P_f/P_i$) of *Meloidogyne chitwoodi*, races 1 and 2, on various *Solanum* species 55 d after inoculating 5000 eggs

	R_f	
Species Code (cv or PI)	Race 1	Race 2
Potato (cv. Russet Burbank	30.4 ab[z]	25.4 ab
S. andreanum 498148.4	3.0 c-g	0.9 f-j
S. andreanum 498148.6	8.8 a-f	2.0 d-i
S. andreanum 498148.7	25.9 abc	7.4 a-e
S. berthaultii 310927.3	35.6 a	21.8 ab
S. berthaultii 310927.5	48.6 a	5.6 a-f
S. berthaultii 310927.8	43.5 a	15.7 abc
S. boliviense 265861.1	1.4 f-i	0.2 jk
S. boliviense 265861.9	10.3 a-f	4.4 a-f
S. boliviense 310974.8	22.7 a-d	0.8 f-k
S. boliviense 310974.10	42.2 a	27.5 a
S. boliviense 310975.1	3.2 c-g	1.6 e-i
S. boliviense 310975.4	2.0 e-h	0.1 jk
S. boliviense 310975.6	2.7 d-g	0.4 h-k
S. boliviense 310975.10	7.4 a-f	1.7 e-i
S. hougasii 161726.1	<0.01 n	0.3 ijk
S. hougasii 161726.2	0.04 kl	0.5 g-k
S. hougasii 161726.5	<0.01 mn	<0.01 l
S. hougasii 161726.7	0.01 lm	<0.01 l
S. acaule 208874.2	1.4 f-i	3.4 b-g
S. acaule 208874.5	0.8 g-j	2.4 c-h
S. canasense 265865.2	16.3 a-e	8.8 a-e

[z] Means of five replicates. Those not sharing a letter are significantly different at 5% level, according to Duncan's Multiple Range Test. Analysis of variance and separation tests were performed on ln(x + 1) transformed egg counts. The R_f values are the geometric means.

suitable hosts to both races, and two were non-hosts to both races. The resistant wild parent, 161726.2, behaved as a non-host to race 1 and as a poor host to race 2. The *S. tuberosum* ssp. *tuberosum* parents, A8341.5 and COO8014.1, were both suitable hosts for races 1 and 2.

The F_1 hybrids show differences in the distribution of R_f values between races 1 and 2 in two ways. First, 10 of the F_1 hybrids were non-hosts for race 1, while two of the R_f values for these same hybrids are non-hosts and the rest of the values lie within poor host or suitable host categories. This stronger expression of resistance to race 1 than to race 2 is similar to the pattern found in the resistant wild parent, 161726.2. Second, the R_f values of race 1 are largely divided discretely between suitable host and non-host categories, while those for race 2 extend the full range of the poor host interval, $0.1 < R_f < 1.0$, and eight hybrids are classified as suitable hosts for race 2. This difference in pattern of expression of resistance to both races was also found among *S. bulbocastanum* Dun. accessions (4), as will be described below. Furthermore, it is apparent that resistance to race 1 is not correlated with resistance to race 2. A more definitive statement of inheritance, and genetic independence of the resistances to the two races, is covered below in the evaluation of backcross progeny. The success in recovering substantial resistance to race 1 and a lower expression of resistance to race 2 in some F_1 hybrids augured well for the transfer

Table 2. Reproductive efficiency ($R_f = P_f/P_i$) of *Meloidogyne chitwoodi* races 1 and 2 on standard, resistant *Solanum hougasii* (hgs), susceptible *S. tuberosum* ssp. *tuberosum* (tbr), and *S. hougasii* x *S. tuberosum* ssp. *tuberosum* hybrids 55 d after inoculating with 5000 eggs

$$R_f = P_f/P_i$$

Genotypes Standard	Race 1 R_f	Race 2 R_f	Host[z] Status
Potato (Russet Burbank)	29.5 a	23.6 a	S/S
Parents			
A8341.5 (tbr)	21.2 a	14.2 ab	S/S
C008014.1 (tbr)	5.5 ab	13.0 ab	S/S
161726.2 (hgs)	<0.01 g	0.13 e	N/N
S. hougasii x *S. tuberosum* ssp. *tuberosum* hybrids			
(161726.2 x A8341.5).2	0.01 def	0.66 b-e	N/P
(161726.2 x A8341.5).3	<0.01 fg	0.08 ef	N/N
(161726.2 x A8341.5).4	<0.01 efg	0.37 de	N/P
(161726.2 x A8341.5).5	<0.01 d-g	0.52 cde	N/P
(161726.2 x A8341.5).6	0.04 cde	12.0 ab	N/S
(161726.2 x A8341.5).7	0.02 def	9.4 a-e	N/S
(161726.2 x A8341.5).9	<0.01 d-g	4.4 a-d	N/S
(161726.2 x A8341.5).10	<0.01 fg	0.8 b-e	N/P
(161726.2 x A8341.5).11	8.7 a	5.4 a-d	S/S
(161726.2 x A8341.5).13	9.05 a	3.1 a-d	S/S
(161726.2 x A8341.5).14	6.0 ab	3.6 a-d	S/S
(161726.2 x A8341.5).15	0.5 bc	<0.01 f	P/N
(161726.2 x A8341.5).16	<0.01 fg	12.1 ab	N/S
(161726.2 x C008014.1).1	0.06 cd	6.5 a-d	N/S

[z]Host status (race 1)/ host status (race 2).
N = non-host, $R_f < 0.1$; P = poor host, $0.1 < R_f < 1.0$; S = suitable host, $R_f > 1.0$.

of this resistance to reproduction of the nematode to the cultivated gene pool through further breeding work (5).

Six of the F_1 hybrids resistant to both races of *M. chitwoodi* were crossed to A8341.5 to create a first generation backcross (BC_1). A total of 132 BC_1 progenies were propagated to produce replicated cuttings and screened for resistance to races 1 and 2 of *M. chitwoodi*. The pattern of resistance is shown in Table 3. Contingency table analysis of the numbers of progeny that fall into non-, poor, and suitable host categories in combination for each race indicate that resistances to the races are independent of each other (chi-square = 1.5, df=4; 0.5 < $\underline{P}$ < 0.9). The pattern of inheritance suggests that resistance to race 1 is controlled by a single dominant gene. Resistance to race 2 is more difficult to define and may be controlled by several genes, displaying a continuous distribution.

Table 3. Combined host suitabilities of races 1 and 2 of *Meloidogyne chitwoodi* on BC$_1$ progenies deriving resistance from *Solanum hougasii*. Marginal values are counts and percents (in parentheses)

	Non-host	Race 2 Poor host	Suit host	Subtotal (Percent Race 1)
Race 1				
Non-host	10	9	23	42 (31.8)
Poor host	6	9	16	31 (23.5)
Suit host	7	16	36	59 (44.7)
Subtotal	23	34	75	132
(% Race 2)	(17.4)	(25.3)	(55.8)	

Resistance from *Solanum bulbocastanum*

Preliminary indications that PI accessions of *S. bulbocastanum* could have resistance to *M. chitwoodi* were investigated further. In replicated tests it was found that clones from several different accessions had resistance to both races (Table 4). The R$_f$ values of *M. chitwoodi* race 1 on *S. bulbocastanum* ranged from 0 to 12.84, with clear distinction between the two suitable hosts and 20 non-hosts. In contrast, the response to race 2 presented many intermediate responses. Out of 22 *S. bulbocastanum* genotypes tested, two were classified as non-hosts for both races of *M. chitwoodi*. Accessions 243508 and 275184 were better hosts for race 2, with mean R$_f$ values of 1.15 and 1.97, respectively, than the other three accessions. There was variation of host suitability within species and within accessions of *S. bulbocastanum*. Single PI seedlots produced seedlings with non-host and suitable host status. Because there was within-species variation in resistance phenotype, it was necessary to use particular clones with non-host status for both races of *M. chitwoodi* as sources of genetic resistance for potato breeding. As with the *S. hougasii* source of resistance, there is no association between resistances to the two races.

Solanum bulbocastanum, 2n=2x=24, is classified as EBN=1 (11). This signifies that some form of ploidy manipulation, such as somatic chromosome doubling or 2n gametes, would be necessary to achieve crosses with cultivated diploid species (EBN=2). Crosses with other EBN=1 wild species, EBN=2 cultivated diploids, and crosses of colchicine doubled *S. bulbocastanum* (presumably EBN=2) with EBN=2 diploids were unsuccessful. The unusual reproductive isolation of *S. bulbocastanum* was also reported by Novy (19).

Table 4. Reproductive efficiency $(R_f = P_f / P_i)$ of races 1 and 2 of *Meloidogyne chitwoodi* on *Solanum bulbocastanum* 55 days after inoculating with 5000 eggs

Identity	Race 1 R_f	Race 2 R_f
Potato	7.26 a-d	2.52 a-f
S. bulbocastanum clones from PI Accessions:		
243505.2	<0.01 jkl	0.50 d-h
243505.4	<0.01 j-m	0.81 b-h
243505.6	0.00 m	0.13 hi
243505.7	<0.01 j-m	0.02 ij
243505.9	12.84 ab	0.68 c-h
243508.2	<0.01 klm	0.25 e-i
243508.4	<0.01 j-m	1.50 b-h
243508.6	<0.01 j-m	1.37 b-h
243508.9	<0.01 j-m	1.42 b-h
255518.5	<0.01 lm	0.36 e-i
255518.6	3.40 a-f	0.19 f-i
255518.7	0.00 m	0.23 f-i
255518.8	<0.01 j-m	0.88 b-h
255518.9	<0.01 j-m	0.40 e-i
275184.4	<0.01 j-m	4.19 a-e
275184.6	<0.01 j-m	0.16 ghi
275184.7	<0.01 klm	2.25 a-h
275184.10	<0.01 j-m	1.26 b-h
275187.1	<0.01 j-m	0.52 d-h
275187.2	<0.01 j-m	1.70 b-h
275187.8	<0.01 lm	0.15 ghi
275187.10	0.00 m	<0.01 jkl

Values are means of 5 replicates. Means not sharing a letter are significantly different (*P* < 0.05) according to Duncan's Multiple Range Test. Separation tests were performed on ln(x + 1) means. The R_f values are geometric means.

Protoplast fusion, a means of overcoming sexual crossing barriers, is achieved by fusing protoplasts of parents which one desires to hybridize. It is additive in nature and produces hybrids that have ploidy that is the sum of the sporophytic chromosome number of the parents. Indeed the entire nuclear and cytoplasmic genetic content of each parent is combined. This procedure (2) was applied successfully to accession 275187.10 (refer to Table 4). A tetraploid *S. t.* ssp. *tuberosum* accession (203900) was combined somatically with 275187.10. Resulting hybrids were tested for reproductive factor (R_f) with races 1 and 2 of *M. chitwoodi* and with *M. hapla*. Rooted cuttings of four somatic hybrids, the susceptible tuberosum parent, PI 203900, and the resistant wild parent, *S. bulbocastanum* 275187.10, were transplanted into buckets containing soil fumigated with methyl bromide. The buckets were inoculated with 25,000 eggs. Tubers were harvested and soil samples were taken 105 days after inoculation. Second stage juveniles (J2) were extracted from soil samples (250 cm^3) (6) to determine R_f values. R_f and tuber damage indices for the resistant wild, the susceptible cultivated parents, and four fusion products are presented in Table 5. *Meloidogyne hapla* completed fewer reproductive cycles than *M. chitwoodi* and caused less tuber damage. Damage ratings are not shown for 275187.10, because it did not tuberize in the buckets. Protoplast fusion products CBP231 and CBP233 showed levels of resistance to reproduction to both races of *M. chitwoodi* and to *M. hapla* equivalent to the level shown by the *S. bulbocastanum* parent. Tuber damage is correlated with R_f values. Genetic diversity among the fusion products is apparent in the greater host suitability of CBP232 and CBP235 to race 2 of *M. chitwoodi* and *M. hapla*.

Epilogue

The discovery of new pests that have considerable economic importance in a major crop can be expected to occur at regular intervals. Strategies to deal with pests in increasingly chemical-free agricultural production systems will benefit greatly from increases in host resistance that result from breeding. As nematode control strategies evolve, attempts will be made to use toxic soil treatments in environmentally safer applications and formulations (See Weingartner and McSorley, this volume). Other non-chemical suppression strategies, including rotation cropping with unsuitable host crops and green manure practices (See G. S. Santo, this volume), that suppress nematodes may be more successful if future potato varieties have significantly greater genetic nematode resistance. The wide host range of Columbia root-knot nematode, which includes cereals and alfalfa limits severely the latitude of crop rotation options. The geographical distribution of *M. chitwoodi* has also been reported to have expanded to The Netherlands, thus magnifying the importance from that of a somewhat restricted regional pest to one with worldwide distribution in important production areas (7). Also, as reported above, the virulence

Table 5. Reproductive efficiency (R_f) and tuber damage index of resistant *Solanum bulbocastanum* (blb), susceptible cv. Russet Burbank, susceptible *S. tuberosum* ssp. *tuberosum* parent (203900), and protoplast fusion hybrids (CBP)[w].

Clone	M. chitwoodi (r1)		M. chitwoodi (r2)		M. hapla	
	R_f	Tuber damage[x]	R_f	Tuber damage	R_f	Tuber damage
RB	56.74 ab[y]	5.88 a	39.61 a	4.26 b	74.32 a	2.52 cd
203900	13.83 ab	4.95 ab	35.70 a	4.48 b	31.70 a	1.60 def
CBP231	0.01 g	0.60 fg	0.27 cde	1.04 efg	0.33 cde	0.32 fg
CBP232	0.02 fg	1.62 def	2.40 bc	3.70 bc	1.51 bcd	0.28 fg
CBP233	0.01 g	0.46 fg	0.10 efg	2.12 de	0.38 cde	0.12 fg
CPB235	0.01 fg	0.46 fg	1.37 bcd	2.20 de	1.48 bcd	0.06 fg
2775187.1 (blb)	0.09 efg	-[z]	0.01 g	-	0.16 def	-

[w]R_f and tuber damage data were analyzed separately. R_f values are geometric means. Mean separation of R_f values was perfromed on ln($x + 1$) means.

[x]Tuber damage: 0 = 0 infection sites per tuber, 1 = 1-10 infection sites per tuber, 2 = 11-30 infection sites per tuber, 3 = 31-50 infection sites per tuber, 4 = 51-75 infection sites per tuber, 5 = 100+ infection sites per tuber, 6 = 200+ infection sites per tuber.

[y]Duncan's Multiple Range Test. Means not sharing the same letter are significantly different at $P < 0.05$ level.

[z]Tuber damage data not available due to lack of tuberization. Values are means of five replicates. Means not sharing a common letter differ significantly ($P < 0.05$) according to Duncan's Multiple Range Test. R_f values are geometric means.

reactions of races 1 and 2 of *M. chitwoodi* and of *M. hapla* on these resistant genotypes is mixed. Resistance to race 1 of *M. chitwoodi* appears to be virtual immunity while that to race 2 is quantitative in nature and somewhat variable in greenhouse pot and field experiments. It is likely that deployment of resistance in nematode populations harboring races and/or species that are reproductively more successful will cause a shift in nematode composition toward predominance of those types (27). This prediction requires the judicious use of multifaceted control measures. The aim would be to prevent selection of nematode populations toward a new genetic composition through use of different methods of control comprising multiple modes of action. Genetic resistance of the host would be only one component of a management strategy that will also encompass rotation with unsuitable host crops, and suppression by nematicidal action of plant by-products and/or acceptable chemical nematicides.

The identification of resistance to Columbia and Northern root-knot nematodes in wild *Solanum* species, and the introduction of these traits into the cultivated potato breeding pool is evidence of the significant contribution that research in germplasm enhancement can make to integrated pest management.

Literature Cited

1. Anonymous. 1986. Integrated pest management for potatoes in the Western United States. Pages 110-114 in: Western Regional Publ. 011. Univ. of Calif., Div. of Agric. & Natural Res. Publ. 3316.

2. Austin, S., Baer, M. A., and Helgeson, J. P. 1985. Transfer of resistance to potato leaf roll virus from *Solanum brevidens* into *Solanum tuberosum* by somatic fusion. Plant Sci. Lett. 39:75-82.

3. Brown, C. R. 1990. Modern Evolution of the Cultivated Potato Gene Pool. Pages 1-11 in: The Molecular and Cellular Biology of the Potato. M. E. Vayda and W. D. Park, eds. CAB Internatl., Wallingford, UK.

4. Brown, C. R., Mojtahedi, H.. and Santo, G. S. 1989. Comparison of reproductive efficiency of *Meloidogyne chitwoodi* on *Solanum bulbocastanum* in soil and in vitro tests. Plant Dis. 73:957-959.

5. Brown, C. R., Mojtahedi, H., and Santo, G. S. 1991. Resistance to Columbia root-knot nematode in *Solanum* ssp. and in hybrids of *S. hougasii* with tetraploid cultivated potato. Am. Potato J. 68:445-452.

6. Byrd, D. W., Barker, K. R., Ferris, H., Nusbaum, C. J., Griggin, W. E., Small, R. H., and Stone, C. A. 1976. Two semi-automatic elutriators for extracting nematodes and certain fungi from soil. J. Nematol. 8:206-212.

7. Evans, K., and Trudgill, D. L. 1992. Pest aspects of potato production Part 1, The nematode pests of potatoes. Pages 438-475 in: The Potato Crop. P. Harris ed. Chapman and Hall, London.

8. Golden, A. M., O'Bannon, J. H., Santo, G. S., and Finley, A. M. 1980. Description and SEM observation of *Meloidogyne chitwoodi* n. sp. (Meloidogynidae), a root-knot nematode on potato in the Pacific Northwest. J. Nematol. 12:319-327.

9. Gomez, P. L., Plaisted, R. L., and Brodie, B. B. 1983. Inheritance of the resistance to *Meloidogyne incognita, M. javanica,* and *M. arenaria* in potatoes. Am. Potato J. 60:339-351.

10. Griffin, G. D., Inserra, R. N., Vovlas, N., and Sisson, D. V. 1986. Differential reaction of alfalfa cultivars to *Meloidogyne hapla* and *M. chitwoodi* populations. J. Nematol. 18:347-352.

11. Hanneman R. E., Jr., and Bamberg, J. B. 1986. Inventory of Tuber-bearing *Solanum* species. Wisc. Agric. Exp. Stn., Bulletin 533, 216 pp.

12. Hoyman, W. G. 1974. Reaction of *Solanum tuberosum* and *Solanum* species to *Meloidogyne hapla*. Am. Potato J. 51:281-286.

13. Hartman, K., Sasser, J. N., and Jatala, P. 1982. Evaluation of potato lines for resistance to major species and races of root-knot nematodes (Meloidogyne species). Pages 94-95 in: Proc. Int. Congr. on Research for the Potato in the Year 2000. Int. Potato Center, Lima Peru.

14. Hussey, R. S., and Barker, K. R. 1973. A comparison of methods of collecting inocula of *Meloidogyne* spp. including a new technique. Plant Dis. Rep. 57:1025-1028.

15. Iwanaga, M., Jatala, P., Ortiz, R., and Guevara, E. 1989. Use of FDR 2n pollen to transfer resistance to root-knot nematodes into cultivated 4x potatoes. J. Am. Soc. Hortic. Sci. 114:1008-1013.

16. Mendoza, H. A., and Jatala, P. 1985. Breeding potatoes for resistance to the root-knot nematode *Meloidogyne* species. Pages 217-224 in: An Advanced Treatise on Meloidogyne. Volume I: Biology and Control. J. N. Sasser and C. C. Carter eds. North Carolina State University, Raleigh, NC, USA.

17. Mojtahedi, H., Santo, G. S., and Wilson, J. H. 1988. Host tests to differentiate *Meloidogyne chitwoodi* races 1 and 2 and *M. hapla*. J. Nematol. 20:468-473.

18. Nirula, K. K., Nayar, N. M., Bassi, K. K., and Singh, G. 1967. Reaction of tuber-bearing *Solanum* species to root knot nematode, *Meloidogyne incognita*. Am. Potato J. 44:66-69.

19. Novy, R. G. 1988. Hybridization between Group *Tuberosum* haploids and 1EBN wild potato species. M.S. Thesis, Univ. of Wisconsin, 88 pp.

20. Oostenbrink, M. 1966. Major characteristics of the relation between nematodes and plants. Meded. Landbouwhogesch. Wageningen 66:3-46.

21. Pinkerton, J. N., Mojtahedi, H., and Santo, G. S. 1987. Reproductive efficiency of Pacific Northwest populations of *Meloidogyne chitwoodi* on alfalfa. Plant Dis. 71:345-348.

22. Plaisted, R. L., and Hoopes, R. W. 1989. The past record and future prospects for the use of exotic potato germplasm. Am. Potato J. 66:603-627.

23. Ross, H. 1986. Potato Breeding Problems and Perspectives. Advances in Plant Breeding, Supplement 13. 132 pp.

24. Santo, G. S., Mojtahedi, H., and Pinkerton, J. N. 1985. A second race of *Meloidogyne chitwoodi* discovered in Washington State. Plant Dis. 69:361.

25. Sasser, J. N., Carter, C. C., and Hartman, K. M. 1984. Standardization of host suitability studies and reporting of resistance to root-knot nematodes. Crop Nema. Res. & Control Proj., NCSU/USAID, Dept. of Plant Path., NCSU, Box 7616, Raleigh, NC, 27695, USA. 7 pp.

26. Sasser, J. N., Hartman, K. M., and Carter, C. C. 1987. Summary of preliminary crop germplasm evaluations for resistance to root-knot nematodes. Crop Nema. Res. & Control Proj., NCSU/USAID, Dept. of Plant Path., NCSU, Box 7616, Raleigh, NC, 27695, USA. 88 pp.

27. Trudgill, D. L. 1991. Resistance to and tolerance of plant parasitic nematodes in plants. Annu. Rev. Phytopathol. 29:167-192.

HOST RESISTANCE FOR MANAGEMENT OF POTATO LATE BLIGHT

G. A. Forbes
International Potato Center
P.O. 17-16-129 C.E.Q.
Quito, Ecuador

M. C. Jarvis
Department of Chemistry
University of Glasgow, Glasgow, G128QQ, United Kingdom

Potato late blight, caused by *Phytophthora infestans* (Mont.) De Bary, has had major social and economic consequences and has stimulated an enormous amount of research in plant pathology. The historical role of late blight in the birth of plant pathology (3) and many of the scientific advancements associated with the disease have been documented (8).

In the developed world, and some parts of the developing world, late blight is a disease under control. Where late blight is a potential problem and resources permit, fungicide applications have became routine in production. In these situations, host resistance is an economically and ecologically advantageous substitute for chemical control. Yield loss due to foliage and tuber damage is severe in developing countries when fungicides are not used or used improperly. Interest in host resistance has varied in the past but this control tactic may soon become an undeniable necessity as fungicides are banned in developed countries or become increasingly more expensive.

In this review we address some of the problems of late blight control on potato through the utilization of host resistance. Resistance to late blight is not a new topic; several reviews already exist, some quite recent (11,38,47,52). Thus, we are presented with the formidable task of complementing the thorough and insightful work that has already been done. To accomplish this, we refer readers to other authors when possible and focus on two areas which we feel merit more thorough analysis. The first concerns the nature, or more precisely, types of host resistance which are available, with emphasis on two important types of polygenic resistance currently in use. The second area of interest is that of R-gene expression in the field, a major limitation to the successful identification and measurement of durable, polygenic resistance.

BACKGROUND

It is generally believed that edible potato (e.g., *Solanum tuberosum* ssp. *tuberosum* , *S. tuberosum* ssp. *andigena* and *S. phureja*) did not co-evolve with *P. infestans*. Edible potatoes, probably *S. tuberosum* ssp. *andigena*, were taken to Europe by Spanish in the 16th century. Cultivation increased, with potato becoming a staple in many parts of Europe, until the disastrous introduction of *P. infestans* in the early 1840's and the initiation of disease in 1845 (2,52).

The origin of *S. tuberosum* ssp. *tuberosum* has two explanations in the literature. One is that it was selected from *S. tuberosum* ssp. *andigena* over centuries of cultivation in Europe (see 52) and the other is that it was introduced directly from Chile in the late 1800's where it replaced the original *S. tuberosum* ssp. *andigena* introductions, which had been practically eliminated by blight (19). The latter hypothesis is supported by DNA analyses.

Most evidence indicates that *P. infestans* originated in Mexico on wild *Solanum* species (16,37). We may take the pre-1845 European potato cultivars or the pre-1900 *S. tuberosum* ssp. *andigena* cultivars in South America as being susceptible. However, they have the genetic potential for a type of resistance. In Europe, selection pressure and intense, if not scientific, breeding activity after the 1845 epidemic soon produced relatively resistant cultivars without the introduction of any new genetic material which had co-evolved with the pathogen. If *S. tuberosum* ssp. *tuberosum* was introduced from Chile, there was no good reason to suspect that it expressed high levels of resistance since it had not yet been exposed to the pathogen.

We shall call the post-epidemic resistance of European cultivars the '*tuberosum*' type. This resistance confers partial protection on both foliage and tubers, is inherited polygenically, and appears to be horizontal (i.e., not specific to races of *P. infestans*.)

The potato (*S. tuberosum*), the tomato (*Lycopersicon esculentum* Mill), and their South American ancestors have no major genes (R-genes) for vertical resistance of the hypersensitive type. This type of R-gene is present in some of the Central American species which co-evolved with *P. infestans* (17,46). Around the turn of the century Radcliffe Salaman introduced R-gene resistance into cultivated potatoes by crossing with *S. demissum* around 1900. *S. demissum* also shows various non-hypersensitive types of resistance, and one of these, which we call '*demissum*' type, has been widely used in potato breeding. It gives partial protection to the foliage, but not to other parts of the plant. It is apparently horizontal and is inherited polygenically. Other non-hypersensitive types of resistance are probably present in *S. demissum* and in other Central American species but these have not been introduced into commercial cultivars on any scale, and much less is known about their expression.

Terminology utilized in the study of host resistance has been varied. Thurston (38) lists some of the different terms used to describe types of resistance. For example, the terms 'partial', 'polygenic', 'horizontal' and 'field' resistance have been used almost interchangeably in the past, referring to what we shall call non-hypersensitive types of resistance.

TYPES OF RESISTANCE

Before describing the principal types of resistance in use, it is important to explain further what is meant by 'type'. A 'type' of resistance has a unique mechanism at the cellular level, which can hinder the development of the fungus at one or more stages in its life cycle. If the impedance is at one stage only, penetration of the leaf surface, for example, then a type corresponds with a component of resistance as normally defined. Two or more types of resistance may be expressed in one component, and one type of resistance, for example the *tuberosum* type, may have a number of components all under the control of a single biochemical factor. In the latter case, the components all vary together when the overall level of resistance is changed; i. e., a 'type' of resistance behaves as a unit in its phenotypic expression. There may be a number of genes, or sets of genes, that can each specify resistance of the same type. This is the normal situation with major gene resistance; it is naturally inevitable with polygenic resistance, but here the genes are additive in effect.

Hypersensitive Resistance

The hypersensitive resistance of potatoes to *P. infestans* determined by the major genes R1-R11 in a gene-for-gene relationship with the pathogen, is a classic example of hypersensitivity on which many of the current ideas are based (32). Most of its features, including host cell death and antifungal consequences, also appear when potatoes are infected by non-pathogenic fungi able to penetrate surface barriers (21), or when *P. infestans* mycelium is killed within the potato tissue, or when 'elicitors' (polysaccharides or glycoproteins of fungal origin) are brought into contact with potato cells. Hypersensitive resistance typically results in microscopic lesions but with some genes (e.g. R10) it is only partially expressed. A recent assessment of some of the questions still surrounding host-pathogen interactions was given by Friend (15).

Non-hypersensitive Resistance

There is no obvious reason why all types of resistance other than hypersensitivity should be horizontal, but the two that have been most widely used in breeding, which we have called the *tuberosum* and *demissum* types, are approximately horizontal in effect. Attempts to determine a cultivar x race interaction have given conflicting results but generally support the hypothesis of little or no interaction.

Vanderplank (49) and Thurston (38) have both argued that general (non-hypersensitive) resistance has been stable over time, based on constant relative levels of resistance of older cultivars. Turkensteen (unpublished) recently tested a number of old European cultivars and found that they had maintained their ranking of resistance levels. Other studies have shown some pathogen adaptation to specific cultivars after successive culturing on potato tubers (5,23) and for incubation periods on detached leaves (23). Field studies have demonstrated a small isolate x cultivar interaction for epidemic rate (26), or were unable to measure any such interaction (22,30).

The stability of general resistance has most certainly been confounded at times by climatic and other environmental effects. Climatic conditions highly favorable to the pathogen may create epidemic conditions which are too severe for existing levels of general resistance. This is especially true if cultivars from temperate regions are planted in the upland tropics where long nights and continuous potato cropping results in high disease pressure year round. In many areas in the upland tropics, fungicide sprays begin immediately after emergence.

Pathogen x environment interactions probably occur when isolates are introduced into an area (30). These effects should be cultivar-non-specific and can be seen as an effect of environment on aggressiveness, the level of disease caused by the pathogen on all cultivars. Major shifts in the population structure of the pathogen may lead to increased pathogenic fitness (16), which could be interpreted as loss of resistance.

Tuberosum Resistance

The *tuberosum* type may be termed an artificially constructed type of resistance, as it has been assembled by selection pressure on a gene pool of susceptible cultivars without the introduction of any resistant wild material. *Tuberosum* type resistance: (a) is expressed in all parts of the plant: foliage, tubers and stems (10,28); (b) is dependent on day length responses; (c) is dependent on plant age; and (d) can be divided into a number of components.

The potato is basically a short-day plant, as befits its tropical, South American origin. Cultivars selected for the long days of temperate summer have lost some of their daylength sensitivity, otherwise they would not form tubers until the days shortened to around 12 hours in the autumn. The early maturing cultivars are quite insensitive.

It seems that the *tuberosum* type of resistance can only be assembled in a cultivar that retains some sensitivity to daylength (41), and reaches high levels only if the plants are grown where the days are long enough in midsummer for the resistance to respond (43). The resistant cultivars in temperate countries are late-maturing, and lose their resistance as well as their lateness when grown under short-day conditions in the tropics. Some cultivars bred for tropical countries show some resistance of this type, but these are excessively late when grown in the temperate zone.

There is a correlation, therefore, between the *tuberosum* type of resistance and late maturity. Resistant, early cultivars have not been bred, but susceptible, late cultivars have, many before 1846. However, there is considerable selection pressure against the latter as they receive the full weight of the disease epidemic at the end of the season. In temperate regions, the susceptibility of early cultivars, and of others at the seedling stage, has not been important because the epidemic does not build up until later in the season. It is only in parts of the upland tropics that the disease epidemic occurs year round.

Plant age. *Tuberosum* resistance is not present in seedlings, and in this respect resembles 'adult plant resistance' to cereal disease. *Tuberosum* resistance is also lost at the end of the growing season, with peak resistance at flowering (4,43,51). The age dependence also applies to individual leaves on a plant; the maximal resistance is in leaves that are mature but not close to senescence (20,27). Some late cultivars produce new stems well into the growing season, and the leaves on many of these will be at the most resistant stage when the disease epidemic is at its height.

Components of expression. *Tuberosum* resistance may involve resistance to penetration into the leaf, retarded fungal growth through both leaf and tuber tissue, long latent period, and reduced sporulation. Nonetheless, these components usually vary together when overall resistance varies (12); they all diminish together when a resistant cultivar is crossed with a susceptible one, or when daylength, growth stage or nutrition level is altered. This is why we are justified in calling it a single type of resistance, albeit its many components and behavior as a single genetic and physiological unit.

Many researchers have studied these components to find the highest correlation with overall resistance (see 38, 50 and 52). Conclusions drawn in these studies have varied to such a degree that it is difficult to establish a general pattern. Van Oijen (50) accredited much of the variation to the use of different genotypes and suggested that a standard group should be used in future studies. An important source of variation in most studies on components of resistance may have been the combination of *demissum, tuberosum*, and perhaps other resistance types in cultivars of unknown pedigree.

There have been many theories about the mechanism of *tuberosum* resistance at the biochemical level. The following factors have been correlated with resistance when cultivars, or growth stages, have been compared: (a) starch and free sugar levels in relation to structural carbohydrates (18); (b) soluble nitrogen compounds (1,6); (c) levels of soluble phenolic compounds (35); (d) sterols (12); (e) aspects of nucleoside metabolism (7); and (f) soluble peroxidase activity, which is highly correlated with resistance if cultivars, growth stages, daylength or different plant parts are compared (13,24,44).

The measurement of soluble peroxidase nearly became one of the few biochemical tests to be used in resistance screening. It was abandoned for two reasons: (a) a strong leaf maturity effect that made it difficult to use on rapidly growing plants; and (b) a report in which a large number of commercial German cultivars were compared and demonstrated a poor correlation between resistance and soluble peroxidase (24). With hindsight we can say that this was probably because many of the cultivars tested had the *demissum* type of resistance and not the *tuberosum* type.

There is obviously much disagreement about the mechanism of the *tuberosum* type. One possible explanation lies in the experiments of Weindlmayr (53) in Austria and Umaerus (45) in Sweden. They found a correlation between resistance and natural gibberellin levels when cultivars, daylengths and nutrition levels were compared. Moreover, they showed that the application of gibberellin A3 to plants increased the resistance, since most of the components tested were enhanced. Results of experiments with growth hormones are notoriously hard to interpret, and a simple effect of gibberellins seems unlikely. Fehrmann and Dimond (14) showed a small increase in resistance with IAA, and interactions are probable. However, it does seem an attractive possibility that this type or resistance is controlled by various aspects of a basic change in the growth form and metabolism of the plant, resulting from the varietal response to environmental conditions such as daylength and subject to hormonal modulation.

If this is true, it is inevitable that almost everything we can measure, such as carbohydrate levels, amino acids, soluble peroxidase, etc., will be affected at the same time. Correlations are inevitable, but we cannot decide which, if any, may be the cause(s) of the resistant response. Correlative evidence of any sort would not be very satisfactory for elucidating mechanisms in this kind of system, though it may be quite effective in screening trials when the type of resistance that it indicates is understood.

The *Demissum* Type of Resistance

There are three main characteristics of this type of resistance. First, it is composed primarily of one component; impedance to leaf penetration resulting in fewer lesions, particularly if the time from inoculation to drying of the leaves is restricted (46). No resistance is conferred on tubers. Second, it is related to formation of appressoria (25) (fine hyphae that penetrate host tissue, formed at the point of contact of long germ tubes with the plant surface). The mechanism is uncertain but the formation of appressoria seems to be retarded. No differences in cuticle structure are known, but diffusible inhibitors are possible. Lastly, it is unaffected by daylength or age of plant. Therefore, selection at the seedling stage favors this type of resistance over the tuberosum type.

Much less research has been done on this type of resistance, but it has been used extensively by breeders. Wastie (52) has noted that *S. demissum* has been used in some of the resistant clones developed at the Scottish Crop Research Institute. Ross (33) estimated that 85% of German cultivars contain *S. demissum* genes. The East African cultivar 'Seseni' is believed to have come from the Scottish program and may also owe its resistance to *S. demissum*. Many of the Mexican cultivars that have had a major impact in Mexico and around the world probably rely mostly on *demissum* resistance.

Assumptions about the type of resistance in a cultivar should not be made unless the exact pedigree is known. Many of the materials tested in Mexico involve several species. A good example is 'Cruza 148', which we now believe is a cross between *S. phureja* and 'Monserrate', itself a hybrid of *S. tuberosum* ssp. *andigena* and *S. tuberosum* ssp. *tuberosum*.

Resistance in *S. tuberosum* ssp. *andigena* and *S. phureja*

If the origins of the Andean species *S. tuberosum* ssp. *andigena*, *S. phureja*, and *S. tuberosum* ssp. *tuberosum* were identical, we could expect similar types of non-hypersensitive resistance. It is generally believed that cultivated potato in Europe derived from *S. tuberosum* ssp. *andigena* materials brought in from Andean countries by the Spaniards (52). As noted above, this has recently been questioned by Grun (19) who used molecular techniques to determine a much closer relationship between the cultivated ssp. *tuberosum* group and the ssp. *tuberosum* from Chile and Argentina.

This implies that the 'type' of non-hypersensitive resistance in ssp. *andigena* and *S. phureja* might differ from that of ssp. *tuberosum*. Our observations in Ecuador support this belief, at least for *S. phureja*. We found a very wide genetic variability in a sample of the Ecuadorian national collection tested in 1991 (Figure 1.). Several of the clones in this relatively small sample of 50 were more resistant than the advanced cultivars 'Monserrate' and 'Superchola', which were bred for resistance to late blight. More importantly for a discussion of resistance types, the resistant *S. phureja* clones appeared to have high levels of resistance at all stages of plant growth, unlike that of the *tuberosum* resistance type. Thurston et al. (40) also reported high levels of resistance in accessions of *S. phureja*.

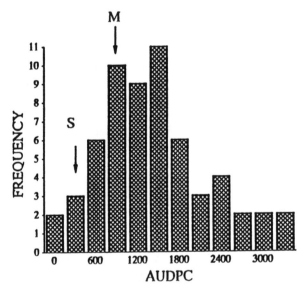

Figure 1. Histogram of resistance levels based on the area under disease progress curve (AUDPC) of a sample (n=50) of *S. phureja* clones from the Ecuadorian national collection. 'M' indicates level of cv. 'Monserrate' (AUDPC = 670) and 'S' indicates level of cv. 'Superchola' (AUDPC= 473). Standard error of the difference between the two clones = 270 AUDPC units.

S. phureja is considered one of the primary sources of resistance to bacterial wilt caused by *Pseudomonas solanacearum* E.F.Smith but has not been widely used for resistance to late blight. Nonetheless, recent findings (L. Turkensteen, personal communication) indicate that the primary source of resistance in cv. 'Cruza 148' may be a *S. phureja* clone. 'Cruza 148', one of most resistant, tropically-adapted cultivars we know of, is widely grown in East Africa.

It is valid to question why resistant materials such as *S. phureja* may go unnoticed by researchers interested in resistance to late blight. Part of the answer may be that this species has no major genes for resistance and has traditionally been evaluated solely on the value of its non-hypersensitive resistance. This resistance probably has appeared unattractive in many instances when compared with segregating materials or clones containing unidentified R-genes that interfere with the expression of non-hypersensitive resistance. R-gene expression is a complex phenomena which is still not fully understood. The second part of this chapter attempts to deal with this problem, which we feel has been a crucial factor limiting success of resistance breeding for many years.

R-GENE INTERFERENCE

Plant Breeding

Before moving on the the problem of R-gene interference per se., we would like to make a comment about plant breeding. Non-hypersensitive resistance appears to be a quantitatively inherited trait for which long-established breeding procedures should be very effective. Simmonds (36) demonstrated that a susceptible population of *S. tuberosum* ssp. *andigena* could consistently be moved toward greater resistance through recurrent selection. This work was done in the UK, out of the natural habitat of the plant species. Many other *Solanum* species have been evaluated for non-hypersensitive resistance and highly-resistant accessions have been identified (9). Several authors discuss sources of resistance to late blight (9,11,47,52).

Regardless of the efficacy of breeding tactics, successes will be reduced or nil if the desired trait can not be measured. This is the crux of the problem today, especially for developing countries where potato production relies so heavily on resistance to late blight.

Immunity

The most conspicuous and, therefore, least dangerous form of R-gene interference is hypersensitivity, often manifested as immunity at the plant level. A good example is illustrated by comparing data from trials in East Africa and Bolivia involving the two cultivars, 'Sangema' and 'Cruza 148' in 1989 and 1990, respectively (Table 1). Both are grown widely in East Africa where 'Cruza 148' has maintained a high level of resistance and 'Sangema' a moderate level. When both were assessed Bolivia, 'Cruza 148' performed as expected but 'Sangema' was not infected. 'Cruza 148' has no R-genes; 'Sangema' is believed to have only one or two of the more common R-genes R1 through R4 (L. Turkensteen, personal communication). In most parts of the world, these R-genes would be matched by virulent races, but virulent races apparently were not present in Bolivia. In Rionegro, Colombia, 'Sangema' is always infected early and has not expressed incompatibility with the predominant local races.

Table 1. An example of hypersensitivity in cultivar Sangema in Bolivia

Country	Clone	Weekly Readings CIP Scale[1]	AUDPC[2]
RWANDA	Cruza-148	2 2 3 5 5	665
	Sangema	2 4 5 7 9	1776
BOLIVIA	Cruza-148	2 3 3 4 4	236
	Sangema	1 1 1 1 1	0

1 The CIP scale ranges from 1 to 9, where 1 = no infection and 9 = 100% foliage infected.
2 AUDPC refers to area under the disease progress curve, where percentage infection is ploted against time.

Unidentified R-genes in Segregating Populations

Probably one of the most potentially confusing effects of hypersensitive resistance is its phenotypic interaction with non-hypersensitive resistance when R-genes are present in segregating populations. At CIP, we have recently begun analyzing populations of this type grown in Rionegro, Colombia, where complex races with virulence for R-genes R1-R4, R6,R7,R10 and R11 are frequently found, but simpler races are also found, especially early in the season. The predominant race is not known, if one exits.

Histograms of grouped frequency distributions based on the 'area under disease progress curve' (AUDPC) of populations containing unidentified R-genes are of many different patterns. A random sample of four families presented here illustrates this heterogeneity (Figure 2). In some cases, such as family D, the hypersensitive or nearly-hypersensitive members of the family separate out distinctly, leaving a seemingly normal distribution of resistance levels. In many other cases, however, the separation between different types of resistance is less obvious (see families A, B and C, Figure 2).

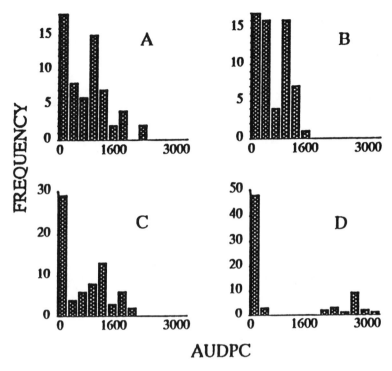

Figure 2. Histograms of resistance levels based on the area under disease progress curve (AUDPC) of four families (A-D) suspected of having unidentified R-genes.

In any case, these families usually have different distributions for AUDPC than do those with no R-genes, which segregate more as one would expect for a quantitatively inherited trait (Figure 3). Small numbers of plants in these families sometimes appear as outliers, which may represent escapes or contamination of pollen from plants with R-genes.

These histograms help identify potential mixtures of populations within families that are almost impossible to distinguish in the field. This points to what may be one of the greatest fallacies in the historical endeavor to control late blight with host resistance, that hypersensitive and non-hypersensitive resistance types can be easily sorted out in the field. In fact, the hypersensitive "type" of resistance resembles high levels of non-hypersensitive resistance under many circumstances. Furthermore, hypersensitive resistance often interacts with non-hypersensitive resistance in ways that generally lead to an overestimation of the latter. A few of the ways this may happen are discussed below.

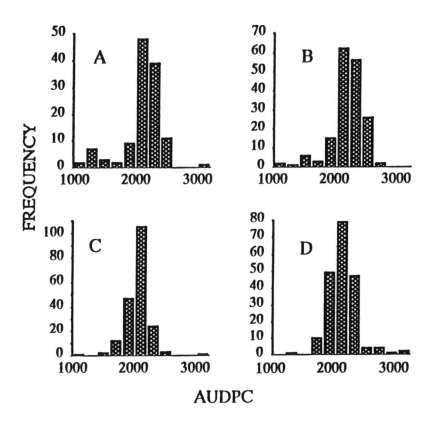

Figure 3. Histograms of resistance levels based on the area under disease progress curve (AUDPC) of four families (A-D) assumed to have no R-genes.

Impartial Expression of Major Genes

It is now known that some of the major genes (R2,R4,R10,R11) do not prevent infection with incompatible races, at least under certain conditions. The real epidemiological effects of this partial incompatibility have not been quantified, but at least one case has been documented where very susceptible cultivars were erroneously selected for high levels of non-hypersensitive resistance. These cultivars were released and rapidly succumbed to compatible races (29).

The problem of interactions between non-hypersensitive and hypersensitive resistance types (horizontal and vertical) was discussed by Vanderplank in his first book on epidemiology (48). He warned about the problems of screening with mixed or unidentified races and suggested that these problems would occur even in the Toluca valley of Mexico. Our experiences in CIP substantiate his warning. In small plots in Toluca, segregates often are not infected until late in the season and may remain uninfected throughout the season. In one experiment reported by Turkensteen (42), the late blight differential R10 was not infected in Toluca until late in the season.

Turkensteen (42) outlined several of the ways in which incompatibility between R-genes and races present in the field can lead to erroneous measures of non-hypersensitive resistance. These include dilution of inoculum, epidemic delay and what he termed "mimesis of horizontal resistance" which refers to the partial incompatibility described above. Experimental data for the epidemiological effects of some of these interactions are lacking for late blight but have been given by Parlevliet (32) for other pathosystems. Clearly, knowledge of R-gene expression should be the foundation upon which all late blight breeding programs are based.

Unfortunately, in developing countries where interest in resistance breeding has been greatest, there has also been an information gap, probably related to insufficient means of communication and language barriers. Several recent cases of boom and bust cycles in developing countries (Table 2) suggest that there has not been a clear understanding of factors affecting the selection of non-hypersensitive resistance.

Table 2. Several recent cases where cultivars selected for resistance have rapidly been overcome by compatible races.

Cultivar	Country or Region	Non-hypersensitive resistance level
Capiro	Colombia	Low
Esperanza	Ecuador	Moderate
Muziranzara	E. Africa	Low
Muruta	E. Africa	Low
Kinigi	E. Africa	Low

451

Such failures appear to be fewer in developed countries. It is easy to build a case, however, for a general lack of interest in resistance to late blight in developed countries, which has reduced the intensity of resistance breeding. The efficacy and cost effectiveness of fungicides underlie the fact that the most popular cultivars grown in the U.S. and Western Europe, for example, are not very resistant to late blight (39,52).

In principle, the presence of R-genes appears to have minimized the ability of researchers to select non-hypersensitive resistance. The most resistant cultivars currently in use in East Africa are 'Cruza 148', from the Mexican program, and 'Seseni', an old European variety of uncertain origin. Both are free of R-genes and are probably excellent examples of the improved efficacy of selecting for non-hypersensitive resistance when there is no interference of R-genes.

A simple examination of these and several other cultivars originally selected for resistance indicates a pattern of susceptibility associated with rare or incompatible R-genes (Table 3). Three of the cultivars in Table 3, 'Muruta', 'Muziranzara' and 'Kinigi', were selected in East Africa from crosses involving a resistant Mexican clone which has one or more relatively rare R-genes, evidenced by the fact that it is still immune in Colombia. The three cultivars in question apparently were selected more for the expression of R-gene(s) than for non-hypersensitive resistance and are perfect examples of Vertifolia effect (48).

Psychological Interference of R-genes.

The variability of phenotypic expression of R-genes has undoubtedly played a role in the way potato researchers conceive of resistance. Late appearances of compatible races, inoculum dilution, and partial incompatibility lead to ultimate disease levels much lower than that of the best non-hypersensitive resistance currently available. Under high levels of disease, 'Cruza 148' can be killed by late blight in East Africa. This type of resistance is visually less attractive than R-gene resistance which may result in 10 or 15% infection under the same conditions. A potential for false expectations of resistance is created under high disease pressure. Materials with non-hypersensitive resistance have certainly been discarded as "susceptible" relative to spurious levels of R-gene resistance as it is manifested on experiment station farms.

Table 3. A comparison of level of non-hypersensitive resistance and the rarity of R-genes in some important tropically adapted cultivars.

Cultivar	Non-hypersensitive resistance[1]	R-Gene rarity[2]
East Africa		
Cruza 148*	(R)	No R-genes
Seseni	(R)	No R-genes
Uganda 11*	(MR)	Common (R1)
Sangema*	(MR)	Common (?)
Nseko	(MR)	Rare
Muruta	(MS)	Rare
Roslyn Eburu	(S)	Rare
Muziranzara	(S)	Rare
Kinigi	(S)	Rare
Latin America		
Monserrate	(MR)	No R-genes
Capiro	(S)	?[3]

[1]Compiled from conversations with CIP workers in East Africa and from tests in Rionegro, Col.
[2]Rare = currently hypersensitive in Rionegro, Col., and assumed to be hypersensitive when selected in East Africa; Common = no hypersensitivity ever noticed in Rionegro, Col.
[3]Was hypersensitive when selected in Colombia, now susceptible in Rionegro, Col.
*Selected for resistance in Mexico.

Future Considerations

The clue to the needs of the immediate future may lie in the past. The two primary ways of controlling problems of hypersensitivity are simple in principle: (a) inoculating with compatible races; and (b) eliminating those R-genes from breeding populations which are not matched by the local pathogen population. One of these approaches should be utilized at all times with the realization that neither is without pitfalls. Inoculation with compatible races is feasible and is done routinely in the Netherlands (9). For it to work well, the race must be virulent on all materials in the field and background infections must be epidemiologically insignificant.

Elimination of R-genes is easier, especially for multi-site evaluations, because there is no need for pathogen purification, evaluation, maintenance or inoculation. R-gene elimination may require that certain desirable, advanced materials not be used as progenitors. Crosses should be strictly controlled so that R-genes are not inadvertently introduced into populations.

R-gene Free Breeding

CIP has adopted a strategy of eliminating R-genes from its late blight resistance program. This is being done primarily by identifying plants free of R-genes with field or greenhouse inoculations of the plants in question. Putative R-gene free progenitors are verified with progeny tests to insure that resistance segregates in a quantitative manner. Procedures are also being developed to identify R-gene free progeny at the seedling stage from crosses involving advanced materials with unidentified R-genes.

Epilogue

Most of the information presented above can be distilled into the following observation: potato researchers cannot effectively select for non-hypersensitive resistance to late blight unless there is a clear understanding of the types of resistance involved and their respective phenotypic expressions. Furthermore, the complexity of interactions between environment and non-hypersensitive resistance will only be clearly elucidated if the source of resistance is considered. Finally, non-hypersensitive resistance cannot be identified and measured if the effects of R-genes are not controlled.

Acknowledgment

We wish to thank the researchers of the Ecuadorian national potato program of the Instituto Nacional de Investigacion Agropecuaria (INIAP) for their assistance in the evaluation of the *S. phureja* clones.

Literature Cited

1.   Birnbaum, D. 1962. Untersuchungen uber den Stickstoffaushalt von Kartoffelblattern und seine Beziehungen zum *Phytophthora* Befall. Biol. Zentralblatt. 3:355-370.

2.   Bourke, A. 1991. Potato blight in Europe in 1845: the scientific controversy. Pages 12-24 in: Phytophthora. J.A. Lucas, R.C. Shattock, D.S. Shaw, L.R. Cooke, eds. Cambridge Univ. Press, Cambridge. 447 pp.

3.   Buczacki, S.T. 1991. The reverend Miles Berkeley. Pages 1-11 in Phytophthora. J.A. Lucas, R.C. Shattock, D.S. Shaw, L.R. Cooke, eds. Cambridge Univ. Press, Cambridge. 447 pp.

4. Carnegie, S.F. and Colhoun, J. 1982. Susceptibility of potato leaves to *Phytophthora infestans* in relation to plant age and leaf position. Phytopath. Z. 104: 157-167.

5. Caten, C. E. 1974. Intra-racial variation in *Phytophthora infestans* and adaptation to field resistance for potato blight. Ann. Appl. Biol. 77:259-270.

6. Child, J.J. and Fothergill, P.G. 1967. The amino acid content of potato plant varieties and their resistance to attack by *Phytophthora* species. J. Science of Food and Agric. 18:3-7.

7. Clark, M.C. 1974. Metabolism of adenine in healthy and blighted potato leaves. J. Exper. Botany. 25:309-319.

8. Clarke, D.D. 1983. Potato late blight: a case study. Pages 3-17 in Biochemical Plant Pathology. J.A. Callow, ed. John Wiley & Sons Ltd., New York.

9. Colon, L.T. and Budding, D.J. 1988. Resistance to late blight (*Phytophthora infestans*) in ten wild Solanum species. Euphytica S:77-86.

10. Deahl, K.L., Gallegley, M.E., and Young, R.J. 1974. Laboratory testing of potato tubers for multigenic resistance to late blight. Am. Potato J. 51: 324-329.

11. Dowley, L.J., O'Sullivan, E., and Kehɔe, H.W. 1991. Development and evaluation of blight resistant potato cultivars. Pages 373-382 in: Phytophthora. J.A. Lucas, R.C. Shattock, D.S. Shaw, L.R. Cooke, eds. Cambridge Univ. Press, Cambridge. 447 pp.

12. Elliot, C.G. and Knights, B.A. 1969. Interactions between steroids in the growth of *Phytophthora*. J. Science of Food and Agric. 20:406-408.

13. Fehrmann, H. and Dimond, A.E. 1967. Peroxidase activity and *Phytophthora* resistance in different organs of the potato plant. Phytopathology 57:69-72.

14. Fehrmann, H. and Dimond, A.E. 1967. Relation of indole-acetic acid to some physiological processes in pathogenesis. Phytopathology 59:105-121.

15. Freind, J. 1991. Host-plant interactions: current questions. Pages 46-49 in. Phytophthora. J.A. Lucas, R.C. Shattock, D.S. Shaw, and L.R. Cooke eds. Cambridge Univ. Press. Cambridge. 447 pp.

16. Fry W. E. and Spielman L. J. 1991. Population biology. Pages 171-192 in: Advances in Plant Pathology - vol 7. Academic Press Ltd.

17. Graham, K.M. 1963. Inheritance of resistance to Phytophthora infestans in two diploid Mexican species. Euphytica 12:35-40.

18. Grainger, J. 1956. Host nutrition and attack by fungal parasites. Phytopathology 46:445-456.

19. Grun, P. 1990. The evolutions of cultivated potatoes. Econ. Botany 44:39-45.

20. Guzman-N, J. 1964. Nature of partial resistance of certain clones of three *Solanum* species to *Phytophthora infestans*. Phytopathology 54: 1398-1404.

21. Henniger, H. and Bartel, W. 1963. Die Eignung des Peroxydaseaktivitat-Testes zur Bestimmung der relativen *Phytophthora* "resistenz". Zuchter 33:86-91.

22. James, R. V. and Fry, W. E. 1983. Potential for *Phytophthora infestans* to adapt to potato cultivars with rate reducing resistance.

23.   Jeffery, S. I. B., Jinks, J. L., and Grindle, M. 1962. Intraracial variation in *Phytophthora infestans* and field resistance to potato blight. Genetica 32:323-338.

24.   Kedar, N. 1959. The peroxidase test as a tool in the selection of potato varieties resistant to late blight. Am. Potato J. 36: 315-324.

25.   Lapwood, D.H. 1968. Observations on the infecton of potato leaves by *Phytophthora infestans*. Trans. British Mycol. Sco. 51: 233-240.

26.   Latin, R.X., MacKenzie, D.R., and Cole, H., Jr. 1981. The influence of host and pathogen genotypes on the apparent infection rates of potato late blight epidemics. Phytopathology 71:82-85.

27.   Main, C.E. and Gallegley, M.E. 1964. The disease cycle in relation to multigenic resistance of potato to late blight, Am. Potato J. 41: 387-400.

28.   Melard, V. 1961. L'Amelioration de la resistance a *Phytophthora* de la pomme de terre en Belgique. European Potato J. 4:40-51.

29.   Mooi, J. C. 1977. Host infection in incompatible interactions between R10 genotypes of potato and races of *Phytophthora infestans*. Potato Res. 20:272.

30.   Parker, J. M. 1989. Stability of disease expression in the potato late blight pathosystem. PhD thesis, Cornell University, Ithaca, New York.

31.   Parleviet, J. E., Identification and evaluation of quantitiative resistance. 1989. Pages 215-247 in Plant Disease Epidemiology. Vol. 2: Genetics, Resistance, and Management. McGraw-Hill, NY.

32.   Person, C. O. 1959. Gene-for-gene relationships in host:pathogen relationships. Can. J. Bot. 37:1101-30.

33.   Ross, H. 1986. Potato Breeding - Problems and perspectives. Advances in Plant Breeding. 13. Parey, Berlin.

34.   Rotem, J. and Sari, A. 1983. Fertiliztion and age controlled predisposition of potatoes to sporulation of and infection by *Phytophthora infestions*. Z. Pflanzenkrankh. Pflanzenschutz 90: 83-88.

35.   Schober, B. 1971. Physiologische Veranderungen in der Kartoffelknolle nach Verletzung and Infektion mit *Phytophthora infestans*. Potato Res. 14:39-48.

36.   Simmonds, N.W. 1966. Studies of the tetraploid potatoes 3. Progress in the experimental recreation of the Tuberosum group. J. of the Linnean Society (Botany) 59:279-288.

37.   Spielman, L.J., Drenth, A., Davidse, L.C., Sujkowski, L.J., Gu, W., Tooley, P. W. and Fry, W. E. 1991. A second world-wide migration and population displacement of *Phytophthora infestans*. Plant Pathology. 40:422-430.

38.   Thurston, H.D. 1971. Relationship of general resistance: late blight of potato. Phytopathology 61:620-627.

39.   Thurston, H.D. 1978. Potentialities for pest management in potatoes. Pages 117-136 in: Pest Control Strategies. Academic Press, Inc.

40.   Thurston, H.D., Heidrick, L.E. and Guzman J.N. (1962). Partial resistance to *Phytophthora infestans* De Bary within the coleccion central colombiana. Am. Potato J.. 39:63-69.

41.   Toxopeus, H.J. 1958. Some notes on the relations between field resistance to *Phytophthora infestans* in leaves and tubers and ripening time in *Solanum tuberosum* subsp. *tuberosum*. Euphytica 7: 123-130.

42.   Turkensteen, L.J. 1989. Interaction of R-genes in breeding for resistance of potatoes against *Phytophthora infestans*. Pages 85-96 in: Fungal

Diseases of the Potato, Report of the Planning Conference on Fungal Diseases of the Potato, International Potato Center, Lima 212 pp.

43.   Ullrich, J. and Krug, H. 1965. Der einfluss von Tageslange und Temperatur auf die relative resistenz einiger Kartoffelsorten gegenuber *Phytophthora infestans* Mont. de Bary. Phytopath. 52: 295-303.

44.   Umaerus, V. 1959. The relationship between peroxidase activity in potato leaves and resistance to *Phytophthora infestans*. Am. Potato Journal. 36:124-131

45.   Umaerus, V. 1971. Studies on field resistance to *Phytophthora infestans*. Z. Pflanzenzuchtung 63:1-23.

46.   Umearus, V., and Stalhammer, M. 1969. Studies on field resistance to *Phytophthora infestans*. 3. Screening of *Solanum* species for field resistance to *P.infestans*. Z. Pflanzenzuchtung 62: 6-19.

47.   Umearus, V., Umaerus, M., Erjefalt, L., and Nilsson, B. A. 1983. Control of *Phytophthora* by host resistnce: Problems and progress. Pages 315-326 in. Phytophthora: Its Biology, Taxonomy, Ecology, and Pathology D. C. Erwin, S. Bartnicki-Garcia, and P.H. Tsao, eds. Am. Phytopath. Society. St. Paul, Mn. 392. pp.

48.   Vanderplank, 1963. Plant Disease: Epidemics and Control. Academic Press, New York, 344 pp.

49.   Vanderplank, J. E. 1971. Stability of resistance to *Phytophthora infestans* in cultivars without R-genes. Potato Res. 14: 263-270.

50.   Van Oijen, M. 1991. Identification of the major characteristics of potato cultivars which affect yield loss caused by late blight. PhD thesis. Agricultural University, Wageningen.

51.   Warren, R.C., King, J.E. and Colhoun, J. 1973. Reaction of potato leaves to infection by *Phytophthora infestans* in relation to position on the plant. Trans. British Mycol. Soc. 57: 501-514.

52.   Wastie, R. E. 1991. Breeding for resistance. Pages 193-224 in: Advances in plant pathology - vol 7. Academic Press Ltd.

53.   Weindlmayr, J. 1963. Untersuchungen uber eine Beeinflussung der *Phytophthora* Anfalligkeit von Kartoffelpflanzen durch Gibberellin Behandlung. Z. Pflanzenkrankheit Pflanzenschutz 70:599-609.

PART IX

Modeling and Expert Systems in Potato Pest Management

MODELING THE EFFECTS OF COLORADO POTATO BEETLE AND EARLY BLIGHT DEFOLIATION ON POTATO GROWTH AND YIELD

E. E. Ewing[1], K. P. Sandlan[2],
and A. G. Nicholson[3]
Cornell University
Ithaca, New York 14853

A crop growth model that contains physiological detail is needed for integrated pest management (IPM) studies with potato (*Solanum tuberosum* L.). Such a model, when linked with pest models, will simulate the effects of damage from pests under various soil and climatic conditions. The linked models could then be used for optimization studies to improve management strategies (3). In this chapter we summarize studies with a crop growth model and preliminary efforts to use it for simulating the effects of defoliation of potato by the Colorado potato beetle (CPB), *Leptinotarsa decemlineata* Say, and by early blight, *Alternaria solani* (Ellis & Martin) Sorauer.

A model is by definition a simplification of the "real thing." Complex relationships must be simplified to be inserted into the code of a simulation model. Furthermore, it is inevitable that any attempt to construct a detailed, physiological model of a growing plant will reveal enormous gaps in our knowledge of the processes involved. Theoretically, by identifying the gaps in knowledge one can plan experiments that will provide the missing information and permit the modeler to establish valid relationships. However, if the information gaps are too extensive, the modeler may decide to proceed in the absence of data by inserting hypothetical relationships into the code. To be sure that the simplifications and the untested hypotheses have not led to errors, validations must be performed with field data to test whether the model is reliable over the range of conditions for which it is intended.

---

[1]Department of Fruit and Vegetable Science
[2]Department of Plant Pathology
[3]Program on Ethics and Public Life

It is our experience that the reactions of the potato plant to CPB defoliation are exceedingly complex. We have information about the qualitative nature of the reactions, but very limited quantitative data under field conditions. Variables to consider include degree of defoliation, portion of the plant defoliated, stage of plant development, previous defoliation history, subsequent defoliation, presence of other pests, cultivar, and a host of environmental factors. Interactions among these variables must also be studied. Thus a huge data base is required to simulate the effects of CPB defoliation on plant development.

Lacking such data for constructing and testing individual hypotheses, we have inserted our hypotheses, run the model with weather data from a CPB defoliation experiment, and compared model output to field data. Although the general nature of the relationships have been based upon experimental observation, by necessity the numerical values chosen have been arbitrary. Only in a few instances were experimental data available upon which to construct hypotheses. When the agreement with field data was poor, we have modified the hypotheses and repeated the runs. Because the hypotheses adopted are interdependent, many iterations were required to find a set of modifications that were consistent with the field observations. Eventually two versions of the model were selected that fit the CPB field data reasonably well. These two were tested against the data from a second CPB experiment that had not been previously used for model development.

With such a methodology it is obvious that agreement of model output with field observations is no assurance that the individual hypotheses leading to the output were correct. Much more extensive validation would be required, and we expect that many modifications to the model would prove necessary.

The approach taken to simulate the effects of early blight was similar to the CPB model, except that the available data sets were less complete in terms of model requirements. For example, no data were available for dry weights of leaves, stems, and tubers at intervals during the growing season. Therefore the early blight simulation is even more tentative than the CPB simulation.

Our purpose in this chapter is not to claim that we have accomplished the goal of developing a model that simulates the effects of pest defoliation, but rather to identify factors that should be considered in developing such a model, to emphasize the complexities, and to outline approaches for solving the problems. We present only a descriptive summary of the code changes for modeling CPB and early blight. The actual codes are available from the authors upon request.

Model Selection

We have chosen the model 'POTATO' (7) to be used for IPM studies. Of the many published models of the potato crop, POTATO contains the most physiological detail. Unlike most other potato models, simulation in POTATO is at the level of individual main stem leaves and branch leaves rather than at the canopy level only. This presents the option of simulating pest damage to leaves of different ages and of following the progress of each damaged leaf through growth, maturation, and senescence. The fact that the model accounts for branching permits simulation of increased branching in response to certain types of defoliation.

Changes to the Model

Many changes were necessary before we could use POTATO for IPM studies in New York. The model was developed for the 'Russet Burbank' cultivar under Idaho conditions. The original version was designed for crops grown at optimal levels of soil moisture and fertility and in the absence of pests. We have made extensive modifications to the original model, changing hypotheses related to carbon assimilation, the partitioning of dry matter to various organs, and the responses to temperature and photoperiod (1). Subsequently we combined our new version with a second new version (9), which was developed in the laboratory of one of the originators of POTATO, and which simulates the effects of soil moisture on plant growth. The combined model was calibrated for New York under conditions of well watered soils, but it is yet to be validated with respect to soil moisture responses.

Simulation of Defoliation

We added the ability to use consecutive estimates of the percentage of canopy defoliated by a pest to compute the leaf dry weights consumed (4). The resulting model incorporated the effect of defoliation on decreased ability to carry out photosynthesis because of decreases in leaf area.

Simulating the effect of loss of photosynthetic area was necessary but not sufficient to model the effects of pest defoliation. Still required was the simulation of compensatory leaf growth, a response that has been observed repeatedly in potato after artificial defoliation (2) and defoliation by CPB (6). Factors responsible for the compensatory leaf growth include increased axillary branching, delayed leaf senescence, more rapid leaf expansion, and higher rates of photosynthesis per unit leaf area compared to undefoliated plants (5).

These effects were added to the revised model and were made to depend upon the severity of defoliation and upon how recently defoliation occurred. Defoliation of young and old leaves is tracked separately. The effects of defoliation increase with increasing defoliation levels, and they decay exponentially with time.

Effect of Defoliation on Leaf Age

In POTATO the age of a leaf affects, among other traits, the leaf's growth rate, its ability to carry on photosynthesis, and the time of its death (7). In our version of POTATO, leaf age is counted in modified degree days (1). The observed effects of defoliation on delaying "aging" of leaves is simulated by subtraction from the age of the leaf.

The fraction of dry weight of each leaf that was consumed by CPB is obtained from the estimate of pest defoliation as described in Heym et al. (4). This value is calculated for each leaf. The extent to which this value affects the age of a given leaf is made to depend upon how old the leaf was at the time of defoliation and how recently the defoliation occurred.

Effect of Leaf Loss on Photosynthesis

We have evidence that under some conditions, defoliation stimulates the photosynthetic rate of the remaining leaf tissue (5). Because leaf age affects photosynthesis in the original model, the above effects of defoliation on leaf age exert an indirect effect on photosynthesis. We have also added a more direct effect on photosynthesis that operates at the canopy level. The effect is at a maximum between 5 and 7 days after each defoliation event occurred, increasing from 0 on day 0 and decreasing to 0 by day 14. This relationship is based upon data (5) which indicate that the stimulation of photosynthesis is optimal about one week after the defoliation occurs.

Effect of Defoliation on Branching

It is a common observation that axillary branching tends to decrease as stem density increases, or as irradiance levels decrease, suggesting a negative relationship between competition for light by individual leaves and branch initiation. Some of the hypotheses in the original version of POTATO (7) and in our modified version (1) indirectly produced such a relationship, but only weakly. We have made the relationship more direct by connecting the rate of branch initiation to the leaf area, which is in turn affected by defoliation. We have also installed an effect of early defoliation on the earliness of branch initiation.

Effects of Defoliation on the Relation Between
Percent Age Reserves and Leaf and Stem Growth

Partitioning in POTATO is partially controlled through the effects of the concentration of assimilate in the reserve pool on the growth rates of the various organs (1). This concentration is expressed as a percentage of the total dry weight of the plant. We have caused defoliation to produce a shift in partitioning of assimilate away from tubers toward leaves and stems when the concentration of assimilate in the reserve pool is limiting leaf growth. Thus heavy defoliation favors more leaf growth at the expense of tuber and root growth. In a parallel manner but to a lesser extent, stem growth is favored by defoliation.

Effect of Defoliation on Reserves

We hypothesize that CPB damage causes wound respiration, interferes with translocation, and in other respects may tend to reduce the effective level of assimilate. Therefore we introduced an effect of defoliation on the concentration of assimilate in the reserve pool, which in turn affects many aspects of growth in POTATO.

Simulation of Field Data
From CPB Experiments

Data from a 1987 experiment (5) with varying degrees of defoliation by the CPB were used to develop the above hypotheses on the effects of defoliation, and data from a similar experiment in 1988 (5) were used for a partial validation. The validation was limited because two versions of the model that fit the 1987 data equally well were compared, and a choice was made between the two based upon the 1988 data.

The field experiments will be described in detail elsewhere (Nicholson, Ewing, and Tingey, in preparation). Briefly, they consisted of three treatments each year: 1) low defoliation, accomplished by season-long application of permethrin; 2) medium defoliation, accomplished by application of permethrin only after emergence of the second CPB brood; 3) and high defoliation, where there was either no permethrin (1987), or it was applied very late in the season (1988).

Simulation of leaf dry weights in the absence of CPB. Before considering the ability to simulate CPB damage, it is useful to examine the ability of the model to simulate leaf production in the absence of the pest. Insect defoliation in the 'low' treatment was minimal both years, so the data from these treatments can be used for this test. Unlike the defoliation routines, the basic model was developed without reference to the data of 1987; thus the data from both years are suitable for validation of the model in the absence of defoliation.

In 1987 leaf dry weights were underpredicted at four of the five biomass harvests, with a discrepancy of about 15% at the peak (Fig. 1A). In 1988 agreement with the first three harvests was excellent, but simulations for the leaf dry weights at the last three harvests were seriously in error (Fig. 2A). Leaves senesced very slowly in 1988, a season of exceptionally warm temperatures, and the model failed to predict the slow senescence.

Simulation of leaf dry weights with CPB present, 1987. For ease of comparison the simulation for zero defoliation (results expected if plots had been completely free from defoliating pests) is reproduced beside the simulation curve for each of the three treatments (Fig. 1). The simulations for leaf dry weights in the zero and low defoliation differed only slightly from each other (Fig. 1A). The medium (Fig. 1B) defoliation treatment caused only slightly more deviation from the no defoliation line. Even though CPB feeding in the medium treatment had caused more than 20% defoliation by the time permethrin was applied (5), measured leaf weight at the fifth harvest was fully as high as in the low defoliation treatment, indicating compensatory leaf growth. The latter effect can be seen to a small degree in the simulated curve 85-95 days after emergence (compare Fig. 1A with 1B). The absence of any permethrin application to the high defoliation treatment caused its defoliation to diverge from the medium treatment after day 59, and a decrease in leaf weight caused by heavy feeding of the CPB can be seen shortly thereafter in both the simulated and field data (compare Fig. 1B with 1C).

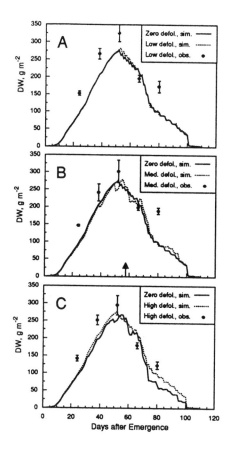

Fig. 1. Leaf dry weights (g m⁻²) measured in field plots from three levels of CPB control compared with simulated results, 1987. Low defoliation (A) was obtained by season-long application of permethrin; medium defoliation (B), by permethrin application on 4 August (marked by arrow); and high defoliation (C) by the absence of permethrin. The measured dry weight is shown for each biomass harvest, with a bracket indicating the S.E. at $P = 0.05$. The solid line (presented in all three treatments to facilitate comparisons among treatments) shows the results predicted in the complete absence of pest defoliation. The broken lines show the simulated leaf dry weights for the respective treatments. The absicissa represents days after 50% plant emergence, 6 June 1987.

Simulation of leaf dry weights with CPB present, 1988. The defoliation pressure in 1988 was more severe than in 1987; but by making 11 applications of permethrin, the CPB population was well controlled in the low defoliation treatment (5). Consequently, the simulations for zero and low defoliation were again virtually identical (Fig. 2A). Just as the rate of senescence was badly underestimated in the low defoliation treatment (Fig. 2A), predictions were similarly in error in the medium (Fig. 2B) and high (Fig. 2C) defoliation treatments. Once the permethrin was applied to the medium defoliation treatment, leaf growth recovered and there was evidence of compensatory growth in plants harvested 84 days after emergence (compare Fig. 2A with 2B). Simulated leaf weights for the medium treatment were somewhat higher than in the low defoliation treatment after the time of permethrin application, but the compensatory leaf growth simulated at the end of the season was less than that measured in the field (Fig. 2A,B). In contrast to the results at the end of the season for the medium treatment (Fig. 2B), neither the field data nor the simulated values for the high defoliation treatment were consistently higher in leaf weight than the equivalent data in the low defoliation treatment (compare Fig. 2A and 2C). One explanation is that the absence of insecticide in the high defoliation treatment until 2 weeks after initial application had begun in the medium treatment permitted considerably more CPB damage to the high treatment (Fig. 2C).

Predictions of yield loss from CPB. Simulations of tuber yields (dry weights) in the low defoliation treatment were 10.5 t/ha in 1987 and 8.3 t/ha in 1988 (Table 1). Dry matter yields estimated from observed fresh weights from the low defoliation treatment were only 6.8 t/ha in 1987 and 6.3 t/ha in 1988. One explanation for the discrepancies is that simulations are based upon hand-harvested yields of healthy plants from small plots. Machine-harvested yields of large plots produce 10-20% lower yields, both because recovery of tubers is less and because of weak or missing plants. A second reason for the lower measured yields may be associated with a certain amount of aerial blackleg (*Erwinia* stalk rot) and other disease problems that were noted in the low defoliation plots toward the end of the season. Even allowing for these two explanations, it seems clear that the simulated values were too high, especially in 1987.

However, for purposes of evaluating the model's ability to simulate defoliation it is useful to examine the relative yield changes that were associated with the CPB defoliation treatments. Therefore fresh weight yields of tubers in the medium and high defoliation treatments are presented as percentages of the low defoliation yields (Table 1); and simulated yields of tuber dry weights are presented in the same manner (Table 1).

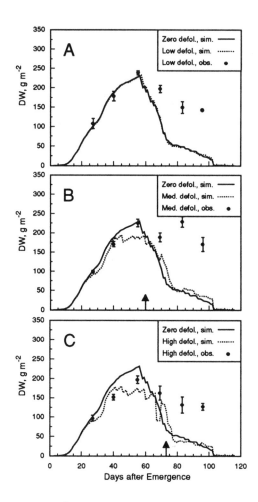

Fig. 2. Leaf dry weights (g m⁻²) measured in field plots from three levels of CPB control compared with simulated results, 1988. Low defoliation (A) was obtained by season-long application of permethrin; medium defoliation (B), by delaying permethrin applications until 2 August (marked by arrow); and high defoliation (C) by delaying permethrin applications until 15 August (marked by arrow). The date of 50% plant emergence was 3 June 1988. Other details are as described for Fig. 1.

There was good agreement between the effects of the two CPB treatments on tuber dry weight and the observed effects on tuber fresh weight for the 1987 data that were used in developing the model (Table 1). In 1988 there was again good agreement between the simulated and measured effects. Measured yields in the medium defoliation treatment

Table 1. Simulated and observed tuber yields in the medium and high defoliation treatments as percentages of the tuber yields in the low defoliation treatment.

Year	Treatment	Simulated[a]	Observed[b]
1987	Medium	97%	99%
	High	87%	86%
1988	Medium	104%	111%
	High	90%	88%

[a]Simulated dry matter yields in the low defoliation treatment were 10.5 t/ha in 1987 and 8.3 t/ha in 1988.
[b]Fresh weight yields ($\pm$ S.E.) measured in the field were 37.0 $\pm$ 0.9 t/ha and 32.5 $\pm$ 3.0 t/ha, respectively, in 1987 and 1988. Based upon estimates derived from specific gravities (10), the observed dry matter yields would be 6.8 $\pm$ 0.2 t/ha in 1987 and 6.3 $\pm$ 0.6 t/ha in 1988.

were 11% higher than in the low defoliation treatment, though the difference was not significant at $P = 0.05$ (5). The simulation showed a 4% difference in the equivalent values (Table 1) as a result of the simulation of compensatory leaf growth (Fig. 2B). In the high defoliation treatment the reductions in measured yields and in simulated yields were in even better agreement than in the medium defoliation treatment (Table 1). The additional CPB feeding at the end of the season prevented the relative increase in leaf dry weight present in the medium defoliation plots (Fig. 2) and caused a reduction in tuber yields (Table 1).

Simulation of early blight. Another goal was to add the ability to simulate effects of early blight. A convenient measure of disease severity in early blight is the degree of defoliation caused by the disease. However, as commonly used, the rating for the fraction defoliated reflects defoliation from natural senescence as well as defoliation caused by early blight. We have devised a method to take this into account when calculating disease severity from scouting reports.

Because old leaves are most affected, we do not expect that defoliation leads to compensatory leaf growth. On the contrary, senescence is accelerated. Therefore to simulate attack by early blight we advance the age of leaves on infected plants, with oldest leaves most affected. When estimates of defoliation call for leaf death, this is simulated by causing the leaves to die in order of age, the oldest first.

The effect on leaf senescence is accomplished by adjusting upward the age (in modified degree days) of an individual leaf in proportion to the severity of the defoliation caused by the disease, and in proportion to the difference between the present age of the leaf and the age which separates young leaves from old leaves.

We assumed that there is a net loss of assimilate through reduced rates of photosynthesis and/or metabolic use by the causal fungus, so we cause the disease to diminish the concentration of assimilate in the reserve pool. This tends to reduce growth of all organs of the plant.

Simulations of hypothetical canopy losses caused by early blight produced losses in tuber yield that appeared consistent with generally observed effects, but no attempts have been made to validate the early blight routine. A difficulty of using actual scouting reports is that small errors in predicting defoliation caused by natural senescence may produce large errors in estimating the severity of defoliation caused by early blight. We have investigated the feasibility of linking POTATO with a simple early blight model (8). Because of limitations in the way the early blight model treated plant development, we concluded that linkage of the two models was not the best approach. Instead the hypotheses concerning disease progress will be transferred from the simple model into the modified POTATO.

Epilogue

It is generally acknowledged that highly explanatory models are less successful than simple regression models at predicting yields in the particular location and environment used to develop the models. Adherents of highly explanatory models usually argue that this disadvantage is offset by the greater flexibility and transportability of their models. It is difficult to see how a simple regression model could cope with the variety of responses to be expected from multiple pest attacks, some of which would elicit compensatory growth.

An obvious disadvantage of a highly explanatory model is the complexity of inserting correct hypotheses to achieve reliable simulations. We began our studies with POTATO more than ten years ago, and there are still a number of improvements that must be made before we can utilize it effectively in an IPM program. Soil moisture regimes are simulated, but responses have not been validated. We have made no attempt to model soil nitrogen or other aspects of soil fertility. The model badly overestimated the rate of leaf senescence in control plots in 1988. In plots defoliated by the CPB, the degree of compensatory leaf growth appears to have been underestimated in 1988. Early blight responses have not been tested against field data, and the work of inserting hypotheses from the early blight model into the code of POTATO is only started. Also underway (by other workers) is the linkage of our version of POTATO to a CPB model.

One of the most difficult aspects of modeling is the limited availability of data sets suitable for use in the formulation and validation of hypotheses. Work on modeling pest defoliation should benefit greatly if modelers and those who cooperate with them will plan in advance the kind of data that are needed, and if ways can be found to share data sets among all interested parties.

Although a great deal of work must still be done, there has been progress. Hypotheses have been inserted into the code of POTATO which provide a framework for dealing with defoliation by such pests as the CPB and early blight. The simulation of relative yield loss caused by varying degrees of defoliation by the CPB was encouraging. It might be expected that a highly explanatory model will be more successful in predicting *relative* effects of pests on yields than in predicting the actual yields. However, even the prediction of relative effects could be useful in designing IPM strategies.

Acknowledgments

We thank Dr. W. E. Fry for advice on the effects of early blight on plant development and yield, and Dr. K. S. Yourstone for preparing the figures. Dr. W. M. Tingey provided facilities and advice for carrying out the field experiments. Paper No. 23 of the Department of Fruit and Vegetable Science, Cornell University. Supported by USDA Grants 86-CRSR-2-2791, 88-34103-3356, and 90-34103-5103; and Hatch Projects NYS161-475 and NYS161-590.

Literature Cited

1. Ewing, E. E., Heym, W. D., Batutis, E. J., Snyder, R. G., Ben Khedher, M., Sandlan, K. P., and Turner, A. D. 1990. Modifications to the simulation model, 'POTATO' for use in New York. Agric. Syst. 33:173-192.

2. Ewing, E. E., McMurry, S. E., Nicholson, A. G., and Heym, W. D. 1987. Effects of repeated defoliations on the growth and development of the potato plant. (abs.) Pages 111-112 in: Abstracts of Conference Papers and Posters of the 10th Triennial Conference of the European Association of Potato Research. 449 pp.

3. Haith, D. A., Farmer, G. S., and White, G. B. 1987. Models for systems analysis of potato integrated pest management. Agric. Syst. 24:183-197.

4. Heym, W. D., Ewing, E. E., Nicholson, A. G., and Sandlan, K. P. 1990. Simulation by crop growth models of defoliation, derived from field estimates of percent defoliation. Agric. Syst. 33:257-270.

5. Nicholson, A. G. 1991. Compensatory growth of potatoes (*Solanum tuberosum* L.) in response to defoliation. Ph.D. thesis. Cornell University, Ithaca, NY. 201 pp.

6. Nicholson, A. G., and Ewing, E. E. 1989. Assessing compensatory growth following defoliation by the Colorado potato beetle for a potato growth simulation model. (Abs.) Am. Potato J. 66:535-536.

7. Ng, E., and Loomis, R. S. 1984. Simulation of growth and yield of the potato crop. Pudoc, Wageningen, Simulation Monographs. 147 pp.

8. Pelletier, J. R. 1987. Computer simulation of cultivar resistance and fungicide effects on epidemics of potato early blight. Ph.D. thesis. Cornell University, Ithaca, NY. 127 pp.

9. Pinto, P. J. 1988. Computer simulation modeling of the growth and development of the potato crop under different water regimes. Ph.D. thesis. University of California, Davis, CA.

10. Ross, A. F., Jenness, L. C., and Hilborn, M. T. 1959. Determination of total solids in raw white potatoes. Pages 465-468 in: Potato Processing. W. F. Talburt and O. Smith, eds. Avi, Westport. 475 pp.

MANAGING THE POTATO CROP
WITH COMPUTER SOFTWARE

W. R. Stevenson
Department of Plant Pathology
University of Wisconsin-Madison
Madison, WI 53706

The commercial production of potato (*Solanum tuberosum* L.) has never been more challenging. Today's growers are besieged with societal demands to reduce the use of pesticides, fertilizers and irrigation, to produce an environmentally benign crop, to be better stewards of the land, all while improving production efficiency and maintaining a sustainable farming enterprise that will provide livelihood for future generations. Wisconsin growers cultivate approximately 68,000 acres of potatoes with the largest concentration of producers on irrigated sandy loam soils in the central part of the state. Productivity and the risks faced by growers are largely dependent on environmental conditions that vary from year to year. During 1990, Wisconsin growers produced some 23 million hundredweight (cwt) of tubers worth $120 million dollars. A typical grower produced 400 acres of potatoes and, before the season was over, had invested in excess of $1,200 per acre in the production of long season cultivars. The management decisions confronted by an average Wisconsin grower are typical of those experienced by growers in the eastern half of the United States. Those decisions ranging from planting, pest control, and irrigation to harvesting, storage and marketing can be represented as a mosaic with each tile of the mosaic representing a group of closely allied decisions that interact with each of the other decision groups (Fig. 1). Careful consideration of each decision and implementation of the best response will hopefully lead to the harvest of a quality product using the most environmentally benign practices in a manner that is sustainable. Decisions that lead to overuse of pesticides, fertilizer or irrigation, inadequate pest control or crop injury do not meet these criteria.

Ten years ago the typical Wisconsin grower of Russet Burbank potatoes (a long season russet type) sprayed the foliage with fungicide as often as 12 (and sometimes more) times for control of early blight and late blight, applied a systemic insecticide at planting, treated the foliage with

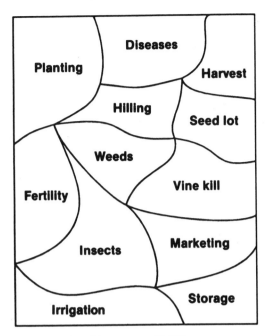

Fig. 1. Production decisions faced by growers.18,000 acres.

insecticide four or more times from emergence to vinekill, treated at least once with herbicide for grass and broadleaf weed control, applied 240+ lb nitrogen per acre, sprayed the foliage with 1-2 applications of growth regulator (maleic hydrazide), killed the vines with 1-2 sprays of vine desiccant in preparation for harvest and storage and irrigated up to three times each week with weekly applications of two or more inches of water, often supplying water in excess of crop needs. Excessive irrigation increases the risk of leaching pesticides and fertilizer into the groundwater and the risk of diseases such as bacterial stem decay, white mold and early blight. Given the detection of insecticides, herbicides and nitrate in the ground-water, pesticide oversprays and drift from field application sites and increased public scrutiny, potato growers soon became the targets for intensive groundwater sampling, pesticide use surveys and pesticide application restrictions. Clearly the industry was ready for and needed a different approach to calendar based, prophylactic and traditional pesticide, irrigation and fertilizer applications.

The Wisconsin Integrated Pest Management (IPM) Program began in 1979 (2) with the goals of improving specific aspects of pest and crop management, reducing crop inputs such as pesticide, irrigation, and fertilizer to economic, environmentally safe and essential levels and maintaining crop profitability. The potato crop received intensive attention in the form of research and extension activities that helped to build strong inter-disciplinary teams as well as a spirit of cooperation between growers and university personnel. After 3 yr of building a program that involved a system of intensive crop and pest scouting combined with regional and in-field weather monitoring, the scouting program was turned over to private enterprise where it continues to thrive. Responses to recent surveys of Wisconsin potato growers indicate that 46% of Wisconsin growers now employ an IPM consultant to scout at least a portion of their acreage while 97% of the growers either scout their own acreage or employ a scouting service.

Computer Technology and Software Development

Computer technology played an important role in the delivery of IPM information and grower acceptance of an IPM philosophy. While our initial focus included the forecasting and improved control of late blight (*Phytophthora infestans* [Mont.] de Bary), a potentially devastating disease of potato, the focus has broadened considerably with time. The concept of disease forecasting was introduced to Wisconsin growers in 1980 through the use of the BLITECAST program (1,3) on a mainframe computer and release in 1983 of software entitled Potato Disease Management (PDM) for forecasting late blight and early blight (*Alternaria solani* [Ell. & Mart.]). The PDM program was used on 40 acres of commercial potatoes in 1983 and by 1985, use expanded to 18,000 acres. Based in part on the success of the disease forecasting and control software and at the request of growers, additional programs were developed that predicted potato emergence, scheduled irrigation and calculated degree days. A version of the PDM software was developed for IBM-compatible microcomputers using MS-DOS in 1985 (6) and by 1987, the PDM soft-ware was used on at least 27,645 acres in a multistate area. As potato growers and the IPM consultants serving them began to adopt computer technology for rapid analysis of environmental and crop surveillance data and decision-making tools, they began to ask for software enhancements to improve ease of use and integration of production components. In 1987 field testing began to evaluate integrated decision support software that used environmental data and information on crop and pest development to predict crop emergence, schedule irrigation, monitor insect development, and forecast and treat the crop for early and late blight control. Based on successes in large field plot evaluations, an integrated program entitled Potato Crop Management (PCM) was released for grower use in 1989

(4,5). The program, designed for IBM-compatible microcomputers using MS-DOS, required 640KB RAM for basic performance and a hard disk with color monitor for optimum performance.

The Potato Crop Management Program

The current PCM program (Ver. 1.2) (Fig. 2A) consists of four primary modules entitled 1) Disease Management, 2) Emergence Prediction, 3) Insect Management and 4) Irrigation Scheduling, plus additional secondary modules that include 1) File Information Data, 2) Data Entry, and 3) Notebook of Field Activities. Each module is accessed through a menu screen (Fig. 2B) where the appropriate module is selected. The program also provides three levels of on-line context sensitive help throughout each module and menu that is accessed by pressing the <F1> key. Much of the information in the printed documentation that accompanies the program is included in the on-line help.

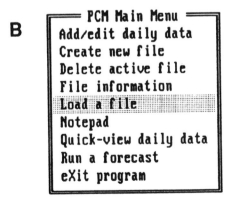

Fig. 2. The opening screen (A) and the PCM Main Menu (B).

Data required for program operation include daily maximum and minimum temperatures, amount of rainfall and water applied by irrigation, estimates of evapotranspiration, density of canopy cover, duration of relative humidity periods at 90% or above, and the maximum and minimum temperatures during these high humidity periods (Fig. 3). Data are collected on the farm by the grower, or in the case of evapotranspiration data used for irrigation scheduling, data are available on a statewide basis by dialing a toll-free telephone number. Most of the growers using the program own recording hygrothermographs that are used in the fields during summer months and in potato storages during the winter months. In some cases, independent crop consultants own and maintain hygrothermographs for individual growers on a fee basis. Data entry is in the format of a spreadsheet with cursor movement between cells located in rows and columns. Files may be updated each day, but it is more common that files are updated every 2-3 days as growers make management decisions.

	7/15	7/16	7/17	7/18	7/19	7/20	7/21
Max. Temp.	87.0	88.0	83.0	88.0	88.0	76.0	77.0
Min. Temp.	67.0	62.0	68.0	68.0	62.0	50.0	53.0
Rainfall	0.30	3.70	0.00	0.00	0.00	0.00	0.40
Irrigation	0.00	0.00	0.00	0.00	0.00	0.00	0.50
ET Estimate	0.16	0.06	0.19	0.11	0.17	0.12	0.13
% Cover	80	80	80	80	80	80	80

Enter data if relative humidity is above 90%

# of Hours	0.0	0.0	0.0	19.0	10.0	14.0	16.0
Max. Temp.	0.0	0.0	0.0	88.0	67.0	68.0	73.0
Min. Temp.	0.0	0.0	0.0	68.0	62.0	50.0	53.0

Fig. 3. Example of data entry screen for the week of July 15.

The disease management module relates specifically to the management of late blight and early blight and is divided into separate screens for each disease (Fig. 4). While late blight is observed about one year in five, early blight appears every year and can become yield limiting if control measures are inadequate. It is critical that fungicide sprays be used when environmental conditions favor disease development. It is also important to reduce or eliminate fungicide sprays when the disease is not present and weather conditions are unfavorable to disease development. Late blight forecasting and spray scheduling continues to use the BLITECAST (1) approach based on the accumulation of severity values and rainfall/irrigation. Early blight forecasting and control recommendations are based on the accumulation of physiological days (P-Days) and the influence of temperature, relative humidity and irrigation/rainfall on disease development.

```
Late blight observed ? N          P-Day threshold : 300
Dates used : 5/22 to 7/19
Choose data display : Forecast
Do you accept these values ? Y


LATE  BLIGHT (Phytophthora infestans) FORECAST
                    ‾‾‾‾‾‾‾‾‾‾   ‾‾‾‾‾‾
                  7/13 7/14 7/15 7/16 7/17 7/18 7/19
Severity Values..|  0 |  3 |  0 |  0 |  0 |  4 |  1 |
Favorability.....|  + |  + |  + |  + |  + |  + |  + |

As of 7/19, late blight severity values TOTAL = 18
( 8 severity values added in the last seven days)

A 5 day spray schedule is recommended at this time
for LATE BLIGHT control.




EARLY  BLIGHT (Alternaria solani) FORECAST
                    ‾‾‾‾‾‾‾‾‾‾   ‾‾‾‾‾‾
                 7/13 7/14 7/15 7/16 7/17 7/18 7/19
P-Day Values   | 7.4 | 7.7 | 7.1 | 9.1 | 8.2 | 9.8 | 9.1 |

As of 7/19, P-Day values TOTAL = 418.9
( 57.5 values added in the last seven days)

Based on environmental factors for the last seven days--
A 7 day spray schedule is recommended at this time
with a mid-range rate of fungicide.
```

[Recommendations based on physiological age of plants]			
Potato Maturity Group	Early-Mid	Late	Very Late
Fungicide Rate	High	Mid	Low
Spray Interval	7 Day	7 Day	7 Day

Fig. 4. Examples of PCM screens related to early and late blight management.

Weed management decisions often revolve around the time of "row cracking" when the soil above a planted seedpiece begins to crack open due to pressure exerted by the potato sprout and the time of 50% emergence when a small green sprout appears aboveground from approximately half of the planted seedpieces. Application of herbicides after emergence may cause plant injury, while careful hilling just prior to expected emergence delays actual emergence and protects the tender potato sprout from herbicide injury. Accurate prediction of "row crack" or emergence improves the timing of cultural and chemical weed management practices. The weed management module uses maximum and minimum temperatures to predict the time of "row crack" and 50% emergence (Fig. 5). The module is tailored for the Wisconsin environment and the cultivars most commonly grown in the state. Evaluation in other states, however, indicates a reasonable correlation between predicted and actual emergence dates.

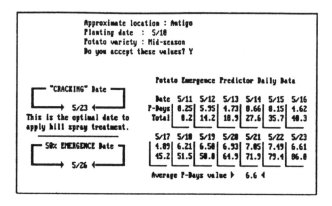

Fig. 5. Example of the weed management screen showing the predicted dates of "row crack" and 50% emergence.

Insect management depends upon the accurate identification of insect species, careful sampling of insect populations and implementation of cultural, biological and chemical controls. Degree day accumulations provide a convenient and effective method for predicting the development of certain insect species such as the Colorado potato beetle. The insect management module of the PCM program utilizes the daily maximum and minimum temperature data to calculate degree days (Fig. 6), thereby permitting the user to predict the appearance of life stages of specific insect species. The method of degree day calculation, base temperatures used for calculation, and the beginning and ending dates for the calculation period are selected by the user. The insect management module also contains an extensive database of insect profiles that detail biological, scouting and control information on potato insects most commonly observed in the Midwest.

The majority of potato acreage in Wisconsin is irrigated to provide a uniform supply of water throughout the growing season. Over-irrigation may lead to leaching of fertilizer and pesticides as well as enhanced disease development while under-irrigation leads to poor

```
View Insect Profiles : N
Computation method   : Arnolds
Dates used :  7/ 1 to  7/12
Lower threshold is  :   52.0

Choose data display : Current TOTAL
Do you accept these values? Y
```

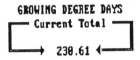

```
        GROWING DEGREE DAYS
     ┌─── Current Total ───┐
     └──┐         ┌──
        └──→ 238.61 ◄──┘
```

Fig. 6. Example of the insect management screen showing the calculation of degree days.

yields and loss in quality. The irrigation scheduling module of PCM uses information on daily rainfall, irrigation, estimates of evapotranspiration and percent crop cover to access water loss and crop needs (Fig. 7). An allowable water deficit (AD) based on crop and soil characteristics is entered at the start of the growing season. As water is added or lost from the field and as the crop canopy increases or decreases each day of the growing season, the program calculates the AD balance and the percentage of the initial AD (% AD Left) that remains. Growers then modify their irrigation practices so that the % AD Left falls between 0 and 100%.

```
AD value for soil : 0.70    Beginning day of data :  5/22
Initial AD BAL :  0.50      Last day of data used :  7/23
Choose data display : Last seven days
Do you accept these values? Y
```

	7/17	7/18	7/19	7/20	7/21	7/22	7/23	Season Totals	Projected AD BAL=
Rainfall	0.00	0.00	0.00	0.00	0.40	0.00	0.00	7.6	
Irrigation	0.00	0.00	0.00	0.00	0.50	0.00	0.00	12.0	7/24 7/25
ET	0.19	0.11	0.17	0.12	0.13	0.22	0.22	12.37	0.00 -0.18
% Cover	80	80	80	80	80	80	80		
Adjusted ET	0.19	0.11	0.17	0.12	0.13	0.22	0.22	10.41	=uses mean ET, last
AD BAL	0.51	0.40	0.23	0.11	0.70	0.40	0.26		4 non-rain
AD Left %	73	57	33	16	126	69	37		days.

Fig. 7. Example of the irrigation management screen showing the calculated AD balance and the % AD left.

Benefits of Adoption

The real test of the software is whether it is used by the clientele for which it was developed and whether it is accomplishing the original goals that spurred its development. Wisconsin growers were surveyed in 1990 to determine production practices. They reported use of management software (PDM and PCM) on an estimated 28,000 acres. It now appears that an additional 20-30,000 acres outside of Wisconsin also benefit from use of this software (Fig. 8). Growers are also reporting an economic benefit from using the software in the range of $700,000 to $900,000 per year for reduced fungicide inputs, a 10-15% reduction in irrigation inputs and improved timing of herbicide and insecticide treatments, often at reduced rates and numbers of sprays. The typical Wisconsin grower who grows Russet Burbank potatoes and uses the PCM software now treats the crop with 8 - 10 sprays of fungicide beginning at 300 P-Days for control of early blight and late blight and applies insecticide sprays to the foliage twice at the minimum rates and at the optimum time to insure highest efficacy. This same typical grower now treats 1 - 2 times with herbicide at the lowest rates needed for weed control while minimizing the potential for crop injury, applies nitrogen fertilizer in split applications in amounts designed to

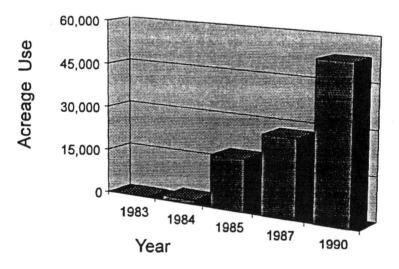

Fig. 8. Adoption of the Potato Disease Management (PDM) and Potato Crop Management (PCM) software by growers. PDM was introduced in 1983 and PCM was introduced in 1989.

meet but not exceed crop requirements, applies 1 - 2 sprays of a growth regulator during mid season, applies a vine desiccant before harvest and irrigates up to 3 times per week with sufficient water to match crop needs and water lost through evapotranspiration. Growers who plant shorter season cultivars and use the PCM program also use substantially less fungicide, insecticide and other inputs than used 10 years ago.

Economics and reductions in crop inputs are important benefits derived from using the PCM software. However, other important long-term benefits have been realized that bode well for future program initiatives. While definitive data have not been collected, it appears that growers who implement the PCM program on their farms tend to be more accepting of the overall IPM philosophy related to reduced reliance on pesticide use and the integrated use of alternative crop and pest management methodology. These same growers appear to be more willing to evaluate new pest and crop management technology as it is developed. There is also a general feeling of partnership and close cooperation between university faculty involved in the development of PCM and those growers adopting this form of technology.

Future Directions

The informal team of university personnel and growers involved in the development of the PCM program have continued to collaborate on integrated multidisciplinary research projects. While initial focus of this research involved the integration of components of potato management with the management of specific pests, current and future focus of research involves specific topics related to potato management plus integrated topics related to the broader farming enterprise. Research projects include crops such as snap bean, sweet corn, red clover and sorghum-sudan that might be grown in rotation with potato and that may provide benefits or liabilities to potato production. From these ongoing and future research projects, the PCM team anticipates development of program modules that relate to additional management decisions which confront growers. Research and module development currently includes those areas listed below:

Seedpiece decay/plant emergence	Soil fertility/plant nutrition
Emergence of weed species	Yield/yield loss projection
Loss of herbicide efficacy	Pest identification
Potato canopy development	Potato storage ventilation
Integration of management thresholds	Economic decision aids
Refined irrigation for improved management of early dying	

Epilogue

Practices used in the production of the potato crop are changing rapidly. To a degree societal issues are driving these changes, but growers themselves are anxious to evaluate and adopt new practices that increase the likelihood of producing a quality crop without risk to the environment. The PCM program provides growers with timely information needed to make accurate management decisions. As growers share in future enhancements of this technology and adopt the software for on-farm use, additional benefits will accrue for both the producer and society.

Acknowledgements

Software development in this project was possible only through the cooperation and assistance of D. Curwen, L. K. Binning, K. A. Kelling, J. A. Wyman, G. J. Rice, R. Schmidt and J. Zajda, The University of Wisconsin, Madison, WI. Their efforts are gratefully acknowledged. This interdisciplinary effort was supported by the USDA NC-IPM Research Program (Project #3128), The College of Agricultural and Life Sciences, University of Wisconsin-Madison, the UW-Extension Integrated Pest Management Program and the Wisconsin Potato and Vegetable Growers Association.

Literature Cited

1. Krause, R.A., Massie, L.B., and Hyre, R.A. 1975. BLITECAST, a computerized forecast of potato late blight. Plant Dis. Rep. 59:95-98.

2. Shields, E.J., Hygnstrom, J.R., Curwen, D., Stevenson, W.R., Wyman, J.A., and Binning, L.K. 1984. Pest management for potatoes in Wisconsin - A pilot program. Am. Potato J. 61:508-515.

3. Stevenson, W.R. 1983. An integrated program for managing potato late blight. Plant Dis. 67:1047-1048.

4. Stevenson, W.R., Binning, L.K., Wyman, J.A., Curwen, D., Rice, G.J., Zajda, J.R., Smidl, J.E., Thorson, B.M., and Schmidt, R.W. 1989. PCM - The Integrated Systems Approach To Potato Crop Management. User Guide For IBM and IBM-Compatible Personal Computers, Ver. 1.1. University of Wisconsin-Madison, IPM Program. 150 pp.

5. Stevenson, W.R., Curwen, D., Binning, L.K., Wyman, J.A., Koenig, J.P., Rice, G.J., Schmidt, R., and Zajda, J. 1989. Management of potato production using integrated computer software (Abstr.) Am. Potato J. 66:547.

6. Stevenson, W.R., Pscheidt, J.W., and Thielman, D.G. 1985. Potato Disease Management - WISPLAN User Guide. 34 pp.

DEVELOPMENT OF AN EXPERT SYSTEM FOR POTATO INTEGRATED PEST MANAGEMENT

P.R. Weisz, Z. Smilowitz, B. Christ and M. Saunders
Departments of Entomology and Plant Pathology
The Pennsylvania State University
University Park, PA 16802

To make integrated pest management (IPM) decisions which are biologically effective, environmentally prudent, socially responsible and still economical, the commercial potato grower must consider a complex of interacting variables. Potato yields are negatively affected by an array of individual pests and abiotic factors whose impact varies as the crop develops. Many of these stresses can occur simultaneously, resulting in even more complex crop responses than those associated with the presence of an isolated pest. These considerations alone make IPM a challenging business for the commercial grower, but the development of pesticide resistance in many potato growing areas has added even further complexity to effective pest management.

Information to assist growers in making IPM decisions has traditionally come from cooperative extension and agricultural supply companies. Other sources of information come from the pesticide industry technical and sales staff, and other producers. Extension service sponsored meetings are typically the only place where growers have an opportunity to meet with more than one specialist at a time. Even then, it is typically left to the grower to develop their own IPM plan. As a result, on farm spray decisions are often based on what the pesticide salesman says worked on a neighbor's farm last week.

There is a large body of IPM knowledge and expertise available in scientific and extension literature and in the form of human experts. Unfortunately, these knowledge sources are rarely available to the majority of growers on a day to day basis. The goal of this project was to organize this expertise on potato pest management into an electronic decision support tool, or expert system. This system is to make both research results and specialists' expertise available to the grower, consultant and others in the industry in a form that can effectively address all types of potato pest management problems.

Expert Systems

An expert system is a computer program designed to emulate the problem solving abilities of a human expert in a specific subject area (5). A human agricultural expert, consulting on IPM, has general knowledge and experience in the problem area. During consultation, the expert goes through a process of gathering information and through an analytical or perhaps intuitive process, formulates advice. In an analogous fashion, an expert system captures the accumulated wisdom of a human specialist into a "knowledge base". The expert system also gathers information about the user's particular problem, and then through a process of inference arrives at a recommendation.

Agriculture computer applications in the form of crop (3,4) or pest (7,8) simulation models and data bases are not new. While being valuable in research, simulation models are not designed as tactical tools to deal with the wide array of problems faced by growers on a daily basis. The information required as input for simulation models is not commonly available to a grower, and their output typically requires interpretation by experts. Simulations are valuable for representing quantitative knowledge and implementing structured problem solving, but are rarely able to handle qualitative information or the ad hoc types of problems faced by growers. This limitation is inherent in the nature of simulation modeling, where the modeler is concerned with the precision with which a model describes the process being simulated. In IPM, precision of correctness is rarely as important as the number of times a correct decision is made (1).

Unlike simulation models or data bases, which primarily manipulate data or information, an expert system deals with integration and delivery of knowledge in the form of specific and personalized advice. Like a human expert, an expert system can apply this knowledge to structured quantitative types of problems, unstructured qualitative formulations, and even to situations where complete information is absent or unknown. Additionally, an expert system can be queried to explain how it formulated it's advice. Compared to simulation models, these features makes expert systems highly flexible, interactive and powerful tools for on farm problem solving.

The Potato Expert System

The potato expert system (PotatoES) has been developed at The Pennsylvania State University primarily to assist northeastern commercial potato growers and others in the industry with IPM decision support. PotatoES employs the expertise of entomologists and plant pathologists, the predictive power of two simulation models, a farm level data base and user

486

supplied quantitative and qualitative field level information. PotatoES presently provides IPM advice for controlling five potato pests: Colorado potato beetle (*Leptinotarsa decemlineata* [Say]), green peach aphid (*Myzus persicae*), potato leafhopper (*Empoasca fabae* [Harris]), early blight (*Alternaria solani*) and late blight (*Phytophthora infestans* [Mont.] de Bary). Other crop pest and production modules will be added to PotatoES in the future.

PotatoES specifically seeks to: 1) prevent unnecessary pesticide applications; 2) reduce the development of pesticide resistance by targeting selected types of pesticides at specific pest life stages and by encouraging the grower to rotate classes of pesticides at each application; 3) maximize pesticide effectiveness by providing the grower with up to date information on pesticide efficacies against local pest populations and by timing applications for maximum benefit; 4) encourage and guide the grower in developing an effective scouting program; and 5) assist the grower in maintaining consistent and accurate pest management records.

PotatoES Design And Structure

PotatoES is divided into three main sections: a facts base, the knowledge base and a recommendations module (Fig. 1). The facts base is the computer analog to the human investigator, gathering and cataloging evidence to be used in solving a problem. The human experts' experience and knowledge is formalized in the knowledge base which orchestrates the investigation and draws the final conclusions. Lastly, these conclusions are passed to the recommendations module which formulates PotatoES' responses for the user.

The facts base. The facts base stores historical and current information about the grower's farm, maintains a library of registered pesticides and assists the grower in preparing appropriate on-farm spray records. Historical information relevant to IPM is stored in "profiles". Profiles are typically created at the beginning of the growing season and contain farm level data (e.g., geographical location, other crops being grown, pest infestation history, past pesticide practices) and specific crop information (e.g., potato cultivar, market objective, pest susceptibility). PotatoES stores profiles for each field for an entire season so the grower need not repeatedly re-enter static information at every consultation.

In contrast to historical data stored in profiles, current information such as forecasted weather, crop phenology or pest densities change between consultations. Just as a human consultant focuses their investigation to maximize their time, PotatoES only elicits current information from the grower which is specifically relevant to the problem at hand.

The facts base also contains a pesticide library. This data base contains label information on all pesticides which are registered for use against potato pests and which are recommended by the local experts. This allows PotatoES to make pesticide recommendations which are both legal and consistent with local guidelines.

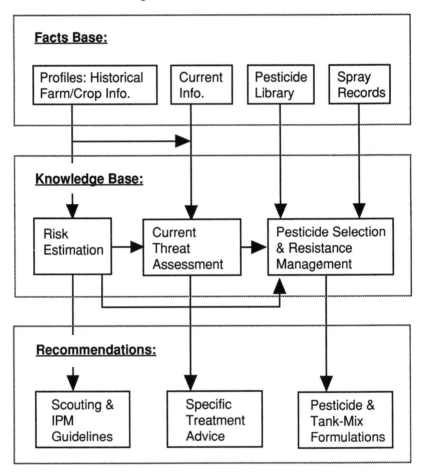

Fig. 1. PotatoES expert system structure and flow chart showing three main modules; the facts base, the knowledge base and the recommendations module.

Knowledge base. The knowledge base contains the formalization of the entomology and plant pathology experts' IPM knowledge. In developing the knowledge base, three main areas of human expertise emerged: pest risk estimation, current threat assessment and pesticide selection and resistance management (Fig. 1).

Pest risk estimation. Pest risk estimation for a farm or individual field defines a general pest management strategy and lays the guidelines for an over-all IPM program. It is determined from historical farm, crop and pest information contained in the farm profile. Pest risk determines when scouting for each pest will be initiated, how frequently scouting will be repeated and the expected level of pesticide resistence for local pest populations. In the case of EB and Colorado potato beetle (CPB), risk estimation also determines the type of early season management program to be recommended.

Since each pest requires different management tactics, risk estimation for each pest is also unique. For the sake of brevity, only one example of pest risk, the highest of three categories of CPB risk, is described here. A field with a "High CPB Risk", is expected to have substantial CPB pressure starting at ground crack and continuing throughout the season. Furthermore, this CPB population is assumed to be highly resistant to synthetic organic pesticides. Consequently, the grower will be strongly encouraged to initiate scouting immediately at ground crack, and to continue scouting at 3 to 5 day intervals until the first flush of first instar larva occurs. At that point a *Bacillus thuringiensis* subsp. *san diego* spray will be advised and the scouting interval extended to 5 to 7 days. Furthermore, in accordance with local conditions for resistance, the knowledge base devalues the efficacy of many registered insecticides resulting in fewer alternatives being available for control.

CPB risk estimation depends on three factors (Fig. 2). The first two, crop rotation (9) and the number of CPB spray applications the grower has historically applied each season, are on-farm indicators of the magnitude of the potential CPB problem. If the grower has historically applied four or more CPB spray applications per season (wide solid line, Fig. 2) the field is assumed to be at high risk. If two or less applications have been previously applied, the field is assigned a lower risk estimate not described here. Finally, if the grower typically applies an average of three CPB sprays per season, crop rotation and a third factor are considered. This third factor, a complex variable called regional risk, assesses the over-all CPB problem in the grower's general geographical area.

Current threat assessment. In contrast to risk estimation which sets general IPM guidelines, threat assessment determines immediate and specific action based on current pest, crop and weather information. Current threat assessment is the most detailed module in the knowledge base and represents the majority of the experts' knowledge about each of the five potato pests. Consequently, detailed discussion in the space provided is impossible and only a small portion of the current CPB threat assessment will be outlined.

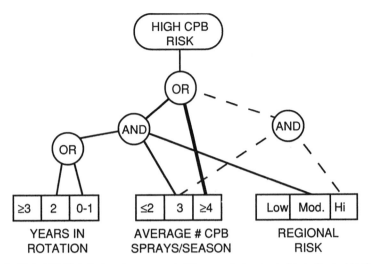

Fig. 2. High CPB Risk Estimation network. The case being tested is indicated in the oval at the top of the diagram. The variables determining the case are depicted in rectangles. The circles are logical connectors between values of these variables. For the case to be true, a logical path leading to it must be evaluated as true including all paths leading into each AND node and any single path leading to an OR node. Three possible pathways are indicated; solid lines, dashed lines, wide solid line.

Current CPB threat assessment is based on a general philosophy for controlling CPB. Early in the season, the grower is encouraged to apply *B. thuringiensis* as close to the first flush of first instar larvae as possible. PotatoES supports this application by recommending frequent early scouting (defined by the CPB risk estimation) and by providing the grower with egg hatch predictions based on the current density of egg masses in the field and predicted weather information.

Once a larval population has developed, specific strategies for controlling small, medium and large larvae are employed. Small larvae (defined as less than 3.2 mm), are controlled with *B. thuringiensis*. Medium larvae (3.2 to 6.4 mm) are controlled with cryolite[1]. Large larvae (greater than 6.4 mm) are controlled with a synthetic organic or rotenone. This strategy of targeting different classes of insecticides against specific CPB age stages is intended to maximize the efficacy of *B. thuringiensis* and cryolite while minimizing the development of pesticide resistance. Finally, emphasis on controlling adults is very high at plant emergence and again

---

[1]Cryolite is only recommended if it is registered or if a special exemption (Section 18) exists.

when first generation adults emerge. In both cases, however, this emphasis decreases as the population ages.

Based on this general philosophy, the knowledge base recognizes 10 types of CPB threats. These are listed in hierarchical order along with their corresponding action requirements in Table 1. Using the risk estimate and the data in the facts base, the CPB threat module scans this list of threats until it finds the first one that exists in the grower's field. Thus, PotatoES first checks to see if the crop is not vulnerable to CPB damage (Table 1). If, for example, the crop is pre-emergence, PotatoES would simply recommend that the grower follow the scouting guidelines determined by the risk estimate. If the crop is vulnerable, PotatoES checks if a spray for large larvae or adults is required now or expected in the near future (items 3 and 4, Table 1). If large larva are not a threat, the system checks medium larvae, small larvae and then the likelihood of an egg hatch in that order (items 5 through 8, Table 1). Finally, if none of these threats are present, PotatoES advises the grower when to scout this field again.

As an example of how PotatoES assesses CPB threat, the first step in determining if small or medium larva require immediate control (threats 5 and 6, Table 1), is illustrated in Fig. 3. Small or medium larva threat is dependent on the crop phenology and three complex variables: late season CPB hazard, the large larva and adjusted adult density and the total CPB density.

TABLE 1. Colorado potato beetle threat priorities.

	Threat Type	Associated Action
1.	Crop not vulnerable	Follow scouting guidelines
2.	Ground crack threat	Spray adults ASAP
3.	Large larvae and adult threat	Spray ASAP
4.	Large larvae and adults close to threshold	Scout in 1 day shorter time interval
5.	Medium larvae threat	Spray Cryolite ASAP
6.	Small larvae threat	Spray *Bacillus thuringienses* ASAP
7.	Egg hatch threat	Spray *Bacillus thuringienses* ASAP
8.	Approaching egg hatch	Run developmental model: act accordingly
9.	Small and medium larvae, close to threshold	Scout in 1 day shorter time interval
10.	All threats low	Follow scouting guidelines

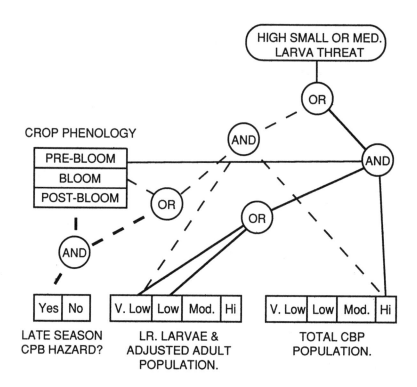

Fig. 3. High small or medium Colorado potato beetle larva threat network. See Fig. 2 for key to network diagrams.

Crop-phenology. The potato crop response to CPB defoliation varies with crop phenological age (6). During pre-bloom (solid lines, Fig. 3), *B. thuringiensis* or cryolite is recommended when the total CPB population is "high" and the large larvae and adjusted adult population is either "very low" or "low". While the crop is blooming (dashed lines), a more conservative stance is taken toward the softer sprays and their use is restricted to when the large larvae and adult population is "low". During post-bloom (wide solid lines), CPB control can sometimes be delayed or eliminated (10). This is determined by the complex variable "late season hazard".

Large larvae and adjusted adult population. Large larvae and adults are controlled with the same types of insecticides. Consequently, PotatoES pools these two life stages into one population. Additionally, the number of adults is adjusted to consider their seasonal feeding pattern. Shortly after emergence, adult and large larva have similar feeding rates (2) and

PotatoES assigns equal weight to each age-stage. As the adults age, their feeding rates decrease and PotatoES reduces their contribution to the CPB population's projected impact on the crop. After adjusting the number of adults, PotatoES estimates the general categories ("low", "moderate", etc.) based on crop phenology and numerical thresholds set by the local entomological experts.

Total CPB population. The total population is the sum of the adjusted adults plus the number of CPB larvae found in the scouting sample. As above, the general categories of "low", "moderate", etc. are determined using crop phenology and numerical thresholds.

CPB late season hazard.Late season hazard estimates the potato crop's post-bloom ability to tolerate CPB defoliation. The purpose of this variable is to encourage the grower to consider delaying or foregoing unnecessary spray applications when the crop yield would be insignificantly affected by CPB damage. Post-bloom, there are a number of situations when insecticide application can be eliminated (10). If the grower indicates that currently developed tuber quality and quantity is satisfactory, PotatoES will forego further spray applications. Additionally, spray applications are not recommended if the canopy nitrogen status is too low to support adequate photosynthetic rates. Finally, if the crop is healthy, having high nitrogen status, low seasonal defoliation, and there is no current or predicted drought, PotatoES will advise delaying foliar insecticide treatments. It is assumed that late in the season, under these conditions the crop can withstand a degree of CPB defoliation without loss in yield. When these conditions exist, the grower is given two options: a) delay CPB control until defoliation levels increase (strongly recommended) or b) direct PotatoES to over-ride this delay advice and proceed with making a spray recommendation.

If a high, small or medium larva threat is found to exist (Fig. 3), PotatoES determines whether to recommend *B. thuringiensis* or cryolite (Fig. 4). Pre-bloom, *B. thuringiensis* is recommended if at least 50% of the CPB population consists of small larvae. During crop bloom, a more conservative stance is taken toward *B. thuringiensis* applications and this percentage is reduced to 40%. When the small larvae population is less than these values a cryolite application is advised.

Pesticide selection and resistance management. Colorado potato beetle small and medium larvae are exceptional cases in that PotatoES recommends a specific pesticide for controlling them (*B. thuringiensis* or cryolite). In the majority of cases, a large number of pesticides with varying degrees of effectiveness are available for treating a given pest. Pesticide selection and resistance management scans the pesticide library for registered chemicals active against each pest which the current threat assessment indicates require treatment. An effectiveness rating is assigned to each chemical based on the risk estimate for the pests involved. PotatoES queries the grower to determine which class/es of pesticides were last applied to this field and eliminates these classes. This elimination encourages the grower to alternate different pesticides and thereby avoid resistance buildup. PotatoES presents the grower with a menu of all remaining pesticides active against the pests requiring treatment. As pesticides are selected from this menu, PotatoES builds a tank-mix, checking chemical compatibilities and the over-all tank-mix effectiveness. The final tank-mix presented to the grower includes label rates and warnings for each pesticide.

Recommendations module. The recommendations module manages the majority of interactions with the user. It relays all management advice in the form of general scouting and IPM guidelines, specific pest treatment advice and pesticide and tank-mix formulations. Additionally, this module can be queried to explain how PotatoES arrived at its recommendations. In explaining itself, PotatoES describes the information it used (from the facts base), and the logical processes it followed through the knowledge base. This permits the grower access to both advice and the reasoning process itself. Furthermore, this module provides the user with assistance with pest identification and scouting methods.

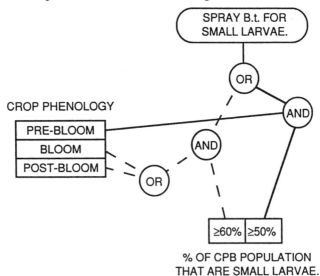

Fig. 4. Spray *Bacillus thuringiensis* for small CPB larvae network. See Fig. 2 for key to network diagrams.

Epilogue

PotatoES is an expert system for assisting commercial potato growers, consultants and others in making effective IPM decisions. It provides decision support for control of three important insect pests, CPB, potato leaf hopper, and green peach aphid, and two diseases early blight and late blight. PotatoES is a flexible system designed to make local expert/extension knowledge available to regional growers, keeping them informed of advanced management practices and changes in pesticide efficacy.

Preliminary field tests of PotatoES were conducted in 1991 at the Russell E. Larson Research Farm at Rock Springs, Pennsylvania. The objectives of these experiments were to test the software performance and determine the degree of agreement between the recommendations given by PotatoES and those given by human experts. Three-year on-farm field trials of PotatoES will be initiated in 1992.

Literature Cited

1. Calvin, D.D., Knapp, M.C., Xingquan, K., Poston, F.L., and Welch, S.M. 1988. Influence of European corn borer (Lepidopetera: Pyralidae) feeding on various stages of field corn in Kansas. J. Econ. Entomol. 81:1203-8.
2. Ferro, D.N., Logan, J.A., Voss, R.H., and Elkinton, J.S. 1985. Colorado potato beetle (Coleoptera: Chrysomelidae) temperature-dependent growth and feeding rates. Environ. Ent. 14:343-348.
3. MacKerron, D.K.L., and Waister, P.D. 1985. A simple model of potato growth and yield. Part I. Model development and sensitivity analysis. Agr. Forest. Meteorol. 34:241-252.
4. Ng, E., and Loomis, R.S. 1979. A simulation model of potato crop growth. Final report for cooperative agreement No. 12-14-5001-287 with USDA Snake River Conservation Research Center, Kimberly, ID.
5. Parsaye, K., and Chignell, M. 1988. Expert systems for experts. John Wiley and Sons, Inc., New York.
6. Shields, E.J., and Wyman, J.A. 1984. Effect of defoliation at specific growth stages on potato yields. J. Econ. Entomol. 77:1194-9.
7. Smilowitz, Z. 1981. GPA-CAST: A computerized model for green peach aphid management on potatoes. Pages 193-203 in Advances in Potato Pest Management. J.H. Lashomb and R. Casagrande, eds. Hutchinson Ross Publishing Co., Philadelphia.
8. Tamaki, G. 1981. Biological control of potato pests. Pages 178-192 in Advances in Potato Pest Management. J.H. Lashomb and R. Casagrande, eds. Hutchinson Ross Publishing Co., Philadelphia.
9. Wright, R.J. 1984. Evaluation of crop rotation for control of Colorado potato beetle (Coleoptera: Chrysomelidae) in commercial potato fields on Long Island. J. Econ. Entomol. 77:1254-1259.
10. Zehnder, G.W., and G.K. Evanylo. 1989. Influence of extent and timing of Colorado potato beetle (Coleoptera: Chrysomelidae) defoliation on potato tuber production in eastern Virginia. J. Econ. Entomol. 82:948-953.

PART X

Application of Biotechnology in Potato Pest Management

ENGINEERED RESISTANCE AGAINST POTATO TUBER MOTH

J. Van Rie, S. Jansens and A. Reynaerts
Plant Genetic Systems
J. Plateaustraat 22, B-9000
Gent, Belgium

The potato tuber moth, *Phthorimaea operculella* (Zeller) (PTM), is widely distributed and is one of the most damaging pests of potato in storage and in the field. The larvae mine the foliage and infest the tubers. Tuber infestation causes dramatic losses, as damaged tubers are attacked by different secondary pests and diseases. PTM is reported as a pest of potato mainly in hot tropical and subtropical areas, but severe infestations have also been reported in cooler areas (e.g. the highlands of Peru, Columbia, Kenya and Nepal). PTM is the most important pest on potato in the Middle East and in North and Central Africa. Losses amount to over 80 % in Turkey, Tunesia, Algeria, Rwanda, Burundi, and Eastern Zaire, despite the use of insecticides.

In some areas, the potato crop can only be protected through applications of insecticides at high rates, due to development of resistance in PTM populations to these chemicals. In addition, some of these insecticides are highly toxic and may be banned from agricultural use.

Attempts at biological control (e.g., the use of parasites and sex pheromone traps) have been successful in some areas, and will be important elements in integrated pest management (IPM) approaches. However, additional tools are needed to increase the effectiveness of IPM. Genetic resistance will likely be an important element in future pest control strategies. The occurrence of bacterial genes coding for insecticidal proteins allows the development of such resistance by genetic engineering methods.

Crystal Proteins of *Bacillus thuringiensis*

Upon sporulation, *Bacillus thuringiensis* produces crystalline inclusions, consisting of insecticidal crystal proteins (ICPs). Different classes of such proteins have been described based on their insecticidal activity and sequence homology: CryI ICPs are active against Lepidoptera; CryII ICPs have dual activity (Lepidoptera and Diptera);

CryIII ICPs are Coleoptera-specific; and CryIV ICPs are Diptera-specific (6). Based on amino acid homology, different ICP subclasses have been recognized. Within the CryI ICPs, the subtypes show marked differences in insecticidal activity when tested against a range of caterpillar species. Some of the proteins are produced as a 60-70 kd molecule, while most are present in the crystals as a protoxin of about 130 kd, which is cleaved in the insect midgut to yield a toxic fragment of about 60 kd. This toxic domain is located in the N-terminal half of the protoxin.

Different insecticidal materials based on formulations of *B. thuringiensis* spore-crystal mixtures have been introduced to the market. High cost and short field stability have been major limitations for large scale applications. Furthermore, application may be very ineffective against species like PTM that penetrate plant tissues as young instars.

Transforming Plants for Insect Resistance

The availability of a variety of insecticidal crystal proteins active against PTM has enabled us to engineer PTM resistance into different potato varieties. The gene encoding CryIA(b) has been cloned from *B. thuringiensis* var. *berliner* (12). The sequence coding for the active toxin has been identified and introduced into an *Agrobacterium* T-DNA vector under the control of the wound-stimulated TR2' promotor derived from *Agrobacterium tumefaciens* wild type plasmids (16). A number of potato varieties (e.g., Bintje, Berolina, Desiree, Kennebec, Kathadin, Yesmina, Spunta) have been transformed with this construct. Transgenic plants were first screened in a bioassay using *Manduca sexta* L. neonate larvae and detached potato leaves. When high mortality of this insect was observed (>70%), corresponding transgenic plants were then screened for resistance to PTM in a bioassay using leaf shoots derived from greenhouse grown plants (7). The results showed that transgenic plants that effectively control a laboratory strain of PTM could be obtained at a low frequency in all varieties (Table 1). Storage experiments using field grown tubers of these potato clones indicated a significant decrease in tuber damage (Fig. 1). Due to low or nonexistent PTM infestations in most countries where regulations for testing genetically modified organisms have been established, field performance of these new potato clones under natural infestation conditions has not yet been evaluated.

Table 1. Insect control in first generation transgenic potato plants expressing CryIA(b)

Variety	No. of transgenic clones	No. of clones showing good control of *M. sexta* larvae (>70% mortality)	No. of clones showing good control of PTM larvae (>70% mortality)
Desiree	44	13	10
Spunta	47	7	1
Kennebec	56	14	10
Yesmina	19	9	3

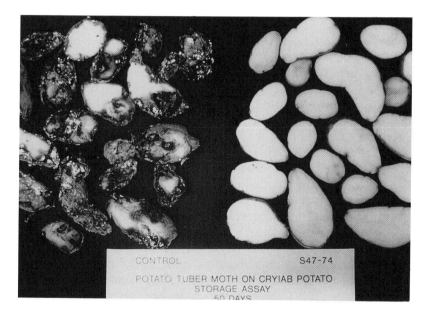

CONTROL   S47-74
POTATO TUBER MOTH ON CRYIAB POTATO
STORAGE ASSAY
50 DAYS

Fig.1. Storage assay : Control (left) and potatoes expressing CryIA(b) (right) artificially infested with PTM larvae.

Similar transformation experiments have been performed using another Cry gene, CryIB (6). In this case, no transgenic plants displaying effective control of PTM have been obtained. In general, expression levels of the bacterial Cry genes in transgenic plants are relatively low. Consequently, the frequency of transformants showing high levels of insect resistance is also low. In many of the transformants, only very low levels of CryIA(b) protein could be detected although they contain the intact cry gene. To develop insect-resistant crop varieties, higher levels of Cry gene expression must be obtained.

Modifying CryIA(b) Vectors for Enhanced Expression

Our experimental results indicated that the low ICP content of transgenic plants was mainly associated with the coding region of the CryIA(b) and CryIB genes which would be suboptimal for plant expression. Transformation experiments using other Cry genes demonstrated that the low expression levels were not unique to these two genes, but shared by most if not all of the Cry genes.

Perlak et al. (9) showed that ICP levels expressed in plants can be significantly increased by introducing translationally neutral substitutions that lower the adenine-thymine (AT) content and that correspond to the preferred plant codon usage. We have introduced different silent mutations into the coding region of the CryIA(b) gene. An experimental system was developed using transient expression in tobacco protoplasts, which allows accurate comparison of expression levels of different mutated coding sequences (3). The different expression vectors used all carry the same reference gene in order to normalize expression data. Mutant coding regions displaying significantly increased transient expression in comparison to the wild type CryIA(b) gene were then introduced into T-DNA vectors and evaluated in stable transformation in tobacco. A mutant CryIA(b) gene, CryIA(b)6, that has a partially modified coding region, directs significantly higher expression in tobacco than the wild type cry region and has been chosen for transformation experiments in other crops.

The CryIA(b)6 coding region has been introduced into the genome of the potato cultivar 'Yesmina', under the control of either the wound stimulated TR2' or the constitutive 35S promotor. Using both vectors a range of transgenic potato clones has been obtained. Transformants were screened for PTM resistance in the lab using a bioassay on detached foliage. In contrast to plants containing the wild type CryIA(b) gene, up to 90 % of the plants expressing CryIA(b)6 show high levels of protection against insect damage in this assay (Table 2).

Table 2. PTM control in 'second generation' transgenic 'Yesmina' potato plants expressing a modified CryIA(b) gene.

Vector	No. of transgenic clones	Clones showing good control of PTM larvae (>70% mortality)
p35S-cryIA(b)6	28	23
pTR2'-cryIA(b)6	39	35

CryIA(b) protein content in leaves of these transformants was measured by ELISA. To ensure full and reproducible induction of the TR2' promotor, protoplasts were prepared from *in vitro*-grown plants and were used as the source of the protein extracts. The 'Yesmina' transformant with the highest expression of the wild type CryIA(b) gene (PDS20-2) was used as a reference. From 36 transgenic lines, all expressing CryIA(b)6 under control of the TR2' promotor, 27 had higher CryIA(b) levels, 4 had equal levels, and only 5 scored lower than PDS20-2. The mean CryIA(b) content was 44 ng/mg protein; the highest-scoring transformant contained 3 times this amount.

Different lines showing varying amounts of CryIA(b)6 levels in the leaf have been multiplied in the field in Belgium (permit B/B/92/V/17 A) and in France. The availability of a wide range of plants with acceptable expression levels allowed further screening of the material on the basis of their agronomic performance. Lines showing less desirable agronomic characteristics (e.g., early senescence of leaves, irregular shape of tubers, decreased yield), that probably originated during the tissue culture phase (somaclonal variants), have been discarded.

Harvested tubers have been analyzed extensively for their performance in storage using artificial PTM infestation. All analyzed lines completely inhibited PTM development and hence showed no damage after several months of storage (Jansens et al., unpublished). Further research to similarly optimize the expression of the CryIB gene is in progress.

Avoiding Insect Adaptation

To warrant continued success of insect control with plants expressing Cry genes, we should anticipate problems of insect resistance and develop strategies to decrease the probability of resistance development. Indeed, selection experiments in the laboratory and studies to monitor insect field populations exposed to *B. thuringiensis* sprays have indicated that insects have the ability to develop resistance against *B. thuringiensis* ICPs (8,11). Analysis of these adapted insect populations and research into the mode of action of the ICPs may provide a basis to design resistance management strategies.

A number of factors have been put forward as determinants governing insect specifity of individual ICPs. Insect species can differ in their ability to solubilize crystals, and in the specificity and efficiency of gut proteases active in processing the solubilized protoxin into the active toxin (6). The highly selective action of the ICPs suggests that specific receptors in the insect may be involved in their mode of action. Indeed, saturable, high affinity binding has been demonstrated initially for CryIB on *Pieris brassicae* brush border membrane vesicles, and subsequently for a number of other ICP-insect combinations (5,13,14). Binding to midgut receptors proved to be a key determinant in the host range of insecticidal crystal proteins and a necessary step towards toxicity. Many insects are sensitive to more than one ICP type. In these insects, ICPs may bind either to distinct receptor types or to a single receptor.

The study of the resistance mechanism in a population of diamondback moth, *Plutella xylostella*, that acquired field resistance to the bacterial insecticide Dipel, suggests that the use of transgenic plants expressing different ICPs which bind to different categories of receptors represents a viable strategy to delay resistance (15). Toxicity and binding of three different ICP types were studied in the resistant strain (R strain) and an unchallenged laboratory strain (S strain) (4). In contrast to CryIA(b), the two other proteins in this study, CryIB and CryIC, are not present in Dipel crystals. All three ICPs were toxic to the S strain, although with varying degree. The R strain was found to be as susceptible to CryIB and CryIC as the S-strain, but at least 200 times less susceptible to CryIA(b). Binding studies using the ^{125}I-labeled proteins and increasing concentrations of brush border membrane vesicles from either the R strain or the S strain revealed a virtually identical binding pattern in the two strains for CryIB and CryIC. This result was confirmed quantitatively for CryIC by performing homologous competition experiments. No significant differences in binding affinity (K_d) or receptor site concentration (R_t) between the two strains could be observed. In contrast, while brush border membranes of the S strain specifically bound CryIA(b) protein, no such binding could be detected in the R strain. Because of this almost complete lack of binding, no quantitative binding data could be obtained for the R strain. Consequently, it was impossible to discriminate between altered affinity or receptor site concentration as the origin of the altered binding characteristics of the protein (the R strain had completely lost the binding capacity for CryIA(b), while the binding characteristics for

CryIB and CryIC were unchanged). Heterologous competition experiments indicated that all three proteins recognize a different receptor in *P. xylostella*, only one of which had undergone an alteration in the resistant strain. An important observation with respect to resistance management is that resistance to one ICP does not automatically imply cross resistance to other ICPs. Thus, to implement a strategy using transgenic plants expressing different ICPs in pest management, knowledge about the interaction between the different proteins and the insect midgut is required.

Three types of ICPs are known to be active against PTM larvae: CryIA(b), CryIB and CryIC (Table 3). Binding characteristics for all three proteins have been determined (10, Escriche et al., submitted). Binding parameters for CryIA(b) and CryIC were determined using ^{125}I-labeled proteins and brush border membranes prepared from larval midguts. For CryIA(b), a K_d (dissociation constant of the receptor-ICP complex) of 0.43 nM and a receptor concentration of 3.5 pmol/mg vesicle protein were calculated from homologous competition experiments. CryIC bound with a somewhat lower affinity ($K_d = 1.7$ nM) to a receptor with a calculated concentration (R_t) of 19.1 pmol/mg vesicle protein. Heterologous competition experiments demonstrated that these two proteins bind to different receptors. For CryIB, no quantitative binding data are available. However, binding experiments on fixed gut tissue sections (1,2) demonstrated that neither CryIA(b) nor CryIC competes with bound CryIB, indicating that CryIB recognizes yet another category of receptors.

Table 3. Toxicity of solubilized, purified crystal proteins against PTM larvae

ICP Type	LC_{50}[a]
CryIA(b)	4-20
CryIB	0.8-4
CryIC	20-100
CryID	>300
CryIE	>300

[a] Toxicity determined by dipping potato chips in a toxin solution; LC_{50} is expressed in µg/ml ICP protein.

To summarize these results, radioligand and immunocytochemical assays have shown that all three PTM-active ICPs bind to distinct receptors (Fig. 2). Accordingly, transgenic potato plants expressing two or all three proteins may provide a valuable approach towards resistance management. Other possible tactics for delaying the development of resistance include alternating transgenic crops expressing different ICPs, mixing of transgenic and non-transgenic plants, creating refuges and using the transgenic plants with other IPM strategies. Tactics for delaying development of resistance are discussed in more detail in Gould et al. (this volume). Further genetic and biochemical analysis of resistant insect strains and research into the biology of insect-crop interactions will help to design the optimal resistance management strategy.

Epilogue

Our results have shown that genetic modification can contribute to the development of new potato lines resistant to potato tuber moth. Insecticidal crystal protein (ICP) genes cloned from *Bacillus thuringiensis* have been used to produce new potato lines which demonstrate

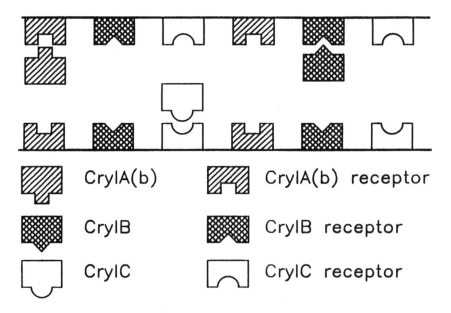

Fig.2. Schematical representation of the PTM brush border membrane. Toxicity of insecticidal crystal proteins is determined by the presence of specific receptors in the midgut epithelium. PTM is sensitive to CryIA(b), CryIB and CryIC because the larvae have receptors for these toxins.

substantial protection against this pest, both in greenhouse conditions and in simulated storage conditions. Introduction of wild-type ICP genes into crops is a relatively straightforward process leading to 'first generation' products. However, to ensure long-term success in agriculture, the development of new varieties of insect resistant crops may be more complex. Researchers developing 'Second generation' material may need to consider factors such as identification and characterization of novel ICP types, ICP mode of action, gene expression technology and resistance management. If these factors are considered, we are confident that the development and use of transgenic plants containing *B. thuringiensis* ICP genes will make a valuable and significant contribution to insect management.

Literature Cited

1.   Bravo A., S. Jansens and M. Peferoen. 1992. Immunocytochemical localisation of *Bacillus thuringiensis* insecticidal crystal proteins in intoxicated insects. J. Invert. Pathol. 60:237-246.

2.   Bravo A., K. Hendrickx, S. Jansens and M. Peferoen. 1992. Immunocytochemical analysis of specific binding of *Bacillus thuringiensis* insecticidal crystal proteins to lepidopteran and coleopteran midgut membranes. J. Invert. Pathol. 60:247-253.

3.   Denecke J., V. Gosselé, J. Botterman and Cornelissen M. 1989. Quantitative Analysis of transiently expressed genes in plant cells. Meth. Mol. Cel. Biol. 1:19-27.

4.   Ferré J., M.D. Real, J. Van Rie, S. Jansens, and M. Peferoen. 1991. Resistance to the *Bacillus thuringiensis* bioinsecticide in a field population of *Plutella xylostella* is due to a change in a midgut membrane receptor. Proc. Natl. Acad. Sci. USA 88:5119-5123.

5.   Hofmann C., P. Lüthy, R. Hütter and V. Pliska. 1988. Binding of the delta endotoxin from *Bacillus thuringiensis* to brush-border membrane vesicles of the cabbage butterfly (*Pieris brassicae*). Eur. J. Biochem. 173:85-91

6.   Höfte H. and H. Whiteley. 1989. Insecticidal crystal proteins of *Bacillus thuringiensis*. Microbiol. Rev. 53:242-255.

7.   Peferoen M., S. Jansens, A. Reynaerts and J. Leemans. 1990. Potato plants with engineered resistance against insect attack. In M.E. Vaeda and W.C. Park [eds.], Molecular and cellular biology of the potato. C.A.B. International, Wallingford U.K. pp.193-204.

8.   McGaughey, W.H. 1985. Insect resistance to the biological insecticide *Bacillus thuringiensis*. Science 229:193-195.

9.   Perlak F., R. Deaton, T. Armstrong, R. Fuchs, S. Simson, J. Greenplate and D. Fishoff. Insect resistant cotton plants. Biotechnology 8:939-943.

10.   Silva, F.J., Escriche, B., Martinez-Ramirez, A.C., Real, M.D. and Ferré, J. (1991). Characterization of receptors for insecticidal Bt activity in *Phthorimaea operculella*. First International Conference on *Bacillus thuringiensis*, Oxford (United Kingdom).

11. Tabashnik B., N. Cushing, N. Finson and M. Johnson. 1990. Field development of resistance to *Bacillus thuringiensis* in diamondback moth (Lepidoptera: Plutellidae). J. Econom. Entomol. 83:1671-1676.

12. Vaeck M., A. Reynaerts, H. Höfte, S. Jansens, M. De Beuckeleer, C. Dean, M. Zabeau, M. Van Montagu and J. Leemans. 1987. Transgenic plants protected from insect attack. Nature 327:33-37.

13. Van Rie J., S. Jansens, H. Höfte, D. Degheele and M. Van Mellaert. 1989. Specificity of *Bacillus thuringiensis* delta-endotoxins: importance of specific receptors on the brush border membranes of the mid-gut of target insects. Eur. J. Biochem. 186:239-247.

14. Van Rie J., S. Jansens, H. Höfte, D. Degheele and H. Van Mellaert. 1990. Receptors on the brush border membrane of the insect midgut as determinants of the specificity of *Bacillus thuringiensis* delta-endotoxins. Appl. Environ. Microbiol. 56:1378-1385.

15. Van Rie, J. 1991. Insect control with transgenic plants: resistance proof? Tibtech 9:177-179.

16. Velten J., L. Velten, R. Hain and J. Schell. 1984. Isolation of a dual promotor fragment from the Ti-plasmid of *Agrobacterium tumefaciens*. EMBO J. 12:2723-2730.

GENETIC TRANSFORMATION OF POTATO FOR INSECT RESISTANCE

Reynaldo V. Ebora and Mariam B. Sticklen
Departments of Entomology and Crop and Soil Sciences
202 Pesticide Research Center
Michigan State University
East Lansing, MI 48824-1311

Recent advances in genetic engineering techniques make it possible to transform different plant species with genes from totally different organisms. At present, several techniques to introduce foreign genes into potato (*Solanum tuberosum L.*) have been developed (28, 51, 56, 57, 61, 62, 81, 83). In conventional breeding techniques, the success of introgressing genes of economic interest from wild to cultivated gene pools generally depends on the crossability among wild and cultivated plant species (66). In some cases, it has not been possible to introduce resistance by this means due to the lack of variation in insect resistance in sexually crossable material (6). The production of insect resistant potato by traditional plant breeding techniques is the most widely used approach in the improvement of commercial cultivar. However, the process of varietal improvement via traditional breeding methods is complicated by tetrasomic segregation patterns and incomplete fertility in many tetraploid commercial cultivars (59). A major goal of plant genetic engineering is the introduction of agronomically desirable traits into crop plants in situations where conventional breeding methods have been unsuccessful (35). Genetic transformation can rapidly accelerate plant breeding efforts for crop protection and enhanced yield (69). After a desirable gene is transferred to a crop, it could be transferred into its crossable relatives via conventional breeding techniques. Dean (12) indicated that a primary goal of agricultural genetic engineering concerns the control of insects. Fraley (24) estimated that in the next 10 to 20 years, introduced genes will probably provide a large percentage of insect control in annual crops and vegetables allowing reduced insecticide usage.

This chapter will focus on developments in potato insect resistance associated with recombinant DNA technology with emphasis on potatoes transformed with *Bacillus thuringiensis* Berliner.

Potato Transformation and Regeneration

Agrobacterium tumefaciens (Smith and Townsend) mediated transformation is the most commonly used procedure for the production of transgenic potato which rely on cocultivation of various tissues or organ explants with the bacteria engineered to various selectable marker and reporter genes harbored in the Ti plasmid vector (55, 57, 59, 61, 62, 70, 83). An efficient transformation of potato using *A. rhizogenes* has also been reported (81). *Agrobacterium* constitutes an excellent system for introducing genes into plant cells since DNA can be introduced into whole plant tissue and the integration of T-DNA is a relatively precise process (26). This system was found to work well in different genotypes and varieties of potato using various plant parts (3, 5, 10, 11, 28, 34, 39, 41, 42, 56, 57, 59, 61, 62, 70, 74, 75, 80). In 1988, Sheerman and Bevan (71) reported a rapid transformation method for potato using binary *A. tumefaciens* vectors and tuber discs. Wenzler *et al.* (83) reported a rapid and efficient transformation and regeneration system which uses leaf explants from axenically grown shoots. These methods allow the production of large numbers of transformed potato plants which are necessary for the critical evaluation of foreign gene expression in the potato genome. Another technique involves the use of PEG (polyethylene glycol) to transform potato leaf protoplasts (17, 44, Helgeson this volume).

In order for genetic modification via *Agrobacterium* or any other systems to be successful, both a reproducible and efficient regeneration system directed towards those cells capable of regeneration are mandatory (59). For practical commercial use, it is desirable to have an efficient means of gene transfer to any commercial cultivars (34).

Transformation of Potato With *Bacillus thuringiensis* Cry Genes

Bacillus thuringiensis (Bt) is a gram positive bacterium that produces crystals (Cry) (also called protoxin, insecticidal crystal protein or delta endotoxin) (8) during sporulation. The crystals are solubilized and degraded to a biologically active toxin in the insect gut (82, 84). Bt has been registered as commercial insecticide in the U.S. for over 30 years beginning with "Thuricide" in 1957 (7). A large number of distinct Bt Cry genes have now been cloned and sequenced. In 1989, Hofte and Whiteley (38) grouped Bt crystal protein genes into 4 major classes based on amino acid sequence and host range. The classes were CryI (Lepidoptera-specific, 130-140 kDa), CryII (Lepidoptera- and Diptera-specific, 65 kDa), CryIII (Coleoptera specific, 73 kDa) and CryIV (Diptera-specific, 72-135 kDa) (29). Recently, Feitelson *et al.* (18) added two new major classes of nematode active toxins, Cry V and Cry VI and other new subclasses have also been added to the existing classes. Over 40 Cry genes have been cloned and sequenced (29) and at least four genes encoding Lepidoptera-specific proteins have been expressed at insecticidal levels in transgenic plants of tomato (14, 22, 77), tobacco (1, 2, 77, 78), cotton (4, 64, 76, 78) and potato (9, 77). In addition, Coleoptera-specific CryIII genes have also been expressed in potato (D.A. Fischoff et al., unpublished, cited by MacIntosh et al. (50)). To obtain plants expressing useful levels of Bt protein, it is necessary to engineer the plant to produce the activated toxin, rather than the entire protoxin (30).

The first transformation of potato with Lepidoptera-specific Bt Cry genes was reported by researchers from Plant Genetics Systems (PGS, Ghent, Belgium) (77, and Reynaerts et al. this volume) using Cry genes isolated from *B.thuringiensis* subsp. *berliner*. The CryI(b) gene was fused to neomycin phosphotranferase II (NPTII) from the *E. coli* transposon Tn5. The NPTII gene (also referred to as neo gene) is a selectable marker that confers kanamycin resistance to transformed plants. The gene fusion was driven by a TR promoter (i.e. a region of DNA involved in binding of RNA polymerase to initiate transcription) of the *Agrobacterium* 2' gene. Another construct was composed of a modified toxin gene which encodes 610 amino-terminal amino acids of Bt protein and contains the entire active toxin. Transformation was carried out using *Agrobacterium*. Transformed shoots were selected on kanamycin- containing medium and rooted on nonselective medium. Bioassays using whole plants and first instar tobacco hornworm (*Manduca sexta*) showed that transgenic plants are protected from feeding damage. The insecticidal activity expressed in leaves from transgenic plants was correlated with the amount of Bt protein detected in leaf tissue. Plants exhibiting the most efficient insecticidal activity expressed the highest level of Bt protein. In transgenic plants that killed all insects, the levels of Bt protein varied between 90 and 150 ng per gram of leaf tissue (77). Recently, PGS researchers also transformed potato with CryIA(a) and CryIA(b) toxin genes (M. Peferoen, personal communication). Cheng *et al.* (9) were also able to transform potato FL1607 with binary plasmid pWB139 which contains the CryIA(c) gene encoding the 68 kDa toxin from *B. thuringiensis* subsp. *kurstaki* HD-73 translationally fused to NPTII. This fused gene is regulated by the cauliflower mosaic virus 35S promoter and the 3' region of the tomato proteinase inhibitor I gene. This cassette is further flanked by the nopaline synthase promoter and terminator (i.e., a sequence of DNA represented at the end of the transcript that causes RNA polymerase to stop transcription). This plasmid is based on a broad host range vector pRK252 (15). Leaf sections were inoculated with *A. tumefaciens* strain Wag11 containing pWB139, and shoots were regenerated and then rooted in medium containing 50 ug/ml kanamycin. Kanamycin-resistant plantlets were acclimated to the greenhouse and grown to maturity.

DNA was isolated from the plants and then analyzed by polymerase chain reaction to amplify specific fragments of the translational fusion. Gene integration was confirmed by Southern blot hybridization of restricted DNA from transformed plants using the CryIA(c)-NPTII gene as a probe. Reconstruction analysis indicated that 5 to 10 copies of the gene fusion were integrated into the potato genome, possibly in tandem fashion without any structural alterations within the translational fusion. The transformed potato was found to be resistant to *M. sexta* in a leaf disk assay. Neonate larvae consumed significantly more leaf disk area from the untransformed potato plant than from leaf disks taken from the transgenic plant. Also, less frass was collected from Petri dishes containing transgenic leaf disks than from dishes containing the nontransformned leaves, indicating a reduction in feeding on the transformed potato plant (9).

Second generation transgenic plants grown from tubers showed some resistance to potato tubermoth (*Phthorimaea operculella* (Zeller) and European corn borer (*Ostrinia nubilalis [Hübner]*) (Ebora and Sticklen, unpublished data). Potato tubermoth is one of the most damaging pests of potato and is generally of greatest importance in warmer climates (19, 23, 65), while European corn borer can utilize potatoes as secondary hosts. No significant difference in insect leaf area consumption between transformed and untransformed plant treatments was observed after 11 days of feeding. However, dry weight of frass was significantly higher on the untransformed plants. Other bioassays indicated that European corn borer larvae were significantly less capable of surviving on transgenic potato than on control plants. Preference tests also showed that leaf disks of transgenic plants were less preferred than the control plants by third instar European corn borer after 24 hours of exposure. Expression of the CryIA(c) gene in transgenic potato plant is quite low and below the level of detection of northern analysis or immunoassay (9), a result that was also observed in other plants transformed with Bt Cry genes (14, 78).

Recent studies by MacIntosh (50) showed that many of the agronomically important lepidopteran pests in the U.S. are more sensitive to CryIA(c) protein than to CryIA(b) protein. Padidam (63) also showed that CryIA(c) was highly toxic to *Heliothis armigera* (Hubner) and that CryIA(c) protoxin was more toxic than either CryIA(b) or CryIA(a). Similarly, CryIA(c) was 10 times more toxic towards *H. virescens* and *Trichoplusia ni* than CryIA(a) (27). These results suggest that it is important to consider which kind of gene(s) should be used in the transformation of potato for resistance against a specific pest. Vaeck *et al.* (77) noted that the cloning of distinct types of Bt genes and their simultaneous expression in plants may be an important step towards the engineering of crop varieties that are resistant against whole insect complexes.

Murray *et al.* (58) showed that the low levels of lepidopteran toxin CryIA(b) gene expression in plants and cells were due to RNA instability. It has also been reported that degrees of insect resistance of transgenic plants are correlated with Bt mRNA levels in transgenic plants (78). This indicates that more efficient expression constructs need to be developed for a higher level of gene expression in transgenic potato. Present results support previous findings that transgenic plants with low Bt gene expression still have substantial tolerance to tobacco hornworm and other target insects (14, 78). One approach to increase the level of gene expression uses a more efficient promoter or modifies the nucleotide sequence of the gene without altering the encoded amino acid. This approach was found to work well in transgenic cotton (64).

Another class of Bt protein active against Coleoptera has been isolated from *B.thuringiensis* subsp. *tenebrionis* (45, 46, 53) and *B.thuringiensis* subsp. *san diego* (32, 33). These strains have been shown to be identical (47) and share the same H antigens as subsp. *morrisoni* (serotype 8a:8b) (13). The genes encoding their protoxins have been cloned and sequenced (32, 37, 43, 53, 68) and shown to be identical. Donovan et al. (16) isolated and characterized a new Bt toxic to coleopteran larvae in 1988. However, the nucleotide sequence of the toxin gene was found to be identical to those isolated from subsp. *tenebrionis* and subsp. *san diego*, alhough the strains differed in several ways. Their protoxin is designated CryIIIA (38) and is used for the control of Colorado potato beetle, *Leptinotarsa decemlineata* (Say) (20, 21, 40, 87, 88). The CryIIIA gene has also been expressed at insecticidal levels in plants (D.A. Fischoff et al., unpublished, cited by MacIntosh (50)) and has protected potato plants from Colorado potato beetle defoliation in the greenhouse and field (24). Colorado potato beetle is one of the most destructive pests of potato in many U.S. potato-growing regions and has developed resistance to a wide range of insecticides. (20, 21, 40, 86, 88). This makes the use of Bt-based insecticides or transgenic plants an attractive alternative.

Several other isolates of Bt belonging to different subspecies have been found to be toxic to Coleoptera. Sick *et al.* (72) reported the nucleotide sequence of a coleopteran-active toxin gene from a new isolate of *B.thuringiensis* subsp. *tolworthi* . Similarly, Rupar *et al.* (67) found isolates of *B.thuringiensis* subsp. *tolworthi* and *B.thuringiensis* subsp. *kumamotoensis* that each contained a unique gene coding for a protein toxic to Colorado potato beetle. Recently, Lambert et al. (48) reported an isolate of *B.thuringiensis* subsp. *kurstaki*, containing a gene that encodes a CryIIID which is more active against Colorado potato beetle than other CryIII toxins. Ohba et al. (60) also reported a unique isolate of *B.thuringiensis* subsp. *japonensis* with a high larvicidal activity specific for scarabaeid beetles. There is no doubt that more isolates of Bt and different types of

Cry genes will be identified in the future, making more genes available for genetic transformation of potato and other plants.

Transgenic Potato and Integrated Pest Management

The development of transgenic potato with inherent resistance to insect pests will be an important tool for integration into pest management programs. Transgenic plants have the potential to overcome the stability problems associated with conventional applications of Bt, and may result in improved control of pests that feed on plant parts or tissues (52). Transgenic plants might also significantly reduce the cost of insect control (79). The use of transgenic plants may be a key component of integrated pest management, and will enhance the trend toward environmentally compatible insect control strategies (36). It has been suggested that widespread cultivation of transgenic crops that express high constitutive levels of the lepidopteran specific Bt endotoxin will lead to selection for insects resistant to the toxin (85). Obviously, any control agent that is not properly managed may stimulate the development of resistance to the target organism. In the case of transgenic potatoes, modification at the molecular level can be done so that the toxin is produced only in specific plant parts or at specific stages of growth. Williams *et al.* (85) devised a system to temporally control the expression of the Bt endotoxin in transgenic tobacco by using a chemically responsive promoter. Gould *et al.* (this volume) provides a more detailed discussion on management of resistance in transgenic crops.

Spore-crystal or purified crystal preparations of Bt were shown to be compatible with other control agents. Gailce Leo Justin *et al.* (25) showed that treatment with Bt increased the suceptibility of *H. armigera* and *Spodoptera litura* to chemical insecticides. Bt was also shown to be compatible with nuclear polyhedrosis virus (54). The potentiation of Bt insecticidal activity by serine protease inhibitors has also been reported (49). These results may also occur in transgenic potato, and further study of the effects of other insect control agents on Bt activity in transgenic plants is needed.

The discovery of different Bt isolates with different types of Cry genes would increase the number of genes that could be used to genetically transform potato. Simultaneous transformation of potato with both Lepidoptera- and Coleoptera-specific Bt Cry genes will produce a plant that is resistant to major potato pests belonging to these insect orders. Gleave (29) noted that increasing the diversity of available genes for microbial insecticides or transgenic plants would facilitate the simultaneous use of genes encoding insecticidal protein which bind to different membrane receptors in the insect midgut cells, and should increase the efficacy of pest control and delay the onset of resistance. The different strategies for effective use of transgenic potato in IPM programs are similar to those proposed for other transgenic plant systems, as discussed by Gould (31, and this volume), Sticklen (73), McGaughey and Whalon (52) and Brunke and Meeusen (7).

Acknowledgment

R. V. Ebora is a Ph.D. student supported by the Rockefeller Foundation. Insect bioassays with transgenic potato at M.B. Sticklen's laboratory are supported by US-AID. (AID CA#: DAN-4197-A-00-1126-00).

Literature Cited

1.   Adang, M.J., E. Firoosabady, J. Klein, D. De Boer, V. Sekar, J.D. Kemp, E. Murray, T.A. Rocheleau, K. Rashka, G. Staffeld, C. Stock, D. Sutton, and D.J. Merlo. 1987. Expression of a *Bacillus thuringiensis* insecticidal crystal protein in tobacco plants. *In* Molecular Strategies for Crop Protection. (C.J. Arntzen and C. Ryan, eds.) Alan R. Liss, Inc. New York. pp. 345-354.

2.   Barton,K.A., H.R. Whiteley, and N.G. Yang. 1987. *Bacillus thuringiensis* δ-endotoxin expressed in transgenic *Nicotiana tabacum* provide resistance to lepidopteran insects. Plant Physiol. 85:1103-1109.

3.   Be Block. M. 1988. Genotype independent leaf disc transformation of potato *Solanum tuberosum* using *Agrobacterium tumefaciens*. Theor. Appl. Genet. 75: 767-774.

4.   Benedict, J.H., D.W. Altman, P.F. Umbeck, and D.R. Ring.1992. Behavior, growth, survival, and plant injury by Heliothis *virescens* (F.) (Lepidoptera: Noctuidae) on transgenic Bt cottons. J. Econ. Entomol. 85: 589-593.

5.   Bones, A. 1991. Transformation of *Solanum tuberosum* plants. 16th Congress of the Scandinavian Society for Plant Physiology. Physiol. Plant. 82: 113-117.

6.   Boulter, D., J.A. Gatehouse, A.M.R. Gatehouse, and V.A. Hilder. 1990. Genetic engineering of plants for insect resistance. Endeavour, New Series. 14: 185-190.

7.   Brunke K.J., and R.L. Meeusen. 1991. Insect control with genetically engineered crops. TIBTECH. 9:197-200.

8.   Chambers, J.A., A. Jelen, M. Pearce Gilbert, C.S. Jany, T.B. Johnson, and C. Gawron-Burke, 1991. Isolation and characterization of a novel insecticidal crystal protein gene from *Bacillus thuringiensis* subsp. *aizawai*. J. Bacteriol. 173: 3966-3976.

9.   Cheng, J. M.G. Bolyard, R.C. Saxena, and M.B. Sticklen. 1992. Production of insect resistant potato by genetic transformation with a δ-endotoxin gene from *Bacillus thuringiensis* var. *kurstaki* Plant Science. 81:83-91.

10.   Chung, S.H., and W.S. Sim. 1987. Transformation of potato *Solanum tuberosum* L. tuber cells with *Agrobacterium tumefaciens* and Ti plasmid DNA. Korean Biochem. J. 20: 389-398.

11. Conner, A.J., M.K. Williams, R.C. Gardner, S.C. Deroles, M.L. Shaw and J.E. Lancaster. 1991. *Agrobacterium* mediated transformation of New Zealand potato cultivars. N. Z. J. Crop Hortic. Sci. 19: 1-8.

12. Dean, D.H. 1984. Biochemical genetics of the bacterial insect-control agent *Bacillus thuringiensis*: Basic principles and prospects for genetic engineering. *In* Biotechnology and Genetic Engineering Reviews. (G.E. Russell, ed.) Intercept, Newcastle upon Tyne.vol.6. pp341-363.

13. de Barjac, H., and E. Frachon. 1990. Classification of *Bacillus thuringiensis* strains. Entomophaga. 35: 233-240.

14. Delannay, X., B. J. LaVallee, R. K. Proksch, R.L. Fuchs, S. R. Sims, J.T. Greenplate, P. G. Marrone, R.B. Dobson, J.J. Augustine, J.G. Layton and D. A. Fischhoff. 1989. Field performance of transgenic tomato plants expressing the *Bacillus thuringiensis* var. *kurstaki* insect control protein. Biotechnology. 7: 1265 - 1269.

15. Ditta, G., T. Schmidhauser, E. Yakobson, P. Lu, X. Liang, D.R. Finlay, D. Guiney, and D.R. Helinski, 1985. Plasmids related to the broad host range vector, pRK290, useful for gene cloning and for monitoring gene expression. Plasmid, 13:149-153.

16. Donovan, W.P., J.Jr., M. Gonzalez, M.P. Gilbert, and C. Dankocsik. 1988. Isolation and characterization of EG2158, a new strain of *Bacillus thuringiensis* toxic to coleopteran larvae, and nucleotide sequence of the toxin gene. Mol. Gen. Genet. 214:365-372.

17. Feher, A., K. Felfoldi, J. Preiszner, and D. Dudits. 1991. PEG-mediated transformation of leaf protoplasts of *Solanum tuberosum L.* cultivars. Plant Cell Tissue Organ Cult. 27:105-114.

18. Feitelson, J.S., J. Payne, and L. Kim. 1992. *Bacillus* thuringiensis: Insects and Beyond. Bio/Technology. 10:271-275.

19. Fenemore, P.G. 1980. Susceptibility of potato cultivars to potato tuber moth, *Phthorimaea operculella* Zell. (Lepidoptera: Gelechiidae). N.Z. J. Agric. Res. 23:539-546.

20. Ferro, D.N., and W.D. Gelernter. 1989. Toxicity of a new strain of *Bacillus thuringiensis* to colorado potato beetle Coleoptera: Chrysomelidae).J. Econ. Entomol. 82:750-755.

21. Ferro, D.N., and S.M. Lyon, 1991. Colorado potato beetle (Coleoptera: Chrysomilidae) larval mortality: Operative effects of *Bacillus thuringiensis subsp. san diego*. J. Econ. Entomol. 84:806-809

22. Fischhoff, D.A., K. S. Bowdish, F. J. Perlak, P.G. Marrone, S.M. McCormick, J.G. Niedermeyer, D.A. Dean, K. Kusano-Kretzner, E.J. Mayer, D.E. Rochester, S.G. Rogers, and R.T. Fraley. 1987. Insect tolerant transgenic tomato plants. Biotechnology. 5:807 - 813.

23. Foot, M.A. 1979. Bionomics of the potato tuber moth, *Phthorimaea operculella* (Lepidoptera: Gelechiidae), at Pukekohe. New Zealand J. Zool. 6:623-636.

24. Fraley, R..1992. Sustaining the food supply. Bio/Technology. 10:40-43.

25. Gailce Leo Justin, C., R.J. Rabindra, and S. Jayaraj, 1989. Increased insecticide susceptibility in *Heliothis armigera* (Hbn) and *Spodoptera litura* F. larvae due to *Bacillus thuringiensis* Berliner treatment. Insect Sci. Applic. 10: 573-576.

26. Gasser, C.S., and R.T. Fraley, 1989. Genetically engineering plants for crop improvement. Science 244:1293-1299.

27. Ge.,A.Z., D. Rivers, R. Milne, and D.H. Dean. 1991. Functional domains of *Bacillus thuringiensis* insecticidal crystal proteins. J. Biol. Chem. 266:17954-17958.

28. Gilissen, L.J.W., K.S. Ramulu, E. Flipse, E. Meinene, and W.J. Stiekema. 1991. Transformation of diploid potato genotypes through *Agrobacterium* vectors and expression of transfer DNA markers in root clones regenerated plants and suspension cells. Acta Bot Neerl. 40:53-62

29. Gleave, A.P., R.J. Hedges, and A.H. Broadwell. 1992. Identification of an insecticidal crystal protein from *Bacillus thuringiensis* DSIR517 with significant sequence differences from previously described toxins. J. Gen. Microbiol. 138:55-62.

30. Goldburg, R.J., and G. Tjaden. 1990. Are B.t.k. plants really safe to eat. Biotechnology. 8:1011-1015.

31. Gould, F., and A. Anderson, 1991. Effects of *Bacillus thuringiensis* and HD 73 delta-endotoxin on growth, behavior,and fitness of susceptible and toxin-adapted strains of *Heliothis virescens* (Lepidoptera: Noctuidae). Environ. Entomol. 20:30-38.

32. Herrnstadt, C., T.E. Gilroy, D.A. Sobieski, B.D. Bennet, and F.H. Gaertner. 1987. Nucleotide sequence and deduced amino acid sequence of a coleopteran-active delta-endotoxin gene from *Bacillus thuringiensis subsp.san diego.* Gene 57:37-46.

33. Herrnstadt, C., G.G. Soares, E.R. Wilcox, and D.L. Edwards. 1986. A new strain of *Bacillus thuringiensis* with activity against coleopteran insects. Bio/Technol. 4, 305-308.

34. Higgins, E.S., J.S. Hulme, and R. Shields, 1992. Early events in transformation of potato by *Agrobacterium tumefaciens*. Plant Science, 82:109 - 118.

35. Hilder, V.A., A.M.R. Gatehouse, S.E. Sheerman, R.F. Barker, and D. Boulter. 1987. A novel mechanism of insect resistance engineered into tobacco. Nature 300: 160-163.

36. Hodgson, J. 1992. Plant or bacterial B.t.? Bio/Technology. 10:274.

37. Hofte, H., J. Seurinck, A. Van Houtven, and M. Vaeck. 1987. Nucleotide sequence of a gene encoding an insecticidal protein B. thuringiensis var.tenebrionis toxic against coleoptera. Nucleic Acids Res., 15:71-83.

38. Hofte, H., and H.R. Whiteley, 1989. Insecticidal crystal proteins of *Bacillus thuringiensis*. Microbiological Reviews. 53:242-255.

39. Hogan, P.S., S.E. Ruzin, C.J. Boyes, and R.G. Hadley. 1989. Transformation of *Solanum tuberosum* cultivars russet burbank and atlantic using binary vectors. 18th Annual UCLA Symposia on Molecular and Cellular Biology, Park City, Utah, USA, April 1 - 7, 1989. J. Cell Biochem. Suppl. (13 part D).

40. Hough-Goldstein, J., A.M. Tisler, G.W. Zehnder, and K.A. Uyeda, 1991. Colorado potato beetle (Coleoptera: Chrysomelidae) consumption of foliage treated with *Bacillus thuringiensis var. san diego* and various feeding stimulants. J. Econ. Entomol. 84:87-93.

41. Ishida, B.K., G.W. Jr. Snyder, and W.R. Belknap. 1989. The use of *in vitro* grown microtuber discs in *Agrobacterium* mediated transformation of russet burbank and lemhi russet potatoes. Plant Cell Rep. 8:325-328.

42. Ishige, T., M. Ohshima and Y. Ohashi. 1991. Transformation of Japanese potato cultivars with the beta glucuronidase gene fused with the promoter of the pathogenesis-related 1A protein gene of tobacco. Plant Sci. (Limerick) 73:167-174.

43. Jahn, NN., W. Schnetter, and K. Geider, 1987. Cloning of an insecticidal toxin gene of *Bacillus thuringiensis subsp. tenebrionis* and its expression in *Escherichia* cells. FEMS Microbiol. Lett. 48:311-315.

44. Karp, A., M.G.K. Jones, G. Ooms, and S.W.J. Bright. 1987. Potato protoplasts and tissue culture in crop improvement. In Biotechnology and Genetic Engineering Reviews (G.E. Russell, ed.) 5:1-26.

45. Krieg, H., A.M. Huger, G.A. Langenbruch, and W. SchNetter. 1983. *Bacillus thuringiensis* var. *tenebrionis*, a new pathotype effective against larvae of coleoptra. Z. Angew. Entomol. 96:500-508.

46. Krieg, A., W. Schnetter, A.M. Huger, and G.A. Langenbruch. 1987. *Bacillus thuringiensis* subsp. *tenebrionis* strain Bl 256 - 82: A third pathotype within the H-serotype 8a:8b. Syst. Appl. Microbiol. 9, 138-141.

47. Krieg, A., A.M. Huger, and W. Schnetter, 1987. *"Bacillus thuringiensis var. san diego"* strain M-7 is identical to the formerly isolated in Germany *B. thuringiensis subsp. tenebrionis* strain Bl 256-82, which is pathogenic to coleopteran insects. J. Appl. Entomol. 104:417-424.

48. Lambert, B., W. Theunis, R. Aguda, K. Van Audenhove, C. Decock, S. Jansens, J. Seurinck, and M. Peferoen. 1992. Nucleotide sequence of gene cryIIID encoding a novel coleopteran-active crystal protein from strain BTI109P of *Bacillus thuringiensis subsp. kurstaki*. Gene. 110:131-132.

49. MacIntosh, S.C., G.M. Kishore, F.J. Perlak, P.G. Marrone, T.B. Stone, S.R. Sims, and R.L. Fuchs. 1990. Potentiation of *Bacillus thuringiensis* insecticidal activity by serine protease inhibitors. J. Agric. Food Chem. 38:1145-1151.

50. MacIntosh, S.C., T.B. Stone, S.R. Sims, P. L. Hunst, J.T. Greenplate, P.G. Marrone, F.J. Perlak, D.A. Fischhoff, and R.L. Fuchs. 1990. Specificity and efficacy of purified *Bacillus thuringiensis* proteins against agronomically important insects. J. Invertebr. Pathol. 56:258 - 266.

51. Masson, J., D. Lancelin, C. Bellini, M. Lecerf, P. Guerche, and G. Pelletier. 1989. Selection of somatic hybrids between diploid clones of potato *Solanum tuberosum L.* transformed by direct gene transfer. Theor. Appl. Genet. 78:153-159.

52. McGaughey Wm.H., and M.E. Whalon, 1992. Potential for insect resistance to *Bacillus thuringiensis. B. t.* Resistance Scientific Conference. January 22-23, 1992. Agricultural Research Institute, Washington, D.C. 48 p.

53. McPherson, S.A., F.J. Perlak, R.L. Fuchs, P.G. Marrone, P.B. Lavrik, and D.A. Fischhoff. 1988. Characterization of the coleopteran-specific protein gene of *Bacillus thuringiuensis var. tenebrionis*. Biotechnology. 6:61 - 66.

54. McVay, J.R., R.T. Gudauskas,and J.D. Harper, 1977. Effects of Bacillus thuringiensis Nuclear-polyhedrosis Virus mixtures on Trichoplusia ni larvae. J. Invertebr. Pathol. 29:367 - 372.

55. Meeusen, R.L. and G. Warren, 1989. Insect control with genetically engineered crops. Annu. Rev. Entomol. 34:373-381.

56. Mitten, D.H., M. Horn, M.M. Burrell, and K.S. Blundy. 1991. Strategies for potato transformation and regeneration. *In* Biotechnology in Agriculture (3). The Molecular Biology of Potato. 260 p. C.A.B. International, Wallingford, England, UK.; Tucson, Arizona, USA. (M.E. Vayda & W.D. Park, eds). pp. 181 - 192.

57.   Mlynarova, L., and M. Bauer. 1991. Transformation of a recalcitant potato cultivar by an *Agrobacterium* binary vector. Acta Bot. Neerl. 40:217-22

58.   Murray, E.E., T. Rocheleau, M. Eberle, C. Stock, V. Sekar, and M. Adang. 1991. Analysis of unstable RNA transcripts of insecticidal crystal protein genes of *Bacillus thuringiensis* in transgenic plasnts and electroporated protoplasts. Plant Mol. Biol. 16: 1035 -1050.

59.   Newell, C.A., R. Rozman, M.A. Hinchee, E.C. Lawson, L. Haley, P. Sanders, W. Kaniewski, N.E. Tumer, R.B. Horsch, and R.T. Fraley, 1991. *Agrobacterium*-mediated transformation of *Solanum tuberosum L.* cv. "Russet Burbank". Plant Cell Reports 10:30 - 34.

60.   Ohba, M., H. Iwahana, S. Asano, N. Suzuki, R. Sato, and H. Hori. 1992. A unique isolate of *Bacillus thuringiensis serovar japonensis* with a high larval activity specific for scarabaeid beetles. Lett. Appl. Microbiol. 14:54-57.

61.   Ooms, G. 1991. Development of vectors and transformation systems with reference to potatoes. *In* Prospects For Transgenic Plants in Agriculture, held at the meeting of the agriculture group of the Society of Chemical Industry, London, England, UK, March 20, 1990. J. Sci. Food Agric. 54:157-158.

62.   Ooms, G., M.M. Burrell, A. Karp, M. Bevan, and J. Hille. 1987. Genetic transformation in two potato cultivars with T-DNA from disarmed *Agrobacterium*. Theor. Appl. Genet. 73:744-750.

63.   Padidam, M., 1992. The insecticidal crystal protein CrylA(c) from *Bacillus thuringiensis* is highly toxic to *Heliothis armigera.* J. Invertebr. Pathol. 59:109 - 111.

64.   Perlak, F.J., R.W. Deaton, T. A. Armstrong, R.L. Fuchs, S.R. Sims, J.T. Greenplate, and D. A. Fischhoff. 1990. Insect resistant cotton plants. Biotechnology. 8:939 - 943. Entomol. 85(2):589 - 593.

65.   Raman, K.V., and M. Palacios. 1982. Screening potato for resistance to potato tuberworm.J. Econ. Entomol. 75:47-49.

66.   Ross, H.1986. Potato Breeding-Problems and Perspective, Verlag Paul Parley, Berlin and Hamburg, 130p.

67.   Rupar, M. J., W. Donovan, R.G. Groat, A A.C. Slaney, J.W. Mattison, T. B. Johnson, J.F. Charles, V.C. Dumanoir, and H. de Barjac. 1991. Two novel strains of *Bacillus thuringiensis* toxic to coleopterans. Appl. Environ. Microbiol. 57:3337-3344.

68.   Sekar, V., Q.V. Thompson, M.J. Maroney, R.G. Bookland, and M.J. Adang. 1987. Molecular cloning and characterization of the insecticidal crystal protein gene of *Bacillus thuringiensis var. tenebrionis.* Proc. Natl. Acad. Sci. USA, 84, 7036-7040.

69.   Shah, D.M., N.E. Tumer, D.A. Fischhoff, R.B. Horsch, S.G. Rogers, R.T. Fraley, and E.G. Jaworski. 1987. The introduction and expression of foreign genes in plants. *In* Biotechnology and Genetic Engineering Reviews (G.E. Russell ed.). 5:81-106.

70.   Shahin, E.A., and R.B. Simpson, 1986. Gene transfer system for potato *Solanum tuberosum.* Hort. Sci. 21:1199-1201.

71.   Sheerman, S., and M.W. Bevan, 1988. A rapid transformation method for *Solanum tuberosum* using binary *Agrobacterium tumefaciens* vectors. Plant Cell Rep. 7:13-16.

72. Sick, A., F. Gaertner, and A. Wong.1989. Nucleotide sequence of a coleopteran-active toxin gene from a new isolate of *Bacillus thuringiensis subsp. tolworthi.* Nucleic Acids Research 18:1305.

73. Sticklen, M.B. 1990. Genetic engineering of plants: An alternative to pesticides and a new component of integrated pest management.*In* Pesticides in the Next Decade: The Challenges Ahead, Proceedings of the Third National Research Conference on Pesticides, November 8-9, 1990. (D.L. Weigmann ed.).pp 552 - 566.

74. Stiekema, W.J., F. Heidekamp, J.D. Louwerse, H. A. Verhoeven, and P. Dijkhuis. 1988. Introduction of foreign genes into potato cultivars Bintje and Desiree using an *Agrobacterium tumefaciens* binary vector. Plant Cell Reports. 7:47-50.

75. Tavazza, R., M. Tavazza, R.J. Ordas, G. Ancora, and E. Benvenuto. 1989. Genetic transformation of potato *Solanum tuberosum* an efficient method to obtain transgenic plants. Plant Sci. (Shannon). 59:175-1182.

76. Umbeck, P., G. Johnson, K. Barton, and W. Swain. 1987. Genetically transformed cotton *(Gossypium hissutum L.)* plants. Bio/Technology, 5:263-266.

77. Vaeck, M., A. Reynaerts, and H. Hofte. 1989. Protein engineering in plants: Expression of *Bacillus thuringiensis* insecticidal protein genes. *In* Cell Culture and Somatic Cell Genetics of Plants. Vol. 6. (J. Schell and I.K. Vasil, eds). Academic Press, Inc. New York. pp. 425-439.

78. Vaeck, M., A. Reynaerts, H. Hofte, S. Jansens, M. De Beuckeleer, C. Dean, M. Zabeau, M. Van Montagu, and J. Leemans.1987. Transgenic plants protected from insect attack, Nature, 328:33-37.

79. Van Rie, J. 1991. Insect control with transgenic plants: resistance proof?. TIBTECH. 9:177-179.

80. Visser, R.G.F., E. Jacobsen, A. H. Meinders, M.J. Schans, B. Witholt, and W.J. Feenstra. 1989. Transformation of homozygous diploid potao with an *Agrobacterium tumefaciens* binary vector system by adventitious shoot regeneration on leaf and stem segments. Plant Mol. Biol. 12:329-338.

81. Visser, R.G.F., E. Jacobsen, B. Witholt, and W.J. Feenstra. 1989. Efficient transformation of potato *Solanum tuberosum L.* using a binary vector in *Agrobacterium rhizogenes.* Theor. Appl. Genet. 78(4):594-600.

82. Visser, B., E. Munsterman, A. Stoker, and W.G. Dirkse. 1990. A novel *Bacillus thuringiensis* gene encoding a *Spodoptera exigua* specific crystal protein. J. Bacteriol. 172(12):6783-6788.

83. Wenzler, H. G. Mignery, G. May & W. Park. 1989. A rapid and efficient transformation method for the production of large numbers of transgenic potato plants. Plant Science. 63:79-85.

84. Whiteley, H.R. and Schnepf, H.R., 1986. The molecular biology of parasporal crystal body formation in *Bacillus thuringiensis* Ann. Rev. Microbiol. 40:549-576.

85. Williams, S., L. Friedrich, S. Dincher, N. Carozzi, H. Kessman, E. Ward and J. Ryals. 1992. Chemical regulation of *Bacillus* d-endotoxin expression in transgenic plants. Bio/Technology. 10:540-543.

86. Zehnder, G.W. and G.K. Evanylo. 1989. Influence of extent and timing of colorado potato beetle (Coleoptera: Chrysomelidae) defoliating on potato tuber production in eastern virginia. J. Econ. Entomol. 82: 948 -953.

87.   Zehnder, G.W., and W.D. Gelernter. 1989. Activity of the M-ONE formulation of a new strain of *Bacillus thuringiensis* against the Colorado potato beetle (Coleoptera: Chrysomelidae): Relationship between susceptibility and insect life stage. J. Econ. Entomol. 82:756 -761.

88.   Zehnder, G.W., G.M. Ghidiu, and J. Speese III. 1992. Use of the occurrence of peak colorado potato beetle (Coleoptera: Chrysomelidae) egg hatch for timing of *Bacillus thuringiensis* spray applications in potatoes. J. Econ. Entomol. 85:283 - 288.

DEVELOPMENT OF *BACILLUS THURINGIENSIS*-BASED PESTICIDES FOR THE CONTROL OF POTATO INSECT PESTS

Cynthia Gawron-Burke and Timothy B. Johnson
Ecogen Inc.
Langhorne, PA 19047-1810

Bacillus thuringiensis, or BT, is a soil-inhabiting microorganism primarily distinguished by its ability to produce proteinaceous crystalline inclusions upon sporulation. The proteins which comprise these crystalline inclusions are toxic when ingested by susceptible insects, and diverse insecticidal crystal proteins (ICPs) exhibiting toxicities against lepidopteran, dipteran, and coleopteran species have been characterized from a variety of BT strains (12).

The genes encoding ICPs have been categorized into four major classes (*CryI-CryIV*) based upon both the amino acid sequence homology and the insecticidal activity of the encoded crystal proteins (12). The *cryI* genes encode lepidopteran-active proteins of 130-140 kDa (CryI ICPs) that form bipyramidal crystalline inclusions and are significantly related (> 50 % positionally identical) in amino acid sequence. In contrast, the *cryIII* genes encode coleopteran-active proteins of approximately 74 kDa (CryIII ICPs) that differ in amino acid sequence from CryI ICPs and form crystals of distinct morphologies (e.g., rhomboid-shaped). Interestingly, despite highly related amino acid sequences, even ICPs of the same class can possess distinctly different insecticidal specificities against a particular insect pest. The CryIA(c) and CryIA(b) ICPs, for example, are greater than 80% identical in amino acid sequence, yet they differ dramatically (100-fold) in their toxicity to *Heliothis virescens* (Fabricius) larvae (12). Much research has been focused on elucidating the structure/function relationships of ICPs (8, 13, 21) and the recent determination of the atomic structure for the CryIIIA protein significantly increases our fundamental understanding of ICP structure and mode of insecticidal action (17). Recent reviews provide additional detailed discussions of BT molecular genetics and ICP mode of action (7, 12, 16).

ICP-encoding genes have been localized to large (>30 MDa) extrachromosomal elements termed plasmids (10), and it is not uncommon to find several plasmids harboring ICP genes residing in the same bacterial cell. These plasmids may encode one or more ICPs with varying insecticidal activities against a specific target insect (12, 15). Certain of these ICP-encoding plasmids can transfer from one cell to another by a bacterial genetic transfer process known as conjugation (9) and conjugal transfer has been used to derive novel combinations of ICP-encoding plasmids (see below).

A variety of BT-based biopesticide products are currently available for numerous agricultural applications, including the control of potato crop insect pests. The focus of this chapter will be the development of Ecogen Inc.'s Foil® OF BT bioinsecticide product, with a specific emphasis on genetic improvements of insecticidal potency and spectrum. Both the laboratory evaluation and the field efficacy of the Foil® OF bioinsecticide product will be discussed. We will also address future prospects for the development of BT-based bioinsecticide products for potato application through genetic manipulation, including approaches involving recombinant DNA technology.

Development of Foil® OF Bioinsecticide

The insecticidal activity of a BT strain is largely determined by the sum of the individual insecticidal activities of the ICPs produced by that strain. Altering the strain's genetic information with respect to its ability to produce certain ICPs, therefore, can have a profound effect on the strain's insecticidal activity. Ecogen's approach to BT strain improvement has been to couple a strain isolation and bioassay screening program with the use of microbial genetic approaches that can alter the BT strain's plasmid content. Knowing which ICP-encoding plasmid to add to, or subtract from, a given strain background in order to achieve optimal insecticidal potency and spectrum, requires both the identification and the characterization of ICP-encoding plasmids in the bacterial strain. Most important is the quantification of the inherent insecticidal activity of the individual ICPs encoded by each plasmid against the specific target of interest. The microbial genetic approaches of subtracting (through plasmid curing) or adding (via conjugal transfer) ICP-encoding plasmids have been used to derive BT strain EG2424, the active ingredient in the Foil® OF bioinsecticide product marketed by Ecogen Inc. for potato crop application.

More specifically, plasmids encoding ICPs with activity against the European corn borer (*Ostrinia nubilalis* (Hübner)), an occasional lepidopteran pest of potatoes in the mid-Atlantic region, were combined with a plasmid encoding an ICP with activity against the Colorado potato beetle (*Leptinotarsa decemlineata* (Say)). The plasmid compositions of the parental and intermediate strains used in the construction of strain EG2424 are illustrated in Figure 1. Initially, an

88 MDa native plasmid encoding the coleopteran-active CryIIIA protein was transferred via conjugation from a novel BT var. *morrisoni* isolate, EG2158 (4), to BT strain HD-263-8, a plasmid cured derivative of the BT var. *kurstaki* strain HD-263. Since strain HD-263-8 harbored a native 60 Mda plasmid encoding the lepidopteran-active CryIA(c) protein, the product of the mating event, transconjugant strain EG2421, harbored both the 60 MDa and the 88 MDa plasmids and encoded both the lepidopteran and the coleopteran-active ICPs. Subsequently, a 44 MDa native plasmid encoding an additional CryIA(c) gene, originally derived from strain HD-279-1, was introduced into strain EG2421 resulting in the transconjugant strain EG2424. Thus, strain EG2424 contains three ICP-encoding plasmids, the 88 MDa CryIIIA-encoding plasmid from strain EG2158, and the 44 MDa and the 60 MDa CryIA(c)-encoding plasmids from strains HD-279-1 and HD-263-8, respectively. Strain EG2424 produces both CryIIIA and CryIA(c) proteins, and as expected, contains both rhomboid and bipyramidal shape crystalline inclusions (Figure 2).

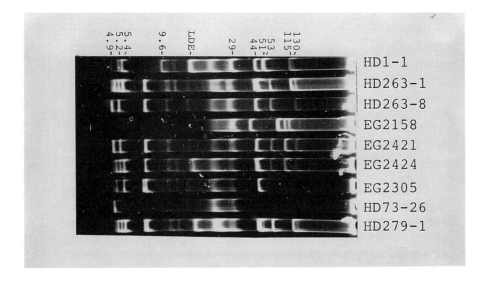

Figure 1. Construction of *Bacillus thuringiensis* var. *kurstaki* strain EG2424 via conjugal transfer. Ethidium bromide-stained agarose gel resolving plasmid DNA prepared from BT strains as indicated above each lane. Numbers at left indicate approximate plasmid mass in megadaltons. LDE, linear DNA element.

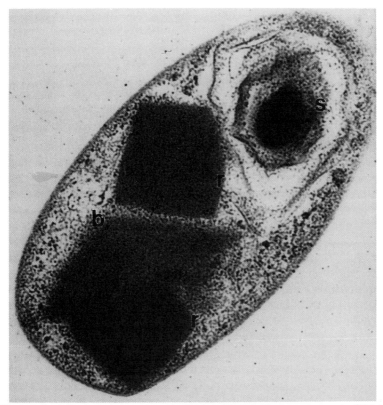

Figure 2. Crystalline inclusions produced by BT strain EG2424. Electron micrograph of BT strain EG2424 displaying spore (s), rhomboid (r) crystals containing CryIIIA protein, and bipyramidal (b) crystal containing CryIA(c) protein. Total magnification 60,000 X.

Laboratory evaluation of Foil® OF (EG2424) bioinsecticide. The Foil® OF bioinsecticide containing spores and crystals of BT strain EG2424, was evaluated in the laboratory using standard bioassay techniques with insects fed artificial agar-based diets (Table 1). Commercial samples of Foil® OF (lot OY-00223), M-One® (containing BT var. *san diego*), and Trident®, (containing BT var. *tenebrionis*), were tested against first-instar Colorado potato beetle in diet-surface-contamination bioassays. A modified version of Bio-Serve's #9380 agar-based diet was used as the test substrate and each assay consisted of eight doses with 32 larvae tested per dose. All products were evaluated simultaneously in four separate assays with data pooled for composite probit analyses (3, 6). The activity of Foil® OF against neonate European corn borer was illustrated in comparative bioassays with DiPel® 2X (containing BT subsp. *kurstaki* strain HD-1), a product marketed for the control of Lepidoptera. Neither M-One® nor Trident®

have activity against Lepidoptera. Bioassay techniques for European corn borer were as with Colorado potato beetle, except that a diet for Lepidoptera was used (14).

Recently, new techniques have been developed that allow BT-based product comparisons on an ICP-specific basis in addition to LC_{50} or International Unit comparisons. At Ecogen Inc., we measure the inherent potency of ICPs by multiplying LC_{50} values by the percent of ICP in the sample as determined by an SDS-PAGE technique (2) and refer to this value as the protein LC_{50} or PLC_{50}.

Table 1. Comparative insecticidal activity of Foil® OF, M-One®, Trident®, and DiPel®2X

Product[a]	% CryIIIA[b]	% CryIA[b]	CPB[c]		ECB[c]	
			LC_{50}	PLC_{50}	LC_{50}	PLC_{50}
Foil®OF	2.61	4.3	9.5	0.25	0.18	0.008
M-One®	2.37	0.0	40.9	0.97	NOT ACTIVE	
Trident®	0.53	0.0	233.7	1.24	NOT ACTIVE	
DiPel®2X	0.0	13.4	NOT ACTIVE		0.09	0.012

[a]Product lots tested were Foil®OF (OY-00223), M-One® (8205480), Trident® (1950979), and DiPel®2X (91-124BJ).
[b]Percent protein determined by SDS-PAGE (2) and includes both CryIA and CryIIA proteins for DiPel®2X.
[c]LC_{50} units are in ng product per mm^2 diet surface. PLC_{50} units are in ng CryIIIA protein per mm^2 diet surface for CPB (Colorado potato beetle) and in ng CryIA protein per mm^2 diet surface for ECB (European corn borer).

Due to the unique nature of the EG2424 strain, Foil®OF is toxic to both Lepidoptera and Coleoptera in contrast with other BT-based products that are toxic to only one order of insect (Table 1). Of particular interest is the greater Colorado potato beetle insecticidal activity of Foil®OF compared with the M-One® lot tested, as illustrated by both the LC_{50} and PLC_{50} values, even though the products contain similar amounts of CryIIIA protein as determined by SDS-PAGE.

Field efficacy of Foil®OF (EG2424) bioinsecticide. The field efficacy of Foil®OF for control of Colorado potato beetle and European corn borer larvae on potatoes has been demonstrated in both small plot research trials and in large commercial fields. In a small plot research trial located in Delmar, Delaware, USA, Foil®OF was applied at three rates and compared in efficacy to a commercial rate of Vydate®2L (oxamyl) (Table 2). Treatments were applied as broadcast sprays with a tractor mounted compressed air sprayer. Foil®OF provided significant control of both Colorado potato beetle and European corn borer infestations at all three rates tested and the level of control did not differ statistically from that observed with Vydate®2L. There was a strong numerical rate response for the control of Colorado potato beetle larvae with Foil®OF and a weaker rate response observed against European corn borer larvae. Foil®OF at 9.3 L/ha provided Colorado potato beetle control numerically equal to Vydate®2L. All rates of Foil®OF resulted in reduced European corn borer larval numbers, compared with Vydate®2L.

Table 2. Control of Colorado potato beetle and European corn borer on Red Norland potatoes[a]

| Treatment[a] | Rate | CPB larvae/ 10 plants | | ECB larvae/ 100 stems |
		6/1	6/8	6/18
Untreated	-	96 b	293 b	39 b
Vydate®2L	1.12 kg AI/ha	1 a	5 a	25 a
Foil®OF	2.3 L/ha	7 a	27 a	10 a
Foil®OF	4.7 L/ha	7 a	12 a	8 a
Foil®OF	9.3 L/ha	1 a	2 a	6 a

[a]Four weekly broadcast applications were applied in a total spray volume of 234 L/ha. Dates represent peak populations of 3-4th instar CPB (Colorado potato beetle) and a single count of ECB (European corn borer) at the conclusion of the trial. Means sharing a common letter are not significantly different (DMRT $P=0.05$).

An operational trial was conducted on three commercial farms in Accomac County, Virginia, USA, to compare the efficacy of Foil®OF to standard chemical insecticides. Treatment plots were 2 ha and were arranged in a randomized complete block design with five replications. Each block consisted of paired treatments (i.e., Foil®OF and standard chemical) separated by a 30 m buffer. Foil®OF was applied with a Piper Pawnee aircraft on a 5-7 day schedule for a total of five applications. The aircraft operated at 185 km/h and applied 4.7 L/ha of Foil®OF in a total spray volume of 47 L/ha. The cooperating growers selected standard insecticides for comparison based on their own management decisions. Seven different chemical insecticides, including carbofuran, azinphosmethyl, fenvalerate, oxamyl, esfenvalerate, permethrin, and parathion were used at label rates using ground and aerial equipment following a variable schedule. In limited cases, tank mixes of two or more chemicals were applied by the growers. Density of Colorado potato beetle adults, small larvae (first and second instars), and large larvae (third and fourth instars) was measured weekly starting in mid-May and continuing through mid-July. The sample unit was five potato stems and auxiliary branches surveyed at 10 sites per replicate. Visual estimates of defoliation were rated on 50 plants per replicate on a weekly basis. Data were analyzed as a two-factor (treatment X factor) analysis of variance for a randomized complete block design. The null hypothesis of comparable efficacy between Foil®OF and the chemical standards was tested by the significance of the treatment by date interaction in the ANOVA. A non-significant interaction would support the null hypothesis, while a significant term ($P=0.05$) would support the alternative hypothesis of superior efficacy from either the Foil®OF or chemical standards.

Measurement of small and large Colorado potato beetle larval and adult seasonal populations indicated similar and acceptable levels of control between Foil®OF and the chemical standards in the study (Figure 3). Defoliation estimates for both treatment regimes were below 20% throughout most of the trial, with defoliation reaching 20-30% at the trial's end, which is below defoliation thresholds corresponding to yield loss.

Future Development of BT Bioinsecticide Products for Potato Application

The development of future BT bioinsecticide products for potato crop application requires the consideration of additional important product development challenges. One such development challenge is to achieve significant reductions in the cost of production of the bioinsecticide, whether by increasing the yields of ICP produced during fermentation and/or by developing a more potent bioinsecticide that allows for a reduction in the product use rate. Another development challenge would be to improve the product's efficacy against a broader range of larval instars and possibly adults. Lastly, the incorporation of additional ICPs with different modes of action against the target pest would expand available resistance management strategies. We have recently made progress in addressing several of these product development challenges through the discovery of novel CPB-active ICPs and the use of BT strain improvement approaches that include the application of recombinant DNA technology.

The use of radioactively-labeled *cryIII* genes as hybridization probes in BT strain isolation has enabled the discovery of novel BT strains encoding CryIII proteins that are distinct from CryIIIA, the CPB-active protein contained in BT var. *kurstaki* strain EG2424 (4), BT var. *tenebrionis* (20), and BT var. *san diego* (11). One such isolate, BT var. *tolworthi* strain EG2838, was recently shown to contain a 100 MDa plasmid encoding a 74 kDa protein (CryIIIB) with activity against CPB larvae (19). Yet another novel isolate, BT var. *kumamotoensis* strain EG4961, was found to contain a 95 MDa plasmid encoding a similar-sized, but unique, protein (CryIIIC) with insecticidal activity against both CPB and southern corn rootworm (*Diabrotica undecimpunctata howardi*) larvae (19). The cloning and characterization of the *cryIII* genes encoding these novel proteins has confirmed the distinct amino acid sequence of CryIIIB and CryIIIC (subsequently termed CryIIIB2) from that of CryIIIA and from each other (5).

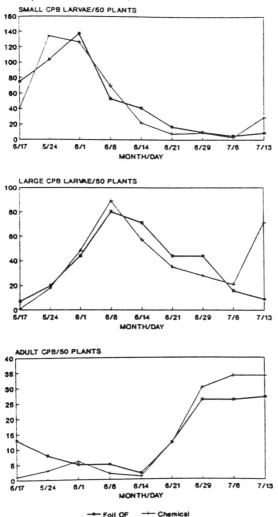

Figure 3. Comparison of Foil®OF and synthetic chemical insecticides for the control of Colorado potato beetle in commercial potatoes, Accomac County, Virginia, USA.

The construction of recombinant BT strains harboring each of these novel *cryIII* genes enabled insect bioassay evaluation of crystalline inclusions comprised solely of the novel CryIII protein against Colorado potato beetle larvae (Table 3). The CryIIIA and CryIIIB2 proteins are the most active of the CryIII proteins tested against Colorado potato beetle larvae. These proteins display similar levels of potency despite their distinct amino acid sequences. (CryIIIB2 is approximately 69% positionally identical to CryIIIA in amino acid sequence.) Interestingly, the CryIIIB protein, which is greater than 94% identical to CryIIIB2 at the level of amino acid sequence, is significantly less potent than CryIIIB2 and CryIIIA. Thus, minimal changes in critical regions of the CryIII proteins can result in significant differences in insecticidal activity, as has been observed for the lepidopteran-active CryI and CryII proteins (8, 21).

Table 3. Insecticidal activity of CryIII proteins against Colorado potato beetle larvae

Protein	PLC_{50}[a]	95% C.I.[a]
CryIIIA	0.34	0.30-0.39
CryIIIB	1.26	1.07-1.46
CryIIIB2	0.29	0.26-0.34

[a] Values are in ng CryIII protein per mm^2 diet surface. Freeze-dried powders of BT strain HD-73-26 containing recombinant plasmids encoding each of the CryIII proteins were assayed against first-instar Colorado potato beetle.

Since not all ICP-encoding genes are located on transferable plasmids, the ability to incorporate novel ICPs into various BT strain backgrounds for the purposes of BT bioinsecticide development is greatly aided by the use of recombinant DNA technology. The recent development of an improved transformation procedure for BT (18), as well as the construction of a family of compatible BT-*Escherichia coli* shuttle vectors (pEG597, pEG853, and pEG854 (1)) derived, in part, from native BT plasmids, enables greater flexibility in producing novel combinations of native and/or modified ICP genes in BT. The design of shuttle vectors such as pEG853 permits the construction of small, stable, recombinant plasmids encoding various ICP genes. These plasmids can be introduced into a variety of BT strain backgrounds including those harboring native ICP-encoding plasmids (1).

Ecogen Inc. has used the BT shuttle vector system to construct the recombinant BT strain EG7618, which produces a novel combination of ICPs useful in the control of the European corn borer and the Colorado potato beetle on potatoes, the original target pests of the Foil®OF bioinsecticide product. In fact, BT strain EG7618 was derived using the host-background of BT strain EG2424, the active ingredient in the Foil®OF bioinsecticide product. More specifically, the recombinant plasmid, pEG894, consisting of a native BT replication origin (*ori60*), a *crylIIB2* gene, an antibiotic resistance marker (Cm^R), and a silent copy of the *Escherichia coli* beta-galactosidase gene was introduced into a plasmid cured derivative of EG2424. With the exception of the *lacZ* coding region and the antibiotic resistance marker incorporated for field monitoring, there is no genetic information foreign to BT in BT strain EG7618. BT strain EG7618 produces both CryIIIA and CryIIIB2 coleopteran-active proteins as well as the lepidopteran-active CryIA(c) protein and, as expected, produces both a bipyramidal crystal (CryIA(c)) and a second irregular shaped crystal (CryIIIA and CryIIIB2). Since the ratio of CryIII/CryI encoding genes has been increased in strain EG7618, the strain produces a greater amount of CryIII protein than that produced by strain EG2424, improving the yield of CPB-active protein during fermentation.

The recombinant BT strain EG7618 was evaluated for control of Colorado potato beetle larvae on potatoes at two field locations in 1991 (Table 4). At both locations, small-plot research trials were conducted comparing Foil®OF and EG7618 formulated as a non-aqueous flowable, containing 5.5% CryIII crystal protein. Foil®OF was applied at 4.7 and 7.0 L/ha, while EG7618 was applied at 3.5 L/ha. Note that the 7.0 L rate of Foil®OF results in an equivalent amount of CryIII protein applied per ha as 3.5 L of EG7618.

Table 4. Control of Colorado potato beetle larvae on potatoes with Foil®OF and EG7618

Treatment	Rate (L/ha)	% CryIII	Painter, VA[a] CPB/stem 6/3	Germansville, PA[b] CPB/stem 8/13	8/20
Foil®OF	4.7	2.75	1.8 b	3.9 b	4.3 b
Foil®OF	7.0	2.75	0.8 b	4.1 b	2.3 b
EG7618	3.5	5.50	0.5 b	2.2 b	2.0 b
Untreated	-	-	13.7 a	13.1 b	12.0 b

[a]Five applications were applied weekly with a backpack sprayer in a total volume of 514 L/ha. Date represents the peak population of 3-4th instar CPB (Colorado potato beetle). Means sharing a common letter are not significantly different (Ryan's Q-Test $P=0.05$).

[b]Eight weekly applications were applied with a backpack sprayer in a total volume of 327-411 L/ha. Dates represent peak populations of 3-4th instar CPB (Colorado potato beetle). Means sharing a common letter are not significantly different (DMRT $P=0.05$).

In both experiments, all bioinsecticide treatments resulted in statistically reduced larval populations, compared with the untreated control, with no significant differences noted among BT treatments. Overall, CPB numbers in the 7.0 L Foil®OF treatment were lower than in the 4.7 L Foil®OF treatment. Although not statistically significant, EG7618 at 3.5 L/ha provided slightly better control than the 7.0 L rate of Foil®OF. Interestingly, in both experiments, fewer adult Colorado potato beetles were observed in EG7618 plots compared with the Foil®OF plots (data not shown).

These field trials demonstrate the potential of using recombinant DNA technology to produce improved BT-based bioinsecticide products for potatoes with reduced usage rates, while retaining a dual activity against both lepidopteran and coleopteran insects.

Epilogue

The genetic manipulation of *Bacillus thuringiensis* strains has played a significant role in the development of BT-based biopesticides for potato crop application. The ability to combine ICP-encoding plasmids using the non-recombinant approaches of plasmid curing and conjugal transfer has enabled the development of BT strain EG2424, the active ingredient in the Foil®OF biopesticide product marketed by Ecogen Inc. for the control of the Colorado potato beetle and the European corn borer. The BT strain EG2424 produces both coleopteran-active (CryIIIA) and lepidopteran-active (CryIA(c)) insecticidal crystal proteins, resulting in the Foil®OF bioinsecticide product with a wider insecticidal spectrum and improved insecticidal potency.

In addition, the development of BT transformation and plasmid vector systems enables the application of recombinant DNA technology for the development of improved BT bioinsecticide products. Recombinant DNA technology has been used to develop a derivative of BT strain EG2424, BT strain EG7618, that produces a novel ICP protein (CryIIIB2) with significant activity against the Colorado potato beetle. With the exception of the *lacZ* coding region and the antibiotic resistance marker incorporated for field monitoring, there is no genetic information foreign to BT in BT strain EG7618. BT strain EG7618 demonstrated effective control of the Colorado potato beetle on potatoes in small-scale field trials in 1991.

Acknowledgements

We gratefully acknowledge the many contributions of our colleagues in Research and Development at Ecogen Inc., in particular Jose González, William Donovan, James Baum, Richard Daoust, Annette Slaney and Marion Burgwin. We also acknowledge the contribution of Anthony Macaluso during his tenure at Ecogen Inc. We thank Bridget Stemberger of the Electron Microscope Facility at The Pennsylvania State University for the electron micrograph depicted in Figure 2, and William Donovan, James Baum, and Bruce Carlton for critical review of the manuscript. The secretarial assistance of Barbara Stakes is much appreciated.

Literature Cited

1. Baum, J. A., Coyle, D. M., Gilbert, M. P., Jany, C. S. and Gawron-Burke, C. 1990. Novel cloning vectors for *Bacillus thuringiensis*. Appl. Environ. Microbiol., 56:3420-2328.

2. Brussock, S. M. and Currier, T. C. 1990. Use of sodium dodecyl sulfate-polyacrylamide gel electrophoresis to quantify *Bacillus thuringiensis* delta-endotoxins. In: Analytical chemistry of *Bacillus thuringiensis* (Hickle, L. A., and Titch, W. L., eds.), American Chemical Society, Washington, D.C.

3. Daum, R. J. 1970. Revision of two computer programs for probit analysis. Bull. Entomol. Soc. Amer., 16:10-15.

4. Donovan, W. P., Gonzalez, J. M., Gilbert, M.P. and Dankocsik, C. 1988. Isolation and characterization of EG2158, a new strain of *Bacillus thuringiensis* toxic to coleopteran larvae, and nucleotide sequence of the toxin gene. Mol. Gen. Genet., 214:365-372.

5. Donovan, W. P., Rupar, M. J., Slaney, A. C., Malvar, T., Gawron-Burke, M. C., and Johnson, T. B. 1992. Characterization of two genes encoding *Bacillus thuringiensis* crystal proteins insecticidal for Coleoptera species. Applied and Environmental Microbiology. 58:3921-3927.

6. Finney, D. J. 1971. Probit analysis. Cambridge University Press, London, England.

7. Gawron-Burke, C. and Baum, J. A. 1991. Genetic manipulation of *Bacillus thuringiensis* insecticidal crystal protein genes in bacteria. In: Genetic Engineering, Vol. 13. (Setlow, J. K. ed.), pp. 237-263, Plenum Press, New York.

8. Ge, A. Z., Shivarova, N. I., and Dean, D. H. 1989. Location of the *Bombyx mori* specificity domain on a *Bacillus thuringiensis* delta-endotoxin protein. Proc. Nat. Acad. Sciences, U.S.A., 86:4037-4041.

9. González, J. M. Jr., Brown, B. J., and Carlton, B. C. 1982. Transfer of *Bacillus thuringiensis* plasmids coding for delta-endotoxin among strains of *B. thuringiensis* and *B. cereus*. Proc. Nat. Acad. Sciences, U.S.A., 79:6951-6955.

10. González, J. M. Jr., Dulmage, H. T., and Carlton, B. C. 1981. Correlation between specific plasmids and delta-endotoxin production in *Bacillus thuringiensis*. Plasmid, 5:351-365.

11.   Herrnstadt, C., Gilroy, T. E., Sobieski, D. A., Bennet, B. D., and Gaertner, F. H. 1987. Nucleotide sequence and deduced amino acid sequence of a coleopteran-active delta-endotoxin gene from *Bacillus thuringiensis* subsp. *san diego*. Gene, 57:37-46.

12.   Höfte, H., and Whiteley, H. R. 1989. Insecticidal crystal proteins of *Bacillus thuringiensis*. Microbiological Reviews, 53:242-255.

13.   Honëe, G., Convents, D, Van Rie, J., Jansens, S., Peferoen, M., and Visser, B. 1991. The C-terminal domain of the toxic fragment of a *Bacillus thuringiensis* crystal protein determines receptor binding. Molecular Microbiol., 5:2799:2806.

14.   King, E. G., and Hartley, G. G. 1985. *Heliothis virescens*, In: Handbook of insect rearing, Vol. 2, (Singh, P. and Moore, R. F., eds.) pp. 323-328, Elsevier Science Publishers, B. V. Amsterdam.

15.   Kronstad, J. W. and Whiteley, H. R. 1986. Three classes of homologous *Bacillus thuringiensis* crystal protein genes. Gene, 43:29-40.

16.   Lereclus, D., Bourgouin, C., Lecadet, M.-M., Klier, A. and Rapaport, G. 1989. Role structure and molecular organization of the genes coding for the parasporal delta-endotoxins of *Bacillus thuringiensis*. In: Regulation of Prokaryotic Development (Smith, I., Slepecky, R. A., and Setlow, P., eds.), pp. 255-276, American Society for Microbiology, Washington, D.C.

17.   Li, J., Caroll, J., and Ellar, D. J. 1991. Crystal structure of insecticidal delta-endotoxin from *Bacillus thuringiensis* at 2.5 Å resolution. Nature, 353:815-821.

18.   Macaluso, A., and Mettus, A.-M. 1991. Efficient transformation of *Bacillus thuringiensis* requires non-methylated plasmid DNA. J. Bacteriol., 173:1353-1356.

19.   Rupar, M. J., Donovan, W. P., Groat, R. G., Slaney, A. C., Mattison, J. W., Johnson, T. B., Charles, J.-F., Dumanoir, V. C., and de Barjac, H. 1991. Two novel strains of *Bacillus thuringiensis* toxic to coleopterans. Appl. and Environ. Microbiol., 57:3337-3344.

20.   Sekar, V., Thompson, D. V., Maroney, M. J., Bookland R.G., and Adang, M. J. 1987. Molecular cloning and characterization of the insecticidal crystal protein gene of *Bacillus thuringiensis* var. *tenebrionis*. Proc. Nat. Acad. Sciences, U.S.A., 84:7036-7040.

21.   Widner, W. R., and Whiteley, H. R. 1990. Location of the dipteran specificity region in a lepidopteran-dipteran crystal protein from *Bacillus thuringiensis*. J. Bacteriol.,172:2826-2832.

BIOTECHNOLOGY AND RESISTANCE TO POTATO VIRUSES

Philip H. Berger
Department of Plant, Soil and
Entomological Sciences
University of Idaho
Moscow, ID 83843

It is probably fair to state that the amount of information obtained about plant viruses, at the molecular level, in the last ten years equals or surpasses the entire sum of our knowledge prior to 1980. These recent advances can be traced to discoveries in two related areas of research: recombinant DNA technology and genetic engineering of higher plants. Consequently, experiments are being performed today that were unimaginable prior to the early 1970's. As a consequence, the nucleotide sequence of many plant viruses has been determined. This information, combined with a multitude of additional analyses, has contributed to our understanding of the replicational and translational strategies used by many plant viruses.

Perhaps one of the more interesting and useful discoveries derived from these advances is that viral genetic information can be used to control virus infection and replication, and has been useful in both experimental and practical bases. Currently, there are a number of strategies that are available for this purpose. Some have already been demonstrated to be effective while others may be potentially useful. The purpose of this review is to discuss the various real or potential strategies that are or may be useful for the control of potato viruses. A number of other, useful reviews have also been published recently (5,27,30,39,54,100,106).

Many of the advances in the area of transgenic resistance can be traced back to two fundamental discoveries. The first dates back many years with the observation that, in some cases, host infection with a 'mild' strain of a virus will prevent superinfection with a 'severe' strain of that virus, i.e., "cross-protection" (68). 'Classical' cross-protection thus requires identification of mild strains of a virus and a practical method for delivery in the field. There is an inherent risk in using live virus for crop protection due to the probability of some finite loss in yield due to the protecting virus alone. Furthermore, the protecting strain may be severe on other species or may mutate to a more severe form. The mechanism by which cross-protection functions is still unknown and a number of hypotheses have been put forward to explain this phenomenon (66). Nonetheless, the existence of cross-protection provides the background for using viral genetic information as a control device.

The second and more recent discovery is that foreign genes can be inserted into and stably expressed as part of a higher plant genome. As long as one pays attention to the requirements of higher plants in terms of coding and regulatory sequence needs, many genes can be inserted into and expressed by the plants' genome. These include genes from other eukaryotes and even many genes of prokaryotic origin. It is now apparent that these two avenues of investigation have essentially opened up a new field of research: Transgenic or pathogen-derived resistance (PDR) to plant viruses.

As of this writing, several different approaches have been used successfully to generate genetically engineered plants that express genes conferring resistance to specific plant viruses. These, as well as other approaches which may be promising, will be discussed below.

Potato Viruses

With a few exceptions, all of the viruses known to infect *Solanum tuberosum* (L.) are single-stranded positive-sense RNA viruses. These are listed in Table 1. Note that this list is not comprehensive and that the genome structure of some viruses has not as yet been determined or confirmed. The viruses are arbitrarily divided into those of "major" or "minor" importance. This division is probably justified on the basis of the amount of effort expended towards controlling certain virus diseases, but the relative economic impact of any particular virus will vary from year to year and by region. Perhaps one way to justify classifying certain viruses as responsible for causing a major impact on potato production is to consider the research effort towards understanding, detecting and controlling these disease agents. Thus, in the Pacific Northwest, potato leafroll virus (PLRV) is considered to be the most significant problem (see Mowry this volume) and is followed closely by potato virus Y (PVY). Potato viruses S and X (PVS, PVX) are included because of their ubiquitous presence. During the 1991 growing season, PVY was probably the major problem. A more complete overview of potato viruses can be found in de Bokx and van der Want (16).

Table 1. Viruses known to infect potato.

1. Viruses of "Major" Importance:

Virus Name	Abbrev.	Genome	Group	Vector
Potato Leafroll Virus	PLRV	ss(+)RNA	Luteovirus	aphids *
Potato Virus Y	PVY	ss(+)RNA	Potyvirus	aphids
Potato Virus X	PVX	ss(+)RNA	Potexvirus	mechanical
Potato Virus S	PVS	ss(+)RNA	Carlavirus	aphids
Potato Spindle Tuber Viroid	PSTVd	viroid	mechanical	

2. Viruses of "Minor" Importance:

Virus Name	Abbrev.	Genome	Group	Vector
Alfalfa Mosaic Virus	AIMV	ss(+)RNA	AIMV group	aphids
Andean Potato Mottle Virus	APMV	ss(+)RNA	Comovirus	mech/beetles?
Andean Potato Latent Virus	APLV	ss(+)RNA	Tymovirus	mech./beetle
Beet Curly Top Virus	BCTV	ssDNA	Geminivirus	leafhopper
Cucumber Mosaic Virus	CMV	ss(+)RNA	Cucumovirus	aphids
Potato Aucuba Mosaic Virus	PAMV	ss(+)RNA	Potexvirus	aphids**
Potato Moptop Virus	PMTV	ss(+)RNA	Tobamovirus	mechanical
Potato Virus A	PVA	ss(+)RNA	Potyvirus	aphids
Potato Virus M	PVM	ss(+)RNA	Carlavirus	aphids
Potato Virus T	PVT	ss(+)RNA	Closterovirus?	?
Potato Yellow Dwarf Virus	PYDV	ss(-)RNA	Rhabdovirus	leafhopper
Potato Yellow Vein Virus	PYVV	?		?
Solanum Apical Leaf Curling Virus	SALCV	ssDNA?	Geminivirus?	?
Tobacco Mosaic Virus	TMV	ss(+)RNA	Tobamovirus	mechanical
Tobacco Necrosis Virus	TNV	ss(+)RNA	Necrovirus	fungus
Tobacco Rattle Virus	TRV	ss(+)RNA	Tobravirus	nematodes
Tobacco Ringspot Virus	TRSV	ss(+)RNA	Nepovirus	nematodes
Tobacco Streak Virus	TSV	ss(+)RNA	Ilarvirus	thrips, pollen?
Tomato Blackring Virus	TBRV	ss(+)RNA	Nepovirus	nematodes
Tomato Spotted Wilt Virus	TSWV	ss(+)RNA	Tospovirus	thrips

*Primarily *Myzus persicae*.

**When plants are also infected with PVA or PVY.

However, we must consider any virus capable of causing disease in potato, particularly those that can be transmitted via seed pieces, as a potentially serious threat. It is little consolation to a farmer to know that his crop was severely damaged by an unimportant virus. All of the viruses considered to be of major importance and many of the less economically important ones are or can be seed-borne and a few may be transmitted via true potato seed. Although not a true virus, potato spindle tuber viroid (PSTVd) is included on the list because much of what is discussed below in terms of genetic engineering for virus resistance, may also apply to PSTVd.

A primary basis for control is through the use of virus-free seed. This is accomplished by limited generation of foundation seed and culling seed lots that, based on serological and field tests, exceed a certain pre-determined level of virus infection. Subsequent control measures include a number of cultural practices such as appropriate vector control, soil fumigation, sterilization of cutting tools, etc. Obviously, any additional treatment during seed or crop production increases input costs and reduces return to the grower. Furthermore, many chemical treatments such as fumigants or pesticides are environmentally hazardous; the decrease in availability of some of these treatments has resulted in a reduction in our ability to control viral diseases and other plant diseases.

Genetic Engineering of Higher Plants

Perhaps the most effective means of disease control is through the use of resistant cultivars. However, because of lack of suitable sources of resistance or difficulty of transfer of traits to agronomically useful cultivars, the use of resistance genes has not been particularly effective as an overall control strategy for virus diseases of potato. Genetic engineering now provides an alternative control strategy, because it has been demonstrated that foreign genes can be stably inserted into the genomes of higher plants which are subsequently inherited in a Mendelian fashion. This was accomplished by utilizing the inherent abilities of the soil-borne plant pathogen, *Agrobacterium tumefaciens*, which can transfer a portion of its genetic information to its host (see, 2). The *A. tumefaciens* strains used were modified so that they are no longer capable of causing disease yet still retain the ability to transfer genetic information as occurs naturally following infection. The process that is used today, on a routine basis, is relatively straightforward; e.g., a gene of interest is inserted into a Ti-based plasmid vector (e.g., 2,90). This plasmid contains a multiple cloning cassette, a selectable marker gene conferring antibiotic or herbicide resistance flanked by necessary control elements, and the border regions from *A. tumefaciens*. The multiple cloning cassette is also usually flanked by a promoter and terminator/polyadenine[poly(A)] addition recognition sequences, so that the gene of interest will be expressed properly and at acceptable levels. This new chimeric plasmid, after all necessary manipulations have been performed in *E. coli*, is used to transform an appropriate strain of *A. tumefaciens*. For potato, either leaf disks, stem internodes or microtubers are co-cultivated with the *A. tumefaciens* harboring the new plasmid, generally for two days. At this point the plant tissues are placed onto tissue culture media which induces shoot formation and contains the selection agent. For potato and most dicots the phytotoxic antibiotic kanamycin is used. Cells expressing the neomycin phosphotransferase (NPTII) gene, which was part of the chimeric plasmid used for transformation, will detoxify the antibiotic. Only kanamycin resistant cells will grow and divide. Using appropriate tissue culture methods, whole plants can be obtained from these explants. The presence of new genes as well as the number of insertion events can be assayed using standard biochemical techniques (e.g., Southern and northern blotting). The level of protein expression can be determined by western blotting or ELISA. Regulatory elements for gene expression and choice of a selectable marker can greatly influence the subsequent level of expression of a given gene. More importantly, the organization and arrangement of the inserted gene can also have a great effect. Care must be taken to insure that the gene(s) of interest will be properly expressed at desired levels (e.g., 29). A number of reviews discussing *Agrobacterium*-mediated plant transformation as well as other approaches have been published, including Goodman (37), Hooykaas (49), Potrykus (82), Weising et al. (105), and Zambryski (107).

Although the commonly used *Agrobacterium*-mediated plant transformation is an efficient means by which transgenic potato plants can be generated, alternative approaches are also available. These include electroporation of protoplasts and the biolistic process, among others (for a recent review, see (89)). The biolistic process, although perhaps not as efficient for potato as *Agrobacterium*-based approaches, may have certain advantages when it becomes desirable to insert multiple genes (e.g., 38).

Plant Virus Genes and Genomes

Plant viruses have evolved a number of strategies for utilization and expression of their genetic information. Generally, ss(+) RNA plant virus genomes encode genes for structural protein(s), proteins involved in cell-to-cell movement and vector transmission, and enzymes involved in the replication process. Energy and raw materials for the processes required for replication and translation are provided by the host. Discussed below are genome organizations and translation strategies of two of the most important potato viruses.

Potyviruses. Potyviruses have a single-stranded RNA (ssRNA) genome of approx. 9.6 kb with a genome-linked viral protein (VPg) at the 5'-end and a polyadenine tail at the 3'-end. The VPg is thought to play a role in replication. The genome is translated as a large polyprotein which is then autocatalytically cleaved to produce the mature viral proteins (1,18,19). The proteinases involved in this processing are part of the polyprotein, although the entire sequence of events involved in autocatalysis has yet to be completely elucidated (13). The only translation initiation codon present in the potyvirus genome is approx. 220 bases upstream from the 5'-end. Thus, with the exception of the first cistron, none of the other cistrons contain an in-frame initiation codon, so an AUG codon must be engineered for plant expression. Also, one must keep in mind principles that have been formulated regarding the context in which the AUG codon exists (58,63,97). The three bases upstream and two bases downstream of AUG codon are critical in terms of *in planta* translational efficiency, particularly the bases at the -3 and +4 positions (relative to A of AUG). Interestingly, the 'natural' AUG used by potyvirus genomes would not be predicted to be particularly efficient.

Luteoviruses. The situation with luteoviruses, which include potato leafroll virus (PLRV) is somewhat different from potyviruses. These viruses have a ssRNA genome of ca. 5.6 kb. Like the potyviruses, the 5'-end contains a VPg, but the 3'-end has a long untranslated region ending in an -OH group. There is no indication of a tRNA-like structure, which is found in a number of other non-polyadenylated viruses. Luteoviruses use a translational frameshift mechanism for expression of an RNA-dependent RNA polymerase from the 5'-half of the genome, and a subgenomic RNA for expression of the 3'-half of the genome (67,101). Within the subgenomic RNA of PLRV are two open reading frames; one (17 K) is internal to and in a different reading frame of the coat protein (CP) (23 K). Downstream and in-frame with the CP cistron is another cistron coding for a 56 K protein that is expressed as a fusion protein with CP as a result of readthrough of a leaky stop codon. There are two functional translation initiation codons in the subgenomic RNA, the second of which is 25 bases downstream from the CP AUG but in a different reading frame. (In fact, in PLRV there are two in-frame AUG codons, separated by a UCA (serine) codon, either of which is potentially capable of initiating translation of the 17 K cistron. It is still an open question as to which of these is the true initiation codon, although one might expect the first AUG encountered by ribosomes to be more effective.) This gene arrangement, due to preferential translation initiation at the 17 K AUG, may result in a less than desirable level of CP expression, unless modifications are made to the CP and/or 17 K AUG codons (95).

Limited data also suggest that the 17 K protein may play a role in regulating expression of CP (94).

Other Viruses. Between the potyvirus and luteovirus groups, many of the translation and replication strategies used by ss(+)RNA plant viruses are represented. Therefore, much of what is discussed above for the luteo- or potyviruses will also apply to other viruses infecting potato. For example, in cases where expression of a specific protein-encoding cistron is desired, there may already be a useful intitiation codon, it may be desirable to modify the initiation codon, or it may be necessary to insert one where it did not previously exist. A similar approach should also be applicable to negative-strand RNA viruses such as tomato spotted wilt or potato yellow dwarf viruses, keeping in mind that the non-encapsidated positive strand codes for protein but the negative strand is the source of the open reading frame(s) (e.g., 35).

Methods for Obtaining Transgenic Resistance

A number of approaches have been developed that have produced genetically engineered potato plants that resist virus infection. There are also several additional strategies that are potentially useful. Typically, transgenic resistance is manifested by either an amelioration in symptom severity, a delay in the onset of symptoms, a reduction in the rate of virus replication (i.e., virus titer), or a combination of these characteristics.

Coat protein-mediated resistance. The use of virus coat protein genes was the first demonstration of transgenic resistance and currently is the most widely used strategy. The first experimental application was the insertion of tobacco mosaic virus coat protein gene into tobacco. In this experiment, it was clearly shown that many of the transformants had much milder symptoms than the control plants and that the onset of symptoms was significantly delayed. There appeared to be high correlation between gene dose and resistance. Inoculation with high concentrations of inoculum or with naked RNA could overcome the resistance (85). This phenomenon has been termed coat protein-mediated resistance (CP-MR) and has been recently reviewed by Beachy et al. (6).

Since the first report of this phenomenon, much effort has been expended to try to determine the mechanism(s) behind CP-MR as well as to utilize this effect for practical purposes. It is sometimes tempting to equate CP-MR with "classical cross-protection". However, it should be kept in mind that it is still not entirely clear how classical cross-protection functions, and it may be erroneous to try to equate the two phenomena. Nonetheless, several possible explanations emerge that may or may not be the same for both CP-MR and classical cross-protection. Recent data strongly suggest that prevention of uncoating of incoming inoculum plays an important role in reducing or eliminating infection or virus accumulation and that re-encapsidation is not responsible for CP-MR (78,86). This concept is supported by work using two strains of tobacco rattle virus (TRV) whose CPs can encapsidate RNAs of either strain (103). It is clear that the CP itself and not CP-RNA sequences are required (84,87).

In the tobamoviruses, there appears to be a positive correlation between the amount of CP homology and the level of CP-MR, suggesting a structural requirement (75). Between different strains, however, expression of TMV-CP in tobacco afforded some protection against heterologous viruses including PVX and PVY (3,74); the reasons for this remain obscure. Indeed, expression of soybean mosaic potyvirus CP results in plants resistant to heterologous potyviruses (tobacco etch virus-TEV and PVY) (91). In addition, expression of tobacco vein mottling potyvirus (TVMV) CP affords higher levels of resistance to TEV than to TVMV itself (65). These reactions would not be predicted based on what is known in terms of relatedness of these coat proteins or "cross-protection".

Using protoplasts from TMV-CP(+) plants, Osbourn et al. (78) demonstrated that 93-99% of the inoculum (TMV) did not disassemble. Since the remaining 1-3% of the virions that did disassemble were probably capable of initiating a successful infection, it would appear that other factors beyond simple inhibition of disassembly are involved. What this factor(s) is remains to be determined although these data as well as work by others suggest an effect at the level of virus replication. In addition, this concept is supported by the occurrence of a number of exceptions to the situation with protection mediated by TMV-CP, some of which are mentioned above. For example, inoculation of transgenic tobacco expressing PVX-CP were resistant to challenge by PVX RNA (45). We must resist, for the present time at least, the temptation of extending conclusions or inferences based on tobamovirus work to other systems. Thus, although CP-MR is an interesting and extremely useful phenomenon, much yet remains to be discovered.

Antisense RNA-mediated resistance. Significant progress has been made in the last few years in the use of antisense technology, particularly as a means of regulation of gene expression (96). The use of antisense RNA constructs, i.e., viral genomes or portions of the genome inserted into plants in the 'opposite' orientation to produce complementary RNA, is an attractive alternative or adjunct to CP-MR. Here again, however, it is not entirely clear as to how this approach functions. One of the first examples of an antisense RNA, in this case a naturally occuring one from *E. coli* ("micRNA" or mRNA-interfering complementary RNA), was shown to function by inhibiting mRNA translation by blocking the ribosome binding site (71). Although the use of antisense RNAs to plant viruses has been demonstrated to reduce levels of virus in plants, it is not clear if this is the mechanism for *in planta* virus resistance. It is possible that an antisense construct, directed against the 3'-end of a viral genome, may inhibit replication by binding to the origin of replication (i.e., polymerase-binding site). It is also possible that an antisense construct could act as a competitor with virus negative strand, thus reducing the rate of replication.

In the cases of PVX and TMV, antisense-mediated resistance was disappointing (45,83). On the other hand, inhibition of cucumber mosaic virus (CMV) was effective with an antisense construct directed against the virus polymerase gene, but not the movement protein or 3'-end containing the replicase binding site (88). Another construct, directed against the CP region of CMV was only partially effective (14). Antisense constructs containing the PLRV-CP cistron region have been shown to be as effective against PLRV infection as sense, CP-expressing constructs (57). Because these constructs also contain a portion of the upstream noncoding region, which is presumably involved in synthesis and/or regulation of subgenomic RNA synthesis, it is difficult to determine how the antisense RNA may be functioning. Indeed, due to the extremely low levels of CP produced in transgenic potatoes using current gene constructs [Berger et al., unpublished; (56,57,102)], it is suggested that transgenic resistance, at least in the case of luteoviruses may be due to inhibition of replication and not to inhibition of incoming virus disassembly. Thus, it may be possible that CP-MR and transgenic resistance to PLRV may be due to interference in some way with replication rather than virus uncoating, and act more like a 'defective-interfering RNA' (see Sense RNA-mediated Resistance, below). By similar analogy, an antisense construct covering the same region of the viral genome is therefore also likely to interfere with replication rather than translation.

In the case of potyviruses, antisense-mediated resistance has been effective against infection of tobacco by tobacco etch virus (TEV) and bean yellow mosaic virus (BYMV). In the former case, an antisense construct of only the TEV-CP sequence was used while for BYMV the antisense construct was to the C-terminal half of BYMV-CP and included the entire 3'-end nontranslated region. In both cases resistance levels were equal to or exceeded CP-MR (W. Dougherty, personal communication; J. Hammond, personal communication).

Sense RNA-mediated resistance. As inferred above, a sense-RNA construct is simply one that includes a viral RNA construct in the sense, or (+) orientation. In a transgenic context, these constructs are intended to generate RNA transcripts but not necessarily to encode a protein. These can possibly be considered analogous to "defective-interfering" RNAs, which may or may not encode proteins (73). The possibility of using a sense orientation construct was suggested by Morch et al. (72), who demonstrated inhibition of turnip yellow mosaic virus (TYMV) replication *in vitro*. As long as the construct included the 3'-end of the genome, which presumably included the replicase recognition site, TYMV replication was reduced. Using TEV and a sense orientation CP construct, but with stop codons closely following the engineered CP AUG codon, very high levels of transgenic resistance were observed (W. Dougherty, personal communication). It may be that an RNA:RNA hybrid is formed between the sense transcript and negative strand virus RNA which results in inhibition of virus replication, as may be the case with defective-interfering particles.

Ribozyme-mediated resistance. The discovery that small RNA molecules, or "ribonucleic acid enzymes" (Rz's), are capable of specifically cleaving other RNA molecules in a catalytic manner has opened up a potentially fruitful area of research (80). The basic design for ribozymes originates with sequences found in the satellite RNA of tobacco ringspot virus (TobRSV) as well as certain other satellite RNAs and some viroids (43). These agents replicate via a rolling circle mechanism and the internal Rz sequence is responsible for cleaving the initial multimer into monomers. Depending on whether (+) or (-) strand is being cleaved, the 'hammerhead' or 'hairpin' Rz may be involved (10,24,25,40,41,44,51,93). (The first ribozyme discovered, from *Tetrahymena*, and characterized by Cech and co-workers, is a very different molecule and has not as of yet been utilized for possible plant protection.) Ribozymes, as they would be used to effect virus resistance, are essentially antisense molecules containing a catalytic, ribonuclease domain.

Since target (substrate) sequence requirements for a Rz are relatively flexible, there are numerous potential cleavage sites within a viral sequence. Thus, there are possible advantages to the ribozyme-mediated approach, including: 1) antisense-Rz constructs can be designed with more than one catalytic domain; 2) antisense-Rz's can be targeted against virtually any portion of the target virus sequence;

and 3) a sequence can be targeted that is highly conserved among virus isolates and strains, thus providing resistance to many strains and/or reducing the potential for resistance-breaking strains to occur.

There are now numerous examples of *in vitro*-tested Rz's, in plant and animal systems, but whether Rz-mediated resistance will reach its potential remains to be determined. In one of the very few *in vivo* experiments to date, Gerlach and colleagues inserted three hammerhead Rz's into an antisense construct (about 1 kb) directed against the 5'-end of TMV. In this example they observed a reduction in infection vs. the comparable antisense construct containing no Rz's (31). In contrast, Galasinski et al. (28) reported little difference in an antisense-hairpin Rz to TMV and an appropriate control. These studies point out the need for further research to determine: 1) the optimal size of a Rz in terms of the number and/or composition of bases complementary to the target (23,46); 2) optimal design of the catalytic domain so as to achieve the highest rate of cleavage under ambient conditions and; 3) optimal Rz design in terms of *in vivo* stability and longevity. Work to date indicates that a 'large' ribozyme, such as the one tested by Gerlach and colleagues may not in fact be catalytic because the enzyme will be unable to release from its substrate. On the other hand, while 'small' ribozymes (i.e., those with less than about 8-10 bases of complementarity) may have favorable reaction kinetics, the specificity of the reaction may also decrease proportionally and perhaps also *in vivo* stability may be adversely affected.

Resistance derived from nonstructural virus genes. Golemboski et al. (36) made a startling discovery while working with the putative 54 K gene of TMV, which is thought to play a role in virus replication. When this cistron was engineered into tobacco, the subsequent transformants were highly resistant to TMV infection regardless of whether virions or virus RNA were used as inoculum. Subsequent work indicated a very low level of virus replication in protoplasts from transgenic tobacco (12). Their results suggest that expression of the 54 K protein or its RNA inhibit virus replicase activity *in vivo*. A similar experiment has been performed where the entire putative polymerase gene of PVX was cloned into tobacco. Levels of resistance were obtained that equalled or exceeded CP-MR, although plants expressing only portions of the PVX polymerase gene were susceptible (9). This is an interesting contrast to the TMV 54 K situation in that the 54 K construct includes the GDD amino acid sequence motif common to many RNA-dependent RNA polymerases, yet a similar construct including this motif from PVX had no effect. Nevertheless, the result with PVX is still striking since the levels of resistance to PVX using CP-MR were very high (45).

Although the mechanism by which this functions is unknown, Carr & Zaitlin (12) suggest that expression of the 54 k cistron inhibits virus replication. It is possible that the mechanism of action in these cases is analogous to sense-mediated resistance and/or to defective-interfering RNAs, although this remains to be determined.

Resistance derived from plant virus satellites. Satellite RNAs are small molecules that require a helper virus for replication, but have no homology to and are not required for helper virus replication (26,98). Satellite viruses are similar, except that they are encapsidated in their own CP and have larger genomes (approximately 350 bases vs 800-1100 bases) and encode their own coat protein. It is not uncommon for the presence of satellite RNAs to correlate with an amelioration of symptoms. This effect may also be host dependent, whereby in one host symptoms are attenuated while in another they are exacerbated. Although the major viruses of potato do not appear to support satellite viruses or RNAs, the expression of DNA copies of certain satellite RNAs in transgenic plants has resulted in [helper] virus resistant plants. The most notable examples of satellite-mediated resistance come from cucumber mosaic virus (CMV) and TobRSV (32,42,52). Resistance appears to be effective against several virus strains using either RNA or intact virus as inoculum and did not appear to be affected by the concentration of inoculum. Note that in the cases of beet western yellow (BWYV) and barley yellow dwarf (BYDV) luteoviruses, a satellite RNA has been detected and thus it may also be possible that one also exists in association with PLRV (22,70). Although this is a viable strategy there may be certain risks associated with this approach. Some satellite RNAs can increase symptom severity rather than decrease it, and the sequence determinants that appear to mediate symptom expression are minimal, providing the potential for a possible detrimental mutation (e.g., 59,79).

Potential Approaches Towards Transgenic Resistance

The various strategies discussed above have examples supporting their utility *in vivo*. A number of other approaches have been proposed. The practical application of these other approaches remains to be established, however.

Certainly, there are sources of virus resistance to be found in certain potato cultivars, wild potato or other *Solanum* spp., e.g., *Solanum brevidens* Phil. (34,53). Several groups have used somatic hybridization to transfer desirable traits from *S. brevidens* to cultivated potato (e.g., 4). Traditional breeding of potato for certain desired traits has its own set of problems, however, and the ubiquitous cultivar Russet Burbank is particularly recalcitrant to traditional breeding techniques. Genetic engineering may provide a means whereby a specific gene can be cloned from a given source plant and inserted into an agronomic variety. Unfortunately, this is easier said than done and there are no known examples of isolated, characterized host-encoded virus resistance genes. Even if specific, single genes were identified (e.g., 81), the cloning, characterizing, and sequencing, etc. of such a gene is not a trivial task.

The use of pathogenesis-related (PR) protein genes is thought to have promise because they are produced by host plants in response to virus infection or other stress situations. PR proteins, of which there are at least 17 (8), are synthesized after induction by pathogen infection. They were first shown to accumulate in tobacco leaves responding hypersensitively to TMV infection (33,104). Not all of the PR proteins have been characterized, but some have been shown to have chitinase, ß-1,3-glucanase or have proteinase inhibition activity. Since TMV will induce PR protein synthesis in hypersensitive hosts, and there appears to be a correlation between PR protein presence and increasing disease resistance, it is logical to hypothesize that constitutive expression of one or more of these genes in a transgenic plant may protect the plant from virus infection. However, experiments conducted where intentional expression of a number of PR protein genes in tobacco was effected failed to result in appreciable levels of resistance to TMV and thus provide no evidence that these have antiviral activity (15,61). In addition, there is no correlation between PR proteins and transgenic CP-MR (11).

The immune response in higher animals is an essential component of their defense against infectious disease. It was recently demonstrated that immunoglobulin genes can be expressed in transgenic plants and functional molecules can be obtained (7,20,47). This is done by synthesizing complementary DNA (cDNA) from heavy- or light-chain immunoglobulin G (IgG) mRNA (typically using spleens from immunized mice as a source). By a series of manipulations one can obtain plants that contain heavy or light chain molecules, or both. The latter may result in IgG-like antigen-binding proteins. It is important to note that, in practice, appropriate signal peptides are also required so that the nascent chain is directed to the endoplasmic reticulum; this is necessary for assembly of heavy and light immunoglobulin chains (7). Thus, cloning of anti-virus [monoclonal] antibody genes, their insertion into plants, and retention of antigen-binding functionality is feasible. Whether this approach will be effective for transgenic resistance remains yet to be determined (92).

A further extension of this approach might be the use of anti-idiotypic antibodies. Anti-idiotype antibodies are those which are directed against the antigen-binding site of another antibody. It was suggested by Mernaugh et al. (69) and Gadani et al. (27) that expression of anti-idiotype antibodies, generated from anti-coat protein antibodies, could mimic CP structural epitopes and thus may mimic CP-MR. Although this approach may be applicable to animal virus systems where host receptors are usually directly involved in the infection process, it would appear unlikely that this tact would be effective for resistance to most plant viruses. Current data suggest that a functional or nearly functional CP is required to effect CP-MR and therefore mimicking a single CP epitope would be insufficient.

Finally, it has been proposed that interferon or interferon-like molecules might be effective in protecting plant cells from virus infection. Interferons (IFN) are a class of low molecular weight proteins secreted by [virus] infected, mammalian host cells which are capable of protecting non-infected cells from viral infection. Whether IFN is effective against (+) RNA plant viruses is still unclear at this time. Different groups have variously reported a lack of a detectable effect of IFN against TYMV or alfalfa mosaic virus (AlMV) (50,62), while two groups have reported that IFN had a significant inhibitory effect on TMV multiplication (76,77). A recent report suggests that certain antiviral proteins from tobacco share a structural relationship with IFN, although the significance of this is still uncertain (21).

Nevertheless, expression of IFN in a transgenic context, with the exception of expression by a recombinant cauliflower mosaic virus (CaMV), has not been reported to date (17). Thus, it is not yet possible to fully assess the potential for this approach; it remains to be seen whether expression of IFN will truly provide useful antiviral activity.

Transgenic Resistance to Potato Viruses and Prospects for the Future

There are currently a number of examples of transgenic resistance successfully applied to viruses capable of infecting potato, either in suitable host plants (usually tobacco) or in potato itself. These include resistance to the major virus diseases of potato, PLRV, PVS, PVX, and PVY (45,48,55-57,60,64,99,102). Most of these utilyze CP-MR, although antisense-mediated resistance is also used in some cases. In several cases, limited field-based testing has been conducted and will continue over the next few years. Assuming approval from the appropriate regulatory agencies, it is likely that commercial release of transgenic plants may occur by 1996 or perhaps earlier. However, much remains to be done at both the basic and applied levels. Many laboratories are trying to understand the mechanisms underlying the various phenomena discussed above, while a serious effort is underway to apply genetically engineered host plant resistance, on a practical level, to plant viruses as well as to other pathogens and insect pests.

Each of the approaches discussed above has advantages and disadvantages. Perhaps the greatest limitation at the present time is lack of control over the stable insertion of desired genes into plants. Admittedly, the technology has advanced significantly in a relatively short period of time. Yet it becomes difficult and eventually impractical when one wishes to insert multiple genes into a particular plant. This is an acute problem when one wishes to insert genes conferring resistance to multiple viruses, as is currently the case with potato. In the only example of resistance to more than one virus in the same plant, the inherent problems become evident. In this case Lawson et al. (60) demonstrated that it was possible to insert both PVY and PVX coat protein genes. This was done by creating a large, tandem construct for *Agrobacterium*-mediated plant transformation that contained three gene cassettes, one for each CP and the third for the selectable marker. Each cassette therefore contained its own promoter, terminator/poly(A) addition site and the gene of interest. Although they successfully generated plants resistant to both viruses and one line in particular (line 303) appeared especially promising (55,60) transformants were generated that resisted neither virus and/or expressed only one of the coat proteins. Even the transformant with good resistance to both viruses (60) expressed PVY-CP at extremely low levels.

A major factor in current plant transformation technology is one of diminishing returns in terms of the number of primary transformants relative to agronomically useful ones. No more than perhaps 10-20% of the primary transformants are likely to survive a breeder's selection process up to and including the first field test (and even this may be a very liberal estimate). When inserting multiple genes, this problem becomes exacerbated. It is hoped that as transformation technology improves during the near future, this will become much less of a problem. Possibly this will be effected by specific gene targeting methods rather than current methods which rely on random gene insertion.

Nevertheless, the most likely area for significant improvement will be in generation of potato plants that not only resist more than one virus but also resist individual viruses by more than one mechanism. History has demonstrated the inherent risk in 'single gene' resistance and there is no reason to assume that transgenic resistance will be any more risk-free than resistance obtained using a conventional approach.

Furthermore, it is reasonable to assume that, if more than one strategy is applied, then the subsequent level of resistance might be additive.

Literature Cited

1. Allison, R., Johnston, R. E., and Dougherty, W. G. 1986. The nucleotide sequence of the coding region of tobacco etch virus genomic RNA: evidence for the synthesis of a single polyprotein. Virology 154:9-20.
2. An, G. 1987. Binary Ti vectors for plant transformation and promoter analysis. Meth. Enzymol. 153:292-305.
3. Anderson, E. J., Stark, D. M., Nelson, R. S., Powell, P. A., Tumer, N. E., and Beachy, R. N. 1989. Transgenic plants that express the coat protein genes of tobacco mosaic virus or alfalfa mosaic virus interfere with disease development of some nonrelated viruses. Phytopathology 79:1284-1290.
4. Austin, S., Baer, M. A., and Helgeson, J. R. 1985. Transfer of resistance to potato leafroll virus from *Solanum brevidens* into *Solanum tuberosum* by somatic fusion. TIG 5:56-60
5. Baulcombe, D. 1989. Strategies for virus resistance in plants. TIG 5:56-60.
6. Beachy, R. N., Loesch-Fries, S., and Tumer, N. E. 1990. Coat protein-mediated resistance against virus infection. Annu. Rev. Phytopathology 28:451-474.
7. Benvenuto, E., Ordàs, R. J., Tavazza, R., Ancora, G., Biocca, S., Cattaneo, A., and Galeffi, P. 1991. 'Phytoantibodies': a general vector for the expression of immunoglobulin domains in transgenic plants. Plant Mol. Biol. 17:865-874.
8. Bol, J. F., Linthorst, H. J. M., and Cornelissen, B. J. C. 1990. Plant pathogenesis-related proteins induced by virus infection. Annu. Rev. Phytopathology 28:113-138.
9. Braun, C. J., Weiss, J. D., and Tumer, N. E. 1991. Alternate strategies for viral protection. *In* 3rd Int. Congr. Plant Mol. Biol. Tucson, AZ,
10. Bruening, G. 1989. Compilation of self-cleaving sequences from plant virus satellite RNAs and other sources. Meth. Enzymol. 180:546-558.
11. Carr, J. P., Beachy, R. N., and Klessig, D. F. 1989. Are the PR1 proteins of tobacco involved in genetically engineered resistance to TMV? Virology 169:470-473.
12. Carr, J. P., and Zaitlin, M. 1991. Resistance in transgenic tobacco plants expressing a nonstructural gene sequence of tobacco mosaic virus is a consequence of markedly reduced virus replication. Mol. Plant-Microbe Interact. 4:579-585.
13. Carrington, J. C., Freed, D. D., and Oh, C. S. 1990. Expression of potyviral polyproteins in transgenic plants reveals three proteolytic activities required for complete processing. EMBO J. 9:1347-1353.
14. Couzzo, M., O'Connel, K. M., Kaniewski, R.-X., Fang, R. H., Chua, N.-H., and Tumer, N. E. 1988. Viral protection in transgenic plants expressing the cucumber mosaic virus coat protein or its antisense RNA. Biotechnology 6:549-557.
15. Cutt, J. R., Harpster, M. H., Dixon, D. C., Carr, J. P., Dunsmuir, P., and Klessig, D. F. 1989. Disease response to tobacco mosaic virus in transgenic plants that constitutively express the pathogenesis-related PR1b gene. Virology 173:89-97.
16. de Bokx, J. A., and Van der Want, J. P. H. 1987. Viruses of potatoes and seed-potato production. Pudoc, Wageningen. 259 pp.

17. De Zoeten, G. A., Penswick, J. R., Horisberger, M. A., Ahl, P., Schultze, M., and Hohn, T. 1989. The expression, localization and effect of a human interferon in plants. Virology 172:213-222.

18. Domier, L. L., Franklin, K. M., Shahabuddin, M., Hellmann, G. M., Overmeyer, J. H., Hiremath, S. T., Siaw, M. F. E., Lomonosoff, G. P., Shaw, J. G., and Rhoads, R. E. 1986. The nucleotide sequence of tobacco vein mottling virus RNA. Nucl. Acids Res. 14:5417-5430.

19. Dougherty, W. G., and Carrington, J. C. 1988. Expression and function of potyviral gene products. Annu. Rev. Phytopathology 26:123-143.

20. Düring, K., Hippe, S., Kreuzaler, F., and Schell, J. 1990. Synthesis and self-assembly of a functional monoclonal antibody in transgenic Nicotiana tabacum. Plant Mol. Biol. 15:281-293.

21. Edelbaum, O., Ilan, N., Grafi, G., Scher, N., Stram, Y., Novick, D., Tal, N., Sela, I., and Rubinstein, M. 1990. Two antiviral proteins from tobacco: Purification and characterization by monoclonal antibodies to human ß-interferon. Proc. Natl. Acad. Sci. USA 87:588-592.

22. Falk, B. W., Chin, L.-S., and Duffus, J. E. 1989. Complementary DNA cloning and hybridization analysis of beet western yellows luteovirus RNAs. J. Gen. Virol. 70:1301-1309.

23. Fedor, M. J., and Uhlenbeck, O. C. 1990. Substrate sequence effects on "hammerhead" RNA catalytic efficiency. Proc. Natl. Acad. Sci. USA 87:1668-1672.

24. Feldstein, P. A., Buzayan, J. M., and Bruening, G. 1989. Two sequences participating in the autolytic processing of satellite tobacco ringspot virus complementary RNA. Gene 82:53-61.

25. Forster, A. C., and Symons, R. H. 1987. Self-cleavage of plus and minus RNAs of a virusoid and a structural model for the active sites. Cell 49:211-220.

26. Francki, R. I. B. 1985. Plant virus satellites. Annu. Rev. Microbiol. 39:151-74.

27. Gadani, F., Mansky, L. M., Medici, R., Miller, W. A., and Hill, J. H. 1990. Genetic engineering of plants for virus resistance. Arch. Virol.115:1-21.

28. Galasinski, S., Zinnen, T., and Hauptmann, R. 1991. In vivo targeting of tobacco mosaic virus by a hairpin ribozyme. 3rd Int. Congr. Plant Mol. Biol. Tucson, AZ. (abstr.)

29. Gallie, D. R., Lucas, W. J., and Walbot, V. 1989. Visualizing mRNA expression in plant protoplasts: Factors influencing efficient mRNA uptake and translation. Plant Cell 1:301-311.

30. Gasser, C. S., and Fraley, R. T. 1989. Genetically engineering plants for crop improvement. Science 244:1293-1299.

31. Gerlach, W. L., Haseloff, J. P., Young, M. J., and Bruening, G. 1990. Use of plant virus satellite sequences to control gene expression. Pages 177-186 in: Viral Genes and Plant Pathogenesis. (T.P. Pirone and J.G. Shaw, eds.). Springer-Verlag, New York.

32. Gerlach, W. L., Llewellyn, D., and Haseloff, J. 1987. Construction of a plant disease resistance gene from the satellite RNA of tobacco ringspot virus. Nature 328:802-805.

33. Gianinazzi, S., Martin, C., and Vallée, J. C. 1970. Hypersensiblité aux virus, température et protéines solubles chez le Nicotiana Xanthi nc. Apparition de nouvelles macromolécules lors de la répression de la synthèse virale. C.R. Acad. Sci. (Paris) D270:2383-2386.

34. Gibson, R. W., Pehu, E., Woods, R. D., and Jones, M. G. K. 1990. Resistance to potato virus Y and potato virus X in Solanum brevidens. Ann. Appl. Biol. 116:151-156.

35. Gielen, J. J. L., de Haan, P., Kool, A. J., Peters, D., van Grinsven, M. Q. J. M., and Goldbach, R. W. 1991. Engineered resistance to tomato spotted wilt virus, a negative-strand RNA virus. Biotechnology 9:1363-1367.

36. Golemboski, D. B., Lomonosoff, G. P., and Zaitlin, M. 1990. Plants transformed with a tobacco mosaic virus nonstructural gene sequence are resistant to the virus. Proc. Natl. Acad. Sci. USA 87:6311-6315.

37. Goodman, R. M. 1989. Genetic transfer in crop improvement. Pages 70-76 in: Biotechnology, Biological Pesticides and Novel Plant-Pest Resistance for Insect Pest Management. (D.W. Roberts and R.R. Granados, eds.). Boyce Thompson Inst., New York.

38. Gordon-Kamm, W. J., Spencer, T. M., Mangano, M. L. Adams, T. R., Daines, R. J., Start, W. G., O'Brien, J. V., Chambers, S. A., Adams, W. R. Jr., Willetts, N. G., Rice, T. B., Mackey, C. J., Krueger, R. W., Kausch, A. P., and Lemaux, P.G. 1990. Transformation of maize cells and regeneration of fertile transgenic plants. Plant Cell 2:603-618.

39. Grumet, R. 1990. Genetically engineered plant virus resistance. Hort. Sci. 25:508-513.

40. Hampel, A., and Tritz, R. 1989. RNA catalytic properities of the minimum (-) sTRSV sequence. Biochemistry 28: 4929-4933.

41. Hampel, A., Tritz, R., Hicks, M., and Cruz, P. 1990. 'Hairpin' catalytic RNA model: evidence for helices and sequence requirement for substrate RNA. Nucl. Acids Res. 18:299-304.

42. Harrison, B. D., Mayo, M. A., and Baulcombe, D. C. 1987. Virus resistance in transgenic plants that express cucumber mosaic virus satellite RNA. Nature 328:799-802.

43. Haseloff, J., and Gerlach, W. L. 1988. Simple RNA enzymes with new and highly specific endoribonuclease activities. Nature 334:585-591.

44. Haseloff, J., and Gerlach, W. L. 1989. Sequences required for self-catalysed cleavage of the satellite RNA of tobacco ringspot virus. Gene 82:43-52.

45. Hemenway, C., Fang, R.-X., Kaniewski, W. K., Chua, N.-H., and Tumer, N. E. 1988. Analysis of the mechanism of protection in transgenic plants expressing the potato virus X coat protein or its antisense RNA. EMBO J. 7:1273-1280.

46. Herschlag, D. 1991. Implications of ribozyme kinetics for targeting the cleavage of specific RNA molecules in vivo: More isn't always better. Proc. Natl. Acad. Sci. USA 88:6921-6925.

47. Hiatt, A., Cafferkey, R., and Bowdish, K. 1989. Production of antibodies in transgenic plants. Nature 342:76-78.

48. Hoekema, A., Huisman, M. J., Molendijk, L., van dan Elzen, P. J. M., and Cornelissen, B. J. C. 1989. The genetic engineering of two commercial potato cultivars for resistance to potato virus X. Biotechnology 7:273-278.

49. Hooykaas, P. J. J. 1989. Transformation of plant cells via Agrobacterium. Plant Mol. Biol. 13:327-336.

50. Huisman, M. J., Broxterman, H. J. G., Schellekens, H., and van Vloting-Doting, L. 1985. Human interferon does not protect cowpea plant cell protoplasts against infection with alfalfa mosaic virus. Virology 143:622-625.

51. Hutchins, C. J., Rathjen, P. D., Forster, A. C., and Symons, R. H. 1986. Self-cleavage of plus and minus RNA transcripts of avocado sunblotch viroid. Nucl. Acids Res. 14:3627-3640.

52. Jacquemond, M., Amselem, J., and Tepfer, M. 1988. A gene coding for a monomeric form of cucumber mosaic virus satellite RNA confers tolerance to CMV. Mol. Plant-Microbe Interact. 8:311-316.

53. Jones, R. A. C. 1979. Resistance to potato leafroll virus in *Solanum brevidens*. Pot. Res. 22:149-152.

54. Joshi, R. L., and Joshi, V. 1991. Strategies for expression of foreign genes in plants. Potential use of engineered viruses. FEBS Lett. 281:1-8.

55. Kaniewski, W., Lawson, C., Sammons, B., Haley, L., Hart, J., Delannay, X., and Tumer, N. E. 1990. Field resistance of transgenic Russet Burbank potato to effects of infection by potato virus X and potato virus Y. Biotechnology 8:750-754.

56. Kawchuk, L. M., Martin, R. R., and McPherson, J. 1990. Resistance in transgenic potato expressing the potato leafroll virus coat protein gene. Mol. Plant-Microbe Interact. 3:301-307.

57. Kawchuk, L. M., Martin, R. R., and McPherson, J. 1991. Sense and antisense RNA-mediated resistance to potato leafroll virus in Russet Burbank potato plants. Mol. Plant-Microbe Interact. 4:247-253.

58. Kozak, M. 1989. The scanning model for translation: an update. J. Cell. Biol. 108:229-241.

59. Kuwata, S., Masuta, C., and Takanami, Y. 1991. Reciprocal phenotype alterations between two satellite RNAs of cucumber mosaic virus. J. Gen. Virol. 72:2385-2389.

60. Lawson, C., Kaniewski, W., Haley, L., Rozman, R., Newell, C., Sanders, P., and Tumer, N. E. 1990. Engineering resistance to multiple virus infection in a commercial potato cultivar: Resistance to potato virus X and potato virus Y in transgenic Russet Burbank potato. Biotechnology 8:127-134.

61. Linthorst, H. J. M., Meuwissen, R. L. J., Kauffmann, S., and Bol, J. F. 1989. Constitutive expression of pathogenesis-related proteins PR-1, GRP, and PR-S in tobacco has no effect on virus infection. Plant Cell 1:285-291.

62. Loesch-Fries, L. S., Halk, E. L., Nelson, S. E., and Krahn, K. J. 1985. Human leukocyte interferon does not inhibit alfalfa mosaic virus in protoplasts or tobacco tissue. Virology 143:626-629.

63. Lütcke, H. A., Chow, K. C., Mickel, F. S., Moss, K. A., Kern, H. F., and Scheele, G. A. 1987. Selection of AUG initiation codons differs in plants and animals. EMBO J. 6:43-48.

64. MacKenzie, D. J., and Tremaine, J. H. 1990. Transgenic *Nicotiana debneyii* expressing viral coat protein are resistant to potato virus S infection. J. Gen. Virol. 71:2167-2170.

65. Maiti, I. B., Murphy, J., Shaw, J. G., and Hunt, A. G. 1991. Expression of the tobacco vein mottling virus coat protein (CP) and cylindrical inclusion protein (CI) in tobacco. 3rd Int. Congr. Plant Mol. Biol. Tucson, AZ. (abstr.)

66. Matthews, R. E. F. 1991. Plant Virology. 3rd ed. Academic Press, San Diego. 835 pp.

67. Mayo, M. A., Robinson, D. J., Jolly, C. A., and Hyman, L. 1989. Nucleotide sequence of potato leafroll luteovirus RNA. J. Gen. Virol. 70:1037-1051.

68. McKinney, H. H. 1929. Mosaic diseases in the Canary Islands, West Africa and Gibralter. J. Agric. Res. 39:557-578

69. Mernaugh, R. L., Durand, D. P., and Hill, J. H. 1987. Generation of anti-idiotype hybridoma antibodies to soybean mosaic virus rabbit polyclonal antibodies. Phytopathology 77:1765 (abstr.).

70. Miller, W. A., Hercus, T., Waterhouse, P. M., and Gerlach, W. L. 1991. A satellite RNA of barley yellow dwarf virus contains a novel hammerhead structure in the self-cleavage domain. Virology 183:711-720.

71. Mizuno, T., Chou, M.-Y., and Inouye, M. 1984. A unique mechanism regulating gene expression: Translational inhibition by a complementary RNA transcript (micRNA). Proc. Natl. Acad. Sci. USA 81:1966-1970.

72. Morch, M. D., Joshi, R. L., Denial, T. M., and Haenni, A. L. 1987. A new 'sense' RNA approach to block viral RNA replication *in vitro*. Nucl. Acids Res. 15:4123-4130.
73. Morris, T. J., Knorr, D. A. 1990. Defective interfering RNAs associated with plant virus infections. Pages 123-127 in: New Aspects of Positive-Strand RNA Viruses. (M.A. Brinton and F.X. Heinz, eds.) Am. Soc. Microbiol., Washington, D.C.
74. Nejidat, A., and Beachy, R. N. 1990. Transgenic tobacco plants expressing a coat protein gene of tobacco mosaic virus are resistant to some other tobamoviruses. Mol. Plant-Microbe Interact. 3:247-251.
75. Nejidat, A., and Beachy, R. N. 1989. Decreased levels of TMV coat protein in transgenic plants at elevated temperatures reduce resistance to TMV infection. Virology 173:531-538.
76. Ogarkov, V. I., Kaplan, I. B., Tal'yanskii, M. É., and Atabekov, J. G. 1984. Supression of the multiplication of potato viruses by human leukocyte interferon. . Dokl. Akad. Nauk. SSR 276:743-745.
77. Orchansky, P., Rubinstein, M., and Sela, I. 1982. Human interferons protect plants from virus infection. Proc. Natl. Acad. Sci. USA 79:2278-2280.
78. Osbourn, J. K., Watts, J. W., Beachy, R. N., and Wilson, T. M. A. 1989. Evidence that nucleocapsid disassembly and a later step in virus replication are inhibited in transgenic tobacco protoplasts expressing TMV coat protein. Virology 172:370-373.
79. Palukaitis, P. 1988. Pathogenicity regulation by satellite RNAs of cucumber mosaic virus: Minor nucleotide sequence changes alter host responses. Mol. Plant-Microbe Interact. 1:175-181.
80. Perriman, R. J., and Gerlach, W. L. 1990. Manipulating gene expression by ribozyme technology. Curr. Opinion Biotech. 1:86-91.
81. Ponz, F., Glascock, C. B., and Bruening, G. 1988. An inhibitor of polyprotein processing with the characteristics of a natural virus resistance factor.. Mol. Plant-Microbe Interact. 1:25-31.
82. Potrykus, I. 1991. Gene transfer to plants: assessment of published approaches and results. Annu. Rev. Plant Physiol. Plant Mol. Biol. 42:205-225.
83. Powell, P. A., Stark, D. M., Sanders, P. R., and Beachy, R. N. 1989. Protection against tobacco mosaic virus in transgenic plants that express tobacco mosaic virus antisense RNA. Proc. Natl. Acad. Sci. USA 86:6949-6952.
84. Powell, P. A., Sanders,P.R., Tumer, N., Fraley, R. T., and Beachy, R. N. 1990. Protection against tobacco mosaic virus infection in transgenic plants requires accumulation of coat protein rather than coat protein RNA sequences. Virology 175:124-130.
85. Powell-Abel, P., Nelson, R.S., De, B., Hoffmann, N., Rogers, S.G., Fraley, R. T., and Beachy, R. N. 1986. Delay in disease development in transgenic plants that experess the tobacco mosaic virus coat protein gene. Science 232:738-743.
86. Register, J. C., and Beachy, R. N. 1988. Resistance to TMV in transgenic plants results from interference with an early event in infection. Virology 166:524-532.
87. Register, J. C., and Beachy, R. N. 1989. Effect of protein aggregation state on coat protein-mediated protection against tobacco mosaic virus using a transient protoplast assay. Virology 173:656-663.
88. Rezaian, M. A., Skene, K. G. M., and Ellis, J. G. 1988. Anti-sense RNAs of cucumber mosaic virus in transgenic plants assessed for control of the virus. Plant. Mol. Biol. 11:463-471.
89. Rogers, S. G. 1991. Free DNA methods for plant transformation. Curr. Opin. Biotech. 2:153-157.

90. Schardl, C. L., Byrd, A. D., Benzion, G., Altschuler, M. A., Hildebrand, D. F., and Hunt, A. G. 1987. Design and construction of a versatile system for the expression of foreign genes in plants. Gene 61:1-11.

91. Stark, D. M., and Beachy, R. N. 1989. Protection against potyvirus infection in transgenic plants: Evidence for broad spectrum resistance. Biotechnology 7:1257-1262.

92. Swain, W. F. 1991. Antibodies in plants. TIBTECH 9:107-109.

93. Symons, R. H. 1989. Self-cleavage of RNA in the replication of small pathogens of plants and animals. TIBS 14:445-450.

94. Tacke, E., Prüfer, D., Salamini, F., and Rohde, W. 1990. Characterization of a potato leafroll luteovirus subgenomic RNA: differential expression by internal translation initiation and UAG suppression. J. Gen. Virol. 71:2265-2272.

95. Tacke, E., Prüfer, D., Schmitz, J., and Rohde, W. 1991. The potato leafroll luteovirus 17K protein is a single-stranded nucleic acid binding protein. J. Gen. Virol. 72:2035-2038.

96. Takayama, K. M., and Inouye, M. 1990. Antisense RNA. Crit. Rev. Biochem. Mol. Biol. 25:155-184.

97. Taylor, J. L., Jones, J. D. G., Sandler, S., Mueller, G. M., Bedbrook, J., and Dunsmuir, P. 1987. Optimizing the expression of chimeric genes in plant cells. Mol. Gen. Genet. 210:572-577.

98. Tien, P., and Wu, G. 1991. Satellite RNA for the biocontrol of plant disease. Adv. Virus Res. 39:321-339.

99. Tumer, N. E., Lawson, C., Hemenway, C., Weiss, J., Kaniewski, W., Nida, D., Anderson, J., and Sammons, B. 1991. Engineering resistance to potato leafroll virus in Russet Burbank potato. 3rd Int. Congr. Plant Mol. Biol. Tucson, AZ. (abstr.)

100. van den Elzen, P. J. M., Huisman, M. J., Posthumus-Lutke Willink, D., Jongedijk, E., Hoekema, A., and Cornelissen, B. J. C. 1989. Engineering virus resistance in agricultural crops. Plant Mol. Biol. 13:337-346.

101. van der Wilk, F., Huisman, M. J., Cornelissen, B. J. C., Huttinga, H., and Goldbach, R. 1989. Nucleotide sequence and organization of potato leafroll virus genomic RNA. FEBS Lett. 245:51-56.

102. van der Wilk, F., Posthumus-Lutke Willink, D., Hiusman, M. J., Huttinga, H., and Goldbach, R. 1991. Expression of the potato leafroll luteovirus coat protein gene in transgenic potato plants inhibits viral infection. Plant Mol. Biol. 17:431-439.

103. Van Dun, C. M. P., and Bol, J. F. 1988. Transgenic potato plants accumulating tobacco rattle virus coat protein resist infection with tobacco rattle virus and pea early browning virus. Virology 167:649-652.

104. Van Loon, L. C., and Van Kammen, A. 1970. Polyacrylamide disc electrophoresis of the soluble leaf proteins from Nicotiana tabacum var. 'Samsun' and 'Samsun NN'. Changes in protein constitution after infection with TMV. Virology 40:199-201.

105. Weising, K., Schell, J., and Kahl, G. 1988. Foreign genes in plants: Transfer, structure, expression, and applications. Annu. Rev. Genet. 22:421-477.

106. Wilson, T. M. A. 1989. Plant viruses: A tool-box for genetic engineering and crop protection. BioEssays 10:179-186.

107. Zambryski, P. 1988. Basic processes underlying Agrobacterium-mediated DNA transfer to plant cells. Annu. Rev. Genet. 22:1-30.

APPLICATION OF PROTOPLAST FUSION TECHNOLOGY TO POTATO DISEASE MANAGEMENT

John P. Helgeson
USDA/ARS Plant Disease Resistance Research Unit
Dept. of Plant Pathology, Univ. of Wisconsin
Madison, Wisconsin, 53706

Disease resistance genes within the potato crop can provide very effective means of controlling many diseases. Ideally, genetic resistances could eliminate the need for expensive sprays or soil fumigations; however, that state of affairs has not yet been reached. Several factors have resulted in today's heavy need for pesticides. One of these is the high grower demand for specific varieties that meet certain agronomic criteria. For example, 'Russet Burbank' is susceptible to many disease but is still the dominant potato variety in the U.S., particularly in the Northwest. As long as chemical and agronomic treatments are available to protect the crop from pest damage, other varieties that are more resistant, but less desirable for processing, will occupy only a small part of the market.

Another factor in the current dependence on older varieties is the tremendous amount of work required to generate a new variety. A new cultivar should be comparable in most agronomic respects but clearly superior in some others. Because potato is a tetraploid this may occur in only one in 100,000 or a million seedlings and, even then, the superior characteristic may not be recognized by the breeder. Because of a great deal of effort, breeders have been able to present new candidates for replacing older varieties each year. However, these must meet very stringent agronomic tests before their resistance potential is even considered.

A final, and particularly serious problem, is the lack of available genes in the gene pool that breeders can manipulate. Good durable resistances to Colorado potato beetle, *Leptinotarsa decemlineata* (Say), Columbia River rootknot nematode (*Meloigyne chitwoodii*) or tuber soft rot caused by *Erwinia* spp. are very hard to find in *Solanum tuberosum* L. and sexually compatible *Solanum* species. Biotechnologies of various types can be of substantial help in this solving this problem.

One application of biotechnology that is receiving attention today is the *Agrobacterium*-mediated introduction of bacterial genes into potato, such as those that encode for Bt toxin from *Bacillus thuringiensis*, or viral coat proteins from viruses such as potato leaf roll virus (PLRV). These experiments are covered in detail elsewhere in this volume. It is important to note here, however, that these genes are not from higher plants. The DNA sequences for disease resistance genes are not yet known and therefore the full capabilities of transformation have not yet been realized.

An alternative biotechnology is the use of somatic hybridization to combine cells of species that carry disease resistance with those from potato breeding lines. This procedure can provide a means for bringing genes from sexually incompatible plants into breeding lines. Consider, for example, the species and disease resistances that are listed in Table 1. These are diploid *Solanum* species that are extremely difficult to cross with *S. tuberosum*, even when ploidies are adjusted. They constitute untapped reservoirs of genes that might be highly useful for new resistances. The difficult question is how do we tap these reservoirs?

Table 1. Potentially valuable resistances in 1EBN wild *Solanum* species incompatible with potato.[a]

S. brachistotrichum - late blight, green peach aphid
S. brevidens - potato leaf roll virus (PLRV), frost and Erwinia spp.
S. bulbocastanum - late blight and *M. chitwoodii*
S. cardiophyllum - black leg and late blight
S. chancayense - Verticillium, potato aphid
S. commersonii - bacterial wilt
S. etuberosum - Potato virus X and Y, PLRV
S. fernandezianum - golden nematode
S. jamesii - Verticillium, root knot nematode
S. mochicense - Verticillium.
S. pinnatisectum - late blight, ring rot
S. polyadenium - G. pallida and late blight
S. trifidum - Wart, late blight, Verticillium

---

[a] Information from Hanneman and Bamberg (8)

Some of the species in Table 1 have been used in bridge crosses with potato but, in general, they do not cross with either diploid or tetraploid potato lines. These are the materials upon which our efforts at somatic hybridization have been focused.

Somatic Hybridization of *Solanum* Species

Somatic hybridization involves the fusion of cells, generally leaf-derived protoplasts, of different plants. The fusions may be either intraspecific (e.g., fertile with infertile lines of potato) or interspecific hybridizations (e.g., two sexually incompatible species). In our work, we have concentrated on fusing cells from diploid wild species and either diploid or tetraploid potato lines. Regardless of the source materials being used, certain common procedures must be employed in the fusions. These include the preparation of viable protoplasts, development of effective fusion protocols, regeneration of fusion hybrids, and verification of their hybridity. After these steps, one can evaluate the vigor, fertility and disease resistances of the hybrids.

We are fortunate that *Solanum* species tend to be particularly amenable to tissue culture procedures and protoplast preparation. In the 1970s, Shepard developed very useful protocols, first with tobacco and then with 'Russet Burbank' potato (13). These procedures are still used, albeit with substantial modification in some cases. We have found that a number of *Solanum* species will produce viable protoplasts that can often be differentiated into plants (7). A key factor for success in producing somatic hybrids is to have at least one of the partners produce plants after the fusion protocols (4). The lack of differentiation from another line can be used to screen out undesirable self-fusions.

After obtaining procedures that will give viable protoplasts, experiments can be done to devise protocols for fusion. The first decision involves whether to perform asymmetric or symmetric fusions. In the former, nuclei of one species may be inactivated (e.g. by radiation) while organelles of the other may be inactivated (e.g. by iodoacetate). This procedure can be used to exchange organelle components while retaining a known nuclear genome. In contrast, symmetrical hybridizations use intact, viable cells of both partners. Our experience has been mostly with the latter procedures and I will restrict my comments below to that procedure.

Somatic hybridizations of protoplasts can be obtained by a variety of methods. Two that are now in common use are electrofusion (12) and chemical fusions in polyethylene glycol (PEG) (1). We have found both procedures to be effective, particularly if combined with a good selection scheme and differentiation medium (11). In electrofusion, an alternating current is applied to protoplasts between two electrodes in order to line them up in a chain. A direct current shock is then applied to cause the cells to bump together and fuse. Fusion efficiencies of up to 5% can be obtained by these procedures.

With PEG, no special apparatus need be purchased or constructed. The slow addition of PEG (approximately 8,000 molecular weight, e.g. Sigma P2139) in solution until about 20% PEG is obtained appears to neutralize cell charges. Then, during a period of 20 minutes while cells are stationary in the medium, a low percentage (1-5%) can fuse. Differential florescent dyes (e.g., flourescein and Rhodoamine) can be effective in determining fusion efficiency.

The regeneration of the fused cells into hybrid plants presents the next challenge. As with protoplast isolation and fusions, a number of experiments must often be done to find the best procedures. *Solanum* species often vary substantially in the conditions that result in differentiation. Even variations between cultivars or accessions are common. Although initially viewed as a problem, this variation can be turned to one's advantage. By manipulating the differentiation media one can control the type of cell that differentiates and substantially reduce the number of non-hybrids that are recovered (4). Clearly, this is an advantage when only 5% or so of the cells actually fuse. Thus, it is very useful to do experiments on single cell types that have been through fusion conditions rather than merely on cells that have been freshly isolated, particularly because some cell lines may not survive the fusion conditions unless they fuse with another line.

If one obtains plants after possible fusions, the next task is to verify that the plants are actually hybrids. Both morphological inspections and molecular probes are useful in this regard. In the former case, leaves and flowers can show clear evidence of both species (1,3). For example, fusion hybrids between *S. brevidens* (no tubers, purple flowers) and *S. tuberosum* (PI 203900, white flowers) formed tubers and had varying degrees of flower pigmentation. In an intraspecific fusion, complementary pigmentation was obtained when a line producing purple-splotched tuber with yellow flesh was fused with a line with red skin and flesh. The purple pigment predominated in the hybrids, both on the skin and in the flesh (2).

The ultimate test of whether or not the plants obtained from fusion mixtures are indeed hybrids is by the use of molecular probes (either isozymes or DNA). Restriction fragment length polymorphism (RFLP) analyses are particularly useful in this regard. If probes that clearly differentiate between the two fusion partners are used, the fusion products will show both sets of bands, thus clearly demonstrating that DNA from both parents is present. A typical result with RFLPs is shown in Figure 1. With sufficient numbers of chromosome-specific probes, one can determine the numbers of chromosomes from each parent which are present in the hybrids (14).

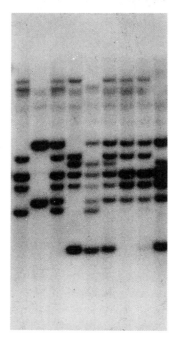

Figure 1. RFLPs of *S. tuberosum* PI 203900, *S. brevidens* PI 218228, their somatic hybrid, and the progeny from crosses with a potato cultivar 'Katahdin'. A probe specific for chromosome 6 (TG 115; obtained from Steve Tanksley, Cornell University) was used. The bands from both of these parents are seen in the somatic hybrid. The somatic hybrid was crossed with 'Katahdin', which also has unique bands, and the sexual progeny show segregation.

Potential for New Resistances from Somatic Hybrids

We have found that somatic hybrids often express the disease resistances of both parent species. In one of our initial hybridizations, we combined *S. brevidens*, which has very good resistance to potato leafroll virus (PLRV) but no resistance against late blight, with a late blight differential line, PI 203900, which is very susceptible to PLRV. The somatic hybrids were resistant to both late blight and PLRV (10). The tubers from the hybrid plants showed no evidence of rotting in the field, but the PI 203900 seed tubers rotted. This led us to examine the resistance of these somatic hybrids to tuber soft rot. The hybrids clearly are resistant to all three of the *Erwinia* species that cause tuber soft rot. In addition, progeny of crosses of the hybrids with 'Katahdin' segregated for resistance, with some of the progeny being as resistant to soft rot as the parents (5). As indicated above, the somatic hybrids of *S. brevidens* and *S. tuberosum*, PI 203900, were fertile when crossed with tetraploid cultivars (6). This is in spite of the fact that the original wild species parent was sexually incompatible with potato. The somatic hybrids were hexaploids; the sum of the chromosome complements of the diploid species, *S. brevidens*, with the tetraploid potato line. Progeny of the hexaploids with 'Katahdin' were pentaploids (60 chromosomes). It appears that the pentaploids retain most of the *S. brevidens* chromosomes and that some crossing over probably occurs (14). This is consistent with the multivalent pairings seen with both tetraploid and hexaploid somatic hybrids (6). Detailed RFLP analyses of the pentaploids are currently underway. These should allow us to determine the extent of genetic exchange that we can expect with crosses. Since our data indicate that there is some crossing over, the exchange of genes to agronomically improved lines should be possible.

The fertility of somatic hybrids is very encouraging. However, it appears that careful selection of materials for fusions should be made if the highest degree of fertility is to be obtained. Both *S. brevidens* and *S. tuberosum* PI 203900 are highly fertile. Their somatic hybrids are also quite fertile. In contrast, hybrids between *S. brevidens* and a sterile haploid line from cv 'Superior' gave no fertile hybrids. This was disappointing because the hybrids were extremely vigorous. An intermediate result was obtained with *S. brevidens* and 'Russet Burbank'. In this case, six of 100 somatic hybrids showed some fertility.

In addition to somatic hybrids with *S. brevidens* and various potato lines, we have been able to hybridize with *S. bulbocastanum*, *S. polyadenium* and *S. cardiophyllum*. Results with *S. etuberosum* and *S. commerosonii* also look promising. Thus, it appears that it will be possible to obtain somatic hybrids with a number of wild species. We anticipate that these hybrids will also express the disease resistances of both parents. We believe that somatic hybridization can be an effective means of capturing new genes for resistance to many of the most serious potato diseases (9).

Problems and Prospects

Although somatic hybridization of potato with sexually incompatible, wild *Solanum* species appears to be one way of obtaining new genes for resistance breeding, it is not without some drawbacks. The procedure is extremely labor intensive and grossly inefficient when compared with conventional crosses. Thus, somatic hybridization is practical only when other techniques fail. However, when one considers that hundreds of millions of dollars are lost each year due to soft rot, hybridization procedures to develop resistance may well be worth the effort.

Somatic hybrids also require a fair degree of breeding before they yield tubers of cultivar standard. In this sense they give breeders the same problems that they encounter in cultivar development. One cannot expect that the fusion of a very wild species with a commercial cultivar will immediately yield a line that produces acceptable tubers. Intraspecific fusions of two lines that do bear reasonable tubers have resulted in hybrids which produce tubers of equivalent quality. Thus, the procedure alone does not always result in a reduction in tuber quality.

Somatic hybrids show substantial somaclonal variation even though the parent materials were exact clones on each side. This can be seen from field evaluations of hybrids between *S. brevidens* and potato (3). Preliminary data also indicate that some of these hexaploid parents produce much better tubers than other hexaploids when crossed with potato cultivars. Therefore, all the problems that breeders face with their crosses may also be expected with the somatic hybrids. Fortunately, one also may expect that success will follow from the effort.

Epilogue

The use of bacterial and viral genes to give new resistances to our potato crop has a great deal of potential for disease management. However, there are many other possibilities for resistances that are present in wild *Solanum* species. To the extent that crossing has been possible, breeders have tapped these sources. Somatic hybridization may allow us to extend the reach of the breeder into new areas of protection. Also, another benefit may result. By combining the divergent DNAs of two species, and by using probes like RFLPs, it may eventually be possible to tag and then to isolate the genes providing disease resistances. Such advances would have far-reaching benefits.

Potato is an almost ideal crop plant for these efforts. The techniques for inserting genes are well advanced. Once the genes are available, it should be possible to develop new resistant cultivars with little more change to phenotype than is seen in Bt toxin- or coat protein-producing cultivars. Having the genes and gene products that are actually associated with disease resistances could provide us with much more information on plant defence mechanisms. In turn, this may provide us with new weapons against pests. Clearly, this is a fertile area for future research efforts. Working together, biotechnologists, breeders, plant pathologists, and entomologists all can contribute to develop new, more environmentally responsible and, in the long term, less costly control measures.

Literature Cited

1. Austin, A., M. A. Baer and J. P. Helgeson. 1985. Transfer of resistance to potato leaf roll virus from *Solanum brevidens* into *Solanum tuberosum* by somatic fusion. Plant Science 39:75-82.
2. Austin, S., M. Baer, M. Ehlenfeldt, P. J. Kazmierczak and J. P.Helgeson. 1985. Intra-specific fusions in *Solanum tuberosum*. Theor. Appl. Genet. 71:172-175.
3. Austin, S., M. Ehlenfeldt, M. Baer and J. P. Helgeson. 1986. Somatic hybrids produced by protoplast fusion between *S. tuberosum* and *S. brevidens*: phenotypic variation under field conditions. Theor. Appl. Genet. 71:682-690.
4. Austin, S. and J. P. Helgeson 1987. Interspecific somatic fusions between *Solanum brevidens* and *S. tuberosum*. pp. 209-222. *In* Plant Molecular Biology. D. von Wettstein and N-H Chua, [Eds.] Plenum Publishing Corp, N.Y.
5. Austin, S., E. Lojkowska, M.K. Ehlenfeldt, A. Kelman and J.P. Helgeson 1988. Fertile Interspecific Somatic Hybrids of *Solanum*: A Novel Source of Resistance to *Erwinia* Soft Rot. Phytopathology 78:1216-1220.
6. Ehlenfeldt, M. K. and J. P. Helgeson. 1987. Fertility of somatic hybrids from protoplast fusions of *Solanum brevidens* and *S. tuberosum*. Theor. Appl. Genet. 73:395-402.
7. Haberlach, G. T., B. A. Cohen, N. A. Reichert, M. A. Baer, L. E. Towill, and J. P. Helgeson. 1985. Isolation, culture and regeneration of protoplasts from potato and several related *Solanum* species. Plant Science 39: 67-74.
8. Hanneman, R. E., Jr. and J. Bamberg. 1966. Inventory of tuber-bearing *Solanum* species. Bull 533, Wisconsin Agr. Expt. Station, 216pp.
9. Helgeson, J. P. 1989. Somatic hybridization of wild *Solanum* species with potato: a potential source of diversity for breeders. pp. 87-94. *In* Parental line breeding and selection in potato breeding. K. Louwes, H. Toussant and L. Dellart, [Eds.] Pudoc, Wageningen.
10. Helgeson, J. P., G. J. Hunt, G. T. Haberlach and S. Austin. 1986. Somatic hybrids between Solanum brevidens and *Solanum tuberosum*: Expression of a late blight resistance gene and potato leaf roll resistance. Plant Cell Reports 3:212-214.

11.   Hunt, G. J. and J. P. Helgeson. 1989. A medium and simplified procedure for growing single cells from *Solanum* species. Plant Science 60:251-257.

12.   Puite, K. J. S. Roest, and L. P. Pijnacker. 1986. Somatic hybrid potato plants after electrofusion of diploid *Solanum tuberosum* and *Solanum phureja*. Plant Cell Reports 5: 262-264.

13.   Shepard, J. F. and R. E. Totten. 1977. Mesophill cell protoplasts of potato: Isolation, proliferation and plant regeneration. Plant Physiol. 60: 313-316.

14.   Williams, C. E., G. Hunt and J. P. Helgeson. 1990. Fertile somatic hybrids of *Solanum* species: RFLP analysis of a hybrid and its sexual progeny from crosses with potato. Theor. Appl. Genet. 80:545-551.

DOUBLE-STRANDED RNA-ASSOCIATED CYTOPLASMIC HYPOVIRULENCE IN *RHIZOCTONIA SOLANI*: PROSPECTS FOR DEVELOPING A RELIABLE, TARGET-SPECIFIC BIOCONTROL SYSTEM

Stellos M. Tavantzis
Department of Plant Biology and Pathology
University of Maine, Orono, ME 04469-0118

One of the greatest challenges facing modern agriculture is to find new ways of production that cease or decelerate environmental deterioration, and rely on renewable resources. Present plant disease management depends heavily on chemicals that lead to increased production costs, use of fossil-fuel energy, water pollution, deleterious effects on non-target organisms, and development of tolerance by the target organism. The genetic and biochemical mechanisms regulating virulence in plant pathogens and disease resistance in plants are now amenable to analysis thanks to the availability of the powerful tools of molecular biology and computer technology. Understanding the factors that control the degree of pathogenicity (e.g., virulence) in the pathogen could lead to the development of biocontrol strategies that will fulfill the need for sustainable and pollution-free agriculture.

Rhizoctonia solani attacks potato and numerous other important crops (4). Rhizoctonia disease of potato occurs wherever potato is grown, but is most severe where soils are moist and cool (16-23°C). Quantitative and qualitative yield losses vary considerably (4). Carling and coworkers (14) reported that total and US grade no.1 yields were reduced by 19% and 35%, respectively, on plots planted with tubers carrying tuber-borne inoculum. Plant emergence was reduced by 24%, and more than 90% of the plants had stems with large girdling lesions. Similar yield losses have been reported by other groups (8). Seed potato treatment with pentachloronitrobenzene (PCNB) is used routinely to control rhizoctonia disease. However, PCNB is one of the most persistent soil fungicides, it has a wide spectrum of antimicrobial activity (22), and it is harmful to beneficial microorganisms living in the rhizosphere of potato or other crop plants (40). Colonization of potato with plant growth-promoting rhizobacteria (PGPR) resulted in a 17% increase in yield, compared with plants not colonized by PGPR (31).

Therefore, there is a need to develop biorational methods for management of rhizoctonia which conserve or enhance beneficial microorganisms.

Association of Hypovirulence and Double-stranded RNA in Plant Pathogenic Fungi

The discovery of fungal viruses in the 1960s added a new dimension in plant pathology, as double-stranded RNA (dsRNA) was thought to be responsible for some of the abnormalities exhibited by fungi (for a recent review see 36). The possibility that dsRNA with adverse effects on phytopathogenic fungi could be exploited as a means of biological control was pursued by several research groups. Double-stranded RNA elements have been found in all major classes of fungi (36), but sufficient correlative evidence linking such elements to the expression of virulence is available only for the following systems. During the first part of this century, the ascomycete *Cryphonectria (Endothia) parasitica* devastated the American chestnut throughout its range in eastern hardwood forests, and caused a similar annihilation of the European chestnut (1). Biological control programs have been developed in Europe where hypovirulent strains of *C. parasitica* are used to curtail blight epidemics (26). Following hyphal anastomosis, cytoplasmic hypovirulence and dsRNA are transmitted simultaneously from a hypovirulent dsRNA-containing strain to a virulent dsRNA-free isolate of *C. parasitica* (20). Hypovirulent strains of the chestnut blight pathogen have been used to cure or arrest the expansion of canker incited by virulent strains in the U.S. (3). Considerable variation exists among hypovirulent strains with regard to dsRNA electrophoretic patterns and sequence homology (21, 33, 38). The complete nucleotide sequence of the L-dsRNA from strain EP113 has recently been reported (41). Transformation of virulent *C. parasitica* with a complementary DNA copy of the above dsRNA conferred the hypovirulence phenotype (19). A virulent form of the causal fungus of Dutch elm disease, the ascomycete *Ophiostoma (Ceratocystis) ulmi*, is transmitted by extrachromosomal determinants (d-factors). Normal and diseased (virulent) cultures of the fungus carry up to 10 dsRNAs, but the virulent state is correlated with a deficiency in cytochrome aa_3, and three specific dsRNAs located in the mitochondria (39). Suppression of virulence in the oat blight incitant, *Helminthosporium victoriae*, is associated with mycelial lysis and reduced production of the phytotoxin Victorin. Co-transmission of the virulent state and dsRNA viruses to normal cultures was reported by Ghabrial (25).

dsRNA-associated Cytoplasmic Hypovirulence in *Rhizoctonia solani*

Rhizoctonia solani (teleomorph *Thanatephorus cucumeris*) consists of several anastomosis groups (AG) (37). Each AG is considered an evolutionary unit in the sense that it is a genetically isolated, noninterbreeding population with a distinct host range (4). AG 3 is the sole incitant of black scurf and the major cause of damping-off of potato (6). The significance of the AG concept is that hyphal fusion occurs only between vegetatively compatible isolates from the same AG. A cytoplasmically controlled degenerative disease of *R. solani* was reported in 1978 (15, 16, 17). The above condition referred to as *Rhizoctonia* decline was characterized by loss of mycelial pigmentation, reduced rate of growth and sclerotia production, and association of dsRNA and hypovirulence similar to that of *C. parasitica*. Healthy, virulent cultures lacking dsRNA could be recovered from a diseased strain (189a) at a low frequency by hyphal-tip isolation (culture 189HT5). Hypovirulence and dsRNA were co-transmitted from 189a to 189HT5. The cured isolate (189HT5) caused 23% postemergence and 79% preemergence damping-off of sugar beet seedlings, but when both 189HT5 and the hypovirulent 189a were added to the soil, no significant damping-off occurred, suggesting that biological control occurred (16). Only 3 out of 13 strains had dsRNA and were hypovirulent, whereas the 10 virulent isolates included in the study contained no detectable dsRNA.

The above findings motivated me to study the potential association of dsRNA and hypovirulence in *R. solani*. Biocontrol of *R. solani* effected by dsRNA-conferred hypovirulence offers a number of advantages over other biocontrol schemes involving various species of *Gliocladium* or *Trichoderma*. Effectiveness of these biocontrol agents is burdened by their dependence on physicochemical properties of the soil, potential lack of adaptation to regions which are ecologically different from that of their origin, poorly understood and non-specific antibiotic activity, and complex relationships with soil microbiota (for a recent review, see 28). Of course, more work is needed to overcome some of the above drawbacks. At the same time, however, the importance of exploiting the phenomenon of dsRNA-conferred hypovirulence in *R. solani* should be recognized.

The ultimate goal of this project is to attain biocontrol of rhizoctonia disease of potato by treating seed potatoes with propagules of genetically manipulated, hypovirulent isolates of *R. solani*. It is expected that these isolates will transmit the hypovirulence-conferring dsRNA to soil- and tuber-borne virulent isolates (through hyphal anastomosis), thereby converting them to a hypovirulent state. This biocontrol system is target-specific, and simpler (with regard to the mechanism involved) than schemes based on the use of biocontrol agents such as *Trichoderma* spp. or *Gliocladium* spp. Essential for the success of the hypovirulence-mediated biocontrol strategy is the development of a transformation system for *R. solani*. This will allow introduction of cloned dsRNA into AG 3 isolates representing a wide spectrum of vegetative compatibility groups. Treatment of seed potatoes with such a mixture of hypovirulent isolates will minimize potential obstacles associated with transmission of dsRNA due to somatic incompatibility among AG 3 isolates. Notably, vegetative incompatibility does not prevent transmission of dsRNA by hyphal anastomosis in *C. parasitica* (2).

The initial objectives of this project were to: 1) examine whether a correlation exists between dsRNA or specific dsRNA species and hypovirulence in naturally-occurring isolates of *R. solani*; 2) study the origin and nature of dsRNA or dsRNA-associated moieties; and 3) conduct field experiments to determine whether hypovirulence-mediated biocontrol of this potato pathogen is feasible.

Although the presence of dsRNA has been associated either with hypovirulence (17) or with virulence (23), my research group has provided strong correlative evidence suggesting that it is the genetic information, as opposed to the mere presence or absence, that determines the biological role of dsRNA in *R. solani* (11, 12, 45). Hyakumachi and coworkers (30) also observed that dsRNA was quite prevalent among Japanese isolates of *R. solani* in which the degree of pathogenicity varied from hypovirulent to highly virulent. Our results suggest that the role of dsRNA in *R. solani* is more complicated than previously thought (17, 23). The conflicting reports on the association of hypovirulence or virulence and dsRNA in this plant pathogen may be attributed to the genetic diversity of dsRNA occurring in natural populations of the fungus, as well as to the complex genetics of *R. solani*. We addressed the first part of the above hypothesis by studying potential genetic relationships among dsRNA species from 51 isolates belonging to 5 AGs and of different degrees of pathogenicity and geographic origins. Individual dsRNA bands were selected as probes on the basis of frequency of occurrence (with respect to size), AG, and virulence of the fungal isolates from which they were derived. The results showed that a relatively high degree of genetic heterogeneity exists among dsRNAs from a single isolate or isolates from the same AG (11). A total of 45 Northern blot hybridization experiments were carried out to determine whether dsRNA populations from different AGs were related. The lack of sequence homology observed in these studies was expected, considering that the *R. solani* AGs are genetically isolated (4). In spite of this genetic isolation, however, strong cross hybridization occurred (under high strigency conditions) among dsRNA species of varying sizes from the hypovirulent isolates Rhs 47 (AG 2) (1.8 kb), Rhs 1A1 (AG 3) (L-RNA and a series of smaller dsRNAs), and Rhs 1 (AG 5) (2.3 kb) (11 and Fig. 1). Rhs 47 (isolated from peanuts) originated from Georgia, whereas Rhs 1A1 (tuber-borne) and Rhs 1 (soil-borne) were obtained from two distant Maine locations (250 miles apart). The fact that all three isolates are hypovirulent suggests that the dsRNA sequence they share might be responsible for their hypovirulence, and may have been present in an ancestral genotype from which the three corresponding AGs (AG 2, AG 3, and AG 5) evolved in a divergent manner.

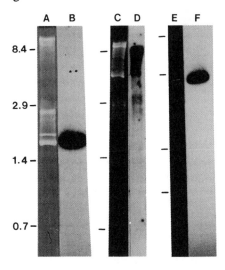

Figure 1. Genetic relatedness of dsRNA elements from three hypovirulent isolates of *R. solani* belonging to three different AGs. Lanes A, C, and E show fractionated dsRNAs from isolates Rhs 47 (AG 2), Rhs 1A1 (AG 3), and Rhs 1 (AG 5), respectively. Membranes containing electrophoretically transferred dsRNAs were hybridized to the radiolabeled 6.4-kb dsRNA from Rhs 1A1. Lanes B, D, and F depict corresponding autoradiograms. Bars to the left of lanes A, C, and F mark positions of dsRNA standards. Numbers on the left indicate sizes (kb) of dsRNA standards (8.4 kb from *Helminthosporium maydis*, 2.9 kb and 0.7 kb from *Penicillium chrysogenum*, and 1.4 kb from *P. stoloniferum*). Data from Bharathan and Tavantzis (11).

A case of a potential dsRNA deletion leading to hypovirulence was observed in *R. solani* isolates belonging to AG 5. When the large (L)-dsRNA band of Rhs 19 was used as a probe, it hybridized to the L-dsRNAs of all the virulent isolates except that of Rhs 59. The same probe hybridized to the much smaller dsRNA bands (2.3 kb and 0.45 kb) of Rhs 1 which contains no detectable amounts of L-dsRNA (11 and

Fig. 2). Rhs 1 is nonpathogenic on three different hosts (potato, tomato, and lupin), whereas all of the other five "cross-hybridizing" isolates (Rhs 9, Rhs 10, Rhs 19, Rhs 22 and Rhs 53) are virulent on all three hosts (5, 11).

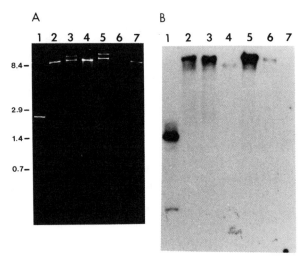

Figure 2. Fractionation of dsRNAs from AG 5 isolates of R. solani in a 7.5% SDS-polyacrylamide gel stained with ethidium bromide (panel A). DsRNA was transferred electrophoretically to a nylon membrane which was hybridized to the largest dsRNA from isolate Rhs 19 (panel B). Lanes 1-7 show dsRNAs from isolates Rhs 1, Rhs 22, Rhs 10, Rhs 53, Rhs 19, Rhs 9, and Rhs 59, respectively. Positions and sizes (kb) of dsRNA standards are indicated on the left. Data from Bharathan and Tavantzis (11).

Hyphal tipping of the moderately virulent AG 3 isolate Rhs 41 resulted in elimination of 3 out of 4 dsRNA bands in two hyphal-tip cultures (Rhs 41-2 and Rhs 41-3) (Fig. 3). Both of these hyphal-tip cultures were more virulent than the original isolate. In fact, Rhs 41-3 was four times more virulent than Rhs 41, and more virulent than any of the field isolates tested to date (Table 1).

The hypovirulent AG 3 culture Rhs 1A1 originated as a sector of the virulent, tuber-borne Rhs 1AP which contains two dsRNA species. Appearance of hypovirulent Rhs 1A1 was associated with five nascent dsRNA species in addition to the two dsRNAs occurring in Rhs 1AP (Tavantzis et al., unpublished). The data described above suggests that dsRNA is involved in expression of virulence in *R. solani*, and that certain dsRNA species are associated with hypovirulence.

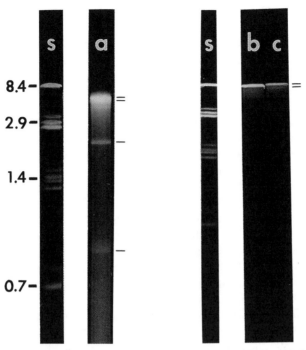

Figure 3. Fractionation of dsRNAs from the AG 3 *R. solani* isolate Rhs 41 (a), its hyphal tip derivatives Rhs 41-2 (b), and Rhs 41-3 (c), and dsRNA standards (s). Numbers on the left indicate sizes (kb) of dsRNA standards.

TABLE 1. Virulence of AG 3 isolates of *R. solani*

Isolate	Virulence[a]
Rhs 41-3	16.2 a
Rhs 27	12.4 ab
Rhs 2	10.7 abc
Rhs 12	7.0 bcd
Rhs 41-2	6.5 bcd
Rhs 6	6.2 bcd
Rhs 42	4.9 cd
Rhs FC	4.2 cd
Rhs 41	4.0 cd
Rhs 14	3.9 cd
Rhs 45	3.7 cd
Rhs 50	3.6 cd
Rhs 43	2.9 cd
Rhs 44	2.2 cd
Rhs 1A1	0 d
None	0 d

[a]Potato cv. 'Katahdin' sprouts with roots attached and free of lesions were planted in sterilized soil in individual pots and inoculated with mycelial plugs from a PDYA culture. Virulence was determined after 2 weeks and was expressed as percent necrotic, lesioned stem tissue of the total stem area covered by soil. Values represent the mean of ten replications. Means followed by the same letter are not significantly different (P=0.05; Duncan's multiple range test).

Nature of dsRNA Moieties in *R. solani*

What is the origin and nature of these dsRNAs? How do they bring about the hypovirulence condition in *R. solani*? These are some of the important questions that must be addressed to design a thoughtful biocontrol strategy to effectively utilize the hypovirulence phenomenon under modern agricultural conditions.

Isometric (33 nm) virus particles were purified to apparent homogeneity from mycelial tissue of Rhs 717 (AG 2/Georgia) and characterized physicochemically (43). The two dsRNA species (2.1 kb and 2.2 kb) isolated from CsCl-purified virions were the same size as and cross hybridized to the two dsRNAs that were phenol-extracted directly from mycelial tissue. Virus particles and RNA-dependent RNA polymerase (RdRp) activity cosedimented as a single peak in isopycnic CsCl gradients, and the RdRp activity was characterized. Thus, the dsRNAs from Rhs 717 and other isolates (23) appear to be encapsidated and of typical mycoviral nature. Furthermore, centrifugal analysis of subcellular fractions in a number of *R. solani* isolates showed that dsRNA is associated primarily with the mitochondrial fraction and the 120,000xg pellet of the cytoplasmic fraction. It appears that dsRNA is not located in the nuclei of this fungus, and does not occur in the soluble cytoplasmic fraction in free plasmid-like form (10).

We carried out Southern blot hybridization analyses of *Eco* RI-digested total DNA from *R. solani* cultures belonging to AGs 1 through 5 to examine whether genetic relationships exist between dsRNA and DNA primarily from the same culture or other cultures belonging to the same or different AG. Interestingly, sequence homology exists between dsRNA elements and DNA from the same *R. solani* isolate or isolates of the same AG (10). It appears that some dsRNA elements might use a retroviral or retroposon mode of replication involving a chromosomal (or mitochondrial) copy of their respective sequence (29).

We believed (12) that a L-dsRNA from the AG 1 culture 189a might be responsible for the debilitating condition described by Castanho and Butler (15). An L-dsRNA element from this isolate shares a common sequence with a 3.8-kb *Eco* RI fragment from mitochondrial (mt) DNA. Interestingly, the majority of the L-dsRNA components are associated with the mitochondrial fraction in 189a (10). Using dot hybridization of mtDNA with a radiolabeled dsRNA probe, Rogers and coworkers (39) did not detect copies of Log1/3-8d^2 dsRNAs in the mtDNA of *O. ulmi*. In contrast, sequence homology between dsRNA and mtDNA occurs in yeast (9).

572

Biological Control Studies

Before conducting a biocontrol experiment, we carried out a survey to determine which AG(s) attacked potato in the field in Maine. Anastomosis grouping of the 219 isolates showed that 100% of the tuber-borne, and over 82% of the lesion-causing isolates (stem, stolons, roots) belonged to AG 3, whereas 13.4% of the lesion-causing isolates were members of AG 5 (6). Field experiments were conducted in 1985 and 1986 to determine whether a hypovirulent AG 3 isolate (Rhs 1A1) could reduce rhizoctonia disease caused by a virulent AG 3 isolate. The hypovirulent isolate Rhs 1A1 causes a slight discoloration of potato stem tissue at the point of entry, unlike the dark, sunken necrotic lesions caused by virulent isolates. A second "hypovirulent" isolate, Rhs 44, was used. However, although Rhs 44 was weakly virulent in greenhouse tests, it was moderately virulent in the field experiment (Table 2). Rhs 27, the most virulent AG 3 culture obtained from potato field soil in Maine, was used as the virulent inoculum. Seed potatoes were disinfected with formaldehyde to eliminate interference by tuber-borne sclerotia of the fungus. Approximately 20 g of wheat grains colonized by hypovirulent inoculum, or 1 g of grains colonized by the virulent inoculum, were applied to each seed piece at planting. In plants inoculated with Rhs 1A1 and Rhs 27, disease severity (% area of underground stem tissue lesioned) was significantly ($P=0.05$) reduced by 56% compared with plants inoculated with Rhs 27 alone (Table 2). Furthermore, in plants co-inoculated with Rhs 27 and Rhs 1A1, the number of stolons was significantly ($P=0.05$) higher (double) than that of plants inoculated with Rhs 27 (Table 3). The ability of hypovirulent *R. solani* to significantly reduce disease caused by virulent isolates of the pathogen was confirmed in greenhouse experiments. Ten g of hypovirulent inoculum or 2 g of virulent inoculum were added per pot near the seed tuber during planting. Co-inoculation with hypovirulent Rhs 1A1 reduced the size of stem lesion caused by virulent Rhs 27 by as much as 60% (Table 2). In fact, biological control was almost complete because lesion size incited by Rhs 27 and Rhs 1A1 (in combination) was similar to that caused by Rhs 1A1 alone (8.0 mm^2 vs. 5.7 mm^2, respectively). The average lesion size incited by Rhs 27 (20.3 mm^2) was 2.5 times greater than that of the co-inoculation treatment (8.0 mm^2), but due to lesion size variability this difference was not statistically significant (7). A second field test was performed with seed tubers that were not disinfected. Tuber-borne inoculum, apparently comprised of AG 3 isolates belonging to different somatic incompatibility groups, interfered with the outcome of this experiment. Thus, a successful biocontrol strategy will require: 1) a mixture of hypovirulent AG 3 isolates of different somatic compatibilities; and 2) a formulation containing an adhesive carrier to coat seed tubers, and thus bring the hypovirulent inoculum into close proximity with the tuber-borne *R. solani* sclerotia.

Table 2. Reduction of Rhizoctonia disease severity in potato effected by a hypovirulent isolate of *R. solani* under field and greenhouse conditions.

Treatment	Field test Percentage of stem area infected[a]	Greenhouse test Lesion area per stem (mm^2)[b]
Untreated	---	0 b
Sterile grain	1.0 c	0.4 b
PCNB, 50 mg/ml	1.5 c	---
Rhs 1	4.0 c	5.7 b
Rhs 27	54.3 a	20.3 a
Rhs 44	28.9 b	---
Rhs 1/Rhs 27	---	8.0 ab
Rhs 1/Rhs 27/Rhs 44	24.1 b	---

Means followed by the same letter are not significantly different (P=0.05; Duncan's Multiple Range Test). Data from Bandy and Tavantzis (7).
[a]Means of 3 replications with 3 'Katahdin' potato plants sampled per replication 10 weeks after planting. Numbers indicate lesioned area as a percentage of the subterraneous portion of stem.
[b]Values are means from 10 'Katahdin' potato plants.

Hypovirulent *R. solani* Enhances Potato Plant Growth

Surprisingly, plants inoculated with hypovirulent Rhs 1A1 alone exhibited a significantly greater growth response. This was expressed as a 4-fold increase in the dry weight of stolons (yield predictor), a 1.7-fold increase in the dry weight of stems (including foliage) (Table 3), and attainment of full bloom (onset of tuberization) one week to 10 days earlier than their respective controls (7). An 18% yield increase (over that of control) of U.S. grade no. 1 tubers in plots treated with Rhs 1A1 was not statistically significant due to the small size of the samples (caused by the unexpected midseason collecting of plants to document enhanced growth) (Table 3). Sneh and coworkers (42) reported increased growth responses induced by nonpathogenic *R. solani* (AG 4). R. solani has been known to have symbiotic relationships with orchids (45), and is one of the mycorrhizal fungi found in roots of grassland (13) or alpine vegetation plants (27).

Table 3. Effect of a hypovirulent AG 3 isolate of *R. solani* on growth and yield of 'Katahdin' potato plants under field conditions.

Treatment	No. of stolons per plant[a]	Dry weight (g/plant)[b]			Yield/plot (Kg)[c]	
		Stem	Stolon	Root	Total tubers	US #1 tubers
Sterile grain	25.3 a	16.3 b	0.6 b	1.7 a	20.1 a	11.1 a
PCNB, 50 mg/ml	21.2 ab	17.4 ab	0.8 b	2.3 a	22.2 a	11.9 a
Rhs 1A1	27.6 a	27.4 a	2.6 a	2.2 a	22.0 a	13.1 a
Rhs 27	13.2 b	14.0 b	0.3 b	1.6 a	18.1 ab	11.8 a
Rhs 44	21.9 ab	11.5 b	0.4 b	1.4 a	16.9 ab	ND
Rhs 1A1/Rhs 27/ Rhs 44	26.6 a	12.5 bc	0.3 b	1.4 a	19.4 a	ND

Means followed by the same letter(s) are not significantly different (P=0.05; Duncan's Multiple Range Test). Data from Bandy and Tavantzis (7).
ND: Not Determined
[a]Means of 3 replications with 3 plants sampled per replication 10 weeks after planting.
[b]Means of 3 replications with 3 plants sampled per replication 6 weeks after planting.
[c]Tuber yields are the means from 3 plots (same number of plants).

The increased growth response of potato to the hypovirulent isolate Rhs 1A1 appeared to be induced by a phytohormone. Earlier work has shown that *in vitro* cultures of *R. solani* produce phenylacetic acid (PAA) which is capable of causing the same disease symptoms on potato as the pathogen itself (24). PAA acts as a plant growth regulator (auxin) at low concentrations, whereas at high concentrations it acts as a toxin (18, 24, 31, 34, 35). Because of these results, a collaborative study (with Prof. Rodney Bushway, Dept. of Food Science) was initiated to determine the amount of PAA and derivatives produced by AG 3 isolates representing a wide spectrum of virulence. When grown in malt extract broth, the amount of PAA (µg/g dry weight of mycelium) produced by hypovirulent Rhs 1A1 was about 10 times lower than that produced by virulent AG 3 isolates (44).

Epilogue

Double-stranded RNA elements have a significant impact on the biology of yeasts and plant pathogenic fungi such as *C. parasitica*, *H. victoriae*, or *O. ulmi*. Experimental evidence suggests that dsRNA is ubiquitous in natural populations of *R. solani*, and certain dsRNA species appear to impede the virulence of the host culture. Three independent groups have shown that hypovirulent isolates can provide a potentially effective biocontrol of this cosmopolitan plant pathogen.

Moreover, two research teams demonstrated that hypovirulent *R. solani* isolates from two different AGs promote plant vigor.

Enhancing our understanding of the dsRNA-conferred hypovirulence in plant pathogenic fungi will enable us to design a biocontrol strategy based on a solid scientific basis. Direct experimental evidence demonstrating that particular dsRNA elements confer hypovirulence has not been furnished to date for *R. solani*. Thus our future research goals include cloning of the dsRNA species associated with hypovirulence. This will allow: 1) introduction of these dsRNAs into appropriate *R. solani* cultures to verify their role in hypovirulence; and 2) sequencing of the cloned dsRNAs to determine the genetic organization and information carried by these entities. Cloning of hypovirulence-conferring dsRNAs and development of a transformation system for *R. solani* also will comprise the technological basis for development of a biocontrol strategy for this plant pathogen. Efficient transformation of AG 3 isolates of diverse somatic compatibilities will be an important element of a practical dsRNA/hypovirulence-mediated biocontrol scheme.

Acknowledgment

I thank B. P. Bandy, N. Bharathan, T. Syminis, and D. H. Zanzinger for contributing parts of the research described here, and R. F. Bozarth for providing the dsRNA standards. This work was supported in part by U.S.D.A. grants 82-CRSR-2-1011 and 84-CRCR-1-1430, the Maine Agricultural Experiment Station, and the University of Maine Faculty Research Fund.

Literature Cited

1. Anagnostakis, S. L. 1982. Biological control of chestnut blight. Science 215:466-471.
2. Anagnostakis, S. L., and P. R. Day. 1979. Hypovirulence conversion in *Endothia parasitica*. Phytopathology 69:1226-1229.
3. Anagnostakis, S. L., and R. A. Jaynes. 1973. Chestnut blight control: Use of hypovirulent cultures. Plant Dis. Rep. 27: 225-226.
4. Anderson, N. A. 1982. The genetics and pathology of *Rhizoctonia solani*. Ann. Rev. of Phytopath. 20:329-347.
5. Bandy, B. P., D. H. Zanzinger, and S. M. Tavantzis. 1984. Anastomosis group 5 of *Rhizoctonia solani* Kuhn isolated from potato-cultivated soils in Maine. Phytopathology 74:1220-1224.
6. Bandy, B. P., S. S. Leach, and S. M. Tavantzis. 1988. Anastomosis group 3 of *Rhizoctonia solani* is the major cause of Rhizoctonia disease in Maine. Plant Disease 72:596-598.

7.   Bandy, B. P., and S. M. Tavantzis. 1990. Effect of hypovirulent *Rhizoctonia solani* on Rhizoctonia disease, growth, and development of potato. Am. Potato J. 67:189-199.

8.   Banville, G. J. 1989. Yield losses and damage to potato plants caused by *Rhizoctonia solani* Kuhn. Am. Potato J. 66:821-834.

9.   Beilharz, M. W., Cobon, G. S., and Nagley, P. 1982. A novel species of double stranded RNA in mitochondria of *Saccharomyces cerevisiae*. Nucl. Acids Res. 10:1051-1069.

10.   Bharathan, N., T. Syminis, and S. M. Tavantzis. Sequence homology between double-stranded RNA elements and total or mitochondrial DNA in *Rhizoctonia solani*. (In Preparation).

11.   Bharathan, N., and S. M. Tavantzis. 1990. Genetic diversity of double-stranded RNAs in *Rhizoctonia solani*. Phytopathology 80:631-635.

12.   Bharathan, N., and S. M. Tavantzis. 1991. Assessment of genetic relatedness among double-stranded RNA components from *Rhizoctonia solani* isolates of diverse geographic origin. Phytopathology 81:411-415.

13.   Campbell, R., E. I. Newman, R. A. Lawley, and P. Christie. 1982. Relationship of a Rhizoctonia species and grassland plants. Trans. Br. Mycol. Soc. 79:123-127.

14.   Carling, D. E., R. H. Leiner, and P. C. Westphale. 1989. Symptoms, signs and yield reduction associated with Rhizoctonia disease of potato induced by tuberborne inoculum of *Rhizoctonia solani* AG-3. Am. Pot. J. 66: 693-701.

15.   Castanho, B., and E. E. Butler. 1978. Rhizoctonia decline: a degenerative disease of *Rhizoctonia solani*. Phytopathology 68:1505-1510.

16.   Castanho, B., and E. E. Butler. 1978. Rhizoctonia decline: studies on hypovirulence and potential use in biological control. Phytopathology 68:1511-1514.

17.   Castanho, B., E. E. Butler, and R. J. Shepherd. 1978. The association of double-stranded RNA with Rhizoctonia decline. Phytopathology 68:1515-1518.

18.   Chamberlain, V. K., and R. L. Wain. 1971. Studies on plant growth-regulating substances-The influence of ring substituents on the plant growth regulating activity of phenylacetic acid. Ann. Appl. Biol. 69: 65-72.

19.   Choi, G.H. and D.L. Noss. 1992. Hypovirulence of chestnut blight fungus conferred by an infectious viral cDNA. Science 257: 800-803.

20.   Day, P. R., J. A. Dodds, J. E. Elliston, R. A. Jaynes, and S. L. Anagnostakis 1977. Double-stranded RNA in *Endothia parasitica*. Phytopath. 67:1393-1396.

21.   Dodds, J. A. 1980. Revised estimates of the molecular weights of dsRNA segments in hypovirulent strains of *Endothia parasitica*. Phytopathology 70:1217-1220.

22.   Edwards, C. A. 1976. Persistent pesticides in the environment. CRC Press, Cleveland.

23.   Finkler, A., Y. Koltin, I. Barash, B. Sneh, and B. Pozniak. 1985. Isolation of a virus from virulent strains of *Rhizoctonia solani*. J. Gen. Virol. 66:1221-32.

24.   Frank, J. A., and S. K. Francis. The effect of a *Rhizoctonia solani* phytotoxin on potatoes. Can. J. Bot. 54:2536-2540.

25.   Ghabrial, S. A. 1986. A transmissible disease of *Helminthosporium victoriae*: evidence for a viral etiology. In "Fungal Virology" ed. K. W. Buck, pp. 163-176. CRC Press, Boca Raton, FL.

26.   Grente, J., and S. Berthelay-Sauret. 1979. Biological control of chestnut blight in France. In "Proceedings of the American Chestnut Symposium" ed. by W. L. McDonald, F. L. Chech, J. Luchok, and C. Smith, pp. 30-37. West Virginia Univ. Press, Morgantown.

27.   Haselwontder, K., and D. J. Read. 1980. Fungal association of roots of dominant and subdominant plants in high alpine vegetation systems with special reference to mycorrhiza. Oecologia 45:57-62.

28.   Howell, C. R. 1990. Fungi as biological control agents. In: "Biotechnology of Plant-Microbe Interactions". J. P. Nakas and C. Hagedorn, Eds. pp. 257-286. McGraw-Hill Publ. Co., N.Y.

29.   Hull, R., and Covey, S. N. 1986. Genome organization and expression of reverse transcribing elements: Variations and a theme. J. Gen. Virol. 67:1751-1758.

30.   Hyakumachi, M., Sumino, A., Ueda, I., and Shikata, E. 1985. Relationship between the presence of dsRNA in Rhizoctonia solani and the pathogenicity. Ann. Phytopath. Soc. Japan 51:372-373.

31.   lacobellis, N. S., and J. E. DeVay. 1987. Studies on pathogenesis of Rhizoctonia solani in beans: an evaluation of the possible roles of phenylacetic acid and its hydroxy derivatives as phytotoxins. Physiol. Mol. Plant Path. 30: 421-432.

32.   Kloepper, J. W., M. N. Schroth, and T. D. Miller. 1980. Effects of rhizosphere colonization by plant growth-promoting rhizobacteria on potato plant development and yield. Phytopathology 70:1078-1082.

33.   L'Hostis, B., S. T. Hiremath,, R. E. Rhoads, and S. A.Ghabrial. 1985. Lack of sequence homology between double-stranded RNA from European and American hypovirulent strains of Endothia parasitica. J. Gen. Virol. 66:351-355.

34.   Mandava, B. N., R. G. Orellana, J. D. Warthen, Jr., J. F. Worley, S. R. Dutky, H. Finegold, and B. C. Weathington. 1980. Phytotoxins in Rhizoctonia solani: Isolation and biological activity of m-hydroxy- and m- methoxyphenylacetic acids. J. Agric. Food Chem. 28:71-75.

35.   Milborrow, B. V., J. G. Purse, and F. Wightman. 1975. On the auxin activity of phenylacetic acid. Ann. Bot. 39: 1143-1146.

36.   Nuss, D. L., and Y. Koltin. 1990. Significance of dsRNA genetic elements in plant pathogenic fungi. Annu. Rev. Phytopath. 28: 37-58.

37.   Ogoshi, A. 1987. Ecology and pathogenity of anastomosis and intraspecific groups of Rhizoctonia solani Kuhn. Ann. Rev. Phytopath. 25: 125-154

38.   Paul, C. P., and D. W. Fulbright. 1988. Double-stranded RNA molecules from Michigan hypovirulent isolates of Endothia parasitica vary in size and sequence homology. Phytopathology 78:751-755.

39.   Rogers, H. J., K. W. Buck, and C. M. Brasier. 1987. A mitochondrial target for double-stranded RNA in diseased isolates of the fungus that causes Dutch elm disease. Nature 329:558-560.

40.   Schroth, M. N., and J. G. Hancock. 1982. Disease-suppressive soil and root-colonizing bacteria. Science 216: 1376-1381.

41.   Shapira, R., Choi G. H., and Nuss D. L. 1991. Virus-like genetic organization and expression strategy for a double-stranded RNA genetic element associated with biological control of chestnut blight. The EMBO J. 10:731-739.

42.   Sneh, B., M. Zeidan, M. Ichielevich-Auster, I. Barash, and Y. Koltin. 1986. Increased growth responses induced by a nonpathogenic Rhizoctonia solani. Can. J. Bot. 64:2372-78.

43. Tavantzis, S. M. and B. P. Bandy. 1988. Properties of a mycovirus from *Rhizoctonia solani* and its virion-associated RNA polymerase. J. Gen. Virol. 69:1465-1477.

44. Tavantzis, S. M., B. L. Perkins, R.J. Bushway, and B. P. Bandy. 1989. Correlation between *in vitro* synthesis of phenylacetic acid and virulence in *Rhizoctonia solani* (Abstr.) Phytopathology 79:1199.

45. Warcup, J. H. 1985. Pathogenic *Rhizoctonia* and orchids. *In*: "Ecology and management of soil-borne pathogens". C. A. Parker, A. D. Rovira, K. J. Moore, P. T. W. Wong, and J. F. Kollmorgen, Eds. pp. 69-70. APS, St. Paul, MN.

46. Zanzinger, D. H., B. P. Bandy, and S. M. Tavantzis. 1984. High frequency of finding double-stranded RNA in naturally occurring isolates of *Rhizoctonia solani*. J. Gen. Virol. 65:1601-5.

PART XI

Potato Pest Management:
A Global View

POTATO PEST MANAGEMENT IN DEVELOPING COUNTRIES

K.V.Raman[1]
Program Leader, Integrated Pest Management
International Potato Center, Apartado 5969
Lima,Peru

Potato is the fourth most widely produced food crop worldwide. Approximately 282 mt are produced each year. Developing countries grow about 30 percent of this amount. It is in the developing world, however, where increases in production have been among the most rapid for all the major food crops. In Asia, production has increased 165% over the past 30 years (27). Production in other parts of the developing world is also significant. As a result, potato farming is becoming an increasingly important source of rural employment, income, and food. In value, potato currently ranks fourth in the developing world (11). Despite its potential as an effective and equitable means for increasing food supplies and income for the rural and urban populations problems in sustainability of potato production remain. Among these are some of the most serious losses caused by pests and diseases and the high cost of chemical pesticides. Of all the major food crops, potato is the heaviest user of chemical pesticides. Costs of pesticide use often total up to 20% of production. A conservative estimate of insecticide costs for developing country potato production exceeds $ 300 million per year (13).

Overuse of insecticides not only increases production costs, but poses serious threats to farm workers, consumers, and the environment. In many locations, farmers apply insecticides up to twenty times per season to avoid catastrophic crop .failures. The most commonly used chemicals include such highly toxic compounds as ethyl parathion, DDT, aldrin, dieldrin, endrin, toxaphene, lindane and chlordane. Most of these compounds are banned in the industrialized world because they are reported to be known carcinogens and accumulate in the food chain and in ground water. In much of the developed world, these insecticides have been linked to the deaths of birds and wildlife and a decrease in

---

[1]Current address: ISAAA, 260 Emerson Hall, Cornell University, Ithaca, NY 14853-1902.

the numbers of natural enemies (parasitoids and predators) that constitute a natural control on many insect pests. Children and pregnant and lactating women are also particularly vulnerable to the harmful effects of these insecticides. For more information on the problems associated with the unilateral and indiscriminate use of insecticides the reader is referred to the following papers (2,5,19,21).

Recognizing that sustainable production cannot be achieved as long as pest and disease control depend on chemical pesticides, the International Potato Center (CIP) has focused its activities on the development of integrated pest management (IPM) strategies to help potato producers in developing countries substantially reduce their use of insecticides and fungicides. IPM is based on the concept that pesticide use can be reduced to minimum levels through a combination of control practices, including the use of resistant or tolerant varieties; the introduction or enhancement of biological control by natural enemies; the use of cultural practices to manipulate crop and pest environments; and the careful selection and timing of chemical applications (5). These control components must be integrated in farmers' fields. Interdisciplinary cooperation between biological and social scientists facilitates this process (6,7).

The objective of this chapter is to provide an update on the advances made in the development of IPM technologies at CIP in collaboration with national agricultural research systems (NARS) around the world.

Major Insect Pests

The potato ecosystem is inhabited by numerous insect and mite species. The greatest diversity of insect pests that attack potato is found in South America. These pests frequently damage the plant by feeding on leaves; reducing photosynthetic area and efficiency by attacking the stems; weakening the plant and inhibiting nutrient transport; and by attacking potato tubers destined for consumption or use as seed.

Present knowledge from developing countries indicates that the potato tuber moth (PTM), *Phthorimaea operculella* (Zell.), the Andean potato weevil (APW), *Premnotrypes* spp., the green peach aphid (GPA), *Myzus persicae* (Sulz.), and leafminer flies (LMF), *Liriomyza huidobrensis* (Blanch.), are all major pests. CIP's research in Peru focuses primarily on these four key pests. Research on other pests (not important to Peru) that can colonize and attack potato, e.g., thrips, mealybugs, red ants, and mites, is conducted in collaboration with national programs or through contract research. For more information on the economic importance, distribution, biology, nature of damage, and yield losses by major pests on a global basis refer to Raman and Radcliffe (21).

Host Plant Resistance

As a control tactic, varietal resistance remains the first defense in the control of insect pests. The development of resistant varieties represents a major research effort involving entomologists and plant breeders from many developing countries. CIP began studying host plant resistance in the early 1970's, but was unsuccessful for many years to identify a suitable source of resistance. Although many species proved resistant to insect pests, most contained high levels of glycoalkaloids. In 1976, however, several wild species with high densities of glandular trichomes and low concentrations of glycoalkaloids were found to be capable of trapping, immobilizing, and eventually killing most insect pests (Tingey and Yencho, this volume). One species, *Solanum berthaultii*-- a wild diploid tuber bearing potato from Bolivia--proved particularly promising. The discovery of resistance in *S.berthaultii* led to the development of a cultivated potato with high yields, good horticultural characteristics, and high levels of resistance. After nearly 12 years of testing, advanced hybrids are now available. These materials have been extensively tested in Latin America, in Asia and Africa, and in several industrialized countries. Thus far, they have proven effective under a variety of growing conditions. Because of the physical-chemical nature of their resistance, the development of insect biotypes that can overcome this resistance is considered unlikely for the immediate future. To date, field testing has shown that glandular trichome clones are highly resistant to the GPA, PTM, thrips, *Thrips palmi*, CPB, leafhoppers, *Empoasca fabae* (Harris), flea beetles, *Epitrix* spp., mealybugs, *Planococcus citri* (Risso), red spider mite (RSM), *Tetranychus urticae* (Koch) and broad mite, *Polyphagotarsonemus latus* (Banks) and LMF. For more details on insect resistance mechanisms provided by glandular trichomes and the advances made in the breeding of insect resistant cultivars, refer to Tingey and Yencho (this volume). The effects of glandular trichomes on pests of economic importance in the tropics have been evaluated at CIP. Glandular trichome clones of the K series developed at Cornell University, USA were highly effective in controlling the immature stages of GPA, RSM, PTM and LMF. Mortalities in these clones ranged from 70-90% (Fig 1). These clones and other hybrids developed at CIP are now being used as progenitors for developing populations with high densities of glandular trichomes. The resistance provided by glandular trichomes is not only effective against the physical damage caused by insects, but also in reducing the

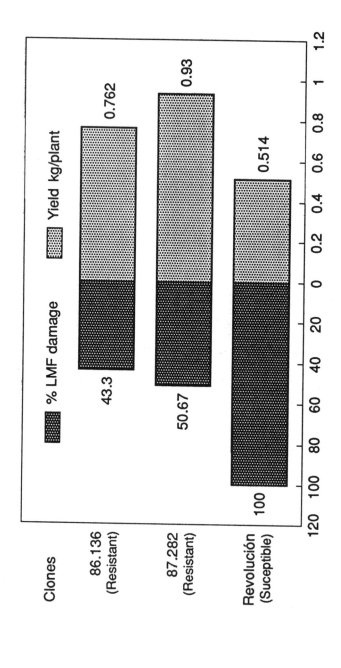

Fig. 1   Effects of glandular trichomes in "K clones" on immature stages of four major potato pests.

viruses transmitted by aphids (8,24). Viruses are a major factor in the reduction of seed quality and seed vigor in many developing countries (Salazar, this volume). In addition, Canadian and Italian researchers have reported that *S.berthaultii* and its hybrids reduce late blight, *Phytophthora infestans*, infection, in some instances by up to 40 % (10). In the developing world, farmers spray an estimated $300 million in fungicides to protect their crop against late blight (12).

In other studies conducted at CIP, tuber resistance to PTM has been identified (19). This work was initiated in 1979 by screening 3,747 accessions of primitive native cultivars maintained in CIP's world germplasm collection. Also included in this work were the wild species in the IR-1 collection obtained from Sturgeon Bay, Wisconsin. Several accessions of *S. andigena, chaucha, stenotomum, sucrense, tarijense, vernei, venturii, pinnatisectum, spegazzinii, commersonii, gandarillasii, megistacrolobum, multiinterruptum, sparsipilum, tarijense, sucrense*, and *oplocense* were identified as highly resistant (4,15). The resistance of thediploids has been transfered into tetraploids through 2x - 4x crosses. After several cycles of selection and screening, a base population with high level of resistance has been created (13,28). Clones from this population act as good transmitters of PTM resistance and can be used as progenitors in breeding NARS programs to transfer PTM resistance in commonly grown tropical cultivars. PTM resistance in three of these potato clones is presented in Fig 2. Each exhibits high levels of antibiosis under both laboratory and storage conditions. Resistance to APW has also been identified in advanced hybrid populations developed for resistance to late blight. In other studies, high levels of resistance have been identified for LMF. Thirteen advanced clones have been selected. Of these, five are from the true potato seed (TPS) populations. Resistance and yield data for two of the resistant clones, CIP 86.136 and 87.282, are presented in Fig.3. Both resistance and yield are significantly higher when compared to the commonly grown susceptible Peruvian cultivar Revolucion. A population with multiple pest resistance has been developed by crossing advanced PTM resistant genotypes, glandular trichome progeny, and LMF resistant clones with high yielding varieties with broad adaptation and good horticultural characteristics. Tuber families from this broad based population will be evaluated in the future by NARS for possible selection as cultivars (13).

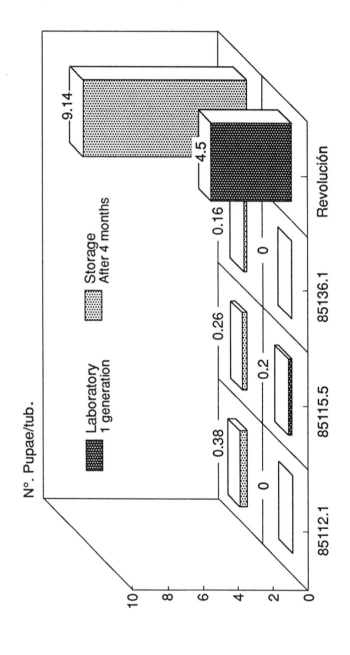

N°. Pupae/tub.

Fig. 2 Resistance of three potato clones to PTM in the laboratory and storage.

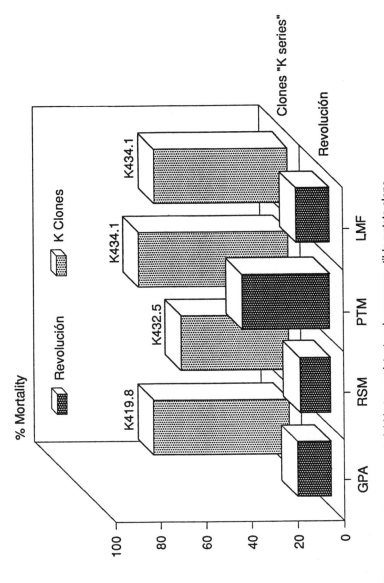

Fig. 3   LMF damage and subsequent yield in two resistant and one susceptible potato clone.

CIP also collaborates with several institutions in industrialized countries to develop transgenic potatoes with resistance to PTM. The goal is to insert the gene for production of *Bacillus thuringiensis* (Bt) and its endotoxin into potato plants. Transformed potato plants have now been tested for resistance to PTM in Belgium and at Michigan State University, USA (13). The availablity of such cultivars should greatly reduce the need for insecticides, but there is concern that this approach will pose considerable selection for Bt resistance in plants. Other genes of interest include the use of a cowpea trypsin inhibitor (CpTi) gene.

Biological and Behavioural Control

Fungi. *Beauveria brogniartii*(Sacc)Petch., a naturally-occurring entomopathogenic fungus is now being used in Peru, Colombia, and Bolivia to control the APW, the most serious insect pest of potato in the Andean highlands. The pest is responsible for average crop losses of 30%. It is most prevalent among small, resource-poor farm families (21).

The fungus is grown on barley husks and is applied in areas where farmers store their potatoes. It is effective against larvae, pupae, and adult weevils. Mortality can reach a maximum of 97% in the larval stage under storage conditions three months after inoculum application. Cottage-level industries to produce the fungus have been established in Peru and are being developed in other countries. The technology is inexpensive, effective, and has been warmly received by farmers and their families. In one pilot community, a law was passed mandating that all village farmers use IPM for this pest. The fungus is particularly attractive because it relieves farmers of the need to apply expensive, highly toxic insecticides in storage areas close to their homes, and thus has a beneficial effect on the health of children and pregnant women. The fungus has been shown to be safe to humans and wildlife. For more information refer to other reports (1,13,29).

Baculovirus. CIP has identified several strains of a granulosis type baculovirus. This naturally occurring organism has been effective in controlling the PTM, the most damaging insect pest of potato in developing countries. PTM causes losses ranging from 30 to 100% when not adequately controlled. It is particularly important in warm climates, areas where potato production is now expanding and where growers are looking to potato as a cash crop and as a new food source (21). The virus is effective against all larval stages of the pest and can be multiplied using low-cost rustic facilities for use in fields and stores. It is a perfect candidate for cottage-level enterprises, as well as for industry. In Peru, it is being used on a wide scale in seed stores. More than 50 mt of potato seed were treated in Peru in 1991. Based on experiences in Peru, NARS in Bolivia, Tunisia, Egypt, and Kenya have identified locally-occurring strains of the virus and are developing mass production methods for on-farm use. Results thus far have been highly positive. For more information on the identification of the virus, formulation procedures, effect on PTM in field and stores, the reader is referred to other reports (12,13,20,21,30 and 31).

Bacteria. Several strains of *Bacillus thuringiensis* Berliner that are pathogenic against PTM have been identified in Peru and Tunisia. In the early 1980's, it was a common practice for farmers in Tunisia, Egypt, Morocco, and Algeria to treat their market potatoes with the deadly insecticide parathion. This insecticide has now been banned in Tunisia, and replaced with Bt and much safer insecticides, such as synthetic pyrethroids. These products are relatively inexpensive and have a short persistence on the foliage. It is now possible to insert the gene sequence from Bt into a different bacterium which can then be killed with the cell remaining intact, encapsulating the toxin. This approach could increase toxin yields and produce a more environmentally stable product. For more information on the effect of Bt strains on PTM control see (7,13,23,32).

Parasitoids and predators. To date, nine parasitoids of PTM, eleven parasitoids of LMF, and one parasitoid of GPA, have been recorded. The most successful have been *Copidosoma koehleri*(Blanchard) and *Chelonus phthorimaeae*(Gahan) which are tiny wasps that control PTM. Copidosoma koehleri has been used with good success in Kenya, India, Tunisia, Colombia, Peru, and Bolivia. Wherever the parasites have been released, they have established themselves and seem to provide good control. In one instance, in the Ancash Valley of Peru, the parasite *Copidosoma koehleri* provided 80% control, and significantly reduced the need for insecticides (13). Reports from other countries are also encouraging. For more information on the progress in the use of parasitoids for control of PTM, GPA, LMF,APW and other pests of importance in tropics see (3,21,22).

Sex pheromones. The sex pheromone of PTM has been found to be a useful tool for monitoring PTM populations under field and storage conditions. The PTM pheromone consists of two components, trans-4,cis-7-tridecatrien-1-ol acetate (PTM-1) (26) and trans-4,cis-7,cis-10-tridecatrien-1-ol acetate (PTM 2) (16). CIP has developed a low-cost formulation process to make this pheromone available to farmers in developing countries. Growers in Mexico, Costa Rica, Peru, Bolivia, India, the Philippines, Tunisia, and Egypt have been able to significantly reduce insecticide use by using pheromones (14).

The pheromone is used in low-cost traps to monitor PTM populations and time insecticideapplications so that they are only applied when needed. For example, in Costa Rica, a threshold of 100 moths per trap per week signals the need for an insecticide treatment (25). In many instances, this technology has helped farmers to reduce their insecticide use by up to 80%. This, in turn, has helped to restore the natural biological balance found in many farmers' fields. In Costa Rica, farmers who use pheromones had previously treated tubers with insecticides just prior to marketing. This is no longer necessary. In addition, Costa Rican cooperatives are marketing the pheromone to farmers for PTM control. For additional information on the use of PTM sex pheromone in monitoring, mass trapping and mating disruption refer to Raman (18).

Repellent plants and botanical insecticides. For centuries, farmers protected their crops with natural insecticides found in the leaves of certain plant species. For example, the Incas used the dried leaves of Muña (*Minthostachys sp.*) in their potato stores. Andean farmers burn dried capsicum fruits to fumigate potato stores to obtain clean, healthy potatoes. Unfortunately, because of social upheaval and a preference for modern technologies, much knowledge about these plants has been forgotten or lost. CIP is promoting the use of these plants for controlling PTM and aphids in storage. These efforts have proven particularly effective in India, Peru, Bangladesh, Thailand, Colombia, and Mexico. For more details on the effect of local plants on insect pests see Raman and Radcliffe (21). Recent attention has also focused on the botanical insecticide neem, which is extracted from the kernel of the neem tree, *Azadirachta indica*. Neem extracts have been used in India for PTM control. PTM exposed to low doses of neem have reduced fecundity (17).

Other important control methods include the use of cultural practices. The most important are use of clean seed, intercropping, irrigation, hilling, early harvest, rapid handling, and storage in well designed stores (21). A total of 43 countries are presently evaluating the use of non-chemical approaches developed by CIP. For more details on the use of CIP-developed IPM strategies the reader is referred to another report (14). The use of innovative pest management approaches in developing countries is summarized in Fig. 4.

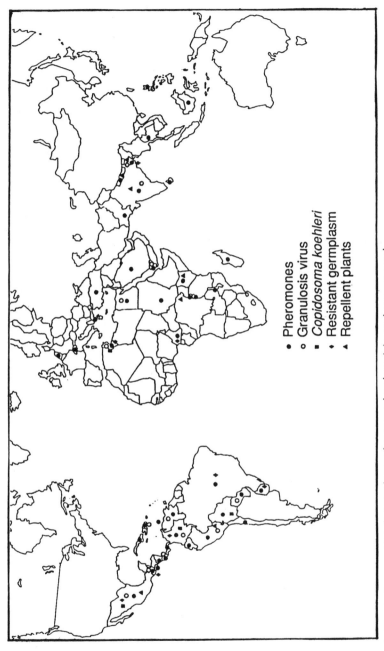

Fig.4. Developing countries that use innovative appraches in potato pest management.

Epilogue

CIP will continue working in collaboration with NARS to improve screening and evaluation protocols that will lead to the development of pest resistant germplasm with improved horticultural quality. Both conventional and non-conventional breeding methods will be emphasized. Programs with this goal will be increasingly multidisciplinary in nature (Mendoza, this volume). Advances in biotechnology have shortened the time for developing transgenic potatoes with resistance to PTM. The safety aspects of Bt-engineered potato plants are not completely known. The key to the success in this area is the availability of information and adequate discussion by all sectors of the community. Some developing countries have already agreed on biosafety guidelines and have begun their implementation. CIP will work in close collaboration with all parties involved in adapting and endorsing biosafety guidelines in developing countries.

An issue that demands attention is the role of private and public sector organizatons in the development and marketing of new biological control agents, such as the baculovirus, entomopathogenic fungi, and parasitoids.

In the tropics, IPM must be tailored to fit the specific conditions. Once a package of improved IPM practices is available, its adoption depends largely on the successful demonstration of its attributes to farmers. Best results usually occur in areas where growers are organized and where there is a system to provide information and technical assistance.

On farm research, surveys, and on-farm monitoring have important roles to play in facilitating the adoption of IPM (7,8). Considerable knowledge has been developed for the formulation of practical IPM programs. CIP's strategy for IPM implementation includes: 1) widespread on-farm dissemination of existing IPM technologies; 2) large-scale international testing of promising IPM practices; 3) awareness building among policymakers and national program personnel about the importance of IPM; and 4) development of regional and national capacities to use and disseminate IPM technologies in farmer's fields. Both national and international programs should encourage such activities.

Literature Cited

1.   Alcazar, J., Raman, K.V., Torres, H. and Yabar, E. (1990). *Beauveria sp.* Hongo amigo del agricultor. Rev. Medio Ambiente. No. 45:44-46.
2.   Barbosa, S. (1983). Potato insect pests in Brazil: present status and future trends. p. 64-65. *In* W.J. Hooker (ed.), Research for the potato in the year

2000. Proc. Intl. Cong., Lima, Peru, Feb. 22-27, 1983. Lima: International Potato Center.

3. Bennett, F.D. (1984). Biological control in IPM. *In* Report of Planning Conference on Integrated Pest Management, June 4-8, 1984. Int. Potato Cent. (CIP), Lima, Peru, 189-197.

4. Chavez, R. (1984). The use of wide crosses in potato breeding. Ph.D. thesis, Univ. Birmingham.

5. Cisneros, F.M. (1984). The need for integrated pest management in developing countries. *In* Report of the XXII Planning Conference on Integrated Pests Management, Jun. 4-8, 1984. Int. Potato Cent. (CIP), Lima, Peru, 19-30.

6. Ewell, P.T. (1990). Socio-economic aspects of farmer-oriented research for potato IPM. In:eds. S.K.Hahn and E.F. Caveness. Proceedings of the Workshop on the Global Status of and Prospects for Integrated Pest Management of Root and Tuber Crops in the Tropics, 25-30 october 1987, International Institute of Tropical Agriculture, Idaban, Nigeria. 108-124.

7. Ewell, P.T., Fuglie, K.O. and Raman, K.V. (1993). Farmers' Perspectives on Potato Pest Management in Developing Countries: Interdisciplinary Research at CIP. (this volume).

8. Gunec, Y. and Gibson, R.W. (1980). Effects of glandular foliar hairs on the spread of potato virus Y. Potato Res. 23:345-51.

9. Hahn, S.K. and Caveness, F.E.(1990). Integrated Pest Management for Tropical Root and Tuber Crops. International Institute of Tropical Agriculture, Idaban, Nigeria.

10. Holley, J.D., King, R.R. and Singh, R.P.(1987). Glandular trichomes and the resistence of *Solanum berthaultii* (PI 473340) to infection from *Phytophtora infestans*. Can. J. Plant Pathol., 9(4): 291-418.

11. Horton, D. (1987). Potatoes: Production, Marketing, and Programs for Developing Countries. Colorado: Westview Press.

12. International Potato Center (1992). Annual Report, International Potato Center, (CIP), Lima, Peru.

13. International Potato Center (1991). Annual Report, International Potato Cent. (CIP), Lima, Peru.

14. International Potato Center, (1989). An Assessment of CIP's Programs: Achievements, Impact, and Constraints. A Working Paper, Lima, Peru.

15. Ortiz, R., Iwanaga, M., Raman, K.V. and Palacios, Mara (1990). Breeding for resistance to potato tuber moth, *Phthorimaea operculella* (Zeller), in diploid potatoes. Euphytica, 50:119-125.

16. Persoons, C.J., Voerman, S., Verwiel, P.E.J-, Ritter, F.J., Nooyen, W.J., Minks, A.K. (1976). Sex pheromone of the potato tuberworm moth, *Phthorimaea operculella*: isolation, identification and field evaluation. Entomol. Exp. Appl. 20, 289-300.

17. Raj, B.T. (1991). Potato tuber moth with special reference to India. Central Potato Research Institute, Technical Bulletin No.16, 16 pp.

18. Raman, K.V. (1988a). Control of potato tuber moth *Phthorimaea operculella* (Zeller) with sex pheromones in Peru. Agric. Ecosys. Environ. 21: 85-99.

19. Raman, K.V. (1988b). Integrated Insect Pest Management for Potatoes in Developing Countries, CIP Circular, Vol. 16, 1, 1-8. Int. Potato Cent. (CIP), Lima, Peru.

20. Raman, K.V. and Alcazar, J. (1988). Biological control of potato tuber moth, *Phthorimaea operculella* (Zeller) using a granulosisi virus in Peru. Asian

Potato Assoc. Proc. Second Triennial Conf., Kunming, China, Jun. 12-26, 1988, pp. 173-174.

21. Raman, K.V. and Radcliffe, E.B. (1992). Pest aspects of potato production, Part 2. Insect pests. *In* The Potato Crop: the scientific basis for improvement (ed. P.M. Harrie), Chapman and Hall, London, pp. 476-506.

22. Raman, K.V. and Redolfi, I. (1984). Progress on biological control of major potato pests. In Report of XXII Planning Conference on Integrated Pest Management, Jun. 4-8, 1984. Int. Potato Cent. (CIP), Lima, Peru. 199-208.

23. Raman, K.V., Booth, R.H. and Palacios, M. (1987). Control of potato tuber moth, *Phthorimaea operculella* (Zeller) in rustic potato stores. Trop. Sci. 27: 175-194.

24. Rizvi, S.A.H and Raman, K.V. (1983). Effect of glandular trichomes on the spread of potato virus Y (PVY) and potato leafroll virus (PLRV) in the field. *In*: Proceeding International Congress "Research for the Potato in the Year 2000", Lima, Peru, 22-27 February, 1982. 162-163.

25. Rodriguez, C.L. and Lepiz, C.S. (1988). Manejo adecuado de las feromonas de la polilla de la papa. Bol Divulgatorio 90, Min. Agric. Gan., Dpto. Entomol., San José, Costa Rica, 1-13.

26. Roelofs, W.L., Kochansky, J.P. and Card,R.T. (1975). Sex pheromone of the potato tuberworm moth, *Phthorimaea operculella*. Life Sci. 17: 699-706.

27. Scott, G.J. (1991). Transforming traditional food crops: The case for product development of roots & Tubers. Paper presented at the workshop "Product Development for Root and Tuber Crops" co-sponsored by CIAT, CIP, IITA, VISCA held at VISCA, Leyte The Philippines 22nd. May 1991 (Proceedings in Press).

28. Scurrah, M. and Raman, K.V. (1984). Breeding and Screening for Resistance to Major Potato Pests. In Report of the XXII Planning Conference on Integrated Pest Management, Jun. 4,8, 1984. Int. Potato Center, (CIP), Lima, Peru. 103-113

29. Torres, H., Alcazar, J. and Vittorelli, C. (1989). Incremento masivo de Beauveria sp. controlador biolgico del gorgojo de los andes de la papa. Resmenes XV Reunin de la Asociacin Latinoamericana de la Papa, Marzo 5-11, Mar del Plata, argentina, p 58.

30. Vickers, J.M. Cory, J. S. and Entwistle, P.F. (1991). DNA characterization of eigth geographic isolates of granulosis virus from the potato tuber moth *Phthorimaea operculella* (Lepidoptera: Gelechiidae). Journal of Invertebrate Pathology, 57, 334-342.

31. Von Arx, R. and Gebhandt, F. (1990). Effects of granulosis virus and *Bacillus thuringiensis* on life-table parameters of the potato tubermoth, *Phthorimaea operculella*. Entomophaga 35: 151-159.

32. Von Arx, R., Goueder, J., Cheikh, M. and Ben Temine, A. (1987). Integrated control of potato tubermoth *Phthorimaea operculella* (Zeller) in Tunisia. Insects Sci Appl. 8, 989-994.

FARMERS' PERSPECTIVES ON POTATO PEST MANAGEMENT IN DEVELOPING COUNTRIES: INTERDISCIPLINARY RESEARCH AT THE INTERNATIONAL POTATO CENTER (CIP)

Peter T. Ewell
Regional Social Scientist, International Potato Center (CIP),
Region III, P.O. Box 25171, Nairobi, Kenya.

Keith O. Fuglie[1]
Economist, International Potato Center (CIP), Region IV,
11 rue des Orangers, 2080 Ariana, Tunisia.

K.V. Raman[2]
Leader, Integrated Pest Management Program,
International Potato Center (CIP)
Apartado Postal, 5969, Lima, Peru.

Potatoes are a high-value, perishable crop with high costs of production. The plants and the tubers are attacked by many insect pests and diseases, both in the field and in storage. Farmers throughout the developing world have developed a range of strategies to deal with pests. The use of chemical insecticides and fungicides is increasing rapidly, particularly in areas where farmers are intensifying their production methods to sell potatoes in urban markets, and where the crop is expanding into new areas outside of its traditional range.

Pesticides can be dramatically effective in the short run. Nevertheless, it is widely recognized that over-reliance on chemicals is not a sustainable pest control strategy. Pest populations develop resistance; predators, parasites and other natural control mechanisms are disrupted; and what

[1]Current address: 1106 Seaton Lane, Falls Church, VA 22046, U.S.A.
[2]Current address: Director, ISAAA, Cornell University, Ithaca, NY 14853, U.S.A

were secondary pests can become serious problems. Costs go up as farmers apply higher doses of more expensive chemicals. A wide diversity of commercial pesticides, many of which have been banned or restricted in industrialized countries, are aggressively promoted by multinational companies, national distributors, and local outlets. Many of these products are dangerous to handle and store, and their residues have serious long-term effects on public health and on the environment.

The International Potato Center (CIP) is developing component technologies for the control of the major pests of potatoes world-wide with the goal of reducing losses within the context of integrated pest management (IPM), without over-reliance on chemical control. Components include: resistant or tolerant varieties; the use of pheromones, repellant plants, and biological control agents; and cultural control practices. Promising technologies developed by CIP are tested and adapted by national agricultural research systems (NARS) as they develop IPM programs for specific areas (8).

Ultimately, it is the farmers who must do the "integrating" of IPM, adapting component technologies to their own conditions and resources. Interdisciplinary cooperation between entomologists and social scientists is an important part of CIP's strategy for bringing the perspectives of these final users into the process of research and development. At CIP, this is called the "farmer-back-to-farmer" approach (9).

This paper summarizes some key results of several years of interdisciplinary research on the major insect pests of potatoes in Peru and in Tunisia. The goals of the research have been as follows: 1] documentation of farmers' perceptions and knowledge of pest problems; 2] documentation of farmers' current pest control practices; 3] adaptive on-farm research on promising component technologies, their effectiveness under local environmental and socioeconomic conditions; 4] assessment of the economic value of pest losses to farmers and consumers; and 5] assessment of the impact of research and development programs carried out by CIP in collaboration with national research and extension organizations.

POTATO PEST MANAGEMENT IN THE HIGHLANDS OF PERU

Potatoes were first domesticated in the highlands of Peru and are now grown by almost all rural households, both as a staple food for home consumption and as a cash crop for sale in either local or urban markets. The crop is attacked by a range of pests and diseases in this, its center of origin[1].

Farmers' Ranking of Pest Problems

As a first stage of the research process, a survey was carried out to document the distribution and severity of the major pests. A box of insect specimens, with pinned adults and larvae in alcohol, proved to be useful research tool. The farmers and their families gathered to examine the specimens, and talked freely about their control practices. They were asked if each insect was a problem in their area and if so, to rank the severity of the damage from 0 (for not a problem) to 3 (for serious damage) (Table 1). Five types of insects -- Andean weevils (*Premnotrypes spp.*), cutworms (*Agrotis spp.* and other Noctuids) and other soil pests, potato tubermoth (*Pthorimaea operculella*) and flea beetles, (*Epitrix spp.*) -- are problems in many areas in most years and were the focus of pest management strategies[2].

Farmers' Pest Management Practices

A survey of pest management practices revealed several different types of control.

Rites and ceremonies. Andean agriculture has a long history in a traditional society, and a number of religious and magical rites and ceremonies associated with the annual cycle of potato production are believed to protect the crop. This traditional knowledge incorporates hundreds of years of empirical experience, and can be tapped as a guide to how scientific research can complement rather than replace local technologies.

Organization of farming systems. The way agricultural production is organized has important effects on pest populations and damage, even if pest control is not the primary purpose of particular practices. For example, communities in the Peruvian highlands traditionally practice long-fallow sectorial rotations as a group. This is done primarily to keep field crops and livestock separate, but it also ensures an adequate fallow. Individual households commonly plant potatoes in widely separated plots in different micro-environments, which ensures that at least some of them will survive until the harvest.

Control methods with direct effects. A number of practices are carried out specifically to control pests. About a third of the farmers in the sample reported placing aromatic plants, particularly a native mint, muña (*Minthostachys sp.*)., in their stores to repel insects; a smaller number were using eucalyptus leaves, hot peppers, and other plants.

Table 1. Farmers' Ranking of Principal Potato Pest Problems in the Mantaro Valley And Cuzco Regions of Peru

Pest	Average Rank (1 - 3)[1]	% of Farmers Who Recognized Specimen[2]
1. Andean weevil larvae (*Premnotrypes spp.*)	2.4	100
2. Soil worms (primarily of the family *Noctuidae*)	2.4	100
3. Fungus diseases, primarily late blight (*Phytopththora infestans*)	2.3	—
4. Potato tubermoth (*Phthorimaea operculella*)	2.0	91
5. Flea beetle adults (*Epitrix spp.*)	1.9	100
6. Stem borers (*Symmetrischema plaesiosema*)	1.9	65
7. Blister beetle (*Epicauta spp.*)	1.7	100
8. Flea beetle larvae (*Epitrix spp.*)	1.7	100
9. Andean weevil adults (*Premnotrypes spp.*)	1.4	68
10. Viral diseases (various)	1.4	—
11. Nematodes (various)	1.3	60
12. Diabrotica (*Diabrotica spp.*)	1.1	57
13. Aphids (*Myzus persicae* and other aphidae)	1.0	75
14. Slugs (*Helix spp.*)	.9	75
15. Leafhoppers (*Empoasca spp.*)	.6	85
16. Thrips (*Frankliniella tuberosi*)	.6	43

1/ Mean score of farmers' assessments of relative severity in the 1984-85 season: 0 = not a problem;   1 = slight problem;   2 = moderate problem;   3 = serious problem

2/ Percent of farmers who could provide some name for a specimen of the insect, and describe its damage.

Source: Interviews with 74 potato farmers in Junin and Cuzco, Peru

Other examples of direct control include the application of lime or ashes around the base of young plants to repel soil worms and slugs, and the release of chickens in the field at weeding and at harvest to find and eat insect larvae. Cultural practices, such as early planting to avoid periods of high infestation and an extra hilling to prevent larvae from finding their way down to the tubers through cracks in the soil, were widely reported.

The use of pesticides. Pesticides were introduced in the 1940's, and have been widely adopted throughout the highland region. This process has been associated with the intensification of agriculture: the reduction in fallow periods, and the adoption of new varieties, fertilizers, and other purchased inputs. Potatoes are the most profitable crop grown by many farmers; thus, they invest what they can in inputs to increase production. An additional expenditure on pesticides is viewed as insurance to protect cash investments made during the growing season.

The survey compared two regions; the Mantaro valley, a major supplier of the urban market in Lima; and Cuzco, where a majority of farmers grow potatoes primarily for home consumption (Figure 1). There were notable differences between the regions in the use of hired labor, the use of tractors for land preparation, and the planting of modern varieties on at least some of their land. Animal manure is usually obtained from one's own or nearby farms. Even so, 88 percent of the farmers sampled in the Mantaro valley and 64 percent of those in Cuzco applied additional chemical fertilizers. Chemical pesticides were the most commonly-used purchased input, reported by 97 and 94 percent of the farmers in the two regions respectively.

Although virtually all of the farmers applied at least some pesticide, the products used, the rate and frequency of application, and the costs, varied significantly. At one extreme, a farmer in Cuzco made a single application of the relatively inexpensive and highly persistent insecticide aldrin, diluted in a can filled with water, splashing it on with a home-made brush made of twigs. The estimated cost was $18 US per ha. At the other extreme, a large seed producer in the Mantaro valley applied carbofuran, a more expensive and more dangerous chemical, at planting and then sprayed the crop ten times with mixtures of insecticides, fungicides, and foliar fertilizers. The total estimated cost in products alone was $1,300 US per ha. A total of 140 farmers surveyed throughout Peru reported using 46 different insecticides and 18 different fungicides.

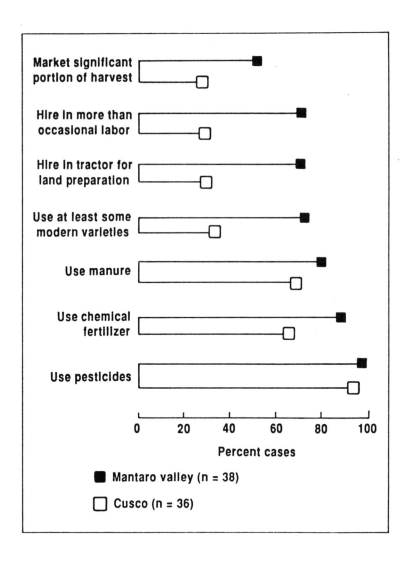

Fig. 1. Key characteristics of potato production systems of sample farmers in the Mantaro Valley and Cuzco regions of Peru

Andean Potato Weevil

Life cycle of the pest. Several weevil species of the genus *Premnotrypes* are important insect pests of potatoes throughout the Andean region. The life cycle of the insect closely tracks the annual production calendar of the potato crop, which means that weevils are difficult to escape. The adults emerge from the soil starting at planting time at the beginning of the rainy season, in October and November, and seek out the leaves of the young potato plants as food. The females lay their eggs under dead vegetation around the base of plants. The larvae emerge about 30 days later and burrow into young tubers, which are just forming. The larvae pass through four instars inside the tubers. They excavate serpentine galleries through the flesh, in which they leave trails of blackish excrement. The larvae move out into the soil to pupate, and overwinter as pupae until the beginning of the next rainy season, when the cycle begins again. More details on the biology of this pest have been previously reported (1).

Strategies of tolerance and chemical control. Weevils cause significant damage to the crop in the ground, particularly if the harvest is delayed, and can be carried into stores in the tubers. When conditions favor the pest, particularly in dry years, field losses of over 50 percent have been reported (3). Nevertheless, weevils are an endemic pest which have co-evolved with potatoes, and farmers have learned to tolerate them.

Traditional management practices, particularly long rotations and wide separation between potato plots, restrain the build-up of pest populations below catastrophic levels. Partially damaged tubers may not be "marketable," but they are used in various ways in Andean households: for home consumption, for processing into freeze-dried chuño, as seed, and for animal feed.

As fallow periods have been reduced and quality standards in the market have gone up, farmers have become increasingly dependent on chemical control, particularly applications of carbofuran to the soil at planting. This practice has been heavily promoted by the chemical companies, and was practiced by over 80 percent of the farmers sampled in two successive seasons. Additional spray applications of mixtures of insecticides and fungicides are made through the growing season.

The median expenditure on insecticides in the year studied was $70 US per ha, second only to fertilizers; the extreme value was over $400 (Figure 2). Chemical control is reasonably effective in the short run; damage varies from year to year, but average weevil damage has not prevented a significant intensification of the crop. Nevertheless, there is experimental evidence that the common pattern of application is wasteful. In any case, this level of insecticide use is not sustainable. The economic costs to the farmers are too high, and the residues are causing significant damage to public health and to the environment.

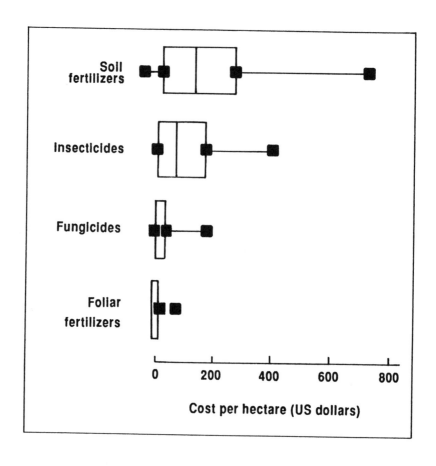

Fig. 2. Expenditures on inputs for potato production by sample farmers in the Mantaro Valley of Peru

Note: The "box and whiskers diagrams" are constructed as follows: the vertical line in the middle of each box is the median value. The box encloses the upper and lower qualities, and the horizontal lines extend out to the extreme values.

IPM Project in Cuzco, Peru. An interdisciplinary approach to integrated control of the Andean weevil has shown very promising results in the farmer community in Chincheros, Cuzco, Peru.

The government authorities in this Peruvian village have passed a law mandating the use of a native fungus for control of this pest. Until recently, farmers in this area controlled this pest with a cocktail of insecticides. The law was passed following the successful introduction of an entomopathogenic fungus, *Beauveria brogniartii* by CIP. Other integrated pest management strategies used by farmers of this area include the use of natural predators (domestic chickens), and better storage and cultural practices (2). This program is particularly timely as there is evidence that the Andean potato weevil is forcing a great many farmers to abandon large tracks of land. Evidence of this can be found in virtually every potato growing area in the Andes above 2,500 m.

Leafminer Fly In The Cañete Valley: A Pesticide Treadmill

The Cañete valley is an irrigated area on the coast of Peru, where potato production in the cool winter season expanded in the 1950's and 1960's to meet off-season demand in the Lima market. The leafminer fly, *Liriomyza huidobrensis*, was found in the 1940's, but it was secondary pest of minor importance. Insecticides were applied to potatoes to control a species of potato tubermoth, *Scrobipalpula absoluta*, which caused some damage as a leaf and shoot miner. These applications disrupted the natural enemies of the leafminer fly, which then became a major pest. When infestations are severe, this insect can defoliate entire fields (7,11).

Cañete is an isolated irrigated valley in the desert. Widespread spraying of virtually all green plants with insecticides throughout the year puts insect populations under heavy selection pressure. The local populations of the leafminer fly have developed resistance to all classes of insecticides, forcing farmers to progressively increase the dosage of more expensive chemicals. This was a major factor leading to a precipitous decline in the area planted with potatoes, starting in the late 1970's.

In their pest management decisions, farmers must juggle unpredictable levels of insect attack and yield reduction, a range of insecticides with very different costs, and unpredictable prices at the time of harvest. The population of the insect is controlled by its natural enemies in the hot summer months, builds up rapidly in the cool season from May through August, and then drops off again (Figure 3). Potato prices in the Lima market fall to their annual low at the end of June, the major harvest period in the highlands. They rise gradually through the rest of the year, as stocks are depleted. The precise shape of both of these curves varies from one year to another.

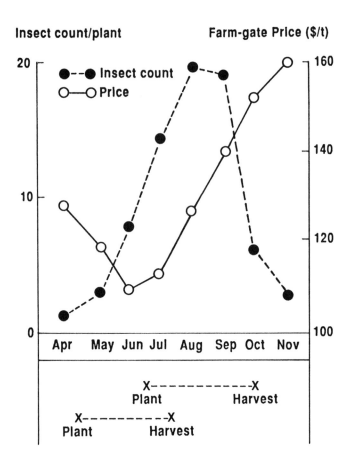

Fig. 3. Expected patterns of potato leafminer fly infestation and farm-gate prices in the Cañete Valley of Peru

A two-year study was carried out to understand how farmers make decisions in this context. If they can find seed, they can plant potatoes in Cañete as early as the end of April. This early crop will avoid the worst period of attack by the leafminer fly, but market prices are likely to be low at harvest. Hence, farmers plant in June or July. Their fields are exposed to high population densities of the pest, and farmers spray repeatedly in the hope that high prices at harvest will compensate their costs.

The number of applications in the sample ranged from three to twelve; the largest number of farmers sprayed seven to eight times with cocktails of insecticide mixtures, including insect growth regulators. Total expenditure on insecticides ranged from $9.50 US over $1,000 US per ha (Figure 4). Costs of insecticides were the highest input. While it is widely recognized that all farmers would benefit if they reduced their applications, it has proved very difficult to organize IPM programs. Potatoes are produced by many independent small farmers and are sold through informal channels to the Lima market. The short-term interests of the individual farmers, rather than the potential benefit to the community as a whole, have dominated pest management decisions.

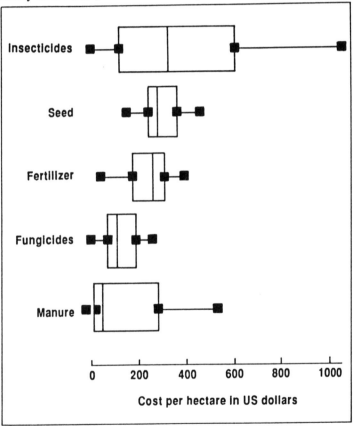

Fig. 4. Expenditures on inputs for potato production by sample farmers in the Cañete Valley of Peru
Note: The "box and whisker diagrams" are constructed as follows: the vertical line in the middle of each box encloses the upper and lower quartiles, and the horizontal lines extend out to the extreme values.

SOCIOECONOMIC CONTRIBUTIONS TO
POTATO IPM IN TUNISIA[3]

The potato tubermoth (*Phthorimaea operculella* [Zeller]) is the most significant insect pest of potato in Tunisia. Populations of the insect begin to rise in mid-June with the onset of the hot and dry summer weather, and remain high until October or November. They infest the spring season potato crop (harvested in June and July) in the field, and are carried into the rustic, non-refrigerated stores. These stores are the source of potatoes in the market throughout the hot summer period, when there is no production.

Interdisciplinary pest management research has sought to reduce or eliminate farmers' dependence on chemical insecticides for potato tubermoth control. Work has focused on finding cultural practices that can reduce infestation in fields, particularly early harvest, supplemental irrigation up to harvest, and hilling. Biological insecticides (*Bacillus thuringiensis* and a granulosis virus) are being formulated and tested as a way to provide effective and safe pest control in rustic stores. The social scientists on the team have helped to answer three questions important to the development of IPM technology: 1] how does the market value potatoes with PTM damage? 2] do farmers use IPM technology? and 3] how does new technology perform under farm conditions?

Market Value of Potatoes with PTM damage. Tubermoth larvae damage potatoes by tunnelling galleries in the tubers. In the market, consumers may tolerate some level of damage, or they may be willing to buy damaged potatoes at a reduced price. The relationship between quality and price depends on market conditions. Understanding how the market tolerates damage is an essential part of an economic assessment of pest management technology. If the market is tolerant of damage and prices do not go down, then there will be little motivation for farmers to invest in improved pest control technology. On the other hand, if quality standards are stringent, then farmers may invest heavily in pest management measures which offer the highest assurance of total control, and may reject cheaper methods which can only keep pest damage low.

In Tunisia, some damage is tolerated in retail markets, but there is zero tolerance in the export trade to Europe. How local markets discount PTM-damaged potatoes was studied in a survey of retail vegetable markets in Tunis. Seventy samples of potatoes from several retail markets were purchased over a two-month period (August and September, 1990). Tubermoth damage in each sample was measured by counting the percentage of tubers in the sample with visible holes. The degree of damage was also assessed by counting the number of holes per tuber. We also took other measures on factors that affect quality, such as average tuber size, shape, color, and losses from rot or greening. With retail market price as the dependent variable, multiple regression analysis was used to quantify the relationship between these quality variables and the price.

These results showed that tubers with one tubermoth hole are generally sold at full market value, but potatoes with two or three holes are sorted out and sold in separate lots at discount of between 30 to 50 percent. Heavily damaged tubers (with four or more holes per tuber) are usually discarded and were rarely found in the market. The implication is that because low levels of damage are tolerated in the market, farmers will probably accept pest management measures which offer good but not necessarily total control of pest damage. It is likely that this kind of pest management technology can be developed and applied at relatively low cost.

Although farmers may not be penalized for low levels of infestation (i.e., one insect gallery per tuber), at the other end of the marketing chain, consumers may be forced to absorb these costs. We interviewed consumers about their attitudes toward potatoes with insect damage. While some responded that they would throw out tubers with any damage, most said that they would simply cut out the damaged parts and use the rest. Some consumers (usually low-income people) seek out low quality potatoes, taking advantage of the lower prices.

Table 2 presents estimates of how well consumers who buy damaged potatoes are compensated for the losses, assuming they cut out and discard damaged parts. While consumers are forced to absorb the losses from low insect infestation, since these are sold in the same lots as non damaged potatoes at the full market price, consumers who buy low priced potatoes with more visible damage appear to be fully compensated for these losses.

Do farmers use IPM technology? Social science participation in interdisciplinary research has documented to what extent and how well farmers are using key component technologies. Surveys of the practices that farmers were using to control PTM infestation in their potato fields were carried out in 1986 and 1990. Over these four years, there was a decline in the use of insecticides and an increase in the use cultural of practices, especially late season irrigation (Figure 5). In 1990, a total of fifty-nine farmers were surveyed over a six week period during the spring crop harvest. Two types of data were collected: 1] socioeconomic data on the farmer's production practices, including

Table 2: Weight Losses and Price Discounts for Damaged Potatoes in Retail Markets in Tunis, Tunisia

Level of Damage	Weight Loss (%)	Price Discount[1] (%)
Low insect infestation (1 gallery per tuber)	5 - 10	Insignificant
High insect infestation (2 or more galleries per tuber)	10 - 30	31 - 52
Other damage[2] (rotting or greening)	10	9 - 14

1/ Price discounts are derived from a regression model. The range is one standard deviatiation above and below the mean value of the regression coefficient

2/ For illustrative purposes, it is assumed that 10% is unusable due to other types oif damage, Measured losses in 77 samples ranged from 0 to 30% by weight.

timing of planting, hilling, irrigation, harvesting, and use of seed, fertilizer and pesticides; and 2] direct measurement of field infestation at harvest.

The relationship between farmers' pest management practices and the level of infestation found in their fields at harvest has been studied (11). Nearly all fields sampled during the first three weeks of the survey had low levels of infestation. But toward the end of the survey period there was a marked increase.

In some cases the damage exceeded twenty percent of the tubers harvested. The farmers' pest management practices other than date of harvest (e.g., the timing of their last irrigation, hilling, and whether or not they used insecticides) were modeled as "slope-dummy" variables. The three practices were found to be effective at reducing the rate of infestation development across the farm sample (Figure 6). The most effective technique to avoid PTM infestation is to complete harvest

Farmers using this technique (%)

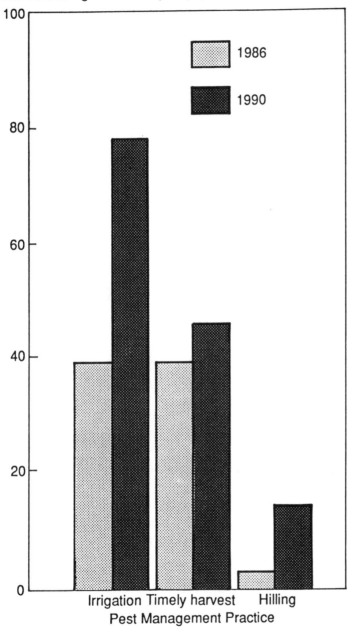

Fig. 5. Adoption of Cultural Practices for the control of potato tubermoth in Tunisia,
1986 - 1990

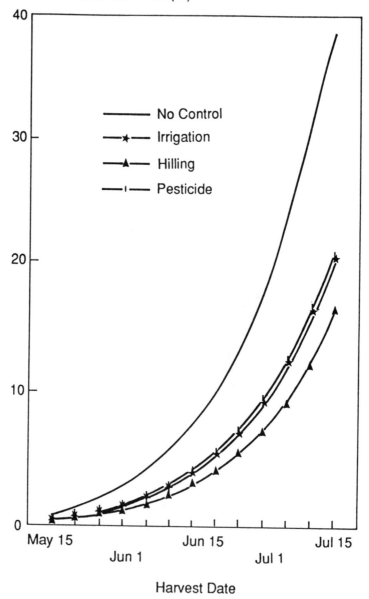

Tubers Infested with PTM (%)

— No Control
—∗— Irrigation
—▲— Hilling
—ı— Pesticide

May 15   Jun 15   Jul 15
    Jun 1   Jul 1

Harvest Date

Fig. 6. Effects of farmers' pest management practices on potato tubermoth damage in Tunisia

before mid-June. For those farmers who had to delay their harvest, irrigation, hilling and insecticide use significantly reduced insect damage. Presumably even greater pest control could be achieved by combining two or more of these practices, but limitations on the number of observations prevented us from testing this hypothesis.

How does this new technology perform under farm conditions? A third area where the social sciences have contributed is interdisciplinary on-farm research to test the efficacy of new biological insecticides in rustic stores. Farmers store potatoes under a wide variety of conditions, such as under shelters, in pits, under trees, or simply in the open air. They cover their potato heaps with whatever materials they find handy (potato haulms, straw, paper sacks, tree branches, or dried seaweed). They apply chemical insecticides in both powder and liquid form. The level of insect infestation brought into the stores from the field varies depending on the prior field management practices and on how carefully the potatoes are sorted before being put into storage.

While biological insecticides have been found to be effective substitutes for chemical insecticides in laboratory experiments, on-farm trials were carried out to test the "robustness" of the technology under the range of storage conditions. Social scientists worked with entomologists to set trials with 20 farmers over a two year period (1990 and 1991). Farmers were purposely selected to provide a cross section of storage conditions. Two small heaps of 100 kilograms were set up next to the farmer's store and kept under identical conditions. One of the heaps was treated with two biological insecticides, a formulation of Bacillus thuringiensis and a granulosis virus. Conventional chemical insecticides were applied to the second heap.

Observations were taken at monthly intervals over a three month period. Results were summarized previously (6). The biological insecticide performed as well as or better than the chemical insecticide treatment. The farm trials also demonstrated the need to integrate insecticide treatments with good storage practices. In two of the trials, the farmers didn't place their stores in shady areas and neither the chemical nor biological insecticides were effective at limiting insect damage in these cases. However, with good storage management, the biological insecticides are effective, and can provide a sustainable alternative to chemical insecticides if they can be produced and distributed at a competitive price.

Epilogue

The goal of IPM research is to develop component technologies which farmers will be able to integrate under their own conditions. Reliance on chemical control alone is not a sustainable pest management strategy. There is an urgent need for the development of more effective and economical technologies that will avoid the familiar problems of the "pesticide treadmill." Success depends on better knowledge both of the pests and of the conditions under which farmers make pest management decisions. It is critical to involve farmers in the research process from the very beginning, using a "farmer-back-to-farmer" approach.

This paper has reviewed examples of this interdisciplinary research approach, in which entomologists and social scientists work together with farmers. The methodologies were flexible, combining surveys, trapping and other kinds of direct monitoring of insect populations and damage, and on-farm research. Assessment of the losses from pests and the potential benefits of IPM required analysis of storage, marketing, and consumption as well as of production.

The research in Peru and in Tunisia has been carried out in collaboration with the two national potato programs. A key goal has been to build capacity for interdisciplinary field research in the NARS. It is important to recognize that personnel and budget are limited. It is critical to develop simple, flexible methodologies which obtain a maximum of useful information from well-planned and efficiently executed field research. The organization of effective linkages with extension are critical if the technologies are to reach the farmers, who are the ones who will integrate the components into effective integrated pest management.

Notes

1/ The research reported in following sections on Peru was carried out by an interdisciplinary team from CIP and the Peruvian National Agricultural Research Institute (INIAA). We would like to acknowledge the contributions of H. Fano, J. Alcazar, M. Palacios, and J. Carhuamaca. The findings are discussed in more detail in other reports (3,4).

2/ Fungal and bacterial diseases are also important problems, but these studies focused on insect pest management.

3/ The research reported in the following section on Tunisia was carried out in collaboration with research scientists at the Tunisian National Agricultural Research Institute (INRAT). The contributions of H. Ben Salah, M. Essamet, A. Ben Temime, A. Rahmouni, and H. Merji were crucial. N. Ferroni of the Zurich Polytechnic Institute also assisted in carrying out market and consumer surveys. The findings are discussed in more detail in other reports (5,6,10,11).

Literature Cited

1. Alcalá, P. and Alcázar,J. 1976. Biología y comportamiento de Premnotrypes suturicallus Kuchel (Col: Curculionidade). Revista Peruana de Entomología. 19: 49-52.
2. CIP. 1992. CIP Annual Report 1992. International Potato Center, Lima, Peru.
3. Ewell, P.T. 1990. Socio-economic aspects of farmer-oriented research for potato IPM. Pages 108-124 in S.K. Hahn and F.E. Caveness, Eds. Integrated Pest management for Tropical Root and Tuber Crops. (International Institute of Tropical Agriculture (IITA), Ibadan, Nigeria.
4. Ewell, P.T., Fano, H., Raman, K.V., Alcázar, J., Palacios, M., Carhuamaca, J. 1990. Farmer Management of Potato Insect Pests in Peru. Food Systems Research Series No. 6. International Potato Center (CIP), Lima, Peru.
5. Fuglie, K. 1991. The demand for potatoes in Tunisia. Social Science Working Paper No. 1991-6. International Potato Center (CIP), Lima, Peru.
6. Fuglie, K., Ben Salah, H., Essamet, M., Ben Temime, A., Rahmouni, A. 1991. The development and adoption of integrated pest management of the potato tubermoth in Tunisia. Social Science Working Paper. International Potato Center (CIP), Lima, Peru.
7. Herrera, J. 1963. Problemas insectiles del cultivo de la papa en el valle de Cañete. Revista Peruana de Entomología Agrícola. 6:1-9.
8. Raman, K.V. 1988. Integrated pest management for potatoes in developing countries. CIP Circular 16:1-8.
9. Rhoades, R.E. and Booth, R.H. 1982. Farmer-back-to-farmer: A model for generating acceptable agricultural technology. Agricultural Administration 11: 121-137.
10. Von Arx, R., Goueder, J., Cheikh, M., Ben Temine, A. 1987. Integrated control of the potato tubermoth Phthorimaea operculella (Zeller), Insect Sci. Applic. 8:989-994.
11. Von Arx, R., Ewell, P.T., Gouder, J., Essamet, M., Cheikh, M. Ben Temime, A. 1988. Management of the potato tuber moth by Tunisian farmers: A report of on-farm monitoring and socioeconomic survey. International Potato Center (CIP), Lima, Peru.
12. Yábar, E. 1988. La mosca minadora de la papa en el Perú. Instituto Nacional de Investigación Agraria y Agroindustrial (INIAA), Lima, Peru.

POTATO DISEASE MANAGEMENT
IN LATIN AMERICA

O.S. Malamud, T. Ames de Icochea, and H. Torres
The International Potato Center,
Santo Domingo, Dominican Republic and Lima, Peru

Potato production in Latin America in 1989 was estimated at 12 million tons, which represented 5% of the world production. In contrast, North America produced 20 million tons. Latin America is the center of origin of the potato, and several secondary centers of diversification exist. The two major cultivated subspecies of *Solanum tuberosum* L. (*tuberosum* and *andigena*), are grown in this region. Potatoes are cultivated at high elevations, in cold, cool and temperate zones, in dry regions, and in areas of heavy precipitation. They are planted in a single season in high latitude countries, in one or more seasons in subtropical-temperate zones, and continuously close to the equator. As a consequence, most of the important pathogens known to attack potatoes are found in Latin America, and a wide range in crop loss occurs.

Disease Distribution and Importance

The importance of potato diseases, based on estimated yield losses, can be placed in five categories: reported only (no yield loss); sporadic (<2% yield loss); moderate (2-10% yield loss); important (11-30% yield loss) and very important (>30% yield loss). In Latin America and the Caribbean, which represent 22 countries, 45 fungal diseases of potatoes are known, and all have been reported to limit yield. In 93 cases only the disease has been reported, but in 24 cases, yield losses exceeded 30% (Table 1). The most important disease is late blight with yield losses in excess over 30% reported for 18 countries.

Three bacterial diseases are known to occur. Bacterial wilt, caused by the soilborne and tuberborne bacterium, *Pseudomonas solanacearum*, is the most prevalent and important. In 20 cases (disease by country), no yield losses were reported. Whereas, in 12 cases, yield losses were considerable (Table 1).

Table 1. Importance of fungal and bacterial diseases of potato in Latin America.

Yield loss	Number of reports		
	South America	Central America, Mexico, Caribbean	Total
Fungal diseases			
Reported only*	37	93	130
Sporadic (<2%)	53	1	54
Moderate (2-10%)	26	4	30
Important (10-30%)	20	5	25
Very important (>30%)	16	8	24
TOTAL	152	111	263
Bacterial diseases			
Reported only*	12	8	20
Sporadic (<2%)	2	0	2
Moderate (2-10%)	2	1	3
Important (10-30%)	3	2	5
Very important (>30%)	4	3	7
TOTAL	23	14	37

*Disease has been reported in scientific papers but no losses were given.

Ranking of the diseases according to relative crop loss and frequency of presence in the region indicates that nine fungal diseases have reached general distribution, whereas 17 are localized (Table 2).

In South America, late blight, Rhizoctonia canker, and early blight are the most widespread and cause the most damage, whereas common rust, smut, and black rot are localized but still cause significant crop losses.

For Central America, Mexico and the Caribbean, limited information on crop losses is available due to smaller plantings and the lesser importance of potato. However, late blight is as great or greater a problem in this region than in South America. Rhizoctonia canker and early blight are also of importance. Updated surveys are needed for this region to assess the status of the different diseases because the total production of potato has doubled in the last decade.

Diseases caused by bacteria in South America include bacterial wilt and soft rot; however, only the former is of economic importance (Table 3).

Table 2. Rank of fungal diseases by crop loss in South America and Latin America.

Distribution/Disease/Pathogen	South America	Central America, Mexico, Caribbean
WIDESPREAD DISTRIBUTION		
Late blight (*Phytophthora infestans*)	40	41
Rhizoctonia canker (*Rhizoctonia solani*)	28	17
Early blight (*Alternaria solani*)	21	12
Powdery scab (*Spongospora subterranea*)	13	
Vertillium wilt (*Verticillium albo-atrum*)	11	
Wart (*Synchytrium endobioticum*)	10	
Fusarium wilt (*Fusarium oxysporum*)	10	
Verticillium wilt (*Verticillium dahliae*)	9	
Stem rot (*Sclerotium rolfsii*)	9	
LOCALIZED DISTRIBUTION		
Common rust (*Puccinia pittieriana*)	7	
Smut (*Thecaphora* [*Angiosorus solani*])	7	
Black rot (*Rosellinia necatrix*)	7	
White mold (*Sclerotinia sclerotiorum*)	6	
Fusarium wilt (*Fusarium solani* var. *caeruleum*)	6	
Powdery mildew (*Erysiphe cichoracearum*)	5	
Grey mold (*Botrytis cinerea*)	4	
Silver scurf (*Helminthosporium solani*)	4	
Black dot (*Colletotrichum atramentarium*)	4	
Leaf spot (*Phoma andina*)	3	
Fusarium wilt (*Fusarium solani* var. *eumartii*)	3	
Dry rot (*Fusarium* sp.)	2	
Phoma leaf spot (*Phoma exigua*)	2	
Septoria leaf spot (*Septoria lycopersici*)	1	
Pink rot (*Phytophthora erythroseptica*)	1	
Powdery mildew (*Oidium* sp.)	1	

For the highland tropics, potatoes are grown from 1000 to 4000 m. Most of the farmers cultivate commercial varieties of *Solanum tuberosum* ssp. *andigenum* or other native species such as *S. phureja*, *S. stenotomum* and *S. gonyocalix*.

Table 3. Rank of diseases by crop loss in Latin America

Disease/Pathogen	South America, Caribbean	Central America, Mexico
Bacterial wilt (*Pseudomonas solanacearum*)	19	22
Blackleg and tuber soft rot (*Erwinia*		
carotovora subsp. *atroseptica*	18	only reported
and *E.c. carotovora*)	4	only reported
Common scab (*Streptomyces scabies*)	9	

Torres has reviewed the status of the most important diseases in the Andean highlands (35). Among the foliar diseases, late blight is considered very severe throughout the region. Depending on the season, altitude, variety, and crop management, disease incidence has reached 100% and has resulted in a total crop loss. Late blight is most severe in the mid to high elevations of Venezuela, Colombia and Ecuador and is less severe and more sporadic in Peru and Bolivia (25,31,39).

Phoma leaf spot, Septoria leaf spot and early blight can be present and in some instances losses caused by these diseases can be severe. Potato rust is common in Ecuador, Colombia, Peru and Bolivia but is only important in Ecuador and certain areas of Colombia (5).

Thirteen soilborne diseases are present in the region and the incidence and severity varies from country to country (13,35). Despite the interchange of seed between regions, there are still some areas within countries which are free from particular diseases. Powdery scab is most important in southern Peru and in the Altiplano of Bolivia (31,36). Black wart is more prevalent and damaging in Bolivia at altitudes of 3500-3800 m (37). Pink rot is important in Peru and Bolivia and is mainly associated with poorly drained soils and high precipitation. Potato smut is prevalent in soils of Peru, Bolivia, Colombia and Ecuador (36,41).

Verticillium wilt is present in all of the Andean zone up to 4,000 m. *Verticillium dahliae* appears to be more prevalent pathogen, but in cool environments, *V. albo-atrum* is the more prevalent species. In Colombia losses up to 100% were recorded in 1984-86 for this disease (23,34,39,40). Rosellinia black rot is a limiting factor in some areas of Ecuador and Southern Colombia. In Ecuador losses have reached 100% (3,30). This rot occurs mainly in soils with a high organic matter content and high humidity (33). Gray mold and white mold are only of local importance (35-39).

Rhizoctonia wilt and canker are present in all countries but wilt occurs occasionally. The severity of the disease and crop losses are influenced by anastomosis groups (2,35).

Other wilts and tuber dry rots associated with *Fusarium* are present in the Andes but their importance is minimal and very localized (38).

In the Southern Cone, most of the potato crop is planted with cultivars derived from *Solanum tuberosum*, except small areas in northern Argentina and Chile where it is also possible to find local, Andean-type varieties. In the last decade, most of the varieties grown were either bred in Canada, the United States, Holland and other European countries or were released locally. As a result of an active germplasm interchange program among countries, germplasm from CIP and other breeding programs that has increased genetic resistance to diseases and pests have been introduced to farmers over the last 10-15 yr with substantial success (18).

Similarities between the Southern Cone in latitude, altitude and the climatic conditions of North America and European countries, may explain the difference in incidence and severity of diseases for this area compared with other regions of Latin America.

Late blight is the most important foliar disease for the Andean Region, southern Brazil, localized provinces of northwestern Argentina and Paraguay. It is endemic, but in some years the disease reaches the level of an epidemic (6,9,21). Early blight is the second most important disease, especially in Brazil, Uruguay and central and southeastern Argentina. Defoliation of the plants and yield loss can reach 80% especially after the flowering stage of the plants. The disease is less prevalent in Chile and Paraguay (6,21).

Among the soilborne diseases caused by fungi, Rhizoctonia wilt and canker, Fusarium wilt and dry rot, and Verticillium wilt are the most conspicuous and important in the region (4,6,8,20). Due to the presence of one or several of them in the major potato growing areas, the lack of fast detection methods, and the somewhat similar symptomatology, the correct evaluation of their incidence and severity is erratic. In general, tuber end rot, Verticillium wilt, scurf are the most prevalent in Argentina. Another that is common but not significant for that country is silver scurf. In Brazil, apart from *Rhizoctonia*, *Rosellinia necatrix* and a complex of *Fusarium* spp. *Cylindrocladium clavatum* was reported to be a problem to potatoes.

In central Brazil and in Chile important diseases include powdery scab, Fusarium tuber rot, and Rhizoctonia scurf (2).

In Central America, late blight can be extremely severe in parts of Mexico, Guatemala, Costa Rica and Panama and less severe in Cuba,

Nicaragua, Haiti, Honduras, El Salvador and Jamaica and sporadic in the Dominican Republic (29). Early blight is severe in Cuba, less severe in Guatemala, Costa Rica, Panama and sporadic in the rest of the region.

The incidence of diseases caused by soilborne fungi are seldom reported, except for Rhizoctonia scurf in Costa Rica, Nicaragua, Guatemala and Cuba and very recently, this disease plus Fusarium wilt and Verticillium wilt have been reported in the state of Guanajuato in Mexico (7). There, losses of 40 to 83% were reported for scurf, 17% for Fusarium wilt in spring and up to 100% in summer for Fusarium wilt and Verticillium wilt.

In the Andean Region, bacterial wilt is present and causes considerable damage in Peru, in regions of Ecuador, Colombia and northern Chile, parts of Bolivia, particularly at lower elevations and warmer climates, and in central and eastern Venezuela (1,13,36). Brazil is affected the most, followed closely by Uruguay. The disease is also present in central and northern Argentina, and northern Chile but occurs only sporadically (6,9, 21,22,25). In Central America, this disease is present in Guatemala, Nicaragua, El Salvador, Haiti, Cuba and some eastern Caribbean Islands (Guadaloupe and Trinidad). It also was reported in Puerto Rico and Honduras (32,35).

In Costa Rica, bacterial wilt was a limiting factor for potato cultivation in the past. Through clean seed selection and planting, the use of resistant germplasm, correct crop sanitation and strict adherence to quarantine regulations, the disease has been almost completely eradicated. In Panama and Mexico, bacterial wilt has caused damage, but it is not present in the main potato growing areas. Recent findings by USA and CIP researchers, utilizing of RFLP analysis, have reported the existence and classification of new strains of Race 3 from lower elevations of Peru and Brazil (11,17).

Diseases caused by the soft rot erwinias are present in Argentina, Colombia, and Peru, but are of limited importance (6,39).

Disease Management

In general terms, foliar diseases are being controlled by a combination of chemical treatments and the planting of resistant varieties. Despite the extreme variability in ecology and climates, types of farmers and their economic capabilities, most farmers except for those who live in very remote areas and or are very poor, apply fungicides. In the latter cases, availability of resistant varieties, either bred or naturally selected from native stocks, has been crucial to producing a crop. This is well exemplified in Mexico, Guatemala,

Colombia, Ecuador, Peru and Bolivia. In tropical areas, where rainfall favors disease development and prevents spraying of fungicides, potatoes are grown in dry seasons to escape disease.

Late blight is the most important disease throughout Latin America. In the last 25 yr national and international research programs have searched for durable and stable plant resistance to the disease.

It is recognized that the fungus probably originated in Mexico or in a neighboring country. In addition, the Toluca Valley, until recently, was the only place where the sexual stage of the pathogen existed and where varieties from the world over could be tested for resistance. Since the demonstration of the breakdown of the resistance provided by "major genes" in the 50's and early 60's, researchers from Mexico, the Rockefeller Foundation Potato Program, Cornell University, Sweden, Holland and CIP have continued the search for field resistance to this disease (15,16,26-28).

The involvement of CIP in late blight research since 1973 has added a strong input toward that goal, especially considering the resources made available to CIP and the worldwide reach of its regional layout.

In the last decade, the participation of Mexico in a Cooperative Research Network in Central America and the Caribbean provided a strong base for interchange and adaptation of new varieties with resistance. Since 1974 this program has provided seven or eight new varieties of which two or three are being extensively grown in several countries (29). Colombia, Ecuador and Peru have each released several varieties with excellent resistance and adaptability to the Andean highlands.

CIP's short-term research priority is to combine field and race-specific resistance. The long term strategy is to produce breeding lines with general or field resistance to the late blight fungus identified through international testing. Resistant lines bred by CIP have been selected at sites in Bolivia, Colombia and Mexico. Bolivia, Colombia, Costa Rica, Chile, Ecuador, Guatemala, Mexico, Nicaragua, Peru and Venezuela have received resistant clones for further selection and variety release.

Most other foliar diseases are controlled mainly through the application of fungicides. However, early blight control is particularly difficult because the fungicides commonly used for late blight are not effective (6).

Resistant clones from CIP's germplasm are being tested in Peru, Brazil and Uruguay. For control of soilborne and tuberborne pathogens the general procedure is to use clean seed and to practice crop rotation.

Only where possible through irrigation, or when economics allow, fumigation or soil fungicides are applied, especially to control *Verticillium, Fusarium* and *Rhizoctonia*. Resistant clones and cultivars are becoming available for control of powdery scab, Verticillium wilt (24), smut, Rosellinia rot, and black wart. Control of pink rot is achieved through a combination of systemic and contact fungicides.

Breeding and selection for resistance to bacterial wilt continues to be emphasized with full collaboration between the countries in Latin America where the problem exists, and the CIP and its collaborators (10,12,14,19). Resistance alone does not always control the disease as it is only one component of an integrated strategy (12). The combination of resistant clones, strict measures of seed sanitation, and proper crop rotations produced a decline in the incidence of the disease and led to the reestablishment of potato in these previously heavily infested areas.

Over the last 5 yr, rapid advances have been made in biotechnology to assist in the control of bacterial diseases through transformation technology and gene transfer. They include the use of *Agrobacterium rhizogenes* to introduce genes from the defensive mechanism of insects, known as immuno proteins, with high antibacterial effect. This procedure, tested by CIP and US collaborators has the potential to introduce resistance to *Pseudomonas* and *Erwinia* in potato (10,11).

Epilogue

This review of the potato diseases is only a small example of what is currently being studied throughout Latin America. At this time of increased international cooperation, open commerce, potential free exchange of products, produce and raw materials, particularly within the Americas, the potential danger of the spread of diseases and pests is great. However, there also may be the unusual chance of further germplasm interchange and seed commerce for improvement of the potato crop, since governments play a big role in quarantine-sanitation regulations, sometimes not necessarily backed by science.

Quarantine regulations vary in Latin America, some too strict, and some too lax, often as a result of lack of knowledge of present and potential problems with diseases and pests associated with introduced germplasm. Most quarantine regulations are inadequate, since they do not cover all categories of potatoes introduced, especially table stocks, which are often used as seed in developing countries. Not all the countries have the technical, financial and human resources to properly develop and enforce sound phytosanitary regulations.

Literature Cited

1. Aley, P., and French, E. R. 1990. Rapidez de marchitamiento por *Pseudomonas solanacearum* y su efecto estructural en papa (Abstr) Congreso Peruano de Fitopatología. Fitopatología (Perú) 25:15.
2. Andrade, S. N., and Gutierrez A. N. 1990. Determinación de grupos de anastomosis (G.A.) de *Rhizoctonia solani* en papas del sur de Chile. Simiente (Chile) 60:192.
3. Ayala, L. 1987. Resistencia varietal, rango de hospederos e identificación del agente causal de la "lanosa" de la papa. BS Thesis. Pontificia Universidad del Ecuador. Np. 129 pp.
4. Bolkan, H. A., and Ribeiro, W. R. C. 1985. Anastomosis groups and pathogenicity of *Rhizoctonia solani* isolates from Brazil. Plant Dis. 69:599-601.
5. Buritica, P., and Orjuela, J. 1968. Estudios fisiológicos de *Puccinia pittieriana* Henn., causante de la roya de la papa (*Solanum tuberosum* L.). Fitotécnica Latinoamericana 5:81-88.
6. Calderoni, A. V. 1978. Enfermedades de la papa y su control. Editorial Hemisferio Sur S.A. Buenos Aires, Argentina. 143 pp
7. Castrejón, A. S., and Rocha, R. 1991. Principales enfermedades fungosas del cultivo de la papa en el área de León Guanajuato, Mexico. Pages 96-97 In: Programa, XV Reunión Asociación Latinoamericana de la Papa (ALAP). Lima, Perú.
8. Castro, C., and Taváres, F. N. 1986. Caracterizacao de isolados de *Rhizoctonia* spp., no Brasil. Summa Phytopathologica 12:26.
9. Chiampi-Panno, L. 1987. Phytopatological problems produced by the introduction of vegetables in Chile. Pages 139-144 In: Proceedings Fitogenetic Resources Symposium: International Board for Genetic Resources (IBPGR). Universidad Austral de Chile.
10. Chiampi-Panno, L. 1989. Biological control of bacterial wilt of potatoes caused by *Pseudomonas solanacearum*. Am. Potato J. 66:315-332.
11. Dodds, J. H. et al. 1990. Potato transformation for confering disease resistance. Pages 86-92 In: Proceedings, Caribbean Food Crop Society 26th Annual Meeting. Mayaguez, Puerto Rico.
12. Elphinstone, J. G. 1989. Reducción de la *Marchitez bacteriana* por aplicación de varias prácticas agronómicas. Fitopatología (Perú) 24:42.
13. French, E. R. et al. 1977. Enfermedades de la papa en el Perú, IDIA, Perú. Boletín Técnico No. 77. 36 pp.
14. French, E. R., and Lindo, L. 1985. Sources of resistance in tuberous *Solanum* sp. to soft rot by *Erwinias*. Page 79 In: Report of the International Conference on Potato Blackleg Disease. D. C. Graham and M. Harrison (eds). Potato Marketing Board (UK), and Potato Assoc. of America (USA).
15. Fry, W. E. 1989. The importance of the perfect stage of *Phytophthora infestans* from the standpoint of epidemiology and adaptation. Pages 17-30 In: Report of the Planning Conference on Fungal Disease of the Potato. The International Potato Center, Lima, Perú.
16. Gallegly, M. F., and Niederhauser, J. S. 1959. Genetic controls of host-parasite interactions in the Phytophthora late blight disease. Pages 168-182 In: Plant Pathology: Problems and Progress 1908-1958. C. S. Holton et al. (eds). University of Wisconsin Press, Madison. 588 pp.
17. Hayward, A. C. et al. 1991. Variante Tropical del biovar 2 de *Pseudomonas solanacearum*. Page 92 In: Programa, XV Reunión de la Asociación Latinoamericana de la Papa (ALAP), Lima, Perú.

18. Hidalgo, O. A. 1991. Consideraciones sobre un programa para analizar datos de campo del Tizón Tardío (*Phytophthora infestans*) y correlaciones entre los valores resultantes. Pages 93-94 In: Programa XV Reunión de la Asociación Latinoamericana de la Papa (ALAP), Lima, Perú.

19. Huamán, Z. 1989. Screening for resistance to Fusarium dry rot in progenies of cultivars of *S. tuberosum* spp. *andigena* with resistance to *Erwinia chrysanthemi*. Am. Potato J. 66:357:364.

20. Inchausti, M. 1991. Control de la sarna negra de la papa (*Rhizoctonia solani*, Kuhn). Page 97 In: Programa, XV Reunión Asociación Latinoamericana de la Papa (ALAP), Lima, Perú.

21. Lopes, C. A., and Reifschneider, F. J. 1982. Batata, identificacao de doencias e controle. Instrucoes tecnicas CNPHortalicas EMBRAPA (Brazil), 4:1-2.

22. Lopes, C. A. 1991. Resistencia: Bacterial wilt Brazil. Potato germplasm evaluation for bacterial wilt resistance: present status of the CNPH/EMBRAPA-CIP research contract. Page 70 In: Programa XV Reunión de la Asociación Latinoamericana de la Papa (ALAP), Lima, Perú.

23. Malamud, O. S. 1989. Research on *Verticillium dahliae*. Pages 139-158 In: Fungal diseases of the potato. Report of the Planning Conference on Fungal Diseases of the Potato held at CIP. The International Potato Center, Lima, Perú.

24. Malamud, O. S. 1975. Inheritance of the reactions to *Verticillium* and *Fusarium* wilts in tuber-bearing *Solanum* species and species-hybrids. Ph.D Thesis. University of Nebraska. 175 pp.

25. Marcano, D. 1988. Principales enfermedades fungosas y bacterianas de la Papa en Venezuela. Pages 161-184 In: Producción de semilla de papa y transferencia de tecnología en Venezuela. FONAIAP-PRACIPA, Venezuela.

26. Mills, W. R., and Niederhauser, J. S. 1953. Observations on races of *Phytophthora infestans* in Mexico. Phytopathology 43:454-455.

27. Niederhauser, J. S., and Cervantes, J. 1959. Anita, Bertita, and Conchita, three new blight-resistant potato varieties developed in Central Mexico. Am. Potato J. 36:301.

28. Niederhauser, J. S. 1961. Genetic studies of *Phytophthora infestans* and *Solanum* species in relation to late blight resistance in the potato. Pages 491-497 In: Recent advances in Botany, Proceedings IX International Botanical Congress. University of Toronto Press, Toronto, Ontario.

29. Niederhauser, J. S. 1972. Late blight resistance (East Africa and high elevation tropics, Mexico). Pages 125-152 In: International Symposium on Key Problems and Potential for Greater Use of the Potato in the Developing World. French, E. R. (ed). The International Potato Center, Lima, Perú.

30. Orellana, A. H. 1978. Estudio de la enfermedad "lanosa" de la papa en Ecuador. Fitopatologia (Perú), 13:61-66.

31. Parker, J. 1991. Diagnóstico de enfermedades en tubérculo de papa en Cochabamba, Chuquisaca y Potosí. Page 97 In: Programa, XV Reunión de la Asociación Latinoamericana de la Papa (ALAP), Lima, Perú.

32. Prior, P., and Steva, H. 1990. Characteristics of strains of *Pseudomonas solanacearum* from the French West Indies. Plant Dis. 74:13-17.

33. Rodríguez, R. A. 1958. "Torbo", una enfermedad de las papas que se presenta en Costa Rica. Turrialba (Costa Rica) 8:55-63.

34. Torres, H. 1981. *Verticillium dahliae* Kleb., identificación y síntomas que produce en seis cultivares comerciales de papas peruanas. Fitopatología (Perú) 16:60-68.

35. Torres, H. 1989. Soil-borne and foliar diseases in the highland tropics. Pages 169-180 In: Report of the Planning Conference on Fungal Diseases of the Potato. The International Potato Center, Lima.

36. Torres, H., and Elphinstone, J. 1990. Control of soil-borne pathogens in the mid-elevation tropical jungle of Perú. Am. Potato J. 67:583-584.
37. Torres, H., and Pacheco, M.A. 1991. "Gabriela" y "Esperanza" dos cultivares de papa resistentes a roña (*Spongopora subterranea*). Page 96 In: Programa, XV Reunión Asociación Latinoamericana de la Papa (ALAP), Lima, Perú.
38. Turkensteen, L. J. 1979. *Choanephora* blight of potatoes and other crops grown under tropical conditions in Perú. Neth J. Plant Pathol. 85:85-86.
39. Turkensteen, L. J, and Nieto, L.E. 1984. Report on a survey on potato diseases in Colombia. Research Institute for Plant Protection. Wageningen. 9 pp.
40. Turkensteen, L. J., and Nieto, L.E. 1986. Report on a survey on potato diseases in Colombia. Research Institute for Plant Protection, Wageningen. 10 pp.
41. Zachmann, R., and Baumann, D. 1975. *Thecaphora solani* on potatoes in Perú: Present distribution and varietal resistance. Plant Dis. Rep. 59:928-931.

DEVELOPMENT OF POTATOES WITH MULTIPLE RESISTANCE TO BIOTIC AND ABIOTIC STRESSES: THE INTERNATIONAL POTATO CENTER APPROACH

H.A. Mendoza
Department of Breeding and Genetics
International Potato Center, P.O Box 5969, Lima,Peru

The potato, the fourth most important food crop worldwide, is grown from 55°N to 50°S, at elevations between sea level up to 4000 meters, and under a wide range of temperature and humidity regimes. Potato is vulnerable to many devastating pathogens and insect pests (11). The most important and widely distributed diseases are late blight, *Phytophthora infestans*, the potato leafroll viruses X and Y, bacterial wilt, *Erwinia* spp., soft rot, *Pseudomonas solanacearum,* and to a lesser extent, early blight *Alternaria solani*. The most important insect and nematode pests are potato tubermoth, *Phthorimaea operculella*, Colorado potato beetle, *Leptinotarsa decemlineata*, Andean potato weevil, *Premnotrypes* spp., potato cyst nematode, *Heterodera* spp., and root knot nematodes, *Meloidogyne* spp. Other less important insects pests in developing countries are various species of aphids, leafhoppers, leaf miners, and flea beetles. The potato is also frequently affected by abiotic stresses such as drought, heat, frost, and salinity. Additionally, its growth may be significantly affected by daylength and the interaction of daylength and temperature. Thus, due to diverse agroecologies, the crop constantly encounters several important yield constraints, and a potato breeding programs should respond to these needs.

Genetic resistance provides the crop with sufficient protection against late blight, leafroll X and Y viruses, cyst and root knot nematodes and early blight. Resistance to insect pests such as tubermoth, Colorado potato beetle, aphids and leafhoppers is not present at the same levels as is resistance to diseases or nematodes. To obtain high yields, farmers depend heavily on toxic chemicals to control disease and insect pests, but their recurrent use has resulted in the development of insect populations with resistance to several chemical pesticides. In addition, the chemicals used for potato crop protection have contributed to increasing environmental deterioration. For these reasons, a major objective of our research programs is to decrease the dependency on chemical pesticides for control of diseases, insects, and nematodes and to develop alternative approaches for managing these pests. This paper discusses the role of genetic resistance and tolerance to the main biotic and abiotic stresses alone, and in combination with other control measures, for developing a more sustainable potato production system.

Major Yield Constraints

Studies conducted by the International Potato Center (CIP) indicated that 98% of the potato production in developing countries is distributed in four major agroecological zones (2). Table 1 presents the main biotic and abiotic stresses in each zone. Late blight is important in all the zones, but is most damaging in cool and humid environments. Leafroll, X and Y viruses represent major yield constraints in three of the four zones. Bacterial wilt is very important in two zones. Potato tubermoth is devastating in the subtropical lowlands as well as in the arid-Mediterranean.

Table 1. Diseases, pests, abiotic stresses, normal day length during the growing season, and potato production (%) by agroecological zone.

Sub-Tropical Lowlands	Temperate	Highlands	Arid Mediterranean
% POTATO PRODUCTION			
38.7%	26.1%	19.1%	14.6%
BIOTIC AND ABIOTIC STRESSES			
PLRV,PVY,PVX	PLRV,PVY,PVX	Late blight	Tuber moth
Tuber moth	Late blight	Bacterial wilt	PLRV,PVY,PVX
Late blight	Cyst nematode	PLRV,PVY,PVX	Heat
Heat	Drought	Cyst nematode	Early + late blight
Bacterial wilt	Frost	Frost	Salinity
Drought	Aphids	Andean weevil	Drought
Salinity			
Short days	Long days	Short, long days	Short to long
			Long to short

Table 2. Heritability (h²) for important agronomic and tuber qualtity traits.

Character	h²
Yield	medium-low
Tuber number	medium
Tuber weight	medium
Earliness	medium
Dry matter	medium
Reducing sugars	low

In developed countries, late blight is mainly controlled by use of expensive fungicides. In developing countries, late blight causes serious damage due to the limited use of expensive fungicides and the scarcity of cultivars with sufficient resistance. A significant limitation in the use of chemical fungicides may provide impetus for potato breeding programs to give a high priority to selection for resistance to late blight.

Virus diseases are effectively controlled in developed countries by planting certified seed. In developing countries, the scarcity of certified seed or the high cost of the imported seed has contributed to viruses becoming serious yield constraints. In this case, virus resistance is the most effective and economic control method.

Bacterial diseases such as bacterial wilt, blackleg and bacterial soft rot hinder potato production and use. With no practical chemical control methods available, these diseases are partially controlled by integrating the use of relatively resistant or tolerant cultuvars, seed certification, and crop rotation.

Genetic resistance also confers adequate control of nematode pests. Resistance against insect pests has either not been fully used and/or occurs at low level. Thus, control of insects depends largely on chemical insecticides. In some cases, such as with Andean weevil and potato tubermoth, the use of integrated control programs is effective.

Genetic Research on Biotic and Abiotic Yield Constraints

Since CIP was founded, the Breeding and Genetics Department has conducted basic research on the genetic variability of potato, and the heritabilities of the most important attributes of potato (Tables 2 and 3). This information is needed to identify the most effective breeding strategies for use with our genetic resources, and to determine the most efficient methods for combining various traits.

Heritability (h^2) for yield varied from 0 to 0.65 in the populations studied, however estimates ranging from 0.1 to 0.25 are more common. Heritabilities of two yield components, tuber number and tuber weight, were between 0.5 to 0.7; h^2 for tuber initiation, a component of earliness, was ca. 0.65. In crosses of early-maturing progenitors, 96% had tuberized within 30 days after transplanting; in crosses of early- x medium-maturing lines, 78.6% had tuberized within the same time period; in crosses between medium-maturity progenitors, 63.6% had tuberized. Progress in selection studies for earliness has been rewarding because many clones with a growing cycle of 75-85 days have been selected (10). Heritability was estimated at 0.5 for dry matter content and 0.10 for reducing sugars. Phenotypic recurrent selection for yield did not ressult in significant progress. Recurrent selection with progeny testing to select progenitors for the next cycle of selection has led to significant gains in yield.

Resistances (immunities) to viruses X and Y are monogenic, dominant, and highly heritable. Despite this, they are considered durable. Virus Y is composed of three groups, PVY^O, PVY^N and PVY^C. Potato progenitors with virus Y immunity were challenged at CIP with a broad spectrum of isolates from the three strains. Results confirmed that the immunities to PVY from *S. tuberosum* ssp. *andigena* and from *S. stoloniferum* were effective (5).

Almost all strains of virus X belong to pathotype 1, and most do not break the immunity in potato conferred by dominant genes from *S. tuberosum* ssp. *tuberousum* and *andigena* and *S. acaule*. However, pathotype HB from Bolivia, present only in the Titicaca lake area, breaks these immunities (5).

Resistance to leafroll virus has several components (resistances to infection, multiplication, translocation, hypersensitivity, aphid antibiosis and antixenosis or non preference). No immunity has been found in cultivated or wild *Solanum* species. Resistance to infection is the most utilized component. However, the durability of resistance to infection, multiplication, and translocation can significantly decrease with simultaneous infection of viruses X and Y with which leafroll strongly interacts (8). The resistance to leafroll virus is polygenically controlled with a low estimate of heritability, $h^2 = 0.24$ (5).

For late blight, two types of resistance are known. Vertical resistance, known as hypersensivity, is controlled by major R-genes derived from *S. demissum*. It is highly heritable but not durable because it acts against non-matching races of the pathogen (the genes for virulence of the pathogen do not match the R-genes for resistance of the host). This resistance is overcome by mutation or sexual recombination of the fungus, which produces the matching virulent races (the genes for virulence of the pathogen match the R-genes for resistance of the host which then becomes susceptible). The second type is horizontal or polygenic resistance and is non-race specific and conceptually durable. A shortcoming is the interaction of this resistance with some environmental components such as day length, temperature, and light intensity. A cultivar with an adequate level of resistance in one environment may be more susceptible in a different environment (20).

Resistance to early blight has a high heritability, $h^2 = 0.7$ to 0.8, suggesting that few genes with additive effects might be responsible for the genetic variability (14). The durability of this resistance has not been adequately tested.

Table 3. Heritability (h^2) and efficiency of screening procedures for various biotic and abiotic stresses affecting potato yield.

Character	h^2	Screening procedure
Late blight (vertical)	high	good (screenhouse)
Late blight (horizontal)	medium-low	good (field)
Early blight	high	good (field)
Bacterial wilt	medium-low	acceptable(screenhouse)
Soft rot	medium-low	good (laboratory)
PVY, PVX	very high	good (screenhouse)
PLRV	low	acceptable (field)
Day length	high-medium	-
Frost	medium-low	good(growth from field)
Heat tolerance	medium	good (field)
Salinity	medium-low	acceptable (field)
Potato tuber moth	high-low	good (storage, lab.test)
Leaf miner fly	appears high	good(field,screenhouse,lab.)
Andean potato weevil	low	acceptable (storage, lab.)
Cyst nematodes	high-medium	good(screenhouse,lab.,field)
Root knot nematodes	high	good (screenhouse, field)

Races 1 and 3 of *Psuedomonas solanacearum*, the causal agent of bacterial wilt, seriously damage potatoes. Race 1 attacks a wide range of species in the lowland tropics. Race 3, which includes isolates adapted to cooler climates, attacks potatoes and a few alternate hosts in the tropics and subtropics. The cultivated diploid *S. phureja* was the first source used to breed for bacterial wilt resistance. This resistance was found to be strain-specific and temperature dependent (6). Although few dominant genes confer resistance to any one isolate, many dominant genes would be required for a broad spectrum of resistance (18). Bacterial wilt and late blight tetraploid cultivars, derived from *S. phureja* and *S. demissum*, held their resistances in the highlands, but failed in warmer environments. Crossing bacterial wilt- and late blight-resistant clones to heat tolerant materials permitted selection of bacterial wilt-resistant cultivars adapted to warmer environments (6).

To widen the genetic base for resistance, a new population that combined resistance to root knot nematode and bacterial wilt was assembled in 1977. This population was composed of *S. phureja*, *S. sparsipilum* and *S. chacoense* (12). Progenies from the first and third cycles of selection for *M. incognita* resistance were screened for bacterial wilt resistance. Eighty three genotypes were resistant to three isolates of race 1 and one isolate of race 3 (7). Schmiediche (18) utilized all these materials plus clone AVRDC 1287.19, derived from *S. chacoense* and *S. raphanifolium*. New cultivars with bacterial wilt resistance in warmer environments were selected. However, it appears that durable resistance might be difficult to achieve. Moreover, Anguiz (1) found a low heritability ($h^2 = 0.18$) in a screenhouse seedling test. The population challenged with the isolate 148 (race 3) was composed of hybrid progenies derived from *S. phureja* and crosses of these with clone AVRDC 1287.19. The cultivar with the best general ability for combined resistance was BR-63.76.

Resistance to potato tubermoth has been reported in both cultivated and wild *Solanum* species. Interspecific hybrids with high levels of resistance to tuber damage have been reported in Colombia (4). Resistance was identified in clones of an CIP interspecific hybrid population composed of *S. phureja*, *S. sparsipilum*, and *S. chacoense* (3). This population, called MBN, was previously developed for resistance to root knot nematode and bacterial wilt(7,12). The resistance was transferred to hybrids between the resistant accessions and susceptible cultivated diploid and tetraploid potatoes (3). Another study (16) reported that the resistance of *S. sparsipilum* was due to antibiosis and antixenosis; that the resistance was simply inherited; and that it could be easily transferred to commercial cultivars via 4x-2x matings. Interspecific potato tubermoth-resistant *tuberosum* x S. sparsipilum hybrids were crossed to resistant *andigena* accessions or their F, hybrids. A sample of 1,577 genotypes were screened twice for resistance and 98 (6%) showed resistance (19). Although these reports are encouraging, there is no information on the level of tubermoth resistance after a few breeding cycles to improve the negative traits contributed by wild *S. sparsipilum*.

Breeding potatoes at the tetraploid (4n) level presents some problems due to tetrasomic inheritance. Changes in genotypic frequencies in a 4n population under selection are slower than in 2n (11). For example, consider two populations, 4n and 2n, in equilibrium with two allelic forms, A and a, with the same frequencies [f(A)=p=f(a)=q=1/2] that are subjected to selection with a high level of efficiency to screen out recessive genotypes. The genetic progress in one generation of selection in the 2n population will be five times greater than that in the 4n. (13).

CIP's Breeding Strategy

Given the vulnerability to stresses of the potato, a breeding strategy oriented to select sustainable cultivars must include durable resistance (when possible) and/or tolerance as major components. If W represents a cultivar's performance in a given agroecological zone, the selection process should concentrate on four major blocks of genes responsible for performance. W = f(A,Y,Q,R) where A,Y,Q,R represent genes for adaptation, yield per se, tuber quality factors, and stress resistance or tolerance, respectively. Fortunately, sufficient genetic variability for most of these characters is available in the cultivated potato and its wild relatives.

CIP's breeding strategy emphasizes the production of advanced populations with the following characteristics: 1) a wide genetic variability; 2) increased frequency of genes controlling adaptation, yield, tuber quality, and resistance or tolerance to the main biotic and abiotic stresses; and 3) combination of these desirable attributes (10).

To make this strategy viable, an adequate breeding methodology had to be developed. The traditional pedigree or back cross breeding methods were not suitable to effectively manage a very large gene pool. Because some of the very important characteristics have a medium to low heritability (Tables 2 and 3), a group of characteristics had to be improved as an ensemble. Thus, an effective methodology was recurrent selection with progeny testing (11). Breeding separately for individual resistances or tolerances for later combination is not effective due to the complexities of tetrasomic inheritance and the low heritability of several resistance traits.

CIP's mandate for breeding is to produce advanced genetic materials for use in the national agricultural research systems (NARS) of developing countries. The breeding strategy delivers two types of products for the NARS use; 1) advanced populations for selection of cultivars better suited for sustainable agricultural systems in developing countries located in the four major potato producing agroecological zones; and 2) highly selected clones and progenitors to be used in NARS for either selection of cultivars or in breeding programs. These progenitors possess a high general combining ability for yield and tuber quality characters and transmit combined disease resistance to a significant portion of their progenies. For example, there are progenitors which transmit high yield, earliness, and heat tolerance. In addition, 70% of the progenies are immune to both viruses X and Y. If these progenitors are crossed to others with resistance to bacterial wilt and root knot nematode, the likelihood of selecting individual clones combining good agronomic characters with several resistances or tolerances to biotic stresses is high.

Attempting to breed for combined resistance or tolerance to all the stresses listed in Table 1 would be utopian. Heritability values for several of them indicate that, in some cases, the progress would be slow. In these cases, the strategy should include using even low levels of resistance as a component of an integrated control program.

Specific Breeding Strategies to Develop
and Test for Individual Resistances

CIP's strategy is to combine resistance, but for the purpose of clarity, breeding for resistance or tolerance to individual major constraints will be discussed. However, individual resistances that depend on their combination with other resistance for durability or effectiveness are also considered.

Strategy for breeding resistance to late blight. CIP has created two populations resistant to late blight (9). Population A combines specific (R-genes) and non-specific resistances and is the oldest of CIP's populations. This population was originally assembled with two main components; 1) *S. demissum*-derived materials from various origins (Mexico, India and Europe) which were provided by the Mexican potato program; and 2) accessions of *S. tuberosum* ssp. *andigena* and to a lesser extent *S. phureja* from CIP's gene bank. More recently, to improve earliness and heat tolerance, early maturing progenitors (some combining virus X and Y immunity) have been included. This population is subjected to a process of R-gene elimination by screening with race 0 and then with the race complex 1,2,3,4,5,6,7,10,11. The surviving individuals are then field-evaluated under high late blight pressure.

The second population, population B, was recently assembled and contains only non-specific horizontal resistance. It is composed of *andigena* R-gene free *tuberosum* and the diploid *S. phureja*. This population is screened with race 0 and then field- evaluated under high late blight pressure. Selected clones after progeny testing are used as progenitors to generate a new cycle of selection with increased gene frequency. The level of protection conferred by this resistance still has not been determined. At present, CIP is looking for new sources of durable resistance in wild *Solanums* that may upgrade the resistance that is already available in population B.

Late blight testing strategy. CIP's testing strategy is a systematic process that involves several steps (Fig. 1). First, at CIP's headquarters in

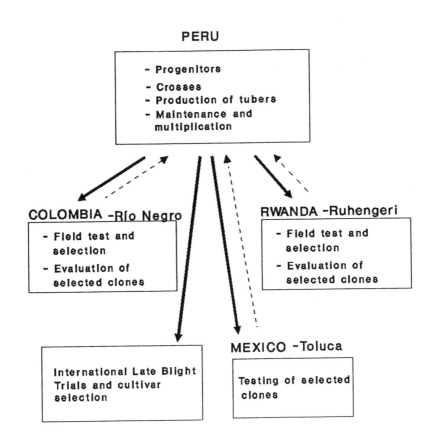

PERU

- Progenitors
- Crosses
- Production of tubers
- Maintenance and
  multiplication

COLOMBIA -Río Negro

- Field test and
  selection
- Evaluation of
  selected clones

RWANDA -Ruhengeri

- Field test and
  selection
- Evaluation of
  selected clones

International Late Blight
Trials and cultivar
selection

MEXICO -Toluca

Testing of selected
clones

Fig. 1. CIP methodology for testing and selection of late blight resistant potato lines.

Peru, maintenance of progenitors, crossing, seedling screening, production of tubers, and maintenance of duplicates under strict quarantine conditions is conducted. Second, simultaneous field tests and selection under high late blight pressure are conducted in Rionegro, Colombia and Ruhengeri, Rwanda. Selected materials are then re-evaluated for resistance and agronomic traits in the same locations, and selected clones are subsequently multiplied in Lima. These clones selected in step 2 are then tested in the Toluca valley in Mexico under high late blight pressure and a wide spectrum of physiological races. Clones are selected for resistance, agronomic characters, and adaptation to intermediate day length. Lastly, the materials selected in the previous steps are multiplied and sent to several countries in the different agroecological zones for further testing, selection and use as new cultivars.

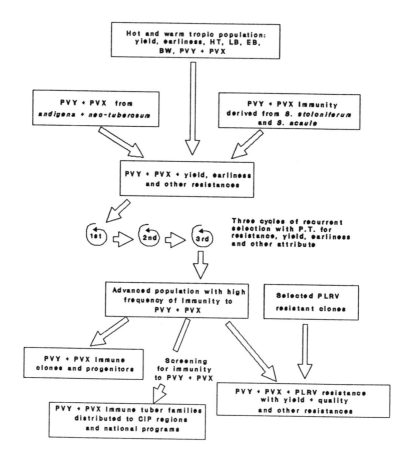

Fig. 2. CIP strategy for breeding combined virus-resistant potato clones (PVY and PVX are potato virus Y and X, respectively; PLRV is potato leafroll virus).

Strategy for breeding resistance to viruses. In most developing countries, viruses are still important yield constraints due to insufficient or nonexisting seed production programs. An important interaction among leafroll and X and Y viruses has been recently found (8). The original level of leafroll resistance decreased significantly when a leafroll-resistant clone became infected with either virus X or Y or both. Thus, the strategy to enhance the durability of resistance to leafroll is to combine it with immunity to both X and Y viruses (Fig. 2). Clones with good agronomic and tuber quality traits that combine the three resistances are available (15). Selection of progenitors with increased gene frequency for durable resistance (immunity) to both X and Y viruses or to virus Y alone is underway. Progenitors with a duplex structure for joint immunity to Y and X viruses have been identified at CIP (i.e., XXxx YYyy). Intercrossing these progenitors produces progenies with 94.5% immunity to both viruses. When these are crossed with clones susceptible to both X and Y viruses but resistant to leafroll virus or other diseases, about 70% of the progeny are immune to both viruses, and a variable percentage of progeny combine immunity to X and Y viruses plus resistance to leafroll. Virus Y immune progenitors with a triplex and quadruplex structure, i.e., YYYy and YYYY, respectively, will be available soon. These clones will produce all virus Y immune progenies when crossed to any progenitor susceptible to virus Y (15).

Strategy for breeding resistance to bacterial wilt. The level of resistance to bacterial wilt exhibited by some cultivars is moderate and breaks down when challenged by another race or isolate of *P. solanacearum* (4). Hence, selecting cultivars with durable resistance across all agroecological zones is not likely. CIP's new bacterial wilt breeding strategy focuses on races of *P. solanacearum* present in specific zones and within regions or countries within zones. Efforts at combining resistance were directed to combine bacterial wilt resisance with resistance to root knot nematode because this nematode may break resistance to bacterial wilt. Bacterial wilt- and root knot-resistant accessions of the species *S. phureja*, *S. sparsiphilum* and *S. chacoense* are all very susceptible to viruses X and Y and late blight. Therefore, these resistances must also be incorporated to protect these cultivars. Combining bacterial wilt resistance with root knot nematode resistance is simple because the sources of resistance are the same. Heritability for root knot resistance is high ($h^2 = 0.78$); the screening procedure is efficient (12); and resistances to the bacterium and the nematode appear to be correlated (7). Combining root knot nematode resistance with X and Y virus immunities was also simple because both traits are highly heritable. Joint selection for bacterial wilt resistance and X and Y virus immunities has been successful despite the reduction in frequency of genotypes resistant to bacterial wilt (1). Combined resistance to late blight and immunity to X and Y viruses is already available. Combining all these resistances is more complicated but feasible despite the medium to low heritabilities of bacterial wilt and durable late blight resistances. At present, the most efficient means for control of bacterial wilt is by an integrated strategy. Rueda (17) used a scale from 0 to 10 to compare the relative values of the various components of an integrated control approach. Seed scheme and soil rotation were given 10 points each; rouging of diseased plants, six points; and host resistance, three points. It is expected that the relative value of the resistance component to the integrated program should increase significantly.

Strategy for breeding for resistance to potato tubermoth. At present, there are no cultivars with resistance to tubermoth grown extensively where this pest is a serious constraint. Thus, control of this insect is based on an integrated pest management (IPM) program that combines several components: 1) use of sex pheromone traps and biological agents that decrease tubermoth populations; 2) use of hilling and, when available, cultivars that set tubers deep in the soil; and 3) prevention of tuber infestation in storage by using insect-repellent plants, biological control agents, and properly selected tubers.

Breeding strategy for potato tubermoth should use several available components: 1) selection for clones that express antibiosis and antixenosis or non-preference; 2) potential use of clones with type A and B glandular trichomes from *S. berthaultii* (see Tingey and Yencho, this volume), and 3) use of biotechnological tools to transfer *Bacillus thuriengensis* genes that are toxic to this pest (see Ebora and Sticklen, Van Rie et al., this volume). This integrated strategy could provide a durable resistance to potato tubermoth.

Present and Future Output of CIP's Breeding Strategy

Some of the available combinations of resistance or tolerance to the main yield constraints, and a time frame for full development, are presented below as a function of needs within the agroecological zones:

-       Combination of adaptation to short, medium and long days, earliness, heat tolerance, X and Y virus immunity, and resistance to leafroll virus for subtropical lowlands, temperate, and arid-mediterranean zones now exist. The frequency of this combination will be increased significantly in the following five years.
-       Combination of short to medium day length adaptation, late blight resistance and X and Y virus immunity is now available.
-       As above, with adapatation to long days (temperate zones). This objective will be achieved within the next five years.

- Combined adaptation to short and intermediate day lengths and resistance to late blight and cyst nematode (P4A, P5A, P6A) is now available for the highlands.
- Combined resistance to late blight, cyst nematode (P4A, P5A, P6A) and X and Y virus immunity for the highlands will be available in the next five years.
- Combined adaptation to short and intermediate day lengths and resistance to cyst nematode (P4A, P5A, P6A) and frost tolerance is now available for the highlands.
- Combination of adaptation to short and intermediate day lengths, resistances to bacterial wilt (race 3), late blight, and X and Y virus immunity is currently underway for the subtropical lowlands and highlands. The evaluation of this population may require up to five years.
- Development of insect resistance, in particular potato tubermoth, may require five years or more.
- The need for advanced genetic materials to release cultivars adapted to zones with drought problems could be partially solved with early-maturing cultivars that combine the additional resistance factors needed in the particular agroecological zone.

Utilization of Genetic Materials Distributed by CIP

CIP has been distributing advanced genetic materials to developing countries since 1973. These materials were a selected group of clones from Mexico, Argentina, Peru and the United States. Clones that had resistance to one or two stresses were cleaned of pathogens and widely distributed. Later, as CIP's own breeding program developed, segregating populations as tuber families or true seed progenies were distributed. Recently, CIP has produced materials that combine resistance or tolerance to two or more stresses.

The number of cultivars released by developing countries is rapidly increasing. Thus far, 135 new cultivars have been released in 36 developing countries (Table 4). The relatively slow diffusion of potato cultivars is due to their vegetative propagation. The rate of multiplication is much slower than is that of the cereal crops, and the seed tubers may carry virus diseases that rapidly degenerate the crop thereby reducing its productivity.

Most developing countries have limited resources and/or do not have environments with low incidence of insect virus vectors to facilitate production of their own healthy seed. The introduction of virus resistance in CIP breeding populations facilitates seed production and favors a more rapid diffusion of new cultivars.

Future Prospects in Potato Breeding at CIP

Breeding work was initially centralized at CIP headquarters in Lima, Peru. In the last five years, four potato breeders have been located in South East Asia, East Africa, and in the Southern Cone of South America to reinforce the Regional Germplasm Distribution Centers (RGDC) in the Philippines, Kenya, and Chile. These RGDC's should have the full capacity to perform breeding activities for production of adapted populations and to clean selected clones of pathogens before shipment. These materials will be distributed to the countries of the region or other regions located in similar agroecological zones. With this effort, CIP expects to enhance the impact of its breeding activities to help increase food production in the developing world.

Table 4. Potato cultivars released or named by NARS in devoloping countries from CIP distributed genetic materials (1973 to 1992).

Region	No. of Countries	No. of Cultivars	Main attributes
South America	5	24	LB,BW,PCN,PVY,PVX,frost
Central America	4	11	LB,PVY,PVX
Africa	13	62	LB,BW,PLRV,PVY,PVX, RKN,heat
West Asia	4	11	LB,BW,PLRV,PVY,PVX
South East Asia	3	12	LB,PLRV,PVY,heat
South Pacific	6	9	PLRV, heat, earliness
China	1	6	LB, PLRV, heat
Total	36	135	

Literature Cited

1. Anguiz, R. 1992. General and specific combining abilities for resistance to bacterial wilt (*Pseudomonas solanacearum*) in autotetraploid potato populations with immunity to PVX and PVY. M. Sc. Thesis. Universidad Nacional Agraria La Molina. Lima,Peru. 70 p.
2. CIP. 1991. Meeting the Challenge: The International Potato Center's Strategy for the 1990's and Beyond. The International Potato Center, Lima. 93 p.

3. Chavez, R., Schmiediche, P., Jackson M.T., and Raman, K.V. 1988. The breeding potential of wild potato species resistant to the potato tuber moth, *Phthorimaea operculella*, Euphytica 39:123-132.

4   Estrada, R.N., and Valencia, L. 1988. Development of potato cultivars resistant to tuber moth, *Phthorimaea operculella*, in Colombia. Rev. Latinoamericana Papa (Colombia). 1 (1):64-73.

5. Fernandez-Northcot, E.N., 1989. Variability of PVX and PVY and its relationship to genetic resistance. pp. 131-139. *In*: Control of virus and virus-like diseases of potato and sweet potato. International Potato Center, Lima,Peru.

6. French, E.R. 1985. Interaction between strains of *Pseudomonas solanacearum*, its hosts and environments. *In* G.I. Perseley [ed], Bacterial wilt diseases in Asia and the South Pacific. Canberra, Australia.

7. Jatala, P., Martin, C., and Mendoza, H.A., 1983. Relationship of resistance to *M. incognita* and *P. Solanacearum* in potatoes. p. 106. *In*: Proceedings of the International Congress on Research for the Potato in the year 2000. International Potato Center, Lima,Peru.

8. Jayasinghe, U. 1989. Variability of and resistance of potato leafroll virus (PLRV). pp. 141-153. *In*: Control of virus-like diseases of potato and sweet potato. International Potato Center, Lima,Peru.

9. Landeo, J. 1989. Late blight breeding strategy at CIP. pp. 57-73. *In*: Fungal diseases of the potato. International Potato Center, Lima,Peru.

10. Mendoza, H.A. 1980. Development of lowland tropic populations. pp. 40-55. *In*: Utilization of the genetic resources of the potato III. International Potato Center, Lima,Peru.

11. Mendoza, H.A. and Sawyer, R.L., 1985. The breeding program at the International Potato Center. pp. 117-137. *In*: Russell, G.E. [ed.] Progress in Plant Breeding. Butterworths, U.K.

12. Mendoza, H.A. and Jatala, P. 1985. Breeding potatoes for resistance to root knot nematodes, *Meloidogyne* spp. pp. 217-224. *In*: Sasser & Carter [eds.] An advanced treatise on *Meloidogyne*. North Carolina State University, Raleigh, North Carolina.

13. Mendoza, H.A. 1988. Progress in resistance breeding in potatoes as a function of efficiency of screening procedures. pp. 39-64. *In*: Bacterial diseases of the potato. The International Potato Center, Lima, Peru.

14. Mendoza, H.A., and Martin, C. 1989. Breeding for resistance to early blight (*Alternaria solani*). pp. 119-137. *In*: Fungal diseases of the potato. International Potato Center, Lima, Peru.

15. Mendoza, H.A., Fernandez, E., Jayasinghe, U., Salazar, L.F., Chuquillanqui, C., and Galvez, R. 1989. Breeding for resistance to potato viruses Y, X, and leafroll: Research strategy, selection procedures, and experimental results. pp. 155-171. *In*: Control of virus and virus-like diseases of potato and sweet potato. International Potato Center, Lima,Peru.

16. Ortiz, R., Iwanaga, M., Raman, K.V. and Palacios, M., 1990. Breeding for resistance to potato tuber moth, *Phthorimaea opercullela*, in diploid potatoes. Euphytica. 50:119-125.

17. Rueda, J.L. 1990. Seed potato improvement under bacterial wilt (*Pseudomonas solanacearum* E.F. Smith) pressure: an integrated approach. Ph.D. Thesis. University of Reading, U.K.

18. Schmiediche, P. 1985. Breeding potatoes for resistance to bacterial wilt caused by *Pseudomonas solanacearum*. *In*: G.I. Persley [ed.] Bacterial wilt disease in Asia and the South Pacific. CSIRO, Canberra, Australia.

19. Scurrah, M. 1986. One cycle of selection for resistance to potato tuber moth. Am. Potato J. 63:454.
20. Turkensteen, L.J. 1989. Interaction of R-genes in breeding for resistance of potatoes against *Phytophthora infestans*. pp. 85-96. *In*: Fungal diseases of the potato. International Potato Center, Lima,Peru.

VIRUS DETECTION AND MANAGEMENT IN DEVELOPING COUNTRIES

Luis F. Salazar
Department of Plant Pathology
The International Potato Center
P.O. Box 5969
Lima, Peru.

In developing countries, potato virus diseases are one of the major causes of lower yields in potato and their control requires the development of appropriate technology for the region. Developing countries are located in the tropics and the ecology and epidemiology of viruses in tropical areas are quite different than in temperate regions of the world. For example, viruses and viroids in the tropics might have a larger number of alternate hosts, whether wild or cultivated plant species, and their vectors might be more abundant and variable than in the temperate zones. The latter is especially true for aphid vectors of viruses, which in the tropics reproduce primarily by parthenogenesis and rarely undergo sexual reproduction. Sub-zones resembling the characteristic temperatures of the temperate zones may be found in the tropics at higher elevations, as in the Andean region of South America. However, during most of the day there is high solar radiation, even in the coldest seasons, resulting in different virus ecology than in temperate regions of the world.

There is no doubt that one of the best approaches for control of virus diseases in potato is through the development of efficient seed programs. There are some strong seed potato programs in the developing countries, but their technological development is always less than ideal, mainly due to the lack of resources or lack of knowledge in specific technologies. Another effective virus control measure relies on the development of cultivars with resistance to viruses. However, this process is rather slow because traditional breeding technology is used. Although recent developments in molecular biology show that the process can be accelerated, the number of viruses that must be controlled given the favorable environment that exists makes the task rather difficult for developing countries.

All methods of virus control will only be possible and effective when two fundamental aspects in virology are met: (1) the development of sensitive, simple, and economical virus detection methods; and (2) the identification of all viruses in the region. At the International Potato Center (CIP), efforts have been directed at helping developing countries fulfill these needs. In addition, three planning conferences have been held to analyze virus problems in developing countries (11).

Potato Viruses in the Tropics

The nature and characteristics of the principal potato viruses in the tropics do not differ greatly from those in other parts of the world. Potato leafroll (PLRV), potato virus Y (PVY), potato virus X (PVX) and potato virus S (PVS) are, in general, the most important viruses in the region. However, there are important differences among typical isolates of each virus. In addition, there are several other viruses that periodically achieve greater importance in some tropic regions than those mentioned above. These are briefly described below:

Potato leafroll virus (PLRV). In the non-Andean regions, isolates appear to be similar or closely related (at least serologically) to those reported elsewhere, but isolates from the Andean region of South America appear to be different. The most typical example is the "enanismo amarillo" disease (17) known in Colombia, Peru, and Bolivia, which is caused by a strain of leafroll in native cultivars. The symptomatology differs significantly from the typical leafrolling observed in cultivars of *Solanum tuberosum* spp. *tuberosum*. Even though there is not a large serological difference between "enanismo amarillo" and the typical leafroll isolates when polyclonal antibodies are used, infectivity of "enanismo amarillo" and effects on certain hosts differ.

Potato virus Y (PVY) group. The three main strains (Y^O, Y^C, and Y^N) are found in the tropics; the Y^N strain is the most widespread (4). Several other isolates related to or different from PVY have been found. One of these, potato virus V (PVV), appears to have a high incidence and distribution (5).

Potato virus X (PVX). Strains of PVX have been grouped into two serotypes: PVX^O, the common serotype around the world, and PVX^A, the Andean serotype (4). Strain PVX_{HB} (16), known to overcome genes for immunity from *S. acaule*, is found in the Andean region and belongs to the PVX^A serotype. In some regions, several other isolates were found that differ serologically, and in their effects on potato. One example is PVX-GUA which appears to be the most widely distributed strain of PVX in Central America and the Caribbean.

Potato virus S (PVS). PVS is found worldwide. A strain that systemically infects *Chenopodium quinoa* is the most common in the Andes (8). Unfortunately, there have been no studies on the effects of PVS strains on potato.

Other viruses. Several other viruses and strains seem to be important to potato in developing countries. Potato mop-top virus (PMTV) is common on potato in many countries, including in the Andes, due to the high prevalence of its vector *Spongospora subterranea* (18).

Andean potato mottle virus (APMV) (6) and Andean potato latent virus (APLV) (14) cause severe damage to potato in the Andes where they spread rapidly in seed stocks. These two viruses are transmitted mechanically, but the importance of their suspected insect vectors is not yet known. Some viruses, such as PVT (19), potato black ringspot virus (PBRV) (20) or *Solanum* apical leaf curling virus (SALCV) (10) are not very common but can be important where they occur. PVT is especially serious because of its ability to be transmitted through true seed (19).

There are other, suspected virus diseases which deserve attention such as the deforming mosaic from Argentina (2) and probably Uruguay and Brazil, and yellow vein from Ecuador and Colombia (1). In some countries, there are other viruses that do not depend on potato for survival and spread, such as tobacco streak (3), tomato spotted wilt virus, sugar beet curly top virus in Brazil, and alfalfa mosaic virus in Andean countries (unpublished). A virus resembling AMV in morphology and other biological characteristics, but unrelated serologically, has recently been reported tentatively as potato yellowing virus (7). Table 1 lists thirty-three viruses found in potatoes (24).

Development of Virus Detection Technology

Approaches for use in developing countries. Before 1970, the detection of viruses in developing countries was almost entirely performed by observation of symptoms; a very inaccurate procedure especially when detection was required in mother plants. Because of high cost, techniques such as the use of indicator hosts were used only to a limited extent. Only a few developing countries used the serological techniques of chloroplast agglutination and microprecipitation with antisera. However, two main limitations of these techniques were noted: (1) the antisera were too expensive for generalized use; and (2) the antisera at times failed to detect strains of viruses prevalent in the region.

Table 1. Plant virus and virus-like agents affecting potato[a]

Virus Group	Typical member in potato	No. viruses in potato	Particle size (nm)	Type/No. nucleic acid strands	Natural transmission
Alfalfa mosaic virus	AMV	2	58,52,42X18	RNA(3)	Aphids
Capilloviruses	PVT	1	640x10	RNA(1)	True Seed
Carlaviruses	PVS	2	640x11	RNA(1)	Mechanical, Aphids
Comoviruses	APMV	1	28	RNA(2)	Beetles
Cucumoviruses	CMV	1	30	RNA(4)	Aphids
Furoviruses	PMTV	1	300x18	RNA	Fungi
Geminiviruses	BCTV	2	17(pairs)	DNA	Leafhopper
	SALCV	1	17(triplets)	DNA	
Ilarviruses	TSV	1	28	RNA(4)	Thrips
Luteoviruses	PLRV	2	25	RNA(1)	Aphids
Necroviruses	TNV	1	26	RNA(1)	Fungi
Nepoviruses	PBRV	4	28	RNA(2)	Nematodes
Potexviruses	PVX	2	520x13	RNA(1)	Mechanical
Potyviruses	PVY	4	740x11	RNA(1)	Aphids
Rhabdoviruses	PYDV	2	380x18	RNA(1)	Leafhopper
Tobamoviruses	PMV	1	300x18	RNA(1)	Mechanical
Tobraviruses	TRV	1	190-45x22	RNA(2)	Nematodes
Tomato spotted wilt virus	TSWV	1	80	RNA(1)	Thrips
Tymoviruses	APLV	2	28	RNA(1)	Beetles
Viroids	PSTVd	1	-	RNA(1)	Mechanical

[a]From: L.F. Salazar (23)

CIP developed the latex agglutination test in 1974, and in 1977 CIP developed an enzyme-linked immunosorbent assay (ELISA). Both techniques were made available to developing country detection programs as field kits containing all the chemicals and reagents needed to perform the test. The double-antibody sandwich ELISA (DAS-ELISA) is still in use, but in recent years ELISA on nitrocellulose membranes (NCM-ELISA) has also become available (21). However, this approach was not the best solution because the demand for antisera increased rapidly beyond CIP's capabilities of production. To obviate this problem, CIP designed a three stage plan. In stage 1, CIP provided crude antisera for the most important viruses to selected countries for use in ELISA. Antisera for PLRV, PVX, PVY, and PVS were distributed to all countries, but antisera for APLV and APMV were also provided to countries in the Andean region from the beginning of the program. Training of personnel in these countries was done by CIP. Reagents were produced to help other countries in the region. In stage 2, some countries started to produce their own virus antisera under continuous advice and supervision by CIP. Stage 3 was designed to interest and involve private companies in the development of reagents for detection.

Presently, Brazil, Thailand, Korea, Tunisia, and China have already accomplished stages 1 and 2. Stage 3 was initiated in Argentina in 1990. Countries such as Peru and the Programa Regional Cooperativo de Papa (PRECODEPA) network contracted specialized persons to develop antisera at CIP facilities. This approach enhanced the use of more advanced technology for virus detection in potato in several developing countries, and also served as a model for other crops.

Background research at CIP. Serological procedures are continuously evaluated at CIP to improve their sensitivity and specificity and lower their cost. For instance, virus isolates used as antigens to produce polyclonal antisera have been revised for PVX, PVY, and PLRV. Those isolates producing antibodies with broad specificity are used for routine antisera production. This type of analysis requires the collection and study of viruses from different geographical sources.

Research to reduce the cost of serological testing has facilitated the development of procedures for reuse of plates, antibodies, and conjugates. Also, the expensive enzyme alkaline phosphatase has been replaced with less expensive enzymes such as penicillinase for use in ELISA.

Detection of the potato spindle tuber viroid. Another important disease agent is the potato spindle tuber viroid (PSTVd)(22). PSTVd has been found sporadically on potato in most developing countries, although it has been found in other host species such as avocado (*Persea americana* L.) in Peru (M. Querci et al., unpublished). The high incidence of PSTVd observed in some provinces in China may have resulted from its introduction and spread by true potato seed in the last 20-30 years.

Until 1978, detection of PSTVd was accomplished by inoculation of tomato and observation of symptoms. This procedure was complicated and could only be used in countries with greenhouse facilities. A new technique using electrophoresis of nucleic acid extracts was begun alone or in combination with inoculation of tomatoes. Although this procedure was more efficient than the tomato test, it was still not sufficiently sensitive. Nucleic acid spot hybridization (NASH) was adopted in 1983 after the development of appropriate probes at the USDA Plant Pathology and Microbiology Laboratory in Beltsville, Maryland. Detection of PSTVd is performed at CIP on nitrocellulose membranes spotted with the samples and hybridized with radio-labelled probes (23). A non-radioactive, enzymatic probe has now been developed and its use is being implemented in some countries.

Development of Virus-resistant Cultivars

The development of cultivars with resistance to most important viruses is a major goal of virus management in developing countries (15). The first step taken to accomplish this goal was to search for genes for virus resistance among CIP's large germplasm collection. Genes conferring extreme resistance to PVX were found in *Solanum tuberosum* ssp. *andigena* (Rx and), *S.acaule* (Rx acl), and *S. tuberosum* (Rx tub). The resistance conferred by these dominant genes acts against all strains of PVX (pathotype 1) except the strain HB (pathotype HB). Recently, however, a high level of resistance to strain HB was found in CIP's germplasm in an accession of *S. sucrense*. Because PVX^{HB} is not widely distributed in potatoes (15) there seems to be no immediate advantage to development of cultivars with resistance to this virus strain.

Resistance genes conferring immunity to PVY were obtained from *S. stoloniferum* and *S. tuberosum* ssp. *andigena*. These genes not only act against PVY, but also against other related potyviruses, such as PVA, PWMV or PTV (4).

The combination of PVX and PW resistance was successful, and at present, genotypes having immunity to both viruses in available. These resistant materials have been evaluated under field conditions in several countries to determine their stability. After six consecutive exposures, no infection with PVX or PW has been detected in these genotypes (4).

The search for resistance to PLRV proved to be more complicated. Initial work in 1974 was devoted to the search for resistant genotypes. Some genotypes had high levels of resistance initially, but became infected with PLRV after several years of field exposure (12). For this reason, we endeavored to increase our knowledge of the mechanisms of resistance to this virus. Our work revealed that resistance to PLRV is multicomponent in nature with each component acting separately (12). These components included resistance to viral infection and multiplication, antixenosis, and antibiosis. The first two components act on the virus, whereas the others act on the vector, *Myzus persicae* (Sulzer). We also found that the overall resistance to PLRV is broken by infection with other viruses, namely PVX and PVY (11). We are now attempting to introduce genes for more than two of the components of resistance to PLRV into potato genotypes with immunity to PVX and PVY. The development of potato lines with resistance to other viruses is not being attempted at present. However, one project is underway to combine virus resistance with resistance to three important pathogens, *Phytophthora infestans, Alternaria solani* and bacterial wilt (*Pseudomonas solanacearum*). We are presently in the process of evaluating this combined resistance at CIP under different ecological conditions.

Exclusion Measures

The development of potato programs in developing countries has increased the exchange of germplasm between countries. This international movement of germplasm increases the risk of inadvertant introduction of harmful pathogens, particularly viruses. To prevent the spread of viruses, CIP developed a "virus-conscious" attitude in developing country programs, in which virus detection technology has become the key element. Distribution of potato genetic materials in developing countries now follows the guidelines used in developed countries. At present, the most important virus disease that should be prevented from spreading is yellow vein, which occurs in Ecuador and Colombia. Its whitefly vector, *Trialeurodes vaporariorum* (Westwood), is present in many countries and therefore the risk of yellow vein spread is high.

Outlook for Virus Management in Developing Countries

Management of virus diseases of potato in developing countries is promising in view of the knowledge obtained about these viruses, the availability of highly sensitive virus detection technology, and the development of virus-resistant cultivars. Virus detection is a prerequisite in any attempt to control virus diseases by any means. For large-scale application of virus detection technology, there is a need for commercial kits for virus detection and/or diagnostic services. Ideally, these should be provided by the private sector. For example, in Argentina, virus detection on potato seed farms is offered by private companies. Private companies have been interested in providing this service in other countries, but their cost analysis apparently did not forecast a profitable return. Because the highest cost associated with these techniques is the purchase of antisera, there is a need for the National Agricultural

Research System (NARS) to initiate a collaborative venture with the private sector to enhance economic success.

Because most developing countries are located in tropical regions, dissemination of newly recognized, or still unknown, virus diseases is likely to occur. This is because the exuberant vegetation in this region harbors viruses and vectors year round. NARS should be prepared to tackle these problems and, after identification of the causal agents, diagnostic methods should be developed.

The development of virus resistant cultivars has great possibilities for application in developing countries either by NARS or by the private sector. In this regard, the availability of transgenic plants with resistance to the most important viruses may become an important tool in management of virus diseases. This technology, however, should be carefully evaluated before application, even though it may be approved for use in developed countries. Because tropical regions harbor diverse vegetation with yet unidentified pathogens, the interaction of genes used in transforming plants with these many pathogenic agents cannot be predicted.

Literature Cited

1. Alba, V.E. 1950. Viropatógenos. Conf. Lat. de Espec. en Papa. Bogotá, Colombia. p.52-58.
2. Calderoni, A. 1965. An unidentified virus of deforming mosaic type in potato varieties in Argentina. Am. Potato J. 42:257 (Abst.)
3. Costa, A.S.; A. B. Carvahlo and J. Deslandes. 1964. Ocorrencia do virus de necrose branca do fumo em plantaoes de batatinha. Bragantia 23:1-8.
4. Fernandez-Northcote, E.N. 1990. Variability of PVX and PVY and its relationship to genetic resistance, pp. 131-139. In. International Potato Center. Control of virus and virus-like disease of potato and sweet potato. Report of the 3rd. Planning Conference. Lima, Peru, CIP, Lima.
5. Fribourg, C.E. and J. Nakashima. 1984. Characterization of a new potyvirus from potato. Phytopathology 74:1363-1369.
6. Fribourg, C.E.; R.A.C. Jones and R. Koening. 1978. Un nuevo virus de la papa. Moteado Andino de la papa (APMV). Fitopatología 13:28 (Abst.)
7. Fuentes, S. 1991. Identification and characterization of a baciliform virus isolated from potato (Solanum tuberosum L.) .M.S. Thesis. Lima, Peru.
8. Hinostroza, A.M. 1973. Isolation of infectious ribonucleic acid from leaves of Chenopodium quinoa infected with potato virus S. Phytopathology. 76:149-152.
9. Hooker, W. J. and L. F. Salazar. 1983. A new plant virus from the high jungle of the eastern Andes; Solanum apical leaf curling virus (SALCV). Ann. Appl. Biol. 103:449-454.
10. International Potato Center (CIP). 1990. Control of virus and virus-like diseases of potato and sweet potato. Report of the 3rd Planning Conference, CIP. Lima, Peru. 228pp.

11. Jayasinghe, U. 1990. Variability of, and resistance to potato leafroll virus (PLRV), pp. 141-153. *In* International Potato Center (CIP). Control of virus and virus-like diseases of potato and sweet potato. Report of the 3rd Planning Conference, CIP, Lima, Peru.

12. Jayasinghe, U., C. Chuquillanqui and L. F. Salazar. 1989. Modified expression of virus resistance in potato mixed virus infections. Am. Potato J. 66:137-144.

13. Jones, R.A.C. and C.E. Fribourg. 1978. Symptoms induced by Andean potato latent virus in wild and cultivated potatoes. Potato Res. 21:121-127.

14. Mendoza, H., E. Fernandez-Northcote, U. Jayasinghe, L.F. Salazar, R. Galvez and C. Chuquillanqui. 1990. Breeding for resistance to potato virus Y, X and leafroll. Research strategy, selection procedures and experimental results, pp. 155-171. *In* Control of virus and virus-like diseases of potato and sweet potato. Report of the 3rd Planning Conference, CIP, Lima, Peru.

15. Moreira, A., R.A.C. Jones and C. E. Fribourg. 1980. Properties of a resistance-breaking strain of potato virus X. Ann. Appl. Biol. 95:93-103.

16. Rodríguez, A. and R. A. C. Jones. 1975. Incidencia y Síntomas del virus del enrollamiento de la papa en el Peru. Fitopatología 10:80-81.

17. Salazar, L. F. and R. A. C. Jones. 1975. Some studies on the distribution and incidence of potato mop-top virus in Peru. Am. Potato J. 52:143-150.

18. Salazar, L. F. and B. D. Harrison. 1978. Host range, purification and properties of potato virus T. Ann. Appl. Biol. 89:223-235.

19. Salazar, L. F. and B. D. Harrison. 1978. The relationship of potato black ringspot virus to tobacco ringspot and allied viruses. Ann. Appl. Biol. 90:387-394.

20. Salazar, L. F. 1989. Producción de antisueros para el diagnóstico de virus. pp. 115-118. *In* H. Rincón and 0. Hidalgo [eds.]. Avances en la producción de tubérculos-semillas de papa en los países del Cono Sur. CIP, Lima, Perú.

21. Salazar, L. F. 1989. Potato spindle tuber. pp. 155-167. *In* R. P. Kahn [ed.]. Plant Protection and Quarantine. Vol. II. CRC Press. Boca Raton, Florida.

22. Salazar, L. F.; R. A. Owens and I. Balbo. 1988. Comparison of four radioactive probes for the diagnosis of potato spindle tuber viroid by nucleic acid spot hybridization. Potato Res. 31:431-442.

23. Salazar, L. F. 1990. Main virus diseases of potato. *In* Report of the 3rd Planning Conference. CIP, Lima, Peru.

THE POTATO'S GLOBAL POTENTIAL

Peter Gregory
Deputy Director General for Research
The International Potato Center
P.O. Box 5969, Lima, Peru

The purpose of this chapter is to put the research associated with the International Potato Pest Management Conference (Jackson Hole, Wyoming, October, 1991) in a global development context. My intention is to demonstrate that our work can make a substantial contribution to global survival. But this can only happen if we make some new initiatives - now.

Global Challenges for Agriculture: Today and Tomorrow

The central question is how to feed the 80 to 100 million children born in the world each year. This translates into a doubling of the planet's population within the next 20 to 30 years. Nine out of 10 of these newborn children will begin life in the developing world, where the highest rates of population increase are often found, and where there is already a severe shortage of good land to bring into production. How are we going to achieve sustainability as we intensify land use and bring marginal land into use in these countries?

By "sustainability" I mean the successful management of resources for agriculture to satisfy changing human needs while maintaining or even enhancing the environment. Indeed, we know that most of the foods and fibers needed for the 21st Century must be grown on the arable land already under production. We must determine the shifts that can be made from extensively produced crops, such as rice and wheat, to the more intensively produced crops: vegetables, and root and tuber crops. But it is not sufficient to think only in terms of food production. We already have serious environmental problems throughout the world, and relatively little has been done about it. Unless we factor these concerns into our future efforts, the benefits attained through improved food production will be shortlived.

The Potential Role of the Potato

The potato is well suited to address the challenges facing agriculture over the next two decades. It is currently ranked as the fourth most important food crop in the developing world in terms of economic value. It has been a staple food in many parts of the world for many decades. This highly productive crop, which fits well into cereal-based farming systems, produces more calories and high-quality protein per unit area and per unit time than any other food plant, and is the best balanced nutritionally. Potatoes are fast growing and their good ground cover helps prevent erosion.

We must augment the productivity and utilization of potato within sustainable farming systems to make use of the crop's full potential in boosting income, employment, and nutrition. Although production of potatoes has been increasing more rapidly than that of any other major food crop in both Asia and Africa, there are still many challenges that face potato scientists within global agriculture for the next 20 years. Among these are the need to: (1) increase potato production in cereal- and agroforestry-based farming systems; (2) increase productivity of quality food per unit area and time; (3) increase the efficiency of utilization of inputs such as fertilizers and water; and (4) sustain these increases in productivity in a way that is friendly to the environment.

These challenges are based on the assumptions that cereals will continue to be the mainstay for food security, even as other more productive foods increase in importance; that most of the increases in production needed over the coming years must be on the land presently cultivated; and finally, that the fragile soils of the highland and lowland tropics must be protected. The comparative advantage of agroforestry as a mechanism to achieve this goal will become increasingly important for food production.

Constraints to be Removed

Which constraints must be overcome to realize the full potential of potato in the 21st Century? Although consumption trends show that potatoes are a popular food around the developing world, greater consumption is constrained by high prices resulting from insufficient supply. Although production has risen markedly, potatoes remain less affordable in most developing countries than in industrialized economies. Price fluctuations resulting from supply, storage, and transportation problems are important in many areas. But perhaps the most important constraints to attaining the full global potential of potatoes are the serious losses caused by many pests and diseases, and the high financial and environmental costs of chemical pesticides used to control them. Potato is the greatest user of chemical pesticides among the major food crops.

The cost of these chemicals can reach up to 20% of the total cost of production in many developing countries! The high cost of imported chemical pesticides, several of which have been banned in developed countries, has been a large drain on the foreign reserves of developing countries. Also, overuse of these toxic chemicals has resulted in the development of resistant pest populations, and the subsequent use of even more toxic chemicals to control them. In many developing countries, farmers spray chemicals indiscriminately on a routine basis to protect the potato crop, often in desperate attempts to earn a reasonable profit. The damage to the health of farmers and consumers is incalculable. The irreversible damage to flora and fauna in the environment is likewise alarming.

Realizing the Potential: The Job to be Done

We must recognize that potato production cannot be made sustainable in developing countries if it is to rely on costly and toxic chemicals. We must promote the extensive use of economically viable and environmentally sound IPM technologies to control the pests of potato. This will not only arrest the damage to the environment and to human health, but will also make potato affordable to resource-poor farmers and consumers. To this end, we must develop strong linkages in developing countries with farmers and farmer groups, national extension services, crop protection technical services, national R&D institutions, national governments and non-governmental organizations.

Our particular challenge is to fully realize the enormous potential of the potato. Research such as that reported in this book is a vital element that must be sustained. But research must be complemented with strong efforts to help national governments break away from policies that emphasize monocropping of cereals to meet soaring food needs. Developing countries must realize that policies based solely on the strategy of the Green Revolution will not be enough for the 21st Century. Also, national policy makers need to be informed of the technological advances that we achieve. Lastly, researchers must emphasize to policy makers and international funding institutions that the full exploitation of the potato's potential can truly make a difference in a world facing overpopulation and food shortages in the 21st Century.

Why have policy makers waited so long to fully exploit the potato and other root and tuber crops? One reason is that researchers generally do a poor job of communicating, except with each other. Communication must become one of our improved technologies. A two-pronged approach is needed: we must continue our research, and we must promote widespread awareness of the importance of our research and its products.

Agricultural scientists are already moving in the right direction. There is increased awareness among the international scientific community that potato can play an even bigger role than it does now. But there are many national policy makers who are relatively unaware of the full potential of this crop. In the future, symposia such as this Potato Pest Management Conference should focus not only on research, but also on the improvement of information flow. Increased participation of the private sector must be encouraged because it is highly probable that the mix of products that industry will contribute to IPM in the future will change markedly as a result of biotechnology. For example, the use of pesticides is likely to decrease as gene products conferring resistance are rapidly incorporated into improved potato cultivars.

I believe that potato can play a major role in fueling a broad-based industrial revolution in developing countries in the 21st Century, much as it did in the already developed world decades ago. Let us keep doing the research work that is so well demonstrated in this fine symposium, but let us also ensure that the world's policy makers hear about our work. Only in this way will we tap the full global potential of the potato.